FOURTEENTH EDITION

Readings *for* Writers

Jo Ray McCuen-Metherell

Anthony C. Winkler

WADSWORTH
CENGAGE Learning·

Australia · Brazil · Japan · Korea · Mexico · Singapore · Spain · United Kingdom · United States

WADSWORTH
CENGAGE Learning

**Readings For Writers,
Fourteenth Edition**
Jo Ray McCuen-Metherell,
Anthony C. Winkler

Senior Publisher: Lyn Uhl

Publisher: Monica Eckman

Acquiring Sponsoring Editor:
Kate Derrick

Senior Development Editor:
Leslie Taggart

Development Editor:
Karen Mauk

Editorial Assistant:
Maggie Cross

Marketing Manager:
Melissa Holt

Marketing Coordinator:
Brittany Blais

Marketing Communications
Manager: Linda Yip

Content Project Manager:
Dan Saabye

Art Director: Marissa Falco

Print Planner: Betsy Donaghey

Rights Acquisition Specialist:
Tom McDonough

VP, Director, Advanced and
Elective Products Program:
Alison Zetterquist

Editorial Coordinator, Advanced
and Elective Products Program:
Jean Woy

Production Service:
PreMediaGlobal

Text Designer:
Nesbitt Graphics, Inc.

Cover Designer:
Nesbitt Graphics, Inc.

Cover Image:
The Bridgeman Art Library

Compositor: PreMediaGlobal

For product information and
technology assistance, contact us at **Cengage Learning
Customer & Sales Support, 1-800-354-9706**

For permission to use material from this text or product,
submit all requests online at **www.cengage.com/permissions.**
Further permissions questions can be emailed to
permissionrequest@cengage.com.

Library of Congress Control Number: 2011945793

ISBN-13: 978-1-133-30847-8

ISBN-10: 1-133-30847-3

Wadsworth
20 Channel Center Street
Boston, MA 02210
USA

Cengage Learning is a leading provider of customized learning solutions with office locations around the globe, including Singapore, the United Kingdom, Australia, Mexico, Brazil and Japan. Locate your local office at **international.cengage.com/region.**

Cengage Learning products are represented in Canada by Nelson Education, Ltd.

Cengage Learning products are represented in high schools by Holt McDougal, a division of Houghton Mifflin Harcourt

For your course and learning solutions, visit
www.cengage.com.

To find online supplements and other instructional support, please visit **www.cengagebrain.com.**

Instructors: Please visit **login.cengage.com** and log in to access instructor-specific resources.

Printed in the United States of America
2 3 4 5 6 7 16 15 14 13 12

*This edition is dedicated to the teachers who will illumine
its content with their wisdom as they interact with students.*

Jo Ray Metherell and Anthony C. Winkler

Contents

4 The Writer's Voice   95

7 Developing Good Paragraphs   202

11 Illustration/Exemplification 370

12 Definition   409

13 Comparison/Contrast   456

14 Division/Classification   510

PART THREE
Rewriting Your Writing   693

The Editing Booth   695

PART FOUR
Special Writing Projects   719

Thematic
Table of Contents

● Literature and the Arts

● Man and Woman

● Philosophy and Religion

● Portrait of the Individual

● Science

● Social Problems

● Thinking

Preface

Since its first publication in 1974, *Readings for Writers* has established a strong track record. To think that in its first edition students were admonished that if they were writing their research papers in ink, they should make sure that their penmanship was legible makes one titter or chuckle. In those days, many students thought they were using advanced technology if they used electric typewriters. You get the picture. Originally, *Readings for Writers* was meant to be the companion reader to a textbook on rhetoric. But something about this reader struck an instant chord with its audience, and before the first year's sales were even added up, it was obvious to the publisher that "the tail was wagging the dog." The two books remained joined through several more editions, when the number of sales of the reader forced them apart. Gradually, the rhetoric was absorbed into the reader as the authors focused on the newest approaches to the process of writing. Thus, you are now looking at the fourteenth edition of the reader.

The main reason that *Readings for Writers* has held its own for so long in the highly competitive and volatile market of English composition textbooks is the way the book combines the process of writing with a huge variety of anthologized material to serve as models and inspiration for fledgling writers. There is something in this book for every conceivable taste. Along the way, *Readings for Writers* also offers clear guidelines to critical thinking and to the recursive and laborious process of writing and rewriting. We warn students that learning the craft of good writing is not easy, but it is possible and necessary to success in most careers.

Readings for Writers provides a taste of all kinds of brilliant writing—literary classics, poems, speeches, narratives, and philosophy. Here William Shakespeare and Henry David Thoreau mingle with Martin Luther King and William Golding. The aristocrat Sir Arthur Grimble mixes with the felon Jimmy Santiago Baca. We respect and challenge each one of them. All of the anthologized material is brought together and ordered under the headings of either *advice* or *examples,* giving students, as well as teachers, an idea of the practical emphasis of each selection. It is this unique structure, range of readings, and multifaceted appeal to every conceivable taste that have endowed *Readings for Writers* with its remarkable longevity.

New to This Edition

This **new fourteenth edition** preserves the best features of the previous editions while adding the following items to intrigue teachers and students:

- In Part I, we have added a new Chapter 3, "Synthesis: Incorporating Outside Sources." This new chapter offers students ample practice in effectively synthesizing outside sources, providing numerous models and exercises as well as an extensive synthesis essay assignment that engage students with a range of source materials. This new chapter introduces students to the concepts and skills they will need to do well on the synthesis question of the AP* exam. Along with the rhetoric chapter in Part I and the argumentation chapter in Part II, these three chapters cover the concepts that students need for the three AP* essays on the exam. Throughout Part I, we have deleted unnecessary bulk, but we have expanded the sections on critical thinking and the importance of grammar. We have added or replaced exercises as needed.

- In Part II, we have replaced twelve professional essays with new or updated selections.
- In Part II, we have updated the *Issues for Critical Thinking and Debate* and replaced the following issues:
  1. "Body image," replaced by "Self-image."
  2. "Drug abuse," expanded to "Drugs and society."
  3. "The existence of heaven," replaced by "Online dating."

These new selections also give the students practice in comparing and analyzing differing points of view.

- We have replaced five student essays.
- Throughout the book, we have sprinkled in a new feature titled "Pointer from a Pro" to give students some general advice, written in the language of writers who have perfected their craft—a new teaching prompt that is practical as well as enjoyable.
- In the Image Gallery, we have updated or changed the images where necessary. New images correspond with the new topics explored in the *Issues for Critical Thinking and Debate* in Part II.
- In Part IV, we have updated coverage of MLA and APA documentation styles, helping students correctly apply the latest citation guidelines when writing in various disciplines. We have also replaced the student research paper based on MLA guidelines and added appropriate new annotations. This new paper deals with one of the latest and most influential Internet inventions, the Google Library.
- We have updated or changed the chapter images, including the cartoons, where necessary.

Unchanged in This Edition

For those longtime users of *Readings for Writers* who are worried that we have made too many radical changes and that they will be forced to re-tool their syllabi, let

---

*AP and Advanced Placement Program are registered trademarks of the College Entrance Examination Board, which was not involved in the production of, and does not endorse, this product.

us reassure them that this is not the case as the basic structure and intent of the book remain unchanged.

- Unchanged is the unique labeling system that identifies the intended function of every anthologized piece as either giving **advice** about some fundamental principle of writing or as serving as **examples** of it.
- Unchanged is the broad sweep of topics, styles, and arguments of the included works.
- Unchanged is the popular "Student Corner," which showcases the essays of actual   students, along with their commentary on how they learned to write and the personal tips they offer composition students.
- Unchanged is the "Punctuation Workshop" that drills students in the use of the most common punctuation marks, such as the comma, semicolon, dash, and colon.
- Unchanged is the "Rhetorical Thumbnail," which sketches out the major considerations that went into the writing of the selections.
- Unchanged are the quirky little prompts that send students to the popular "Editing Booth" with its checklist of fundamental rules for editing.
- Each anthologized piece is still followed by key vocabulary terms as well as questions about the Facts, Strategies, and Issues explored, and is bolstered by suggestions for writing.
- Each chapter still ends with Chapter Writing Assignments, Writing Assignments for a Specific Audience, and an Image Gallery Assignment.

All of the changes in this fourteenth edition have one unmistakable aim: to make *Readings for Writers* even easier and more practical to use than before. Combining the advice of its anthologized experts with the authors' commentary, *Readings for Writers* can still be used unaccompanied by any other book.

Ancillaries

- **The Heinle Original Film Series in Literature DVD**—This DVD includes three short films. The first film, Eudora Welty's *A Worn Path*, includes an interview with Eudora Welty conducted by Pulitzer Prize–winning playwright Beth Henley. The second film, John Updike's *A&P*, includes an interview with John Updike conducted by Pulitzer Prize–winning writer Donald Murray. The final film, Raymond Carver's *Cathedral*, includes an interview with Raymond Carver's widow, Tess Gallagher, conducted by Carver scholars William Stull and Maureen P. Carroll.
- **Instructor's Manual**—Prepare for class more quickly and effectively with such resources as suggestions for lively classroom discussion and possible answers to the questions posed at the end of the readings and the Image Gallery

- **Resources for Writers**—Resources for Writers offers a variety of online activities for students to practice and refine their understanding of key concepts via interactive grammar and proofreading exercises, anti-plagiarism tutorials, writing and research modules, multimedia activities, and downloadable grammar podcasts.

- *Salvation* **by Langston Hughes (DVD): The Wadsworth Original Film Series in Literature**—Based on a chapter from Langston Hughes's autobiography, *The Big Sea, Salvation* stars Lou Beatty, Jr., and Ella Joyce. The video also includes interviews with Alice Walker, the novelist, and Arnold Rampersad, the foremost authority on Langston Hughes.

- *Fast Track to a 5:* *Preparing for the AP* English Language and Composition Examination*—This test-preparation guide includes an introduction on taking the exam, a vocabulary of literary terms, detailed preparation guidelines for each type of question found on the exam, and two complete practice exams. Written by Steve Olson and Eveline Bailey, both of La Porte High School, La Porte, Texas.

—For AP* teachers, this book contains 500 multiple-choice practice questions for use in helping students prepare for the exam. Written by Theresa Kanu, Alexander W. Dreyfoos School of the Arts, West Palm Beach, Florida; Carole Hamilton, Cary Academy, Cary, North Carolina; and several contributors.

The Journey Ahead

Learning to write well is comparable to taking a journey. Students travel from topic to topic—picking up tips and techniques as they go, meeting new writers whose art they can study and perhaps try to imitate. If there were a metaphorical equivalent for this book, it would be a field trip, where students learn by observing and by practicing what they have learned. Along the way, we send students to some editing workshops and guide their steps along various road signs, indicating the directions they are to follow. Think of this book, then, not merely as a text with the usual implications of dryness that the word suggests, but as a road map that will rush students off to far-flung destinations and then take them back to their own backyards as better writers than they were when they began.

Acknowledgments

A textbook is always a collaborative work. Many people—including editors, proofreaders, fact checkers, and various supporting personnel—contribute their skills and insights into making a book of this sort what it finally becomes. We thank them all for sharing their minds and talents with us and for making themselves available to us any time we needed them. Specifically, we would like to thank our editor, Karen Mauk, for encouraging us to keep to our time line and for her careful attention to detail, which often included helping us find material we needed and keeping us organized. A special measure of appreciation goes to Gaen Murphree, who wrote Chapter 3 to help students understand, evaluate, and synthesize out-side sources and to successfully incorporate them into their own writing. Her thoughtful expertise has enhanced this textbook. We also wish to thank the fol-lowing strong advisors and providers: Lyn Uhl, Senior Publisher; Kate Derrick, Acquiring Sponsoring Editor; Leslie Taggart, Senior Development Editor; Aimee Chevrette Bear, Content Project Manager; and Stacey Purviance, Executive Mar-keting Manager.

We would like to also gratefully acknowledge those reviewers who helped shape this edition:

Roseanna Almaee, *Darton College*
Daniel Bartlett, *Lamar University*
David Beveridge, *Butte College*
Shelley Bingham, *Darton College*
Rob Blain, *Houston Community College*
Gricelle Cano, *Houston Community College, Southeast*
Helen Ceraldi, *North Lake Community College*
Constance Christophersen, *Homestead High School*
Linda Cohen, *Bridgewater State University*
Eric Decker, *John Marshall High School*
Jane Gamber, *Hutchinson Community College*
Amy Habberstad, *South Anchorage High School*
Mark Howland, *Tabor Academy*
Ferdinand Hunter, *Gateway Community College*
Erica Lara, *Southwest Texas Junior College*
Christine Long, *Bellbrook High School*
Julie Long, *College of the Albemarle*
Caroline Mains, *Palo Alto College*
Deborah Manson, *Georgia Perimeter College*
Shawn Miller, *Francis Marion University*
Vicki Moulson, *College of the Albemarle*
Maureen O'Bryan, *Effingham County High School*
Erika Olsen, *NHTI*
Jamie Pickering, *Pinnacle High School*
Maria Rankin-Brown, *Pacific Union College*
Suzanna Riordan, *Baruch College*
Jill Silos, *Hesser College*
Tina Smith, *West High School*
Michael Sollars, *Texas Southern University*
Valerie Stevenson, *Patrick Henry High School*
Mary Ann Sullivan, *Hesser College*

Andrew Tomko, *Bergen Community College*
Kamana Tshibengabo, *Georgia Perimeter College, Newton*
Victor Uszerowicz, *Miami-Dade College*
Bradley Waltman, *Community College of Southern Nevada*
Bradley Waltman, *Darton College*
Mark Weber, *Buffalo State College*
Lewis Whitaker, *Georgia Perimeter College*
John Williamson, *Highlands High School*
Theodore Worozbyt, *Georgia Perimeter College, Newton*
Anita Wyman, *Hillsborough Community College*
Diana Yeager, *Hillsborough Community College*

Finally, we thank the members of our Advanced Placement advisory board, who offered valuable input for this edition:

Patricia Bond, *Shonomish High School*
John Brassil, *Mt. Ararat High School*
Patricia Cain, *Pasadena Memorial High School*
Debbie Engler, *Llano High School*
Steve Klinge, *Archmere Academy*
Joanne Krajeck, *Canton South High School*
Tania K. Lyon, *Mankato West High School*
Jason P. Thibodeaux, *Westminster Christian Academy*

Jo Ray McCuen-Metherell and
Anthony C. Winkler

PART ONE

Reading and Writing
From Reading to Writing

A veteran English teacher once remarked to us that she had known readers who were not writers, but she had never known writers who were not readers. Neither have we. All writers begin as eager readers and continue to read throughout their lives. Their lifelong pleasure in reading wanes only in the presence of the greater pleasure they take in writing.

You may not be a writer in the sense of making a living from what you write, and you may not even write every day. But like it or not, you read every day, even if it is nothing more than the sign on a passing bus or the words on a billboard. Unless you live in a cave or on a desert island, modern life compels you to read.

All of us begin life as nonreaders. Reading is a skill that is learned in childhood and shapes the growth of our intellect in ways that are still not completely understood. And even though we might have learned to read under peculiarly similar or different conditions, we all more or less share a similar reading history.

It began with the delight we felt when we first were taught to read. And once we were able to read on our own, many of us found ourselves swept away into magical worlds. Books took us on exotic journeys to places that existed only on the page and in our heads. We were visited by cats wearing hats, by talking rabbits, and by children who never grow old. We walked down yellow brick roads, sailed a balloon to the moon, and traveled with a crusty pirate in search of buried treasure on a remote island. Reading had planted in our heads a delightful high-definition TV called *imagination*, and never were colors brighter or images sharper.

But as we grew older, a curious thing happened: Reading became associated with schoolwork as we were forced to read textbooks we disliked on subjects we hated. The very act of opening a book became a labor. Soon we were watching television to relax and reading only when we had to because of schoolwork. For many, reading changed from fun to drudgery. A lucky few retained a deep love of reading and will continue throughout their lives to read for fun. Speaking for them, the famous eighteenth-century British historian Edward Gibbon wrote in his *Memoirs*: "My early and invincible love of reading, I would not exchange for the treasures of India."

If you wish to write, you should develop the habit of reading. The skill of writing well is essentially a kind of mimicry, and the more writers we read, the more examples we can choose to imitate. And although reading voraciously is no guarantee that you will write well, your writing is likely to get better if you continue to be an avid reader.

The first part of this book—*Reading and Writing*—covers the preliminary topics of a writing course. Chapter 1 covers critical reading and introduces us to one of America's most prolific writers, himself an avid reader who devoured hundreds of books each year. Chapter 2 examines the role of rhetoric, an ancient discipline that is much misunderstood today. Chapter 3 illumines the weighty skill of synthesis—that is, imbedding other writers' ideas into your own work, Chapter 4 covers the writer's voice, while Chapters 5, 6, and 7 deal first with the nuts and bolts of choosing a thesis topic and organizing a paper, and then with the indispensable craft of paragraph writing.

Among the lessons Part One teaches is this: Writing is not an isolated skill that exists apart from the intellect of the individual. It is, instead, ingrained in the whole person. Read widely and your writing is likely to get better as your judgment of good writing matures. You are also likely to rediscover pleasures you once derived from memorable storybooks—pleasures that have no box office charge, no crowds, and require no hardware more elaborate than a library card.

1

Reading Critically

KINDS OF READING

There are at least four different kinds of reading. *Casual reading* is the most common. Everyone does it. The casual reader glances at magazines, newspaper headlines, letters, email messages, and roadside signs. Casual readers read not because they want to, but because they must. Many people, if not most, fall into this category.

Reading for pleasure—whether mystery novels, romances, or tales of adventure—is the second common kind of reading. Reading of this kind is relaxed and uncritical. Many readers do it at bedtime to help them fall asleep. Pleasure readers don't worry about grasping the writer's full meaning as long as they get the gist of it and are transported by the writing to an imaginary world.

Reading for information, the third kind of reading, is practiced by information seekers who use reading as a tool. This type of reading is usually done at work or at school. Doing a job well or completing an assignment on schedule is the primary purpose of reading for information. This type of reading requires attention, understanding, and memorization.

Finally, there is *critical reading*—the kind of reading you must do for your college classes and the kind we shall emphasize throughout this book. Critical reading is active reading. You engage in a kind of mental dialogue with the writer. The writer says so-and-so is the case and you reply, "Maybe so, but what about this?" You annotate the margins of the book you're reading with your reactions and comments. You not only try to understand the author's main point, but you also try to deduce any consequences of it. Teachers and parents are forever muttering that students can't read well—that they know what the words say, but they don't know what the words mean. Energetic curriculum creators, abhorring this vacuum in students' minds, recently jumped into the fray and designed freshman composition courses that would encourage students to read critically. So what is critical reading? One way to explain it is to say what it is not. Critical reading is not gullibility—accepting as truth anything you read.

1. **Analysis.** First, students are encouraged to analyze their reading so as to see how ideas are composed, how they are connected to other ideas, and how

they are often based on biases and prejudices. In research, it means to gather numerous sources that support a point. For instance, a student writing a paper on the results of online dating will need to explore journals, books, and Internet sources to see what marriage counselors, psychologists, and ordinary people have reported about online romances and what opinions they have offered on the subject.

2. **Synthesis.** Next, students are encouraged to *synthesize*, which means to absorb or blend the ideas analyzed and forge something new and original—belonging to them alone and reflecting the student's mind. In other words, the critical reader will form his own opinion after studying the opinions of other thinkers. This reaching out for new data from new sources can send students on highly exotic adventures. However, the best part about synthesis is that it tampers down the students' arrogance by demonstrating that on most knotty subjects, more than a single opinion exists. For instance, on the subject of online dating, a student will find through research that while online dating is growing at an amazing speed, with thousands of single men and women placing their profiles on the Internet, the results are not consistent. Some couples are finding a harmonious and lasting relationship, but others discover only sexual chaos and even dangerous liaisons. A student reading on the subject must take into account various attitudes or findings, not just one.

3. **Evaluation.** The final step in critical thinking is to *evaluate*. This step is extremely important because what it does is give students the power to assess and grade the material read. After probing ideas that are for or against a point of view, the student finally must take sides. Is online dating the best answer to finding a mate, or is it hazardous? The student's conclusion might well be that more study on the subject is needed before anyone can state with certainty that marriages arranged through the computer are either good or bad. As one teacher lectured to her class: "Blessed are they who walk in the middle of the road, for they shall avoid extremes."

Throughout this book, we shall encourage you to read critically and to form an educated opinion on various controversies. Should the retirement age be raised to 70, or should it remain at 65? Should the United States continue to spend billions of dollars on foreign aid, or should we use the money to solve our own problems? Should we create a path to citizenship for illegal aliens or should we have them deported? These are topics on which writers disagree, and critical reading will offer you the chance to place your own weight on the seesaw. In a way, this is a complete reversal of teacher-student roles because critical reading requires that students think on their own. Now, not all college professors approve of critical thinking. In fact, some few consider it dangerous because they worry that it invites students to pass judgment on whether they should accept or reject all ideas they confront—even time-honored truths. A few critics believe that within critical thinking lie the germs of revolution, as in the French and American Revolution, Tiananmen Square, Kent State, the 1963 march on Washington, and the Tea Party movement. Fear mongering professors worry that students will ask questions such as these: "Is this class important?" "Does anyone see an inconsistency in this university's policy?" "Why should I conform?" "Shouldn't I be allowed to think on my own and make my own rules?"

This book considers critical reading a boon, not a bane. One of our goals is to have all students using this book learn how to solve problems by shining the beam of analysis on them—to take the facts and compare them with other facts in order to extract (synthesize) the truth. We believe that you are qualified to see the historical and cultural contexts of what you read. With experience, you will realize that you cannot allow your personal experience to judge everything you read, but you must see facts in the appropriate context in which they appear. For instance, if a Libertarian insists that the local fire and police departments should be run by a private owner, you have to understand that Libertarians believe, for better or for worse, that the less the government is involved in our lives, the more we shall flourish. Conversely, if some cultural progressive insists that the government must take care of all of the poor and the weak, you have to understand that progressives encourage government spending, especially on the dispossessed. Regardless of where a writer stands on an issue, you will become a better writer yourself if you read critically. The following guidelines will help you form the correct approach to reading critically.

Steps to Critical Reading

1. **Read actively.** Determine the author's main point as well as any secondary effects that stem from it. Ask yourself whether you agree or disagree with the author's opinions. If you disagree, make a note in the margin saying why. If the author makes a mistake of logic or fact, make a note on the page where it occurred.

2. **Demystify the writer.** Many of us have the tendency to regard writers as godlike and to take everything they say as gospel. But writers are only human and are just as likely to make mistakes as anyone else. Reading critically begins with kicking the writer off the throne of public esteem and regarding the writer's work as you would any other human production—which is to say, prone to error.

3. **Understand what you read.** Reread difficult passages, looking up in a dictionary all the unfamiliar words. You cannot form an opinion about what you have read unless you understand what the author is saying. Some students find it helpful to summarize aloud any difficult ideas they encounter. Reread any difficult chapter or essay whose meaning you didn't completely comprehend. A difficult-to-understand point usually seems clearer the second time around. For example, Tolstoy's massive novel *War and Peace,* on first reading, seems like a tangled plot cluttered by an overwhelming mass of scenes and characters. On second reading, however, the plot will seem clearer and the scenes and characters more understandable.

4. **Imagine an opposing point of view for all opinions.** If the writer says that the Arab punishment of cutting off the hands of a thief is more humane than the American system of imprisonment, reverse the argument and see what happens. In other words, look for reasons that support the other side. For example, if an essayist is passionately against the use of dogs in medical research, try to see the opposing point of view—namely, the benefits of such research to the lives of millions who suffer from terrible diseases. A little digging will reveal that insulin, the use of which has prolonged the lives of millions of diabetics, was discovered through research on dogs. The argument boils down to this question: Does a puppy have the same worth as a human baby?

5. **Look for biases and hidden assumptions.** For example, an atheist arguing for abortion will not attribute a soul to the unborn fetus; a devout Catholic will. To ferret out possible biases and hidden assumptions, check the author's age, sex, education, and ethnic background. These and other personal biographical facts might have influenced the opinions expressed in the work, but you cannot know to what extent unless you know something about the author. (That is the rationale behind the use of biographical headnotes, which accompany the readings in this book.)

6. **Separate emotion from fact.** Talented writers frequently color an issue with emotionally charged language, thus casting their opinions in the best possible light. For example, a condemned murderer may be described in sympathetic language that draws attention away from his or her horrifying crime. Be alert to sloganeering, to bumper-sticker philosophizing about complex issues. To the neutral observer, few issues are as simple as black and white. Abortion is a more complex issue than either side presents. Capital punishment is not simply a matter of vengeance versus mercy. The tendency in public debate is to demonize the opposition and reduce issues to emotional slogans. As a critical reader, you must evaluate an argument by applying logic and reason and not be swayed by the emotionality of either side.

7. **If the issue is new to you, look up the facts.** If you are reading about an unfamiliar issue, be willing to fill in the gaps in your knowledge with research. For example, if you are reading an editorial that proposes raising home insurance rates for families taking care of foster children, you will want to know why. Is it because foster children do more property damage than other children? Is it because natural parents are apt to file lawsuits against foster parents? You can find answers to these questions by asking representatives of the affected parties: The State Department of Social Services, typical insurance agencies, foster parents associations, the county welfare directors association, any children's lobby, and others. To make a critical judgment you must know, and carefully weigh, the facts.

8. **Use insights from one subject to illuminate or correct another.** Be prepared to apply what you already know to whatever you read. History can inform psychology; literature can provide insights into geography. For example, if a writer in psychology argues that most oppressed people develop

a defeatist air that gives them a subconscious desire to be subjugated and makes them prey to tyrants, your knowledge of American history should tell you otherwise. As proof that oppressed people often fight oppression unto death, you can point to the Battle of Fallen Timbers in 1794, to the Battle of Tippecanoe in 1811, and to the Black Hawk War of 1832—conflicts in which the Indians fought desperately to retain their territories rather than go meekly to the reservations. In other words, you can use what you have learned from history to refute a falsehood from psychology.

9. **Evaluate the evidence.** Critical readers do not accept evidence at face value. They question its source, its verifiability, its appropriateness. Here are some practical tips for evaluating evidence:

   • **Verify a questionable opinion by cross-checking with other sources.** For example, if a medical writer argues that heavy smoking tends to cause serious bladder diseases in males, check the medical journals for confirmation of this view. Diligent research often turns up a consensus of opinion among the experts in any field.

   • **Check the date of the evidence.** In science especially, evidence varies from year to year. Before 1987, no one really knew exactly how the immune system worked. Then Susumu Tonegawa, a geneticist at the Massachusetts Institute of Technology, discovered how the immune system protects the body from foreign substances by manufacturing antibodies. In 1980, the evidence would say that the working of the immune system was a mystery, but that evidence would be inaccurate in 1987.

   • **Use common sense in evaluating evidence.** For example, if a writer argues that a child's handwriting can accurately predict his or her life as an adult, your own experience with human nature should lead you to reject this conclusion as speculative. No convincing evidence exists to corroborate it.

10. **Ponder the values behind a claim.** In writing the Declaration of Independence, Thomas Jefferson based his arguments on the value that "all men are created equal." On the other hand, Karl Marx based the arguments of his *Communist Manifesto* on the value that the laborer is society's greatest good. Critical reading means thinking about the values implicit in an argument. For instance, to argue that murderers should be hanged in public to satisfy society's need for revenge is to value revenge over human dignity. On the other hand, to argue that democracy can exist only with free speech is to value freedom of speech.

11. **Recognize logical fallacies.** Logic is not interested in the truth or falsehood of a claim. It is only interested in the method used to reach certain conclusions. Consider this train of thought: "All Italians are musical. Luigi is Italian, therefore Luigi must be musical." It is perfectly logical, but we know that it is not true because the major premise "All Italians are musical" is not true. We have all known Italians who can't sing a note. In other words, sometimes a claim is supported by evidence, but sometimes it is not. Being logical does

not guarantee being right, but avoiding logical fallacies is a requirement of critical thinking. The following logical flaws are among the ones most commonly used in a wide range of arguments: the *ad hominem* attack (attacking the person instead of the point of view or the argument); the *ad populum* appeal (the use of simplistic popular slogans to convince); the *false analogy* (comparing situations that have no bearing on each other); *begging the question* (arguing in circles); *ignoring the question* (focusing on matters that are beside the point); *either/or reasoning* (seeing the problem as all black or all white, with no shades of gray); *hasty generalization* (the mistake of inadequate sampling); and *non sequitur* (drawing a conclusion that is not connected to the evidence given). For a more detailed discussion of logical fallacies, turn to Chapter 16.

12. **Don't be seduced by bogus claims.** Arguments are often based on unsubstantiated statements. For example, a writer may warn that "Recent studies show women becoming increasingly hostile to men." Or, another writer might announce, "Statistics have shown beyond doubt that most well-educated males oppose gun control." You should always remain skeptical of these and similar claims when they are unaccompanied by hardheaded evidence. A proper claim will always be documented with verifiable evidence.

13. **Annotate your reading.** Many of us have the tendency to become lazy readers. We sit back with a book and almost immediately lapse into a daze. One way to avoid being a lazy reader is to annotate your reading—to write notes in the margins as you read. Many students are reluctant to scribble in the margins of a book because they hope to resell it at the end of the term. But this is a penny-wise-and-pound-foolish outlook. Instead of aiming to resell the book, your focus should be on getting the most out of it; annotating is one way to do that. Indeed, to make notes in the margins of books is, in a way, to interact with the reading—almost like chatting with the author. If you can't bring yourself to write directly on the printed page of this book, we suggest you make notes on a separate sheet as you read. Here are some suggestions for annotating your reading:

- **Write down your immediate impression of the essay**.
    a. Did the subject interest you?
    b. Did the reading leave you inspired, worried, angry, amused, or better informed?
    c. Did the reading remind you of something in your own experience? (Cite the experience.)
    d. Did you agree or disagree with the author? (Note specific passages.)
    e. Did the reading give you any new ideas?
- **Note the author's style, especially the words or expressions used**.
    a. What specific passages really made you think?
    b. Where did the writer use an especially apt expression or image? What was it? What made it so good?
    c. Where, if any place, did the author write "over your head"?

d. What kind of audience did the author seem to address? Did it include you or did you feel left out?

- **Make marginal notes that express your response to the author's ideas.**

  a. Supplement the author's idea or example with one of your own.

  b. Underline passages that seem essential to the author's point.

  c. Write any questions you might want to ask the author if he or she were sitting next to you.

  d. Write down any sudden insight you experienced.

  e. Write why you disagree with the author.

  f. Write a marginal explanation of any allusion made by the writer. For example, in the fourth paragraph of this chapter, we wrote, "We were visited by cats wearing hats, by talking rabbits, and by children who never grow old." Did you understand these three allusions? The first is a reference to *The Cat in the Hat* by Dr. Seuss; the second, to *Alice in Wonderland*; the third, to *Peter Pan*.

14. **Finally, be sure you understand the writer's opening context.** The writing may be part of an ongoing debate that began before you arrived and will continue after you've left. Some essays begin by plunging right into an ongoing discussion, taking for granted that the reader is familiar with the opening context. The effect can be mystifying, like hearing an answer but not knowing the question.

Here are the principles of critical reading applied to a brief essay by CBS News commentator Andy Rooney. The annotations in the margins raise questions that we think any reasonable critical reader would ask. At the end of the essay, we provide the answers.

1. What is the opening context of this article?

1   I would choose to have written Fowler's *Modern English Usage*.

2   My book, known far and wide and for all time as Rooney's *Modern English Usage* and comparable in sales to the Bible, would have assured my fame and fortune. Even more than that, if I'd had the kind of command of the language it would take to have written it, I would never again be uncertain about whether to use *further* or *farther*, *hung* or *hanged*, *dived* or *dove*. When I felt lousy and wanted to write about it, I'd know whether to say I felt *nauseous* or *nauseated*.

2. Who is Fowler?

3. What is his book about?

3   If I was the intellectual guru of grammar, as author of that tome, I would issue updated decrees on usage such as an end to the pretentious subjunctive. Not if I were.

4. What do we learn about Fowler's book in this paragraph?

4   I would split infinitives at will when I damn well felt like it, secure in my knowledge that I was setting the standard for when to and when not to. Challenged by some petty grammarian quoting a high school English textbook, I would quote myself and say, as Fowler does, "Those upon whom the fear of infinitive-splitting sits heavy should remember that to give conclusive evidence, by distortions, of misconceiving the nature of the split infinitive is far more damaging to their literary pretensions than an actual lapse could be, for it exhibits them as deaf to the normal rhythm of English sentences."

5. What is Rooney doing here?

5   Never again would I suffer indecision over matters like whether it was necessary for me to use an "of" after "apropos." I would not be looking up "arcane" eight or ten times a year. I would not use "like" when I meant "such as."

6. What does this quotation tell us about Fowler?

6   The fine difference between sophisticated bits of usage such as syllepsis and zeugma would be clear in my mind. ("She ate an omelet and her heart out" is either syllepsis or zeugma. I am unclear which.)

7. What do these terms mean?

7   Having produced the best book on English usage ever written, I would berate the editors of the newly issued *New York Times Manual of Style and Usage* for their insistence that the President of the United States be referred to as merely president except when used as a title immediately preceding his name. In my book he's The President. Corporate chief executives are plain president.

8. What is the best book ever written on English usage?

8   I would conduct a nationwide poll to choose a satisfactory gender neutral replacement for both "he," "she," "him," and "her." This would relieve writers of the cumbersome but socially correct necessity of "he or she," "him or her," or the grammatically incorrect "they" or "their" with a singular precedent. ("Someone left their keys.")

9. What does this paragraph mean?

9   Eventually, I'd expect Oliver Stone to buy the movie rights to Rooney's *Modern English Usage*. His film would prove it was neither I nor me who murdered the English language.

10. What is the significance of either "I nor me"?

Answers to Critical Reading Questions on Andy Rooney

1. If you do not know the opening context of this essay, you're likely to miss the writer's intent—although you could probably reconstruct it from his essay. Rooney's essay initially appeared in the 2000 annual awards issue of the *Journal of the Screenwriters' Guild* as part of a feature called *A Writer's Fantasy— What I Wish I Had Written*. Various writers, Rooney among them, were asked to select the one work they wish they had written and say why.

2. Henry Watson Fowler (1858–1933) was an English lexicographer and philologist—someone who studies linguistics—who, in collaboration with his younger brother Frank, published in 1906 *The King's English*, a witty book on English usage and misusage. After the death of his brother, Fowler completed the classic Rooney wished he had written, *A Dictionary of Modern English Usage* (1926). Fowler was known for being definitive and blunt in his grammatical and literary opinions.

   He wrote, "Anyone who wishes to become a good writer should endeavor, before he allows himself to be tempted by the more showy qualities, to be direct, simple, brief, vigorous, and lucid"—certainly good advice for anyone who writes.

3. Many people consider *A Dictionary of Modern English Usage* to be the definitive book on English usage and grammar. Grammarians often consult it to settle arguments over the fine points of acceptable usage.

4. We learn in this paragraph that Fowler's book sold as well as the Bible and that its popularity ensured fame and fortune to its writer.

5. He's mocking the rule of the subjunctive, which many people think is an ugly Latin holdover.

6. It gives us a glimpse of the sometimes starchy writing style of Fowler, who is capable of going from clarity and plainness to a scholastic denseness in a single page.

7. These are examples of the kind of arcane topics that Fowler deals with in his book. *Syllepsis* refers to the use of a word in the same grammatical relationship with two other words while disagreeing in case, gender, number, or sense with one of them. An example is "Neither she nor they are coming," where *are* agrees with *they* but not with *she*. Syllepsis is also a figure of speech in which a single word is linked to two others but in different senses, as in this use of *write:* "I write with enthusiasm and a pen." *Zeugma* refers to the linking of one word to two, one of which it does not grammatically fit, as in this use of *were:* "The seeds were devoured but the banana uneaten."

8. Obviously Fowler's, in Rooney's opinion.

9. Rooney is referring here to the quest for a nonsexist, third-person pronoun so that a sentence like "A doctor should take care of his patients" can be written without the sexist bias implicit in the use of "his." In 1858, Charles Crozat Converse, of Erie, Pennsylvania, proposed the use of *thon,* a shortened form of *that one,* as a neutral, third-person pronoun—"A doctor should take care of thon patients"—but the word never caught on.

10. Again, Rooney is spoofing another fusty rule from English grammar—namely, that the verb "to be" takes no object. Rigorous practice of this rule is responsible for the snooty construction one hears over the telephone occasionally: "It is I" or "This is he."

Hidden within Technology's Empire, a Republic of Letters

SAUL BELLOW

Rhetorical Thumbnail

Purpose: to convince us that more people read than we realize

Audience: educated readers

Language: standard English

Strategy: to cite evidence of readership

Saul Bellow (1915–2005), an American author of novels, essays, and dramas, was born in Quebec of Jewish Russian immigrant parents. As a child, Bellow studied French and Hebrew as well as English. When he was nine, his family moved to Chicago, a city to which he remained devoted throughout his long writing career. His first two novels were autobiographical: *Dangling Man* (1944) and *The Victim* (1947). After World War II, he joined the top ranks of fiction writers with the publication of his picaresque novel about a Jewish boy growing up in Chicago, *The Adventures of Augie March* (1953), which was much admired for its comic zest. His 1955 novel *Humboldt's Gift* (1955) won him a Pulitzer and Nobel Prize.

If you have been tempted to wait until a new novel comes out as a movie so that you can watch it on the screen rather than thumbing through the pages of a book, rethink your outlook and continue to discover the age-old pleasure of reading. You might be in a social minority, but you will be enriched. Also, remember that most good writers are also good readers.

• • •

1   When I was a boy "discovering literature," I used to think how wonderful it would be if every other person on the street were familiar with Proust and Joyce or T. E. Lawrence or Pasternak and Kafka. Later I learned how refractory to high culture the democratic masses were. Lincoln as a young frontiersman read Plutarch, Shakespeare and the Bible. But then he was Lincoln.

2   Later when I was traveling in the Midwest by car, bus and train, I regularly visited small-town libraries and found that readers in Keokuk, Iowa, or Benton Harbor, Michigan, were checking out Proust and Joyce and even Svevo and

Andrey Bely. D. H. Lawrence was also a favorite. And sometimes I remembered that God was willing to spare Sodom for the sake of ten of the righteous. Not that Keokuk was anything like wicked Sodom, or that Proust's Charlus would have been tempted to settle in Benton Harbor, Michigan. I seem to have had a persistent democratic desire to find evidences of high culture in the most unlikely places.

3   For many decades now I have been a fiction writer, and from the first I was aware that mine was a questionable occupation. In the 1930s an elderly neighbor in Chicago told me that he wrote fiction for the pulps. "The people on the block wonder why I don't go to a job, and I'm seen puttering around, trimming the bushes or painting a fence instead of working in a factory. But I'm a writer. I sell to *Argosy* and *Doc Savage*," he said with a certain gloom. "They wouldn't call that a trade." Probably he noticed that I was a bookish boy, likely to sympathize with him, and perhaps he was trying to warn me to avoid being unlike others. But it was too late for that.

4   From the first, too, I had been warned that the novel was at the point of death, that like the walled city or the crossbow, it was a thing of the past. And no one likes to be at odds with history. Oswald Spengler, one of the most widely read authors of the early '30s, taught that our tired old civilization was very nearly finished. His advice to the young was to avoid literature and the arts and to embrace mechanization and become engineers.

5   In refusing to be obsolete, you challenged and defied the evolutionist historians. I had great respect for Spengler in my youth, but even then I couldn't accept his conclusions, and (with respect and admiration) I mentally told him to get lost.

6   Sixty years later, in a recent issue of the *Wall Street Journal*, I come upon the old Spenglerian argument in a contemporary form. Terry Teachout, unlike Spengler, does not dump paralyzing mountains of historical theory upon us, but there are signs that he has weighed, sifted and pondered the evidence.

7   He speaks of our "atomized culture," and his is a responsible, up-to-date and carefully considered opinion. He speaks of "art forms as technologies." He tells us that movies will soon be "downloadable"—that is, transferable from one computer to the memory of another device—and predicts that films will soon be marketed like books. He predicts that the near-magical powers of technology are bringing us to the threshold of a new age and concludes, "Once this happens, my guess is that the independent movie will replace the novel as the principal vehicle for serious storytelling in the 21st century."

8   In support of this argument, Teachout cites the ominous drop in the volume of book sales and the great increase in movie attendance: "For Americans under the age of 30, film has replaced the novel as the dominant mode of artistic expression." To this Teachout adds that popular novelists like Tom Clancy and Stephen King "top out at around a million copies per book," and notes, "The final episode of NBC's *Cheers*, by contrast, was seen by 42 million people."

9   On majoritarian grounds, the movies win. "The power of novels to shape the national conversation has declined," says Teachout. But I am not at all certain that in their day *Moby-Dick* or *The Scarlet Letter* had any considerable influence

on "the national conversation." In the mid-nineteenth century it was *Uncle Tom's Cabin* that impressed the great public. *Moby-Dick* was a small-public novel.

10   The literary masterpieces of the twentieth century were for the most part the work of novelists who had no large public in mind. The novels of Proust and Joyce were written in a cultural twilight and were not intended to be read under the blaze and dazzle of popularity.

11   Teachout's article in the *Journal* follows the path generally taken by observers whose aim is to discover a trend. "According to one recent study 55 percent of Americans spend less than 30 minutes reading anything at all . . . It may even be that movies have superseded novels not because Americans have grown dumber but because the novel is an obsolete artistic technology.

12   "We are not accustomed to thinking of art forms as technologies," he says, "but that is what they are, which means they have been rendered moribund by new technical developments."

13   Together with this emphasis on technics that attracts the scientific-minded young, there are other preferences discernible: It is better to do as a majority of your contemporaries are doing, better to be one of millions viewing a film than one of mere thousands reading a book. Moreover, the reader reads in solitude, whereas the viewer belongs to a great majority; he has powers of numerosity as well as the powers of mechanization. Add to this the importance of avoiding technological obsolescence and the attraction of feeling that technics will decide questions for us more dependably than the thinking of an individual, no matter how distinctive he may be.

14   John Cheever told me long ago that it was his readers who kept him going, people from every part of the country who had written to him. When he was at work, he was aware of these readers and correspondents in the woods beyond the lawn. "If I couldn't picture them, I'd be sunk," he said. And the novelist Wright Morris, urging me to get an electric typewriter, said that he seldom turned his machine off. "When I'm not writing, I listen to the electricity," he said. "It keeps me company. We have conversations."

15   I wonder how Teachout might square such idiosyncrasies with his "art forms as technologies." Perhaps he would argue that these two writers had somehow isolated themselves from "broad-based cultural influence." Teachout has at least one laudable purpose: He thinks that he sees a way to bring together the Great Public of the movies with the Small Public of the highbrows. He is, however, interested in millions: millions of dollars, millions of readers, millions of viewers.

16   The one thing "everybody" does is go to the movies, Teachout says. How right he is.

17   Back in the '20s children between the ages of eight and twelve lined up on Saturdays to buy their nickel tickets to see the crisis of last Saturday resolved. The heroine was untied in a matter of seconds just before the locomotive would have crushed her. Then came a new episode; and after that the newsreel and *Our Gang*. Finally there was a western with Tom Mix, or a Janet Gaynor picture about a young bride and her husband blissful in the attic, or Gloria Swanson and Theda Bara or Wallace Beery or Adolphe Menjou or Marie Dressler. And of course there was Charlie Chaplin in *The Gold Rush*, and from *The Gold Rush* it was only one step to the stories of Jack London.

18   There was no rivalry then between the viewer and the reader. Nobody supervised our reading. We were on our own. We civilized ourselves. We found or made a mental and imaginative life. Because we could read, we learned also to write. It did not confuse me to see *Treasure Island* in the movies and then read the book. There was no competition for our attention.

19   One of the more attractive oddities of the United States is that our minorities are so numerous, so huge. A minority of millions is not at all unusual. But there are in fact millions of literate Americans in a state of separation from others of their kind. They are, if you like, the readers of Cheever, a crowd of them too large to be hidden in the woods. Departments of literature across the country have not succeeded in alienating them from books, works old and new. My friend Keith Botsford and I felt strongly that if the woods were filled with readers gone astray, among those readers there were probably writers as well.

20   To learn in detail of their existence you have only to publish a magazine like *The Republic of Letters.* Given encouragement, unknown writers, formerly without hope, materialize. One early reader wrote that our paper, "with its contents so fresh, person-to-person," was "real, non-synthetic, undistracting." Noting that there were no ads, she asked, "Is it possible, can it last?" and called it "an antidote to the shrinking of the human being in every one of us." And toward the end of her letter our correspondent added, "It behooves the elder generation to come up with reminders of who we used to be and need to be."

21   This is what Keith Botsford and I had hoped that our "tabloid for literates" would be. And for two years it has been just that. We are a pair of utopian codgers who feel we have a duty to literature. I hope we are not like those humane do-gooders who, when the horse was vanishing, still donated troughs in City Hall Square for thirsty nags.

22   We have no way of guessing how many independent, self-initiated connoisseurs and lovers of literature have survived in remote corners of the country. The little evidence we have suggests that they are glad to find us, they are grateful. They want more than they are getting. Ingenious technology has failed to give them what they so badly need.

● Vocabulary

refractory (1)	majoritarian (9)	alienating (19)
obsolete (5)	superseded (11)	antidote (20)
evolutionist (5)	discernible (13)	utopian (21)
atomized (7)	numerosity (13)	connoisseurs (22)
vehicle (7)	idiosyncrasies (15)	ingenious (22)

● The Facts

1. What technology does the author emphasize? Why does he place such importance on it?

2. Do you agree with his analysis of its importance? Explain your answer.

3. What statistics does the author use to emphasize his point? Do you believe these statistics still hold true today? Or have they either increased or decreased? Give evidence to support your answer.

4. What does the title of the essay suggest? Give your interpretation of the terms *empire* and *republic* in the context in which they are used.

5. Who are the authors discovered by Bellow when he was young? What characteristics do these authors share? If you have read any of these authors, what do you think of them? Would you recommend them to your friends?

6. In paragraph 9, what does the author say about the movies? Do you agree or disagree with him? Explain your answer.

● The Strategies

1. How does the author begin his essay? What is the purpose of his opening paragraph?

2. What technique used in the essay tells the reader that the writer is a literary person?

3. What evidence does Bellow use to support the argument that art forms are becoming technologies? What response, if any, do you propose to counter this assertion?

4. What is the point of making paragraph 16 so brief and undeveloped? What effect does it have?

5. How does the essay end? How effective is the ending? Would you change it if you could? Explain your answer.

● The Issues

1. What does the author's essay tell us about majorities versus minorities in our country? Expand his view with your own opinion, using examples from your past.

2. Do you think the author came to his realization about the importance of reading for certain minorities only after he observed the popularity of the movies, or was he aware of minority readers earlier? Support your answer with evidence from Bellow's essay.

3. Why do you think the book *Uncle Tom's Cabin*, which is rarely mentioned in today's literary circles, was so popular when it was published? If you are not familiar with this work, look it up on the Internet. Why are those kinds of books no longer influential?

4. Although you may not be familiar with the magazine *The Republic of Letters*, what is your opinion of a magazine whose purpose is to give aspiring writers an audience for their work? Why would aspiring writers want an audience? Is it worth the cost of publishing such a periodical? Explain your answer.

5. The author makes the point that in our country we have huge minorities. What is the purpose of drawing attention to this fact? What are some of the "minorities of millions" to which the author alludes? In your opinion, what role do these minorities play?

● Suggestions for Writing

1. Write an essay in which you analyze the part played by reading in your everyday life. Describe your reading habits, and specify what you particularly like to read and what you don't.

2. Consider a book you have read that influenced your life in significant ways. In an essay, describe the book briefly and give examples of its lasting effect on you.

For tips on how to revise your work, exit on page 696 to the **Editing Booth!**

2

Rhetoric: The Art of Persuasion

Rhetoric is the art of putting one's case in the strongest and best possible way. All of the strategies of communicating in speech and writing that we use daily in an attempt to sway each other come under its heading, with practical effects so lasting and widespread that we take them for granted. For instance, when we open a popular cookbook, we expect it to be written clearly, with ordinary words framed into speakable sentences. We do not expect it to be dense and wordy like a piece of legislation. Because of rhetoric, cookbooks are not written like legal contracts; insurance policies do not read like a comic's jokes; and love letters do not sound like State of the Union speeches.

Yet, there is no law requiring that this should be so. It is merely the effect of rhetoric—a combination of audience expectation and writers' desire to please—that operates like a force of nature. No doubt there are badly written cookbooks, but few are either published or read; flippant insurance companies go bankrupt; and pompous lovers have trouble finding mates. This desire of writers to please—to communicate with their audiences—is the basic law of rhetoric.

Grammar and Rhetoric

In the minds of some students, grammar and rhetoric are often confused, but they are significantly different. Grammar tells a writer how words should be used and sentences framed. Just as drivers obey the rules of the road, writers follow the rules of grammar. They know that they should not begin a sentence with "one" and then suddenly switch to "you," as in "One must try to do well or you will be embarrassed." That is called a shift in point of view and, like most grammatical lapses, tends to muddy meaning.

In an ideal world, grammar would be strictly neutral and mechanical and would imply nothing about anyone's inner self or social standing. In our grubby world

18

grammar is often the self-serving weapon of the language snob. Some people passionately believe that anyone who says or writes *ain't* instead of *isn't* would not be a suitable guest for tea. Yet as a wise orator from ancient times once remarked, "Nobody ever praises a speaker for his grammar; they only laugh at him if his grammar is bad." Grammar, in short, is a bit like tact: when it is absent we notice it; when it is present we don't.

There are basically two schools of grammar: prescriptive grammar and descriptive grammar. Prescriptive grammar begins with the assumption that the rules of grammar are etched in granite and have the universal application of gravity. People must be taught how to speak and write properly—for their own good and the good of the language. Descriptive grammar, on the other hand, makes no such assumptions. It begins by asking, How do certain people express themselves? How do they say this or that? Without making any value judgments on the usage based on some supposed universal standard of right and wrong, the descriptive grammarian infers the grammar rules that a community of writers and speakers observe. It says, under these conditions people use *ain't*. But since that is what they do, even though it's not what we do, we can still be good neighbors. People not in the prescriptive or descriptive camp fall somewhere between these two extreme positions.

The importance of good grammar, however, in our view, should be based on its useful function of helping us communicate and not on its misuse as a benchmark to sort people into social classes. In some countries, having a certain accent and using a bookish formal grammar are essential for social advancement and acceptance. In the United States, there are pockets of the population that think this way about grammar, but this belief is by no means common or universal.

Everyone knows what grammar is in general, but not everyone agrees that a particular construction is right or wrong. English grammar is in this muddle because its principles were founded by Latin grammarians who tried to superimpose the rules of that dead language on the emerging infant of English. This led to the formulation of some silly rules. Take, for example, the so-called split infinitive rule. Many instructors, editors, and institutions would damn as incorrect this popular phrase used in the introduction of *Star Trek* episodes: "to boldly go where no man has gone before." This is regarded as wrong because it puts the adverb *boldly* between the infinitive *to go*. In other words, it splits the infinitive as if it were a banana. According to the orthodox view, this should read "to go boldly" or "boldly to go." Why is this splitting wrong? Because since the infinitive in Latin is a single word that cannot be split, its equivalent in English, even though it consists of two words, should likewise never be split. On the basis of that silly line of reasoning was sculpted a rule of grammar that has bedeviled generations of writers and speakers.

However we arrived at our present state of confusion, the fact is that grammar is undeniably important because the world at large will judge you by your use or nonuse of it. The hard fact is that if you are applying for a job with a company sensitive about its image, you are less likely to be hired if your English is ungrammatical. Like it or not, the way you write and talk reveals your inner person as definitively as the way you dress or act. This concept of the inner man dates back to ancient Greece where, as the story goes, a rich merchant had taken his son to a philosopher who he hoped would accept the boy as a student. The philosopher glanced at the boy who was standing four feet away in broad daylight, and said, "Speak, so I can see you." We do not have on record what followed. But if there had been two boys, one of whom replied something like, "I ain't getting your point," and the other, "I don't quite understand what you mean," which boy do you think would have been chosen?

LETTING THE HABITS OF LITERATE WRITERS BE THE FINAL REFEREE

Call it being snobbish and promoting class distinctions, but the truth is that if you want to achieve top-level jobs, you will have a better shot at doing so if you follow the grammar of people considered literate—those who write editorials in magazines like *Time, Harper's*, and *The New Yorker*, or in newspapers that influence public thinking, such as *The New York Times, The Wall Street Journal*, and *The Washington Post*. What we would like students to do is follow the grammatical rules observed by the best writers when they write unselfconsciously and regularly. All good writers make an occasional grammatical goof, and when someone corrects them, they are grateful. The most important rules to follow are those whose violations will stigmatize you as a person who uses substandard English. Here are some of the most grating errors committed by thousands of writers:

1. Double negatives: **Wrong:** He had hardly no clothes to wear in cold weather. **Right:** He had hardly any clothes to wear in cold weather. **Wrong:** I don't know nothing about baseball. **Right:** I don't know anything about baseball.

2. Nonstandard verbs: **Wrong:** Pete **knowed** the name of each bird. **Right:** Pete knew the name of each bird. **Wrong:** Melanie should've **wrote** an apology. **Right:** Melanie should've **written** an apology.

3. Double comparatives: **Wrong:** If you climb over the fence, you'll get there **more faster. Right:** If you climb over the fence, you'll get there **faster**.

4. Adjective instead of adverb: **Wrong:** That was a **real** stupid answer. **Right:** That was a **really** stupid answer. **Wrong:** She types good without looking at the keyboard. **Right:** She types **well** without looking at the keyboard.

5. Incorrect pronoun: **Wrong:** The coach never chooses him or **I. Right:** The coach never chooses him or **me. Wrong: Her** and **me** might get married. **Right: She** and **I** might get married.

6. Subject-verb disagreement: **Wrong:** They **was** always late. **Right:** They **were always late. Wrong:** That **don't** matter in the least. **Right:** That **doesn't** matter in the least.

These and numerous other grammatical errors we could have listed belong to the category of mistakes that literate writers never knowingly make. By the way, literate writers will instantly notice when another writer makes such errors, but not making these errors is simply taken for granted. Don't expect to garner special kudos if you avoid them. The rules we hope you will learn and obey are those that help you avoid being stigmatized as "illiterate." If you think your knowledge of correct grammar is weak, then we suggest you purchase a compact grammar handbook, such as *Grammar Matters* or *The Least You Should Know About Grammar*, to review or brush up on the rules.

● Exercises

1. Write a paragraph in which you express your views about the rules of grammar with which you are familiar. Do you consider their observance important, or do you see them as a way of segregating people?

2. Write a paragraph in which you describe your reaction to people who seem to disregard grammatical rules. Does their lack of grammatical sense affect your attitude toward them, or is it irrelevant to your attitude?

THE IMPORTANCE OF RHETORIC

While grammar speaks in terms of rules, rhetoric speaks only in terms of effectiveness—and effectiveness is a relative judgment. If you are writing to a child, for example, you must use simple words and short sentences if you wish to be understood. However, simple words and short sentences may be entirely inappropriate in a paper explaining a complex process to an audience of specialists. When you know the rules of grammar, it is easy to compare two versions of a writing assignment and say if one is more conventionally grammatical than the other. It is far harder to say whether one version is more effectively written than the other.

Judging the effectiveness of a work is, in fact, the chief business of rhetoric. For example, consider this student paragraph:

> During high school, my favorite English course was English literature. Literature was not only interesting, but it was also fun. Learning about writers and poets of the past was enjoyable because of the teachers I had and the activities they scheduled. Teachers made past literature interesting because they could relate the writers back to the time in which they lived. This way I learned not only about English writers but also about English history.

Grammatically, this paragraph is correct; rhetorically, it is empty. It cries out for examples and supporting details. Which writers and poets did the student find so interesting? What activities did the teacher schedule to make them seem so? Without such details, the paragraph is shallow and monotonous.

Here is a paragraph on the same subject, written by a student with a strong sense of rhetoric:

> Picture a shy small-town girl of eighteen, attending college for the first time in a large city. She is terrified of the huge campus with its crowds of bustling students, but she is magnetically drawn to a course entitled "Survey of English Literature," for this awkward girl has always been an avid reader. College for me, this alien creature on campus, was the sudden revelation of a magical new world. I now could read the great English literary masterpieces—Milton's *Paradise Lost*, Shakespeare's *Othello*, Jane Austen's *Pride and Prejudice*. Then I could discuss them in class under the watchful eye of my professor, who encouraged me to dig for ideas and interpret them on my own. As the teacher asked questions, and the students responded to them, I received exciting flashes of insight into the human condition: I understood the loneliness of Jude the Obscure, the hardness of life in *Oliver Twist*, and the extravagant beauty of nature as detailed by the Romantic poets. English literature also led me into the mazy paths of history. I learned about the greed for political power as I read about the War of the Roses. I saw how the Magna Carta, so reluctantly signed by King John, influenced our present democracy. And Chaucer's tales convinced me that the pageantry of people has not changed much since medieval times. English literature educated me without my being aware of the act of acquiring knowledge. I learned through falling in love with English literature.

The second paragraph is rhetorically more effective than the first because it tells us in richer detail exactly how the author was affected by her English classes.

Audience and Purpose

To write well, you must bear in mind two truths about writing: It has an audience and it is done for a purpose. Many students think that the audience of their writing is a single instructor whose tastes must be satisfied, but this viewpoint is too narrow. The instructor is your audience only in a symbolic sense. The instructor's real job is to be a stand-in for the educated reader. In this capacity, the instructor represents universal standards of today's writing. An English instructor knows writing, good and bad, and can tell you what is good about your work and what is not so good. In this capacity, your instructor can be compared to the working editor of a newspaper, and you, to a reporter.

Purpose, on the other hand, refers to what you hope to accomplish with your writing—the influence you intend your work to exert on your reader. Contrary to what you might think, earning a grade is not the purpose of an essay. That might be its result, but it cannot be its purpose. A freelance writer who sits down to do an article has expectations of earning money for the effort, but that is not the writer's primary purpose. Instead, purpose refers to the intention—be it grand or simple—the writer had in mind when pen first touched paper. If you are writing an essay about the funniest summer vacation you have ever had, your purpose is to amuse. If you are writing an essay about how amino acids are necessary for life, your purpose is to inform. If you are writing an essay urging mandatory jail terms for sellers of child pornography, your purpose is to persuade.

It follows from this discussion that you must understand the audience and purpose of an assignment if you are to have a context for judging the effectiveness of your words and sentences. Context hints at what might work and what might flop; it warns of perils and points to possible breakthroughs. Anyone knows that a love letter should not be written in the dense sentences of a bank report and that a note of sympathy to a grieving friend should not tell jokes—anyone, that is, who thinks about the audience and the purpose of the written words. As the English writer W. Somerset Maugham put it, "To write good prose is an affair of good manners." Like good manners, good prose is always appropriate. It fits the audience; it suits the purpose. This fitting and suiting of one's writing to audience and purpose are among the chief concerns of rhetoric.

The Internal Reader/Editor

The basic aim of any instruction in rhetoric is to teach you how to distinguish between what is appropriate and inappropriate for different audiences and purposes. You develop a sixth sense of what you should say in an essay for an English instructor, a note addressed to your mother, or an ad seeking a new roommate. We call this sixth sense the internal reader/editor. One writer defined it this way: ". . . as it is for any writer, there are two characters in my head: the Writer (me) and a Reader/Editor (also me), who represents anyone who reads what I write. These two talk to each other."

Your internal reader/editor is your sense for judging aptness and effectiveness in writing. This sense improves with practice and exposure to assignments intended for different audiences and purposes. Whether you are penning an essay for a psychology instructor or a letter to a creditor asking for more time to repay a debt, the same internal reader/editor judges the rhetorical and grammatical appropriateness of what you have written.

By the time you are old enough to read this book, your internal reader/editor is already in place and functioning with some sophistication. For example, your reader/editor surely knows that obscenities have no place in an essay, that "ain't" is not appropriate in a formal exam paper, and that a wealth of personal jokes and anecdotes do not belong in an objective paper on science.

Levels of English

Virtually all writing can be divided into three levels of English: formal, informal, and technical. Each has its place in the various assignments you will be asked to do. It is your internal reader/editor who must decide on the appropriateness of each for a specific assignment.

Formal English is characterized by full, complex sentences and the use of standard and consistent grammar. It states ideas in an orderly fashion and with an educated vocabulary. It avoids the "I" point of view and does not use contractions such as "can't," "don't," "he'd," or "wouldn't." Here is an example of formal English:

> As the sun rose higher that morning, swarms of canoes, or *canoas* as they were called in the Arawak language, were pushed out to sea through the surf breaking over the glistening white sands of Long Bay. They were all full of excited, painted Indians carrying balls of cotton thread, spears and vividly colored parrots to trade with the vessels lying a short distance off-shore. The Indian craft, probably painted as colorfully as their occupants, must have given the atmosphere of a festive regatta, and trading was brisk and lasted all day until nightfall.
>
> —D. J. R. Walker, *Columbus and the Golden World of the Island Arawaks*

The aim of formal writing is to make a case or present an argument impartially rather than to relate the writer's own views on a subject. The writer takes special care to eliminate the "I" reference and to remain discreetly in the background. Examples are either generalized or in the third person, but never personal. Note the following differences:

Generalized: "All of the participants agreed to publish their notes on the laboratory experiment."

Third person: "Murdoch, the director of the experiment, came to a different conclusion."

Personal: "I was delighted with the results of the study because it promised hope for diabetes patients."

In formal English the personal example would be disallowed because it seems too biased or emotional and therefore unscientific. In formal writing, the facts are allowed to speak for themselves; the writer's task is to present them with objectivity.

Formal English is the staple of college writing. You should use it in research papers, scholarly papers, written examinations, and serious letters. Unless instructed to do otherwise, you should also use it in your essays.

Informal English is based on the familiar grammatical patterns and constructions of everyday speech. You should use it in journalistic writing and in personal letters, diaries, and light essays. The following student essay is a typical example:

> I drive a truck for a living, and every other week I'm assigned to a senior driver called Harry. Now, Harry is the dirtiest person I've ever met. Let's start with the fact that he never takes a bath or shower. Sitting in the closed cab of a diesel truck on a hot August day with Harry is like being

shut up in a rendering plant; in fact, the smell he emanates has, on many occasions, made my eyes water and my stomach turn. I always thought Harry was just dark-complexioned until it rained one day and his arms started to streak—I mean, this guy is a self-inflicted mud slide. In fact, I could've sworn that once or twice I saw Harry scratch his head and a cloud of dust whirled up above him.

This point of view is unabashedly personal and relaxed. The "I" point of view is mixed with contractions, such as "I've," "I'm," and "could've." However, in many fields, the strict standards for using formal over informal English are easing. Even some scientific journals today allow the investigator to use the "I" pronoun, especially if the writer was heavily involved in the research. Consider this paragraph about a revolution in Nepal, reprinted from an article in *National Geographic*:

> From the teahouse I can see the police station, a broken concrete shell daubed with Maoist graffiti. The police have fled from here, as they have from most of rural Nepal, and the village is now the front line, the first community I've seen that is openly controlled by the rebels. When photographer Jonas Bendiksen and I arrived in Babiyachour, we noticed a few Maoist soldiers buying aluminum plates and sacks of rice for hundreds of new recruits training on a hill above the village. One of the highest ranking Maoists, Comrade Diwakar, was said to have arrived for their "graduation." We sent our letters of introduction up the hillside, asking to meet him. Nobody seemed in a hurry to respond.

In brief: Use formal English in most papers you submit to your teacher. Use informal English in your personal writing and in those special circumstances where you are free to express yourself in your own individualistic style.

Technical English is formal English that uses the vocabulary of a specialized field. It is written most often by engineers, technicians, and scientists. It commonly suffers from wordiness, overuse of abstract nouns, misuse of the passive voice, and improper subordination. Nevertheless, some technical writers are experts at their craft. Here is an example of technical writing:

Using a style set to change line spacing for an entire document

1. Go to the **Home** tab, in the **Styles** group, and click **Change Styles.**
2. Point to **Style Set** and point to the various style sets. Using the live preview, notice how the line spacing changes from one style set to the next.
3. When you see spacing that you like, click the name of the style set.

The level of English you should use in any specific essay will depend on its audience and purpose; that is a judgment your internal reader/editor must make.

Let us take an example. Your English teacher asks you to write an essay on the most unforgettable date you've ever had. One student wrote this paragraph:

> My most unforgettable date was with Carolyn, whom I took to a drive-in movie. I chose the drive-in movie as the site of our date because Carolyn was nearly a foot taller than I, and I was embarrassed to be seen out in the open with her. What I did not expect was that my car would break down and I would not only have to get out and try to fix it, but that we would end up walking home side by side like Mutt and Jeff.

The tale that followed was a funny one about the writer's mishaps at the drive-in with Carolyn. He wrote the paragraph and the essay in an informal style because that is exactly what this assignment called for.

If, however, your sociology teacher asks you to write an essay on dating as a courtship ritual in America, you must write a formal essay. Instead of saying what happened to you personally on a date, you must say what is likely to happen on a date. Instead of airing your personal views, you must express the researched ideas and opinions of others. You should not use the pronoun "I" to refer to yourself nor attempt to impose your personality on the material. This does not mean that you should have no opinions of your own—quite the opposite—but you should base your expressed opinions on grounds more substantial than personal experience or unsupported belief. Here is an example of a student paper that follows the rules of objectivity:

> Dating is a universal courtship experience in the life of most American adolescents. The ritual goes back to the earliest chaperoned drawing-room meetings between eligible couples and has evolved to the present-day social outing. But the greatest impact on the ritual, so far as its American practice goes, has been the introduction and popularization of the automobile.

The writer supported her thesis—that the automobile has had a drastic impact on the dating ritual in America—throughout the paper and amply supported it with statistics, facts, and the testimony of experts. Her examples are also generalized rather than personal. Instead of writing that so-and-so happened to me on a date, she wrote that so-and-so is likely to happen to an American couple dating.

All writers will similarly adapt their language to suit the audience and purpose of their writing, using the principles that spring from common sense and the ancient discipline of rhetoric. While much of this adapting may be done unconsciously, it still must be done by all who sincerely wish to communicate with an audience.

Writing as a Process

Learning to write well cannot be mastered by rote, the way you might absorb facts about the anatomy of a fish or the chemistry of a nebula. It involves learning a process, and that is always harder to do than memorizing a set of facts. The parts of a bicycle can be memorized from a manual, but no one can learn to ride a bicycle merely by reading a book about it. *Scribendo disces scribere*, says the Latin proverb: "You learn to write by writing." Here, then, are some truths about the writing process uncovered by laboratory research:

- **Composing is a difficult, back-and-forth process.** Many writers compose in a halting, lurching way. A writer will pen a few sentences, pause to go back and revise them, compose several new sentences, and then pause again to reread and further edit before continuing with the paragraph. "In their thinking and writing," says one researcher, "writers 'go back' in order to push thought forward."

  Any professional writer will recognize the truth of this observation, but often it comes as a revelation to students who tend to worry when their own compositions emerge by similar fits and starts. Be assured that this back-and-forth movement is a healthy and normal part of composing. The research even suggests that writers who accept the halting, stumbling nature of composing actually have an easier time with this necessary process of "waiting, looking, and discovering" than those who fight against it. Because of this circularity in composing, writing is often described as a recursive process, meaning that results are achieved by a roundabout rather than a straight-line path. Often it is necessary to retrace one's trail, to go back to the beginning of a work, or to revise earlier sentences and paragraphs before writing new ones. If you find yourself doing something similar in your own writing, be heartened by this truth: That is how the vast majority of writers work. You are merely going through the normal cycle of composing.

- **The topic can make a difference in your writing.** Professional or amateur, few writers are entirely free to choose their own topics. Most are assigned topics by employers, professors, or circumstances. Yet, when choice does exist, the lesson from common sense and research is that you should always pick the topic you like best. The fact is that most people write better when they write about a subject that appeals to them. It is no mystery why this should be so. We all try harder when we are engaged in a labor of love—whether building our dream house or writing an essay. Unfortunately, in a classroom setting, many students are content to settle for a topic that seems simplest to research or easiest to write about, regardless of whether they find it appealing. This is a mistake. When you write for your own enjoyment, you will behave more like an experienced writer than when you force yourself to write about a subject you find boring.

- **Your writing will not automatically improve with each essay.** Writing does not automatically get better with every paper. It is realistic to compare writing to, say, archery. The first arrow might hit the bull's-eye, while the tenth might entirely miss the target. An archer's overall accuracy will gradually improve with practice, but never to the point of absolute certainty for any one arrow. In practical terms, this simply means that you shouldn't brood if you find a later essay turning out worse than an earlier one. Your overall writing skills are bound to improve with experience, even if the improvement isn't reflected in any single essay.

The gist of this chapter may be summed up thus: You can learn to write well, and rhetoric can teach you how. Writing well means doing more than simply scribbling down the first idea that pops into your head. It involves thinking about your audience and purpose and choosing between this level of language and that. It means developing a rhetorical sense about what techniques are likely to work for a particular assignment. All of these skills can be learned from a study of rhetoric.

Writing about Visual Images

Visual images range from works of art found only in museums to photographs published in daily newspapers. They include television images, line drawings, sketches, computer graphics, and a bewitching gallery of exotic scenes and pictures of beautiful people from advertising. So widespread and influential are visual images that many instructors use them as essay topics. This book, for example, contains an image gallery on pages IG-1–IG-32 whose exhibits you will be asked to interpret or evaluate in the context of the various readings they are meant to illustrate.

If you've never done this kind of writing before, don't worry. Writing about an image is not that different from writing about a pig, a poem, or an adventure. Here are some techniques for writing about artwork, news photographs, cartoons, and advertising images.

Writing about Artwork You do not have to be an art critic to write about a work of art, and you do not have to try to write like one. As in all kinds of writing, it is better for a writer to write from an honest self than to pretend to be someone else. In other words, be yourself always, whether you're writing about a real plum or one in a still-life painting. Here are some steps you can take to write about a work of art:

- **Study the work carefully**. Is it realistic or is it an abstract work with a distorted and imaginary vision? If it is a realistic work—say, a painting of a rural scene—take note of the colors and the way the paint is applied. An artist, by using drab colors and bold strokes of the brush, can suggest a negative feeling about a scene. On the other hand, a scene can be idealized with the use of bright colors and fine brushstrokes. After studying the work carefully, sum up in a single sentence your overall impression of it. This single sentence will be your thesis.
- **Pay attention to the title of the work.** Many Expressionist painters create images that are purely imaginary and have no equivalent in reality. It often takes a title to help us understand what the images mean. Figure 2.1 is a dramatic example of the importance of title. The painting shows a sinister

Bildarchiv Preussischer Kulturbesitz/Art Resource, NY/Art Resource, Inc.

● **FIGURE 2.1** *The Pillars of Society, 1926, by George Grosz.*

How admirable are these pillars of society?

assembly of men, two of whom have half a skull crammed with what looks like excrement and miscellaneous garbage. In the background are an ugly priest and a Nazi soldier with a bloody sword. It is only after we know the title of the painting, *The Pillars of Society,* that we grasp who these revolting men are meant to be—the emerging Nazi rulers whom the artist was satirizing.

Another example can be found in Figure 2.2, a lithograph by Kathe Kollwitz of a woman whose hand is raised in a gesture explained by the work's title, *Never Again War!*

- **Use the Internet to research background about the artist and the work.** For example, before writing the paragraph about The *Pillars of Society,* we entered the name of the artist George Grosz and the title of his painting in the search engine Google, which gave us the information we needed about the work and its creator. Another example is the lithograph of the anti-war woman. Through the Internet we learned that losing a son in World War I and a grandson in World War II made the artist, German Expressionist Kathe Kollwitz (1867–1945), into a committed pacifist and explains much of her work.

- **Check your response to the work of art against the responses of art critics.** We all have a unique eye. If beauty is in the eye of the beholder, so is much of art. Some modernists argue that one reaction to a work of art is as valid as another. Traditionalists take just the opposite point of view, arguing that it is possible for one reaction to be "right" and another "wrong." Most likely the truth lies somewhere in between. It is possible for an interpretation of an artwork to be so farfetched and unprovable as to come entirely from the viewer's mind rather than from the artwork itself. It is also possible for two contrary interpretations of the same artwork to exist side by side, one no more "right" than the other. In situations like this one, art critics can be helpful. They have the experience and background in evaluating artistic works that enable them to spot what is unique about an artwork and what is imitative.

- **Support your opinions or interpretations of the artwork.** Any opinion you have about an artwork should be supported by details drawn from the work itself. If you say that the portrait of a certain person reflects an air of gloom, you should say why you think that. In support of this opinion, you can point to background colors, a grim facial expression, or perhaps the way the figure slumps.

- **Say how the work made you feel.** Artwork is meant to appeal both to the mind and to the heart. Don't be afraid to express how the work made you

Bildarchiv Preussischer Kulturbesitz/Art Resource, NY/Art Resource, Inc.

● FIGURE 2.2
*Never Again War!
(Nie Wieder Kreig),
1924, by Kathe
Kollwitz*

Mothers united
against the killing
fields of war.

feel or to say why you think it affected you as it did. That kind of admission will help a reader better understand your opinions of the work. It is also perfectly allowable to use "I" in an essay interpreting a visual image. As a matter of fact, writing on such a personal topic without the use of "I" would be very difficult to do. You are, after all, expected to say how the work affected you and how you feel about it. You should not necessarily feel any obligation to like the artwork just because you're writing an essay about it. You may find that you heartily dislike the work. In such a case, what you have to do is to say why. If you did like the work, you should also say why.

In review, here are the steps involved in writing about artwork:

1. State your overall impression of the work in a single sentence.
2. Ground your opinions and impressions of the artwork in details drawn from it.
3. Say how the work affected you.

● Writing Assignment

Find and make a copy of a work of art that you like. Write three paragraphs about it, interpreting the work of art and saying what about it you especially appreciate. Include a copy of the work of art with your essay.

Writing about News Photographs News photographs, a staple of newspapers and magazines, range from the serene to the horrific. In the hands of a good photographer, the camera can seem to totally capture a subject. That uncanny ability to seemingly x-ray the human soul, coupled with the spontaneity missing in more formal artworks such as paintings, has made photography into a universal language. A photograph of people leaping to their death from a burning skyscraper is globally understandable and universally wrenching, no matter what language we speak. Here are some tips on how to approach writing about a news photo:

- **Begin by researching and describing the context of the photograph.** When was it taken and by whom? Under what circumstances was it shot? Knowing its context puts a photograph in historical perspective and affects your interpretation of it.
- **Describe the news photograph by clearly stating its details**. Sum up, as well as you can, the importance of the scene depicted. Figure 2.3, for example, catches a spectacular moment in mountain rescuing.

In review, here are the steps involved in writing about news photos:

1. Establish the context of the photograph, when and where it was taken, and why.
2. Describe the photo in detail.
3. Compose a thesis for the photo.
4. Develop evidence from the photo and its context to support your thesis.

Andreas Strauss/Getty Images

● **FIGURE 2.3**

A helicopter rescues a man lost in the French Alps.

● **Writing Assignment**

Write a couple of paragraphs about a news photograph, explaining its context and giving your interpretation of it. Include a copy of the photo with your written work.

Writing about Cartoons Nothing captures the spirit of an age better than a collection of its best cartoons. They seem to sum up in shorthand the idiosyncrasies of the time. The political cartoon, particularly the caricature—which is a cartoon that exaggerates physical appearance—is actually a good measure of how a particular person is regarded at a particular time. To get an idea of how Teddy Roosevelt was perceived in his day, for example, you need only go to the collection of cartoons that depict him. Here are some tips for writing about cartoons:

- **Make sure you understand the message of the cartoon.** Some cartoons, of course, are merely intended to amuse and have no particular message. Many cartoons mix sugar (humor) with medicine (a message). Look at Figure 2.4, for example. It is reprinted from a French Canadian newspaper. Here, we see a young boy with his pants at half mast, revealing the top of his buttocks, which forms a clear "Y." To the left, preceding the image, are the words (in French) "GENERATION." In its January 22, 2008 edition, the Quebec City paper *Le Soleil* introduced the cartoon by grouping generations by age groups, as follows:

> —The Silent Generation, people born before 1945
>
> —The Baby Boomers, people born between 1945 and 1961
>
> —Generation X, people born between 1962 and 1976
>
> —Generation Y, people born between 1977 and 1989

Why do we call the last group "generation Y"? The cartoon gives the answer with eloquent satire. At the same time, it subtly asks the reader to ponder why kids would ever want to follow a dress code meant to shock the elderly and other people with less inhibition than the kids who decided to popularize this fashion in the western part of the world.

Another example of this subtlety is in a cartoon that depicts an English teacher standing angrily in front of her class. Behind her on the chalkboard is scrawled, "Homework due today." In front of the teacher stands a young boy who is saying, "I did my homework, but the dog pressed Control-Alt-Delete." What makes this line funny is that it is the computer-age equivalent of "The dog ate my homework."

- **Be aware of the topsy-turvy world of cartoons.** Many cartoons spoof the accepted and habitual views of society, often by turning the world upside down. For example, one cartoon shows the seats of a movie theater filled with an audience of winged bugs waiting for the feature to begin. On the screen is the name of the upcoming movie: *Return of the Killer Windshield*. Another— one of our favorites—shows a horrible monster scrambling to get dressed. Looking at his watch worriedly, he is complaining to his wife that he's late and should have already been in a certain boy's closet. The caption of the cartoon? "Monster jobs." The humor of both cartoons comes mainly from the inversion of normalcy, giving us an unusual slant on a familiar situation.

GÉNÉRATION

Marc Beaudet/Le Journal de Montréal

● **FIGURE 2.4**
Cartoon lampooning the current fad of boys wearing low-riding pants.

- **State what lesson the cartoon teaches.** Many cartoons teach a lesson. Sometimes the lesson is obvious, as in an old cartoon that shows two males stranded on a tiny tropical island. One fellow looks at the other and suggests that perhaps they should form some simple form of government—reminding the viewer that setting up governments is part of the human instinct for politics. Sometimes the lesson is less obvious. For example, a cartoon featuring two forlorn-looking people standing side by side in the aisle of a library and looking at two different books, one entitled *Self-Improvement*, the other *Self-Involvement*, is teaching a subtle lesson about narcissism. In any case, part of your interpretation of the cartoon is to say what lesson it teaches—if it, indeed, teaches any. Study the cartoon until you get its meaning.

In review, here are the steps involved in writing about cartoons:

1. Make sure you understand the message of the cartoon, if it has one.
2. Be aware of the topsy-turvy world of cartoons.
3. Study the lesson of the cartoon.

● Writing Assignment

Write a few paragraphs about any cartoon that you particularly like. Be sure to include a copy of the cartoon with your work.

Writing about Advertisements Advertising images, although sometimes bewitching, often have an air of unreality. They glamorize persons, settings, and objects. Or they can make products seem to have an exaggerated influence on the world. See Figure 2.5, which asks us to believe that taking an Altoids mint can snap your mind into immediate attention.

Many of the graphic messages in advertisements are either exaggerated or outright lies. We know that it is impossible for anyone to turn a rainy day into a sunny one just by swallowing a pill, that all our worries will not vanish if we take a certain laxative, and that rubbing our faces with a cream will not make wrinkles disappear overnight. Buying a certain mattress will not turn an insomniac into another Rip Van Winkle, nor will driving a new car make you into an overnight sensation with the opposite sex.

Anyone who writes about advertising images has to exercise both common sense and logic. Common sense will enable you to see through the pitch. Logic will help you to sift through the exaggerated claims made by the hype. Writing about an advertising image requires you to take the following steps:

- **Be sure you know the audience at whom the ad is aimed and the product that is being advertised.** An ad directed at women—for a perfume, for example—often comes with a feminized image. On the other hand, masculine images are typically found in a beer advertisement aimed mainly at men. Strange as it may seem, a few advertisements have been oblique rather than blunt in their hype of a product. Probably the most famous example of this is the advertising campaign for a certain Japanese car. The ads show scenes of pastures and mountain brooks—to the accompaniment of philosophical babble that has little to do with owning a car. Ask yourself what the product is, who uses it, and what it does. Sum up this information in a single sentence and you have your thesis.

- **Pay attention to the language that accompanies the image.** Advertising copy is often written in fragments rather than whole sentences. For example, an ad for a trip to Wales uses the following copy: "Suggested itinerary: London-Nirvana-London. It's a stopover in serenity. A side trip to paradise. Where the wonders of nature and the comforts of home live side by side. Wales. Just two hours from London." One sentence and five fragments make up this copy. Notice any poetic touch used to highlight the image. For example, the most successful advertising slogan of all time consists of two rhyming words: "Think Mink." Advertising copy is also often openly romantic, as in this example: "Somewhere she went from the girl of your dreams to the love of your life. A diamond is forever."

AWAKENS

LIKE A

horse whip

ON THE BACKFLESH.

ALTOIDS

A SLAP to the CEREBELLUM

Wm. Wrigley Jr. Company

● **FIGURE 2.5**
Altoid ad with its popular slogan.

- **Notice any inversion of reality.** Advertisers are notorious for turning reality on its head. If a product is bad for you, the advertising may surround it with an aura of health and well-being. For example, cigarette advertisements used to always show smokers as specimens of perfect, robust health. The typical image associated with Marlboro cigarettes was a rugged cowboy shown on the range herding cattle and occasionally pausing for a "healthful" smoke. While those ads have faded from view, they have been replaced by commercials touting creams to cure pimples, baldness, or erectile dysfunction. Can anyone not envy the male who has taken Cialis or Viagra before strolling through a spring meadow planning to make love to his beloved "when the time is right"?

- **Watch out for buzzwords or euphemisms.** A buzzword is a slogan or saying that is associated with the product. The slogan of a certain underarm deodorant was, "Strong enough for a man. But made for a woman." A euphemism is a gentler way of saying something. For example, saying "he passed away" is a euphemism for "he died." Advertisers often combine images with euphemisms as part of their pitch. For example, an advertisement for insurance will talk about sparing your family the heartbreak of final decisions—meaning, finding a place to bury you and a way to pay for it. Personal-hygiene products for women are always euphemistic in their claims. Sometimes, even an image can be euphemistic, as is often the case in some advertisements for laxatives.

- **Use logic to evaluate the extravagant claims of an advertising image.** It is no exaggeration to say that advertisements often tell outright lies. Ad people would probably claim that they do not lie, but merely stress the positives about their product. Yet, anyone with common sense can't help but wonder what to make of a claim like "X toothpaste is used by two out of three dentists." How many dentists were surveyed to come to this conclusion? It might have been three. And what does this claim mean: "Degree antiperspirant deodorant is body-heat activated. Your body heat turns it on." And when an insect repellent advertises that it makes you "invisible to bugs," is that claim meant literally or figuratively?

- **Mention any humor associated with image.** An ad for Toshiba copy machines features a speaking copier: "I print eighty pages per minute and sit near the men's room. She types eighty words per minute and gets the corner office. Is there no balance in the universe?" To discuss this particular image you would have to touch on the humor of the talking copier.

In review, here are the steps involved in writing about advertisements:

1. Be sure you know what's being advertised and to whom.
2. Pay attention to the language that accompanies the image.
3. Notice any inversion of reality.
4. Watch out for buzzwords or euphemisms.
5. Use logic to evaluate the extravagant claims of an advertising image.
6. Mention any humor associated with the image.

Writing Assignments

1. Write two paragraphs on a magazine or newspaper ad that you particularly dislike. Include a copy of the ad with your work.

2. After studying the following passages, suggest the purpose of each and the audience for which it is intended. Give specific examples of language suitable to that audience.

   a. At first, our Greg was a model child. Healthy, happy, unfailingly sweet-tempered, he was a total joy as a baby. When he was one year old, he thought that everything mother and father wanted him to do was wonderful. His second birthday passed, and he remained cooperative and adorable. Aha, I thought, the "terrible twos" that everyone complains about must result from inadequate attention and discipline.

Then Greg turned two and three-quarters. Suddenly we had an obnoxious monster in the house. His favorite word was "No!" and he used it constantly. At the simplest request he would stamp his feet and cry. It took a battle to get him to put on clothing he had previously worn happily. Favorite foods were thrown on the floor. It became almost impossible to take him shopping because he would lie down in the store and refuse to move. There was constant tension in the house, and my husband and I became irritable, too. We felt as if we were living on the slopes of a volcano, and we found ourselves giving in to Greg too much in order to avoid the threatened eruptions.

b. Others will debate the controversial issues, national and international, which divide men's minds. But serene, calm, aloof, you stand as the nation's war guardians, as its lifeguards from the raging tides of international conflict, as its gladiators in the arena of battle. For a century and a half you have defended, guarded, and protected its hallowed traditions of liberty and freedom, of right and justice.

Let civilian voices argue the merits or demerits of our processes of government: whether our strength is being sapped by deficit financing indulged in too long; by federal paternalism grown too mighty; by power groups grown too arrogant; by politics grown too corrupt; by crime grown too rampant; by morals grown too low; by taxes grown too high; by extremists grown too violent; whether our personal liberties are as firm and complete as they should be.

These great national problems are not for your professional participation or military solution. Your guidepost stands out like a tenfold beacon in the night: duty, honor, country.

c. To give Eleanor her due, any suspicion as to the slightest inclination on her part toward Mr. Slope was a wrong to her. She had no more idea of marrying Mr. Slope than she had of marrying the bishop, and the idea that Mr. Slope would present himself as a suitor had never occurred to her. Indeed, to give her her due again, she had never thought about suitors since her husband's death. But nevertheless it was true that she had overcome all that repugnance to the man which was so strongly felt for him by the rest of the Grantly faction. She had forgiven him his sermon. She had forgiven him his low church tendencies, his Sabbath schools, and puritanical observances. She had forgiven his pharisaical arrogance, and even his greasy face and oily vulgar manners. Having agreed to overlook such offences as these, why should she not in time be taught to regard Mr. Slope as a suitor?

d. Earthquakes are often accompanied by a roaring noise that comes from the bowels of the earth. This phenomenon was known to early geographers. Pliny wrote that earthquakes are "preceded or accompanied by a terrible sound." Vaults supporting the ground give way and it seems as though the earth heaves deep sighs. The sound was attributed to the gods and called *theophany*.

The eruptions of volcanoes are also accompanied by loud noises. The sound produced by Krakatoa in the East Indies during the eruption of 1883 was so loud that it was heard as far as Japan, 3,000 miles away, the farthest distance traveled by sound recorded in modern annals.

e. I beg you to excuse a father who dares to approach you in the interests of his son.

> I wish to mention first that my son is twenty-two years old, has studied for four years at the Zurich Polytechnic and last summer brilliantly passed his diploma examinations in mathematics and physics. Since then he has tried unsuccessfully to find a position as assistant, which would enable him to continue his education in theoretical and experimental physics. Everybody who is able to judge praises his talent, and in any case I can assure you that he is exceedingly assiduous and industrious and is attached to his science with a great love.

f. Letters written by a potential customer asking suppliers for free materials, information, or routine services are among the easiest to write. The customer will usually receive what he or she is asking for since it is to the supplier's advantage to provide it. The potential customer need only be clear and courteous. In writing routine request letters, give all the information the supplier will need in order to be really helpful, keep your request as brief as possible without omitting important details, and express your wishes courteously and tactfully.

3. Write two one-page essays explaining the reasons you wish to pursue a certain career. Address the first to the personnel manager of an organization that might hire you and the second to your father. Contrast the language and phrasing of each essay and explain the differences between them.

4. Both of the following letters refuse credit to a potential customer. How does the second differ in purpose from the first?

a. Please accept our regrets that we cannot offer you a 60-day credit for the meeting of your organization here at Pine Lodge in July of 2009. When you held your meeting here last year, we had the embarrassing experience of having to wait six months before you made full payment on your bill. I am sure that you will understand that we cannot take chances on such bad credit risks.

b. Thank you for choosing Pine Lodge again for your 2009 meeting. We consider it a pleasure to have you, although we must ask you to send us a 25% deposit and to make a full settlement when you check out. This is now our standard arrangement with organizations similar to yours. If these arrangements are satisfactory, we shall do our best to make sure that your group is extended every courtesy and service during its stay.

5. A restaurant owner has sent the following memorandum to the waiters and waitresses working for him. Rewrite the memo to create a more positive tone, without destroying its purpose.

> To: All waiters and waitresses. I've had it with you lazy clowns! This month's profits fell 20% below last year's at this same time. Now, any fool can tell that the problem is your sloppy service to the customers, your excessive breaking of china and glassware, and your horsing around instead

of paying attention to such details as keeping the food warm, setting the tables properly, and getting the customer's order straight. So, I'm warning you: either start doing your job right, or you'll find yourselves fired.

6. Assuming an educated audience, label the purpose of each of the following passages: (1) to inspire, (2) to get action, (3) to amuse, or (4) to inform.

   a. Please send us either a check within the next week or an explanation if some problem has arisen. We are eager to cooperate with you.

   b. Conscience is a sacred sanctuary where God alone may enter as judge.

   c. In great straits, and when hope is small, the boldest counsels are the safest.

   d. Men seldom make passes at girls who wear glasses.

   e. The more one comes to know men, the more one admires the dog.

   f. "Gavelkind" is the custom of having all of the sons of an estate holder share equally in the estate upon the death of the father. Most of the lands in England were held in gavelkind tenure prior to the Norman Conquest.

   g. Seek not the favor of the multitude; it is seldom got by honest and lawful means. But seek the testimony of few; and number not voices, but weigh them.

   h. Botticelli isn't a wine, you dunce! Botticelli is a cheese.

   i. The Indus River is approximately 1,900 miles long. It rises in the Kailas range of Tibet, flows west across Kashmir, India, and then moves southwest to the Arabian Sea.

   j. Flaming manifestoes and prophecies of doom are no longer much help, and a search for scapegoats can only make matters worse. The time for sensations and manifestoes is about over. Now we need rigorous analysis, united effort, and very hard work.

7. Label each of the following passages according to its level of English: formal, informal, or technical. In each case, describe the characteristics that identify the level of writing.

   a. Sometimes I wish I were a mountain stream. If I were a mountain stream, I'd flow down a beautiful, green, woodsy, snow-capped mountain. I'd be fed by the cool, melting snow, and I'd shimmer and glisten as the sun warmed my flowing presence. Being a mountain stream, I'd attract only a few select people—those with enough courage and stamina to climb through thickets, across ravines, and up steep paths to my cool, ethereal banks. Those special people could enjoy sitting on my banks to search my clear depths for the solitude, serenity, and peace they're longing to find.

   b. The bony remains of Peking Man all came from a single limestone cave at Chou-k'ou-tien. The bones consist of fifteen crania, six facial bones, twelve mandibles, a miscellaneous collection of postcranial bones, and 147 teeth. Studies of the physical characters of these bones by Davidson Black and Franz Weidenreich disclose that Peking Man was still in an early stage of human development, comparable to the *Homo erectus* of Java.

   The limbs were highly developed and quite modern, indicating that he stood upright and walked on two feet, but the cranium is characterized by low vault, heavy bony features, thick wall, and small cranial capacity (914–1,225 cc., with an average of 1,043 cc., as against Java Man's 860 cc. and modern man's 1,350 cc.). —John T. Meskill

c. Unlike in nature, where the root feeds the plant, in art, the pinnacle makes possible the base. Drama did not begin with a lot of hacks gradually evolving into Aeschylus and Sophocles; the novel did not start with a slew of James Micheners and Leon Urises building up to Dickens and Joyce. Richardson, Fielding, Sterne, and Smollett started things on a pretty high level; it is they who made the Jacqueline Susanns possible, not the other way around. Public funds for the dissemination of culture are necessary, but unless the most difficult and demanding creations on the individual level are subsidized, no amount of grants to public television to put on *The Adams Chronicles* will prevent culture and art from withering away or becoming debased, which is the same thing. —John Simon

8. Remember your last significant writing assignment and answer the following questions:

   a. Who was your audience?
   b. What was your purpose?
   c. What level of English did you use?

9. Assuming that choice of topic affects the quality of your writing, choose the topic that most interests you from the following list. In two or three sentences, state why the topic appeals to you. Describe the audience for whom you would like to write about your chosen topic.

   a. The future of working women
   b. Care for the elderly
   c. The cost of owning a house
   d. The pleasures associated with a particular hobby
   e. Preserving our environment
   f. Some aspect of working with computers
   g. Handicapped children
   h. Some aspect of primitive civilization
   i. A favorite painter, sculptor, dancer, or musician
   j. Business ethics
   k. Political reform

Stumped by wordiness? Exit on pages 700–704, at the **Editing Booth!**

What—and How—to Write When You Have No Time to Write

DONALD MURRAY

Rhetorical Thumbnail

Purpose: provide some practical tips about the daily business of writing

Audience: college students and others who write frequently

Language: a blend of formal and informal English; frequent use of contractions

Strategy: cites his own experience with writing deadlines and schedules

Donald Murray (1924–2006) was a Pulitzer Prize–winning journalist who made it part of his life's work to teach others how to write. He wrote a much-read weekly column for *The Boston Globe* as well as feature articles for a variety of magazines. Many teachers of composition rely on Murray's books for teaching strategies. Among his most influential books are *Shoptalk: Learning to Write with Writers* (1990); *Expecting the Unexpected: Teaching Myself and Others to Read and Write* (1989); *The Craft of Revision* (2007); and *Crafting a Life in Essay, Story, Poem* (1996). Murray was Professor Emeritus of English at the University of New Hampshire.

Murray, who was known for his practical approach to writing, dispenses some sensible advice, which he summarizes into "ten little habits of mind and craft." While his ideas apply particularly to the full-time writer, they are also practical enough to help the student.

• • •

1   The less time I have for writing, the more important it is that I write. Writing gives me a necessary calm, what Robert Frost called "a momentary stay against confusion." Writing slows down the rush of life, forcing awareness and reflection. As writing increases my awareness, language clarifies that vision. What is vague and general becomes concrete and specific as I find the words. These words connect with other words in phrase and sentence, placing the immediate experience in the context of my life. I read the story of my life by writing it. I also receive the gift of concentration and escape the swirling problems of my life as I follow paragraph and page toward meaning.

2   I write fragments in slivers of time, always with interruptions, and yet, when I look back, I am surprised that the writing caught on the fly has produced

a lifetime of productivity. I have come to realize that very little published writing is produced during sustained periods of composition without interruption. You have to arrange a life in which part of your mind is writing all the time; that's when the seeds of writing are sown and then cultivated. The writing is harvested in short periods of time between the busy chores that crowd the day.

3   Graham Greene said, "If one wants to write, one simply has to organize one's life in a mass of little habits." Here are ten little habits of mind and craft that I realize, looking back, made me a productive writer—without long writing days free of interruption.

1. Don't wait for an idea.

4   If you know what you want to say, you've probably said it before, or it's not worth saying. Writing is thinking, and thought begins not with a conclusion but with an itch, a hint, a clue, a question, a doubt, a wonder, a problem, an answer without a question, an image that refuses to be forgotten. Such fragments are caught on the wing, when I think my mind is somewhere else.

5   My four-year-old grandson told his mother, "I know Grandpa is a writer because he's always writing in his wallet." It is not a wallet, but a container for the 3" × 5" cards that are always in my shirt pocket with three pens. In a shoulder case that is not far from me night and day is the spiral daybook in which I talk to myself, capturing and playing with fragments of language that may become a draft.

2. Listen to your own difference.

6   People who want to write look at what is being published, but the writers who are published have looked within themselves, found their own vision of the world, heard their own voices. Sandra Cisneros said, "Write about what makes you different."

7   As I look back, I realize that what made me strange to my family, classmates and teachers, friends and neighbors, colleagues and editors, is what has produced the writing that has been read. In the wonderful way of art, what is most personal, eccentric, individual, becomes most universal. When I have tried to become someone else I have failed; when I have been myself I have succeeded.

3. Avoid long writing sessions.

8   Most people believe, as I once did, that it is necessary to have long, uninterrupted days in which to write. But there are no such days. Life intrudes. I try to follow the counsel of Horace, Pliny, and so many others through the centuries: *nulla dies sine linea*—never a day without a line.

9   How long does it take me to write? My weekly columns take 71 years of living and about forty-five minutes of writing. I write in bursts of twenty minutes, five, fifteen, thirty, sixty; ninety minutes is the maximum amount of writing time that is effective for me.

0   And how much writing do I produce? I've finished a book averaging 300 words a day. These days I try to average 500 words a day.

The important thing is not the time or the words, but the habit, that dailiness of the writing.

4. Break long writing projects into brief daily tasks.

11   Books are written a page at a time, and I find it helpful—essential—to break a book into units that can be finished in a short morning's writing: lead for Ch. 3, scene in court, description of experiment, interview with source, column on writing time.

5. Write in the morning.

12   Most writers write in the early morning before the world intrudes. They harvest the product of their subconscious. Each hour of the day becomes less efficient as the writer is not only interrupted, but increasingly aware of all the professional and family concerns that crowd the mind. An 800-word column I can write in 45 minutes in the morning takes me three hours in the afternoon.

6. Know tomorrow's task today.

13   I set myself a single writing task and know what it is the night before. I don't know what I am going to write, but I assign the writing problem to my subconscious at the end of the morning writing session or before I go to bed, and part of my mind works on it as I go about my living.

7. Seek instructive failure.

14   Effective writing is the product of instructive failure. You try to say what you cannot yet say, but in the attempt you discover—draft by draft—what you have to say and how you can say it. Failure is essential. Failure occurs when the words race ahead of thought, producing insights that may be developed through revision. The writer should seek to fail, not to say what has been said before, but what has not yet been said and is worth saying.

8. Focus on what works.

15   Once failure has revealed what you want to say, you should develop the topic by concentrating on what works, rather than focusing on correcting errors. Most errors will not occur if you develop what works and, at the end of the drafting process, you can solve any problems that remain. I revise mostly by layering, writing over—and over—what has been written.

9. Keep score.

16   As you write, it is important to suspend critical judgment until after a draft is finished. It's helpful to count words—or pages or hours—so that you can tell yourself that you have written without assessing how well you have written until the piece is finished.

10. Let it go.

17   Hardest of all is to let it go. The draft never equals the dream. The draft will expose your private thoughts and feelings to the world, but when you are published, what you most feared would appear foolish, your readers often find most profound. You have given words to their private thoughts and feelings.

18   Writing produces writing. When writing you are more aware of the world and your own reaction to it. As a writer, you relive your life hundreds

of times, and when you are in your seventies, as I am, you'll come to your writing desk and discover you have even more to say than you imagined when you were 7 years old and dreaming of a writing life.

Donald Murray, "What—and How—to Write When You Have No Time to Write." From THE WRITER (September 1996). Reprinted by permission of The Poynter Institute.

● Vocabulary

sustained (2)

daybook (6)

eccentric (9)

suspend (25)

assessing (25)

EXAMPLES

I Have a Dream

MARTIN LUTHER KING, JR.

Rhetorical Thumbnail

Purpose: to draw the attention of American society to the oppressed condition of black people

Audience: the English-speaking world, particularly America

Language: elevated, semi-poetic English

Strategy: uses language with powerful moral overtones

Martin Luther King, Jr. (1929–1968), American clergyman and black civil rights leader, was born in Atlanta and educated at Morehouse College, Crozer Theological Seminary, and Boston University (Ph.D., 1955). Dr. King, a lifelong advocate of nonviolent resistance to segregation, led a boycott of blacks in Montgomery, Alabama (1955–1956) against the city's segregated bus system and organized a massive march on Washington, D.C., in 1963, during which he delivered his famous "I Have a Dream" speech. In 1964, he was awarded the Nobel Peace Prize. Dr. King was assassinated on April 4, 1968, on a motel balcony in Memphis, Tennessee, where he had journeyed in support of the city's striking sanitation workers.

In August 1963, more than 200,000 blacks and whites gathered peacefully in Washington, D.C., to focus attention on black demands for civil rights. The marchers gathered at the Lincoln Memorial, where Dr. King delivered this impassioned speech.

● ● ●

1 Five score years ago, a great American, in whose symbolic shadow we stand today, signed the Emancipation Proclamation. This momentous decree came as a great beacon light of hope to millions of Negro slaves who had been seared in

the flames of withering injustice. It came as a joyous daybreak to end the long night of their captivity.

2   But one hundred years later, the Negro still is not free. One hundred years later, the life of the Negro is still sadly crippled by the manacles of segregation and the chains of discrimination.

3   One hundred years later, the Negro lives on a lonely island of poverty in the midst of a vast ocean of material prosperity. One hundred years later, the Negro is still languished in the corners of American society and finds himself an exile in his own land. So we have come here today to dramatize a shameful condition.

4   In a sense we have come to our nation's capital to cash a check. When the architects of our republic wrote the magnificent words of the Constitution and the Declaration of Independence, they were signing a promissory note to which every American was to fall heir. This note was a promise that all men, yes, black men as well as white men, would be granted the unalienable rights of life, liberty, and the pursuit of happiness.

5   It is obvious today that America has defaulted on this promissory note insofar as her citizens of color are concerned. Instead of honoring this sacred obligation, America has given the Negro people a bad check, which has come back marked "insufficient funds."

6   But we refuse to believe that the bank of justice is bankrupt. We refuse to believe that there are insufficient funds in the great vaults of opportunity of this nation. So we have come to cash this check—a check that will give us upon demand the riches of freedom and the security of justice.

7   We have also come to this hallowed spot to remind America of the fierce urgency of now. This is no time to engage in the luxury of cooling off or to take the tranquilizing drug of gradualism. Now is the time to make real the promises of democracy. Now is the time to rise from the dark and desolate valley of segregation to the sunlit path of racial justice. Now is the time to lift our nation from the quicksands of racial injustice to the solid rock of brotherhood. Now is the time to make justice a reality for all of God's children.

8   It would be fatal for the nation to overlook the urgency of the movement and to underestimate the determination of the Negro. This sweltering summer of the Negro's legitimate discontent will not pass until there is an invigorating autumn of freedom and equality. 1963 is not an end but a beginning. Those who hope that the Negro needed to blow off steam and will now be content will have a rude awakening if the nation returns to business as usual.

9   There will be neither rest nor tranquility in America until the Negro is granted his citizenship rights. The whirlwinds of revolt will continue to shake the foundations of our nation until the bright day of justice emerges.

10   But there is something that I must say to my people who stand on the warm threshold which leads into the palace of justice. In the process of gaining our rightful place we must not be guilty of wrongful deeds.

11   Let us not seek to satisfy our thirst for freedom by drinking from the cup of bitterness and hatred. We must forever conduct our struggle on the high plane of dignity and discipline. We must not allow our creative protest to degenerate

into physical violence. Again and again we must rise to the majestic heights of meeting physical force with soul force.

12   The marvelous new militancy which has engulfed the Negro community must not lead us to a distrust of all white people, for many of our white brothers, as evidenced by their presence here today, have come to realize that their destiny is tied up with our destiny and they have come to realize that their freedom is inextricably bound to our freedom. This offense we share mounted to storm the battlements of injustice must be carried forth by a biracial army. We cannot walk alone.

13   And as we walk, we must make the pledge that we shall always march ahead. We cannot turn back. There are those who are asking the devotees of civil rights, "When will you be satisfied?" We can never be satisfied as long as the Negro is the victim of the unspeakable horrors of police brutality.

14   We can never be satisfied as long as our bodies, heavy with the fatigue of travel, cannot gain lodging in the motels of the highways and the hotels of the cities. We cannot be satisfied as long as the Negro's basic mobility is from a smaller ghetto to a larger one.

15   We can never be satisfied as long as our children are stripped of their selfhood and robbed of their dignity by signs stating "for whites only." We cannot be satisfied as long as a Negro in Mississippi cannot vote and a Negro in New York believes he has nothing for which to vote. No, we are not satisfied, and we will not be satisfied until justice rolls down like waters and righteousness like a mighty stream.

16   I am not unmindful that some of you have come here out of excessive trials and tribulation. Some of you have come fresh from narrow jail cells. Some of you have come from areas where your quest for freedom left you battered by the storms of persecution and staggered by the winds of police brutality. You have been the veterans of creative suffering. Continue to work with the faith that unearned suffering is redemptive.

17   Go back to Mississippi; go back to Alabama; go back to South Carolina; go back to Georgia; go back to Louisiana; go back to the slums and ghettos of the Northern cities, knowing that somehow this situation can, and will be changed. Let us not wallow in the valley of despair.

18   So I say to you, my friends, that even though we must face the difficulties of today and tomorrow, I still have a dream. It is a dream deeply rooted in the American dream that one day this nation will rise up and live out the true meaning of its creed—we hold these truths to be self evident, that all men are created equal.

19   I have a dream that one day on the red hills of Georgia, sons of former slaves and sons of former slave-owners will be able to sit down together at the table of brotherhood.

20   I have a dream that one day, even the state of Mississippi, a state sweltering with the heat of injustice, sweltering with the heat of oppression, will be transformed into an oasis of freedom and justice.

21   I have a dream my four little children will one day live in a nation where they will not be judged by the color of their skin but by the content of their character. I have a dream today!

22   I have a dream that one day, down in Alabama, with its vicious racists, with its governor having his lips dripping with the words of interposition and nullification, that one day, right there in Alabama, little black boys and black girls will be able to join hands with little white boys and white girls as sisters and brothers. I have a dream today!

23   I have a dream that one day every valley shall be exalted, every hill and mountain shall be made low, the rough places shall be made plain, and the crooked places shall be made straight and the glory of the Lord will be revealed and all flesh shall see it together.

24   This is our hope. This is the faith that I go back to the South with.

25   With this faith we will be able to hew out of the mountain of despair a stone of hope. With this faith we will be able to transform the jangling discords of our nation into a beautiful symphony of brotherhood.

26   With this faith we will be able to work together, to pray together, to struggle together, to go to jail together, to stand up for freedom together, knowing that we will be free one day. This will be the day when all of God's children will be able to sing with new meaning—"my country 'tis of thee; sweet land of liberty; of thee I sing; land where my fathers died, land of the pilgrim's pride; from every mountain side, let freedom ring"—and if America is to be a great nation, this must become true.

27   So let freedom ring from the prodigious hilltops of New Hampshire.

28   Let freedom ring from the mighty mountains of New York.

29   Let freedom ring from the heightening Alleghenies of Pennsylvania.

30   Let freedom ring from the snow-capped Rockies of Colorado.

31   Let freedom ring from the curvaceous slopes of California.

32   But not only that.

33   Let freedom ring from Stone Mountain of Georgia.

34   Let freedom ring from Lookout Mountain of Tennessee.

35   Let freedom ring from every hill and molehill of Mississippi, from every mountainside, let freedom ring.

36   And when we allow freedom to ring, when we let it ring from every village and hamlet, from every state and city, we will be able to speed up that day when all of God's children—black men and white men, Jews and Gentiles, Catholics and Protestants—will be able to join hands and to sing in the words of the old Negro spiritual, "Free at last, free at last; thank God Almighty, we are free at last."

● Vocabulary

momentous (1)	invigorating (8)	sweltering (20)
manacles (2)	degenerate (11)	interposition (22)
languished (3)	inextricably (12)	nullification (22)
unalienable (4)	militancy (12)	exalted (23)
gradualism (7)	tribulation (16)	prodigious (27)
hallowed (7)	redemptive (16)	curvaceous (31)

● The Facts

1. The speech begins "Five score years ago . . ." Why was this beginning especially appropriate?

2. What grievances of black Americans does Dr. King summarize in paragraphs 2 and 3 of this speech?

3. What does Dr. King caution his listeners against in paragraph 11?

4. What attitude toward white people does the speaker urge upon his audience?

5. Although Dr. King speaks out mainly against injustices committed against blacks in the South, he is also critical of the North. What can be inferred from this speech about the living conditions of blacks in the North during the early 1960s?

● The Strategies

1. One critic of this speech has written that its purpose was to intensify the values of the black movement. What characteristic of its style can you point to that might be said to have served this purpose?

2. Paragraphs 4 through 6 of the speech are linked through the use of an extended analogy. What is this analogy?

3. What common rhetorical device does the speech frequently use to emphasize its points?

4. It is often said that speakers and writers use paragraphs differently. How are the paragraphs of this speech especially adapted for oral delivery? What is the most obvious difference between these paragraphs and those a writer might use?

5. What is the function of the brief paragraph 32?

● The Issues

1. "Black" is a term widely used in the United States to designate people whose skin color may range from dark brown to sepia; however, what definition of blackness does our society seem implicitly to use?

2. In your opinion, what is the basis of racial prejudice?

3. Will the United States ever have a black president? Defend your answer.

4. Does prejudice in the United States against black men exceed or equal the prejudice against black women? Explain the difference, if there is one, and justify your answer.

5. What stereotypes do you hold about people of other races? Write them down along with an explanation of how you arrived at them. Share them with your classmates.

● Suggestions for Writing

1. Write an essay analyzing the extensive use of metaphors in this speech. Comment on their effectiveness, bearing in mind the audience for whom the speech was intended.

2. Write an essay analyzing the oral style of this speech. Point out specific techniques of phrasing, sentence construction, paragraphing, and so on, that identify this composition as a speech. Suggest how a writer might have phrased some passages if this work had been written to be read rather than heard.

Letter to Horace Greeley

ABRAHAM LINCOLN

Rhetorical Thumbnail

Purpose: to explain the writer's political determination to preserve the Union

Audience: not just Greeley, but all Americans

Language: old-fashioned formal English

Strategy: uses repetition to make emphatically clear that the writer's overwhelming aim is preservation of the Union.

Abraham Lincoln (1809–1865) is ranked by many historians as among the best U.S. presidents ever. Born in a log cabin and reared to work on frontier farms, Lincoln was often poor and given little formal schooling. Before entering the political arena, he worked as a mill manager, grocery store keeper, surveyor, postmaster, and lawyer. His political career began in 1834 with his election to the Illinois state legislature. In 1860, after many debates with his opponents, Lincoln was elected the sixteenth president of the United States.

The letter that follows was written during the turmoil of the Civil War and stands as a classic statement of Lincoln's constitutional responsibilities. Horace Greeley, editor of the influential New York Tribune, had written an editorial implying that Lincoln's administration lacked direction and resolve. Lincoln's response reveals his unshakable commitment to preserving the Union.

• • •

Executive Mansion,
Washington, August 22, 1862.
Hon. Horace Greeley:
Dear Sir,

1   I have just read yours of the 19th. addressed to myself through the New-York Tribune. If there be in it any statements, or assumptions of fact, which I may know to be erroneous, I do not, now and here, controvert them. If there be in it any inferences which I may believe to be falsely drawn, I do not now and here, argue against them. If there be perceptable [sic] in it an impatient and dictatorial tone, I waive it in deference to an old friend, whose heart I have always supposed to be right.

2   As to the policy I "seem to be pursuing" as you say, I have not meant to leave any one in doubt.

3   I would save the Union. I would save it the shortest way under the Constitution. The sooner the national authority can be restored; the nearer the Union will be "the Union as it was." If there be those who would not save the Union, unless they could at the same time save slavery, I do not agree with them. If there be those who would not save the Union unless they could at the same time destroy slavery, I do not agree with them. My paramount object in this struggle is to save the Union, and is not either to save or to destroy slavery. If I could save the Union without freeing any slave I would do it, and if I could save it by freeing all the slaves I would do it; and if I could save it by freeing some and leaving others alone I would also do that. What I do about slavery, and the colored race, I do because I believe it helps to save the Union; and what I forbear, I forbear because I do not believe it would help to save the Union. I shall do less whenever I shall believe what I am doing hurts the cause, and I shall do more whenever I shall believe doing more will help the cause. I shall try to correct errors when shown to be errors; and I shall adopt new views so fast as they shall appear to be true views.

4   I have here stated my purpose according to my view of official duty; and I intend no modification of my oft-expressed personal wish that all men everywhere could be free.

Yours,

A. Lincoln.

● Vocabulary

controvert (1)   perceptable (1)   paramount (3)
inferences (1)   forbear (3)

● The Facts

1. What was Lincoln's motivation for writing this letter?

2. What attitude does Lincoln show in addressing Greeley? What is the tone of the letter?

3. How does Lincoln imply that he detects an impatient edge to Greeley's letter? What is Lincoln's reaction to this tone?

4. In paragraph 2, Lincoln states that he did not intend to leave anyone in doubt about his policies. Were you left in doubt about Lincoln's policies after reading this letter? Explain your answer.

5. What does the date of the letter add to your understanding of its content?

● The Strategies

1. What do you think Lincoln achieved when he used the words "I waive it in deference to an old friend, whose heart I have always supposed to be right"?

2. What is the thesis of the letter? State it in one clear sentence with your own words.

3. What is the most obvious rhetorical strategy used in the letter? Provide examples of the strategy. How effective is it?

4. What tactic had Greeley used to criticize Lincoln's administration? Does his approach seem fair or backhanded? Give reasons for your answer.

5. What is the purpose of the final paragraph of Lincoln's letter? Is this paragraph necessary? Why or why not?

● The Issues

1. How do you react to Lincoln's view that keeping the Union intact was more important than freeing the slaves? How would that opinion be regarded today?

2. In the final paragraph of his letter, Lincoln refers to his "official duty." What is his official duty? Do think that today the "official duty" of U.S. presidents has changed? What, in your opinion, is the president's primary duty while in office?

3. With your advantage of being able to look back at U.S. history, what is your attitude toward Lincoln's view of slavery?

4. What attitude does Lincoln hold toward errors and toward new views? Do you support his attitude or do you believe he is too wishy-washy?

5. What do you think of Lincoln's statement to Greeley that he does not plan to refute any of Greeley's wrong ideas or conclusions and that he will overlook Greeley's impatient voice and dictatorial posture? What advantage, if any, does Lincoln's response present?

● Suggestions for Writing

1. Choosing one of your political points of view with which someone you know strongly disagrees, write a letter meant to justify your opinion with reason and evidence.

2. Write a paragraph or two analyzing the tone of Lincoln's letter.

● CHAPTER WRITING ASSIGNMENTS

1. Select any two paragraphs, one from an article in *Reader's Digest* and another from an article in *The New Yorker*. Analyze the differences in the language (diction, phrasing, sentence style, and paragraph length) and speculate on the intended audience of each magazine.

2. Write an essay on the meaning and practice of rhetoric as exemplified in this chapter.

● WRITING ASSIGNMENTS FOR A SPECIFIC AUDIENCE

1. To an audience of African American readers, write an essay arguing for or against the idea that race relations in America have gotten better since Dr. King delivered his "I Have a Dream" speech.

2. Write an essay aimed at an audience of eighth graders explaining to them what they can expect to encounter later in high school and college writing courses.

Pointer from a Pro **WRITE OFTEN**

No one presumes to give a dance recital without having first mastered the rudiments of dance, to perform Mozart before playing scales, or to enter a weight-lifting contest without first hoisting weights. Yet, because we've been reading since age five, we blithely assume we can read; because we scrawled our signature when six, we glibly aspire to write.

—Nicholas Delbanco, "From Echoes Emerge Original Voices."
Writers on Writing, p. 47.

All students who are serious about wanting to write well should welcome each opportunity to set ideas on paper because the more you write with a desire to improve your writing, the better you will become in honing your craft.

REAL-LIFE STUDENT WRITING

Email from Samoa

The following excerpt is from an actual email written by one student to another. The sender, Mark, is writing from the South Pacific island of Samoa, where he had arrived two months before as a Peace Corps volunteer. He was on the island only a month when he and another volunteer fell afoul of local authorities and were expelled from the Peace Corps—in their opinion, unfairly. To appeal their expulsion would have required a trip to Washington, D.C., which neither could afford. Instead of returning home as his friend did, Mark decided to stay on the island for as long as he could. He took a job teaching English at a local school while he applied for his visa, which would allow him to remain in Samoa for at least another year. Mark sent this email to his friend, Adam. The two had been classmates in a cross-cultural program in British and American studies.

• • •

From: Mark Smith
Sent: Wednesday, January 15, 2009 4:14 PM
To: Adam Johnson
Subject: Hey What's Up

So things got a little out of hand last night. My friend Taui fire danced at this club last night and we made quite an event of the whole thing. I guess I got a little wasted and then found myself in the Peace Corps office and for the first time in weeks I had access to email and just figured I should send something, anything. I guess my typing fluency was a bit shattered with the excessive alcohol abuse.

I still haven't heard about this work permit. My stamp on my passport runs out soon. Tomorrow actually. I probably should have prepared better for this, but I didn't. I just went to the immigration office. Maybe they'll deport me. It's hard to say.

This school year ends in a couple of weeks, and after that I've got a couple of months off to do absolutely nothing I don't feel like doing. I'll have no money, so I can't really go anywhere, but I've got plenty of free places to stay in Samoa.

If I get my work permit I'm going to buy a spear for spear fishing. Basically, you just put on your snorkel gear and carry around this 4-pronged spear with a rubber band on the end of it that wraps around your wrist. It'll be a fun thing to do when I take my boat out every day.

My Samoan language skills are going to hell. I haven't been learning that much because I don't want to spend my precious time (that is, maybe my last month or so here) learning new words that I'll never ever use again. It's more fun to swim in the ocean, drink recklessly, and use the language I'm used to.

But if I stay I'll get my butt back in gear.

1

A new Peace Corps group just showed up. They've heard many stories about me and my fellow, fallen comrade.

They're scared. When we arrived I was told by some friends the only way to get kicked out was to ride up to the Country director's house with a spliff in your mouth on a motorcycle naked with no helmet.

That was true for a while there; now, with the new administration, they're cracking down on this wild summer camp in Samoa called the Peace Corps. I'm not really too bothered by it. I'm still doing it my own way without that childish organization.

Anyway . . .

Post me some literature if you've got any—writing of any sort. I'm reading like a madman, and writing even more. I've started my book. I like where it's going so far. It's time to stop talking about being a writer and actually piece this thing together.

If people like us aren't going to do it, who will?

Well, let me know what you're doing back home?

You've quit the carpet cleaning job, right? What sort of job does a guy with a degree in British and American cultures get?

Well, take care man. Give me a buzz too if you get a phone card and some time.

Rock on, Mark

Oh yeah, for Halloween I grew a moustache. It was absolutely repulsive.

2

3

Synthesis: Incorporating Outside Sources

Today's best writers often absorb other writers' ideas into their own work. In point of fact, outside sources can be brought into almost every kind of writing, from the most objective to the most personal. But drawing from outside sources without being snowed under by them is a complex skill. It means being able to assimilate someone else's information while not losing sight of your own central point. It means skillfully weaving a quotation, a summary, or a paraphrase into your writing without creating a patchwork quilt that leaves your reader baffled. You can learn this important writing skill by studying examples from experienced writers. But first of all, you need to develop a skill called "synthesis," which includes your understanding the other person's ideas before you can incorporate them into your own.

Generally speaking, synthesis is the ability to combine disparate elements into a new whole. In critical reading and writing, synthesis is the ability to take your understanding of outside texts, images, or information and to *combine these disparate elements into a new whole by responding from your own point of view.*

Educational psychologist Benjamin Bloom understood the complexity of synthesis, and many of his ideas about how we build knowledge, first put forward in the 1950s, are still in use. When we learn, Bloom argued, we must first start with basic remembering and understanding skills and then move through successively more complex kinds of thinking—applying, analyzing, evaluating—before we can gain mastery over a particular body of knowledge and be able to synthesize it into something new and fully our own. It's as if learning is a ladder and we need to climb one rung at a time. This idea is often referred to as "Bloom's hierarchy of cognition" or "Bloom's taxonomy of learning."

Bloom's taxonomy (structural classification) has been presented in many different ways. A recent revision by educational researchers Lorin Anderson and David Krathwohl looks something like this:

For our purposes, this multitiered process of synthesis can be boiled down to three essential steps:

Step 1. Comprehend the ideas presented; gain a basic understanding of them.

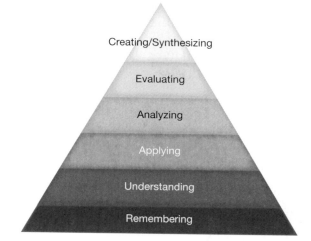

Creating/Synthesizing

Evaluating

Analyzing

Applying

Understanding

Remembering

● **FIGURE 3.1.** *Adapted from Bloom's Taxonomy 1956, as revised by Anderson and Krathwohl 2001.*

Step 2. Analyze and evaluate the ideas; ask questions; wrestle with the information to find where you agree or disagree; notice what ideas you would qualify; make a judgment; begin to formulate your own thoughts and responses.

Step 3. Integrate all of the above into a formal response that is your own; formulate and assert your own thoughts or responses; create something new; write your paper.

As simplified above, this three-step process is what critical reading and writing are all about. Indeed, synthesis—the ability to respond to someone else's ideas, writing, art, or data fully and critically from your own point of view—is perhaps *the* fundamental skill of academic discourse. We make this assertion because academic discourse is fundamentally a dialogue. Every class you take, every book you read, places you at the heart of an ongoing conversation.

This chapter is about building some of the skills that help you take part in this ongoing conversation, especially as it applies to your writing. This chapter looks at both the critical-thinking and the writing skills important to synthesizing and integrating outside sources.

BUILDING BLOCKS FOR INCORPORATING OUTSIDE SOURCES

Paraphrase, summary, and *quotation* are the building blocks for successfully integrating outside sources into your writing.

But before looking closer at each of them, we must consider the conventions for using someone else's ideas correctly and ethically. If you use someone else's creative or intellectual work, you need a citation. If you reference something that can be considered common knowledge, you do not. Quotations, paraphrases, and summaries from outside sources *all* need to be properly acknowledged. This is for two reasons: ethics and argument. Ethically, you must acknowledge the use of someone else's work. In terms of argument, the reader needs to know the source of your information to be able to evaluate what you have to say. For more on documentation and avoiding plagiarism, see the discussion in Part four.

For our discussion of paraphrase, summary, and quotation, we'll refer to Abraham Lincoln's Gettysburg Address, reproduced in full below, as well as to Steve Rushin's "A Nation in Need of Vacation" (pp. 630–632).

Gettysburg Address

ABRAHAM LINCOLN

Address delivered at the dedication of the Soldiers' National Cemetery at Gettysburg, Pennsylvania, November 19, 1863

Fourscore and seven years ago our fathers brought forth upon this continent, a new nation, conceived in Liberty, and dedicated to the proposition that all men are created equal.

Now we are engaged in a great civil war, testing whether that nation, or any nation so conceived and so dedicated, can long endure. We are met on a great battlefield of that war. We have come to dedicate a portion of that field, as a final resting place for those who here gave their lives that that nation might live. It is altogether fitting and proper that we should do this.

But, in a larger sense, we cannot dedicate—we cannot consecrate—we cannot hallow—this ground. The brave men, living and dead, who struggled here, have consecrated it, far above our poor power to add or detract. The world will little note nor long remember what we say here, but it can never forget what they did here. It is for us the living, rather, to be dedicated here to the unfinished work which they who fought here have thus far so nobly advanced. It is rather for us to be here dedicated to the great task remaining before us—that from these honored dead we take increased devotion to that cause for which they gave the last full measure of devotion—that we here highly resolve that these dead shall not have died in vain—that this nation, under God, shall have a new birth of freedom—and that government of the people, by the people, and for the people, shall not perish from the earth.

Paraphrase

To paraphrase is to put a specific passage into your own words. The passage being paraphrased can be as short as a phrase or as long as a paragraph but is typically a sentence or a few sentences. Whereas a *summary* (see below) "sums up" the ideas in a whole book, whole article, whole poem, or even just a section or passage, a *paraphrase* by its very nature is a rewriting on the sentence level. We summarize whole ideas but paraphrase words and sentences.

When you paraphrase an outside source, you must be careful to use your own language, not the author's:

Original: "But, in a larger sense, we cannot dedicate—we cannot consecrate—we cannot hallow—this ground. The brave men, living and dead, who struggled here, have consecrated it, far above our poor power to add or detract."

Paraphrase: We can't make this ground holy because the struggle and sacrifice of the soldiers who died here have already made it holy—far beyond our feeble abilities to do so.

Original: "My fellow citizens are the least vacationing people in the industrialized world. We receive, on average, 14 days of vacation a year, and no legally mandated paid leave. Even the Japanese average 17.5 days off annually, and they have a word—*karoshi*—for working oneself to death."

Paraphrase: Americans take less vacation time (just 14 days) than citizens of any other industrialized nation. Even workers in Japan, where there is an actual word for death caused by overworking, take more vacation time than workers in America.

And you must always acknowledge the source properly when incorporating the paraphrase into your writing:

Paraphrase incorporated into new writing: According to Lincoln, we cannot make this ground holy, because the struggle and sacrifice of the soldiers who died here have already made it holy—far beyond our feeble abilities to do so (58).

Paraphrase incorporated into new writing: Rushin notes that Americans take less vacation time than citizens of any other industrialized nation. And he humorously reminds us that even in Japan, where there is an actual word for death caused by overworking, workers average more vacation time than in America (631).

● Exercises

1. The Gettysburg Address is composed of just ten sentences. Although brief, it is densely packed with meaning. Working your way through the entire speech one sentence at a time, paraphrase each sentence. As in the discussion examples above, first write the original sentence, using quotation marks. Then, write your paraphrase of that sentence. As necessary, use a dictionary or other outside references for words or concepts you do not understand.

2. Evaluate the Gettysburg Address in relation to its audience and purpose (to review these concepts, see pp. 22–23). You may use an outside source or sources of your choosing. Write a paragraph that argues your point of view and that incorporates at least one paraphrase of the address.

Summary

To summarize is to condense the meaning of something to a shortened form. You can summarize almost anything, short or long: a poem, an article, a speech, an entire book, or even an author's entire body of work. While a *paraphrase* restates a passage on the sentence level—and to a certain extent mirrors the language of the original—a *summary* crystallizes its main ideas. We paraphrase words but summarize broader ideas.

When you summarize an outside source, you must be careful to use your own language (never the author's exact wording) and to document the source properly. Here are possible summaries of Lincoln's entire speech and Rushin's whole article:

> Lincoln told the crowd that the best way to honor the soldiers who died at Gettysburg would be to save the union and win the war (58).
> In "A Nation in Need of Vacation," Rushin argues that our national productivity would increase if we took more time off (632).

Note that if we summarize an entire book, citing pages is not required:

> *David Copperfield* charts the eponymous hero's quest from the vulnerability of childhood to the struggles and triumphs of the adult.

Both paraphrase and summary are important critical reading and research skills. To review critical reading skills, see Chapter 1. For more on paraphrase and summary as part of research and note-taking, see Part four.

● Exercises

1. Consider the summary of *David Copperfield* in the discussion above or the kinds of marketing summaries found on book jackets. Summarize your favorite novel in one sentence, conveying the essence of its plot, themes, and/or style. Write two different one-sentence summaries: one using diction appropriate for a college course, and another using diction appropriate for a book jacket.

2. What is the most interesting or significant book-length work of nonfiction you have ever read? How would you describe it to an interested reader? How would you condense its main argument down to the essentials? Conveying as much information about the book's main argument as possible, summarize a favorite book-length work of nonfiction in one to three sentences. Use diction appropriate for a book review in a current periodical.

3. Consider the summary of "A Nation in Need of Vacation" in the discussion above. Choose a short essay in this reader and summarize its main argument in one sentence.

Quotation

A quotation uses an author's writing word for word, be it a phrase, a sentence, an entire paragraph, or sometimes even a word:

> Faced with the enormous losses at the battle of Gettysburg—and indeed with the enormous loss of life over the course of the war thus

far—Lincoln did not shrink from noting the inadequacy of dedicating the National Cemetery on that November day: "We cannot dedicate—we cannot consecrate—we cannot hallow—this ground. The brave men, living and dead, who struggled here, have consecrated it, far above our poor power to add or detract" (58).

As Rushin humorously reminds us, "Even the Japanese average 17.5 days off annually, and they have a word—*karoshi*—for working oneself to death" (631).

As opposed to paraphrase or summary, quotation is especially effective when the original text is so striking or eloquent that conveying the mere sense of the words would fall flat.

When incorporating a quotation, always use quotation marks; be careful to preserve the punctuation, spelling, and capitalization of the original; and always use appropriate documentation. For details and exceptions consult a style manual appropriate to your field of study (or ask your instructor which style manual he or she recommends).

● Exercises

1. Choose some aspect of the Gettysburg Address that interests you. Bolster your understanding of the speech's historical and cultural context by consulting at least two outside sources. Then, develop a clear position and write a three-paragraph essay that incorporates at least one quotation from the Gettysburg Address and one paraphrase and one summary, either of the address itself or of an outside source.

2. Choose a fiction or nonfiction book that interests you and write a three-paragraph book review that evaluates and describes the book's style and content. In your book review, incorporate at least one paraphrase, one summary, and one quotation from the book itself. Use diction appropriate for a contemporary periodical, take a strong point of view, and strive to engage the reader.

3. Choose a contemporary topic that interests you and write a one- to three-paragraph letter to the editor (brevity is essential; the *New York Times,* for example, allows only 150 words per letter). Take a clear position and defend it logically, incorporating at least two outside sources. Acknowledge the sources in the text of your letter and also create a separate list of sources with complete documentation. Make your writing clear, concise, and persuasive.

GUIDELINES FOR EFFECTIVELY SYNTHESIZING OUTSIDE SOURCES

Following specific guidelines, presented in this section, will help you master the complex skill of synthesis.

Guidelines for Thinking and Reading Critically

Having introduced the building blocks for using outside sources in your writing, let's return for a moment to the task of synthesis, as it applies to the critical reading and writing process overall. When you consider any kind of writing assignment that asks you to *engage with, respond to, critique, evaluate, discuss, describe, agree with, disagree with, qualify, incorporate, provide an overview of, review,* or *synthesize* another text, a few guidelines apply. Note, too, that while we've been discussing outside sources primarily as texts, they can also include tables, charts, graphs, and images of all kinds. For more on working with images, see Chapter 2.

First, understand. Understand the assignment and understand the source materials. Read and reread until you have grasped the meaning and requirements of the assignment and have grasped the meanings of the various source materials. As we noted in our initial discussion of Bloom's taxonomy, understanding provides the basis for all further analysis, evaluation, and synthesis. You need that foundation to have something to build on.

Second, allow space for your own thoughts. It's easy to get overwhelmed by all those experts and feel that you have nothing to say. Different students find different approaches work best for them, and if you persist, so will you. One technique many find helpful, especially when working on a research paper or a researched argument paper, is to posit a point of view before you begin your research. Stop to take stock of your own ideas and responses before hearing expert opinion, and continue taking stock of your own ideas and responses while reading and evaluating others' texts and ideas, and while writing about and responding to them. Many find this approach especially helpful on the kind of timed synthesis essays now found on many standardized exams.

Third, make research a dialogue with the material. Listen to yourself and listen to the material. Have a road map, but be open to discovery. This guideline and the previous one can sound contradictory, but they are not. There is a back-and-forth at work here, a conversation ongoing between you and the material. Engaging with outside resources should expand your own thinking. Critical reading and writing should be a voyage of discovery, not a rote regurgitation of "right" answers, not a rigid steamrolling to prove pre-assumed dogma, and not a vague or vapid skimming of the surface just to get by. Every time you engage with a text, truly engage with it, you should come out changed, somehow, even if only a little bit.

Persist, revise, rewrite. A first reading of any text is unlikely to bring you to a place of comprehension, much less a place of being able to analyze, evaluate, and synthesize it for your own purposes. Read and reread and take notes until you've grasped the material; only then will you be able to enter into dialogue with it. By the same token, a first draft of any writing is unlikely to be the strongest, the most interesting, or the most successful. And many writers find that—outlines aside—they only really find what they want to say as they write it. For many, writing itself unlocks the deepest level of engagement on any given topic. So don't just rush through a paper and hand it in. Give yourself time to rewrite if you want to truly figure out what you have to say and find the best way to say it.

Repeat all of the above. Writing is a recursive, not a linear, process. This means, as we say in Chapter 2, that writing is a back-and-forth process. You often find yourself going back to push forward. And you often find that writing is more circular or spiraling than linear. When you read good writing, it pours so straightforwardly off the page that it often feels like it must have been created in as easy and straightforward a manner. But most writers will tell you that they revisit any and all of the steps above, in every possible sequence, before they achieve a final draft with which they can be satisfied.

Many of the most common weaknesses in student writing stem from the failure to fully engage with the above fundamental processes. We began this chapter by discussing how the ability to successfully synthesize and integrate outside sources is both a writing and a critical-thinking skill. Many common student errors—failure to stake out a strong argument, weak point of view, allowing the source to dominate (rather than support) the argument, failure to understand the source entirely, oversimplification of the source, misrepresentation of the source, weak relationship of the source to one's own argument, failure to use the source properly—more often show a weakness in thinking than in writing. Successfully synthesizing and integrating outside sources into your writing requires that you harness critical-thinking and writing skills together. The more you engage with the source materials and with the writing process, the clearer and the more interesting your writing will be.

Commenting on her essay "Body Modification—Think about It!" (pp. 323–328), student writer Shelley Taylor offers some excellent advice about these processes to her fellow writers:

> Before I actually begin writing, I do a lot of reflective thinking and organizing in my mind. I decide what information I am going to include and try to get a rough idea of the order and format I want to use. I usually sketch out an outline that I can follow. . . . After I have finished, I read through my work several times to do further editing.
>
> While working on this piece, I used the Internet to look up a few sites and articles on my subject to get an idea about current research, others' opinions, etc. I searched my memory for incidents in my own experience and illustration that were relevant to the issue. Finally, I synthesized and integrated all of this information to formulate my own thoughts, feelings, and insights.
>
> (329)

To review approaches to critical reading, the writing process, and working with visual imagery, see Chapters 1 and 2.

Guidelines for Improving Your Use of Outside Sources

Whether you are using a quotation, paraphrase, or summary, outside sources have essentially two functions in your writing:

1. to support your argument
2. to enliven your writing

But these two functions can be effectively carried out in varied ways, depending on what you want to say and how you want to say it. As in other writing tasks, different kinds of writing that incorporate outside sources often require different strategies to be effective. Are you writing a personal essay *or* a researched argument? Are you writing for a newspaper or popular magazine *or* for an academic journal? Will your diction need to be formal or informal? Will your piece be humorous or serious? What makes for effective writing depends on your subject matter, genre, venue, audience, and the needs of the particular piece in terms of flow and emphasis. In incorporating outside sources, as in all kinds of writing, understanding the rhetorical situation is important.

That said, a few guidelines apply.

Always keep your argument in the foreground. In any kind of writing, your argument—also termed your thesis—drives content. Your argument drives the essay forward, your argument drives the writing. (This is even true in a narrative essay, in which "argument" becomes "story.") The outside source is used to support your argument, but it never replaces it. A research paper—even one in which most of the information comes from outside—must be filtered and focused through your point of view. It is always up to you, the author, to shape the material. Think of the steel girders bracing a skyscraper—that's your argument, no matter what else gets added floor by floor. A simple percentage count can sometimes be helpful. A paper that consists primarily of quotations, for example, is already in trouble.

Weave the sources into your argument. Don't just drop them in from outer space. One of the most common criticisms of student writing is that outside information is inserted willy-nilly with little to no connection to the writer's argument. As discussed earlier, this kind of weak relationship between source and writing can often be traced to a shallowness in understanding the source and/or a shallowness in thinking through your argument. Moreover, even when you know what you want to say and how you want to use the outside information to support it, successfully weaving outside sources into your argument takes study and practice. An apt metaphor here might be a casserole. What if, instead of a delicious mix of sauce, chopped meat, minced vegetables, and carefully chosen spices, someone handed you a bowl with an uncooked hunk of meat, unchopped vegetables, and a salt shaker? Doubtless you would be perplexed. Believe us, the reader tackling the "uncooked" essay feels the same way.

Consider form as well as function. First strive to make your writing clear, then strive to make it lively. And by "lively" we mean all of the nuances that make someone's writing a pleasure to read. Once you've achieved clarity, you can turn your attention to greater elegance of style. That said, as you'll notice in the examples that follow, what makes a particular piece of writing well written and pleasurable, and what makes the writer's incorporation of an outside source particularly effective, is often as individual as the piece itself. But a few generalizations apply. Good writing often has variation, but not too much. Shifts in tone and diction, variation in wording, and shifts in pace as appropriate often help keep things lively. Too much variation and it's a mess. Too little and the writing is dull and boring. Good writers find the right balance. Good writers know how to use humor (when that's their aim). Good writers know how to make us go silent. They know how to place emphasis and draw the reader's attention where they want it to go. Learning what works to create readable writing is a matter of study and practice.

WRITERS AT WORK: STRATEGIES FOR INCORPORATING OUTSIDE SOURCES

One of the best ways to improve your writing is by studying how experienced writers make things work. So in considering how to successfully synthesize outside sources into your writing, one of the best places to look is at the many essays included in this reader. What kinds of strategies do these writers employ? How do they use quotation, paraphrase, and summary (either separately or in combination) to build persuasive arguments and to enliven their writing?

Writers at Work: Using Paraphrase and Summary

Paraphrase and summary are the real workhorses for integrating outside sources into your writing. Because any paraphrase or summary of another text is itself a synthesis, using paraphrase and summary in your writing keep you—your thoughts, your responses, your unique point of view—in the driver's seat. By paraphrasing a phrase, sentence, or passage or by summarizing an entire book, chapter, article, or idea (however long or short), you've already begun your own process of understanding, analyzing, evaluating, and synthesizing the information. You've already started to digest it.

While paraphrase and summary are in some ways alike, each has a different function and is created differently when you gather your evidence. Paraphrase, to recap, is when you restate a specific phrase, sentence, or passage in your own words. Paraphrase is useful to evoke a writer's language, when for reasons of argument, balance, flexibility, or efficiency you don't want to quote the whole thing. Paraphrase lets you bring in the *sense* of someone's exact statement but in your own words, thus allowing you to highlight only that part of a statement that's important to your argument. Paraphrase is also useful when the original writing *isn't* memorable but you want to convey another writer's information efficiently and succinctly, or when the original is in obscure or archaic language and requires simplifying. Paraphrase is often a useful way to introduce or conclude a quotation.

Summary gives you the greatest degree of flexibility to adapt outside sources to your argument. Because you can summarize anything from a passage to an entire series of books, summary puts you fully in charge of the breadth of scope or level of detail with which you want to discuss a particular idea. Consider these examples of summary:

> The famous storm scene in *David Copperfield* brings to an end the story of David's boyhood friend and hero, Steerforth.
> *David Copperfield* charts the eponymous hero's quest from the vulnerability of childhood to the struggles and triumphs of the adult.
> Dickens's later novels show a repeated obsession with double lives and duplicity.
> Throughout his long career—from the orphaned Oliver Twist of his second novel to the pitiful street urchin Jo in the mature *Bleak House* to Pip's coming-of-age-struggles in the later *Great Expectations*—Dickens returned again and again to the child's struggle against a brutal and seemingly uncaring universe.

A quotation, by contrast, restricts you not just to the original author's words but also to the pace and scope of the original idea. A paraphrase frees you somewhat but, because it operates at the sentence level, doesn't allow the same freedom to zoom in or out as a summary. Whether you want to provide a broad sweeping overview or hone in sharply on a microscopic detail, using a summary puts you in charge. Summary also gives you far more room than either quotation or paraphrase to present an outside idea through the lens of your own interpretation.

Let's consider, then, the following passages to see how some of the writers in this book have used paraphrase and summary to support their ideas and enliven their writing.

Student writer Shelley Taylor's sweeping summary of the history of tattoos gives breadth and depth to her initial observations about the current craze for body modification:

> Actually, through history, people from various cultures have decorated their bodies with piercings and tattoos. In 1992, a 4,000-year-old body of a tattooed man was found in an Austrian glacier. From 4000 to 2000 BC, Egyptians identified tattooing with fertility and nobility. Body piercing has been used as a symbol of royalty and courage, as well as other

lauded attributes. In some societies, body piercing and tattoos have long been used in initiation rites and as socialization symbols.

(323)

Notice that she doesn't document each of these details because she's summarizing from what can legitimately be thought of as common knowledge. (This information can, however, go into a bibliography.)

One of the overall most artful blends of summary, paraphrase, and quotation is found in science writer Natalie Angier's "Of Altruism, Heroism, and Evolution's Gifts" (pp. 414–418). Angier gives a sweeping overview of current scientific research on the biological basis of altruism. But what makes the piece effective— what makes it a piece of stunningly good writing and not just a string of quotes, paraphrases, and summaries—is the way Angier herself remains in control of the storyline. The historical context within which she writes (the piece was published in the *New York Times* within days of the attacks on the World Trade Center) brings tremendous urgency to the topic. And Angier so skillfully interweaves her blend of summary, paraphrase, and quotation with her own thoughts and insights that the overall effect is simply eloquent.

In the following two passages, notice how she nimbly provides an overview of an entire body of knowledge, using summary to zoom *out*. Here she deftly summarizes current research on language and memory:

[M]ost biologists concur that the human capacity for language and memory allows altruistic behavior—the desire to give, and to sacrifice for the sake of others—to flourish in measure far beyond the cooperative spirit seen in other species.

With language, they say, people can learn of individuals they have never met and feel compassion for their suffering, and honor and even emulate their heroic deeds. They can also warn one another of any selfish cheaters or malign tricksters lurking in their midst.

(415–416)

Here, she takes us all the way back to Darwin and zooms over the past century and a half:

The desire to understand the nature of altruism has occupied evolutionary thinkers since Charles Darwin, who was fascinated by the apparent existence of altruism among social insects. In ant and bee colonies, sterile female workers labor ceaseless for their queen, and will even die for her when the nest is threatened. How could such seeming selflessness evolve, when it is exactly those individuals that are behaving altruistically that fail to breed and thereby pass their selfless genes along?

(416)

In this passage, she zooms *in* and focuses on the work of a single scientist, while also moving effortlessly between paraphrase and quotation:

> The concept of inclusive fitness explains many brave acts observed in nature. Dr. Richard Wrangham, a primatologist at Harvard, cites the example of the red colobus monkey. When they are being hunted by chimpanzees, the male monkeys are "amazingly brave." Dr. Wrangham said, "As the biggest and strongest members of their group, they undoubtedly could escape quicker than the others." Instead, the males jump to the front, confronting the chimpanzee hunters while the mothers and offspring jump to safety. Often, the much bigger chimpanzees pull the colobus soldiers off by their tails and slam them to their deaths.
>
> (416)

It's as if we too are in the room, listening to the interview.

One of the most humorous and most effective uses of paraphrase is the one with which Bill Bryson closes his argument (highlighted below). Having begun his essay "Wide-open Spaces" (pp. 445–447) by telling us "Daniel Boone was an idiot," Bryson leaves us in suspense about what this could possibly mean until the next-to-last paragraph:

> Of course, Americans have always tended to see these things in a different way. Daniel Boone famously is supposed to have looked out his cabin window one day, seen a wisp of smoke rising from a homesteader's dwelling on a distant mountain, and announced his intention to move on, complaining bitterly that the neighborhood was getting too crowded.
>
> Which is why I say Daniel Boone was an idiot. I just hate to see the rest of my country going the same way.
>
> (447)

Bryson paraphrases the famous Boone saying ("Too many people! Too crowded, too crowded! I want some elbow room!") to knock this beloved American icon down a peg—and get us to rethink our mythical view of ourselves as Boone-like independent spirits, while bringing his essay to its witty conclusion.

Writers at Work: Using Quotation

Like paraphrases and summaries, quotations can be used to provide evidence. A classic use of quotation for this purpose is when a writer quotes an expert authority to support his or her argument. And, of course, quotations can be used in other ways simply to deliver information. But quotations differ from summaries and paraphrases in that they can be especially useful at providing stylistic flair. Because quotations reproduce another person's speech and writing word for word, they are a flexible and effective way to add emphasis to a particular thought, land a punch, bring your paragraph, section, or entire essay to a walloping conclusion. For this reason, quotations can be particularly effective at or towards the end of a paragraph. But opening and mid-paragraph placements can, of course, also be used effectively.

Quotations are also uniquely suited to writing situations where you want to add depth or breadth to an argument, where you turn to someone else's mullings on your particular topic to allow the reader to dwell more deeply. For this purpose, writers will often use quotations from famous authors, philosophers, artists, or other respected public figures. We expect William Shakespeare or Albert Einstein, for example, to have something to say that is uniquely insightful about the human condition. One final note: Use quotations sparingly. By their very nature, quotations are never in your voice. Consider the following examples of effective use of quotation.

Student writer Shelley Taylor brings "Body Modification—Think About It!" to a well-punched end with a classic, end-placed quotation:

> Remember that this decision [to get a tattoo or body piercing] will most likely affect the rest of your life. That makes it extremely important, wouldn't you say? Whether you are a teenager, a young adult, or a middle-aged person who has always dreamed of doing something fun and outrageous, don't forget to look at all sides of this issue. It will be well worth the trouble. At the risk of being unoriginal, I would like to end with a quotation from one of those very wise anonymous writers for *The College Chalkboard* Web site: "Ponder before you pierce, and think before you ink." I couldn't have said it better myself.
>
> (328)

Readers will likely walk away from this essay with "think before you ink" bouncing around their brains for a few hours at least. The quotation is effective at bringing Taylor's essay to its conclusion because of placement (end of paragraph), because it's funny and memorable (especially with its use of rhyme and alliteration), and because it's an apt and clever summing up of her overall thesis, already nicely clarified in the title and well developed in the overall flow of her argument.

In "Illegal Immigrants Are Bolstering Social Security with Billions" (pp. 441–443), Eduardo Porter uses expert opinion to support and provide evidence for his point of view:

> Illegal immigration, Marcel Suárez-Orozco, codirector of immigration studies at New York University, noted sardonically, could provide "the fastest way to shore up the long-term finances of Social Security."
>
> (442)

His expert, as we would expect in an essay on a current social issue, is someone with recognized professional standing in the field being discussed.

Note, too, that Porter uses this quotation (one of only two in a 15-paragraph article) to cap an argument he's been building over several paragraphs, having first described a single immigrant's typical workday, wages, and contribution to Social Security and then filled in the big picture with a paragraph or so of convincing statistics.

An "expert" quotation can also be from someone who speaks not as a noted authority *on* a particular subject but as someone who *is* the subject. In "Body Image" (pp. 310–315), health professional Cindy Maynard speaks about teenage body image primarily from her own position as a health expert. But she includes a paragraph in which teenagers speak for themselves:

> Some sports can contribute to a negative body image. The need to make weight for a sport like wrestling or boxing can cause disordered eating. But other boys say sports make them feel better about themselves. Jon, a 15-year-old, states, "Guys are in competition, especially in the weight room. They say, 'I can bench 215 lbs.' and the other guy says, 'Well, I can bench 230 lbs.' If you're stronger, you're better." Daniel, age 16, shares, "Guys are into having the perfect body. But if you feel good about your body, you automatically feel good about yourself."
>
> (311–312)

By doing so, she brings a different kind of expertise to her article, she shifts from a professional to a personal point of view and from her own "expert" voice to the boys' personal voices, and she lets her teenage readers know that she's not just an expert talking *at* them; she's willing to listen.

Alfred Lubrano makes a similar shift in voice, but in a different direction, in the deeply personal "Bricklayer's Boy" (pp. 572–577). Over the essay's 28 paragraphs, there are only two brief uses of outside sources. In this one, towards the essay's conclusion, he quotes an expert in men's issues, on the subject of father-son class divides:

> When we see each other these days, my father still asks how the money is. Sometimes he reads my stories; usually he likes them, although he recently criticized one piece as being a bit sentimental: "Too schmaltzy," he said. Some psychologists say that the blue-white-collar gap between fathers and sons leads to alienation, but I tend to agree with Dr. Al Baraff, a clinical psychologist and director of the MenCenter in Washington, DC. "The core of the relationship is based on emotional and hereditary traits," Baraff says. "Class [distinctions] just get added on. If it's a healthful relationship from when you're a kid, there's a respect back and forth that'll continue."
>
> (576)

By bringing in Dr. Baraff's perspective, Lubrano shifts from the truth of his own story to a proposed truth about all such father-son relationships; he shifts from talking about his experience as the white-collar son of a blue-collar man to a society-wide observation about all such relationships. Quoting an expert makes this shift effective and economical.

Cowley begins "The View from Eighty" (pp. 352–356) with the observation that being elderly can feel like playing a part. He then amplifies and expands on this reflection by quoting from Nobel Prize–winning novelist and essayist André Gide:

> Even before he or she is 80, the aging person may undergo another identity crisis like that of adolescence. Perhaps there had also been a middle-aged crisis, the male or the female menopause, but for the rest of adult life he had taken himself for granted, with his capabilities and failings. Now, when he looks in the mirror, he asks himself, "Is this really me?"—or he avoids the mirror out of distress at what it reveals, those bags and wrinkles. In his new makeup he is called upon to play a new role in a play that must be improvised. André Gide, that long-lived man of letters, wrote in his journal, "My heart has remained so young that I have the continual feeling of playing a part, the part of the 70-year-old that I certainly am; and the infirmities and weaknesses that remind me of my age act like a prompter, reminding me of my lines when I tend to stray. Then, like the good actor I want to be, I go back into my role, and I pride myself on playing it well."
>
> (352)

Gide's "expertise" is that of the noted writer providing insight into the human condition, and the quotation helps the reader dwell more deeply on Cowley's already established idea.

In narrative nonfiction, quotation can also become dialogue to great effect. Partway through the excerpt from *Warriors Don't Cry* (pp. 537–540), Melba Patillo Beals talks about what it was like to be invited to the Clinton governor's mansion thirty years after a previous Arkansas governor fostered a climate of violence and hatred to keep Beals and a handful of other young African Americans out of Arkansas high schools:

> During all the fancy ceremonies, some of Arkansas's highest officials and businessmen came from far and wide to welcome us. And perhaps the most astounding evidence that things have indeed changed for the better was the attitude of Governor Bill Clinton.
>
> "Call me Bill," he said, extending his hand, looking me in the eye. "You'll come on up to the house and sit a while." He flashed that charming

grin of his. A few minutes of conversation assured me that his warm invitation was genuine. He is, after all, a man my brother refers to as "good people," based on their working relationship over the years.

(539)

Here the use of quotation as dialogue provides a powerful means of showing—not just telling—how much times had changed.

Finally, a quotation can be used in ways that combine many of the above strategies but that are most noteworthy for providing sheer delight. Steven Rushin uses quotations from Jimmy Buffet and from Shakespeare to provide literary evidence, to place emphasis on his central idea by quoting something memorable, and to bring his essay to its conclusion:

> From the beginning of time, and across cultural boundaries, humans have had wanderlust, often with the emphasis on the second half of that compound word. Jimmy Buffett sees the romantic possibilities when freedom from duty and duty-free booze conspire: "The weather is here, I wish you were beautiful / My thoughts aren't too clear but don't run away / My girlfriend's a bore, my job is too dutiful / Hell nobody's perfect, would you like to play?"
>
> It's a nearly universal human impulse. And so another bard—of Avon, not Margaritaville—was writing the very same sentiments some 400 years earlier in *As You Like It*: "Come woo me, woo me; for now I am in a holiday humour, and like enough to consent."
>
> So humor me—"holiday humor" me—and consent. We are One Nation in Need of Vacation. Studies show that Americans would be more productive with increased time off. Some companies are now mandating that employees take their vacations. In short, it's not just your right to annually abdicate duty. It's your duty.

(632)

Both Buffet and Shakespeare support his assertion that "wanderlust" crosses cultural and temporal boundaries and that holidays are important to our happiness. At the same time, Rushin makes us laugh by the wonderful absurdity of mixing up the disparate worlds of these two artists. Note, too, the fancy wordplay as Rushin goes from his own use of "wanderlust" to these two different examples of lust while wandering: Buffet's "would you like to play?" and Shakespeare's "Come woo me." Then, Rushin takes Rosalind's flirtatious "woo me; for now I am in a holiday humour, and like enough to consent" and asks the reader to consent and humor him, the writer. Here "humour" ping-pongs back and forth from its Elizabethan meaning of a kind of temperament to our meaning of "do me this one little favor" as Rushin prods the reluctant American worker into taking a break. The use of an outside source doesn't get much more fun or more elegant than this!

● CHAPTER WRITING ASSIGNMENT: WRITING A
SYNTHESIS ESSAY

This assignment asks you to write an essay synthesizing at least three out-side sources in support of your argument.

The essay topic is described below. You will find the readings themselves on the pages that follow. Essay prompts can be found on pages 92–93. Suggestions for additional reading can be found on pages 93–94.

Income Disparity, Social Mobility, and the American Dream

Introduction

The "American Dream" has been dismissed as a cliché and upheld as the glue that holds our nation together. It has been variously described throughout our nation's history. In the past decade, a number of studies have documented a rising gap between the incomes of the wealthiest Americans and all other wage earners, alongside a decrease in America's much-touted tradition of social mobility. These findings have many policymakers, journalists, researchers, and ordinary people wondering about our long-held notions of social mobility and the American Dream. The following readings present a number of viewpoints on this topic.

Directions

First, read and annotate each source critically and carefully. Pay attention to the different points of view they each express, the different ways they each express them, and the rhetorical context for each source.

Then, using one of the prompts on pages 92–93, write an essay that synthesizes at least three of the sources in support of your argument.

Make sure to acknowledge sources properly. Strive to make your argument as clear and persuasive as possible, and to make your writing effective and readable.

Sources

1. Commencement speech, "The American Dream." Martin C. Jischke, "The American Dream," *Vital Speeches of the Day* 73, no. 7 (July 2007): 314–15.

2. Magazine article, "The Death of Horatio Alger." Paul Krugman, "The Death of Horatio Alger," *The Nation*, January 5, 2004, 16.

3. Book excerpt, "By Our Own Bootstraps." From W. Michael Cox and Richard Alm, "Chapter 4: By Our Own Bootstraps," *Myths of Rich and Poor: Why We're Better Off Than We Think* (New York: Basic, 1999), 69, 87–89.

4. Book excerpt and statistical overview, "How the U.S. Stacks Up against Other Wealthy, Industrialized Nations." From Richard Wilkinson and Kate

Pickett, *The Spirit Level: Why Greater Equality Makes Societies Stronger* (New York: Bloomsbury, 2009), 17, 20, 148, 160.

5. Online commentary, "Long Live the American Dream." Shikha Dalmia, "Long Live the American Dream," Reason.com, March 1, 2011; originally published at TheDaily.com, February 24, 2011.

6. Book excerpt, "Deer Hunting with Jesus." From Joe Bageant, *Deer Hunting with Jesus: Dispatches from America's Class War* (New York: Crown, 2007), 62–64, 69–74.

7. Magazine article, "The American Dream." From Richard Todd, "Who Me, Rich? What It Takes (and What It Means) to Be Wealthy Today: A Look at the Top 1 Percent," *Worth*, September 1997, 70–84.

8. Book excerpt, "Epilogue: The American Dream." From James Truslow Adams, *The Epic of America* (Boston: Little, 1931), 404–12.

1. The American Dream

MARTIN C. JISCHKE, "THE AMERICAN DREAM," *VITAL SPEECHES OF THE DAY* 73, NO. 7 (JULY 2007): 314–15.

The following reading is excerpted from Martin C. Jischke's commencement speech delivered at Purdue University, May 2007. Jischke was president of Purdue University from 2000 to 2007.

• • •

1   I am the first person in my family to graduate from college. Some of you today know how this feels.

2   My grandfather immigrated to this country from an area that is now part of Poland. He had minimal education. He was a Wisconsin farmer, and he ran a small grocery. My father wanted to be a physician. But there was no money to send him to college during the Great Depression, so he worked in the grocery business in Chicago. I don't remember him ever taking a vacation. With the six kids at home, we spent everything my father made.

3   My father found my experience of going to college quite amazing. . . . I worked. I had scholarships. I took out loans. I financed my own education. When I finished my Ph.D. at MIT, I went home for a visit. I brought with me a copy of my doctoral thesis, and I gave it to my parents. . . . My father opened it. And he saw what I wanted them to see. I had dedicated my thesis to my parents. When my father saw this, he started weeping. I will never forget it. . . .

4   But this story is not about me. I tell you this story because I represent just one of many millions of Americans whose lives and futures have been changed by the power of education. Today we are adding these new graduates to that growing list.

5   Our graduates today are living a promise that was best identified by an American historian named James Truslow Adams. Most people have never heard of him. But we are all very familiar with three words that he wrote: three simple, but powerful words. They might be among the most defining three words in American history, after "We the people."

6   In a widely translated book titled *Epic of America,* James Truslow Adams coined the term "the American dream." Wherever you come from in the world . . . you have all heard of the American dream. It is part of American culture and heritage. It is the essence of what we, as Americans, believe about ourselves and our nation.

7   But the term doesn't come from our Declaration of Independence, our Constitution, or the Bill of Rights. It comes from James Truslow Adams. You might be surprised that he introduced the term in 1931 in the early years of the Great Depression—the Depression that stopped my father's dreams of higher education.

8   In 1931 when the term American dream was introduced, U.S. unemployment exceeded 16 percent. Eight million people were without work. It would get worse. Much worse.

9   Into this, James Truslow Adams introduced the American dream. And people believed it.

10   What is the American dream? What does it mean to you? Is it your own prosperity? Is it becoming more successful than your parents?

11   I can tell you what it meant to James Truslow Adams. He wrote that the American dream is the "dream of a land in which life should be better and richer and fuller for everyone, with opportunity for each according to ability or achievement. It is not a dream of motor cars and high wages merely, but a dream of a social order in which each man and each woman shall be able to attain to the fullest stature of which they are innately capable, and be recognized by others for what they are, regardless of birth or position."

12   Standing here before you—the grandson of a German immigrant with little education, the son of a grocer—I have experienced the incredible opportunity of serving as president of Purdue. I am surely living the American dream.

13   But I believe the American dream is not merely success. The American dream is not the attainment of riches. It is not fame. The American dream is opportunity. And when coupled with desire and hard work, opportunity can fulfill all our greatest dreams.

14   I believe the American dream was the concept Thomas Jefferson was crafting when he wrote: "We hold these truths to be self-evident: That all men are created equal, that they are endowed by their creator with certain unalienable rights, that among these are life, liberty and the pursuit of happiness."

15   I believe the American dream is much more than the dreams of individuals. I believe the American dream is the dream of this nation.

16   I believe the American dream is the opportunity to live in a nation in which diversity is celebrated as the source of strength and beauty.

17   I believe the American dream is the opportunity not only to acquire, but to give and to serve other people in need.

18   I believe the American dream is the opportunity to pursue knowledge freely, through a lifetime of learning, growing, changing, and evolving.

19   I believe the American dream is the opportunity to share these great possibilities with people throughout the world, no matter where they live, no matter what their circumstance.

20   All of this is the American dream to me.

21   Martin Luther King Jr., said: "America is essentially a dream, a dream as yet unfulfilled. It is a dream of a land where [people] of all races, of all nationalities and of all creeds can live together as brothers and [sisters]."

22   Dr. King was right. Even today we struggle to fulfill the incredible full promise of the American dream. But I believe it can be fulfilled. I believe it must be fulfilled. And I believe you are the ones who will do it.

23   There are those today who will tell you the American dream is finished and gone. There are those who will tell you that all dreams are foolish, beyond the harsh realities of life and a waste of our time. Don't believe them. Brooks Atkinson was a 20th century American drama critic who said: "Our nation was built by pioneers who were not afraid of failure, scientists who were not afraid of the truth, thinkers who were not afraid of progress, and dreamers who were not afraid of action."

24   What is the American dream?

25   Ultimately, you are the American dream, this class of 2007. You are the culmination of all the dreams of all the people who have dreamed before you.

26   You are the best-educated generation in the history of the world.

27   Your opportunities are limited only by the depth of your resolve and the height of your ambition. . . .

28   You are our American dream for a better tomorrow.

Reprinted with permission from Martin Jischke.

2. The Death of Horatio Alger

PAUL KRUGMAN, "THE DEATH OF HORATIO ALGER,"
THE NATION 5 (JANUARY 2004): 16.

In the following Nation *article, Paul Krugman discusses the impact of rising inequality on the American Dream. Krugman won the Nobel Prize in Economics in 2008; he is a professor of economics at Princeton and a regular columnist for the* **New York Times**. *He also served on the Council of Economic Advisers for the Reagan administration.*

• • •

1   The other day I found myself reading a leftist rag that made outrageous claims about America. It said that we are becoming a society in which the poor tend to stay poor, no matter how hard they work; in which sons are much more likely to inherit the socioeconomic status of their father than they were a generation ago.

2   The name of the leftist rag? *Business Week*, which published an article titled "Waking Up From the American Dream." The article summarizes recent

research showing that social mobility in the United States (which was never as high as legend had it) has declined considerably over the past few decades. If you put that research together with other research that shows a drastic increase in income and wealth inequality, you reach an uncomfortable conclusion: America looks more and more like a class-ridden society.

3   And guess what? Our political leaders are doing everything they can to fortify class inequality, while denouncing anyone who complains—or even points out what is happening—as a practitioner of "class warfare."

4   Let's talk first about the facts on income distribution. Thirty years ago we were a relatively middle-class nation. It had not always been thus: Gilded Age America was a highly unequal society, and it stayed that way through the 1920s. During the 1930s and '40s, however, America experienced what the economic historians Claudia Goldin and Robert Margo have dubbed the Great Compression: a drastic narrowing of income gaps, probably as a result of New Deal policies. And the new economic order persisted for more than a generation: Strong unions; taxes on inherited wealth, corporate profits and high incomes; close public scrutiny of corporate management—all helped to keep income gaps relatively small. The economy was hardly egalitarian, but a generation ago the gross inequalities of the 1920s seemed very distant.

5   Now they're back. According to estimates by the economists Thomas Piketty and Emmanuel Saez—confirmed by data from the Congressional Budget Office—between 1973 and 2000 the average real income of the bottom 90 percent of American taxpayers actually fell by 7 percent. Meanwhile, the income of the top 1 percent rose by 148 percent, the income of the top 0.1 percent rose by 343 percent, and the income of the top 0.01 percent rose 599 percent. (Those numbers exclude capital gains, so they're not an artifact of the stock market bubble.) The distribution of income in the United States has gone right back to Gilded Age levels of inequality.

6   Never mind, say the apologists, who churn out papers with titles like that of a 2001 Heritage Foundation piece, "Income Mobility and the Fallacy of Class-Warfare Arguments." America, they say, isn't a caste society—people with high incomes this year may have low incomes next year and vice versa, and the route to wealth is open to all. That's where those commies at *Business Week* come in: As they point out (and as economists and sociologists have been pointing out for some time), America actually is more of a caste society than we like to think. And the caste lines have lately become a lot more rigid.

7   The myth of income mobility has always exceeded the reality. As a general rule, once they've reached their 30s, people don't move up and down the income ladder very much. Conservatives often cite studies like a 1992 report by Glenn Hubbard, a Treasury official under the elder Bush who later became chief economic adviser to the younger Bush, that purport to show large numbers of Americans moving from low-wage to high-wage jobs during their working lives. But what these studies measure, as the economist Kevin Murphy put it, is mainly "the guy who works in the college bookstore and has a real job by his early 30s." Serious studies that exclude this sort of pseudo-mobility show

that inequality in average incomes over long periods isn't much smaller than inequality in annual incomes.

8   It is true, however, that America was once a place of substantial inter-generational mobility: Sons often did much better than their fathers. A classic 1978 survey found that among adult men whose fathers were in the bottom 25 percent of the population as ranked by social and economic status, 23 percent had made it into the top 25 percent. In other words, during the first thirty years or so after World War II, the American dream of upward mobility was a real experience for many people.

9   Now for the shocker. The *Business Week* piece cites a new survey of today's adult men, which finds that this number has dropped to only 10 percent. That is, over the past generation upward mobility has fallen drastically. Very few children of the lower class are making their way to even moderate affluence. This goes along with other studies indicating that rags-to-riches stories have become vanishingly rare, and that the correlation between fathers' and sons' incomes has risen in recent decades. In modern America, it seems, you're quite likely to stay in the social and economic class into which you were born.

10   *Business Week* attributes this to the "Wal-Martization" of the economy, the proliferation of dead-end, low-wage jobs and the disappearance of jobs that provide entry to the middle class. That's surely part of the explanation. But public policy plays a role—and will, if present trends continue, play an even bigger role in the future.

11   Put it this way: Suppose that you actually liked a caste society, and you were seeking ways to use your control of the government to further entrench the advantages of the haves against the have-nots. What would you do?

12   One thing you would definitely do is get rid of the estate tax, so that large fortunes can be passed on to the next generation. More broadly, you would seek to reduce tax rates both on corporate profits and on unearned income such as dividends and capital gains, so that those with large accumulated or inherited wealth could more easily accumulate even more. You'd also try to create tax shelters mainly useful for the rich. And more broadly still, you'd try to reduce tax rates on people with high incomes, shifting the burden to the payroll tax and other revenue sources that bear most heavily on people with lower incomes.

13   Meanwhile, on the spending side, you'd cut back on healthcare for the poor, on the quality of public education, and on state aid for higher education. This would make it more difficult for people with low incomes to climb out of their difficulties and acquire the education essential to upward mobility in the modern economy.

14   And just to close off as many routes to upward mobility as possible, you'd do everything possible to break the power of unions, and you'd privatize government functions so that well-paid civil servants could be replaced with poorly paid private employees.

15   It all sounds sort of familiar, doesn't it?

16   Where is this taking us? Thomas Piketty, whose work with Saez has transformed our understanding of income distribution, warns that current policies

will eventually create "a class of rentiers in the U.S., whereby a small group of wealthy but untalented children controls vast segments of the US economy and penniless, talented children simply can't compete." If he's right—and I fear that he is—we will end up suffering not only from injustice, but from a vast waste of human potential.

17   Goodbye, Horatio Alger. And goodbye, American Dream.

"The Death of Horatio Alger" by Paul Krugman. Reprinted with permission from the January 5, 2004 issue of THE NATION. For subscription information, call 1-800-333-8536. Portions of each week's Nation magazine can be accessed at http://www.thenation.com

3. By Our Own Bootstraps

W. MICHAEL COX AND RICHARD ALM, "CHAPTER 4: BY OUR OWN BOOTSTRAPS," *MYTHS OF RICH AND POOR: WHY WE'RE BETTER OFF THAN WE THINK* (NEW YORK: BASIC, 1999), 69, 87–89.

This excerpt from W. Michael Cox and Richard Alm's classic Myths of Rich and Poor: Why We're Better Off Than We Think *articulates their belief in the importance of opportunity versus equality in striving for the American Dream. Cox is Director of the William J. O'Neil Center for Global Markets and Freedom at Southern Methodist University and the former chief economist for the Federal Reserve Bank of Dallas. Alm is a business reporter with the* Dallas Morning News.

• • •

1   "Land of Opportunity." Anywhere in the world, those three words bring to mind just one place: the United States of America.

2   Opportunity defines our heritage. The American saga entails waves of immigrant farmers, shopkeepers, laborers, and entrepreneurs, all coming to the United States for the promise of a better life. Some amassed enormous fortunes—the Rockefellers, the Carnegies, the DuPonts, the Fords, the Vanderbilts, to name just a few. Even today America's opportunity is always on display. Bill Gates in computer software, Ross Perot in data processing, Bill Cosby and Oprah Winfrey in entertainment, Warren Buffett in investing, Sam Walton in retailing, Michael Jordan in sports, and Mary Kay Ash in cosmetics could head a list of the many thousands who catapulted from society's lower or middle ranks to the top. Many millions more, descendants of those who arrived with little more than the clothes on their backs and a few bucks in their pockets, took advantage of an open economic system to improve their lot in life through talent and hard work. . . .

3   That's what the American Dream, a dream of opportunity, is all about. . . .

4   [But] judging from the public debate, at least some Americans would prefer a more equal distribution of income to a less equal one, perhaps on moral grounds, perhaps as a part of an ideal of civic virtue. There's no *economic* reason, however, to prefer one pattern of income distribution over another. In fact, the income statistics do little but confirm what's obvious: America isn't an egalitarian society. It wasn't designed to be. Socialism, a failed and receding

system, sought to impose an artificial equality. Capitalism, a successful and expanding system, doesn't fight a fundamental fact of human nature—we vary greatly in capabilities, motivation, interests, and preferences. Some of us are driven to get ahead. Some of us are just plain lazy. Some of us are willing to work hard so we can afford a lifestyle rich in material goods. Some of us work just hard enough to provide a roof overhead, food, clothes, and a few amenities. It shouldn't come as a surprise that our incomes vary greatly.

5   Income inequality isn't an aberration. Quite the opposite, it's perfectly consistent with the laws that govern a free-enterprise system. In the early 1970s, three groups of unemployed Canadians, all in their twenties, all with at least 12 years of schooling, volunteered to participate in a stylized economy where the only employment was making woolen belts on small hand looms. They could work as much or as little as they liked, earning $2.50 for each belt. After 98 days, the results were anything but equal: 37.2 percent of the economy's income went to the 20 percent with the highest earnings. The bottom 20 percent received only 6.6 percent. This economic microcosm tells us one thing: Even among similar people with identical work options, some workers will earn more than others.

6   In a modern economy, incomes vary for plenty of reasons having little to do with fairness or equity. Education and experience, for example, usually yield higher pay. As industry becomes more sophisticated, the rewards to skilled labor tend to rise, adding to the number of high-income earners. Location matters. New Yorkers earn more than Mississippians. Lifestyle choices play a part, too. Simply by having an additional paycheck, two-income families make more money than those with a single breadwinner. Longer retirements, however, will add to the number of households with low income, even if many senior citizens live well from their savings. Demographic changes can twist the distribution of income. As the Baby Boom enters its peak earning years, the number of high-income households ought to rise. Economic forces create ripples in what we earn. The ebb and flow of industries can shift workers to both ends of the income distribution. Layoffs put some Americans into low-income groups, at least temporarily. Companies with new products and new technologies create jobs and, in most cases, share the bounty by offering workers higher pay. In technology industries, bonuses and stock options are becoming more common. Higher rates of return on investments—with, for example, a stock-market boom—will create a windfall for household with money riding on financial markets.

7   In and of itself, moreover, income distribution doesn't say much about the performance of an economy or the opportunities it offers. A widening gap isn't necessarily a sign of failure, nor does a narrowing one guarantee that an economy is functioning well. As a matter of fact, it's quite common to find a widening of income distribution in boom times, when almost everyone's earnings are rising rapidly. All it takes is for one segment of the workforce to become better off faster than others. However, the distribution can narrow in hard times, as companies facing declining demand cut back on jobs, hours, raises, and bonuses. In fact, we often see a compression of incomes in areas where people are sinking into poverty.

8   There's no denying that our system allows some Americans to become much richer than others. We must accept that, even celebrate it. Opportunity, not equality of income, is what made the U.S. economy grow and prosper. It's most important to provide equality of opportunity, not equality of results. There's ample evidence to refute any suggestion that the economy is no longer capable of providing opportunity for the vast majority of Americans. At the end of the twentieth century, upward mobility is alive and well. Even the lower-income households are sharing in the country's progress. What's more, data suggest that the populist view of American as a society torn between haves and have-nots, with rigid class lines, is just plain wrong. We are by no means a caste society.

4. How the U.S. Stacks Up against Other Wealthy, Industrialized Nations

RICHARD WILKINSON AND KATE PICKETT, *THE SPIRIT LEVEL: WHY GREATER EQUALITY MAKES SOCIETIES STRONGER* (NEW YORK: BLOOMSBURY, 2009), 17, 20, 148, 160.

In The Spirit Level: Why Greater Equality Makes Societies Stronger, *British epidemiologists Richard Wilkinson and Kate Pickett examine the link between income inequality and a range of health and social problems in the world's richest industrialized nations. Based on thirty years of research, data used in the study comes from such sources as the World Bank, the World Health Organization, the United Nations, and the Organization for Economic Cooperation and Development.*

• • •

Income Gaps

● FIGURE 3.2

How much richer are the richest 20 percent than the poorest 20 percent in each country?

Index of:
* Life expectancy
* Math & literacy
* Infant mortality
* Homicides
* Imprisonment
* Teenage births
* Trust
* Obesity
* Mental illness—including drug & alcohol addiction
* Social mobility

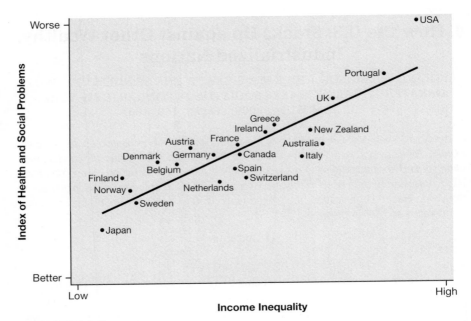

● FIGURE 3.3

Health and social problems are closely related to inequality among rich countries.

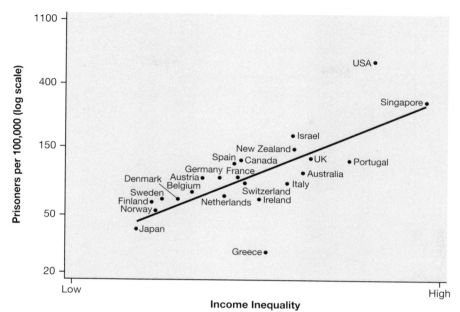

● **FIGURE 3.4**

More people are imprisoned in more unequal countries.

5. Long Live the American Dream

SHIKHA DALMIA, "LONG LIVE THE AMERICAN DREAM," REASON.COM, MARCH 1, 2011; ORIGINALLY PUBLISHED AT THEDAILY.COM, FEBRUARY 24, 2011.

Now a senior policy analyst at the Reason Foundation, Shikha Dalmia emigrated to America from New Delhi, India. Her article "Long Live the American Dream" first appeared online at TheDaily.com. Dalmia analyzes her adopted country's particular strengths by means of comparison against fast-growing India and China.

• • • •

1   Americans, hit first by outsourcing and then a recession, are becoming deeply pessimistic about their country's ability to maintain its economic leadership in a globalized world. America's Aristophanes, Jon Stewart, commented during a recent interview with Anand Giridhardas, author of *India Calling*: "The American dream is still alive—it's just alive in India." Likewise, 20 percent of Americans in a December *National Journal* poll believed that the U.S. economy was no longer the strongest. Nearly half picked China instead.

2   But there are at least five reasons why neither India nor China will knock America off its economic perch any time soon, at least not by the only measure that matters: Offering the best life to the most people.

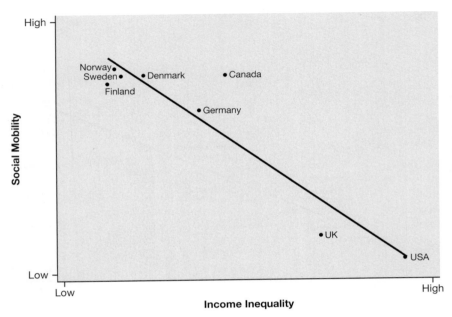

● **FIGURE 3.5**
Social mobility is lower in more unequal countries.

America Wastes No Talent

3 Conventional wisdom holds that America's global competitiveness is driven by geniuses flocking to its shore and producing breathtaking inventions. But America's real genius lies not in tapping genius—but every scrap of talent up and down the scale.

4   A 2005 World Bank study found that the bulk of a people's wealth comes not from tangible capital like raw resources and infrastructure. It comes from intangible wealth: effective government, secure property rights, a functioning judiciary. Such intangible factors put the equivalent of $418,000 at the disposal of every American resident. India and China? $3,738 and $4,208 respectively.

5   America's vast intangible wealth makes everyone more productive and successful. Personal attributes—talent, looks, smarts—matter only on the margins. Having witnessed the life trajectory of many Indian immigrants, what's striking to me is that, with some exceptions, it doesn't matter whether they are the best in their profession in India or just mediocre. Within 10 to 15 years of arriving, they land in a very similar space. They get good jobs, buy homes, have children, send them to decent schools and colleges, and save for their retirement. The differences in their standard of living would have been far greater had they stayed home.

America Does Not Have India's Infrastructure Deficit or China's Civil Society Deficit

6   India's gap with America extends not just to intangible capital but tangible capital as well. Basic facilities in India—roads, water, sewage—remain primitive. For example, a 2010 McKinsey Global Institute report found that India treats 30 percent of raw sewage, whereas the international norm is 100 percent. India provides 105 liters of water per person per day, the minimum standard is 150 liters. It needs to spend twice the slated expenditures over the next 10 years to deliver basic services.

7   China, meanwhile, has a major civil society problem. America has made about $100 trillion in Social Security and Medicare promises to seniors that it can't fund. But American seniors face nothing like the kind of destitution that the Chinese do. China's one-child policy has decimated the natural safety net that old people rely on in traditional societies. And China offers no public safety net to the vast majority of village-born. Worse, many Chinese have invested their nest eggs in various asset bubbles that will wipe out their only means of subsistence if they burst, making the Great Depression look like a beach party.

America Does Not Have Grinding Poverty

8   Despite all the recent hoopla about China becoming the world's second biggest economy and India hoping to follow suit, the reality is that the per capita GDP—even measured by purchasing power parity—in both is pathetic. America's is about $47,000, China's $7,500, and India's $3,290.

9   Worse, both still harbor medieval levels of poverty with 300 million people in each living on less than $1.25 a day. India's IT boom gets big press, but it—along with all the tertiary industries it has spawned—employs 2.3 million people, or 0.2 percent of the population.

10   Neither country is a font of opportunity comparable to America.

American Education Is Superior

11   [The] President . . . claims that America is in an "education arms race" with India and China. Rubbish.

12   Notwithstanding all the horror stories about American kids underperforming on standardized tests compared to Asian kids raised by Tiger moms, things are worse in India and China. India's literacy rate is 66 percent. China puts its at 93 percent—but between 2000 and 2005, China's illiterate population *grew* by 30 million. The same may happen in India, thanks to last year's Right to Education Act whose regulations will cripple India's private school market. The fundamental problem is that both countries put their resources into educating elite kids—and ignoring the rest.

13   College education in both countries, especially in engineering, is also vastly overrated. Harvard researcher Vivek Wadhwa has shown that, contrary to conventional wisdom, not only does America graduate comparable number of engineers to India and China—American engineers are vastly superior.

14   But unless more Indian and Chinese kids get access to a quality education, their countries won't be able to actualize their human potential, precisely what America does so well.

America Doesn't Have a Culture of Hype

15   An important reason why the gloom-and-doom about America is unjustified is precisely that there is so much gloom-and-doom. Indians and Chinese, by contrast, have drunk their own Kool Aid. Their moribund economies have barely kicked into action and they are entertaining dreams of becoming the next global superpower. This bespeaks a profound megalomania—not to mention lopsided priorities. There is not a culture of hope in these countries, as Giridhardas told Jon Stewart. There is a culture of hype.

16   By contrast, Americans are their own worst critics—always looking for lessons to improve what is working and fix what's not. Alexis de Tocqueville observed that although Americans were the freest and most enlightened men placed in the happiest of conditions, "a sort of cloud habitually covered their features." Why? Because "they were constantly tormented by a vague fear of not having chosen the shortest route that can lead to . . . their wellbeing."

17   Indeed, Americans have a grab-the-bull-by-its-horns quality so that they simply don't hang around hoping for things to get better on their own. If the public school monopoly is failing kids, by golly, then they'll homeschool them themselves. (Public schools are dysfunctional virtually everywhere, but which other country has spawned anything equivalent to America's homeschooling movement?) The government responds ineffectually to the recession, modest by historic standards, and Americans go into panic mode. Grass-roots movements such as the Tea Party emerge to rein in the government. Pay Pal founder Peter Theil has even given close to a million dollars to the Seasteading Institute to establish new countries on the sea to experiment with new forms of government. This might be wacky but it puts an outside limit on how out-of-whack Americans will let their institutions get before they start fixing them.

18   This American spirit, ultimately, is the biggest reason to believe that the American dream is and will stay alive—in America.

Reprinted with permission from Shikha Dalmia, Senior Analyst at Reason Foundation.

6. Deer Hunting with Jesus

JOE BAGEANT, *DEER HUNTING WITH JESUS: DISPATCHES FROM AMERICA'S CLASS WAR* (NEW YORK: CROWN, 2007), 62–64, 69–74.

Dubbed "the Sartre of Appalachia," writer Joe Bageant gives a bleak picture of working class life in his hometown of Winchester, Virginia, in Deer Hunting with Jesus: Dispatches from America's Class War.

• • •

1   Like so many heartland working-class folks, Tom is a walking contradiction. At fifty-eight, he is a super at Rubbermaid [a supervisor at the Rubbermaid plant in Winchester] and the wise old man and mentor of younger workers. He is rangy and dressed in denim with a huge cowboy belt buckle accenting his small pot gut (redneck men should never be allowed to accessorize), and his smile is craggy and wry when he says things like: "We will win the war on terrorism when we elect a man with the stones to use our nukes." . . .

2   I have known Tom since 1957, when we were both little hayseeds from out in the sticks, arriving in what is now called middle school in plaid flannel "Monkey Wards" catalog shirts that marked us as poor whites recently removed from our rural estates out in the county. Town and country divisions were much greater back then, before the age of suburbs. Like most Winchester/Frederick County natives, we are "sideways kin." According to genealogical records downtown at the library, Tom and I have common ancestors in this county and town dating back to the 1750s. I wouldn't want to guess about inbreeding in subsequent generations.

3   After high school we did what kids in our caste did and still do: We went into the military. He went to Nam and I went aboard the aircraft carrier USS *America,* CVA 66. After we were discharged, there was a period when we jammed on guitar together a few times and discovered we had more in common than bad imitations of Bob Dylan. . . . Tom is typical of the ironclad, hard-assed people this valley produces. A couple of years ago he had a heart bypass operation. "At first I didn't feel that much better," he says, "but after I was home a couple of days I said to hell with laying around. So I got a shovel, and I dug a ditch and laid pipe for my drainfield. Loosened me right up. What I needed was a good workout." . . .

4   Life is about work for the American redneck. By *redneck,* I mean all kinds of rednecks, not just southern ones, ranging from Polish and Hungarian stock rednecks of the Appalachian coal country to the Scandinavian ones of the logging Northwest. In the South and the Midwest there are even Jewish rednecks who drive muscle cars and brawl and love country music. For all these people work is an obsession and has been for generations stretching back to the textile mills, the homesteads of the West and Midwest, the immigrant labor mines of West Virginia and Colorado and Montana, the subsistence farms of the South. The forebears of today's rednecks were people for whom not working meant their families would starve. Literally. So the work ethic is burned into their genetic code. (Incidentally, I am not talking about white trash here. I am talking about rednecks, the difference being that rednecks work themselves to death and will never accept a handout. White trash folks do not have the same hang-up.) In the redneck mind, lazy is the worst thing a person can be—worse than dumb, drunk, or mean, worse than being a liar and a jailbird or crazy. The absolute worst thing that a redneck can say about anyone is: "He doesn't want to work," which is generally followed by, "Hell, I don't want to either, but I have to." By the same logic, educated liberals who have time to read, who in fact read so much that they join book clubs, are suspect. . . .

5   Getting a lousy education, then spending a lifetime pitted against your fellow workers in the gladiatorial theater of the free market economy does not

make for optimism or open-mindedness, both hallmarks of liberalism. It makes for a kind of bleak coarseness and inner degradation that allows working people to accept the American empire's wars without a blink.

6   Like most of conservative Winchester, Tom believes violence can solve foreign political problems. During political discussion around here, it is not uncommon to hear someone talk about the Middle East or some Asian or European country "getting out of line" and "needing to be put in its place." Any day of the week I can easily show you a hundred people who believe we should bomb France (though I doubt many of them could readily find it on a map). For a certain kind of American, it seems, bombing anyone anywhere helps purge some unarticulated inner rage—rage that the easy truisms that once seemed to lend nobility to the dullest of lives are no longer believable. So long as Americans agreed that they were brave and true and exceptional—people toward whom the entire world looked, for example—and so long as they wrapped themselves in the cloak of that self-anointed goodness, their lives had meaning. No insight required. Just add religious faith. Being an American was something to cherish, something worth defending, preferably on the enemy's turf.

7   So what happens if you are Tom Henderson and you've put in more than twenty years at the plant and let every unique aspect of yourself atrophy so you could do the American Dream by the numbers, only to find that cloak of goodness torn? Twenty years at the same job and the same church, thirty years of good credit, and you look up to find that your wife suffers from chronic depression and that terrorists crashed airplanes into New York. And whispered rumor again has it that Rubbermaid is moving your job to Asia, and television pundits loudly proclaim the impending death of the Social Security system you've been counting on to be there for you, though you'd never admit it openly because, well, it's a handout. An entitlement.

8   "America didn't used to be this way," Tom laments. "People have [messed] up this country." He's not sure who. It certainly wasn't him. But in the harsh new light outside the cloak of goodness there are some very likely suspects, starting with "weirdo university professors, union racketeers, and the rich California ACLU types. People who never worked for a living," he says. "It all started to go to hell during the sixties." . . .

9   Tom and I did not discuss his job at Rubbermaid. The details of being a floor super are not that interesting in print or practice. What haunted me as he spoke was this: Tom is every bit as intelligent as I am. He was a better writer than I was in high school and often said back then that his goal in life was to be a writer, painter, musician. Where did those dreams go? The same place any such dreams go for the children of lower-working-class families. They go out the same door that opportunity for a decent education never walks in through. They vanish along the trails of places like Vietnam or the dusty streets of Iraq. They disappear between high school graduation and the immediate need to earn a living that follows graduation (rednecks are not much for living with mummy and daddy past the age of twelve). It leaves you hardened, and it leaves you standing in the human relations room at Rubbermaid filling out an application to bust yellow wet-floor signs off a hot mold or to work the

night shift snaking electrical wire through conduit in a windowless concrete city. And once you've accepted your lot as a citizen of that nocturnal city, you get even harder.

7. The American Dream

RICHARD TODD, "WHO ME, RICH? WHAT IT TAKES (AND WHAT IT MEANS) TO BE WEALTHY TODAY: A LOOK AT THE TOP 1 PERCENT," *WORTH*, SEPTEMBER 1997, 70–84.

In the conclusion to his September 1997 article in Worth *magazine, "Who Me, Rich?" writer Richard Todd asks if we've lost sight of the true meaning of the American Dream.*

• • •

1   I was sitting at a Washington, D.C., dinner party in the middle of a conversation (a conversation I had initiated) about the rich. As is customary, everyone around the table was pretending that he or she wasn't rich. A nice woman to my left was lamenting the excesses of somebody and then of somebody else, and I was matching her, and we were just generally on the side of fairness. A fellow to her left, an entrepreneur, intervened with a burst of what I took to be candor. "Let's face it," he said. "In this country the destructive behavior is done by the bottom 5 percent. The productive behavior comes from the top 5 percent. Everybody in the middle just eats the food." Stark and ghastly a vision as this may be, it had the virtue of explicitness, of saying something that one often senses at the top ranks of our country but seldom hears: a true abhorrence of the people in the middle. The entrepreneur went on to say that in the end he couldn't take inequality very seriously because of the great saving grace of our society: mobility. The ability of the "productive" to rise to the top. It is an argument, living where and as we do, that has to be taken seriously.

2   The *Wall Street Journal* recently proclaimed the American dream lives, above a piece about a longitudinal study of economic class over some 15 years. Between 1975 and 1991, the story said, almost 30 percent of those in the bottom fifth had risen to the top fifth. About half of the billionaires on the 1996 Forbes 400 list are there by virtue of money they have made, not inherited, and virtually all the very largest fortunes are "first generation." (To be sure, many on the list came from comfortable upper-middle-class upbringings.) This sort of data, and the rags-to-riches anecdotes we encounter almost daily, are seductive. It is important to remember that figures on income inequality are not static, that when you speak of the poor you are speaking about some people, anyway, who one day will be rich.

3   Net worth typically rises over the course of a lifetime, but the median household net worth of those for whom the mobility game is over—people at retirement age—is just $92,000. But debates like these—the American dream is dead; no, the American dream lives—leave something out. Why does one wince a bit at the very phrase—only because it has become such a cliché? I did not fully know what I found so unsatisfying about this argument until I encountered a passage by the late Christopher Lasch, in his book *The Revolt of the Elites and the Betrayal of Democracy*, reminding me that, once, the American dream had meant something nobler, the belief that in a democratic society equality refers to more than opportunity. Lasch refers to the most important choice a democratic society has to make: "Whether to raise the general level of competence, energy, and devotion—'virtue,' as it was called in an older political tradition—or merely to promote a broader recruitment of elites. Our society has clearly chosen the second course . . . generating social conditions in which ordinary people are not expected to know anything at all."

4   In many ways we live in a thrilling society. On a day in spring, I have lunch at a club in San Jose, California, with a man who embodies American opportunity—a Korean-born software entrepreneur just months from taking his fledgling company public. He speaks of the hopeful engineers who came to the valley willing to work for stock options. It is another heartening story of wealth being created by intelligence, initiative, energy. Later, driving to San Francisco, I stop on a ridgetop and look out over Silicon Valley, the bright green hills torn by new construction—a sensuality in that sullied landscape, like a mussed silk blouse—and though the agents of change are technology and money, they seem here as irresistible as nature itself. But the fragile idea that there is an equality based on worth that transcends net worth, the original American dream—what place does it have here? How much success, how many billionaires, how large and prosperous a "mass elite" can it survive? When it disappears entirely, we will all suffer equal loss—the 1 percent no less than the rest of us.

"Who Me, Rich?" by Richard Todd appeared in WORTH Magazine, September 1997. Reprinted with permission from the author.

8. Epilogue: The American Dream

JAMES TRUSLOW ADAMS, *THE EPIC OF AMERICA* (BOSTON: LITTLE, 1931), 404–12.

*Writer and historian James Truslow Adams first coined the term "the American Dream" in his 1931 history of the United States, **The Epic of America**. In this excerpt from the book's conclusion, he asks what the dream should truly mean in terms of American values.*

• • •

1   If, as I have said, the things already listed were all we had had to contribute, America would have made no distinctive and unique gift to mankind. But there

has been also the *American dream*, that dream of a land in which life should be better and richer and fuller for every man, with opportunity for each according to his ability or achievement. It is a difficult dream for the European upper classes to interpret adequately, and too many of us ourselves have grown weary and mistrustful of it. It is not a dream of motor cars and high wages merely, but a dream of a social order in which each man and each woman shall be able to attain to the fullest stature of which they are innately capable, and be recognized by others for what they are, regardless of the fortuitous circumstances of birth or position. I once had an intelligent young Frenchman as a guest in New York, and after a few days I asked him what struck him most among his new impressions. Without hesitation he replied, "The way that everyone of every sort looks you right in the eye, without a thought of inequality." Some time ago a foreigner who used to do some work for me, and who had picked up a very fair education, used occasionally to sit and chat with me in my study after he had finished his work. One day he said that such a relationship was the great difference between America and his homeland. There, he said, "I would do my work and might get a pleasant word, but I could never sit and talk like this. There is a difference there between social grades which cannot be got over. I would not talk to you there as man to man, but as my employer."

2   No, the American dream that has lured tens of millions of all nations to our shores in the past century has not been a dream of merely material plenty, though that has doubtless counted heavily. It has been much more than that. It has been a dream of being able to grow to fullest development as man and woman, unhampered by the barriers which had slowly been erected in older civilizations, unrepressed by social orders which had developed for the benefit of classes rather than for the simple human being of any and every class. And that dream has been realized more fully in actual life here than anywhere else, though very imperfectly even among ourselves.

3   It has been a great epic and a great dream. What, now, of the future? . . .

4   Can we hold to the good and escape from the bad? Are the dream and the idealism of the frontier and the New Land inextricably involved with the ugly scars which have also been left on us by our three centuries of exploitation and conquest of the continent?

5   We have already tried to show how some of the scars were obtained; how it was that we came to insist upon business and money-making and material improvement as good in themselves; how they took on the aspects of moral virtues; how we came to consider an unthinking optimism essential; how we refused to look on the seamy and sordid realities of any situation in which we found ourselves; how we regarded criticism as obstructive and dangerous for our new communities; how we came to think manners undemocratic, and a cultivated mind a hindrance to success, a sign of inefficient effeminacy; how size and statistics of material development came to be more important in our eyes than quality and spiritual values; how in the shifting advance of the frontier we came to lose sight of the past in hopes for the future; how we forgot to *live*, in the struggle to "make a living"; how our education tended to become utilitarian or aimless; and how other unfortunate traits only too notable today were developed.

6   While we have been absorbed in our tasks, the world has also been changing. We Americans are not alone in having to search for a new scale and basis
for values . . . [but] the mere fact that there were no old things to be swept
away here made us feel the full impact of the Industrial Revolution and the effect of machinery, when we turned to industrial life, to a far greater extent than
in Europe, where the revolution originated.

7   It would seem as though the time had come when this question of values
was of prime and pressing importance for us. For long we have been tempted
and able to ignore it. Engaged in the work of building cities and developing the
continent, values for many tended to be materialized and simplified. . . . The
trees had to be chopped, the log hut built, the stumps burned, and the corn
planted. Simplification became a habit of mind and was carried into our lives
long after the clearing had become a prosperous city. . . .

8   We no longer have the frontier to divert us or to absorb our energies. We
shall steadily become a more densely populated country in which our social
ideals will have to be such as to give us civilized contentment. . . . Once the
frontier stage is passed,—the acquisition of a bare living, and the setting up of
a fair economic base,—the American dream itself opens all sorts of questions
as to values. It is easy to say a better and richer life for all men, but what *is* better and what *is* richer?

Essay Prompts

Choose one of the prompts below and write an essay that synthesizes at least
three of the sources in support of your argument. Remember that in addition to using quotations, you can also incorporate sources as paraphrases and
summaries.

1. Using the readings in Income Disparity, Social Mobility, and the American
   Dream, and drawing from your own beliefs and experience, write an essay
   that defends, challenges, or qualifies the claim that anyone can make it in
   contemporary America if he or she is willing to work hard and persevere.

2. Consider James Truslow Adams's statement that the American Dream is "a
   dream of a social order in which each man and each woman shall be able
   to attain to their fullest stature of which they are innately capable." To what
   extent does this ideal depend on individual initiative versus societal support?
   Write an essay discussing to what extent and in what ways a society is responsible for creating fair opportunities for all its citizens.

3. Jischke quotes from the Declaration of Independence, "We hold these
   truths to be self-evident: That all men are created equal, that they are endowed by their creator with certain unalienable rights, that among these are
   life, liberty and the pursuit of happiness." Cox and Alm state that "America isn't an egalitarian society. It wasn't designed to be." How would you
   reconcile the tension between these two statements? Drawing from the

readings and from your own beliefs and experience, write an essay that defends, challenges, or qualifies Cox and Alm's statement that "America isn't an egalitarian society." As part of this essay, you will also need to conduct outside research to define what is meant by "egalitarian" and synthesize this research into your essay.

4. Considering the various sources from a cultural and historical point of view, develop a position on whether and to what extent the American Dream is about individual material success ("high wages and motor cars," as Truslow says in the 1930s) or about some greater national vision (as in Jischke's reference to the Declaration of Independence and Martin Luther King). If the latter, explain what that greater national vision might be. Are these two visions mutually exclusive or complementary? What relation might there be, if any, between the two?

5. Develop a position on what the American Dream means to you, incorporating ideas and evidence from the source materials in Income Disparity, Social Mobility, and the American Dream. Make sure to defend your position by drawing from source materials in support of your argument and to take account of source materials that qualify or challenge your point of view.

6. Consider this statement from the conclusion to Richard Todd's essay:

> But the fragile idea that there is an equality based on worth that transcends net worth, the original American dream—what place does it have here? How much success, how many billionaires, how large and prosperous a "mass elite" can it survive? When it disappears entirely, we will all suffer equal loss—the 1 percent no less than the rest of us.

What does he mean by this? What does Todd believe is at stake? Why does he believe that the conviction "that there is an equality based on worth that transcends net worth" is now at risk? Develop a position on this issue, drawing from the readings and your own beliefs and experience.

7. With your instructor's approval, conduct additional research to bring in at least two additional sources of your own choosing or draw from the list of additional readings below. Write your own prompt, in response to your research, and use this prompt to write an essay that synthesizes the readings in Income Disparity, Social Mobility, and the American Dream and your independent research.

Suggestions for Additional Reading

Ronald Bailey, "The Secrets of Intangible Wealth," *The Wall Street Journal Online* (WSJ.com), September 29, 2007.

Aaron Bernstein, "Waking Up from the American Dream," *Business Week,* December 1, 2003.

Chuck Collins, Mike Lapham, and Scott Klinger, *I Didn't Do It Alone: Society's Contribution to Individual Wealth and Success* (United for a Fair Economy, 2004).

David Kamp, "Rethinking the American Dream," *Vanity Fair,* April 2009.

Erich Origen and Gan Golan, *The Adventures of Unemployed Man* (New York: Little, 2010).

Theodore Roosevelt, "New Nationalism," in *Letters and Speeches* (New York: Library of America, 2004).

Katharine W. Seelye, "What Happens to the American Dream in a Recession?" *New York Times,* May 7, 2009.

Louis Uchitelle, "The Richest of the Rich, Proud of a New Gilded Age," *New York Times,* July 15, 2007.

World Bank, "Where Is the Wealth of Nations? Measuring Capital for the 21st Century" (Washington: World Bank, 2006).

4

The Writer's Voice

Most writers do not sit down to write consciously in a certain style. They do, however, try to project a certain voice onto the page. Sometimes the writer assumes this voice deliberately, but often it is chosen for the writer by the psychology of audience and material—by the need and occasion that make the writing necessary.

Here is an example. You are the boss. You sit down to write a memo to your employees, but being the boss goes to your head, and you write:

> Illumination of the overhead fixtures must be extinguished by the final person exiting the premises.

This notice tells the reader two things: First, it tells the reader to turn off the lights before leaving the room; second, it tells the reader that you are the boss and you say so. That is not the only kind of notice you could have written. You might, for example, have written this equivalent:

The last person to leave this room must turn out the overhead lights.

This makes the point, but you think it also makes you sound more modest than the first version.

The difference between these two is not one of content, but of tone or style. It is tone of voice when you are composing the memo, for what you tried to do was not write in a certain style but to sound like the boss; to the reader, however, it is your style.

Many writing teachers, with some justification, approach voice and style as if they were always related to the writer's psychology. If you had confidence in your authority as the boss, if you really felt comfortable with your power, you wouldn't think it necessary to sound like God in your every memo. If you must sound like the Almighty in your memos, perhaps it is because you really don't feel at ease with the idea of being the boss. Many similar mishaps of voice or style in student papers can be traced to a psychological uncertainty about the material, to a self-doubting attitude, or even to the writer's feelings about the assignment.

The relationship between feelings and tone is slippery but makes sense. It is only natural that our feelings about a subject or person should spill out onto the page and affect our tone. Here is an example:

Dear Monty,

    I'm really sick and tired of your mess. It's embarrassing to walk into our room with a visitor and see your bed unmade, your clothes scattered all over the floor, and your beer cans making sticky rings on the table. I've told you before about this, but now I want you to know that if you don't shape up, I'm moving out.

Bob

Do you hear the angry tone in that note? On the other hand, listen to the difference in the tone of this email:

Hi, Everyone,

    I have just returned from my backpacking trip through Europe. You won't believe the wonderful experiences I had. At one point I even lost my passport, but the American consulate was very helpful in getting me a temporary one. I met some exciting new friends, who, like me, were camping out or riding the second-class compartments of the trains. The world is really a great place. Anyway, I'll wait until I see you to fill in the details. I sure missed you. A bunch.

Irene

The practical effect of tone on our writing is sometimes plainly evident and sometimes not. We would expect, for example, that if we write a letter to a roommate we're mad at, our tone will reflect that anger. Less evident is the effect a feeling of boredom about an assignment might have on our tone. It is only logical to assume that if we're bored with the topic and think it a waste of our time, our tone will be affected for the worse. That is why instructors always urge students to write about topics they like.

Another piece of traditional advice related to tone is the ancient warning instructors often give to student writers to be themselves—and it is genuinely good advice. Don't try to write in a voice that is not truly your own; don't try to put on airs in your writing. If you do, your tone is bound to be affected by the pretense. You will discover, if you have not already, that you do your best writing when you simply sound like your true self.

These psychological considerations aside, we do know—on a more practical level—that voice in writing is influenced by three factors under the writer's control: (1) vocabulary, (2) syntax, and (3) attitude. Before exploring these factors, let's enjoy a bit of humor as we explore a famous question, answered in a variety of voices.

Why did the Chicken Cross the Road?

Politician (self-righteous)

My fellow conservatives, the chicken crossed to steal a job from a decent, hardworking American. That is what these reckless left-wing chickens do.

Children's book writer (nonsensical)
Did the chicken cross the road? Did he cross it with a toad? Yes, the chicken crossed the road, but why he crossed, I've not been told!

Ernest Hemingway (straightforward)
To die. In the rain. Alone. From an idée fixe.

Grandpa (overbearing)
In my day, we didn't ask why the chicken crossed the road. Someone told us that the chicken crossed the road, and that was good enough for us.

Karl Marx (philosophical)
It was a historical inevitability.

Sigmund Freud (psychological)
All chickens cross the road for the same reason: sex.

Albert Einstein (ambiguous)
Did the chicken really cross the road or did the road cross under the chicken?

Colonel Sanders (miffed)
Darn! I missed one!

Vocabulary

The English language is a treasure trove of words. It is bursting with synonyms—words that have the same meaning. As you write, you can express the same idea any number of different ways. Often, the choice seems to boil down to expressing yourself either simply or complexly. You can give the facts without frills while remaining quietly in the background or you can mount the pulpit, take on the grandeur of a bishop, and posture.

The second choice is one that we do not recommend. You will do your reader a kindness if you write without putting on airs or pretending to be a know-it-all. Choose your words to inform, not to impress. Faced with the choice between a big, little-known word and a smaller, better-known equivalent, choose the smaller one because more people will understand it. Your overriding aim is to tell your reader what you know about the subject, not to impress. (Yet, oddly enough, sophisticated readers are generally impressed by writing that is plain and to the point.)

Here's an example of a style of writing that even for its day was pompous:

> It is the fate of those who toil at the lower employments of life, to be rather driven by the fear of evil, than attracted by the prospect of good; to be exposed to censure, without hope of praise; to be disgraced by miscarriage, or punished for neglect, where success would have been without applause, and diligence without reward.
>
> —Samuel Johnson, *Preface to the Dictionary of the English Language (1755)*

Johnson was a noted scholar and conversationalist who had a definite flair for spoken and written pompousness. If we replace some of the words with their more common equivalents, the passage takes on a different tone:

> It is the lot of those who work at the lower jobs of life, to be rather driven by the fear of evil, than drawn by the likelihood of good; to be open to criticism, without hope of praise; to be shamed by mistakes, or punished for neglect, where success would have been without recognition, and hard work without reward.

Even with the changes in vocabulary, this passage is still hard to follow because it suffers from a second problem—knotty syntax.

Syntax

The arrangement of words in a sentence is known as *syntax*. Because English is so flexible, the same idea can be said in many different ways and in many different kinds of sentences. The considerate writer uses only as many sentences as are needed to get the job done. Most of these sentences will be simple subject-verb-object combinations. For the sake of variety, a few will have a different construction, but mainly, the sentences will be short and easy to read and understand.

In constructing a sentence, your aim should be to express your ideas clearly. It should not be to show off your learning or scholarship. The Johnson passage quoted earlier consists of a single sentence punctuated by commas and semicolons. A little alteration in the syntax—mainly in the use of simpler sentences—makes the ideas in the quotation much easier to understand:

> Those who work at the lower jobs of life are driven by the fear of doing wrong, rather than drawn by the likelihood of doing good. They are open to criticism yet have no hope of praise. They are both shamed by their mistakes and punished for their neglect; yet their success wins no recognition, and their hard work no reward.

Now we have a better idea of what Johnson is trying to say. We may agree or disagree with it, but at least we share a common understanding.

Why, then, did Johnson express himself the way he did if he could have written the same idea more clearly? The answer is because of his attitude—the third factor affecting a writer's voice.

Attitude

Your attitude toward yourself and your work is bound to affect your voice. If you regard writing as a means of communication, you will work hard to make your meaning clear. If you regard writing as a reflection of your inner self, you might behave as some people do when they stand in front of a mirror: they preen and strut.

The problem with the Johnson passage is that he does not believe what he says, because he knows it is not true. He is, in fact, pretending to feel a humility and modesty he does not have. It is his attitude toward the work that makes his style so self-inflated and pompous. Here are the next two paragraphs from the preface:

> Among these unhappy mortals is the writer of dictionaries; whom mankind have considered, not as the pupil, but the slave of science, the pioneer of literature, doomed only to remove rubbish and clear obstructions from the paths of Learning and Genius, who press forward to conquest and glory, without bestowing a smile on the humble drudge that facilitates their progress. Every other author may aspire to praise; the lexicographer can only hope to escape reproach, and even this negative recompense has been yet granted to very few.
>
> I have, notwithstanding this discouragement, attempted a dictionary of the English language, which, while it was employed in the cultivation of every species of literature, has itself been hitherto neglected, suffered to spread, under the direction of chance, into wild exuberance, resigned to the tyranny of time and fashion, and exposed to the corruptions of ignorance, and caprices of innovation.

Does Johnson really believe that he is a "drudge," a "slave of science," a garbage man "doomed only to remove rubbish and clear obstructions from the paths of Learning and Genius?" Nothing about the man or his life tells us that he saw himself in such lowly terms. He had just completed, after a massive labor of nine years, a dictionary that defined 43,000 words supported by 114,000 quotations from literature. His was not the first dictionary of the English language, but even today it is ranked as the most important. Part of the problem with his preface is that he uses it to show off his learning and scholarship rather than to communicate facts about his dictionary. His attitude affects his voice.

Vocabulary, syntax, and attitude—these are all factors the writer can control. They are important in developing the voice you can use in factual writing. Naturally, they're less important in some other kinds of writing—poetry and fiction, for example—that aim to do more than merely communicate an idea. The lessons we are teaching are meant only for factual writing, which is to prose what the camel is to the desert. For that kind of writing, you must strive for clarity and readability if you wish to please your reader.

Exercises

1. How would you characterize the tone of the following paragraph that came from a letter a tenant sent to a landlord?

    If you want your rent this month, you'd better do something about the leaky kitchen faucet. I've told you about this at least five times and still you have done nothing. The dripping at night is driving me mad. I don't know what ever possessed me to rent such a pigsty. But if you don't do something about it, I'm going to go to the city and complain and tell them what a roach-infested dump you're renting to innocent people.

2. Change the voice of the preceding paragraph by rewriting it to reflect a softer tone.

3. How would you characterize the voice in the following excerpts? Describe the vocabulary, syntax, and attitude evident in each passage:
   a. I am twenty years of age today. The past year has been crappy—breaking up with my boyfriend, losing my job mixing blended drinks for a local Dutch Boy drive-in, and flunking a math night class at Sierra Community College. What a bummer!
   b. The Internet is a treasure chest of data, facts, statistics, opinions, speculations, and viewpoints—all that comes under the general heading of information.
   c. In clinical psychiatry and psychoanalytical work there are few such heroes, men and women whose intelligence, compassion, and above all, candor, illuminate their deeds, their words, and the failures they inevitably suffer.

4. Write two brief letters on any event that occurred in your school and in which you took part: one to a parent or an authority figure and the other to your best friend.

5. Write a paragraph or two analyzing the differences in the voices you used in the letters you just wrote.

6. What attitude toward medical doctors does the following paragraph reveal? What kind of person might write such a paragraph?

   If I had cancer, I would not submit to chemotherapy. I watched my mom have chemotherapy, and it made her so nauseated and so weak that she often said, "I can't take this anymore." I can't see why it would be beneficial to put what is obviously a strong poison into any human body. Surely, nature has better ways of curing cancer than chemotherapy. Doctors are just too tunnel-visioned to use natural herbs to help cure cancer. They think that only prescriptions you get through pharmaceutical companies can possibly be effective; yet, I know someone who was cured of breast cancer by drinking a quart of carrot juice every day.

7. Which of the two statements that follow reflects the more rational and objective tone toward a photographic exhibit? Identify the vocabulary that makes the difference.
   a. This photographic exhibit is a wonderful gallery of varied portraits—politician, seamstress, drifter, ballet dancer, mother, and much more. Each portrait has been shot against a starkly white background, which seems to allow no place for the subject to hide and therefore suggests a confrontational intimacy between the photographer and the subject. Because of the backlighting involved, each head appears to sprout a halo that contrasts paradoxically with the shadows on the face, lending a beguiling mystery to the facial features in each frame.
   b. After staring at this portrait gallery for almost an hour, I decided that it was all meaningless trash. Who wants to waste time looking at this sort of nightmare? This is not art; it is the revelation of a sick mind. All I could see were men and women photographed against a white wall. Some kind of weird circle of light surrounded their heads, but their faces were dark and wrinkled. The ugliness of these faces really bugged me. I felt depressed to think that this Halloween-type exhibit was considered great modern art and was shown at the local museum.

How to Say Nothing in Five Hundred Words

PAUL ROBERTS

Rhetorical Thumbnail

Purpose: to teach students how to write

Audience: freshman composition students and English instructors

Language: informal English used satirically

Strategy: takes audience through the steps of a typical freshman trying to write an essay

---

Paul McHenry Roberts (1917–1967) taught college English for over twenty years, first at San Jose State College and later at Cornell University. He wrote several books on linguistics, including *Understanding Grammar* (1954), *Patterns of English* (1956), and *Understanding English* (1958).

Freshman composition, like everything else, has its share of fashions. In the 1950s, when this article was written, the most popular argument raging among student essayists was the proposed abolition of college football. With the greater social consciousness of the early 1960s, the topic of the day became the morality of capital punishment. Topics may change, but the core principles of good writing remain constant, and this essay has become something of a minor classic in explaining them.

● ● ●

1   It's Friday afternoon, and you have almost survived another week of classes. You are just looking forward dreamily to the weekend when the English instructor says: "For Monday you will turn in a five-hundred-word composition on college football."

2   Well, that puts a good hole in the weekend. You don't have any strong views on college football one way or the other. You get rather excited during the season and go to all the home games and find it rather more fun than not. On the other hand, the class has been reading Robert Hutchins in the anthology and perhaps Shaw's "Eighty-Yard Run," and from the class discussion you have got the idea that the instructor thinks college football is for the birds. You are no fool. You can figure out what side to take.

3   After dinner you get out the portable typewriter that you got for high school graduation. You might as well get it over with and enjoy Saturday and Sunday. Five hundred words is about two double-spaced pages with normal margins. You put in a sheet of paper, think up a title, and you're off:

Why College Football Should Be Abolished

College football should be abolished because it's bad for the school and also for the players. The players are so busy practicing that they don't have any time for their studies.

This, you feel, is a mighty good start. The only trouble is that it's only thirty-two words. You still have four hundred and sixty-eight to go, and you've pretty well exhausted the subject. It comes to you that you do your best thinking in the morning, so you put away the typewriter and go to the movies. But the next morning you have to do your washing and some math problems, and in the afternoon you go to the game. The English instructor turns up too, and you wonder if you've taken the right side after all. Saturday night you have a date, and Sunday morning you have to go to church. (You can't let English assignments interfere with your religion.) What with one thing and another, it's ten o'clock Sunday night before you get out the typewriter again. You make a pot of coffee and start to fill out your views on college football. Put a little meat on the bones.

Why College Football Should Be Abolished

In my opinion, it seems to me that college football should be abolished. The reason why I think this to be true is because I feel that football is bad for the colleges in nearly every respect. As Robert Hutchins says in his article in our anthology in which he discusses college football, it would be better if the colleges had race horses and had races with one another, because then the horses would not have to attend classes. I firmly agree with Mr. Hutchins on this point, and I am sure that many other students would agree too.

One reason why it seems to me that college football is bad is that it has become too commercial. In the olden times when people played football just for the fun of it, maybe college football was all right, but they do not play college football just for the fun of it now as they used to in the old days. Nowadays college football is what you might call a big business. Maybe this is not true at all schools, and I don't think it is especially true here at State, but certainly this is the case at most colleges and universities in America nowadays, as Mr. Hutchins points out in his very interesting article. Actually the coaches and alumni go around to the high schools and offer the high school stars large salaries to come to their colleges and play football for them. There was one case where a high school star was offered a convertible if he would play football for a certain college.

Another reason for abolishing college football is that it is bad for the players. They do not have time to get a college education, because they are so busy playing football. A football player has to practice every afternoon from three to six and then he is so tired that he can't concentrate on his studies. He just feels like dropping off to sleep after dinner, and then the next day he goes to his classes without having studied and maybe he fails the test.

(Good ripe stuff so far, but you're still one hundred fifty-one words from home. One more push.)

Also I think college football is bad for the colleges and the universities because not very many students get to participate in it. Out of a college of ten thousand students only seventy-five or a hundred play football, if that many. Football is what you might call a spectator sport. That means that most people go to watch it but do not play it themselves.

(Four hundred fifteen. Well, you still have the conclusion, and when you retype it, you can make the margins a little wider.)

These are the reasons why I agree with Mr. Hutchins that college football should be abolished in American colleges and universities.

4   On Monday you turn it in, moderately hopeful, and on Friday it comes back marked "weak in content" and sporting a big "D."

5   This essay is exaggerated a little, but not much. The English instructor will recognize it as reasonably typical of what an assignment on college football will bring in. He knows that nearly half of the class will contrive in five hundred words to say that college football is too commercial and bad for the players. Most of the other half will inform him that college football builds character and prepares one for life and brings prestige to the school. As he reads paper after paper all saying the same thing in almost the same words, all bloodless, five hundred words dripping out of nothing, he wonders how he allowed himself to get trapped into teaching English when he might have had a happy and interesting life as an electrician or a confidence man.

6   Well, you may ask, what can you do about it? The subject is one on which you have few convictions and little information. Can you be expected to make a dull subject interesting? As a matter of fact, this is precisely what you are expected to do. This is the writer's essential task. All subjects, except sex, are dull until somebody makes them interesting. The writer's job is to find the argument, the approach, the angle, the wording that will take the reader with him. This is seldom easy, and it is particularly hard in subjects that have been much discussed: College Football, Fraternities, Popular Music, Is Chivalry Dead?, and the like. You will feel that there is nothing you can do with such subjects except repeat the old bromides. But there are some things you can do which will make your papers, if not throbbingly alive, at least less insufferably tedious than they might otherwise be.

Avoid the Obvious Content

7   Say the assignment is college football. Say that you've decided to be against it. Begin by putting down the arguments that come to your mind: it is too commercial, it takes the students' minds off their studies, it is hard on the players, it makes the university a kind of circus instead of an intellectual center, for most schools it is financially ruinous. Can you think of any more arguments, just offhand? All right. Now, when you write your paper, make sure that you don't use any of the material on this list. If these are the points that leap to your mind, they will leap to everyone else's too, and whether you get a "C" or a "D" may depend on whether the instructor reads your paper early when he is fresh and tolerant or late, when the sentence "In my opinion, college football has become too commercial," inexorably repeated, has brought him to the brink of lunacy.

8   Be against college football for some reason or reasons of your own. If they are keen and perceptive ones, that's splendid. But even if they are trivial or foolish or indefensible, you are still ahead so long as they are not everybody else's reasons too. Be against it because the colleges don't spend enough money on it to make it worthwhile, because it is bad for the characters of the spectators, because the players are forced to attend classes, because the football stars hog all the beautiful women, because it competes with baseball and is therefore un-American and possibly Communist-inspired. There are lots of more or less unused reasons for being against college football.

9   Sometimes it is a good idea to sum up and dispose of the trite and conventional points before going on to your own. This has the advantage of indicating to the reader that you are going to be neither trite nor conventional. Something like this:

> We are often told that college football should be abolished because it has become too commercial or because it is bad for the players. These arguments are no doubt very cogent, but they don't really go to the heart of the matter.

Then you go to the heart of the matter.

Take the Less Usual Side

10   One rather simple way of getting into your paper is to take the side of the argument that most of the citizens will want to avoid. If the assignment is an essay on dogs, you can, if you choose, explain that dogs are faithful and lovable companions, intelligent, useful as guardians of the house and protectors of children, indispensable in police work—in short, when all is said and done, man's best friends. Or you can suggest that those big brown eyes conceal, more often than not, a vacuity of mind and an inconstancy of purpose; that the dogs you have known most intimately have been mangy, ill-tempered brutes, incapable of instruction; and that only your nobility of mind and fear of arrest prevent you from kicking the flea-ridden animals when you pass them on the street.

11   Naturally, personal convictions will sometimes dictate your approach. If the assigned subject is "Is Methodism Rewarding to the Individual?" and you are a pious Methodist, you have really no choice. But few assigned subjects, if any, will fall in this category. Most of them will lie in broad areas of discussion with much to be said on both sides. They are intellectual exercises, and it is legitimate to argue now one way and now another, as debaters do in similar circumstances. Always take the side that looks to you hardest, least defensible. It will almost always turn out to be easier to write interestingly on that side.

12   This general advice applies where you have a choice of subjects. If you are to choose among "The Value of Fraternities" and "My Favorite High School Teacher" and "What I Think About Beetles," by all means plump for the beetles. By the time the instructor gets to your paper, he will be up to his ears in tedious tales about a French teacher at Bloombury High and assertions about how fraternities build character and prepare one for life. Your views on beetles, whatever they are, are bound to be a refreshing change.

13   Don't worry too much about figuring out what the instructor thinks about the subject so that you can cuddle up with him. Chances are his views are no stronger than yours. If he does have convictions and you oppose him, his problem is to keep from grading you higher than you deserve in order to show he is not biased. This doesn't mean that you should always cantankerously dissent from what the instructor says; that gets tiresome too. And if the subject assigned is "My Pet Peeve," do not begin, "My pet peeve is the English instructor who assigns papers on 'my pet peeve.' " This was still funny during the War of 1812, but it has sort of lost its edge since then. It is in general good manners to avoid personalities.

Slip Out of Abstraction

14   If you will study the essay on college football (near the beginning of this essay), you will perceive that one reason for its appalling dullness is that it never gets down to particulars. It is just a series of not very glittering generalities: "football is bad for the colleges," "it has become too commercial," "football is big business," "it is bad for the players," and so on. Such round phrases thudding against the reader's brain are unlikely to convince him, though they may well render him unconscious.

15   If you want the reader to believe that college football is bad for the players, you have to do more than say so. You have to display the evil. Take your roommate, Alfred Simkins, the second-string center. Picture poor old Alfy coming home from football practice every evening, bruised and aching, agonizingly tired, scarcely able to shovel the mashed potatoes into his mouth. Let us see him staggering up to the room, getting out his econ textbook, peering desperately at it with his good eye, falling asleep and failing the test in the morning. Let us share his unbearable tension as Saturday draws near. Will he fail, be demoted, lose his monthly allowance, be forced to return to the coal mines? And if he succeeds, what will be his reward? Perhaps a slight ripple of applause when the third-string center replaces him, a moment of elation in the locker room if the

team wins, of despair if it loses. What will he look back on when he graduates from college? Toil and torn ligaments. And what will be his future? He is not good enough for pro football, and he is too obscure and weak in econ to succeed in stocks and bonds. College football is tearing the heart from Alfy Simkins and, when it finishes with him, will callously toss aside the shattered hulk.

16   This is no doubt a weak enough argument for the abolition of college football, but it is a sight better than saying, in three or four variations, that college football (in your opinion) is bad for the players.

17   Look at the work of any professional writer and notice how constantly he is moving from the generality, the abstract statement, to the concrete example, the facts and figures, the illustrations. If he is writing on juvenile delinquency, he does not just tell you that juveniles are (it seems to him) delinquent and that (in his opinion) something should be done about it. He shows you juveniles being delinquent, tearing up movie theatres in Buffalo, stabbing high school principals in Dallas, smoking marijuana in Palo Alto. And more than likely he is moving toward some specific remedy, not just a general wringing of the hands.

18   It is no doubt possible to be too concrete, too illustrative or anecdotal, but few inexperienced writers err this way. For most the soundest advice is to be seeking always for the picture, to be always turning general remarks into see-able examples. Don't say, "Sororities teach girls the social graces." Say, "Sorority life teaches a girl how to carry on a conversation while pouring tea, without sloshing the tea into the saucer." Don't say, "I like certain kinds of popular music very much." Say, "Whenever I hear Gerber Sprinklittle play 'Mississippi Man' on the trombone, my socks creep up my ankles."

Get Rid of Obvious Padding

19   The student toiling away at his weekly English theme is too often tormented by a figure: five hundred words. How, he asks himself, is he to achieve this staggering total? Obviously by never using one word when he can somehow work in ten.

20   He is therefore seldom content with a plain statement like "Fast driving is dangerous." This has only four words in it. He takes thought, and the sentence becomes:

In my opinion, fast driving is dangerous.

Better, but he can do better still:

In my opinion, fast driving would seem to be rather dangerous.

If he is really adept, it may come out:

In my humble opinion, though I do not claim to be an expert on this complicated subject, fast driving, in most circumstances, would seem to be rather dangerous in many respects, or at least so it would seem to me.

Thus four words have been turned into forty, and not an iota of content has been added.

21   Now this is a way to go about reaching five hundred words, and if you are content with a "D" grade, it is as good a way as any. But if you aim higher, you must work differently. Instead of stuffing your sentences with straw, you must try steadily to get rid of the padding, to make your sentences lean and tough. If you are really working at it, your first draft will greatly exceed the required total, and then you will work it down, thus:

> It is thought in some quarters that fraternities do not contribute as much as might be expected to campus life.
>
> Some people think that fraternities contribute little to campus life.
>
> The average doctor who practices in small towns or in the country must toil night and day to heal the sick.
>
> Most country doctors work long hours.
>
> When I was a little girl, I suffered from shyness and embarrassment in the presence of others.
>
> I was a shy little girl.
>
> It is absolutely necessary for the person employed as a marine fireman to give the matter of steam pressure his undivided attention at all times.
>
> The fireman has to keep his eye on the steam gauge.

22   You may ask how you can arrive at five hundred words at this rate. Simple. You dig up more real content. Instead of taking a couple of obvious points off the surface of the topic and then circling warily around them for six paragraphs, you work in and explore, figure out the details. You illustrate. You say that fast driving is dangerous, and then you prove it. How long does it take to stop a car at forty and at eighty? How far can you see at night? What happens when a tire blows? What happens in a head-on collision at fifty miles an hour? Pretty soon your paper will be full of broken glass and blood and headless torsos, and reaching five hundred words will not really be a problem.

Call a Fool a Fool

23   Some of the padding in freshman themes is to be blamed not on anxiety about the word minimum but on excessive timidity. The student writes, "In my opinion, the principal of my high school acted in ways that I believe every unbiased person would have to call foolish." This isn't exactly what he means. What he means is, "My high school principal was a fool." If he was a fool, call him a fool. Hedging the thing about with "in-my-opinion's" and "it-seems-to-me's" and "as-I-see-it's" and "at-least-from-my-point-of-view's" gains you nothing. Delete these phrases whenever they creep into your paper.

24   The student's tendency to hedge stems from a modesty that in other circumstances would be commendable. He is, he realizes, young and inexperienced, and he half suspects that he is dopey and fuzzy-minded beyond the

average. Probably only too true. But it doesn't help to announce your incompetence six times in every paragraph. Decide what you want to say and say it as vigorously as possible, without apology and in plain words.

25   Linguistic diffidence can take various forms. One is what we call euphemism. This is the tendency to call a spade "a certain garden implement" or women's underwear "unmentionables." It is stronger in some eras than others and in some people than others but it always operates more or less in subjects that are touchy or taboo: death, sex, madness, and so on. Thus we shrink from saying "He died last night" but say instead "passed away," "left us," "joined his Maker," "went to his reward." Or we try to take off the tension with a lighter cliché: "kicked the bucket," "cashed in his chips," "handed in his dinner pail." We have found all sorts of ways to avoid saying "mad": "mentally ill," "touched," "not quite right upstairs," "feebleminded," "innocent," "simple," "off his trolley," "not in his right mind." Even such a now plain word as "insane" began as a euphemism with the meaning "not healthy."

26   Modern science, particularly psychology, contributes many polysyllables in which we can wrap our thoughts and blunt their force. To many writers there is no such thing as a bad schoolboy. Schoolboys are maladjusted or unoriented or misunderstood or in need of guidance or lacking in continued success toward satisfactory integration of the personality as a social unit, but they are never bad. Psychology no doubt makes us better men and women, more sympathetic and tolerant, but it doesn't make writing any easier. Had Shakespeare been confronted with psychology, "To be or not to be" might have come out, "To continue as a social unit or not to do so. That is the personality problem. Whether 'tis a better sign of integration at the conscious level to display a psychic tolerance toward the maladjustments and repressions induced by one's lack of orientation in one's environment or—" But Hamlet would never have finished the soliloquy.

27   Writing in the modern world, you cannot altogether avoid modern jargon. Nor, in an effort to get away from euphemism, should you salt your paper with four-letter words. But you can do much if you will mount guard against those roundabout phrases, those echoing polysyllables that tend to slip into your writing to rob it of its crispness and force.

Beware of Pat Expressions

28   Other things being equal, avoid phrases like "other things being equal." Those sentences that come to you whole, or in two or three doughy lumps, are sure to be bad sentences. They are no creation of yours but pieces of common thought floating in the community soup.

29   Pat expressions are hard—often impossible—to avoid, because they come too easily to be noticed and seem too necessary to be dispensed with. No writer avoids them altogether, but good writers avoid them more often than poor writers.

30   By "pat expressions" we mean such tags as "to all practical intents and purposes," "the pure and simple truth," "from where I sit," "the time of his life,"

"to the ends of the earth," "in the twinkling of an eye," "as sure as you're born," "over my dead body," "under cover of darkness," "took the easy way out," "when all is said and done," "told him time and time again," "parted the best of friends," "stand up and be counted," "gave him the best years of her life," "worked her fingers to the bone." Like other clichés, these expressions were once forceful. Now we should use them only when we can't possibly think of anything else.

31   Some pat expressions stand like a wall between the writer and thought. Such a one is "the American way of life." Many student writers feel that when they have said that something accords with the American way of life or does not they have exhausted the subject. Actually, they have stopped at the highest level of abstraction. The American way of life is the complicated set of bonds between one hundred eighty million ways. All of us know this when we think about it, but the tag phrase too often keeps us from thinking about it.

32   So with many another phrase dear to the politician: "this great land of ours," "the man in the street," "our national heritage." These may prove our patriotism or give a clue to our political beliefs, but otherwise they add nothing to the paper except words.

Colorful Words

33   The writer builds with words, and no builder uses a raw material more slippery and elusive and treacherous. A writer's work is a constant struggle to get the right word in the right place, to find that particular word that will convey his meaning exactly, that will persuade the reader or soothe him or startle or amuse him. He never succeeds altogether—sometimes he feels that he scarcely succeeds at all—but such successes as he has are what make the thing worth doing.

34   There is no book of rules for this game. One progresses through everlasting experiment on the basis of ever-widening experience. There are few useful generalizations that one can make about words as words, but there are perhaps a few.

35   Some words are what we call "colorful." By this we mean that they are calculated to produce a picture or induce an emotion. They are dressy instead of plain, specific instead of general, loud instead of soft. Thus, in place of "Her heart beat," we may write, "Her heart pounded, throbbed, fluttered, danced." Instead of "He sat in his chair," we may say, "He lounged, sprawled, coiled." Instead of "It was hot," we may say, "It was blistering, sultry, muggy, suffocating, steamy, wilting."

36   However, it should not be supposed that the fancy word is always better. Often it is as well to write "Her heart beat" or "It was hot" if that is all it did or all it was. Ages differ in how they like their prose. The nineteenth century liked it rich and smoky. The twentieth has usually preferred it lean and cool. The twentieth-century writer, like all writers, is forever seeking the exact word, but he is wary of sounding feverish. He tends to pitch it low, to understate it, to throw it away. He knows that if he gets too colorful, the audience is likely to giggle.

37   See how this strikes you: "As the rich, golden glow of the sunset died away along the eternal western hills, Angela's limpid blue eyes looked softly and trustingly into Montague's flashing brown ones, and her heart pounded like a drum in time with the joyous song surging in her soul." Some people like that sort of thing, but most modern readers would say, "Good grief," and turn on the television.

Colored Words

38   Some words we would call not so much colorful as colored—that is, loaded with associations, good or bad. All words—except perhaps structure words—have associations of some sort. We have said that the meaning of a word is the sum of the contexts in which it occurs. When we hear a word, we hear with it an echo of all the situations in which we have heard it before.

39   In some words, these echoes are obvious and discussible. The word *mother*, for example, has, for most people, agreeable associations. When you hear *mother* you probably think of home, safety, love, food, and various other pleasant things. If one writes, "She was like a mother to me," he gets an effect which he would not get in "She was like an aunt to me." The advertiser makes use of the associations of *mother* by working it in when he talks about his product. The politician works it in when he talks about himself.

40   So also with such words as *home, liberty, fireside, contentment, patriot, tenderness, sacrifice, childlike, manly, bluff, limpid.* All of these words are loaded with associations that would be rather hard to indicate in a straight-forward definition. There is more than a literal difference between "They sat around the fireside" and "They sat around the stove." They might have been equally warm and happy around the stove, but *fireside* suggests leisure, grace, quiet tradition, congenial company, and *stove* does not.

41   Conversely, some words have bad associations. *Mother* suggests pleasant things, but *mother-in-law* does not. Many mothers-in-law are heroically lovable and some mothers drink gin all day and beat their children insensible, but these facts of life are beside the point. The point is that *mother* sounds good and *mother-in-law* does not.

42   Or consider the word *intellectual.* This would seem to be a complimentary term, but in point of fact it is not, for it has picked up associations of impracticality and ineffectuality and general dopiness. So also such words as *liberal, reactionary, Communist, socialist, capitalist, radical, schoolteacher, truck driver, undertaker, operator, salesman, huckster, speculator.* These convey meaning on the literal level, but beyond that—sometimes, in some places—they convey contempt on the part of the speaker.

43   The question of whether to use loaded words or not depends on what is being written. The scientist and the scholar try to avoid them; for the poet, the advertising writer, the public speaker, they are standard equipment. But every writer should take care that they do not substitute for thought. If you write, "Anyone who thinks that is nothing but a Socialist (or Communist or capitalist)" you have said nothing except that you don't like people who think that,

and such remarks are effective only with the most naïve readers. It is always a bad mistake to think your readers more naïve than they really are.

Colorless Words

44 But probably most student writers come to grief not with words that are colorful or those that are colored, but with those that have no color at all. A pet example is *nice*, a word we would find it hard to dispense with in casual conversation but which is no longer capable of adding much to a description. Colorless words are those of such general meaning that in a particular sentence they mean nothing. Slang adjectives like cool ("That's real cool") tend to explode all over the language. They are applied to everything, lose their original force, and quickly die.

45   Beware also of nouns of very general meaning, like *circumstances, cases, instances, aspects, factors, relationships, attitudes, eventualities*, etc. In most circumstances you will find that those cases of writing which contain too many instances of words like these will in this and other aspects have factors leading to unsatisfactory relationships with the reader resulting in unfavorable attitudes on his part and perhaps other eventualities, like a grade of "D." Notice also what *etc.* means. It means "I'd like to make this list longer, but I can't think of any more examples."

Paul Roberts, UNDERSTANDING ENGLISH, © 1958. Reprinted by permission of Pearson Education, Inc., Upper Saddle River, New Jersey.

● Vocabulary

contrive (5)	vacuity (10)	jargon (27)
bromides (6)	warily (22)	polysyllables (27)
inexorably (7)	diffidence (25)	elusive (33)
cogent (9)	euphemism (25)	induce (35)

EXAMPLES

Tone: The Writer's Voice in the Reader's Mind

MORT CASTLE

Rhetorical Thumbnail

Purpose: to teach the use of tone in writing

Audience: writing students and instructors

Language: snappy, informal English as befitting a writing guru

Strategy: draws details from personal experience to make a convincing case for the meaning of "tone"

Mort Castle (b. 1946) is a dedicated teacher and fiction writer. He has 350 short stories and a dozen books to his credit, including *Cursed Be the Child* (1994), *The Strangers* (1984), and *Moon on the Water* (2000). Castle takes particular pride in the fact that 2,000 of his students, ranging in age from six to ninety-three, have seen their work in print. He is a frequent keynote speaker at writing conferences or workshops. His book, *Writing Horror* (1997), for which he served as editor, has become the "bible" for aspiring horror authors. He is also the executive editor of Thorby Comics, which publishes the popular comic books *Night City, Death Asylum, The Skuler, Blythe: Nightvision,* and *Johnny Cosmic.*

Novice writers often think that tone is used only in speaking, not in writing. By using numerous examples and taking on a humorous tone, Castle convinces us that tone is a key ingredient in the relationship between reader and writer.

● ● ●

1   Johnny, the new kid, walks into third grade, casually waves to his teacher, Ms. Cruth, and says, "How's it goin', Butthead?"

2   "We do not talk that way in this class, Johnny," says Ms. Cruth. Opting for educational strategy #101: neo-traditional negative reinforcement, but not allowed to hit, she sends Johnny to the corner.

3   The next day, Johnny steps into the classroom, with "Hey, what's up, Ms. Bimbo?"

4   "Corner, Johnny," says Ms. Cruth.

5   The day after, Johnny comes into the classroom. He says, "Good morning, Ms. Cruth."

6   "Go to the corner, Johnny," says Ms. Cruth.

7   "Huh?" Johnny's inquiring mind wants to know. "Why are you sending me to the corner? I did not call you 'Butthead' and I did not call you 'Ms. Bimbo,' and I didn't say one word that might be considered pejorative!"

8   "No," says Ms. Cruth, "but I don't like your tone."

9   When we speak to others, our tone of voice is no less important than our actual words. Call your faithful friend, Fido, into the room, for our experiment in tone. Granted, with the difference in the communicative arts as practiced by human being and canine being, the following analogy is not fully apropos, yet 'twill serve:

10   Talk to your dog. Though your tone is a warm one, you know, "praise the pup, I love my wonderful companionate animal, etc.," don't use real words of praise. Try: "Fido, you double ugly moron, you stinky poo puppy, you drecky wretched doggy dastard!"

11   Fido wags his tail. All is well. I may not get the words, but I know what you mean.

12   In speaking, stressed sounds, vocal cadences, pronunciation, rhythm and pauses, repetition, voice pitch, timbre, and volume, etc. help the listener get the message. The "sincere" tone tells the listener "I'm sorry" truly indicates ... "I am sorry." Yet, with a sneering, sarcastic tone, those same two words can

implicitly say, "I am sorry I did not cause you half the grief, misery, agony, and woe I could have had I only been a trace more imaginative."

13 The "listen up" tone is for when the mechanic needs to hear that this time, damn it, he'd better find the oil leak.

14 The "cooing selected little nothings" tone can be well-suited for the prelude to the proposal moment, whether that be a major commitment proposal or a suggestion of serious messing around.

15 Most kids know the tone that signals, "You'd really better cut it out and this time I mean it!"

16 The conspiratorial tone signals it's "true dirt-dishing time."

17 The "ha ha ha ready to happen" tone is for the joke . . .

18 The writer putting words on the page (or computer screen or out there in cyberville) also has a tone of voice. The writer, of course, does not have a speaker's unique tone tools: vocal cords, sinus cavities, lip, tongue, palette, etc. Nor does the writer have a raised eyebrow to provide a hint, nor a smile, nor a broad hand wave. Instead, tone is achieved by choice and arrangement of our prime building blocks: words.

19 The reader hears—and responds to—that tone of voice as he is reading.

20 That voice, that tone, must be suited to the material so that the reader clearly understands what is said, understands on both the literal and the figurative levels.

21 "Let us go then, you and I," T. S. Eliot begins "The Love Song of J. Alfred Prufrock." The tone is somber and formal, made more so, perhaps, by the deliberate grammar fluff of the nominative "I" used instead of the objective "me," an error often made by those hoping to sound "educated": the reader is invited to undertake a desolate and wearying journey. The tone helps to establish the mood of the poem, gives the reader a feeling. But if Eliot had begun (with or without an apology to The Ramones): "Hey ho! Let's go!"

22 Or had he whined in classic Jerry Lewis style, "Look, would you please come on, already? Aw, just come on, okay?"

23 Or in keeping with contemporary "dirty words currently acceptable on Prime Time Network TV": "Let's haul ass!"

24 Well, we would not exactly be anticipating gloom and soul dread as we walk with J. Alfred, would we?

25 Consider the opening of Edgar Allan Poe's familiar "The Tell-Tale Heart":

26 "True!—nervous—very very dreadfully nervous I had been and am, but why will you say that I am mad?"

27 There's an immediate rush of energy with that very first word and exclamation point: A frantic energy. A crazed madman's energy. You hear the protagonist protesting way, way more than a "bit too much" the idea that he is insane. To use today's pseudo-artistic term, the "edgy tone" of the story is established: a barely-in-control-and-soon-to-wig-out tone.

28 The right tone, the proper voice in the reader's mind, lets you say what you want to say the way you want to say it.

29 And the wrong tone . . .

30   In the scene that follows from a deservedly unpublished short story, Mike is visited by his psychopathic brother, Arnold. Mike believes Arnold intends to kill him—and Mike is right.

31   Arnold stepped in. "How are you doing, Mike?" he asked.
32   "I've been doing all right," Mike responded promptly.
33   "That's good," Arnold said.
34   "How about you?" Mike asked.
35   "Well, I guess I have been doing okay," Arnold calmly said.
36   "I'm glad to hear it. It certainly is a snowy day."
37   "I guess everyone talks about the weather but no one does anything about it," Arnold said. "That is my opinion, anyway."
38   "I agree," Mike said.
39   Then Arnold shouted, "It's a perfect day for you to die, you dirty rat!"

40   Except for Arnold's closing outburst, the tone of this passage is mundane, prosaic, no more tense (or interesting) than that of an ordinary, everyday conversation you might overhear in the dentist's waiting room. It is totally unsuited for what is meant to be a moment of high drama.

41   Here's another cutting from a different "wrong tone" story. The protagonist is attempting to get up the nerve to stand before an Alcoholics Anonymous meeting and say for the first time: "My name is Sharon and I am an alcoholic." She sits, biting her nails, and then shakily gets to her feet, ". . . flinging her hair back like a galloping filly tossing its mane . . ."

42   Uh-uh. That "mane tossing filly" gives the scene an inappropriate tone. My Girl Friend Flicka. Lighthearted Retro-Range-Romance: Up rides Dale Evans on Buttermilk, meeting her spunky niece from out East, Manda Llewellyn Travis . . . This lighthearted tone and the upbeat optimism one feels make for what most critics would judge a wrong tone.

43   That is not to say, of course, that only the "comic tone" can be employed for comic writing, that the "romantic tone" must be used for romance writing, that a horrific tone must be used for horror writing.

44   Let's spend a tone moment with the late Charles Beaumont, one of my all-time literary heroes and the writer of many classic short short stories that came to typify what is thought of as "Playboy Magazine horror" in the late 1950s and 1960s.

45   Beaumont's short story is called "Free Dirt":

46   It opens:

"No fowl had ever looked so posthumous."

47   Seven words—and the tone is established. "Posthumous" gives the sentence an overly formal, almost pompous tone. "Fowl," rather than chicken, is likewise formal. The voice that reads this sentence inside the reader's mind is wryly sardonic, not unlike the voice of the late Alfred Hitchcock. There's humor here, but it's dark humor, the laughter we can hear as we stand by the gravesite, and it's perfect for a brief and utterly chilling story, a work of "moral fiction" in the best sense: It teaches in a non-didactic way.

48   The right tone, then, is the one that allows the writer to speak clearly to the reader. The goal, of course, is the essence of the writer–reader relationship: "I get it," the reader implicitly says.

49   You don't want your home builder cracking up with laughter, telling you that you should be swapping one-liners with Leno, when you demand he put the front door in front, just as the blueprints have it, instead of on the roof—and you don't want your reader snickering, giggling, guffawing, and hoo-ha-ing because your voice in his mind cues him to laugh at your sequel to *A Christmas Carol*, in which Tiny Tim dies of consumption, Bob Cratchit is run over by a hansom cab, and Scrooge gets murdered by Marley's ghost!

Mort Castle, "The Writers Voice on the Readers Mind" from WRITERS WRITE: THE INTERNET WRITING JOURNAL, September 2000. Copyright 1997–2000 by Writers Write, Inc. Reprinted by permission.

● Vocabulary

neo-traditional (2)	timbre (12)	mundane (40)
pejorative (7)	conspiratorial (16)	prosaic (40)
apropos (9)	figurative (20)	posthumous (46)
cadences (12)	desolate (21)	sardonic (47)
pitch (12)	pseudo-artistic (27)	non-didactic (47)

● The Facts

1. What kind of student is the author portraying through Johnny? How would you react to having such a student in your class?
2. What was wrong with Johnny's third greeting?
3. What analogy does the author use to illustrate the importance of tone over words in speech? What other analogy can you cite?
4. What elements, not used in writing, can a person use to communicate in speech?
5. What is the only arsenal available to writers to establish tone? Does this limited arsenal curtail good writers? Give examples that support your opinion.

● The Strategies

1. What rhetorical strategy does the author use to persuade us that his view of tone is correct? Are you convinced? Give reasons for your answer.
2. In what paragraph does the author switch from vocal tone to writing tone? Were you able to follow his shift? If no, why not? If yes, why?
3. Why do you think the author uses the opening line of T. S. Eliot's "J. Alfred Prufrock" as an example of setting a definite tone? Do you think this was a good choice? Why or why not?
4. In paragraph 29, the author does not finish his sentence, but leaves you hanging with ellipsis points. How would you finish this sentence?
5. In what paragraph does the author tell you what the right tone is? What will the reader implicitly say if the author has established the right tone?

● The Issues

1. Are there kinds of writing in which no tone is necessary? If you think there are, give examples of this kind of writing.

2. How can mastery of tone help your writing?

3. How can voice and tone be suited to the material on the figurative level? (See paragraph 20.) Explain this idea by using an example.

4. The author assures us that tone does not always need to match the writing genre. For instance, a comic tone might be used for a romance and a romantic tone for a comedy. Cite an example from literature that mixes tone and genre.

5. What tone would most likely suit the following situations?
   a. A mother writes goodbye to her son leaving for war.
   b. A college student thanks her sorority sisters for giving her a wild bachelorette party the week before her wedding.
   c. A minister encourages his congregation to donate money for some new hymnbooks.

● Suggestions for Writing

1. Write a letter to one of the following people, using an appropriate tone:
   a. To your boss, announcing that you are quitting the company for a new assignment
   b. To your father, asking for money to pay your car insurance
   c. To your best friend, describing a recent camping trip
   d. To an acquaintance who borrowed money from you and refuses to pay you back

2. Write an essay in which you define tone as you now understand it.

The Waltz

DOROTHY PARKER

Rhetorical Thumbnail

Purpose: to amuse or entertain

Audience: general magazine readers

Language: conversational English

Strategy: dramatizes the contrast between what a female character says inwardly and what she says outwardly

Dorothy Parker (1893–1967) was an American short-story writer and poet. While serving as drama critic for *Vanity Fair* (1916–1917) and as book reviewer for the *New Yorker* (1927), she became legendary for her sardonic remarks about contemporary manners and attitudes. Her first volume of poetry, *Enough Rope* (1926), brought her instant fame. This was followed by *Death and Taxes* (1931) and *Not So Deep as a Well* (1936). Most of her works are collected in *The Portable Dorothy Parker,* (Ed. Brendan Gill, NY: The Viking Press, 1973).

The short story below is written in a sardonic voice that is typical of Dorothy Parker. Many readers will readily identify with the conflict between surface civility and inward resentment that the narrator expresses.

● ● ●

1   *Why, thank you so much. I'd adore to.*

2   I don't want to dance with him. I don't want to dance with anybody. And even if I did, it wouldn't be him. He'd be well down among the last ten. I've seen the way he dances; it looks like something you do on Saint Walpurgis Night. Just think, not a quarter of an hour ago, here I was sitting, feeling so sorry for the poor girl he was dancing with. And now *I'm* going to be the poor girl. Well, well. Isn't it a small world?

3   And a peach of a world, too. A true little corker. Its events are so fascinatingly unpredictable, are not they? Here I was, minding my own business, not doing a stitch of harm to any living soul. And then he comes into my life, all smiles and city manners, to sue me for the favor of one memorable mazurka. Why, he scarcely knows my name, let alone what it stands for. It stands for Despair, Bewilderment, Futility, Degradation, and Premeditated Murder, but little does he wot. I don't wot his name, either; I haven't any idea what it is. Jukes, would be my guess from the look in his eyes. How do you do, Mr. Jukes? And how is that dear little brother of yours, with the two heads?

4   Ah, now why did he have to come around me, with his low requests? Why can't he let me lead my own life? I ask so little—just to be left alone in my quiet corner of the table, to do my evening brooding over all my sorrows. And he must come, with his bows and his scrapes and his may-I-have-this-ones. And I had to go and tell him that I'd adore to dance with him. I cannot understand why I wasn't struck right down dead. Yes, and being struck dead would look like a day in the country, compared to struggling out a dance with this boy. But what could I do? Everyone else at the table had got up to dance, except him and me. There was I, trapped. Trapped like a trap in a trap.

5   What can you say, when a man asks you do dance with him? I most certainly will *not* dance with you, I'll see you in hell first. Why, thank you, I'd like to awfully, but I'm having labor pains. Oh, yes, *do* let's dance together—it's so nice to meet a man who isn't a scaredy-cat about catching my beri-beri. No. There was nothing for me to do, but say I'd adore to. Well, we might as well get it over with. All right, Cannonball, let's run out on the field. You won the toss; you can lead.

6   *Why, I think it's more of a waltz, really. Isn't it? We might just listen to the music a second. Shall we? Oh, yes, it's a waltz. Mind? Why, I'm simply thrilled. I'd love to waltz with you.*

7   I'd love to waltz with you. I'd love to waltz with you. I'd love to waltz with you. I'd love to have my tonsils out, I'd love to be in a midnight fire at sea. Well,

it's too late now. We're getting under way. *Oh*, Oh, dear. Oh, dear, dear, dear. Oh, this is even worse than I thought it would be. I suppose that's the one dependable law of life—everything is always worse than you thought it was going to be. Oh, if I had any real grasp of what this dance would be like, I'd have held out for sitting it out. Well, it will probably amount to the same thing in the end. We'll be sitting it out on the floor in a minute, if he keeps this up.

8　　I'm so glad I brought it to his attention that this is a waltz they're playing. Heaven knows what might have happened, if he had thought it was something fast; we'd have blown the sides right out of the building. Why does he always want to be somewhere that he isn't? Why can't we stay in one place just long enough to get acclimated? It's this constant rush, rush, rush, that's the curse of American life. That's the reason that we're all of us so—*Ow!* For God's sake, don't *kick*, you idiot; this is only second down. Oh, my shin. My poor, poor shin, that I've had ever since I was a little girl!

9　　*Oh, no, no, no. Goodness, no. It didn't hurt the least little bit. And anyway it was my fault. Really it was. Truly, Well, you're just being sweet, to say that. It really was all my fault.*

10　　I wonder what I'd better do—kill him this instant, with my naked hands, or wait and let him drop in his traces. Maybe it's best not to make a scene. I guess I'll just lie low, and watch the pace get him. He can't keep this up indefinitely— he's only flesh and blood. Die he must, and die he shall, for what he did to me. I don't want to be of the oversensitive type, but you can't tell me that kick was unpremeditated. Freud says there are no accidents. I've led no cloistered life, I've known dancing partners who have spoiled my slippers and torn my dress; but when it comes to kicking, I am Outraged Womanhood. When you kick me in the shin, *smile.*

11　　Maybe he didn't do it maliciously. Maybe it's just his way of showing his high spirits. I suppose I ought to be glad that one of us is having such a good time. I suppose I ought to think myself lucky if he brings me back alive. Maybe it's captious to demand of a practically strange man that he leave your shins as he found them. After all, the poor boy's doing the best he can. Probably he grew up in the hill country, and never had no larnin'. I bet they had to throw him on his back to get shoes on him.

12　　*Yes, it's lovely, isn't it? It's simply lovely. It's the loveliest waltz. Isn't it? Oh, I think it's lovely, too.*

13　　Why, I'm getting positively drawn to the Triple Threat here. He's my hero. He has the heart of a lion, and the sinews of a buffalo. Look at him—never a thought of the consequences, never afraid of his face, hurling himself into every scrimmage, eyes shining, cheeks ablaze. And shall it be said that I hung back? No, a thousand times no. What's it to me if I have to spend the next couple of years in a plaster cast? Come on, Butch, right through them! Who wants to live forever?

14　　Oh. Oh, dear. Oh, he's all right, thank goodness. For a while I thought they'd have to carry him off the field. Ah, I couldn't bear to have anything happen to him. I love him. I love him better than anybody in the world. Look at the spirit he gets into a dreary, commonplace waltz; how effete the other dancers seem, beside him. He is youth and vigor and courage, he is strength and gaiety and—*Ow!* Get off my instep, you hulking peasant! What do you think I am, anyway—a gangplank? *Ow!*

15   *No, of course it didn't hurt. Why, it didn't a bit. Honestly. And it was all my fault. You see, that little step of yours—well, it's perfectly lovely, but it's just a tiny bit tricky to follow at first. Oh, did you work it up yourself? You really did? Well, aren't you amazing! Oh, now I think I've got it. Oh, I think it's lovely. I was watching you do it when you were dancing before. It's awfully effective when you look at it.*

16   It's awfully effective when you look at it. I bet I'm awfully effective when you look at me. My hair is hanging along my cheeks, my skirt is swaddled about me, I can feel the cold damp of my brow. I must look like something out of "The Fall of the House of Usher." This sort of thing takes a fearful toll of a woman my age. And he worked up his little step himself, he with his degenerate cunning. And it was just a tiny bit tricky at first, but now I think I've got it. Two stumbles, slip, and a twenty-yard dash; yes. I've got it. I've got several other things, too, including a split shin and a bitter heart. I hate this creature I'm chained to. I hated him the moment I saw his leering, bestial face. And here I've been locked in his noxious embrace for the thirty-five years this waltz has lasted. Is that orchestra never going to stop playing? Or must this obscene travesty of a dance go on until hell burns out?

17   *Oh, they're going to play another encore. Oh, goody. Oh, that's lovely. Tired? I should say I'm not tired. I'd like to go on like this forever.*

18   I should say I'm not tired. I'm dead, that's all I am. Dead, and in what a cause! And the music is never going to stop playing, and we're going on like this, Double-Time Charlie and I, throughout eternity. I suppose I won't care any more, after the first hundred thousand years. I suppose nothing will matter then, not heat nor pain nor broken heart nor cruel, aching weariness. Well. It can't come too soon for me.

19   I wonder why I didn't tell him I was tired. I wonder why I didn't suggest going back to the table. I could have said let's just listen to the music. Yes, and if he would, that would be the first bit of attention he has given it all evening. George Jean Nathan said that the lovely rhythms of the waltz should be listened to in stillness and not be accompanied by strange gyrations of the human body. I think that's what he said. I think it was George Jean Nathan. Anyhow, whatever he said and whoever he was and whatever he's doing now, he's better off than I am. That's safe. Anybody who isn't waltzing with this Mrs. O'Leary's cow I've got here is having a good time.

20   Still if we were back at the table, I'd probably have to talk to him. Look at him—what could you say to a thing like that! Did you go to the circus this year, what's your favorite kind of ice cream, how do you spell cat? I guess I'm as well off here. As well off as if I were in a cement mixer in full action.

21   I'm past all feeling now. The only way I can tell when he steps on me is that I can hear the splintering of bones. And all the events of my life are passing before my eyes. There was the time I was in a hurricane in the West Indies, there was the day I got my head cut open in the taxi smash, there was the night the drunken lady threw a bronze ash-tray at her own true love and got me instead, there was that summer that the sailboat kept capsizing. Ah, what an easy, peaceful time was mine, until I fell in with Swifty, here. I didn't know

what trouble was, before I got drawn into this *danse macabre*. I think my mind is beginning to wander. It almost seems to me as if the orchestra were stopping. It couldn't be, of course; it could never, never be. And yet in my ears there is a silence like the sound of angel voices . . .

22   *Oh, they've stopped, the mean things. They're not going to play any more. Oh, darn. Oh, do you think they would? Do you really think so, if you gave them fifty dollars? Oh, that would be lovely. And look, do tell them to play this same thing. I'd simply adore to go on waltzing.*

"The Waltz," copyright 1933, renewed © 1961 by Dorothy Parker, from THE PORTABLE DOROTHY PARKER by Dororthy Parker, edited by Marion Meade. Used by permission of Viking Penguin, a division of Penguin Group (USA) Inc.

● Vocabulary

Saint Walpurgis (2)	captious (11)	leering (16)
beri-beri (5)	scrimmage (13)	bestial (16)
acclimated (8)	effete (14)	noxious (16)
unpremeditated (10)	hulking (14)	travesty (16)
maliciously (11)	degenerate (16)	gyrations (19)

● The Facts

1. In paragraph 5, the speaker lists three excuses she might give in order to refuse the man's dance request, claiming that these excuses are not suitable, and therefore she is forced to dance with the man. What appropriate excuse did she leave out that would have saved her from the dance without sounding uncivil or rude? What does her lack of refusal add to the story?

2. What kind of personality does the speaker reveal? How would you describe it in a nutshell? Provide some examples of your dominant impression of her.

3. How does the title of the story fit into the entire scene depicted?

4. How does paragraph 13 add to the portrait of the unfortunate dance partner?

5. What kind of ending occurs? What is its effect on the reader?

● The Strategies

1. Obviously the speaker in this story is neither ignorant nor naïve. What kind of portrait does the author create and how does she accomplish this task?

2. Look up the following references in the story and indicate how they clarify the mind of the main character: St. Walpurgis, Jukes, beri-beri, "Fall of the House of Usher," George Jean Nathan, Mrs. O'Leary's cow, *danse macabre.*

3. In paragraph 4, what is meant by the image "trapped like a trap in a trap? Is it purely redundant, or does it make sense within the context of the speaker's attitude?

4. How does the author distinguish between the speaker's outward and internal voices? What does this strategy accomplish?

5. At several points in the dance the speaker seems almost drawn to her devilish dance partner. What happens each time she begins to admire him?

● The Issues

1. What is the theme of the story? What lesson does it teach concerning society?

2. What is the tone of the story and how does it enhance the theme?

3. Some readers are turned off by the fact that most of the speaker's woes are self-inflicted because she refuses to assert herself and escape a painful situation. How do you feel about this self-perpetuation of misery? Do you believe it is realistic? Do some people really act as does the speaker?

4. What would have happened if the woman had refused to accept another dance with her partner? Did the ending surprise you? Why or why not?

5. Is it ever justified to be dishonest about your antagonistic feelings toward a person or a situation? Defend your answer by providing convincing real-life situations. If you need to qualify your answer, do so by providing appropriate cases.

● Suggestions for Writing

1. Using Dorothy Parker's strategy of alternating between italics and regular type font, write an essay in which you recreate an experience in which you were polite to a person who angered and frustrated you. Like the author, create two distinct voices and make sure your audience can understand the circumstances described.

2. Write an essay in which you defend the notion that people should be tolerant of opinions or traditions that are different from their own. Bolster your views with examples that reveal critical thinking on the subject.

Remarks on the Life of Sacco and on His Own Life and Execution

BARTOLOMEO VANZETTI

Rhetorical Thumbnail

Purpose: to argue for and his and Sacco's innocence

Audience: the court of public opinion in the 1920s

Language: fractured English

Strategy: Vanzetti's strategy was to humanize himself and Sacco; the editors' is to dramatize the power of broken English

Bartolomeo Vanzetti (1888–1927) was born of peasant stock in northern Italy, where he worked as a baker's apprentice. He migrated to the United States in

1908, where he worked as a laborer and became an avowed anarchist. In 1920, along with Nicolo Sacco, another Italian immigrant, Vanzetti was arrested for the murder of a guard during a payroll robbery. While in prison awaiting execution, he wrote his autobiography. Maintaining their innocence to the end, and despite the worldwide public protest mounted in their behalf, Sacco and Vanzetti were executed on August 22, 1927.

These four paragraphs are assembled from Vanzetti's writings and sayings. The first three paragraphs are notes from a speech. Vanzetti intended to deliver them in court before his sentencing, but the judge barred him from doing so. The final paragraph is a transcription from an interview that Vanzetti gave to Philip D. Strong, a reporter for the North American Newspaper Alliance, in April 1927.

● ● ●

1   I have talk a great deal of myself but I even forgot to name Sacco. Sacco too is a worker from his boyhood, a skilled worker lover of work, with a good job and pay, a good and lovely wife, two beautiful children and a neat little home at the verge of a wood, near a brook. Sacco is a heart, a faith, a character, a man; a man lover of nature and of mankind. A man who gave all, who sacrifice all to the cause of Liberty and to his love for mankind; money, rest, mundane ambitions, his own wife, his children, himself and his own life. Sacco has never dreamt to steal, never to assassinate. He and I have never brought a morsel of bread to our mouths, from our childhood to today—which has not been gained by the sweat of our brows. Never. His people also are in good position and of good reputation.

2   Oh, yes, I may be more witful, as some have put it, I am a better babbler than he is, but many, many times in hearing his heartful voice ringing a faith sublime, in considering his supreme sacrifice, remembering his heroism I felt small small at the presence of his greatness and found myself compelled to fight back from my throat to not weep before him—this man called thief and assassin and doomed. But Sacco's name will live in the hearts of the people and in their gratitude when Katzmann's[1] and your bones will be dispersed by time, when your name, his name, your laws, institutions, and your false god are but a deem rememoring of a cursed past in which man was wolf to the man . . .

3   If it had not been for these thing . . . I might have live out my life talking at street corners to scorning men. I might have die, unmarked, unknown, a failure. Now we are not a failure. This is our career and our triumph. Never in our full life could we hope to do such work for tolerance, for joostice, for man's onderstanding of man as now we do by accident.

4   Our words—our lives—our pains—nothing! The taking of our lives—lives of a good shoemaker and a poor fish-peddler—all! That last moment belongs to us—that agony is our triumph.

---

[1]Frederick G. Katzmann was the district attorney who prosecuted the case.

Vocabulary

mundane (1)   sublime (2)

The Facts

1. What kind of man does the excerpt make Sacco out to be?
2. What does Vanzetti claim to be better at than Sacco?
3. According to Vanzetti, how might his life have turned out were it not for his trial and conviction?

The Strategies

1. The author was an Italian with a frail grasp of the American speech idiom. What is the effect of his grammatical errors on the way he expresses himself?
2. How would you characterize the diction of this excerpt? Is it lofty? Plain?
3. Why do some editors include this excerpt in poetry anthologies? What is poetic about it?

The Issues

1. Because of his beliefs, Vanzetti was labeled a philosophical anarchist. What is a philosophical anarchist?
2. In the final paragraph, Vanzetti calls his impending execution with Sacco "our triumph." What do you think he meant by that?
3. The Sacco and Vanzetti trial was made famous mainly because of the intense media attention it drew. What restrictions, if any, do you think should be imposed on media coverage of sensational criminals and trials? Why? Justify your answer.

Suggestions for Writing

1. Copy this excerpt, correcting its grammatical and spelling errors as you go. Add any words that are necessary to make it grammatical. Write a paragraph on which version you think is more effective—the original or the corrected one—giving your reasons.
2. Without doing any further research into Vanzetti, and using this excerpt as your only evidence, write an impressionistic description of the kind of man you think he was. Be specific in your references to passages in the excerpt.

Research Paper Suggestion

Write a research paper on the Sacco-Vanzetti trial. After carefully pondering the evidence and opinions you found, present your own conclusion as to whether the trial was just or unjust. Be sure to evaluate and synthesize your information. Assure that your reader can trace the critical thinking that led to your conclusion.

Salvation

LANGSTON HUGHES

> ## Rhetorical Thumbnail
>
> **Purpose:** to pen his autobiography
>
> **Audience:** general readers
>
> **Language:** standard English
>
> **Strategy:** to recollect and re-create an experience with religion as seen through the eyes of the child he used to be

Langston Hughes (1902–1967) was born in Joplin, Missouri, and educated at Columbia University, New York, and Lincoln University, Pennsylvania. He worked at odd jobs in this country and in France before becoming established as a writer. His lifelong interest was the promotion of black art, history, and causes. In addition to many collections of poetry, Hughes wrote a novel, *Not Without Laughter* (1930), and an autobiography, *The Big Sea* (1940).

In this selection from The Big Sea, Hughes recounts a dramatic incident from his childhood. The incident is narrated from the perspective of a twelve-year-old boy and demonstrates a skillful writer's use of language to re-create the innocent voice of childhood.

• • •

1   I was saved from sin when I was going on thirteen. But not really saved. It happened like this. There was a big revival at my Auntie Reed's church. Every night for weeks there had been much preaching, singing, praying, and shouting, and some very hardened sinners had been brought to Christ, and the membership of the church had grown by leaps and bounds. Then just before the revival ended, they held a special meeting for children, "to bring the young lambs to the fold." My aunt spoke of it for days ahead. That night I was escorted to the front row and placed on the mourners' bench with all the other young sinners, who had not yet been brought to Jesus.

2   My aunt told me that when you were saved you saw a light, and something happened to you inside! And Jesus came into your life! And God was with you from then on! She said you could see and hear and feel Jesus in your soul. I believed her. I had heard a great many old people say the same thing and it seemed to me they ought to know. So I sat there calmly in the hot, crowded church, waiting for Jesus to come to me.

3   The preacher preached a wonderful rhythmical sermon, all moans and shouts and lonely cries and dire pictures of hell, and then he sang a song about the ninety and nine safe in the fold, but one little lamb was left out in the cold. Then he said: "Won't you come? Won't you come to Jesus? Young lambs, won't you come?" And he held out his arms to all us young sinners there on the mourners' bench. And the little girls cried. And some of them jumped up and went to Jesus right away. But most of us just sat there.

4   A great many old people came and knelt around us and prayed, old women with jet-black faces and braided hair, old men with work-gnarled hands. And the church sang a song about the lower lights are burning, some poor sinners to be saved. And the whole building rocked with prayer and song.

5   Still I keep waiting to see Jesus.

6   Finally all the young people had gone to the altar and were saved, but one boy and me. He was a rounder's son named Westley. Westley and I were surrounded by sisters and deacons praying. It was very hot in the church, and getting late now. Finally Westley said to me in a whisper: "God damn! I'm tired o' sitting here. Let's get up and be saved." So he got up and was saved.

7   Then I was left all alone on the mourners' bench. My aunt came and knelt at my knees and cried, while prayers and songs swirled all around me in the little church. The whole congregation prayed for me alone, in a mighty wail of moans and voices. And I kept waiting serenely for Jesus, waiting, waiting—but he didn't come. I wanted to see him, but nothing happened to me. Nothing! I wanted something to happen to me, but nothing happened.

8   I heard the songs and the minister saying: "Why don't you come? My dear child, why don't you come to Jesus? Jesus is waiting for you. He wants you. Why don't you come? Sister Reed, what is this child's name?"

9   "Langston," my aunt sobbed.

10   "Langston, why don't you come? Why don't you come and be saved? Oh, Lamb of God! Why don't you come?"

11   Now it was really getting late. I began to be ashamed of myself, holding everything up so long. I began to wonder what God thought about Westley, who certainly hadn't seen Jesus either, but who was now sitting proudly on the platform, swinging his knickerbockered legs and grinning down at me, surrounded by deacons and old women on their knees praying. God had not struck Westley dead for taking his name in vain or for lying in the temple. So I decided that maybe to save further trouble, I'd better lie, too, and say that Jesus had come, and get up and be saved.

12   So I got up.

13   Suddenly the whole room broke into a sea of shouting, as they saw me rise. Waves of rejoicing swept the place. Women leaped in the air. My aunt threw her arms around me. The minister took me by the hand and led me to the platform.

14   When things quieted down, in a hushed silence, punctuated by a few ecstatic "Amens," all the new young lambs were blessed in the name of God. Then joyous singing filled the room.

15   That night, for the last time in my life but one—for I was a big boy twelve years old—I cried. I cried, in bed alone, and couldn't stop. I buried my head under the quilts, but my aunt heard me. She woke up and told my uncle I was crying because the Holy Ghost had come into my life, and because I had seen Jesus. But I was really crying because I couldn't bear to tell her that I had lied, that I had deceived everybody in the church, and I hadn't seen Jesus, and that now I didn't believe there was a Jesus any more, since he didn't come to help me.

● Vocabulary

gnarled (4)   punctuated (14)   ecstatic (14)

● The Facts

1. How does Westley's attitude differ from the narrator's? Is Westley more realistic and less gullible, or is he simply more callous and less sensitive than the narrator?
2. The narrator holds out to the last minute and finally submits to being saved. What is his motive for finally giving in?
3. Who has been deceived in the story? The aunt by the narrator? The narrator by the aunt? Both the narrator and the aunt by the minister? Everybody by the demands of religion?
4. What insight does the narrator reach at the end of the story? What has he learned?
5. The story is told as a flashback to Hughes's boyhood. What is his attitude toward the experience as he retells it?

● The Strategies

1. The story is narrated from the point of view of a twelve-year-old boy. What techniques of language are used in the story to create the perspective of a boy? How is the vocabulary appropriate to a boy?
2. In his article "How to Say Nothing in Five Hundred Words," Paul Roberts urges the use of specific details in writing. How does Hughes make use of such details?
3. The description in paragraph 4 is vivid but compressed. How does Hughes achieve this effect?

● The Issues

1. Marx wrote that "religion . . . is the opium of the people." What is your view of this sentiment? How does it apply or not apply to this excerpt?
2. The little girls were the first to break down and offer themselves to be saved. The last two holdouts were boys. How do you explain this different reaction of the two sexes?
3. What do you think would likely have happened if the narrator had not gone up to be saved?
4. Religions often use ovine terms (sheep, lamb, flock) to refer to their congregations. What do you think is the origin of this usage? What does this usage imply about the members?

● Suggestions for Writing

1. Describe an experience of your own in which group pressure forced you into doing something you did not believe in.
2. Write a brief biographical sketch of Westley, fantasizing on the kind of man you believe he grew into and the kind of life he eventually led.
3. Defend or challenge the view that to be truly effective, religious belief must be based on emotion.

A Grunt's² Prayer

KEN NOYLE

Rhetorical Thumbnail

Format: dramatic monologue

Genre: modern poem without rhyme

Purpose: to describe the fears felt by soldiers during battle

Ken Noyle (b. 1922) is a professional magician, poet, and novelist who resides in the Monoa Valley in Hawaii. He is the author of twenty eight published works, including a recent novel, *The Magician of Kalipur* (2007), and a book of poetry, *Gone Tomorrow: Zen Inspired Poetry* (1967). Ranging from delicate sensitivity to realistic earthiness, his writing is often inspired by Zen Buddhism.

Although little is known about the specific circumstances that inspired this poem, it could well have been written yesterday because it captures the universal hopes of soldiers.

● ● ●

Oh Lord,
Another day has ended
And I thank you
For not revealing
5 To the other guys
How scared I am.
It's not so much
The fear of being killed,
As the horror
10 Of winding up
Like Pete—
Poor bastard—
Without legs.
Or like Colin who
15 Will always live
(If it is living)
In darkness and in pain.
I thank you, Lord,

---

²U.S. military slang for foot soldier, especially one at the front.

For giving me the will
20 To do as I'm told,
While every fiber
Of my being rebels
And wants to run away—
Away from all the awful sounds of war
25 And the relentless pour of sand
In the hourglass of my life.
Lord, too, I thank you
For the strength you give me
And the sometime mental block
30 That shuts out
The cries, the screams,
Of friend and foe,
And that seditious voice
That cries within me.
35 For those at home—
Lord,
Be kind with time
And fill their hours so full of it
That days will blur to weeks,
40 Weeks to months,
And then be gone
To be replaced by days more easily understood.
For my mother—
Bless her.
45 Lord, let her dream good dreams
And let the time that I'm away
Touch her only gently.
And let her greatest concern be
That I use the powder that she sends
50 To put between my toes
And that I change my shorts.
And, Lord, please—
Just give me time
To get it over with,
55 To do what I must.
And forgive me, please,
For breaking your commandments—
For, if I obey You,

60 Then I am dubbed a coward—
    Or worse, a traitor.
    And, if I obey my leaders,
    Then I must kill
    Or be killed.
    So please
65 Give me the faith to believe
    That any sin approved
    By Act of Congress
    Finds absolution
    And I,
70 A state of grace
    Before my Lord
    —Amen

Reprinted with permission from Tuttle Publishing.

Vocabulary

fiber (21)   absolution (68)
seditious (33)   grace (70)
dubbed (59)

The Facts

1. Who is the speaker in this poem? Whom is he addressing, and what are the circumstances in which the words are spoken?

2. What does this soldier fear more than he fears death? Is his fear realistic? Would you feel the same way? If not, given the same circumstances, what would your worst fear be? Explain your answer.

3. What is the "darkness" and "pain" the speaker's buddy Collin must live through the rest of his life? What can society do to show respect or gratitude for such a war-time sacrifice?

4. What are the particular items for which the speaker thanks God? Of the items listed, which do you think is the most necessary for survival? Explain your answer.

5. What does the speaker request for the people "at home"? What does he request for his mother? What do all of these requests reveal about the speaker?

The Strategies

1. The entire poem develops an important and truthful irony—one that every country declaring war must face. What is this irony? Where is it stated? Is the placement effective?

2. Noyes is known for his contrasting images of delicate sensitivity and earthy plainness. What are some examples of this contrast? Point to specific passages.

3. Compared with other poems, the lines of "A Grunt's Prayer" are short and create a rather skinny-verse effect. Do these short lines complement the purpose of the poem? Or do you think longer lines would make the poem seem intellectually and emotionally more weighty? Explain your answer.

4. How do you know that this poem is partly a monologue? To whom are the speaker's words addressed? Within the context of the poem, is this person the appropriate person to hear the speaker's words? What is the speaker's *voice* as defined in this chapter? What tone does he use throughout the poem?

5. How does the poet reconcile the speaker's fear of breaking God's commandments with his fear of disobeying the commandments of his military leaders?

The Issues

1. In what way does this soldier seem to depart from the Hallmark card view of a patriotic soldier? Does this departure seem real or fabricated? Support your answer with evidence or personal experience.

2. In lines 35–42, the speaker prays that people at home will keep so busy and preoccupied with their own lives that they will not focus on their soldiers' sufferings or struggles to survive. What do you think is the best way for parents to handle their offspring's wartime absence from home?

3. The speaker seems baffled by the paradox of obeying both God and his battle commander. If you were a conscientious objector, how would you reconcile your belief with patriotism and your obligation to defend your country from its enemies?

4. How would you answer the speaker's admittance to God that "every fiber of his being rebels and wants to run away"? What exactly would you say to him?

5. What is the "seditious" voice mentioned in line 33? How do you interpret the label "seditious?" Does it seem recognizable and applicable to a wide range of soldiers? Or do you think the poet is merely reflecting his particular political view? Explain your answer.

Suggestions for Writing

1. Write an essay about the suffering of a soldier of your acquaintance wounded in a recent military conflict. If you don't know of any such soldier, go on the Internet to see photos of soldiers in rehab after losing arms or legs while in combat. Write about what you think might be the lifelong effects of their losses. Use specific examples to strengthen your case.

2. Write an essay in which you analyze the various voices audible in "A Grunt's Prayer." Give specific examples from the poem to support your analysis.

● CHAPTER WRITING ASSIGNMENTS

1. Contrast the voice of the writer of "A Grunt's Prayer" with that of the writer of "Salvation."

2. When you write, do you find yourself deliberately altering your voice for a particular audience? In a paragraph or two, describe how you use your writing voice in different contexts.

● WRITING ASSIGNMENTS FOR A SPECIFIC AUDIENCE

1. Assuming an audience of junior high students, write a couple of paragraphs explaining the concept of voice in a writer's work.

2. Write two letters to the editor of your local newspaper complaining about a problem in your neighborhood. In the first letter, try to sound impatient and angry. In the second, let your voice be that of a reasonable but concerned citizen. State which of the two approaches you consider more effective and likely to garner results.

REAL-LIFE STUDENT WRITING

A Thank-You Note to an Aunt

The thank-you note continues to flourish even in these days of email and instant communication by telephone. Nothing can replace the personal touch found in a handwritten note. Here, for example, is a student's note thanking her aunt for a graduation present.

● ● ●

Thank You . . .

Dear Auntie Jo-Jo:

Thanks tons for the $50.00 graduation present. I didn't place it in a savings account because you said to spend it on something personal. Well, I thought you might want to know how prudently I spent the money. I went to T. J. Maxx, my favorite discount store, where I always get amazing deals. Believe it or not, for $50.00 I bought a smart-looking DKNY argyle sweater and a pair of navy corduroy pants. I'm sure my friends think I have been spending profligately at Neiman Marcus. I wish every college student had an adorable aunt like you. You have been far better than Auntie Mame.

Much love,
Trudi

P.S. I painted this card myself; hope you like it.

Stumped by the passive voice? Exit on pages 705–706, at the **Editing Booth!**

5

The Writer's Thesis

The thesis is a single sentence that announces to your reader exactly what you intend to argue, to prove, to refute, to describe, to tell, or to explain. By convention, it is usually the final sentence of the first paragraph. Of course, this is not the only place a thesis can appear; but the final sentence of the first paragraph has evolved in classroom compositions as the most effective niche for the thesis, especially in the 500-word essay, which students are usually asked to write.

The idea of the thesis is an old one that has survived for the simple reason that it works. Writers generally write better when they know exactly what they have to say, and readers usually are better able to follow a writer's thought development when they know the main point of a written work. For example, consider this thesis statement from an actual student essay:

> Our government must assume the responsibility of caring for the thousands of homeless mentally ill people who are now forced to roam the streets because of changes in governmental policy.

This thesis tells us, in a nutshell, what the student intends to argue. We expect her to show us how changes in governmental policy have caused thousands of the mentally ill to become homeless. We also expect her to argue the moral rightness of helping them.

The thesis, then, is the main point of your essay summed up in a single sentence. In it, you tell the reader where you stand on the issue, what subtopics you intend to cover, and in what order.

Finding Your Thesis

Let us say, for example, your assignment is to write an essay about a sport or recreation you enjoy. You muse and think and finally decide to write about sailing. That is your topic. It is a usable topic because it falls under a general subject. If you had decided to do an essay on the composition of mosaic tile or on the

Roman technique of road building, you would have strayed from the subject, because neither is a sport or recreation.

So sailing will be your topic. You think some more and decide to write an essay on the joys of sailing. Note, by the way, that you could have chosen to write about the boredom and work of sailing; you could also have slanted your essay any number of other ways. But you love sailing and think it a wonderful sport, so you decide to sing its praises in your essay. The joy of sailing will be your main point.

Next you must express this main point in a thesis. One way to do this is to write down the main point on the top of a page either as a sentence or a fragment—sailing is a wonderful sport; sailing is a joy; sailing is a relaxing recreation—and then ask yourself questions about it. Write down the questions as they occur to you. Perhaps you will come up with a list of questions such as these:

Main Point: Sailing is a wonderful sport.

Why do I love sailing as much as I do?

What are the benefits of sailing?

Why is sailing such a popular sport?

Why is sailing so relaxing?

What does sailing teach?

To find your thesis, choose the question that seems most appropriate to your main point, audience, and assignment, and answer it in a single, detailed sentence. This means you must make a decision about whether the instructor wants a personal essay—one heavy with "I" pronouns and emphasizing your own experiences with sailing—or an impersonal essay that presents its ideas in an objective style. For example, you might answer the last question this way:

Sailing is a delightful sport that teaches independence, balance, and navigation.

Now you have a thesis. You also have a sketch of your essay's subtopics. First, you will explain how sailing teaches independence; next, how it teaches balance; finally, how it teaches navigation. You will draw on your personal experiences and anecdotes as a sailor to amplify these points.

Answering a different question will obviously give you another thesis. For example, if your instructor makes it clear that the essay may be based on your own experiences, answering the first question would give you a thesis suitable for a personal essay:

I love the exhilaration, the freedom, and the adventure of sailing.

You now have a thesis that emphasizes your personal views of sailing.

When you do have your thesis, write it on a sticky note and stick it on your computer. It is a promise you make to your reader, and you must be faithful to it in the essay by covering the subtopics in the exact order of occurrence in your thesis. This means, for example, that in writing an essay on the joy of sailing, you must first discuss the exhilaration, and then the freedom, and finally the adventure of sailing. And you should discuss nothing else but these three points.

Key Words in the Thesis

Every thesis contains one or more key words that represent ideas on which the essay will focus. In effect, these key words are ideas that the essay must amplify with definitions, examples, and explanations. Each of the following theses, for example, contains a single key word, which is highlighted:

Pheasant hunting is a tiring sport.

I am a jealous person.

Investing in the stock market is risky.

Most of the time, however, theses will contain several key words:

Good English is clear, appropriate, and vivid.

Studies show that as children the real achievers in our society were independent and spirited.

Riding a bicycle to work has several advantages over driving a car.

Islam requires that women learn obedience, self-discipline, and subordination.

Occasionally, the thesis will contain a proposition that is inseparable from its individual words. The essay will have to amplify the whole statement:

Students should be advised against majoring in subjects in which job prospects are limited.

If the United States is to survive, Americans will have to learn to conserve their country's resources.

Characteristics of a Good Thesis

The precision with which you word your thesis will help determine the quality of your essay. At a minimum, a good thesis predicts, controls, and obligates.

The Thesis Predicts A good thesis will contain a discussible idea while also suggesting to the writer a method of developing it. (For more on methods of development, see Part Two of this book.) Some propositions, however, such as the following, are so self-evident that they warrant no further discussion:

> A relationship exists between excessive eating and gaining weight.
>
> Rich people usually live in big houses.
>
> In our country, movie stars are greatly admired.

None of these statements contains a discussible idea on which one might enlarge in a whole essay; their wording suggests no method of development. They would, therefore, not make good theses. In contrast, the following thesis not only contains discussible assertions but also predicts a likely method of development:

> Being a student reporter for the local paper means conducting interviews at odd hours and in strange places.

One immediately wonders, at what odd hours and in which strange places? The most obvious method of development for such a thesis is by illustration/exemplification (see Chapter 11). The reader expects more particulars about interviews at odd hours and in strange places, and the writer knows that he or she must find examples of these and work them into the essay. This sentence would make a good thesis.

Consider another example of how a properly worded thesis can predict the development of an essay:

> Because of the computer revolution and the premium it places on educational skills, many people over the age of twenty-one are enrolling in colleges today.

This is a "reason why" thesis, one that predicts the development of the essay primarily by an analysis of cause (see Chapter 15).

Common sense tells us that it is easier to write the essay whose method of development is predicted in the wording of its thesis than the one for which some developmental pattern must be found during the actual writing. Wording the thesis so that it predicts not only what you will say, but the pattern of development in which you will say it, can help you write a better essay.

The Thesis Controls The thesis controls the essay by restricting you to a specific order of topics or by presenting an obvious organizing principle for the essay (for more on patterns of organization, see Chapter 6 and the introduction to Chapter 8). Consider this term paper thesis, for example:

> Today, religion is no longer the uncontested center and ruler of human life, because Protestantism, science, and capitalism have brought about a secularized world.

Implicit in this thesis are a certain number and order of subtopics:

1. A description of medieval society when religion was the center of human existence
2. An explanation of how Protestantism secularized the world
3. An explanation of how science secularized the world
4. An explanation of how capitalism secularized the world

The advantage of this thesis is obvious. You do not have to cast around wondering what you should say next, for you know what your subtopics are and in what order they should occur. Moreover, the wording of the thesis tells you the kind of information you need to look up in the library.

Sometimes a thesis will control an essay by presenting the writer with a ready-made scheme of organization. Consider, for example, this thesis:

> My religious outlook has been shaped by three distinct phases of belief and disbelief in my life.

This thesis requires a chronological organization, with the writer detailing her religious beliefs from the earliest to the present. Note, however, that this thesis is suitable only for a personal essay; you could not write an objective essay on it without some drastic rewording.

Consider, on the other hand, this thesis:

> A winning tennis strategy requires a player to have a grasp of the geometry of the playing surface and to work to cut off the angle of an opponent's shots.

This thesis cries out for an essay organized by a spatial pattern. You could divide the playing surface into three zones—backcourt, midcourt, and net—and show how a player might win by maneuvering within them to cut off the angle of an opponent's shots.

The Thesis Obligates When a writer strays from the thesis, the result is often vague, unfocused writing. If the thesis is "Police officers spend more time controlling traffic and providing information than they spend enforcing the law," then you must prove this point in your essay. You should not rhapsodize about the heroism of the police or complain about police brutality. Likewise, if your thesis is "California college students are more sexually liberated than their New York counterparts," then that is the only point you should discuss. You should not write about the disputed intellectual superiority of New York college students or weave in facts about vegetarianism in California, unless these issues are somehow related to the sexual behavior of college students in New York and California.

However, it follows that in a focused essay the wording of the thesis must obligate the writer to discuss a single issue. Consider this thesis, for example:

> Definitions of obscenity change as society changes, and the courts' decisions on censorship reflect the legal profession's confusion on the issue.

This thesis is pulling in two directions. The first part of it requires a discussion of how definitions of obscenity reflect changes in society, while the second part leads to a discussion of the legal profession's confusion on obscenity. An essay based on this thesis would fall into two mismatched parts. The student should rewrite the thesis until it discusses a single issue. Here is a suggested revision of the thesis, which unifies its two parts and commits the writer to a single idea:

> Because definitions of obscenity change as society changes, the courts have handed down some contradictory decisions on censorship.

Although many students worry about making their theses too restrictive, this fault is found only rarely in the essays of beginners. Far more common is the overly broad thesis that cannot be adequately developed in a brief essay. For example, none of the following actual student theses is restrictive enough to be dealt with in a short paper:

> Parachuting is unbelievable!
>
> The war against Iraq was stupid.
>
> Evaluating college teachers is an interesting idea.

Admittedly, these examples are vaguely worded and overly terse, but they are also not restrictive enough to guide a writer's hand. Ambiguous key words like *unbelievable*, *stupid*, and *interesting* need to be replaced. To predict, control, and obligate the course of an essay, a thesis must be unambiguous, structured, and restrictive. Common sense also tells us that the scope of the thesis must be in proportion to the length of the essay. A broad thesis is not suited to a short essay, nor a narrow thesis to a long essay.

Nine Errors to Avoid in Composing a Thesis

1. **A thesis should not be a fragment.** A fragment is a phrase or dependent clause that is punctuated as if it were a complete sentence. Our objection to using a fragment as a thesis, however, is based neither on punctuation nor on grammar, but on the fact that it is usually too limited or sketchy for a writer to elaborate on in an essay. A fragment simply cannot adequately sum

up what your essay will cover, which is what the thesis should do. Here is an example:

Poor: How life is in a racial ghetto.

Better: Residents of a racial ghetto tend to have a higher death rate, a higher infant mortality rate, and a higher unemployment rate than do residents of the suburbs.

2. **A thesis must not be worded as a question** (usually, the answer to the question could be the thesis). The purpose of the thesis is to spell out the main idea of the essay, which is difficult, if not impossible, to do in a question:

Poor: Do Americans really need large refrigerators?

Better: If Americans did their marketing daily, as do most Europeans, they could save energy by using smaller refrigerators.

3. **A thesis should not be too broad.** An overly broad thesis will commit you to write on an idea you may be unable to adequately cover in a short essay. The solution in that case is to rewrite your thesis and begin again for, no matter how hard you work, your essay will otherwise seem labored and abstract:

Poor: The literature of mythology contains many resurrection stories.

Better: One of the oldest resurrection myths is the story of the Egyptian god Osiris.

4. **A thesis should not contain unrelated elements.** The expression of a single and unified purpose should be your overriding aim in drafting your thesis. You are trying to prove one point, make one case, dramatize one situation. Veteran writers can, of course, complete more than one task in an essay, but this is a skill acquired only with much practice. The beginner is better off framing the thesis to commit the essay to making one point or performing one function. One way to do this is to avoid using a compound sentence as a thesis statement.

A compound sentence is two independent clauses joined by a conjunction. An independent clause is a grammatical construction that can be punctuated to make sense on its own. Two independent clauses automatically imply two different ideas, which may be hard for the writer to keep separate or treat fairly in a single essay without making a muddle of both. Here is an example:

Poor: All novelists seek the truth, and some novelists are good psychologists.

Properly punctuated, each clause expresses a different idea and can stand on its own. "All novelists seek the truth" is one idea. "Some novelists are good psychologists" is the other. Writing an essay on this thesis will require the writer to prove two unrelated points.

Better: In their attempt to probe human nature, many novelists become excellent psychologists.

5. **A thesis should not contain phrases like "I think" or "in my opinion" because they weaken a writer's argument.** Use the thesis to tell your reader plainly where you stand, what you think, or what you intend to prove in the essay. This is no place to be wishy-washy or uncertain, as if you are not quite sure about your opinion or viewpoint. Indeed, if you are not sure about the opinion expressed in your thesis, you should rethink it until you are.

   Poor: In my opinion, smoking should be outlawed because of the adverse health effects of "passive smoking."

   Better: Smoking should be outlawed because of the adverse health effects of "passive smoking."

6. **A thesis should not be expressed in vague language.** With only rare exceptions, it is a general truth that the vague thesis will lead to a vague essay. If the thesis is vaguely worded, it is usually because the writer is uncertain of what to say or has not sufficiently thought through the controlling idea. Should that happen to you, rethink your views on the topic.

   Poor: Religion should not be included in the school curriculum because it can cause trouble.

   Better: Religion should not be included in the school curriculum because it is a highly personal commitment.

7. **A thesis must not be expressed in muddled or incoherent language.** If the thesis is incoherent or muddled, the essay is likely to follow suit. Work on your thesis until it expresses exactly the opinion or viewpoint you intend to cover in the essay.

   Poor: The benefits of clarity and easy communication of a unified language compel a state to adopt codes to the effect that make bilingualism possible but preserving a single official language for transacting business and social intercourse.

   Better: The benefits of clarity and easy communication offered by a single official language in a state are compelling and persuasive.

8. **A thesis should not be expressed in figurative language.** Figurative language has a place in factual writing, but not in a thesis statement. As we have stressed, the thesis is where you plainly state the main point of your essay. Figurative language tends to weaken this healthy plainness and should, therefore, never be used in a thesis.

   Poor: The Amazons of today are trying to purge all the stag words from our language.

   Better: Today's feminists are trying to eliminate the use of sex-biased words from public documents and publications.

9. **A thesis must not be nonsensical.** Above all else, your thesis statement must make sense. You cannot defend the indefensible or argue the unarguable, nor should you waste ink on behalf of a thesis that is absurd. For example, consider this sentence:

Poor: A good university education is one that is useful, fulfilling, and doesn't require study.

As a thesis, it is virtually useless, even though it does predict, control, and obligate. The problem is that its proposition is plainly nonsense. We cannot conceive of a good university education that doesn't require study. Only a frivolous essay could be written on such a thesis.

Better: A good university education is one that is useful, fulfilling, and challenging.

We are not suggesting that your theses should always advance narrowly orthodox or boringly conventional ideas, but the ideas they contain should be sensible enough to merit discussion by reasonable people.

The Explicit versus the Implicit Thesis

Anyone who has ever listened to a speaker ramble or read a piece of aimless writing can readily appreciate the usefulness of a thesis statement that sets down clearly the writer's main point. However, not all writers find it necessary to be explicit about their main points. Veteran writers know how to make a main point and stick faithfully to it without broadcasting it in a thesis statement. A conspicuous example of this is the essay "Once More to the Lake," reprinted in Chapter 17. In that essay, the writer sticks to the point without ever expressing it in a single thesis sentence.

As a matter of fact, many veteran writers do not need or use a thesis. Yet they always write with a built-in sense of structure; they do not stray from the point or lose their train of thought. The explicit thesis admittedly has become a requirement of classroom writing, but while it is a useful device for the inexperienced, it can be too simplistic for the professional writer—too much of a formula. Later, as you become a more experienced writer, you, too, might abandon the use of the explicit thesis. But for now, it is a convention that will help you write better essays.

● Exercises

1. Formulate a thesis for one of the following topics. Use the step-by-step method outlined in the chapter.
   a. Adolescence
   b. Women and the military
   c. Obligations of parents
   d. The entertainment world
   e. Spectator sports

2. Find a picture that expresses some aspect of today's society, such as students protesting, someone reading a Kindle, a scene from "Dancing with the Stars," or people attending a church service; then write a thesis that could serve as an appropriate caption.

3. Underline the key words of the following theses:
   a. Memory entails recall, recognition, and revival.
   b. An argument must present both sides of the question being debated.

    c. The Amish people resist public education because they believe that a simple farm life is best and that formal education will corrupt their young people.

    d. A good farmer cooperates with weather, soil, and seed.

    e. Laura in "Flowering Judas" by Katherine Anne Porter is tortured by doubt, guilt, and disappointment.

    f. The racetracks, the ballparks, the fight rings, and the gridirons draw crowds in increasing numbers.

4. Which of the following theses is the best? Support your choice.

    a. Forest fires are enormously destructive because they ravage the land, create problems for flood control, and destroy useful lumber.

    b. Installment buying is of great benefit to the economy, having in mind the consumer to use a product while paying for it and being like forced savings.

    c. Television is a handicap.

5. The following theses are poorly worded. Analyze their weaknesses in terms of the nine errors discussed earlier, and rewrite each to make it clear and effective.

    a. In my opinion, birth control is the most urgent need in today's world.

    b. Just how far should the law go in its tolerance of pornography?

    c. How Christian missionaries were sent to the Ivory Coast of Africa to introduce Western civilization.

    d. The history of psychology had its inception with Plato and came to full term with Freud.

    e. Strip mining is an environmentally destructive solution to the problem of fuel shortage, and the fuel shortage is caused by our government's foreign policy.

    f. In the United States, the press is the watchdog of society.

    g. Three factors may be singled out as militating against the optimum adjustment that partners in the marriage relationship should experience as money, culture, and education.

    h. Homemaking is the most meaningful work a woman can perform.

    i. The problem with sound pollution is: How much longer can our ears bear the noise?

    j. The noteworthy relaxation of language taboos both in conversation and in print today.

    k. My feeling is that educationalists are just as infatuated with jargon as are sociologists.

    l. Retirement homes need not be depressing places which commercial activities can bring residents together in shared experiences.

    m. The city of New York is in bad shape.

6. From the following pairs of theses, pick out the thesis with the discussible issue. Explain your choice.

    a. (1) The Eiffel Tower is located near the center of Paris.

        (2) Three spectacular crimes have been committed near the Eiffel Tower in Paris.

b. (1) Michelangelo's *David* symbolizes the best qualities of youthful manhood.

(2) Michelangelo's *David* is carved out of white marble from Carrara.

c. (1) The Model-A Ford became popular because it was dependable and uncomplicated.

(2) Close to a million people still own Model-A Fords today.

d. (1) In Hemingway's *A Farewell to Arms*, the knee injury suffered by Frederick Henry symbolizes man's wounded spirit.

(2) In Hemingway's novel *A Farewell to Arms*, Frederick Henry is shot in the knee while driving an ambulance truck.

e. (1) The Greek historian Herodotus claimed that the city of Troy was destroyed in 1250 B.C.

(2) Troy was an important city because any fortress built on its site could control all shipping traffic through the Dardanelles.

f. (1) Good grammar is the equivalent of good manners.

(2) According to the rules of grammar, "he don't" is a barbarism.

ADVICE

The Thesis

SHERIDAN BAKER

Rhetorical Thumbnail

Purpose: to teach about the thesis

Audience: freshman composition students

Language: uses a blend of formal and informal language

Strategy: addresses the reader as *you* with a style that is both simple and refreshingly direct

Sheridan Baker (1918–2000) was Emeritus Professor of English at the University of Michigan and has been a Fulbright lecturer. He has edited several works by the eighteenth-century novelist Henry Fielding, including Joseph Andrews, Shamela, and Tom Jones. Baker's two rhetorics, *The Practical Stylist* (1962) and *The Complete Stylist* (1976) have been widely used in colleges throughout the United States.

In this excerpt from The Complete Stylist, Baker advises the student to state clearly, in a sharp-edged thesis, the controlling purpose of the essay.

• • •

1   You can usually blame a bad essay on a bad beginning. If your essay falls apart, it probably has no primary idea to hold it together. "What's the big idea?" we used to ask. The phrase will serve as a reminder that you must find the "big idea" behind your several smaller thoughts and musings before you start to write. In the beginning were the logos, says the Bible—the idea, the plan, caught in a flash as if in a single word. Find your logos, and you are ready to round out your essay and set it spinning.

2   The big idea behind our ride in the speeding car[1] was that in adolescence, especially, the group can have a very deadly influence on the individual.

3   If you had not focused your big idea in a thesis, you might have begun by picking up thoughts at random, something like this:

> Everyone thinks he is a good driver. There are more accidents caused by young drivers than any other group. Driver education is a good beginning, but further practice is very necessary. People who object to driver education do not realize that modern society, with its suburban pattern of growth, is built around the automobile. The car becomes a way of life and a status symbol. When a teenager goes too fast he is probably only copying his own father.

4   A little reconsideration, aimed at a good thesis sentence, could turn this into a reasonably good beginning:

> Modern society is built on the automobile. Every child looks forward to the time when he can drive; every teenager, to the day when his father lets him take out the car alone. Soon he is testing his skill at higher and higher speeds, especially with a group of friends along. One final test at extreme speeds usually suffices. The teenager's high-speed ride, if it does not kill him, will probably open his eyes to the deadly dynamics of the group.

5   Thus the central idea, or thesis, is your essay's life and spirit. If your thesis is sufficiently firm and clear, it may tell you immediately how to organize your supporting material and so obviate elaborate planning. If you do not find a thesis, your essay will be a tour through the miscellaneous. An essay replete with scaffolds and catwalks—"We have just seen this; now let us turn to this"—is an essay in which the inherent idea is weak or nonexistent. A purely expository and descriptive essay, one simply about "Cats," for instance, will have to

---

[1]The example to which the paragraph refers occurred earlier in material that was not printed here.

rely on outer scaffolding alone (some orderly progression from Persia to Siam) since it really has no idea at all. It is all subject, all cats, instead of being based on an idea about cats.

The Argumentative Edge

Find Your Thesis

6   The aboutness puts an argumentative edge on the subject. When you have something to say about cats, you have found your underlying idea. You have something to defend, something to fight about: not just "Cats," but "The cat is really man's best friend." Now the hackles on all dog men are rising, and you have an argument on your hands. You have something to prove. You have a thesis.

7   "What's the big idea, Mac?" Let the impudence in that time-honored demand remind you that the best thesis is a kind of affront to somebody. No one will be very much interested in listening to you deplete the thesis "The dog is man's best friend." Everyone knows that already. Even the dog lovers will be uninterested, convinced that they know better than you. But the cat . . .

8   So it is with any unpopular idea. The more unpopular the viewpoint and the stronger the push against convention, the stronger the thesis and the more energetic the essay. Compare the energy in "Democracy is good" with that in "Communism is good," for instance. The first is filled with platitudes, the second with plutonium. By the same token, if you can find the real energy in "Democracy is good," if you can get down through the sand to where the roots and water are, you will have a real essay, because the opposition against which you generate your energy is the heaviest in the world: boredom. Probably the most energetic thesis of all, the greatest inner organizer, is some tired old truth that you cause to jet with new life, making the old ground green again.

9   To find a thesis and put it into one sentence is to narrow and define your subject to a workable size. Under "Cats" you must deal with all felinity from the jungle up, carefully partitioning the eons and areas, the tigers and tabbies, the sizes and shapes. The minute you proclaim the cat the friend of man, you have pared away whole categories and chapters, and need only think up the arguments sufficient to overwhelm the opposition. So, put an argumentative edge on your subject—and you will have found your thesis.

10   Simple exposition, to be sure, has its uses. You may want to tell someone how to build a doghouse, how to can asparagus, how to follow the outlines of relativity, or even how to write an essay. Performing a few exercises in simple exposition will no doubt sharpen your insight into the problems of finding orderly sequences, of considering how best to lead your readers through the hoops, of writing clearly and accurately. It will also illustrate how much finer and surer an argument is.

11   You will see that picking an argument immediately simplifies the problems so troublesome in straight exposition: the defining, the partitioning,

the narrowing of the subject. Actually, you can put an argumentative edge on the flattest of expository subjects. "How to build a doghouse" might become "Building a doghouse is a thorough introduction to the building trades, including architecture and mechanical engineering." "Canning asparagus" might become "An asparagus patch is a course in economics." "Relativity" might become "Relativity is not so inscrutable as many suppose." You have simply assumed that you have a loyal opposition consisting of the uninformed, the scornful, or both. You have given your subject its edge; you have limited and organized it at a single stroke. Pick an argument, then, and you will automatically be defining and narrowing your subject, and all the partitions you don't need will fold up. Instead of dealing with things, subjects, and pieces of subjects, you will be dealing with an idea and its consequences.

Sharpen Your Thesis

12   Come out with your subject pointed. Take a stand, make a judgment of value. Be reasonable, but don't be timid. It is helpful to think of your thesis, your main idea, as a debating question—"Resolved: Old age pensions must go"—taking out the "Resolved" when you actually write the subject down. But your resolution will be even stronger, your essay clearer and tighter, if you can sharpen your thesis even further: "Resolved: Old age pensions must go because—." Fill in that blank and your worries are practically over. The main idea is to put your whole argument into one sentence.

13   Try, for instance: "Old age pensions must go because they are making people irresponsible." I don't know at all if that is true, and neither will you until you write your way into it, considering probabilities and alternatives and objections, and especially the underlying assumptions. In fact, no one, no master sociologist or future historian, can tell absolutely if it is true, so multiplex are the causes in human affairs, so endless and tangled the consequences. The basic assumption—that irresponsibility is growing—may be entirely false. No one, I repeat, can tell absolutely. But by the same token, your guess may be as good as another's. At any rate, you are now ready to write. You have found your logos.

14   Now you can put your well-pointed thesis sentence on a card on the wall in front of you to keep from drifting off target. But you will now want to dress it for the public, to burnish it, and make it comely. Suppose you try:

> Old age pensions, perhaps more than anything else, are eroding our heritage of personal and familial responsibility.

15   But is this true? Perhaps you had better try something like:

> Despite their many advantages, old age pensions may actually be eroding our heritage of personal and familial responsibility.

16   This is really your thesis, and you can write that down on a scrap of paper too.

Sheridan Baker, THE COMPLETE STYLIST AND HANDBOOK, 3rd ed., © 1984, pp. 22–25. Adapted by permission of Pearson Education, Inc., Upper Saddle River, New Jersey.

● Vocabulary

obviate (5)	inherent (5)	platitudes (8)
replete (5)	affront (7)	multiplex (13)

EXAMPLES

The Grieving Never Ends

ROXANNE ROBERTS

Rhetorical Thumbnail

Purpose: to dramatize the horror of suicide

Audience: newspaper readers

Language: standard English modified by newspeak

Strategy: draws on the example from her father's suicide showing the emotional fallout that eventually affects everyone in the family

---

Roxanne Roberts is an American journalist who occasionally writes for the *Los Angeles Times.*

This essay alerts us to the painful truth about suicide: Often, it can cause lifelong scars that linger to torment those left behind. As the author tells us, twenty years after her father's suicide, she still finds herself cleaning up the emotional debris from that tragic act.

● ● ●

1   The blood was like Jell-O. That is what blood gets like, after you die, before they tidy up. Somehow, I had expected it would be gone. The police and coroner spent more than an hour behind the closed door; surely it was someone's job to clean it up. But when they left, it still covered the kitchen floor like the glazing on a candy apple.

2   You couldn't mop it. You needed a dustpan and a bucket.

3   I got on my knees, slid the pan against the linoleum and lifted chunks to the bucket. It took hours to clean it all up.

4   It wasn't until I finally stood up that I noticed the pictures from his wallet. The wooden breadboard had been pulled out slightly, and four photographs were spilled across it. "Now what?" I thought with annoyance. "What were the police looking for?"

5   But then it hit me. The police hadn't done it. These snapshots—one of my mother, one of our dog and two of my brother and me—had been carefully set out in a row by my father.

6   It was his penultimate act, just before he knelt on the floor, put the barrel of a .22 rifle in his mouth, and squeezed the trigger.

7   He was 46 years old. I was 21. It has been 20 years since his death and I am still cleaning up.

8   By the time you finish this article, another person in the United States will have killed himself. More than 30,000 people do it every year, one every 15 minutes. My father's was a textbook case: Depressed white male with gun offs himself in May. December may be the loneliest month, April the cruelest, but May is the peak time for suicide. No one knows why, but I can guess: You've made it through another winter, but your world is no warmer.

9   This year, thousands of families will begin the process that ours began that night 20 years ago. Studies show that their grief will be more complicated, more intense and longer lasting than for any other form of death in the family. They will receive less support and more blame from others. Some will never really get over it: Children of suicides become a higher risk for suicide themselves.

10   These are the legacies of suicide: guilt, anger, doubt, blame, fear, rejection, abandonment and profound grieving.

11   Shortly after he died, I remember thinking, "I wonder how I'll feel about this in 20 years?"

12   Twenty years later, my father's suicide is, simply, a part of me. Think of your life as a can of white paint. Each significant experience adds a tiny drop of color: pink for a birthday, yellow for a good report card. Worries are brown; setbacks, gray. Lavender—my favorite color when I was a little girl—is for a pretty new dress. Over time, a color begins to emerge. Your personality.

13   When a suicide happens, someone hurls in a huge glob of red. You can't get it out. You can't start over. The red will always be there, no matter how many drops of yellow you add.

14   The call came about 9 P.M. It was a Friday night in suburban Minneapolis; the restaurant was packed. I was racing from the bar with a tray of drinks for my customers when the manager gestured me to the phone. "It's your mother," she said.

15   "Roxanne, he's got a gun. He's in the garage with a gun. You have to come."

16   There had been many, many threats. This was different. There had never been a weapon before.

17   I made many choices that night; some were smart, some stupid, some crazy. I believed my father would indeed kill himself, sooner or later. Looking back, I feel lucky to have survived the night.

18   I drove past the house. He was standing in the shadows of the front yard; I couldn't see if he had the gun. I sped to a phone booth two blocks away and dialed.

19   She answered. "He's in the front yard," I said. "Can you get out?"

20   Five minutes later, she walked up to the car. "He was quiet now," she said. She told him she was going to talk to me but would be back. Then she dropped the bombshell: He had held her at gunpoint for two hours before she called me.

21   We attempted rational conversation. We came to what seemed, at the time, a rational decision. We pulled up to the house, and my father came out the front door without the gun. He wanted to talk.

22   "Give me the gun," I said. He refused. "We can't talk until the gun is gone," we said. He shook his head. "Come inside," he asked my mother. She shook her head.

23   He went back in, we drove to a coffee shop nearby. Frantic, we debated what to do next. To this day, I am still astonished that it never occurred to us to get help.

24   It was almost midnight; exhausted, my mother wanted to go home. She would stay the night if he let her take the gun away.

25   The house was silent; the door to the kitchen was shut. Ominous. My mother reached it first. Opened it.

26   "He did it," she whispered and slumped against the wall.

27   There was a time when suicide was considered a noble act of noble men. There was a time when corpses of suicides were dragged through the streets, refused Christian burial, and all the family's worldly goods were seized by the state. There was a time when romantics embraced suicide as a sign of their sensitivity.

28   Now we have long, impassioned debates about "assisted suicide," which pales beside the much larger issue: How do we feel about suicides when there isn't a terminal disease and a supportive family on hand? How do we feel about suicide if a 46-year-old guy just doesn't want to live anymore?

29   How do we feel about someone who's depressed but won't get help? Who blames all his problems on someone else? Who emotionally terrorizes and blackmails the people he loves? Is that OK too?

30   This is what I will tell you: Suicide is the last word in an argument, maybe an argument you never knew you were having. It is meant to be the last scene of the last act of life. Curtain down. End of story.

31   Except it isn't.

32   Tosca jumps off the parapet and I wonder who finds the shattered body. Romeo and Juliet die with a kiss, and I grieve for their parents.

33   The calls began: first to my father's only brother, who lived three blocks away, then to the police. Officers arrived, then detectives and someone from the coroner's office. Someone came into the living room to ask questions. I answered. Yes, he was depressed. Yes, he had threatened suicide. No, there wasn't a note.

34   This was the night of my brother Mike's high school senior prom. The dance was on a boat—we didn't know where—then there was an all-night party and a picnic the next day.

35   The detectives were still in the kitchen when Mike's car turned slowly onto the street and found a sea of police cars, lights flashing.

36   I watched from the front step as my mother ran to him. "Your father shot himself and he's dead," she said, guiding him to the neighbor's house. I watched as the police took the body out, dripping thick drops of blood. I watched my uncle stare blankly when I asked him to help clean up the kitchen.

37   White-lipped, he watched as I scooped up buckets of blood and flushed them down the toilet. I threw him an old sheet and told him to start wiping.

38   Years later, I learned how angry I made him, how he never forgave me for making him do that.

39   I was alone in the kitchen again when I noticed the pictures from my father's wallet. There were two portraits of his children. He loved both pictures. Everybody knew Mike Roberts loved his kids. So why ruin his son's prom night?

40   "You selfish bastard," I thought. "You couldn't have waited one more night?"

41   My mother was never well liked by my father's sisters, and so they concluded that what had happened was my mother's fault. She was having an affair. That's what my father had told them before he died. The fact that she wore an aqua suit to the funeral was proof, wasn't it? (My mother swears there was no affair.)

42   And I? I was on her side. So it was my fault too.

43   After the funeral, we were simply abandoned by my father's family. My mother was still numb, but I was confused and angry. No calls, no help, no kindness. There were no invitations to dinner, not even Thanksgiving or Christmas.

44   Two years later, I found out why: They thought my mother and I killed him.

45   At one of those little get-togethers just after he died, my father's family decided that perhaps my mother and I had cleverly managed to murder my father and make it look like a suicide.

46   A cousin was so skeptical he went to the coroner and asked to see police photos. It was a suicide, the coroner assured him.

47   I vowed never, ever to speak to any of them again. When a distant member of the family—a devoted wife and mother—found her husband dead, sucking the end of an exhaust pipe, I was almost glad.

48   "Good," I thought fiercely. "Now they'll understand that suicide happens in nice families too."

49   Second-guessing is the devil's game, for there are no answers and infinite questions. But it is an inevitable, inescapable refrain, like a bad song you can't get out of your mind. What if, what if, what if? What if we had forced him to get help? Had him committed? What if we had called the police that night? Why didn't we?

50   Part of it was the natural tendency toward privacy. Part of it was arrogance, believing that we knew father best, or at least we could handle whatever he threw at us. I think I knew my father would have charmed the police, sent them away, leaving him furious with me, furious with my mother, dangerous, armed.

51   Maybe that's why. Maybe it was fear. Maybe not. Maybe I wanted him to die.

52   The police were puzzled by a wand of black mascara they found in my father's pocket. Another woman? Proof of an affair? The answer was simple: He used it to touch up the gray on his temples.

53   I don't think he ever really expected to get old. He was the baby, the youngest of five children. He was a very happy child; it was adulthood that he could never quite grasp.

54   He was charming enough to talk his way into job after job. There was the real estate phase, the radio phase, the political hanger-on phase. (In one photo, he is shaking hands with Hubert Humphrey.) No job lasted long; it never occurred to him to do heavy lifting.

55   Things started out well enough: a beautiful teenage bride, two kids and—after his mother died—his childhood home, a little bungalow, to raise his family in.

56   When did things start falling apart? Or were they ever really together?

57   I remember a night when I was 11. One of our cats streaked across the living room. In his mouth was a hamster that had somehow escaped from its cage. We all jumped to the rescue; my father caught the cat at the top of the basement stairs. He was suddenly, unaccountably livid. He shook the cat, and the hamster fell to the floor and scampered free.

58   I will never forget what came next: With all his might, he threw the cat down the stairs.

59   There was a moment of stunned silence, then tears and regret and an emergency trip to the vet. The cat lived. But I think I never fully trusted my father again.

60   The 10 years that followed were filled with sudden rages, explosions. I found out later that he first hit my mother when she was pregnant with me, and continued on and off for two decades.

61   We begged him to get help. We asked his brother and sisters to talk to him. And when, ultimately, I told my mother I thought she needed to leave for her own safety, my father saw that as a betrayal. He didn't speak to me for two months, until the night he died.

62   I lied to the police.

63   I told them there was no suicide note. In fact, there were three. Two were waiting in the living room as we walked into the house.

64   The note to my mother begged for forgiveness but said he simply could not go on the way things were. She has, to this day, no memory of reading it.

65   The note addressed to me opened with a rapprochement. "All is forgiven," read the first line. My eyes filled. "No," I said silently, all is not forgiven.

66   The rest of the note instructed me to take care of things.

67   When I went to call the police, I found the third note, addressed to my brother. I cannot recall the specific words, but the short message to an 18-year-old boy was this: Son, you can't trust women.

68   My father had asked me to take care of things. And I was going to take care of things.

69   I stuffed all three notes in my purse and went back out to the living room. A week later, I ripped them to pieces and flushed them down the toilet.

70   When I recently told my brother about this, he was angry and hurt. He asked, quietly, "What made you think you could take something Dad left for me?" Fair question.

71   Here is the answer, Mike. It is simple. I hope you can live with it: I had to. The wishes of the dead do not take precedence over the needs of the living.

72   About a year after my father died, I left Minneapolis. I stumbled through my twenties, met a terrific man and got married, and spent a lot of time thinking about what I wanted to be when I grew up.

73   Nine months after the funeral, my brother moved to California. He was reckless, strong, adrift and almost died three times—once in a motorcycle accident, once in a stabbing and once in a heedless dive into a pool that split open his skull. He returned to Minnesota, subdued and gentle, and went on to a successful computer career. He was, surprisingly, never angry at my father or his family.

74   But he cannot bring himself to marry his girlfriend of 16 years. They live together, in a home they bought together, but he simply does not trust marriage.

75   Two years after the suicide, my mother remarried, changing her friends, her religion, even her first name. She was widowed again—a heart attack—and announced a year later that she was getting married again. Her fiancé was my cousin—her nephew by marriage. He was the son of the aunt who had accused us of murder.

76   "I expect you to be civil to her," my mother told me.

77   We had an ugly fight, and my mother didn't speak to me for months. I went to her wedding but fled to the other side of the room when my aunt approached me.

78   My mother tells me my aunt is very hurt by all this. The cycle continues, in ways I will never fully understand.

79   Four years ago, when my son was a month old, I took him to Minnesota to meet my family.

80   "Take me to Father's grave," I told my brother.

81   It's the first time I'd been there since the funeral. I introduced my beautiful new baby to his grandfather, and my father to his only grandchild.

82   Today, when I stare at the boy who takes my breath away, I think about how much my father missed over the past 20 years, and how much more he will miss. I've more sorrow than anger now.

83   A lot of wonderful things have happened in those years, hundreds of shimmering droplets added to the mix. When I stir the paint now, it is a soft dusky rose. A grownup's color, with a touch of sweetness and a touch of melancholy.

● Vocabulary

coroner (1)	legacies (10)	wand (52)
penultimate (6)	ominous (25)	rapprochement (65)

● The Facts

1. What did the author discover in her father's wallet?

2. According to the author, how many people commit suicide annually in the United States?

3. When the author drove past the house after her mother called, what did she see?

4. Where was the author's brother, Mike, when the father committed suicide?

5. Whom did the father's relatives blame for the suicide?

● The Strategies

1. What is the thesis of the essay? Write it in one sentence in your own words.

2. Every once in a while the author interrupts the story of the father's suicide with commentary about suicide in general. Why do you think she does this? Does the technique appeal to you? Why or why not?

3. How important is the reference to "assisted suicide" in paragraph 28? What, if anything, does it add to the development of the author's thesis?

4. What figurative language does the author use in her essay? Point out at least one simile and one metaphor. Do you consider these images effective? Give reasons for your answer.

5. How effective is the author's strategy of relating her father's suicide from her own "I" point of view? What does it add to the essay?

● The Issues

1. What is the purpose of this essay on the gloomy subject of suicide? Do you agree or disagree with its purpose?

2. What does the author mean when she says, "He was 46 years old. I was 21. It has been 20 years since his death and I am still cleaning up"?

3. The author refers to the fact that in the past, suicide was considered a noble act, a sinful act, or a romantic act (see paragraph 27). How do you view suicide today? Should everyone embrace your view? Give reasons for your answer.

4. In your opinion, what consequences of the father's suicide seem the worst?

5. What do you think was the basic cause of the father's suicide?

● Suggestions for Writing

1. Choose one of the following topics and develop a thesis-oriented essay:

   a. Suicide as an act of desperation

   b. Suicide as an act of selfishness

2. Write an essay in which you answer the question, "Can suicide be averted?" Analyze differing sources and synthesize them into a coherent thesis.

A Good Man Is Hard to Find

FLANNERY O'CONNOR

Rhetorical Thumbnail

Purpose: to present the author's Catholic worldview

Audience: educated readers

Language: Southern Creole and its many idioms

Strategy: focuses on characterizing the two children as representatives of the Gothic Southern character; story leads logically with the underpinning of Catholic theology to a gruesome conclusion

Flannery O'Connor (1925–1964) was a Christian humanist writer and a member of the so-called "Southern Renaissance" in American literature. She was born in Savannah, Georgia, and educated at the Woman's College of Georgia and the State University of Iowa. Her best-known stories, written from an orthodox Catholic perspective, are contained in *A Good Man Is Hard to Find and Other Stories* (1953) and *Everything That Rises Must Converge* (1956).

We do not usually think of a story as having a thesis, but we almost always think of a story as having a point. The point of this story—its thesis—is hinted at in its title, from which it proceeds with grim, irresistible logic. Readers should remember that the racist language used in this selection is partly what labeled O'Connor's stories "Southern Grotesque." Moreover, O'Connor wrote at a time when blacks in the South were often treated in a derogatory manner.

• • •

1   The grandmother didn't want to go to Florida. She wanted to visit some of her connections in east Tennessee and she was seizing at every chance to change Bailey's mind. Bailey was the son she lived with, her only boy. He was sitting on the edge of his chair at the table, bent over the orange sports section of the Journal. "Now look here, Bailey," she said, "see here, read this," and she stood with one hand on her thin hip and the other rattling the newspaper at his bald head. "Here this fellow that calls himself The Misfit is loose from the Federal Pen and headed toward Florida and you read here what it says he did to these people. Just you read it. I wouldn't take my children in any direction with a criminal like that aloose in it. I couldn't answer to my conscience if I did."

2   Bailey didn't look up from his reading so she wheeled around then and faced the children's mother, a young woman in slacks, whose face was as

broad and innocent as a cabbage and was tied around with a green headker-
chief that had two points on the top like a rabbit's ears. She was sitting on
the sofa, feeding the baby his apricots out of a jar. "The children have been to
Florida before," the old lady said. "You all ought to take them somewhere else
for a change so they would see different parts of the world and be broad. They
never have been to east Tennessee."

3   The children's mother didn't seem to hear her but the eight-year-old
boy, John Wesley, a stocky child with glasses, said, "If you don't want to go
to Florida, why dontcha stay at home?" He and the little girl, June Star, were
reading the funny papers on the floor.

4   "She wouldn't stay at home to be queen for a day," June Star said without
raising her yellow head.

5   "Yes and what would you do if this fellow, The Misfit, caught you?" the
grandmother asked.

6   "I'd smack his face," John Wesley said.

7   "She wouldn't stay at home for a million bucks," June Star said. "Afraid
she'd miss something. She has to go everywhere we go."

8   "All right, Miss," the grandmother said. "Just remember that the next time
you want me to curl your hair."

9   June Star said her hair was naturally curly.

10   The next morning the grandmother was the first one in the car, ready to
go. She had her big black valise that looked like the head of a hippopotamus
in one corner, and underneath it she was hiding a basket with Pitty Sing, the
cat, in it. She didn't intend for the cat to be left alone in the house for three
days because he would miss her too much and she was afraid he might brush
against one of the gas burners and accidentally asphyxiate himself. Her son,
Bailey, didn't like to arrive at a motel with a cat.

11   She sat in the middle of the back seat with John Wesley and June Star on
either side of her. Bailey and the children's mother and the baby sat in front
and they left Atlanta at eight forty-five with the mileage on the car at 55890.
The grandmother wrote this down because she thought it would be interesting
to say how many miles they had been when they got back. It took them twenty
minutes to reach the outskirts of the city.

12   The old lady settled herself comfortably, removing her white cotton gloves
and putting them up with her purse on the shelf in front of the back window.
The children's mother still had on slacks and still had her head tied up in a
green kerchief, but the grandmother had on a navy blue straw sailor hat with a
bunch of white violets on the brim and a navy blue dress with a small white dot
in the print. Her collars and cuffs were white organdy trimmed with lace and at
her neckline she had pinned a purple spray of cloth violets containing a sachet.
In case of an accident, anyone seeing her dead on the highway would know at
once that she was a lady.

13   She said she thought it was going to be a good day for driving, neither too
hot nor too cold, and she cautioned Bailey that the speed limit was fifty-five
miles an hour and that the patrolmen hid themselves behind billboards and

small clumps of trees and sped out after you before you had a chance to slow down. She pointed out interesting details of the scenery: Stone Mountain; the blue granite that in some places came up to both sides of the highway; the brilliant red clay banks slightly streaked with purple; and the various crops that made rows of green lace-work on the ground. The trees were full of silver-white sunlight and the meanest of them sparkled. The children were reading comic magazines and their mother had gone back to sleep.

14   "Let's go through Georgia fast so we won't have to look at it much," John Wesley said.

15   "If I were a little boy," said the grandmother, "I wouldn't talk about my native state that way. Tennessee has the mountains and Georgia has the hills."

16   "Tennessee is just a hillbilly dumping ground," John Wesley said, "and Georgia is a lousy state too."

17   "You said it," June Star said.

18   "In my time," said the grandmother, folding her thin veined fingers, "children were more respectful of their native states and their parents and everything else. People did right then. Oh look at the cute little pickaninny!" she said and pointed to a Negro child standing in the door of a shack. "Wouldn't that make a picture, now?" she asked and they all turned and looked at the little Negro out of the back window. He waved.

19   "He didn't have any britches on," June Star said.

20   "He probably didn't have any," the grandmother explained. "Little niggers in the country don't have things like we do. If I could paint, I'd paint that picture," she said.

21   The children exchanged comic books.

22   The grandmother offered to hold the baby and the children's mother passed him over the front seat to her. She sat him on her knee and bounced him and told him about the things they were passing. She rolled her eyes and screwed up her mouth and stuck her leathery thin face into his smooth bland one. Occasionally he gave her a faraway smile. They passed a large cotton field with five or six graves fenced in the middle of it, like a small island. "Look at the graveyard!" the grandmother said, pointing it out. "That was the old family burying ground. That belonged to the plantation."

23   "Where's the plantation?" John Wesley asked.

24   "Gone With the Wind," said the grandmother. "Ha. Ha."

25   When the children finished all the comic books they had brought, they opened the lunch and ate it. The grandmother ate a peanut butter sandwich and an olive and would not let the children throw the box and the paper napkins out the window. When there was nothing else to do they played a game by choosing a cloud and making the other two guess what shape it suggested. John Wesley took one the shape of a cow and June Star guessed a cow and John Wesley said, "no, an automobile," and June Star said he didn't play fair, and they began to slap each other over the grandmother.

26   The grandmother said she would tell them a story if they would keep quiet. When she told a story, she rolled her eyes and waved her head and was very dramatic. She said once when she was a maiden lady she had been courted by

a Mr. Edgar Atkins Teagarden from Jasper, Georgia. She said he was a very good-looking man and a gentleman and that he brought her a watermelon every Saturday afternoon with his initials cut in it, E. A. T. Well, one Saturday, she said, Mr. Teagarden brought the watermelon and there was nobody at home and he left it on the front porch and returned in his buggy to Jasper, but she never got the watermelon, she said, because a nigger boy ate it when he saw the initials, E. A. T.! This story tickled John Wesley's funny bone and he giggled and giggled but June Star didn't think it was any good. She said she wouldn't marry a man that just brought her a watermelon on Saturday. The grandmother said she would have done well to marry Mr. Teagarden because he was a gentleman and had bought Coca-Cola stock when it first came out and that he had died only a few years ago, a very wealthy man.

27   They stopped at The Tower for barbecued sandwiches. The Tower was a part stucco and part wood filling station and dance hall set in a clearing outside of Timothy. A fat man named Red Sammy Butts ran it and there were signs stuck here and there on the building and for miles up and down the highway saying, TRY RED SAMMY'S FAMOUS BARBECUE. NONE LIKE FAMOUS RED SAMMY'S! RED SAM! THE FAT BOY WITH THE HAPPY LAUGH! A VETERAN! RED SAMMY'S YOUR MAN!

28   Red Sammy was lying on the bare ground outside The Tower with his head under a truck while a gray monkey about a foot high, chained to a small chinaberry tree, chattered nearby. The monkey sprang back into the tree and got on the highest limb as soon as he saw the children jump out of the car and run toward him.

29   Inside, The Tower was a long dark room with a counter at one end and tables at the other and dancing space in the middle. They all sat down at a board table next to the nickelodeon and Red Sam's wife, a tall burnt-brown woman with hair and eyes lighter than her skin, came and took their order. The children's mother put a dime in the machine and played "The Tennessee Waltz," and the grandmother said that tune always made her want to dance. She asked Bailey if he would like to dance but he only glared at her. He didn't have a naturally sunny disposition like she did and trips made him nervous. The grandmother's brown eyes were very bright. She swayed her head from side to side and pretended she was dancing in her chair. June Star said play something she could tap to so the children's mother put in another dime and played a fast number and June Star stepped out onto the dance floor and did her tap routine.

30   "Ain't she cute?" Red Sam's wife said, leaning over the counter. "Would you like to come be my little girl?"

31   "No I certainly wouldn't," June Star said. "I wouldn't live in a broken-down place like this for a million bucks!" and she ran back to the table.

32   "Ain't she cute?" the woman repeated, stretching her mouth politely.

33   "Aren't you ashamed?" hissed the grandmother.

34   Red Sam came in and told his wife to quit lounging on the counter and hurry up with these people's order. His khaki trousers reached just to his hip bones and his stomach hung over them like a sack of meal swaying under his

shirt. He came over and sat down at a table nearby and let out a combination sigh and yodel. "You can't win," he said. "You can't win," and he wiped his sweating red face off with a gray handkerchief. "These days you don't know who to trust," he said. "Ain't that the truth?"

35   "People are certainly not nice like they used to be," said the grandmother.

36   "Two fellers come in here last week," Red Sammy said, "driving a Chrysler. It was a old beat-up car but it was a good one and these boys looked all right to me. Said they worked at the mill and you know I let them fellers charge the gas they bought? Now why did I do that?"

37   "Because you're a good man!" the grandmother said at once.

38   "Yes'm, I suppose so," Red Sam said as if he were struck with this answer.

39   His wife brought the orders, carrying the five plates all at once without a tray, two in each hand and one balanced on her arm. "It isn't a soul in this green world of God's that you can trust," she said. "And I don't count nobody out of that, not nobody," she repeated, looking at Red Sammy.

40   "Did you read about that criminal, The Misfit, that's escaped?" asked the grandmother.

41   "I wouldn't be a bit surprised if he didn't attact this place right here," said the woman. "If he hears about it being here, I wouldn't be none surprised to see him. If he hears it's two cent in the cash register, I wouldn't be at all surprised if he . . ."

42   "That'll do," Red Sam said, "Go bring these people their Co'-Colas," and the woman went off to get the rest of the order.

43   "A good man is hard to find," Red Sammy said. "Everything is getting terrible. I remember the day you could go off and leave your screen door unlatched. Not no more."

44   He and the grandmother discussed better times. The old lady said that in her opinion Europe was entirely to blame for the way things were now. She said the way Europe acted you would think we were made of money and Red Sam said it was no use talking about it, she was exactly right. The children ran outside into the white sunlight and looked at the monkey in the lacy chinaberry tree. He was busy catching fleas on himself and biting each one carefully between his teeth as if it were a delicacy.

45   They drove off again into the hot afternoon. The grandmother took cat naps and woke up every few minutes with her own snoring. Outside of Toombsboro she woke up and recalled an old plantation that she had visited in this neighborhood once when she was a young lady. She said the house had six white columns across the front and that there was an avenue of oaks leading up to it and two little wooden trellis arbors on each side in front where you sat down with your suitor after a stroll in the garden. She recalled exactly which road to turn off to get to it. She knew that Bailey would not be willing to lose any time looking at an old house, but the more she talked about it, the more she wanted to see it once again and find out if the little twin arbors were still standing. "There was a secret panel in this house," she said craftily, not telling the truth

but wishing that she were, "and the story went that all the family silver was hidden in it when Sherman came through but it was never found . . ."

46   "Hey!" John Wesley said. "Let's go see it! We'll find it! We'll poke all the woodwork and find it! Who lives there? Where do you turn off at? Hey Pop, can't we turn off there?"

47   "We never have seen a house with a secret panel!" June Star shrieked. "Let's go to the house with the secret panel! Hey Pop, can't we go see the house with the secret panel!"

48   "It's not far from here, I know," the grandmother said. "It wouldn't take over twenty minutes."

49   Bailey was looking straight ahead. His jaw was as rigid as a horseshoe. "No," he said.

50   The children began to yell and scream that they wanted to see the house with the secret panel. John Wesley kicked the back of the front seat and June Star hung over her mother's shoulder and whined desperately into her ear that they never had any fun even on their vacation, that they could never do what THEY wanted to do. The baby began to scream and John Wesley kicked the back of the seat so hard that his father could feel the blows in his kidney.

51   "All right!" he shouted and drew the car to a stop at the side of the road. "Will you all shut up? Will you all just shut up for one second? If you don't shut up, we won't go anywhere."

52   "It would be very educational for them," the grandmother murmured.

53   "All right," Bailey said, "but get this: This is the only time we're going to stop for anything like this. This is the one and only time."

54   "The dirt road that you have to turn down is about a mile back," the grandmother directed. "I marked it when we passed."

55   "A dirt road," Bailey groaned.

56   After they had turned around and were headed toward the dirt road, the grandmother recalled other points about the house, the beautiful glass over the front doorway and the candle-lamp in the hall. John Wesley said that the secret panel was probably in the fireplace.

57   "You can't go inside this house," Bailey said. "You don't know who lives there."

58   "While you all talk to the people in front, I'll run around behind and get in a window," John Wesley suggested.

59   "We'll all stay in the car," his mother said.

60   They turned onto the dirt road and the car raced roughly along in a swirl of pink dust. The grandmother recalled the times when there were no paved roads and thirty miles was a day's journey. The dirt road was hilly and there were sudden washes in it and sharp curves on dangerous embankments. All at once they would be on a hill, looking down over the blue tops of trees for miles around, then the next minute, they would be in a red depression with the dust-coated trees looking down on them.

61   "This place had better turn up in a minute," Bailey said, "or I'm going to turn around."

62   The road looked as if no one had traveled on it in months.

63   "It's not much farther," the grandmother said and just as she said it, a horrible thought came to her. The thought was so embarrassing that she turned red in the face and her eyes dilated and her feet jumped up, upsetting her valise in the corner. The instant the valise moved, the newspaper top she had over the basket under it rose with a snarl and Pitty Sing, the cat, sprang onto Bailey's shoulder.

64   The children were thrown to the floor and their mother, clutching the baby, was thrown out the door onto the ground; the old lady was thrown into the front seat. The car turned over once and landed right-side-up in a gulch off the side of the road. Bailey remained in the driver's seat with the cat—graystriped with a broad white face and an orange nose—clinging to his neck like a caterpillar.

65   As soon as the children saw they could move their arms and legs, they scrambled out of the car, shouting, "We've had an ACCIDENT!" The grandmother was curled up under the dashboard, hoping she was injured so that Bailey's wrath would not come down on her all at once. The horrible thought she had had before the accident was that the house she had remembered so vividly was not in Georgia but in Tennessee.

66   Bailey removed the cat from his neck with both hands and flung it out the window against the side of a pine tree. Then he got out of the car and started looking for the children's mother. She was sitting against the side of the red gutted ditch, holding the screaming baby, but she only had a cut down her face and a broken shoulder. "We've had an ACCIDENT!" the children screamed in a frenzy of delight.

67   "But nobody's killed," June Star said with disappointment as the grandmother limped out of the car, her hat still pinned to her head but the broken front brim standing up at a jaunty angle and the violet spray hanging off the side. They all sat down in the ditch, except the children, to recover from the shock. They were all shaking.

68   "Maybe a car will come along," said the children's mother hoarsely.

69   "I believe I have injured an organ," said the grandmother, pressing her side, but no one answered her. Bailey's teeth were clattering. He had on a yellow sport shirt with bright blue parrots designed in it and his face was as yellow as the shirt. The grandmother decided that she would not mention that the house was in Tennessee.

70   The road was about ten feet above and they could see only the tops of the trees on the other side of it. Behind the ditch they were sitting in there were more woods, tall and dark and deep. In a few minutes they saw a car some distance away on top of a hill, coming slowly as if the occupants were watching them. The grandmother stood up and waved both arms dramatically to attract their attention. The car continued to come on slowly, disappeared around a bend and appeared again, moving even slower, on top of the hill they had gone over. It was a big black battered hearselike automobile. There were three men in it.

71   It came to a stop just over them and for some minutes, the driver looked down with a steady expressionless gaze to where they were sitting, and didn't

speak. Then he turned his head and muttered something to the other two and they got out. One was a fat boy in black trousers and a red sweat shirt with a silver stallion embossed on the front of it. He moved around on the right side of them and stood staring, his mouth partly open in a kind of loose grin. The other had on khaki pants and a blue striped coat and a gray hat pulled down very low, hiding most of his face. He came around slowly on the left side. Neither spoke.

72   The driver got out of the car and stood by the side of it, looking down at them. He was an older man than the other two. His hair was just beginning to gray and he wore silver-rimmed spectacles that gave him a scholarly look. He had a long creased face and didn't have on any shirt or undershirt. He had on blue jeans that were too tight for him and was holding a black hat and a gun. The two boys also had guns.

73   "We've had an ACCIDENT!" the children screamed.

74   The grandmother had the peculiar feeling that the bespectacled man was someone she knew. His face was as familiar to her as if she had known him all her life but she could not recall who he was. He moved away from the car and began to come down the embankment, placing his feet carefully so that he wouldn't slip. He had on tan and white shoes and no socks, and his ankles were red and thin. "Good afternoon," he said. "I see you all had you a little spill."

75   "We turned over twice!" said the grandmother.

76   "Oncet," he corrected. "We seen it happen. Try their car and see will it run, Hiram," he said quietly to the boy with the gray hat.

77   "What you got that gun for?" John Wesley asked. "Whatcha gonna do with that gun?"

78   "Lady," the man said to the children's mother, "would you mind calling them children to sit down by you? Children make me nervous. I want all you all to sit down right together there where you're at."

79   "What are you telling us what to do for?" June Star asked.

80   Behind them the line of woods gaped like a dark open mouth. "Come here," said their mother.

81   "Look here now," Bailey began suddenly, "we're in a predicament! We're in . . ."

82   The grandmother shrieked. She scrambled to her feet and stood staring. "You're The Misfit!" she said, "I recognized you at once!"

83   "Yes'm," the man said, smiling slightly as if he were pleased in spite of himself to be known, "but it would have been better for all of you, lady, if you hadn't of reckernized me."

84   Bailey turned his head sharply and said something to his mother that shocked even the children. The old lady began to cry and The Misfit reddened.

85   "Lady," he said, "don't you get upset. Sometimes a man says things he don't mean. I don't reckon he meant to talk to you thataway."

86   "You wouldn't shoot a lady, would you?" the grandmother said and removed a clean handkerchief from her cuff and began to slap at her eyes with it.

87   The Misfit pointed the toe of his shoe into the ground and made a little hole and then covered it up again. "I would hate to have to," he said.

88   "Listen," the grandmother almost screamed, "I know you're a good man. You don't look a bit like you have common blood. I know you must come from nice people!"

89   "Yes ma'am," he said, "finest people in the world." When he smiled he showed a row of strong white teeth. "God never made a finer woman than my mother and my daddy's heart was pure gold," he said. The boy with the red sweat shirt had come around behind them and was standing with his gun at his hip. The Misfit squatted down on the ground. "Watch them children, Bobby Lee," he said. "You know they make me nervous." He looked at the six of them huddled together in front of him and he seemed to be embarrassed as if he couldn't think of anything to say. "Ain't a cloud in the sky," he remarked, looking up at it. "Don't see no sun but don't see no cloud neither."

90   "Yes, it's a beautiful day," said the grandmother. "Listen," she said, "you shouldn't call yourself The Misfit because I know you're a good man at heart. I can just look at you and tell."

91   "Hush!" Bailey yelled. "Hush! Everybody shut up and let me handle this!" He was squatting in the position of a runner about to sprint forward but he didn't move.

92   "I pre-chate that, lady," The Misfit said and drew a little circle in the ground with the butt of his gun.

93   "It'll take a half a hour to fix this here car," Hiram called, looking over the raised hood of it.

94   "Well, first you and Bobby Lee get him and that little boy to step over yonder with you," The Misfit said, pointing to Bailey and John Wesley. "The boys want to ast you something," he said to Bailey. "Would you mind stepping back in them woods there with them?"

95   "Listen," Bailey began, "we're in a terrible predicament! Nobody realizes what this is," and his voice cracked. His eyes were as blue and intense as the parrots in his shirt and he remained perfectly still.

96   The grandmother reached up to adjust her hat brim as if she were going to the woods with him but it came off in her hand. She stood staring at it and after a second she let it fall on the ground. Hiram pulled Bailey up by the arm as if he were assisting an old man. John Wesley caught hold of his father's hand and Bobby Lee followed. They went off toward the woods and just as they reached the dark edge, Bailey turned and supporting himself against a gray naked pine trunk, he shouted, "I'll be back in a minute, Mamma, wait on me!"

97   "Come back this instant!" his mother shrilled but they all disappeared into the woods.

98   "Bailey Boy!" the grandmother called in a tragic voice but she found she was looking at The Misfit squatting on the ground in front of her. "I just know you're a good man," she said desperately. "You're not a bit common!"

99   "No'm, I ain't a good man," The Misfit said after a second as if he had considered her statement carefully. "But I ain't the worst in the world neither.

My daddy said I was a different breed of dog from my brothers and sisters. 'You know,' Daddy said, 'it's some that can live their whole life out without asking about it and it's others has to know why it is, and this boy is one of the latters. He's going to be into everything!'" He put on his black hat and looked up suddenly and then away deep into the woods as if he were embarrassed again. "I'm sorry I don't have on a shirt before you ladies," he said, hunching his shoulders slightly. "We buried our clothes that we had on when we escaped and we're just making do until we can get better. We borrowed these from some folks we met," he explained.

100 "That's perfectly all right," the grandmother said. "Maybe Bailey has an extra shirt in his suitcase."

101 "I'll look and see terrectly," The Misfit said.

102 "Where are they taking him?" the children's mother screamed.

103 "Daddy was a card himself," The Misfit said. "You couldn't put anything over on him. He never got in trouble with the Authorities though. Just had the knack of handling them."

104 "You could be honest too if you'd only try," said the grandmother. "Think how wonderful it would be to settle down and live a comfortable life and not have to think about somebody chasing you all the time."

105 The Misfit kept scratching in the ground with the butt of his gun as if he were thinking about it. "Yes'm, somebody is always after you," he murmured.

106 The grandmother noticed how thin his shoulder blades were just behind his hat because she was standing up looking down on him. "Do you ever pray?" she asked.

107 He shook his head. All she saw was the black hat wiggle between his shoulder blades. "No'm," he said.

108 There was a pistol shot from the woods, followed closely by another. Then silence. The old lady's head jerked around. She could hear the wind move through the tree tops like a long satisfied insuck of breath. "Bailey Boy!" she called.

109 "I was a gospel singer for a while," The Misfit said. "I been most everything. Been in the arm service, both land and sea, at home and abroad, been twicet married, been an undertaker, been with the railroads, plowed Mother Earth, been in a tornado, seen a man burnt alive oncet," and looked up at the children's mother and the little girl who were sitting close together, their faces white and their eyes glassy; "I even seen a woman flogged," he said.

110 "Pray, pray," the grandmother began, "pray, pray . . ."

111 "I never was a bad boy that I remember of," The Misfit said in an almost dreamy voice, "but somewheres along the line I done something wrong and got sent to the penitentiary. I was buried alive," and he looked up and held her attention to him by a steady stare.

112 "That's when you should have started to pray," she said. "What did you do to get sent to the penitentiary that first time?"

113 "Turn to the right, it was a wall," The Misfit said, looking up again at the cloudless sky. "Turn to the left, it was a wall. Look up it was a ceiling, look

down it was a floor. I forget what I done, lady. I set there and set there, trying to remember what it was I done and I ain't recalled it to this day. Oncet in a while, I would think it was coming to me, but it never come."

114   "Maybe they put you in by mistake," the old lady said vaguely.

115   "No'm," he said. "It wasn't no mistake. They had papers on me."

116   "You must have stolen something," she said.

117   The Misfit sneered slightly. "Nobody had nothing I wanted," he said. "It was a head-doctor at the penitentiary said what I had done was kill my daddy but I known that for a lie. My daddy died in nineteen ought nineteen of the epidemic flu and I never had a thing to do with it. He was buried in the Mount Hopewell Baptist churchyard and you can go there and see for yourself."

118   "If you would pray," the old lady said, "Jesus would help you."

119   "That's right," The Misfit said.

120   "Well then, why don't you pray?" she asked trembling with delight suddenly.

121   "I don't want no hep," he said, "I'm doing all right by myself."

122   Bobby Lee and Hiram came ambling back from the woods. Bobby Lee was dragging a yellow shirt with bright blue parrots in it.

123   "Throw me that shirt, Bobby Lee," The Misfit said. The shirt came flying at him and landed on his shoulder and he put it on. The grandmother couldn't name what the shirt reminded her of. "No, lady," The Misfit said while he was buttoning it up, "I found out the crime don't matter. You can do one thing or you can do another, kill a man or take a tire off his car, because sooner or later you're going to forget what it was you done and just be punished for it."

124   The children's mother had begun to make heaving noises as if she couldn't get her breath. "Lady," he asked, "would you and that little girl like to step off yonder with Bobby Lee and Hiram and join your husband?"

125   "Yes, thank you," the mother said faintly. Her left arm dangled helplessly and she was holding the baby, who had gone to sleep, in the other.

126   "Hep that lady up, Hiram," The Misfit said as she struggled to climb out of the ditch, "and Bobby Lee, you hold onto that little girl's hand."

127   "I don't want to hold hands with him," June Star said. "He reminds me of a pig."

128   The fat boy blushed and laughed and caught her by the arm and pulled her off into the woods after Hiram and her mother.

129   Alone with The Misfit, the grandmother found that she had lost her voice. There was not a cloud in the sky nor any sun. There was nothing around her but woods. She wanted to tell him that he must pray. She opened and closed her mouth several times before anything came out. Finally she found herself saying, "Jesus, Jesus," meaning, Jesus will help you, but the way she was saying it, it sounded as if she might be cursing.

130   "Yes'm," The Misfit said as if he agreed, "Jesus thrown everything off balance. It was the same case with Him as with me except He hadn't committed any crime and they could prove I had committed one because they had the

papers on me. Of course," he said, "they never shown me my papers. That's why I sign myself now. I said long ago, you get you a signature and sign everything you do and keep a copy of it. Then you'll know what you done and you can hold up the crime to the punishment and see do they match and in the end you'll have something to prove you ain't been treated right. I call myself The Misfit," he said, "because I can't make what all I done wrong fit what all I gone through in punishment."

131   There was a piercing scream from the woods, followed closely by a pistol report. "Does it seem right to you, lady, that one is punished a heap and another ain't punished at all?"

132   "Jesus!" the old lady cried. "You've got good blood! I know you wouldn't shoot a lady! I know you come from nice people! Pray! Jesus, you ought not to shoot a lady, I'll give you all the money I've got!"

133   "Lady," The Misfit said, looking beyond her far into the woods, "there never was a body that give the undertaker a tip."

134   There were two more pistol reports and the grandmother raised her head like a parched old turkey hen crying for water and called, "Bailey Boy, Bailey Boy!" as if her heart would break.

135   "Jesus was the only One that ever raised the dead," The Misfit continued, "and He shouldn't have done it. He thrown everything off balance. If He did what He said, then it's nothing for you to do but throw away everything and follow Him, and if He didn't, then it's nothing for you to do but enjoy the few minutes you got left the best way you can—by killing somebody or burning down his house or doing some other meanness to him. No pleasure but meanness," he said and his voice had become almost a snarl.

136   "Maybe He didn't raise the dead," the old lady mumbled, not knowing what she was saying and feeling so dizzy that she sank down in the ditch with her legs twisted under her.

137   "I wasn't there so I can't say He didn't," The Misfit said. "I wisht I had of been there," he said, hitting the ground with his fist. "It ain't right I wasn't there because if I had of been there I would of known. Listen lady," he said in a high voice, "if I had of been there I would of known and I wouldn't be like I am now." His voice seemed about to crack and the grandmother's head cleared for an instant. She saw the man's face twisted close to her own as if he were going to cry and she murmured, "Why, you're one of my babies. You're one of my own children!" She reached out and touched him on the shoulder. The Misfit sprang back as if a snake had bitten him and shot her three times through the chest. Then he put his gun down on the ground and took off his glasses and began to clean them.

138   Hiram and Bobby Lee returned from the woods and stood over the ditch, looking down at the grandmother who half sat and half lay in a puddle of blood with her legs crossed under her like a child's and her face smiling up at the cloudless sky.

139   Without his glasses, The Misfit's eyes were red-rimmed and pale and defenseless-looking. "Take her off and throw her where you thrown the others," he said, picking up the cat that was rubbing itself against his leg.

140   "She was a talker, wasn't she?" Bobby Lee said, sliding down the ditch with a yodel.

141   "She would of been a good woman," The Misfit said, "if it had been somebody there to shoot her every minute of her life."

142   "Some fun!" Bobby Lee said.

143   "Shut up, Bobby Lee," The Misfit said. "It's no real pleasure in life."

● Vocabulary

asphyxiate (10)   dilated (63)   ambling (122)
sachet (12)   jaunty (67)   parched (134)
bland (22)   embossed (71)

● The Facts

1. Why didn't the grandmother want to go to Florida? Where did she want to go instead?

2. Why does the family turn off onto the lonely dirt road?

3. What caused the accident?

4. For what crime was The Misfit sent to the penitentiary?

5. Why does he call himself "The Misfit"?

● The Strategies

1. The Misfit is mentioned in the first paragraph. Why does O'Connor introduce him so early?

2. What does the initial dialogue between the grandmother and the children accomplish?

3. In paragraph 70, The Misfit's automobile is described as "a big black battered hearselike automobile." What is O'Connor doing in this description?

4. At a climactic part of the story, the grandmother has a sudden, dramatic recognition of responsibility. When does it occur? Whom does it involve?

5. In paragraph 80, O'Connor writes: "Behind them the line of woods gaped like a dark open mouth." What does this description accomplish? What does it signal to the reader?

● The Issues

1. The Misfit and his cronies commit cold-blooded murder on a family of six. What prerequisite, if any, do you think must exist before a person is capable of murder? If you think there is no prerequisite, do you also think anyone is capable of cold-blooded murder? Justify your answer.

2. What punishment would you regard as just and fitting for The Misfit and his henchmen?

3. Some commentators have said that the children are brats, pure and simple, whereas others have argued that they are rather typical. What is your opinion of the children and their behavior?

4. One interpretation argues that The Misfit is the devil and the grandmother a Christian who confronts him. What is your opinion of this interpretation?

5. What do you think the grandmother meant when she said to The Misfit, "Why you're one of my babies. You're one of my own children!" Why do you think The Misfit killed her when she said that?

● Suggestions for Writing

1. Write an essay analyzing the techniques used by the author to foreshadow the family's fatal encounter with The Misfit. Make specific references to scenes and images and include as many quoted passages as necessary to prove your case.

2. Write an essay interpreting this story. You might begin by asking yourself, "What does the story teach about life?" "Are some people born evil?" "What makes a misfit like the one in the story?" Since the topic of criminal personalities is fraught with questions that are difficult to answer, try to evaluate critically any claims you encounter. Your thesis should contain the main point of the story.

Spring

EDNA ST. VINCENT MILLAY

Edna St. Vincent Millay (1892–1950), a graduate of Vassar and one of the most popular poets of her day, lived a Bohemian life during the 1920s in Greenwich Village, New York, writing satirical columns for *Vanity Fair* under a pseudonym. Her first volume of poetry, *Renascence*, was published in 1917 to glowing praise for its vitality. Subsequent volumes include *A Few Figs from Thistle* (1920) and *The Ballad of the Hat Weaver and Other Poems* (1923; Pulitzer Prize). She also wrote verse dramas, many of which were produced by the Provincetown Players. Later volumes of her work include *Fatal Interview* (1931), *Conversation at Midnight* (1937), and *Make Bright the Arrows* (1940). Her former home, "Steepletop," in Austerlitz, New York, which she shared with husband Eugan Jan Boissevain, is a Registered Historic Landmark and the center of the Edna St. Vincent Millay National Society, founded in 1978.

In many poems, the opening sentence presents a theme around which the rest of the poem is organized. In a way, this opening sentence, although strictly speaking not a thesis, fulfills the function of one. This poem is a classic example of what we mean.

● ● ●

To what purpose, April, do you return again?
Beauty is not enough.
You can no longer quiet me with the redness
Of little leaves opening stickily.

5   I know what I know.
    The sun is hot on my neck as I observe
    The spikes of the crocus.
    The smell of the earth is good.
    It is apparent that there is no death.
10 But what does that signify?
    Not only under ground are the brains of men
    Eaten by maggots.
    Life in itself
    Is nothing,
15 An empty cup, a flight of uncarpeted stairs,
    It is not enough that yearly, down this hill,
    April
    Comes like an idiot, babbling and strewing flowers.

● Vocabulary

crocus (7)   strewing (18)

● The Facts

1. What quality does April bring with it?

2. In what way do little red leaves open "stickily"?

3. According to the author, what is just as obvious as the fact that at death, the human body is eaten by maggots?

4. What keeps the author dissatisfied with spring?

● The Strategies

1. The poem begins with a question. Is the question ever answered? If so, what is the answer?

2. A sharp contrast underlies the poem. What is that contrast?

3. In what way, according to Millay, is the line "brains of men eaten by maggots" symbolic?

4. What metaphors and similes are used in the poem? Explain what they mean.

5. What is the tone of the poem? Is the tone appropriate for the theme?

● The Issues

1. What is the theme (thesis) of Millay's poem? State it in one sentence. What do you think has caused the poet to take such a position? Do you agree with it? Why or why not?

2. What is the meaning of the expression "no longer" in line 3?

3. What concrete aspects of spring please the poet? What do these aspects have in common?

4. Why does the author stress the beautiful aspects of spring?

5. Why is it not enough to experience a beautiful spring? What is your personal answer to this poem?

● Suggestions for Writing

1. Write an essay on spring and what it means to you.

2. Write an essay refuting Millay's comment that "Life in itself is nothing."

● CHAPTER WRITING ASSIGNMENTS

1. Convert one of the following general subjects into a suitable thesis:
   a. college life
   b. the relationship of parents to their offspring
   c. teenage pregnancies
   d. television coverage of crime, war, or natural disasters
   e. finding a meaningful job
   f. youth and age
   g. today's heroes
   h. freedom of speech

2. Select any issue covered in your local news reports, formulate your position on it in a thesis, and then explain and defend your thesis in an essay.

● WRITING ASSIGNMENTS FOR A SPECIFIC AUDIENCE

1. For an audience of junior high students, explain in an essay the concept of a thesis and how you make use of it in your own writing. Hint: Keep your vocabulary simple.

2. Explain to an audience of business executives how the English education you are presently receiving will make you a better employee.

REAL-LIFE STUDENT WRITING

A Eulogy to a Friend Killed in a Car Wreck

Students sometimes have the unenviable duty of saying a few last words at a funeral or memorial service of friends, relatives, and classmates. Here is a brief eulogy, given by a young man whose best friend was killed in an automobile crash.

• • •

He was my best friend. We went to elementary school to-gether, where we drove our teachers crazy. We grew up in North Hollywood, both loving the Giants, the 49ers, and the Lakers. We never missed a Rose Bowl game on TV. We weathered a thunderstorm in our pup tents in the Sierra Nevadas; we played Blind Man's Bluff in my parent's swimming pool; we TP'd our girlfriends' homes; we learned to play the guitar; and we read a lot of science fiction books together. When I was angry at my parents, Brett would calm me down. When I felt nervous about some final exam, Brett encouraged me.

What evil force is this that has taken Brett away without warning?

Yes, I am angry at the driver who mowed him down; I am angry that God didn't save him. But I am also aware that anger won't bring him back. So, I guess we must all live with the knowledge that Brett was a one-of-a-kind friend— loyal, upbeat, and generous. We'll all remember the good times we had with him. And for those of us who believe in life after death—we look forward to some day meeting him again and hearing him say, "Hey man, how's it goin'?"

1

Stumped by noun clusters? Exit on page 708 at the **Editing Booth!**

6

Organizing Ideas

ROAD MAP TO ORGANIZING

Writers and the way they work fall mainly into two major camps: the organic and the mechanical. The organic writer writes from the subconscious. Such writers often go to sleep thinking about an assignment and wake up the next morning knowing exactly what they intend to write. The mechanical writer, like a carpenter building a house, works from a blueprint or plan. These writers organize their thoughts before writing and plot out their ideas and topics before committing a single word to paper.

We raise this distinction to point out that organizing is not for everyone. It is a technique better suited to the working habits of the mechanical writer. For the organic writer whose subconscious does most of the work, organizing offers little benefit and might even interfere with the process of composing.

Organizing the Short Essay

Short essays (about 300 words long) are usually written in class under the pressure of a time limit. An instructor may assign you to write three paragraphs on some topic you have been studying in class, or you may be asked to write an informal essay on a topic such as why an uninformed person should or should not vote. Obviously, you cannot spend a great deal of time planning what to say in such an essay. Yet you think some preliminary sketch would be helpful. What can you do?

Make a Jot List A "jot list" is exactly as it says: a list of those points you mean to cover in the essay. You begin your jot list by scribbling down your main point or thesis. In this case, you think it is better for an ignorant voter to abstain than to cast a vote that amounts to a guess. You express this position in a thesis sentence:

> **Thesis:** To vote for someone whose record you don't know is worse than not voting at all.

Then you add the points you think you ought to cover:

1. If I don't vote, at least the people who know what the candidates stand for will make the decision for me.
2. Uncle John picks candidates by closing his eyes and poking at the ballot with his finger.
3. Voting from ignorance is disrespectful of the democratic process.
4. If I don't know anything about a candidate or an issue, I won't vote. At least that way, I leave the decision up to people who do know.

The jot list has no conventional form. You do not hand it in to your instructor. You can number its entries or arrange them in any other way you please. When you're done writing the essay, you can make a paper plane of the jot list if you like. It is nothing more than a thumbnail sketch of what you want to do.

Sketch out Your Paragraphs   This method of organizing is as simple as a jot list. Sketch out the paragraphs that you intend to write. Most in-class essays require no more than five paragraphs—and usually around three. Here's an example. You have been given the essay topic to write on any aspect of modern popular culture. You choose to write about the movies and why you like them.

Begin by writing down a rough draft of your thesis:

> **Thesis:** The most interesting and entertaining products of modern popular culture are movies.

Next, write down the topics of your beginning paragraphs:

> **First paragraph:** interesting movies. *Hotel Rwanda, Sicko, March of the Penguins.* Why these movies are interesting to me.
> **Second paragraph:** entertaining movies. *Wall-E, Steel Magnolias, Sex and the City.* Why I find these movies entertaining.
> **Third paragraph:** Our movies are global influences. They spread our culture and way of life better than literature does.

You don't want to make this list too long because you still have the actual essay to write. But at least you know what topics you have to cover in upcoming paragraphs.

Make a Flowchart   This is a more graphic variation of the jot list. Simply make a plan of your entire essay, using specially shaped boxes for supporting ideas and main points. In the example given (Figure 6.1), the triangular shapes indicate supporting details. The rectangular shapes indicate main points, and the diamond shape indicates where transitions need to be inserted.

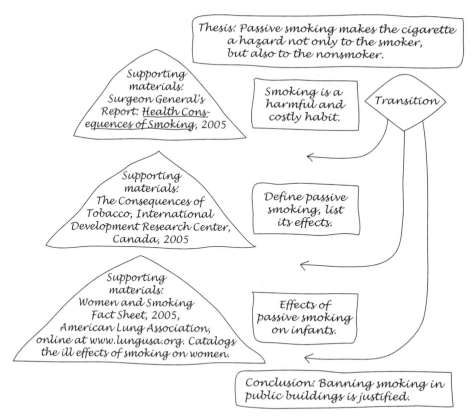

- **FIGURE 6.1**
Example of Essay Flowchart.

Organizing the Long Essay

The long essay might be a weekend assignment or a research paper completed over the course of several weeks. You might be expected to write an essay five to ten pages long with appropriate and accurate documentation on a topic such as the following: "Why the Shark Is Such a Successful Predator;" "Art Therapy;" or "Initial Critical Reactions to Henry Miller's Novels." Writing about such subjects will require library and Internet research as well as reading periodicals or books found in the libraries of friends and relatives.

The plan of such an essay should function as a guide not only to its writing but also to the research you need to do before you are ready to write. You should consult the plan both as you do the research—modifying it if necessary as you accumulate more supporting materials and possibly change your mind about what you want to say—and as you do the writing. If you find yourself going off in a different direction from the plan during the actual writing, never mind. Follow the lead of inspiration. When you have finished, go back over the rough draft and compare it with your original plan. Be sure that you can justify the switch.

Planning by Listing Supporting Materials

If you have a topic, you can often generate a crude outline of the essay by making a list of the supporting materials you will need for reference. How can you know what supporting materials you need? You find out by asking commonsense questions about the topic. These questions are those that any interested reader would likewise ask.

Here is an example: A student who accompanied her parents on a summer trip to Stonehenge, England, decided to do a paper on the area's mysterious monoliths. Her own tourist pamphlets, bolstered by some preliminary background reading in the college library, led her to this thesis:

> **Thesis:** A visit to Stonehenge, England, taught me that some civilizations of the past have left us some challenging mysteries we can't seem to solve.

These are the questions that naturally occurred to her as she thought about what supporting materials she would need:

- Where is Stonehenge? Give its geographical location.
- What is Stonehenge? Describe the stones so that the reader can visualize their size and arrangement. Try to get across the awesome nature of the stones.
- What was Stonehenge used for? What are the theories of its use?
- Summarize the most popular legends surrounding the history of Stonehenge:
  1. Stonehenge as a sanctuary of the Druids. Look up "Druids" in the encyclopedia. See what role they played in the early history of England (probably Celtic).
  2. The Devil's confrontation with a friar. Find out how this exotic legend got started.
  3. A memorial to the slain knights of King Arthur.
  4. An observatory for tracking the heavens, especially the rising of the moon. This seems to be a realistic explanation. Find out if many sources mention this theory.
- Why is Stonehenge so popular even today? Explain the reasons for its popularity.

These rather straightforward questions gave the writer an idea of the supporting materials she needed to complete the assignment. Asking these questions also resulted in a rough outline of the paper.

Organizing with a Formal Outline

The outline is a summary of what you plan to say in your essay. The outline tells you what you have to do, where you have to go, and when you have gotten there. If you tend to get sidetracked by details or bogged down in vast quantities of information, outlining is a handy way of imposing structure on a long essay.

A convention has evolved for the formal outline, based mainly on the desire to make it readable at a glance. The title of the essay is centered at the top of the page, with the thesis below it. Main ideas are designated by Roman numerals. Sub-ideas branching off the main ideas are indented and designated by capital letters. Examples of these sub-ideas are further indented and designated by Arabic numerals. Indented beneath the examples are supporting details, designated by lowercase letters. In theory, this subdividing could go on forever; in practice, it rarely extends beyond the fourth level. Here is the framework for the formal outline:

Title
  Thesis
    I. Main idea
      A. Sub-idea
        1. Division of sub-idea
          a. Part of division of sub-idea

An outline omits introductory materials, transitions, examples, illustrations, and details; it lists only the major ideas and sub-ideas of the essay. This practice makes sense when you remember that the prime purpose of an outline is to condense the major divisions of a long essay into a form that can be read at a glance. To make the outline as long and complex as the essay itself is self-defeating and pointless labor.

To make an outline, begin with the thesis of your essay and divide it into smaller ideas. It is an axiom of division that nothing can be divided into fewer than two parts. From this, it follows that under every main idea that has been divided, at least two sub-ideas must appear. In other words, for every I there must be at least a II; for every A, at least a B. Consider this example:

Temperatures and Mountain Climbers

  Thesis: Extremes in temperatures can have dangerous effects on mountain climbers.
    I. The dangerous effects of excessive heat
      A. Heat exhaustion
      B. Heat stroke
    II. The dangerous effects of excessive cold
      A. Surface frostbite
      B. Bodily numbness

The logic of division will always produce an outline characterized by symmetry. A by-product of this symmetry is evenness in the treatment of all topics. Notice also that each entry is worded in more or less parallel language. This wording underscores the equal importance of the entries and emphasizes the major divisions in the outline.

Creating the Outline Outlining is systematic thinking about your thesis. You examine the essay as a reader might and try to decide what points you need to present, and in what order, to make the topic understandable. For example, let us suppose that you were planning to write an essay on this thesis:

> **Thesis:** Listening is such an important and badly practiced communicative skill that schools should begin offering courses in how to do it better.

The first question a reader is likely to ask is, "Why is listening so important?" The answer should be the development of your first major point.

> I. Listening is an important communicative skill.

What do you mean by "listening is badly practiced"? Common sense suggests that this is the second question likely to occur to an interested reader. The answer could be the development of your second major point.

> II. Listening is a badly practiced communicative skill.

Fill out these two major headings with some secondary points that serve as answers, and you have completed the first part of your outline.

> I. Listening is an important communicative skill.
>   A. We spend most of our communicating time listening.
>   B. We get most of our political information from radio and television.
> II. Listening is a badly practiced communicative skill.
>   A. We typically understand only one-half of what we hear.
>   B. We typically recall only one-quarter of what we hear.

Following this line of thinking, we can deduce some other questions that common sense tells us are likely to occur to a reader: What do you mean by listening? Are all types of listening alike? Answers to these questions can provide us with two more headings:

> III. Listening is an active communicative skill that is divisible into four components.
>   A. Receiving entails decoding the message.
>   B. Attending entails analyzing the message.
>   C. Assigning meaning entails interpreting the message.
>   D. Remembering entails information storage and retrieval.

IV. Listening is grouped into five major types.
   A. Appreciative listening involves acceptance.
   B. Discriminative listening involves selection.
   C. Comprehensive listening involves generalizing.
   D. Therapeutic listening involves relaxation.
   E. Critical listening involves judgment.

Think about the purpose of the assignment and the questions your thesis is likely to evoke in a reader and you will likewise discover the logical divisions of your essay.

Guidelines for Outlining You should observe the following guidelines in making your outline:

1. **Don't make the outline too long.** One page of an outline is the basis for five pages of developed writing. Your aim is to produce a model of the essay that you can inspect for flaws at a glance.
2. **Don't clutter the sentences of your outline.** Make your entries brief. The idea is to make the outline instantly readable.
3. **Use parallel wording for subordinate entries whenever possible.** Parallel entries are easier to read than nonparallel ones.
4. **Align the entries properly.** Do not allow the second line of an entry to go farther toward the left margin than the line above it.

If you observe these simple guidelines, the outline that results should be easy to read. You should be able to glance at its major entries and immediately spot any flaws in the structure of the essay.

Outlining by Topic/Outlining by Sentence Some outlines are topic outlines in which the entries are not complete sentences, but fragments that sum up the topic. Other outlines are sentence outlines in which the entries are complete sentences. Your decision on whether to use a topic or a sentence outline depends on how complete a breakdown you need. If your subject is simple and all you need are key words to serve as guideposts so that you will not get sidetracked, or if you merely wish to set down some major trends, categories, or stages, then you should use a topic outline. If your subject is a difficult one or in an area that is new to you, you should use a sentence outline. Consider the following topic outline:

The Future of Our Cities **Thesis:** An assessment of the future of our cities reveals two emerging trends.

   I. The megalopolis
      A. Definition
         1. Cluster
         2. System

      B. Two major organizational problems
         1. Transcendence
         2. Coordination
   II. Shift in decision making
      A. Local decisions
         1. Facts not known
         2. Outside agencies
      B. Federal government
         1. Increase in power
         2. Local restrictions

    This topic outline is of no value to a person who is not thoroughly familiar with the problems of city government. A student writing a paper based on such a cryptic outline is bound to have difficulty. Now consider the following sentence outline of the same subject:

The Future of Our Cities **Thesis:** An assessment of the future of our cities reveals two emerging trends.

   I. The megalopolis is replacing the city.
      A. Megalopolis can be defined in two ways.
         1. A megalopolis is a cluster of cities.
         2. A megalopolis is a system of interwoven urban and suburban areas.
      B. Two major organizational problems of the megalopolis will need to be solved.
         1. One problem is how to handle questions that transcend individual metropolitan areas.
         2. Another problem is how to coordinate the numerous activities in the megalopolis.
   II. Decision making is shifting from local control to higher echelons of public and private authority.
      A. The growing scale of the urban world often makes local decisions irrelevant.
         1. Local agencies may not know all of the facts.
         2. National policies may supersede local decisions.
      B. The federal government moves into the picture.
         1. The extent of federal involvement increases as the city grows.
            a. Federal long-range improvement plans are used.
            b. Grant-in-aid programs become necessary.

2. Federal assistance imposes restrictions.

    a. Federal policies make sure that no discrimination takes place in the areas of housing, employment, and education.

    b. Federal representatives check on local installations to make sure that they are up to federal standards.

A good sentence outline supplies all of the basic information you need to write your paper. Without an outline, you run the risk of treating major ideas like details and details like major ideas; furthermore, you may find yourself moving forward, then backtracking, and then moving forward again, resulting in an incoherent paper. Because a careful outline takes into account the relationships among ideas and their degrees of importance, it keeps a novice from producing muddled writing.

We do not wish to mislead you into thinking that every essay you write will be just as easily and neatly outlined as our examples may suggest. In fact, you will most likely find it necessary to revise the outline heavily. You might even end up with three or four scratched-up versions before you are satisfied with the result. As you outline, new ideas will occur to you and clamor to be fitted in somewhere. Old headings will strike you as too obvious to be included. Whether you make a formal outline or simply draw up a sketch of your essay, you are still likely to revise heavily before you are happy with your plan.

● Exercises

1. Write a paragraph outline for one of the following theses:

    a. Inflation has a deteriorating effect on the purchasing power of the dollar.

    b. The essay exam has several advantages over the objective test.

    c. The first three months of an infant's life are crucial to the development of his or her personality.

2. Create a flowchart for one of the following theses:

    a. Society often uses language to favor one sex over the other.

    b. Economic inflation has political consequences.

    c. Teachers deserve higher salaries.

    d. English should be made the official language of the United States.

3. List the supporting materials you might use for an essay on one of the following topics:

    a. Why people often don't help in a crisis.

    b. Multiple-choice versus essay exams as tools of education.

    c. Comic strips that have social value.

    d. Why modern products are often shoddy.

4. Identify the key words in the following theses, specifying two or three subtopics into which they may be divided:

    a. Strong diplomatic ties with China would have several advantages for the United States.

    b. An electrical blackout in any major city of the United States would have disastrous results.

    c. The words *disinterested*, *inflammable*, and *fortuitous* are often misunderstood.

5. Delete the entry that destroys the logical order in the following outlines:

   a. *Thesis: Because of their cultural traits, the Dobuans are different from other primitive tribes.*

      I. The location and environment of Dobuan Island make it difficult for the Dobuans to find sufficient food.

      II. The rituals of marriage set the Dobuans apart from other primitive tribes.

      III. The Dobuans' reliance on magic makes them more superstitious than other primitive tribes.

      IV. The fact that the Dobuans value treachery and ill will sets them apart from other primitive tribes.

   b. *Thesis: The purpose of the California missions was to Christianize the Indians and to strengthen Spain's claim to California.*

      I. The mission padres taught the Indians Christian virtues.

      II. The padres were concerned with saving the souls of the Indians.

      III. The missions were constructed in the form of small cities.

      IV. Without its colonists in California, Spain's claim to this territory was weak.

      V. Spain was competing with Russia and England for territory in California.

   c. *Thesis: American political assassins have acted on nonpolitical impulses.*

      I. They are pathetic loners.

      II. Their reality is a fantasy world.

      III. The victim is usually a surrogate parent image.

      IV. The assassin is seeking the same "fame" that the victim has.

      V. European assassinations, unlike ours, have been the results of elaborate plots.

6. Scrutinize the following outline for errors of form as well as content. Correct the errors by producing two improved versions—a sentence outline and a topic outline.

   a. *Thesis: The adult Moses is one of the most commanding and inspirational figures of the Old Testament.*

      I. Moses as a God-intoxicated man.

         A. Moses' faith in God.

         B. He created in the Hebrews a religious faith that was to endure after their life as a nation had died.

            1. The Babylonian and Persian conquests.

            2. The faith endured during the Greek conquest.

            3. The faith endured during the Roman conquest.

            4. Despite their faith, the Hebrews often worshiped foreign gods.

            5. The faith endured during the various diasporas.

      II. Moses was a peerless travel guide.

         A. During the long sojourn in the wilderness, Moses showed endless patience.

            1. Enduring constant grumbling on the part of the tribes.

            2. This period of desert wandering symbolizes the age of innocence of any developing nation.

            3. He settled quarrels with great patience.

   B. His earlier flight in order to escape punishment for having killed an Egyptian made him fully acquainted with the Sinai desert.

     1. He knew where to find water.

     2. He knew how to avoid dangerous enemy territory.

     3. He always followed a magical cloud by day and a pillar of fire by night.

III. Moses was the founder of a complex legal system.

   A. He gave the Hebrews the Torah.

     1. Parts of the Torah dealt with man's relationship to God.

     2. Parts of the Torah dealt with man's relationship to man.

   B. He gave the Hebrews the ordinances.

     1. Some of the ordinances dealt with matters of social justice.

     2. According to one ordinance, a man who knocks out his slave's tooth must let that slave go free.

     3. Others of the ordinances dealt with religious ceremonies.

     4. Some of the ordinances dealt with plans for building a temple.

ADVICE

Write to Be Understood

JIM STAYLOR

Rhetorical Thumbnail

Purpose: to teach the art of plain writing

Audience: anyone who must write as part of a job

Language: mainly standard English but also gives examples of stuffy writing

Strategy: teaches the rules of clear writing by citing examples tinged with humorous exaggeration

Jim Staylor (b. 1958), a media producer, is a graduate of San Diego State University and California State University at Fullerton. Named a "Top-100 Producer" by *AV, Video, Multimedia* magazine in 2000, Staylor is president of a media production company that serves high-tech, health care, hospitality, defense, restaurant, and retail industries. He is in great demand as a motivational speaker.

Without wasting words or concepts, this essay draws the connection between clarity and organization in writing. Follow its simple rules, and your writing will connect with your reader.

• • •

1   Use clear, direct and simple text to be easily understood. In other words, as a proponent of perspicuity one should really espouse eschewing obfuscation in typographical emanations.

2   Good writing (in contrast to the sentence above) is clear, concise, congruent and compelling. Layout and text design may help organize content and guide the reader to what is important, but ultimately, words and their usage often determine the success or failure of your communications. Six guidelines for clarifying text can help you become more perspicuous in your writing.

Perspicuity is the Goal

3   Perspicuity means being clear of statement or expression; easily understood; or lucid.

4   Titles, headlines, sub-headings, captions and body copy all contain text with the power to confuse or clarify.

5   Find more information about writing well by consulting a few reputable style guides in print or on the Internet.

Clarifying Text

6   According to Hartley (1996)*, a writer can generally do six things to make text easier to understand.

1. Follow Simple Sentence Structure

7   Sentences with many subordinate clauses and modifying statements are more difficult to understand. Practice the KISS formula; Keep It Simple and Straightforward.

8   ● Use the fewest possible words to say what you mean.
9   ● Never say "blah, blah" when all you need is "blah."

2. Use Active vs. Passive Voice

10 The active voice is usually more direct and vigorous than the passive voice. Writing in the active voice results in shorter, stronger sentences. The subject doing the action often holds more interest than the object being acted upon. "The hat which is owned by me was thrown on the roof by Peter who is my brother" is better as "My brother Peter threw my hat on the roof." This has half the words and perhaps twice the impact.

3. Choose Positive Terms

11 Using positive terms makes it easier for readers to grasp concepts and paint mental pictures. Readers would rather know about what is than what

---

*Hartley, J. (1996) "Text Design." In D.H. Jonassen (ed.) *Handbook of research for educational communication and technology.*

is not. Therefore it is generally better to express even negatives in positive form.

Not honest	Dishonest
Not important	Trifling
Did not remember	Forgot
Did not pay attention to	Ignored
Did not have much confidence in	Distrusted

4. Avoid Multiple Negatives

12 Double or triple negatives are often confusing. An example by Harold Evans (1972) compares, "The figures provide no indication that costs would have not been lower if competition had not been restricted," with, "The figures provide no indication that competition would have produced higher costs."

5. Personalize Copy

13 Personalizing text or writing in the form of a story helps students recall information. Describing benefits of a medical procedure, for example, comes to life when told from the point of view of a patient receiving treatment as opposed to a clinical step-by-step explanation of the process. "My name is Susie and I'd like to tell you how I discovered I was sick and what my Doctor Steve did about it."

6. Make It Interesting

14 Lively examples and vivid anecdotes also help make text interesting and memorable. Be careful to avoid making the details so seductive they distract from the main point.

15 These six basic guidelines offer a good start toward good writing. Good Luck.

16 *It's your right to be understood, so write to be understood.*

Jim Staylor, "Write to be Understood," located at http://edweb.sdsu.edu/eet/articles/ writeclearly. Reprinted by permission of San Diego State University and Jim Staylor, http://www.staylor-made.com.

● Vocabulary

proponent (1)	obfuscation (1)	congruent (2)
perspicuity (1)	typographical (1)	personalizing (13)
espouse (1)	emanations (1)	anecdotes (14)
eschewing (1)	concise (2)	seductive (14)

● The Facts

1. What kind of writing does the author want his readers to produce? What three adjectives does he use as guiding principles of good writing?

2. According to the author, what is more important than layout and text design? Why?

3. How many rules should be followed to produce easily understood text? To whom does the author give credit for these rules? (See the asterisk at the end of the essay.)

4. What does "KISS" stand for? What will it prevent?

5. Which rules mentioned deal with the avoidance of roundabout writing? Why are these rules important?

● The Strategies

1. How does the layout or text of this essay help the reader to follow the author's ideas? Do you consider this attempt successful? Explain your answer.

2. How does the author capture the reader's attention at the start of the essay? Do you consider this a helpful strategy? Why or why not?

3. In paragraph 6, what does the reference to Hartley add to the paper? Could it have been left out in order to save space?

4. In numbering the rules of good writing, how is the author keeping his own counsel? Be specific in your answer.

5. What is the author's thesis? State it in one simple sentence. Which, if any of the strategies used in the essay, helped you most to understand the thesis?

● The Issues

1. Do you agree with the author that good writing is "clear, concise, congruent, and compelling"? Have you ever read a book or magazine in which the writing was good and also could not be labeled "clear or concise"? Provide an example from your own reading. Where do you find writing that best fits the author's description of good writing? What is your reaction when you read this style of writing?

2. When, if ever, might you be justified in using the passive rather than active voice in a sentence? Give an example.

3. The author encourages writers to use lively examples and vivid anecdotes to enhance their writing. Why do you think examples and anecdotes are useful writing tools? Cite an instance of you or someone else using an example or an anecdote in writing.

4. What does the author mean when he tells writers never to use "blah, blah" when "blah" will do? What point is he stressing?

5. What strikes you about the italicized remark at the end of Staylor's essay? What is its purpose? Do you consider it a strong ending? Explain your answer.

● Suggestions for Writing

1. This essay stresses plain writing as one of the keys to being understood. Write a brief essay in which you analyze what happens when a reader confronts unnecessarily complicated sentences or gobbledygook.

2. Choosing one of the following topics, write an essay in which you use a vivid anecdote to liven up your writing:

   a. A job interview that didn't go well.

   b. A date that turned out to be disastrous.

   c. A telephone conversation that made me furious.

   d. What my best friend brings to my life.

EXAMPLES

My Wood

E. M. FORSTER

> ### Rhetorical Thumbnail
>
> **Purpose:** to make an amusing point about property ownership
> **Audience:** educated readers
> **Language:** British English but not snobby or starchy
> **Strategy:** shows the illusions of property ownership

E. M. Forster (1879–1969) was a British novelist, essayist, and short-story writer whose work first won wide recognition in 1924 with the publication of his book, *A Passage to India*. In 1946, Forster was made an honorary fellow of King's College, Cambridge, where he lived until his death. Among his many other works are *Howard's End* (1910) and *Two Cheers for Democracy* (1951), a collection of his essays.

"My Wood," a superbly organized short essay, investigates the effect of property ownership on the individual and society.

• • •

1   A few years ago I wrote a book which dealt in part with the difficulties of the English India. Feeling that they would have had no difficulties in India themselves, the Americans read the book freely. The more they read it the better it made them feel, and a cheque to the author was the result. I bought a wood with the cheque. It is not a large wood—it contains scarcely any trees, and it is intersected, blast it, by a public footpath. Still, it is the first property that I have owned, so it is right that other people should participate in my shame, and should ask themselves, in accents that will vary in horror, this very important question: What is the effect of property upon the character? Don't let's touch economics; the effect of private ownership upon the community as a whole is another question—a more important question, perhaps, but another one. Let's keep to psychology. If you own things, what's their effect on you? What's the effect on me of my wood?

2   In the first place, it makes me feel heavy. Property does have this effect. Property produces men of weight, and it was a man of weight who failed to get into the Kingdom of Heaven. He was not wicked, that unfortunate millionaire in the parable, he was only stout; he stuck out in front, not to mention behind, and as he wedged himself this way and that in the crystalline entrance and bruised his well-fed flanks, he saw beneath him a comparatively slim camel passing through the eye of a needle and being woven into the robe of God. The Gospels all through couple stoutness and slowness. They point out what is

perfectly obvious, yet seldom realized: that if you have a lot of things you cannot move about a lot, that furniture requires dusting, dusters require servants, servants require insurance stamps,[1] and the whole tangle of them makes you think twice before you accept an invitation to dinner or go for a bathe in the Jordan. Sometimes the Gospels proceed further and say with Tolstoy that property is sinful; they approach the difficult ground of asceticism here, where I cannot follow them. But as to the immediate effects of property on people, they just show straightforward logic. It produces men of weight. Men of weight cannot, by definition, move like the lightning from the East unto the West, and the ascent of a fourteen-stone bishop into a pulpit is thus the exact antithesis of the coming of the Son of Man. My wood makes me feel heavy.

3   In the second place, it makes me feel it ought to be larger.

4   The other day I heard a twig snap in it. I was annoyed at first, for I thought that someone was blackberrying, and depreciating the value of the undergrowth. On coming nearer, I saw it was not a man who had trodden on the twig and snapped it, but a bird, and I felt pleased. My bird. The bird was not equally pleased. Ignoring the relation between us, it took fright as soon as it saw the shape of my face, and flew straight over the boundary hedge into a field, the property of Mrs. Henessy, where it sat down with a loud squawk. It had become Mrs. Henessy's bird. Something seemed grossly amiss here, something that would not have occurred had the wood been larger. I could not afford to buy Mrs. Henessy out, I dared not murder her, and limitations of this sort beset me on every side. Ahab did not want that vineyard—he only needed it to round off his property, preparatory to plotting a new curve—and all the land around my wood has become necessary to me in order to round off the wood. A boundary protects. But—poor little thing—the boundary ought in its turn to be protected. Noises on the edge of it. Children throw stones. A little more, and then a little more, until we reach the sea. Happy Canute! Happier Alexander! And after all, why should even the world be the limit of possession? A rocket containing a Union Jack, will, it is hoped, be shortly fired at the moon. Mars. Sirius. Beyond which . . . But these immensities ended by saddening me. I could not suppose that my wood was the destined nucleus of universal dominion—it is so very small and contains no mineral wealth beyond the blackberries. Nor was I comforted when Mrs. Henessy's bird took alarm for the second time and flew clean away from us all, under the belief that it belonged to itself.

5   In the third place, property makes its owner feel that he ought to do something to it. Yet he isn't sure what. A restlessness comes over him, a vague sense that he has a personality to express—the same sense which, without any vagueness, leads the artist to an act of creation. Sometimes I think I will cut down such trees as remain in the wood, at other times I want to fill up the gaps between them with new trees. Both impulses are pretentious and empty. They are not honest movements towards money-making or beauty. They spring from a foolish desire to express myself and from an inability to enjoy what I have got. Creation, property, enjoyment form a sinister trinity in the human mind. Creation and enjoyment are both very good, yet they are often unattainable without a material basis,

---

[1] In England.

and at such moments property pushes itself in as a substitute, saying, "Accept me instead—I'm good enough for all three." It is not enough. It is, as Shakespeare said of lust, "The expense of spirit in a waste of shame": it is "Before, a joy proposed; behind, a dream." Yet we don't know how to shun it. It is forced on us by our economic system as the alternative to starvation. It is also forced on us by an internal defect in the soul, by the feeling that in property may lie the germs of self-development and of exquisite or heroic deeds. Our life on earth is, and ought to be, material and carnal. But we have not yet learned to manage our materialism and carnality properly; they are still entangled with the desire for ownership, where (in the words of Dante) "Possession is one with loss."

6   And this brings us to our fourth and final point: the blackberries.

7   Blackberries are not plentiful in this meagre grove, but they are easily seen from the public footpath which traverses it, and all too easily gathered. Foxgloves, too—people will pull up the foxgloves, and ladies of an educational tendency even grub for toadstools to show them on the Monday in class. Other ladies, less educated, roll down the bracken in the arms of their gentlemen friends. There is a paper, there are tins. Pray, does my wood belong to me or doesn't it? And, if it does, should I not own it best by allowing no one else to walk there? There is a wood near Lyme Regis, also cursed by a public footpath, where the owner has not hesitated on this point. He has built high stone walls on each side of the path, and has spanned it by bridges, so that the public circulate like termites while he gorges on the blackberries unseen. He really does own his wood, this able chap. Dives in Hell did pretty well, but the gulf dividing him from Lazarus could be traversed by vision, and nothing traverses it here. And perhaps I shall come to this in time. I shall wall in and fence out until I really taste the sweets of property. Enormously stout, endlessly avaricious, pseudo-creative, intensely selfish, I shall weave upon my forehead the quadruple crown of possession until those nasty Bolshies come and take it off again and thrust me aside into the outer darkness.

● Vocabulary

asceticism (2)	Alexander (4)	traversed (7)
antithesis (2)	exquisite (5)	avaricious (7)
Canute (4)	carnal (5)	pseudo (7)

● The Facts

1. What intersects Forster's wood and is a source of annoyance to him?
2. What is the first effect Forster's wood had on him?
3. What or whom did Forster discover on his property when he heard a twig snap?
4. According to Forster, what is the effect of property on its owner?
5. What does Forster think he will eventually do with his wood?

● The Strategies

1. What are the obvious divisions in the topics and subtopics of this essay? Make an outline showing the thesis, main points, and subtopics of the essay.
2. Read the last sentence of paragraph 2. What is the purpose of this sentence?
3. What is the purpose of paragraph 3?
4. What tone does Forster use throughout this essay? Do you regard his tone as mocking, serious, or ironic? Justify your answer.
5. In paragraph 4, Forster writes: "Happy Canute! Happier Alexander!" What is this figure of speech called? Why is Alexander happier than Canute?

● The Issues

1. What point does Forster make obliquely in his discussion about the bird?
2. What effect does ownership have on you? Is Forster exaggerating here, or have you experienced the effects that he describes?
3. What benefits, if any, do you think society gains from ownership of private property?
4. What do you think Dante meant by "Possession is one with loss"? Interpret this statement.
5. "Our life on earth is, and ought to be, material and carnal." What is your opinion of this statement? How do you think our life on earth ought to be?

● Suggestions for Writing

1. Write an essay in which you analyze the effects on an individual of owning nothing.
2. Write an essay in which you either defend or challenge the author's claim that too much property eventually leads to revolution.

Rules for Aging

ROGER ROSENBLATT

Rhetorical Thumbnail

Purpose: to amuse or entertain

Audience: general educated reader

Language: standard English

Strategy: assumes the voice of a wise counselor giving advice on aging

Roger Rosenblatt (b. 1940) is one of *Time's* most respected editorial writers. His insights into politics and society, as well as his wonderful sense of humor, have delighted his readers for close to two decades. Rosenblatt graduated from Harvard, where he earned a Ph.D. and briefly taught English. He has been featured on television reading his eloquent *Time* essays.

• • •

1 Since older people are as close to perfection as human beings get, I thought it would be generous, from time to time, to use this space to offer guidelines for living to those less old to help them age successfully, or at all. The art of aging requires not doing things more than taking positive action, so this is essentially a list of "nots" and "don'ts."

2 **1.** *It doesn't matter.* Whatever you think matters, doesn't. This guideline is absolutely reliable and adhering to it will add decades to your life. It does not matter if you are late for anything; if you're having a bad hair day, or a no-hair day; if your car won't start; if your boss looks at you cockeyed; if your girlfriend or boyfriend looks at you cockeyed; if you are cockeyed; if you don't get the promotion; if you do; if you have spinach in your teeth or if you lose your teeth in your spinach. It doesn't matter.

3 **2.** *Nobody is thinking about you.* Yes, I know. You are certain that your friends are becoming your enemies; that your enemies are acquiring nuclear weapons; that your grocer, garbage man, clergyman, sister-in-law, and dog are all of the opinion that you have put on weight; furthermore, that everyone spends two-thirds of every day commenting on your disintegration, denigrating your work, plotting your murder. I promise you: Nobody is thinking about you. They are thinking about themselves, just like you.

4 **3.** *Do not go to your left.* Going to one's left, or working on going to one's left, is a basketball term for strengthening one's weakness. A right-handed player will improve his game considerably if he learns to dribble and shoot with his left hand, and to move to his left on the court. But this is true only for basketball, not for living. In life, if you attempt to strengthen a weakness, you will grow weaker. If, on the other hand (the right), you keep playing to your strength, people will not notice that you have weaknesses. Of course, you do not believe me. You will go ahead and take singing lessons or write that novel anyway. Trust me.

5 **4.** *Give honest, frank, and open criticism to nobody, never.* The following situation will present itself to you over and over: There is a friend, a relative, an employee, an employer, a colleague, whose behavior flaws are so evident to everyone but themselves, you just know that a straightforward, no-punches-pulled conversation with them will show them the error of their ways. They will see the light at once, and forever be grateful that only as good and candid a person as you would have sufficient kindness and courage to confront them.

6 Better still: From the moment you inform them about their bad table manners, their poor choices in clothing, their hygiene, their loudness, their deafness, their paranoia, they will reform on the spot. Their lives will be redeemed,

and they will owe their renewed selves and all future happiness to you—honest, frank, and open you.

7   I implore you: forget about it. When the muse of candor whispers in your ear, swat it, take a long walk, a cold shower, and clear your head. This guideline relates to guideline number two. Nobody is thinking about you, unless you tell them about their faults. Then you can be sure they are thinking of you. They are thinking of killing you.

8   That's enough wisdom for now. I know younger people will not heed my advice anyway. So the guideline I offer them is: Don't. Go ahead and stay awake worrying what people are thinking about you, work on your weaknesses, and criticize your friends. It doesn't matter.

Excerpt from RULES FOR AGING, copyright © 2000 by Roger Rosenblatt, reprinted by permission of Houghton Mifflin Harcourt Publishing Company.

● Vocabulary

adhering (2)	denigrating (3)	muse (7)
disintegration (3)	paranoia (6)	candor (7)

● The Facts

1. How many rules for aging does Rosenblatt offer? What form do these rules follow?
2. The first rule is pronounced with great authority—"It doesn't matter." What is the author telling us with this rule?
3. In what way is rule #2 related to rule #1?
4. What does the author mean by the image of "going to your left"?
5. What is the implication behind rule #4?

● The Strategies

1. How would you describe the tone of this essay? How does the tone affect the purpose of the essay? Does the essay have a thesis? If so, where is it stated?
2. What is your reaction to the opening sentence of the essay? How did it strike you? Consider such matters as the author's voice, his tone, and his purpose.
3. What is the effect of the "Yes, I know" sentence at the beginning of paragraph 3?
4. Where does the author use parallelism to achieve balance and euphony? Point to specific passages in the essay.
5. Why does the author refer to "the muse of candor" in paragraph 7?

● The Issues

1. What is your personal understanding of the author's statement, "It doesn't matter"? Elaborate on his meaning.
2. Assuming that most human beings are concerned with their own problems more than those of other people, why do they often persist in feeling that their neighbors are plotting against them or making disparaging remarks behind their backs?

3. From the following list of widely admired 20th-Century persons, choose one whose contributions you organize into an essay with a clear thesis. Synthesize any outside sources as taught in Chapter 3.

   Mother Teresa   Helen Keller   Mohandas Gandhi

   Martin Luther King, Jr.   Albert Einstein   Nelson Mandela

4. Which of Rosenblatt's rules do you think is the most difficult to follow? Why?

5. In giving us rule #3, do you think the author is discouraging forays into new and exciting territories? Might he be keeping older people from trying new hobbies or taking on new responsibilities that might enrich the final years of their lives? Explain your answer.

● Suggestions for Writing

1. Write an essay in which you propose your own rules for aging. You can be humorous like Rosenblatt or dead serious, but use a clear method of organization.

2. Choose one of the following comments and turn it into your thesis for a brief essay. Use a clear pattern of organization.

   a. Don't let the opinions of others control your life.

   b. Decide how you will react to unsolicited advice.

The Catbird Seat

JAMES THURBER

Rhetorical Thumbnail

Purpose: to amuse

Audience: educated reader

Language: standard English

Strategy: exaggerates the depiction of the main character

James Thurber (1894–1963) was an American humorist, cartoonist, and social commentator. His contributions to *The New Yorker* made him immensely popular. Among his best-known works are *My Life and Hard Times* (1933), *Fables for Our Time* (1940), and *The Thurber Carnival* (1945), from which this selection was taken.

A conventional, well-behaved office clerk suddenly finds his job threatened by an aggressive, loud-mouthed "special adviser to the president." To protect his job, this unobtrusive little man resorts to a most unusual crime.

● ● ●

1   Mr. Martin bought the pack of Camels on Monday night in the most crowded cigar store on Broadway. It was theatre time and seven or eight men were buying

cigarettes. The clerk didn't even glance at Mr. Martin, who put the pack in his overcoat pocket and went out. If any of the staff at F & S had seen him buy the cigarettes, they would have been astonished, for it was generally known that Mr. Martin did not smoke, and never had. No one saw him.

2   It was just a week to the day since Mr. Martin had decided to rub out Mrs. Ulgine Barrows. The term "rub out" pleased him because it suggested nothing more than the correction of an error—in this case an error of Mr. Fitweiler. Mr. Martin had spent each night of the past week working out his plan and examining it. As he walked home now he went over it again. For the hundredth time he resented the element of imprecision, the margin of guesswork that entered into the business. The project as he had worked it out was casual and bold, the risks were considerable. Something might go wrong anywhere along the line. And therein lay the cunning of his scheme. No one would ever see in it the cautious, painstaking hand of Erwin Martin, head of the filing department at F & S, of whom Mr. Fitweiler had once said, "Man is fallible but Martin isn't." No one would see his hand, that is, unless it were caught in the act.

3   Sitting in his apartment, drinking a glass of milk, Mr. Martin reviewed his case against Mrs. Ulgine Barrows, as he had every night for seven nights. He began at the beginning. Her quacking voice and braying laugh had first profaned the halls of F & S on March 7, 1941 (Mr. Martin had a head for dates). Old Roberts, the personnel chief, had introduced her as the newly appointed special adviser to the president of the firm, Mr. Fitweiler. The woman had appalled Mr. Martin instantly, but he hadn't shown it. He had given her his dry hand, a look of studious concentration, and a faint smile. "Well," she had said, looking at the papers on his desk, "are you lifting the oxcart out of the ditch?" As Mr. Martin recalled that moment, over his milk, he squirmed slightly. He must keep his mind on her crimes as a special adviser, not on her peccadilloes as a personality. This he found difficult to do, in spite of entering an objection and sustaining it. The faults of the woman as a woman kept chattering on in his mind like an unruly witness. She had, for almost two years now, baited him. In the halls, in the elevator, even in his own office, into which she romped now and then like a circus horse, she was constantly shouting these silly questions at him. "Are you lifting the oxcart out of the ditch? Are you tearing up the pea patch? Are you hollering down the rain barrel? Are you scraping around the bottom of the pickle barrel? Are you sitting in the catbird seat?"

4   It was Joey Hart, one of Mr. Martin's two assistants, who had explained what the gibberish meant. "She must be a Dodger fan," he had said. "Red Barber announces the Dodger games over the radio and he uses those expressions—picked 'em up down South." Joey had gone on to explain one or two. "Tearing up the pea patch" meant going on a rampage; "sitting in the catbird seat" meant sitting pretty, like a batter with three balls and no strikes on him. Mr. Martin dismissed all this with an effort. It had been annoying, it had driven him near to distraction, but he was too solid a man to be moved to murder by anything so childish. It was fortunate, he reflected as he passed on to the important charges against Mrs. Barrows, that he had stood up under it so well. He had maintained always an outward appearance of polite tolerance. "Why,

I even believe you like the woman," Miss Paird, his other assistant, had once said to him. He had simply smiled.

5   A gavel rapped in Mr. Martin's mind and the case proper was resumed. Mrs. Ulgine Barrows stood charged with willful, blatant, and persistent attempts to destroy the efficiency and system of F & S. It was competent, material, and relevant to review her advent and rise to power. Mr. Martin had got the story from Miss Paird, who seemed always able to find things out. According to her, Mrs. Barrows had met Mr. Fitweiler at a party, where she had rescued him from the embraces of a powerfully built drunken man who had mistaken the president of F & S for a famous retired Middle Western football coach. She had led him to a sofa and somehow worked upon him a monstrous magic. The aging gentleman had jumped to the conclusion there and then that this was a woman of singular attainments, equipped to bring out the best in him and in the firm. A week later he had introduced her into F & S as his special adviser. On that day confusion got its foot in the door. After Miss Tyson, Mr. Brundage, and Mr. Bartlett had been fired and Mr. Munson had taken his hat and stalked out, mailing in his resignation later, old Roberts had been emboldened to speak to Mr. Fitweiler. He mentioned that Mr. Munson's department had been "a little disrupted" and hadn't they perhaps better resume the old system there? Mr. Fitweiler had said certainly not. He had the greatest faith in Mrs. Barrows' ideas. "They require a little seasoning, a little seasoning, is all," he had added. Mr. Roberts had given it up. Mr. Martin reviewed in detail all the changes wrought by Mrs. Barrows. She had begun chipping at the cornices of the firm's edifice and now she was swinging at the foundation stones with a pickaxe.

6   Mr. Martin came now, in his summing up, to the afternoon of Monday, November 2, 1942—just one week ago. On that day, at 3 P.M., Mrs. Barrows had bounced into his office. "Boo!" she had yelled. "Are you scraping around the bottom of the pickle barrel?" Mr. Martin had looked at her from under his green eyeshade, saying nothing. She had begun to wander about the office, taking it in with her great, popping eyes. "Do you really need all these filing cabinets?" she had demanded suddenly. Mr. Martin's heart had jumped. "Each of these files," he had said, keeping his voice even, "plays an indispensable part in the system of F & S." She had brayed at him, "Well, don't tear up the pea patch!" and gone to the door. From there she had bawled, "But you sure have got a lot of fine scrap in here!" Mr. Martin could no longer doubt that the finger was on his beloved department. Her pickaxe was on the upswing, poised for the first blow. It had not come yet; he had received no blue memo from the enchanted Mr. Fitweiler bearing nonsensical instructions deriving from the obscene woman. But there was no doubt in Mr. Martin's mind that one would be forthcoming. He must act quickly. Already a precious week had gone by. Mr. Martin stood up in his living room, still holding his milk glass. "Gentlemen of the jury" he said to himself, "I demand the death penalty for this horrible person."

7   The next day Mr. Martin followed his routine, as usual. He polished his glasses more often and once sharpened an already-sharp pencil, but not even Miss Paird noticed. Only once did he catch sight of his victim; she swept past him in the hall with a patronizing "Hi!" At five-thirty he walked home, as usual,

and had a glass of milk, as usual. He had never drunk anything stronger in his life—unless you could count ginger ale. The late Sam Schlosser, the S of F & S, had praised Mr. Martin at a staff meeting several years before for his temperate habits. "Our most efficient worker neither drinks nor smokes," he had said. "The results speak for themselves." Mr. Fitweiler had sat by, nodding approval.

8   Mr. Martin was still thinking about that red-letter day as he walked over to the Schrafft's on Fifth Avenue near Forty-sixth Street. He got there, as he always did, at eight o'clock. He finished his dinner and the financial page of *The Sun* at a quarter to nine, as he always did. It was his custom after dinner to take a walk. This time he walked down Fifth Avenue at a casual pace. His gloved hands felt moist and warm, his forehead cold. He transferred the Camels from his overcoat to a jacket pocket. He wondered, as he did so, if they did not represent an unnecessary note of strain. Mrs. Barrows smoked only Luckies. It was his idea to puff a few puffs on a Camel (after the rubbing out), stub it out in the ashtray holding her lipstick-stained Luckies, and thus drag a small red herring across the trail. Perhaps it was not a good idea. It would take time. He might even choke, too loudly.

9   Mr. Martin had never seen the house on West Twelfth Street where Mrs. Barrows lived, but he had a clear enough picture of it. Fortunately, she had bragged to everybody about her ducky first-floor apartment in the perfectly darling three-story red-brick. There would be no doorman or other attendants; just the tenants of the second and third floors. As he walked along, Mr. Martin realized that he would get there before nine-thirty. He had considered walking north on Fifth Avenue from Schrafft's to a point from which it would take him until ten o'clock to reach the house. At that hour people were less likely to be coming in or going out. But the procedure would have made an awkward loop in the straight thread of his casualness, and he had abandoned it. It was impossible to figure when people would be entering or leaving the house, anyway. There was a great risk at any hour. If he ran into anybody, he would simply have to place the rubbing-out of Ulgine Barrows in the inactive file forever. The same thing would hold true if there were someone in her apartment. In that case he would just say that he had been passing by, recognized her charming house, and thought to drop in.

10   It was eighteen minutes after nine when Mr. Martin turned into Twelfth Street. A man passed him, and a man and a woman, talking. There was no one within fifty paces when he came to the house, halfway down the block. He was up the steps and in the small vestibule in no time, pressing the bell under the card that said "Mrs. Ulgine Barrows." When the clicking in the lock started, he jumped forward against the door. He got inside fast, closing the door behind him. A bulb in a lantern hung from the hall ceiling on a chain seemed to give a monstrously bright light. There was nobody on the stair, which went up ahead of him along the left wall. A door opened down the hall in the wall on the right. He went toward it swiftly, on tiptoe.

11   "Well, for God's sake, look who's here!" bawled Mrs. Barrows, and her braying laugh rang out like the report of a shotgun. He rushed past her like a football tackle, bumping her. "Hey, quit shoving!" she said, closing the door behind them. They were in her living room, which seemed to Mr. Martin to be lighted by a hundred lamps. "What's after you?" she said. "You're as jumpy as a goat." He found he was unable to speak. His heart was wheezing in his throat. "I—yes,"

he finally brought out. She was jabbering and laughing as she started to help him off with his coat. "No, no," he said. "I'll put it here." He took it off and put it on a chair near the door. "Your hat and gloves, too," she said. "You're in a lady's house." He put his hat on top of the coat. Mrs. Barrows seemed larger than he had thought. He kept his gloves on. "I was passing by," he said. "I recognized— is there anyone here?" She laughed louder than ever. "No," she said, "we're all alone. You're as white as a sheet, you funny man. Whatever has come over you? I'll mix you a toddy." She started toward a door across the room. "Scotch-and-soda be all right? But say, you don't drink, do you?" She turned and gave him her amused look. Mr. Martin pulled himself together. "Scotch-and-soda will be all right," he heard himself say. He could hear her laughing in the kitchen.

12   Mr. Martin looked quickly around the living room for the weapon. He had counted on finding one there. There were andirons and a poker and something in a corner that looked like an Indian club. None of them would do. It couldn't be that way. He began to pace around. He came to a desk. On it lay a metal paper knife with an ornate handle. Would it be sharp enough? He reached for it and knocked over a small brass jar. Stamps spilled out of it and it fell to the floor with a clatter. "Hey," Mrs. Barrows yelled from the kitchen, "are you tearing up the pea patch?" Mr. Martin gave a strange laugh. Picking up the knife, he tried its point against his left wrist. It was blunt. It wouldn't do.

13   When Mrs. Barrows reappeared, carrying two highballs, Mr. Martin, standing there with his gloves on, became acutely conscious of the fantasy he had wrought. Cigarettes in his pocket, a drink prepared for him—it was all too grossly improbable. It was more than that; it was impossible. Somewhere in the back of his mind a vague idea stirred, sprouted. "For heaven's sake, take off those gloves," said Mrs. Barrows. "I always wear them in the house," said Mr. Martin. The idea began to bloom, strange and wonderful. She put the glasses on a coffee table in front of a sofa and sat on the sofa. "Come over here, you odd little man," she said. Mr. Martin went over and sat beside her. It was difficult getting a cigarette out of the pack of Camels, but he managed it. She held a match for him, laughing. "Well," she said, handing him a drink, "this is perfectly marvelous. You with a drink and a cigarette."

14   Martin puffed, not too awkwardly, and took a gulp of the highball. "I drink and smoke all the time," he said. He clinked his glass against hers. "Here's nuts to that old windbag, Fitweiler," he said, and gulped again. The stuff tasted awful, but he made no grimace. "Really, Mr. Martin," she said, her voice and posture changing, "you are insulting our employer." Mrs. Barrows was now all special adviser to the president. "I am preparing a bomb," said Mr. Martin, "which will blow the old goat higher than hell." He had only had a little of the drink, which was not strong. It couldn't be that. "Do you take dope or something?" Mrs. Barrows asked coldly. "Heroin," said Mr. Martin. "I'll be coked to the gills when I bump that old buzzard off." "Mr. Martin!" she shouted, getting to her feet. "That will be all of that. You must go at once." Mr. Martin took another swallow of his drink. He tapped his cigarette out in the ashtray and put the pack of Camels on the coffee table. Then he got up. She stood glaring at him. He walked over and put on his hat and coat. "Not a word about this," he said, and laid an index finger against his lips. All Mrs. Barrows could bring out was

"Really!" Mr. Martin put his hand on the doorknob. "I'm sitting in the catbird seat," he said. He stuck his tongue out at her and left. Nobody saw him go.

15   Mr. Martin got to his apartment, walking, well before eleven. No one saw him go in. He had two glasses of milk after brushing his teeth, and he felt elated. It wasn't tipsiness, because he hadn't been tipsy. Anyway, the walk had worn off all effects of the whiskey. He got in bed and read a magazine for a while. He was asleep before midnight.

16   Mr. Martin got to the office at eight-thirty the next morning, as usual. At a quarter to nine, Ulgine Barrows, who had never before arrived at work before ten, swept into his office. "I'm reporting to Mr. Fitweiler now!" she shouted. "If he turns you over to the police, it's no more than you deserve!" Mr. Martin gave her a look of shocked surprise. "I beg your pardon?" he said. Mrs. Barrows snorted and bounced out of the room, leaving Miss Paird and Joey Hart staring after her. "What's the matter with that old devil now?" asked Miss Paird. "I have no idea," said Mr. Martin, resuming his work. The other two looked at him and then at each other. Miss Paird got up and went out. She walked slowly past the closed door of Mr. Fitweiler's office. Mrs. Barrows was yelling inside, but she was not braying. Miss Paird could not hear what the woman was saying. She went back to her desk.

17   Forty-five minutes later, Mrs. Barrows left the president's office and went into her own, shutting the door. It wasn't until half an hour later that Mr. Fitweiler sent for Mr. Martin. The head of the filing department, neat, quiet, attentive, stood in front of the old man's desk. Mr. Fitweiler was pale and nervous. He took his glasses off and twiddled them. He made a small, bruffing sound in his throat. "Martin," he said, "you have been with us more than twenty years." "Twenty-two, sir," said Mr. Martin. "In that time," pursued the president, "your work and your—uh—manner have been exemplary." "I trust so, sir," said Mr. Martin. "I have understood, Martin," said Mr. Fitweiler, "that you have never taken a drink or smoked." "That is correct, sir," said Mr. Martin. "Ah, yes." Mr. Fitweiler polished his glasses. "You may describe what you did after leaving the office yesterday, Martin," he said. Mr. Martin allowed less than a second for his bewildered pause. "Certainly, sir," he said. "I walked home. Then I went to Schrafft's for dinner. Afterward I walked home again. I went to bed early, sir, and read a magazine for a while. I was asleep before eleven." "Ah, yes," said Mr. Fitweiler again. He was silent for a moment, searching for the proper words to say to the head of the filing department. "Mrs. Barrows," he said finally, "Mrs. Barrows has worked hard, Martin, very hard. It grieves me to report that she has suffered a severe breakdown. It has taken the form of a persecution complex accompanied by distressing hallucinations." "I am very sorry, sir," said Mr. Martin. "Mrs. Barrows is under the delusion," continued Mr. Fitweiler, "that you visited her last evening and behaved yourself in an—uh—unseemly manner." He raised his hand to silence Mr. Martin's little pained outcry. "It is the nature of these psychological diseases," Mr. Fitweiler said, "to fix upon the least likely and most innocent party as the—uh—source of persecution. These matters are not for the lay mind to grasp, Martin. I've just had my psychiatrist, Dr. Fitch, on the phone. He would not, of course, commit himself, but he made enough generalizations to substantiate my suspicions. I suggested

to Mrs. Barrows, when she had completed her—uh—story to me this morning, that she visit Dr. Fitch, for I suspected a condition at once. She flew, I regret to say, into a rage, and demanded—uh—requested that I call you on the carpet. You may not know, Martin, but Mrs. Barrows had planned a reorganization of your department—subject to my approval, of course, subject to my approval. This brought you, rather than anyone else, to her mind—but again that is a phenomenon for Dr. Fitch and not for us. So, Martin, I am afraid Mrs. Barrows' usefulness here is at an end." "I am dreadfully sorry, sir," said Mr. Martin.

18   It was at this point that the door to the office blew open with the suddenness of a gas-main explosion and Mrs. Barrows catapulted through it. "Is the little rat denying it?" she screamed. "He can't get away with that!" Mr. Martin got up and moved discreetly to a point beside Mr. Fitweiler's chair. "You drank and smoked at my apartment," she bawled at Mr. Martin, "and you know it! You called Mr. Fitweiler an old windbag and said you were going to blow him up when you got coked to the gills on your heroin!" She stopped yelling to catch her breath and a new glint came into her popping eyes. "If you weren't such a drab, ordinary little man," she said, "I'd think you'd planned it all. Sticking your tongue out, saying you were sitting in the catbird seat, because you thought no one would believe me when I told it! My God, it's really too perfect!" She glared at Mr. Fitweiler. "Can't you see how he has tricked us, you old fool? Can't you see his little game?" But Mr. Fitweiler had been surreptitiously pressing all the buttons under the top of his desk and employees of F & S began pouring into the room. "Stockton," said Mr. Fitweiler, "you and Fishbein will take Mrs. Barrows to her home. Mrs. Powell, you will go with them." Stockton, who had played a little football in high school, blocked Mrs. Barrows as she made for Mr. Martin. It took him and Fishbein together to force her out of the door into the hall, crowded with stenographers and office boys. She was still screaming imprecations at Mr. Martin, tangled and contradictory imprecations. The hubbub finally died out down the corridor.

19   "I regret that this has happened," said Mr. Fitweiler. "I shall ask you to dismiss it from your mind, Martin." "Yes, sir," said Mr. Martin, anticipating his chief's "That will be all" by moving to the door. "I will dismiss it." He went out and shut the door, and his step was light and quick in the hall. When he entered his department he had slowed down to his customary gait, and he walked quietly across the room to the W20 file, wearing a look of studious concentration.

● Vocabulary

fallible (2)	patronizing (7)	bruffing (17)
appalled (3)	temperate (7)	exemplary (17)
peccadilloes (3)	red herring (8)	hallucinations (17)
romped (3)	ducky (9)	unseemly (17)
gibberish (4)	monstrously (10)	catapulted (18)
edifice (5)	wheezing (11)	surreptitiously (18)
indispensable (6)	grossly (13)	imprecations (18)
obscene (6)		

● The Facts

1. What is the origin of the colorful expressions that Mrs. Barrows constantly uses?
2. What is Mrs. Barrows's title in the firm of F & S?
3. Why does Mr. Martin finally decide to "rub out" Mrs. Barrows?
4. What shocking disclosures does Mr. Martin make to Mrs. Barrows on his surprise visit to her apartment?
5. What is the outcome of Mrs. Barrows's accusations against Mr. Martin?

● The Strategies

1. The organization of the story falls naturally into four divisions: (a) the trial and verdict of Mrs. Barrows, (b) preparation for the crime, (c) change of plan and perpetration of the crime, and (d) result of the crime. Summarize what happens in each of these segments.
2. Early in the story, the author tells us that Mr. Martin plans to kill Mrs. Barrows. Why does this announcement not eliminate suspense from the story?
3. What is the emotional climax of the story?
4. How does Thurber prepare us for Mr. Fitweiler's incredulous reaction to Mrs. Barrows's story about Mr. Martin? Why are we amused but not surprised at Mr. Fitweiler's reaction?

● The Issues

1. What obvious contrasts between Mr. Martin and Mrs. Barrows does Thurber draw?
2. What is your view of the morality of Mr. Martin's actions? Was he justified in his extreme steps or not? Build a clear case for your opinion.
3. How does Mrs. Barrows's character reinforce an ancient sexual stereotype about women? How would you characterize this stereotype?
4. If this story were set in an office today rather than in the 1940s, would it be as believable? Why or why not?
5. Reverse the characters of Mrs. Barrows and Mr. Martin: She is now the fastidious head of the filing department; he the brassy opportunist who has ingratiated himself in the good graces of the boss, Fitweiler. Does the story still work? Why or why not?

● Suggestions for Writing

1. Write a short caricature about one of your close friends and exaggerate his or her traits.
2. Write an essay analyzing the humorous devices used by Thurber in the story "The Catbird Seat." Pay attention to such factors as character, plot reversal, and style.

That Time of Year (Sonnet 73)

WILLIAM SHAKESPEARE

William Shakespeare (1564–1616) is generally acknowledged as the greatest literary genius of the English language. Born in Stratford-upon-Avon, England, he was the son of a prosperous businessman, and probably attended grammar schools in his native town. In 1582, Shakespeare married Anne Hathaway, who was eight years his senior, and who bore him three children. The legacy of his writing includes 36 plays, 154 sonnets, and 5 long poems.

The English or Shakespearean sonnet is composed of three quatrains of four lines each and a concluding couplet of two lines, rhyming abab cdcd efef gg. There is usually a correspondence between the units marked off by the rhymes and the development of the thought. The three quatrains, for instance, may represent three different images or three questions from which a conclusion is drawn in the final couplet. As a result, the sonnet is one of the most tightly organized poetic forms used.

● ● ●

That time of year thou mayst in me behold
When yellow leaves, or none, or few, do hang
Upon those boughs which shake against the cold,
Bare ruined choirs where late the sweet birds sang.
5   In me thou see'st the twilight of such day
As after sunset fadeth in the west,
Which by and by black night doth take away,
Death's second self, that seals up all in rest.
In me thou see'st the glowing of such fire,
10   That on the ashes of his youth doth lie
As the deathbed whereon it must expire,
Consumed with that which it was nourished by.
This thou perceivest, which makes thy love more strong,
To love that well which thou must leave ere long.

● The Facts

1. What image does the poet focus on in the first quatrain? What relationship does this image have to the speaker?

2. The speaker shifts to another image in the second quatrain. What is it, and what relationship does it bear to him?

3. Yet another image is introduced in the third quatrain. What is the image, and how does it relate to the speaker? What rather complex philosophical paradox is involved?

4. The final couplet states the poet's thesis (or theme). What is that thesis? State it in your own words.

● The Strategies

1. The entire poem is organized around three analogies. State them in three succinct sentences.

2. The three images in the poem are presented in a particular order. Do you see any reason for this order?

3. In lines 3 and 4, what effect do the words "cold,/Bare ruined choirs" have on the rhythm and meter?

4. In line 2, what would be the result of substituting "hang" for "do hang"?

5. What is the antecedent of "this" in line 13?

● The Issues

1. What can you deduce from this poem about the speaker and his frame of mind?

2. Someone once said, "Youth is wasted on the young." How might that witticism be applied to this poem?

3. Why should a student whose major is, say, business and who has no interest whatsoever in literature be forced to take classes in which poems such as this one are studied?

4. Shakespeare has been called surprisingly modern in his outlook. What about this poem would seem to justify that observation?

● Suggestions for Writing

1. In two or three well-developed paragraphs, challenge or defend the claim that too much money is spent on extending the lives of old people.

2. Write an essay about a memorable older person.

● CHAPTER WRITING ASSIGNMENTS

1. Write a well-organized essay in which you describe your conflicting attitudes about some aspect of society that puzzles you or to which you have no clear answer.

2. Write a well-organized chronological autobiography.

3. Write an essay detailing the steps you follow when you have to complete a writing assignment.

4. Detail in a tightly organized essay any particular procedure or process (e.g., how to send digital photographs via email) with which you are intimately familiar.

● WRITING ASSIGNMENTS FOR A SPECIFIC AUDIENCE

1. Write an essay of appreciation directed at your favorite teacher—from any grade—telling how he or she affected your life.

2. Write an essay, after doing the necessary research, telling an audience of high-school dropouts the opportunities available to them for continuing their education.

REAL-LIFE STUDENT WRITING

Note from a Graduate Student to a Department Secretary

The following note was written by a student named Jennifer, who is in the graduate school program of a well-known Catholic university. Katie is the department secretary of the business school. Jennifer is writing to Katie to ask for her help in getting registered in a statistics class. Notice the polite social remarks Jennifer makes before saying what she really wants. Jeff is Katie's new husband. Bailey is Jennifer's boyfriend.

• • •

Hi Katie!

Welcome back from your honeymoon! Hope married life is treating you well. Bailey said he ran into ya'll last night, and Jeff's wig was realistically scary. Wish I could have seen it.

Lucinda sent me to you on an issue I'm having. I keep trying to register for classes in the business school for next quarter, but the system won't let me in! Lucinda said something about how they've changed their criteria. I wonder if I could be using the wrong password. I heard it was due to be changed, but I haven't seen any memo telling us that it had been. Meantime, I need to register for business statistics ASAP! As department secretary, you're my last hope.

Can you help me?

Thanks!

Jennifer

7

Developing Good Paragraphs

From ancient times, the primary use of the paragraph has been to signal the introduction of a new idea or the further development of an old one. Here is an example of a paragraph signaling a new idea:

> In the modern formal bullfight or "corrida de toros" there are usually six bulls that are killed by three different men. Each man kills two bulls. The bulls by law are required to be from four to five years old, free from physical defects, and well armed with sharp-pointed horns. They are inspected by a municipal veterinary surgeon before the fight. The veterinary is supposed to reject bulls that are under age, insufficiently armed or with anything wrong with their eyes, their horns or any apparent disease or visible bodily defects such as lameness.
>
> The men who are to kill them are called matadors and which of the six bulls they are to kill is determined by lot. Each matador, or killer, has a caudrilla, or team, of from five to six men who are paid by him and work under his orders. Three of these men, who aid him on foot with capes and at his orders place the banderillas, three-foot wooden sharps with harpoon points, are called peones or banderilleros. The other two, who are mounted on horses when they appear in the ring, are called picadors.
>
> —Ernest Hemingway, *The Bullfight*

The shift in discussion between the first and second paragraph is obvious: Paragraph 1 is about the bulls; paragraph 2 is about the men who will fight and kill them.

A second use of the paragraph is to add significantly to or elaborate on what has been said in a preceding paragraph. Here is an example:

> The oxen in Africa have carried the heavy load of the advance of European civilization. Wherever new land has been broken they have broken it, panting and pulling knee-deep in the soil before the ploughs, the

long whips in the air over them. Where a road has been made they have made it; and they have trudged the iron and tools through the land, to the yelling and shouting of the drivers, by tracks in the dust and the long grass of the plains, before there ever were any roads. They have been inspanned before daybreak, and have sweated up and down the long hills, and across dungas and riverbeds, through the burning hours of the day. The whips have marked their sides, and you will often see oxen that have had an eye, or both of them, taken away by the long cutting whip-lashes. The waggon-oxen of many Indian and white contractors worked every day, all their lives through, and did not know of the Sabbath.

It is a strange thing that we have done to the oxen. The bull is in a constant stage of fury, rolling his eyes, shovelling up the earth, upset by everything that gets within his range of vision—still he has got a life of his own, fire comes from his nostrils, and new life from his loins; his days are filled with his vital cravings and satisfactions. All of that we have taken away from the oxen, and in reward we have claimed their existence for ourselves. The oxen walk along within our own daily life, pulling hard all the time, creatures without a life, things made for our use. They have moist, limpid, violet eyes, soft muzzles, silky ears, they are patient and dull in all their ways; sometimes they look as if they were thinking about things.

—Isak Dinesen, *Out of Africa*

In the first paragraph the author points out that oxen have played a key role in civilizing the African continent. In the second paragraph she elaborates on the first by reminding us that the oxen's patient subservience has come at a price.

Parts of the Paragraph

A paragraph generally consists of two main parts: a topic sentence and specific details that support it.

The Topic Sentence This is the sentence that tells us what the writer intends to propose, argue, or demonstrate. In the following paragraph, the topic sentence is highlighted.

> To all English-speaking peoples the Bible is a national as well as a noble monument, for much of their history is securely rooted and anchored within it. In 17th century England it nurtured the Puritan revolt and paved the way for the Bill of Rights. In 17th and 18th century America it supplied not only the names of our ancestors but the stout precepts by which they lived. They walked by its guidance; their rough places were made plain by their trust in its compassionate promises. It was a lamp to their feet and a light to their path, a pillar of cloud by day and of fire by night. It was the source of the convictions that shaped the building of this country, of the faith that endured the first New England winters and later

opened up the Great West. It laid the foundations of our educational system, built our earliest colleges, and dictated the training within our homes. In the words alike of Jefferson and Patrick Henry, John Quincy Adams and Franklin it made better and more useful citizens to their country by reminding a man of his individual responsibility, his own dignity, and his equality with his fellow man. The Bible is, indeed, so imbedded in our American heritage that not to recognize its place there becomes a kind of national apostasy, and not to know and understand it, in these days when we give all for its principles of human worth and human freedom, an act unworthy of us as a people.

—Mary Ellen Chase, *The Bible and the Common Reader*

Implied Topic Sentences Some paragraphs have an implied topic sentence, also known as a controlling idea. Here is an example:

At graveside, the casket is lowered into the earth. This office, once the prerogative of friends of the deceased, is now performed by a patented mechanical lowering device. A "Lifetime Green" artificial grass mat is at the ready to conceal the sere earth, and overhead, to conceal the sky, is a portable Steril Chapel Tent ("resists the intense heat and humidity of summer and the terrific storms of winter. . . available in Silver Grey, Rose or Evergreen"). Now is the time for the ritual scattering of earth over the coffin, as the solemn words "earth to earth, ashes to ashes, dust to dust" are pronounced by the officiating cleric. This can be accomplished "with a mere flick of the wrist with the Gordon Leak-proof Earth Dispenser. No grasping of a handful of dirt, no soiled fingers. Simple, dignified, beautiful, reverent! The modern way!" The Gordon Earth Dispenser (at $5) is of nickel-plated brass construction. It is not only "attractive to the eye and long wearing"; it is also "one of the 'tools' for building better public relations" if presented as "an appropriate noncommercial gift" to the clergyman. It is shaped something like a saltshaker.

—Jessica Mitford, *The American Way of Death*

The controlling idea of this paragraph is that the funeral industry is guilty of vulgar commercialism. The details amply support that point, and the writer's focus is clear even though she uses no topic sentence. A writer does not have to telegraph a paragraph's meaning in an explicit topic sentence so long as all its details are linked by some organizing theme or focus.

Supporting Details

Good paragraphs are filled with supporting facts, instances, examples, and details. They make a point and then adequately support it. They do not circle the subject, nor do they repeat at the same level of generality what the writer has already said. Here are two examples. In both examples, the topic sentence is highlighted. We made up the first example as a dramatic illustration of the repetitive writing often found in bad paragraphs, where the main point is restated over and over at the same level of generality:

> Rotten writing is scarcely a new problem. People have always had bad handwriting. Some old manuscripts are difficult to read because they are so badly written. Old letters are also indecipherable. Some writing from the past looks as if a drunken chicken had walked over it. Strain as much as you might, you just can't tell what the writer meant. Inscriptions of various kinds are just as impossible to read.

Has the point of this paragraph—that "rotten writing is scarcely a new problem"—been proved? It has not. The paragraph simply says that people have always written badly but gives no concrete instances or facts to make this assertion believable.

Here, on the other hand, is a paragraph that begins with the same generalization and then proves it with facts and examples drawn from the past:

> Bad handwriting is scarcely a new problem. The original draft of the Declaration of Independence was scribbled over so much that at first glance it is difficult to see its renowned "elegance." Horace Greeley, the venerated 19th-century editor of the *New York Tribune,* had such a terrible handwriting that a note to a reporter, telling him he was fired for gross incompetence, was so indecipherable that for years to come this reporter used it as a letter of recommendation. Robert Frost, one of New England's most celebrated poets, had such bad penmanship, that occasionally it made him seem dyslexic and senseless. It is said that the poet William Butler Yeats couldn't read his own handwriting because it was so illegible. Scholars have spent years trying accurately to transcribe the handwritten manuscripts of famous authors—from David Thoreau to Henry James. The mistakes that keep coming to life in printed page proofs speak of the difficult task involved in reproducing badly written sentences. Usually it takes several eyes to complete the task of transcribing the crabbed and cramped penmanship of important writers.
>
> —Jeffrey O. Sorensen

Paragraphs with a Final Summing-up Sentence Some paragraphs begin and end with a generalization. The first generalization is the topic sentence; the second is a summary. Here is an example:

> A language changes because things happen to people. If we could imagine the impossible—a society in which nothing happened—there would be no changes in language. But except possibly in a cemetery, things are constantly happening to people: they eat, drink, sleep, talk, make love, meet strangers, struggle against natural perils, and fight against one another. They slowly adapt their language to meet the changing conditions of their lives. Although the changes made in one generation may be small, those made in a dozen generations may enormously affect the language.

The big and little phases of history, fashions, fads, inventions, the influence of a leader, a war or two, an invasion or two, travel to a foreign land, the demands of business intercourse—may alter a language so much that a Rip Van Winkle who slept two or three hundred years might have trouble making himself understood when he awoke. Even in a relatively quiet society, linguistic change proceeds inexorably.

—J. N. Hook and E. G. Mathews, *Modern American Grammar and Usage*

Topic Sentence Developed over More Than One Paragraph

A single topic sentence can also be developed over the course of two or more paragraphs. This development usually occurs when the topic sentence is too broad or complex to be adequately covered in a single paragraph or when the presentation of supporting details in several paragraphs is more emphatic. In the following example, a topic sentence is developed over two paragraphs. The topic sentence is highlighted:

There has always been something so fascinating about the mere fact of fatness that men of all nations and of many degrees of wisdom or lack of it have formulated opinions on its state, its origins, and its correction. Shakespeare's characters are at their most eloquent when the topic is obesity. "Make less thy body and hence more thy grace. Leave gormandizing. Know the grave cloth gape for thee thrice wider than for other men." And, of course, to Julius Caesar, the Bard attributed the notion of the harmlessness of fat companions in warning against "the lean and hungry look" of "yon Cassius."

In *Coming Up for Air*, George Orwell has the narrator, himself a fat man, sum it up: "They all think a fat man isn't quite like other men. He goes through life on a light-comedy plane . . . as low farce." Sometimes the situation is just as sad and much less tolerable. When W. D. Howells was consul at Venice, he was told by a tall, lanky man, "If I were as fat as you, I would hang myself." And Osborn in his otherwise lightly satirical picture-essay, *The Vulgarians*, pontificates, "The fat and the fatuous are interchangeable."

—Jean Mayer, *Overweight: Causes, Cost, and Control*

Covering a topic sentence in more than one paragraph allows for a fuller development of the general idea, but it also tempts the writer to stray from the point. Beginning writers will find it safer to use a separate topic sentence for each paragraph.

Position of the Topic Sentence

As the sum of what a paragraph is about, the topic sentence should naturally occupy a prominent position, and in all of our examples so far, the topic sentence has come first. Such a paragraph is said to be organized from the general to the particular: the idea first, followed by the particulars. The reverse of this arrangement is the paragraph organized from the particular to the general: The supporting details come first and the topic sentence last. Here is an example:

> The human population already stands at over 4 billion, and at current growth rates that number will double within thirty-eight years. If the growth rate were to continue unchecked, in fact, the global population would reach about 150 billion within two centuries. Yet nearly two-thirds of the existing inhabitants of the earth are undernourished or malnourished, and they are dying of starvation at the rate of more than 10 million every year. There can be little question that unchecked population growth is the most critical social problem in the modern world, with potential consequences in terms of sheer human misery that are almost unimaginable.
>
> —Ian Robertson, *Sociology*

This arrangement is an uncommon one and somewhat mannered. Before you can cite details in support of an idea, you must first know the idea. Consequently, it has become traditional for writers to first state the general idea of a paragraph and then cite details in support of it—this pattern conforms to the way people usually think. The paragraph in which the topic sentence appears after the supporting details should be used only as a change of pace, not as a matter of course.

Finally, some paragraphs have topic sentences that come not first or last, but second or third. Paragraphs of this kind are usually found in the middle of an essay. The initial sentences are used to ensure a smooth transition from the preceding paragraph, and then the topic sentence makes its appearance. In the following example, the topic sentence is highlighted:

> In our own *way*, we conform as best we can to the rest of nature. The obituary pages tell us of the news that we are dying off, while the birth announcements in finer print, off at the side of the page, inform us of our replacements, but we get no grasp from this of the enormity of scale. There are 3 billion of us on the earth, and all 3 billion must be dead, on schedule, within this lifetime. The vast mortality, involving something over 50 million of us each year, takes place in relative secrecy. We can only really know of the deaths in our households, or among our friends. These, detached in our minds from the rest, we take to be unnatural events, anomalies, outrages. We speak of our own dead in low voices; struck down, we say, as though visible death can only occur for cause, by disease, or violence, avoidably. We send off flowers, grieve, make ceremonies, scatter bones, unaware of the rest of the 3 billion on the same schedule. All that immense mass of flesh and bone and consciousness will disappear by absorption into the earth, without recognition by the transient survivors.
>
> —Lewis Thomas, *Death in the Open*

The first sentence is for transition—to connect this paragraph with the one before. The second sentence is the topic sentence. It contains the assertion that the supporting details prove.

Paragraph Patterns

Paragraphs are often written to conform to certain abstract patterns that are partly rhetorical and partly based on some common operations of thinking. You might, for example, write a paragraph drawing a contrast between two animals, two objects, or two people. Or, you might write a paragraph explaining why an incident occurred or predicting what is likely to happen if something is done or left undone. In the first case, you would develop the paragraph by a pattern of comparison and contrast; in the second, by causal analysis.

In Part Two of this book, we shall focus on how to write paragraphs—even entire essays—by these patterns. We shall explain the paragraph-writing techniques used to compare and contrast, analyze cause, narrate, describe, illustrate, define, classify, and explain process. But for now, we mention these patterns to emphasize this point: No matter what its developmental pattern, any paragraph you write must support its main idea with specific details.

Characteristics of a Well-Designed Paragraph

The characteristics of the well-designed paragraph are unity, coherence, and completeness.

Unity   A paragraph is said to have unity when its sentences stick to the topic and do not stray to secondary issues or deal with irrelevancies. Here's an example of a paragraph that lacks unity:

> (1) A fairy tale is a serious story with a human hero and a happy ending. (2) The hero in a fairy tale is different from the hero in a tragedy in that his progression is from bad to good fortune, rather than the reverse. (3) In the Greek tragedy "Oedipus Rex," for example, the hero goes from highest fortune to lowest misery, but in the end he recognizes his error in judgment and maintains a noble posture despite profound suffering. (4) The audience watching him is purged of pity and fear through what Aristotle labeled a "catharsis." (5) The hero in a fairy tale usually has a miserable beginning. (6) He is either socially obscure or despised as being stupid and lacking in heroic virtues. (7) But in the end, he has surprised everyone by demonstrating his courage, consequently winning fame, riches, and love. (8) We clearly see this bad-to-good-fortune progress in stories like "Cinderella," "Sleeping Beauty," and "The Frog Prince."

The topic sentence of the paragraph promises to give a definition of a fairy tale, but part of the paragraph drifts away from the definition. Sentences 3 and 4 (highlighted) are entirely beside the point. With the fifth sentence, the writer resumes the announced intent of the paragraph—to define a fairy tale.

The possible causes of this fault are several. Some digressions can be traced to a writer's daydreaming; some to boredom with the topic on hand; some to a desire to impress the reader by introducing an interesting but irrelevant point. The cure is not easy to prescribe. The inexperienced writer needs to remember that the purpose of the paragraph is announced in the topic sentence, and it is this purpose that the other sentences of the paragraph must carry out.

Coherence A paragraph has coherence when its sentences are logically connected. However, sentences are not automatically linked simply because they follow one after another on the page. Four devices can be used to ensure paragraph coherence:

1. Transitional words and phrases
2. Pronoun reference
3. Repeated key terms
4. Parallelism

Transitional words and phrases, which point out the direction of the paragraph, are used to link sentences. Here are examples, highlighted:

> In addition to the academic traditionalism in schools, there are other problems. First, there is the problem of coordinating education with the realities of the world of work. Second, there is the question of how long the schooling period should be. Despite evidence to the contrary, a case can be made for the notion that we not only overeducate our children, but also take too long to do it.

The highlighted words and phrases add coherence to the passage. They join sentences and consequently ideas in clear and logical relationships. Without the use of transitional words and phrases, the writing would seem choppy and the relationships between sentences unclear.

Coherence can also be achieved by *pronoun reference*. A noun is used in one sentence or clause and a pronoun that refers to it is used in the next sentence or clause. In the following paragraph the pronouns so used are highlighted:

> Twenty years ago, women were a majority of the population, but they were treated like a minority group. The prejudice against them was so deep-rooted that, paradoxically, most people pretended that it did not exist. Indeed, most women preferred to ignore the situation rather than to rock the boat. They accepted being paid less for doing the same work as men. They were as quick as any male to condemn a woman who ventured outside the limits of the roles men had assigned to females: those of toy and drudge.

Key terms may be repeated throughout the paragraph to link sentences. The key terms in the following paragraph are highlighted:

> Fantasy is not restricted to one sector of the southern California way of life; it is all-pervasive. Los Angeles restaurants and their parking lots are such million-dollar structures because they are palaces of fantasy in which the upward-moving individual comes to act out a self-mythology he or she has learned from a hero of the mass media. Often enough, the establishments of La Cienega Boulevard's Restaurant Row are fantasies of history in their very architecture.

Parallelism is also used to ensure coherence, although not nearly so often as any of the other three devices. The principle behind parallelism is that similar ideas are expressed in structurally similar sentences. Here is a paragraph that uses parallelism to ensure coherence:

> Now, I will not for a moment deny that getting ahead of your neighbor is delightful, but it is not the only delight of which human beings are capable. There are innumerable things which are not competitive. It is possible to enjoy food and drink without having to reflect that you have a better cook and a better wine merchant than your former friends whom you are learning to cold-shoulder. It is possible to be fond of your wife and children without reflecting how much better she dresses than Mrs. So-and-So and how much better they are at athletics than the children of that old stick-in-the-mud Mr. Such-and-Such. There are those who can enjoy music without thinking how cultured the other ladies in their women's club will be thinking them. There are even people who enjoy a fine day in spite of the fact that the sun shines on everybody. All these simple pleasures are destroyed as soon as competitiveness gets the upper hand.
>
> —Bertrand Russell, *The Unhappy American Way*

The repetition of "It is possible" and "There are" add bridges that smoothly connect one thought with another.

Completeness A paragraph is complete when it has provided enough details to support its topic sentence. A paragraph is incomplete when the topic sentence is not developed or when it is merely extended through repetition. In either case, the reader is burdened with useless generalizations. The following paragraph is incomplete:

> Withholding tax is a bad way to go about collecting taxes from the people in our country because this system assumes that the American people are incompetent.

This paragraph hints at an argument but then comes to a dead stop. The reader will automatically ask, "In what way or by what means does tax withholding assume that the American people are incompetent?" Without further evidence, the paragraph goes nowhere. Now read the following paragraph:

> Withholding is a bad way to go about collecting tax money, even though the figures may show that it gets results. It is bad because it implies that the individual is incapable of handling his own affairs. The government as much as says, We know that, if left to your own devices, you will fritter away your worldly goods, and tax day will catch you without cash. Or it says, We're not sure you'll come clean in your return, so we will just take the money before it reaches you, and you will be saved the trouble and fuss of being honest. This implication is an unhealthy thing to spread around, being contrary to the old American theory that the individual is a very competent little guy indeed. The whole setup of our democratic government assumes that the citizen is bright, honest, and at least as fundamentally sound as a common stock. If you start treating him as something less than that, you are going to get into deep water. The device of withholding tax money, which is clearly confiscatory, since the individual is not allowed to see, taste, or touch a certain percentage of his wages, tacitly brands him as negligent or unthrifty or immature or incompetent or dishonest, or all of those things at once. There is, furthermore, a bad psychological effect in earning money that you never get your paws on. We believe this effect to be much stronger than the government realizes. At any rate, if the American individual is in truth incapable of paying his tax all by himself, then he should certainly be regarded as incapable of voting all by himself, and the Secretary of the Treasury should accompany him into the booth to show him where to put the X.

> —E. B. White, "Withholding"

While the reader may not agree with these ideas, the writer has fulfilled his promise to show why he does not like withholding tax. He has provided clear examples and has moved from the general to the specific, keeping in mind the direction of his topic sentence. His paragraph is complete. Make your own paragraphs complete by providing enough detail to support their topic sentences.

It is an essential part of a writer's job to dig up the details necessary to make an essay complete. One source of such details, of course, is the library. Another is the Internet and its various electronic databases.

Writing Your Own Paragraphs

There is no mystery to writing good paragraphs. Begin with a topic sentence that states your opinion or proposes an idea. Back up this sentence with ample supporting details. Stick to the point of the topic sentence. Insert transitions as necessary to keep the text coherent. That, in a nutshell, is all there is to it.

The problems that arise with paragraph writing are usually problems of content rather than of technique. In other words, the writing is affected by the fact that the writer has not done the necessary research and does not understand the topic. Even gifted writers have difficulty writing on topics about which they know little. Writing does not begin when you first sit down in front of a keyboard. It actually begins when you begin to research your topic. If you are thoroughly grounded in the details of your topic, you'll find that writing paragraphs about it will be surprisingly easy.

● Exercises

1. Write a suitable topic sentence for a paragraph that would contain the following supporting details:

   a. (1) Cultivate only the best writers.

   (2) You needn't assume that just because something is in print, it is well-written.

   (3) If you fall into the habit of reading hacks or writers who have only a dulled sense for the right word, then you are not helping yourself to become a writer who is fresh and original.

   (4) Read those authors who appear in *The New Yorker*, who get good reviews in magazines like *Time,* and who haven't faded after writing one book or one play.

   b. (1) In primitive tribes this concern was limited to members of the tribe. If a man was not a member, one need not worry about whether one was behaving ethically or unethically toward him.

   (2) But as man started reflecting on his own behavior and how it affected others, he slowly began to realize that his social concerns—his ethics—must include all human beings with whom he came in contact.

   (3) Thus it can be said that a system of ethics evolved in order to ensure that man would be at peace with himself.

   c. (1) Vaccination for German measles has practically eradicated the incidence of birth defects and other complications resulting from that disease.

   (2) Smallpox vaccination has been so effective that the virus lingers only in special labs.

   (3) In the last thirty years, vaccines have all but wiped out polio in our country.

   (4) While a few people fear that some new and terrible disease will crop up for which no vaccine will be powerful enough, we can rejoice in the fact that at least the major child-killers of the past have been vanquished.

2. Provide four sentences of supporting details for each of the following topic sentences. (Make sure that the details are on a more specific level than is the topic sentence.)

   a. Many people treat their pets with a lack of respect.

   b. Buying items "on sale" often means buying lower quality.

   c. The claim that owning a credit card today adds to a student's prestige and is therefore necessary is bogus, and let me tell you why.

   d. A long commute to work can have some advantages.

   e. Today's newspaper cartoons get to the heart of social concerns.

3. Choose one of the following topics and write a paragraph about it based on a controlling idea rather than on a topic sentence:

    a. Summer camp for disabled children
    b. Typical class reunions
    c. Advantages of coming from a poor family or disadvantages of coming from an affluent family
    d. Stereotyping as revealed in movies
    e. Stopping pollution on an individual level

4. Select one sentence from the following pairs that more clearly consists of supporting details:

    a. (1) Much has been written about the afflictions of growing old.
       (2) The worst aspect of growing old is losing hearing and eyesight.
    b. (1) The average outfit for snow skiing costs $1,000.
       (2) Some popular sports are so expensive that few people can afford to compete in them.
    c. (1) In *Little Red Riding Hood* the wolf pounces on the innocent little girl, devouring her.
       (2) Children's fairy tales are filled with horrible violence.
    d. (1) Some women feel more comfortable being treated by a female rather than a male gynecologist.
       (2) For many women who are modest to begin with, to be checked for such problems as uterine or breast cancer is less traumatic when the physician is also female.
    e. (1) Too many cooks today have no idea how to prepare homemade cornbread, meat casseroles from scratch, or freshly cooked garden peas.
       (2) The market of "prepared" or "frozen" foods is replacing food that really tastes good with food that is barely appealing to the gourmet's taste buds.

5. In the following paragraphs, draw a line through any sentence that weakens paragraph unity.

    a. I agree with Thomas Jefferson that there is a natural aristocracy among human beings, based on virtue and talent. A natural aristocrat is a person who shows genuine concern for his fellow human beings and has the wisdom as well as ability to help them improve the quality of their lives. He is the kind of person to whom you would entrust your most important concerns because his decisions would be honest rather than self-serving. A natural aristocrat cannot be bought or manipulated. He will not promise what he cannot deliver. But when he makes a promise, he has virtue backed up by talent to fulfill it. Unfortunately, few political leaders today are natural aristocrats, because early in their ambitious careers they become beholden to those powers that helped them up the political ladder.

    b. In medieval society, physical strength and animal cunning were the most admired characteristics of human beings, but since the invention of gunpowder, we have come to value other qualities more highly. Now that even a physically weak person can be made strong by carrying a gun, other ingenuities have become the marks of heroic people. Of course, boxing requires physical strength and animal cunning; yet many people today admire good boxers. The qualities most admired today are intellectual acumen, leadership ability, artistic talent, and social adjustment. I find it distressing that we do not prize goodness as much as we should. After all, Lincoln's outstanding feature was goodness. If a person is not good, he is not admirable. The tournament and personal combat have been replaced by the university, the political arena, the stage, and the personality inventory as testing grounds for heroes.

6. Identify the most obvious means used to establish coherence in the following paragraphs:

   a. In general, relevancy is a facet of training rather than of education. What is taught at law school is the present law of the land, not the Napoleonic Code or even the archaic laws that have been scratched from the statute books. And at medical school, too, it is modern medical practice that is taught, that which is relevant to conditions today. And the plumber and the carpenter and the electrician and the mason learn only what is relevant to the practice of their respective trades in this day with the tools and materials that are presently available and that conform to the building code.

      —Harry Kemelman, *Common Sense in Education*

   b. The extent of personal privacy varies, but there are four degrees that can be identified. Sometimes the individual wants to be completely out of the sight and hearing of anyone else, in solitude; alone, he is in the most relaxed state of privacy. In a second situation the individual seeks the intimacy of his confidants—his family, friends, or trusted associates with whom he chooses to share his ideas and emotions. But there are still some things that he does not want to disclose, whether he is with intimates or in public. Either by personal explanation or by social convention, the individual may indicate that he does not wish certain aspects of himself discussed or noticed, at least at that particular moment. When his claim is respected by those around him, he achieves a third degree of privacy, the state of reserve. Finally, an individual sometimes goes out in public to seek privacy, for by joining groups of people who do not recognize him, he achieves anonymity, being seen but not known. Such relaxation on the street, in bars or movies or in the park constitutes still another dimension of the individual's quest for privacy.

      —Alan F. Westin, *Privacy*

   c. The motor car is, more than any other object, the expression of the nation's character and the nation's dream. In the free billowing fender, in the blinding chromium grills, in the fluid control, in the ever widening front seat, we see the flowering of the America that we know. It is of some interest to scholars and historians that the same autumn that saw the abandonment of the window crank and the adoption of the push button (removing the motorist's last necessity for physical exertion) saw also the registration of sixteen million young men of fighting age. It is of deep interest to me that in the same week Japan joined the Axis, De Soto moved its clutch pedal two inches to the left—and that the announcements caused equal flurries among the people.

      —E. B. White, "The Motorcar"

7. Write a provocative introductory paragraph for an essay on one of the following topics:
   a. Female soldiers fighting in combat
   b. Rationing water or gasoline
   c. Automatic capital punishment for terrorists who take hostages
   d. Purging our language of all words with a sexist bias ("he" as a general pronoun—chairman, congressman, businessman, insurance man)
   e. Job prospects for college seniors
   f. One of today's most serious urban problems

8. Write a brief paragraph that would function as a smooth transition from one to the other of the following pairs of paragraphs:
   a. (1) The first paragraph lists activities of a male executive that are the same as activities for which the homemaker is chided (long phone conversations, coffee klatches with colleagues, unnecessary fancy luncheons).
      (2) The second paragraph indicates the differences between the two sets of activities.
   b. (1) The first paragraph provides statistics to demonstrate that thousands of poor people in America live on pet food.
      (2) The second paragraph argues that we must do something in order to solve the problem of hunger and malnutrition in America.
   c. (1) The first paragraph makes the point that many foreign countries consider Americans wasteful, extravagant, and selfish in their insistence on driving big cars.
      (2) The second paragraph holds the automobile industry responsible for shaping America's taste in cars.

ADVICE

Writing Successful Paragraphs

A. M. TIBBETTS AND CHARLENE TIBBETTS

Rhetorical Thumbnail

Purpose: to teach paragraph writing

Audience: freshman composition students

Language: standard English

Strategy: uses examples to teach mastery of the paragraph

Arnold M. Tibbetts (b. 1927) has taught English at the University of Iowa, Western Illinois University, Vanderbilt University, and the University of Illinois, Urbana. His wife, Charlene Tibbetts (b. 1921), has also taught part-time at the University of Illinois, Urbana. The Tibbettses are coauthors of Strategies of Rhetoric (1969), from which this excerpt was taken.

The proverbial warning "Don't promise more than you can deliver" applies to writing as well as to everyday life. The basis of a good paragraph, say the authors, is a promise that is made in the topic sentence and then carried out in the specific details. In this excerpt, the authors demonstrate with examples how to make and keep your "paragraph promises."

• • •

1   A paragraph is a collection of sentences that helps you fulfill your thesis (theme promise). Itself a small "theme," a paragraph should be clearly written and specific; and it should not wander or make irrelevant remarks. Each paragraph should be related in some way to the theme promise. Here are suggestions for writing successful paragraphs:

1. Get to the Point of Your Paragraph Quickly and Specifically

2   Don't waste time or words in stating your paragraph promise. Consider this good example of getting to the point—the writer is explaining the ancient Romans' technique for conquering their world:

> The technique of expansion was simple. Divide et impera [divide and conquer]: enter into solemn treaty with a neighbouring country, foment internal disorder, intervene in support of the weaker side on the pretense that Roman honour was involved, replace the legitimate ruler with a puppet, giving him the status of a subject ally; later, goad him into rebellion, seize and sack the country, burn down the temples, and carry off the captive gods to adorn a triumph. Conquered territories were placed under the control of a provincial governor-general, an ex-commander-in-chief who garrisoned it, levied taxes, set up courts of summary justice, and linked the new frontiers with the old by so called Roman roads—usually built by Greek engineers and native forced labour. Established social and religious practices were permitted so long as they did not threaten Roman administration or offend against the broad-minded Roman standards of good taste. The new province presently became a springboard for further aggression.
>
> —Robert Graves, "It Was a Stable World"

3   Graves makes his promise in the first nine words, in which he mentions the "simple" technique the Romans had for "dividing" and "conquering" in order to expand their empire. Suppose Graves had started his paragraph with these words:

> The technique of expansion was interesting. It was based upon a theory about human nature that the Romans practically invented. This theory had to do with how people reacted to certain political and military devices which . . .

4   Do you see what is wrong? Since the beginning sentences are so vague, the paragraph never gets going. The writer can't fulfill a promise because he hasn't made one. Another example of a poor paragraph beginning:

> The first step involves part of the golf club head. The club head has removable parts, some of which are metal. You must consider these parts when deciding how to repair the club.

5   Specify the beginning of this paragraph and get to the point quicker:

> Your first step in repairing the club head is to remove the metal plate held on by Phillips screws.

6   This solid, specific paragraph beginning gives your reader a clear promise which you can fulfill easily without wasting words. (Observe, by the way, that specifying a writer's stance—as we did in the last example—can help you write clearer paragraph beginnings.)

2. *Fulfill Your Reader's Expectation Established by the Paragraph Promise*

7   Do this with specific details and examples—explain as fully as you can:

> The next thing is to devise a form for your essay. This, which ought to be obvious, is not. I learned it for the first time from an experienced newspaperman. When I was at college I earned extra pocket- and book-money by writing several weekly columns for a newspaper. They were usually topical, they were always carefully varied, they tried hard to be witty, and (an essential) they never missed a deadline. But once, when I brought in the product, a copy editor stopped me. He said, "Our readers seem to like your stuff all right; but we think it's a bit amateurish." With due humility I replied, "Well I am an amateur. What should I do with it?" He said, "Your pieces are not coherent; they are only sentences and epigrams strung together; they look like a heap of clothespins in a basket. Every article ought to have a shape. Like this" (and he drew a big letter S on his page) "or this" (he drew a descending line which turned abruptly upward again) "or this" (and he sketched a solid central core with five or six lines pushing outward from it) "or even this" (and he outlined two big arrows coming into collision). I never saw the man again, but I have never ceased to be grateful to him for his wisdom and for his kindness. Every essay must have a shape. You can ask a question in the first paragraph, discussing several different answers to it till you reach one you think is convincing. You can give a curious fact and offer an explanation of it: a man's character (as Hazlitt did with his fives champion), a building, a book, a striking adventure, a peculiar custom. There are many other shapes which essays can take; but the principle laid down by the copy editor was right. Before you start you must have a form in your mind; and it ought to be a form felt in paragraphs or sections, not in

words or sentences—so that, if necessary, you could summarize each paragraph in a single line and put the entire essay on a postcard.

—Gilbert Highet, "How to Write an Essay"

8   Highet makes a promise in the first three sentences, and in the remaining sentences he specifically fulfills it.

3. Avoid Fragmentary Paragraphs

9   A fragmentary paragraph does not develop its topic or fulfill its promise. A series of fragmentary paragraphs jumps from idea to idea in a jerky and unconvincing fashion:

> My freshman rhetoric class is similar in some ways to my senior English class in high school, but it is also very different.
>
> In my English class we usually had daily homework assignments that were discussed during the class period. If we were studying grammar, the assignments were to correct grammatical errors in the text. If we were studying literature, we were supposed to read the material and understand its ideas.
>
> In rhetoric class, we do basically the same things, except that in the readings we are assigned, we look much deeper into the purpose of the author.
>
> In my English class . . .

10   Fragmentary paragraphs are often the result of a weak writer's stance.

4. Avoid Irrelevancies in Your Paragraphs

11   The italicized sentence does not fit the development of this paragraph:

> We need a better working atmosphere at Restik Tool Company. The workers must feel that they are a working team instead of just individuals. If the men felt they were part of a team, they would not misuse the special machine tools, which now need to be resharpened twice as often as they used to be. *Management's attitude toward the union could be improved too.* The team effort is also being damaged by introduction of new products before their bugs have been worked out. Just when the men are getting used to one routine, a new one is installed, and their carefully created team effort is seriously damaged.

As with the fragmentary paragraph, the problem of irrelevancies in a paragraph is often the result of a vague writer's stance. The paragraph above does not seem to be written for any particular reader.

A. M. Tibbetts and Charlene Tibbetts., STRATEGIES OF RHETORIC, © 1974, pp. 82–85. Reprinted by permission of Pearson Education, Inc., Upper Saddle River, New Jersey.

● Vocabulary

foment (2)   topical (7)

EXAMPLES

Paragraphs with the Topic Sentence at the Beginning

From the Lessons of the Past

EDITH HAMILTON

Edith Hamilton (1867–1963) was an American classicist, educator, and writer. Her writing career began after retirement, and at the age of eighty, she started giving public addresses and lectures. When she was ninety, she was made an honorary citizen of Greece. Among her books are *The Greek Way* (1942), *The Roman Way* (1932), and *Witness to the Truth: Christ and His Interpreters* (1948).

Basic to all the Greek achievement was freedom. The Athenians were the only free people in the world. In the great empires of antiquity—Egypt, Babylon, Assyria, Persia—splendid though they were, with riches beyond reckoning and immense power, freedom was unknown. The idea of it never dawned in any of them. It was born in Greece, a poor little country, but with it able to remain unconquered no matter what manpower and what wealth were arrayed against her. At Marathon and at Salamis overwhelming numbers of Persians had been defeated by small Greek forces. It had been proved that one free man was superior to many submissively obedient subjects of a tyrant. Athens was the leader in that amazing victory, and to the Athenians freedom was their dearest possession. Demosthenes said that they would not think it worth their while to live if they could not do so as free men, and years later a great teacher said, "Athenians, if you deprive them of their liberty, will die."

Excerpt from THE LESSONS OF THE PAST by Edith Hamilton.

● Vocabulary

reckoning	arrayed	Marathon
Salamis	submissively	tyrant
Demosthenes		

● The Facts

1. Were you convinced of the truth of the topic sentence after reading the paragraph? If so, what convinced you?
2. In what way are free men superior to those who are submissively obedient to a tyrant?

● The Strategies

1. What is the topic sentence of the paragraph?
2. Who is the "great teacher" alluded to?

● The Issues

1. Hamilton writes that freedom was basic to the Greek achievement. What does freedom mean to you in a political context?

2. According to Hamilton, it has "been proved that one free man [is] superior to many submissively obedient subjects." Why do you think this is so?

Pain

WILLIAM SOMERSET MAUGHAM

English author William Somerset Maugham (1874–1965) wrote short stories, novels, plays, and books of criticism. His most popular plays include *The Circle* (1921), *Our Betters* (1923), and *The Constant Wife* (1927). His best-known novel is his semiautobiographical account of a young physician with a clubfoot, *Of Human Bondage* (1919).

No more stupid apology for pain has ever been devised than that it elevates. It is an explanation due to the necessity of justifying pain from the Christian point of view. Pain is nothing more than the signal given by the nerves that the organism is in circumstances hurtful to it; it would be as reasonable to assert that a danger signal elevates a train. But one would have thought that the ordinary observation of life was enough to show that in the great majority of cases, pain, far from refining, has an effect which is merely brutalising. An example in point is the case of hospital in-patients: physical pain makes them self-absorbed, selfish, querulous, impatient, unjust and greedy; I could name a score of petty vices that it generates, but not one virtue. Poverty also is pain. I have known well men who suffered from that grinding agony of poverty which befalls persons who have to live among those richer than themselves; it makes them grasping and mean, dishonest and untruthful. It teaches them all sorts of detestable tricks. With moderate means they would have been honourable men, but ground down by poverty they have lost all sense of decency.

● Vocabulary

querulous

● The Facts

1. According to Maugham, why do some people think it necessary to justify pain?

2. What is Maugham's view of pain?

3. Aside from the pain of physical illness, what is another cause of pain?

● The Strategies

1. What analogy does Maugham use in refuting the view that pain elevates?
2. What example does Maugham give to support his view of pain?
3. The paragraph discusses two causes of pain. What transitional word does Maugham use to move the discussion from the one cause to the other?

● The Issues

1. Maugham says that he cannot name a single virtue that pain produces. What virtue is pain generally thought to produce?
2. What is the distinction between pain and suffering?
3. Maugham writes that to say pain elevates is as reasonable as asserting that "a danger signal elevates a train." What is fundamentally false about this analogy?

I Am Tired of Fighting (Surrender Speech)

CHIEF JOSEPH OF THE NEZ PERCÉ

Chief Joseph (1840–1904) was the leader of the Nez Percé tribe of the Sahaptin Indians, who lived along the Snake River in Idaho and Oregon. In 1877, under Chief Joseph, the tribe fought the United States government in a desperate attempt to preserve its land. Eventually, the Indians lost their struggle and were forced to retreat to the border of Canada.

I am tired of fighting. Our chiefs are killed. Looking Glass is dead. Toohulsote is dead. The old men are all dead. It is the young men who say no and yes. He who led the young men is dead. It is cold and we have no blankets. The little children are freezing to death. My people, some of them, have run away to the hills and have no blankets, no food. No one knows where they are—perhaps they are freezing to death. I want to have time to look for my children and see how many of them I can find. Maybe I shall find them among the dead. Hear me, my chiefs, I am tired. My heart is sad and sick. From where the sun stands I will fight no more forever.

● The Facts

1. According to this speech, what nonmilitary factor contributed most to Chief Joseph's decision to surrender?
2. Who was left among the Nez Percé to say "no" and "yes"?

● The Strategies

1. On what word do most of the sentences of this paragraph end? What is the effect of this repeated ending?

2. How would you characterize the language used in this speech? Formal? Informal? Colloquial? What effect do you think the speaker achieves in his diction?

3. What are some examples of poetic constructions that add to the stateliness and dignity of this speech? Translate them literally and say what is lost in the translation.

● The Issues

1. How are American Indians portrayed in popular literature and films? How has this portrayal affected your impression of them?

2. Historians agree that the Indians got short shrift at the hands of the encroaching white settlers. What responsibility, if any, do the descendants of the victors have to the descendants of the vanquished Indians?

Paragraphs with the Topic Sentence at the End

Man against Darkness

W. T. STACE

Walter Terrence Stace (1886–1967) was an English naturalist and philosopher known for his ability to translate complex theories into terms that appealed to a general reader. An authority on Hegel, Stace was the author of numerous books, among them *A Critical History of Greek Philosophy* (1920) and *The Philosophy of Hegel* (1924).

The picture of a meaningless world, and a meaningless human life, is, I think, the basic theme of much modern art and literature. Certainly it is the basic theme of modern philosophy. According to the most characteristic philosophies of the modern period from Hume in the eighteenth century to the so-called positivists of today, the world is just what it is, and that is the end of all inquiry. There is no reason for its being what it is. Everything might just as well have been quite different, and there would have been no reason for that either. When you have stated what things are, what things the world contains, there is nothing more which could be said, even by an omniscient being. To ask any question about why things are thus, or what purpose their being so serves, is to ask a senseless question, because they serve no purpose at all. For instance, there is for modern philosophy no such thing as the ancient problem of evil. For this once-famous question pre-supposes that pain and misery, though they seem so inexplicable and irrational to us, must ultimately subserve some rational purpose, must have their places in the cosmic plan. But this is nonsense. There is no such overruling rationality in the universe. Belief in the ultimate irrationality of everything is the quintessence of what is called the modern mind.

MAN AGAINST DARKNESS AND OTHER ESSAYS, by W. T. Stace, © 1967. Reprinted by permission of the University of Pittsburgh Press.

● **Vocabulary**

positivists   omniscient   subserve   quintessence

● The Facts

1. What is the basic theme of much modern art and literature?
2. How do the most characteristic philosophies of the modern era view the world?
3. Why is there no such thing in modern philosophy as the ancient problem of evil?

● The Strategies

1. Stace is known for expressing complex ideas with clarity. In this example, how does he make clear the complex views of modern philosophy?
2. From which point of view is this paragraph mainly written? How can you tell?
3. "Begging the question" is the logical name given to an argument that assumes as proven the very thing that is in dispute. Is the attitude of modern philosophy toward evil an example of begging the question? Why or why not?

● The Issues

1. What is your opinion of modern philosophy, as Stace summarizes it, that ascribes everything to irrationality? How does this philosophy square with your own beliefs?
2. From your knowledge of various belief systems, what is the most common belief about the origin of evil?
3. What imaginable purpose can evil possibly serve? If evil did not exist, would it have to be invented? Supply evidence for your claim.

What Is a Poet?

MARK VAN DOREN

Mark Van Doren (1894–1973), American poet and critic, was born in Illinois and educated at Columbia University, where he later won renown as a dedicated teacher. He was the author of many books, among them *American and British Literature Since 1890* (1939, written with his brother Carl), *Collected Poems, 1922–1938* (1939, Pulitzer Prize), and *The Last Days of Lincoln* (1959).

Here is the figure we have set up. A pale, lost man with long, soft hair. Tapering fingers at the ends of furtively fluttering arms. An air of abstraction in the delicate face, but more often a look of shy pain as some aspect of reality—a real man or woman, a grocer's bill, a train, a load of bricks, a newspaper, a noise from the street—makes itself manifest. He is generally incompetent. He cannot find his way in a city, he forgets where he is going, he has no aptitude for business, he is childishly gullible and so the prey of human sharks, he cares nothing for money, he is probably poor, he will sacrifice his welfare for a whim, he stops to pet homeless cats, he is especially knowing where children are concerned (being a child himself), he sighs, he sleeps, he wakes to sigh again. The one great assumption from which the foregoing portrait is drawn is an assumption which thousands of otherwise intelligent citizens go on. It is the assumption that the poet is more sensitive than any other kind of man, that he feels more than the rest of us and is more definitely the victim of his feeling.

From Mark Van Doren, "What Is A Poet?"

● Vocabulary

gullible

● The Facts

1. What do we expect a poet to look like?
2. What kind of personality do we expect a poet to have?
3. What one great assumption do we make about poets?

● The Strategies

1. What is Van Doren attempting to do in this paragraph? What single word could you use to describe the type of portrait he is sketching?
2. Van Doren writes: "A pale, lost man with long, soft hair. Tapering fingers at the ends of furtively fluttering arms." Grammatically, what do these two assertions have in common? What effect do they contribute to the description?
3. A catalogue is a list of things or attributes. Where in this paragraph does the author obviously use a catalogue?

● The Issues

1. Given the characteristics traditionally identified as masculine and feminine, which would you expect a poet to be—more masculine than feminine, or vice versa? Why?
2. What, in your mind, is a poet? Does your definition of a poet differ substantially from Van Doren's description? In what way?
3. Of what use is poetry in the modern world?

On Disease

LEWIS THOMAS, M.D.

Lewis Thomas (1913–1993) was born in New York and educated at Princeton and Harvard. Dr. Thomas was a medical administrator of the Memorial Sloan-Kettering Cancer Center in New York and an essayist who has been praised for his lucid style. His essays have been published in collections such as *The Lives of a Cell* (1974, National Book Award), *The Medusa and the Snail* (1979), *Late Night Thoughts on Listening to Mahler's Ninth Symphony* (1983), and *Etcetera Etcetera* (1990).

We were all reassured, when the first moon landing was ready to be made, that the greatest precautions would be taken to protect the life of the earth, especially human life, against infection by whatever there might be alive on the moon. And, in fact, the elaborate ceremony of lunar asepsis was performed after each of the early landings; the voyagers were masked and kept behind plate glass, quarantined away from contact with the earth until it was a certainty that we wouldn't catch something from them. The idea that germs are all around us, trying to get at us, to devour and destroy us, is so firmly rooted in modern consciousness that it made sense to think that strange germs, from the moon, would be even scarier and harder to handle.

● Vocabulary

asepsis   quarantined

● The Facts

1. About what were we all reassured before the first moon landing was made?
2. What idea about germs is firmly rooted in our consciousness?

● The Strategies

1. What specific detail does the author use to support his assertion that an elaborate ceremony of asepsis was performed after each of the lunar landings?
2. Assuming that the paragraph is representative of the style of the whole essay, for what kind of audience do you think the essay was written?

● The Issues

1. Do you trust medical doctors to the extent that you implicitly follow their advice? Why or why not?
2. Which disease do you fear the most? Why?

The Flood

ROBERT FROST

Robert Frost (1874–1963) was a lecturer, poet, and teacher. When he was nineteen and working in a mill in Lawrence, Massachusetts, the *Independent* accepted and published "My Butterfly, An Elegy"—the poem that began Frost's career as one of America's great poets. Rugged New England farm life was the inspiration for many of his poems.

> Blood has been harder to dam back than water.
> Just when we think we have it impounded safe
> Behind new barrier walls (and let it chafe!),
> It breaks away in some new kind of slaughter.

5   We choose to say it is let loose by the devil;
    But power of blood itself releases blood.
    It goes by might of being such a flood
    Held high at so unnatural a level.
    It will have outlet, brave and not so brave.
10 Weapons of war and implements of peace
    Are but the points at which it finds release.
    And now it is once more the tidal wave
    That when it has swept by leaves summits stained.
    Oh, blood will out. It cannot be contained.

From The Poetry of Robert Frost, edited by Edward Connery Lathem. Copyright 1928, 1969 by Henry Holt and Company, 1956 by Robert Frost. Reprinted by permission of Henry Holt and Company, LLC.

● Vocabulary

impounded (2)   chafe (3)

● The Facts

1. What interpretation can be given to Frost's mention of a flood of blood?
2. What is meant by the statement "power of blood itself releases blood"?
3. What is the "tidal wave" to which Frost refers? Why does it leave summits stained?

● The Strategies

1. In poetry, the stanza serves a purpose similar to that of the paragraph. That being the case, what do you consider the topic sentence of this poem? Is it stated more than once?
2. Both water and blood are mentioned in this poem. Which of these words is used literally and which symbolically?

● The Issues

1. What is the theme of this poem?
2. In writing about blood, Frost says: ". . . implements of peace/Are but the points at which it finds release." What can this line possibly mean?

● CHAPTER WRITING ASSIGNMENTS

1. Select one of the following topics and develop it into a unified, coherent, and complete paragraph:
   a. Carelessness can do more harm than lack of knowledge.
   b. Today the prevailing mood of our economy is one of _____ (fill in the words you think apply).
   c. The Global Positioning System (GPS) Is one of the most useful modern inventions.
   d. Kissing is an odd, over-romanticized act.

e. A female bus driver may face some challenges that a male driver will not.

f. Buying a research paper from a commercial source is unethical.

2. List the particular details that you would use to write a convincing paragraph on the following topic sentences:

   a. Sarcastic people are unpleasant to be around.

   b. I like the security of dating the same person. Or: I like the freedom of dating different people.

   c. Many of today's popular rappers have unfairly received bad press and a bad name.

   d. Hiring experts in computer technology from India is good for the U.S. economy.

or

   Hiring experts in computer technology from India is bad for the U.S. economy.

   e. Common sense is _____ (define it).

● WRITING ASSIGNMENTS FOR A SPECIFIC AUDIENCE

1. Write an essay aimed at an audience of unemployed fishermen in Louisiana, arguing that the government should not have to bear the financial responsibility for accidental oil spills.

or

   Write an essay aimed at an audience of environmentalists, arguing for the importance of paying for oil spill cleanups in order to preserve the natural habitats of fish and fowl.

2. Write a blog in which you respond to the person who posted this blog: "Anyone who is stupid enough to invest in a Ponzi scheme like Bernie Madoff's deserves to lose every penny invested. I don't feel sorry for such a greedy idiot."

REAL-LIFE STUDENT WRITING

Letter of Application to an Honors Program

Students who apply to gain entrance to colleges, honors programs, and graduate schools, or for scholarship grants, are usually required to submit a personal essay telling about their goals, motivation, special interests, and the like. The following essay was written as part of an application to a community college honors program. If the tone seems a tad formal and stiff, remember the student was under pressure to look perfect.

● ● ●

The Assignment In a brief essay, state your educational goals and why you want to be in the Honors Program.

Some day I want to be a labor lawyer like my father and his father before him. To achieve this goal will require dedication and focus. I realize that I will have to give up the more frivolous activities of fraternity life, such as beer busts, poker games, and hanging out. I have already tried to get into the habit of getting top grades not only to gain entrance to a good law school, but also because I would really like to know the details of important historical events, such as how Lincoln won the Civil War, what the Watergate Scandal was all about, and why labor unions have become so weak. I also want to read a few more Shakespeare plays and even learn to read and write in French. My short-term educational goal is to receive a B.A. in history with a minor in business administration. Two reasons drive me to join the Honors Program: First, in honors classes I shall be surrounded by students who are highly motivated and serious about their studies. Consequently, it seems to me that the classroom debates and discussions would be on a more challenging level than in regular classes. Second, I know that the top universities in the country give preference to honor students in their acceptance rankings. While some of my college friends think honors programs are elitist, I think they stimulate students to value learning and scholarship. Thank you for considering my application.

Phil Anderson

TERRORISM

MOHAMMED ABED/AFP/Getty Images

● STUDYING THE IMAGE

1. What underlying contradiction do you see in this image? What feelings does it evoke in you?

2. What is the effect of the mask worn by the terrorist? Why is the mask black?

3. What stereotype of terrorism does the photo suggest?

4. How do you think a law-abiding, devout Muslim would feel about this photo? How would you react if you were a Muslim?

● WRITING ASSIGNMENT

Write an essay in which you point out the perils of a religious sect that calls for the elimination of innocent citizens believed to be "infidels."

MAI/Landov

Customers fearful of being shot by the sniper, who for months terrorized the Washington, D.C., area, are given protection via a large blue tarp by one local Texaco station.

● STUDYING THE IMAGE

1. When the "D.C. Sniper," who for months terrorized the Washington, D.C., community by shooting people as they went about their daily routines, was finally caught, the American public was astounded to learn that two males— one older and the other a 17-year-old youth—had managed to kill ten victims whom they had targeted and shot from the trunk of their car. Under the circumstances, how much protection would the blue tarp provide? How would you react if you lived in a neighborhood where a sniper was randomly shooting helpless civilians?

2. As you study the photo of this ordinary Texaco gas station, how do you explain the fact that sometimes a harmless place can suddenly turn into a blood field?

3. What do you consider the major difference between terrorists like the sniper and terrorists who act out of political or religious motivation? What, if anything, do they share in common?

4. What can parents or teachers do to lessen children's fear of terrorists or other predators?

● WRITING ASSIGNMENT

After researching the case of the Washington, D.C., sniper, write an essay in which you describe the two snipers, their relationship, and what the law meted out to each. Give credit to any outside sources you used.

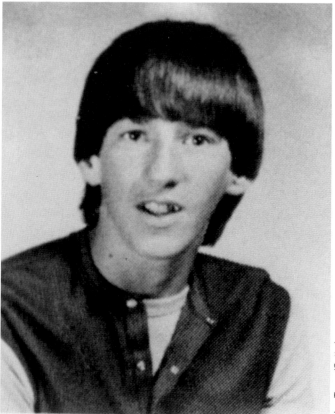

Image of Timothy McVeigh as a young boy.

● STUDYING THE IMAGE

1. How old would you guess Timothy McVeigh to be in this picture?

2. What characteristics strike you most about this portrait? What kind of boy do you imagine Timothy to have been?

3. How do you react to knowing that this youth was destined one day to detonate a bomb that would blow up the Alfred Murrah Building in Oklahoma City, killing 165 people and injuring 450, including some children?

4. What do you think are the strongest forces that affect a child's outlook on life?

● WRITING ASSIGNMENT

After researching the life of Timothy McVeigh, write a paper in which you offer some logical explanation for his unquenchable fury against the U.S. government. Cite any outside source used to bolster your analysis.

SELF-IMAGE

Couperfield/Shutterstock.com

Aleksandr Kurganov/Shutterstock.com

Male in red plaid pants and female in pink revealing dress trying to look "cool."

● STUDYING THE IMAGES

1. What look are both of these young people trying to achieve through their apparel? Does this look have popular appeal today or is it an image of the past? What kind of look do you prefer for mundane activities like shopping, hanging out at the mall, or eating at IHOP? What kind for more formal events, such as attending a concert, church, or a wedding?

2. What self-image has motivated both the young male and the young female to dress in this manner? Project the kind of feeling they have about themselves. For instance, do they both think of themselves as super "cool" and attractive? Or is there some other motivation at work here?

3. If you wanted to have these two young people dress for a dinner date with a traditional family at some elegant restaurant, what modifications would you suggest in their apparel? If you are a male, modify the girl; if you are a female, modify the boy. Make as few changes as possible to make the look more appealing to a conservative audience.

● WRITING ASSIGNMENT

Write an essay in which you clarify the principles that guide you when you dress for public events. Consider such factors as propriety, prevailing custom, attractiveness, practicality, and expense.

© AF archive/Alamy

© London Entertainment/Alamy

Mike Tyson (on left) with facial tattoo, and Lady Gaga (on right) in an outrageous costume and hairdo.

● STUDYING THE IMAGES

1. Describe in detail Mike Tyson's face and Lady Gaga's getup. Make your description vivid enough so that someone unfamiliar with these two celebrities could envision their look.

2. Recently, *HULIQ News* proclaimed the following headline: "Mike Tyson Facial Tattoo Is Newest Craze for Singles on the Prowl." Why do you think Mike Tyson ordered this tattoo for his face? What is your artistic evaluation of the Tyson tattoo? What future do you predict for tattoos? Are they a permanent art form or are they headed for extinction?

3. Lady Gaga has been a polarizing figure in the entertainment world. Her fans adore her whereas her detractors scream that she is crazy. Since both Tyson and Gaga exude an image that some fans consider exotic, do you think they owe it to their followers to reveal a customary self-image or is the outrage they cause a normal aspect of innovative personal styles? Explain your attitude.

4. How important is it for young people to have a good self-image? Which aspects of one's background contribute most strongly to the self-image one acquires?

5. Do you think that famous people like movie stars, athletes, or political leaders have a responsibility to portray a self-image of decency for young people to imitate? Or do you think that every human being should be free to act on his or her instincts and ambitions? Supply a rationale for your opinion.

● WRITING ASSIGNMENT

Focusing on your self-image as you perceive it, write an essay in which you trace the major forces that contributed to who you are at this point in life. Give some specific examples to clarify your claims.

Morales/age fotostock

Bo Zaunders/CORBIS

Obesity in public places: three people on a bench, and a young male strolling in black shorts.

● STUDYING THE IMAGES

1. What is the visual impact made on you by either the people on the bench or the young man strolling along in public? How would you describe them to a close friend?

2. What is our culture's attitude toward obese people? Analyze some of the effects of this attitude—especially among young people who have not formed a good self-image.

3. Which role do motion pictures or fashion magazines play in forming the ideal female or male image? What happens when certain individuals cannot measure up to the image?

4. In the lower grades of school, overweight kids are often bullied by being called names like "fatso," "lard ass," or "balloon butt." What can be done to stop this kind of bullying? If you were the parent of an obese child, what measures would you take to curb your child's appetite and to improve his or her self-image? Suggest a practical plan.

5. In your view, what are the main reasons why so many more Americans are obese today than twenty years ago? How can the trend be reversed? Who should be held most responsible for preventing obesity?

● WRITING ASSIGNMENT

Write an essay describing the process of achieving and maintaining the kind of body you personally admire. If you use an outside source, integrate those ideas into your own writing and assign proper credit.

AGEISM

Tom & Dee Ann McCarthy/CORBIS

● STUDYING THE IMAGE

1. How would you characterize the mood of the dancing couple? What does this photo imply about aging?

2. What strong but rather predictable contrast exists between the man and the woman dancing? (*Hint:* Look at their grooming.) Which one looks younger to you? Why?

3. Judging by her jewelry, his shirt, and the general appearance of the couple, to what level of society do you think they belong? How do you think social class affects people in their old age?

4. How do you feel about people who try desperately to look younger than they really are? How do you think you will feel when you grow old?

● WRITING ASSIGNMENT

Write an essay using this couple as an example of how getting older does not have to stifle all the fun in life. You might add examples of elderly acquaintances in your life who are still active traveling, attending concerts, or throwing parties.

Cynthia Diane Pringle/CORBIS

● STUDYING THE IMAGE

1. Which details in the portrait indicate that the woman is quite old?

2. How would you describe this woman? Do you see beauty in her face? Why or why not?

3. Do you find the portrait depressing or reassuring? What are the reassuring as well as depressing elements?

4. What is your attitude toward old people? Do you take time to visit with them, or do you find them irrelevant to your life? What valuable lessons, if any, can we all learn from the old?

● WRITING ASSIGNMENT

Using your imagination, write a brief biographical sketch of this woman's life, describing her work, her philosophy or religion, and her outlook on her present condition. Your sketch should reflect your personal opinion of the kind of woman you see portrayed.

Jeff Cadge/Getty Images

● STUDYING THE IMAGE

1. Ponder the advantages the older physician might have over the younger ones surrounding him, but think also about some possible disadvantages. Which side do you think outweighs the other?

2. Would you trust an older physician like the one in the image? Why or why not?

3. Why do you think older people often want to continue to work? Do you think it is strictly economic necessity that motivates them? Are there other rewards that come from working?

4. Some observers of the job market say that companies are going out of their way to hire older workers. What do you think is the rationale for this trend? What do you think older workers bring to the table that younger ones do not?

● WRITING ASSIGNMENT

Write an essay arguing that mandatory retirement at the age of 65 is not necessarily a positive factor for our communities. Or, if you prefer, argue that mandatory retirement at age 65 is appropriate.

DRUGS AND SOCIETY

MIKE NELSON/epa/Corbis

People passing by a sign advertising medical marijuana in Venice Beach, California.

● STUDYING THE IMAGE

1. How would you describe the reaction of the passersby to the sign advertising medical marijuana? Considering the polarizing attitudes that prevail in our society concerning the use of marijuana, what emotions are absent?

2. When you read the words "Walk-ins welcome," what popular businesses along strip malls or near shopping areas come to mind? What tone do these words convey? What is the purpose of this tone?

3. What do the words "The doctor is in" add to this sign? Why is no doctor's name, such as "Ernest W. Smith, M.D.," attached to the sign? How professional does this sign look compared with signs on billboards advertising other medical specialists, such as dermatologists, pediatricians, or cosmetic dentists? Speculate on what kinds of patients would walk into this clinic.

4. Do you consider marijuana for medical purposes the same as herbal supplements or prescription pain medications? Or do you think it belongs in the category of street drugs? Support your opinion with verifiable facts.

● WRITING ASSIGNMENT

Argue the case for legalizing the use of marijuana or for keeping it illegal. Regardless of what side you take, find at least three expert opinions to support your argument. Use MLA format to cite your sources.

Fernando Castillo/LatinContent/Getty Images

U.S. soldiers and police at checkpoint for drugs in Apatzingan, Mexico—within the zone of influence of the La Familia drug cartel.

● STUDYING THE IMAGE

1. What is your emotional reaction to this image of a conflict between law enforcement and crime? Imagine if any of the males in the photo were your father or brother. How would you feel about him, caught in this perilous setting?

2. In your social circle, what role do smoking, drinking, or drugs play? Does it make any difference in being accepted whether or not a person participates in these activities?

3. Recently, several world leaders (including the former President of Mexico, Vincent Fox) have suggested that one way to solve the problem of drug violence is to decriminalize the use of drugs the way we legalized smoking and drinking. What new problems, if any, might we face if we voted for such a stance?

4. Most college students know someone in their social circle or family who had to go through rehab due to some addiction. To which major cause do you attribute the continuing problem with drug addiction in our country? Select the one that seems the most directly connected to addiction as you have observed it.

● WRITING ASSIGNMENT

Write an essay in which you argue for the protection of children whose parents are addicted to drugs. What role, if any, should the government play in this matter? What remedial action do you recommend? Spending some time doing research on the Internet, studying what experts have to say about children and drug abuse, may be helpful in completing this assignment.

● STUDYING THE IMAGE

1. With so much public information in the media about the dangers of smoking, what do you think motivates young children to smoke?

2. As you study the expressions on the faces of these young boys, what do you think the one offering the cigarette is telling the other boy? What does the other boy's facial expression tell you about his thoughts? Do you think he will accept or reject the cigarette offered him?

3. What role do grownups play in the upsurge or prevention of youthful smoking?

4. Experts agree that smoking for the beginner is a harsh and unpleasant experience to which the body violently reacts. Why do people persist in smoking in spite of the initial unpleasantness? Do you think that cigarettes are a drug? Why or why not?

● WRITING ASSIGNMENT

Various commercials and ad campaigns have tried to persuade children not to pick up smoking, but with only marginal success. Write an essay in which you discuss an appeal to children not to smoke that is likely to work. How would you word such an appeal? What facts and specific details would you bring up? Personalize your appeal by directing it to a specific child that you know.

IMMIGRATION

Todd Bigelow/Getty Images

Illegal immigrants climbing over a wall at sunset to get into the United States.

● STUDYING THE IMAGE

1. What makes this image seem almost unreal?
2. How does the picture preserve the anonymity of the illegal immigrants? Why?
3. How do you personally regard these men? Be specific in whether you view them as a good source of labor, unwanted intruders, or otherwise.
4. Aside from providing the United States with a source of manual labor, what other good do illegal immigrants contribute to American society? Think of the intangibles that such men and women bring to the culture.

● WRITING ASSIGNMENT

Write an essay in which you explain the causes that lead certain people to risk their lives to enter the United States. Try to keep your personal biases out of the essay.

© Bettmann/CORBIS

Early immigrants entering the United States through Ellis Island.

● STUDYING THE IMAGE

1. What general impression of these immigrants does this old photo give?

2. Why do all the immigrants, even the children, seem glum? Why is there no frivolity along the line?

3. Contrast the placidity of this scene with the frantic depiction of the illegal immigrants climbing the wall that blocks them from entry into the United States. What differences can you see between the people shown here and those climbing over the wall? What part do you think racial differences play in the society's attitude toward the two groups?

4. Where is Ellis Island? What reputation does it have in its treatment of immigrants?

● WRITING ASSIGNMENT

Write an essay comparing and contrasting the Ellis Island immigrants with the illegal immigrants entering our country today. Consider such differences as their countries' histories, ethnic differences, and levels of poverty.

Inti St Clair/Getty Images

● STUDYING THE IMAGE

1. For many years, American couples looking to adopt, traveled to China and found some wonderful adoptive daughters. However, adopting Chinese girls has become increasingly difficult in recent years. Why do you think most of the Chinese children were female? Why has it become more difficult to adopt in China?

2. With many children in the United States waiting to be adopted, why do individuals and families continue to go outside the United States to adopt? What is your opinion of this choice?

3. What is your opinion of interracial adoption? What advantages or difficulties are inherent in such adoptions?

4. What seems to be the relationship between the mother and daughter as revealed in the image above?

● WRITING ASSIGNMENT

Write an essay in which you state your feelings about parents who choose to adopt children from China, Russia, Mexico, and other foreign countries. Try to be fair in your evaluation of the rewards or hardships of such an adoption, taking into account the parents, the adopted child, and the community.

ONLINE DATING

© timtim.com

● STUDYING THE IMAGE

1. Which emotional aspects of online dating does this cartoon capture?

2. What fantasy is at work in this image?

3. If you were single and searching for a companion, would you consider online dating? Why or why not?

4. One common reason given for online dating is that singles who are busy pursuing a career can't find the time to meet appropriate dates. What is your reaction to this rationale?

5. How has propaganda increased the number of people seeking companionship online? Is this a good trend? Explain your answer.

● WRITING ASSIGNMENT

Write an essay in which you argue for or against the growing trend of online dating. Analyze and synthesize at least two outside sources.

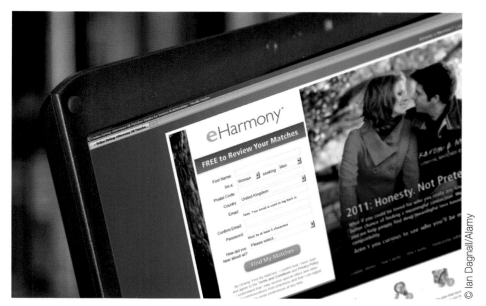

eHarmony advertisement.

● STUDYING THE IMAGE

1. What is this advertisement trying to achieve with its viewers? Consider such matters as trust, enthusiasm, and the promise of romance or companionship.

2. How significant is the physical appearance of the couple portrayed in the ad? Do you find them attractive? Why or why not?

3. What is the meaning of the heading "Free to review your matches"? How does that kind of freedom help the success of the service?

4. Do you consider the TV or computer ads created by the multitude of online dating services influential in shaping today's society? Are they a blessing or a curse to personal relationships?

● WRITING ASSIGNMENT

After interviewing your grandparents or some other couple not of your generation, write an essay reflecting their attitudes toward the modern trend of online dating.

William Archie/Detroit Free Press/MCT

A middle-aged couple who met online and got married—having dinner at a restaurant.

● STUDYING THE IMAGE

1. The middle-aged couple portrayed above are Larry and Cheryl Bond, who met online in 2007 and married in 2009. As you study their appearance and demeanor, what is your reaction to them as a couple? Do they seem comfortable and confident, or do they seem nervous and worried? What does their clothing tell us about them? Use your imagination to create a word picture of this couple.

2. Larry and Cheryl Bond belong to the 50+ crowd of web daters, who are said to be the fastest growing group of people trying to find companionship and romance online. What effect does age have on the risk factor of online dating? Weigh the advantages and disadvantages of youth versus maturity.

3. What is the cause of the recent impulse on the part of singles to rush online and entrust their entire personality profiles to agents who will match them up with an appropriate partner? Is this a good or bad trend? Explain your estimation.

4. The Internet, newspapers, and magazines are full of admonitions about how to avoid meeting a dangerous partner online. Of all the rules, which one do you consider crucial to a person's safety—especially that of a vulnerable woman?

● WRITING ASSIGNMENT

Write a well-researched essay about online dating as a helpful way to connect with people of your own social class, intellectual interests, and entertainment tastes. If you find no value in online dating, develop an essay clarifying your negative position and supporting it with evidence from your experience or that of experts.

RACISM

Old ink sketch of black woman on auction block, being sold as a slave.

● STUDYING THE IMAGE

1. How do you think this picture would make you feel if you were a member of a race for whom enslavement, as depicted in this scene, is a historical truth? If your ancestors were once slaves, how do you react to this picture?

2. What do you think the woman to whom the child clings for help is feeling? What does her body language reveal?

3. Many Southern white women insisted that house slaves were often treated like family members. Based on the cruelty implicit in this picture, what is your opinion of that assertion?

4. What effect might a history of enslavement have on the descendents of slaves? How do you feel about the proposal that is occasionally brought up to pay financial reparations to those whose ancestors were once slaves?

5. Why are there no Southern white women in this sketch?

● WRITING ASSIGNMENT

Write an essay on the proposal to pay reparations to the descendents of slaves in the United States. Take a position for or against the proposal and explain the reasons behind your stand. You may need to do a little research on this topic in order to strengthen your assertions.

Painting by Norman Rockwell of Ruby Bridges, the first girl to attend a desegregated school in New Orleans, Louisiana, over the objections of whites, first published in Look magazine in 1964.

● STUDYING THE IMAGE

1. This painting, by one of America's most beloved artists who is known for his realistic but patriotic depiction of people and events, offended vast numbers of people when it was first published. What do you think so many people who had formerly admired Rockwell's work found offensive in this painting?

2. Who are the men accompanying Ruby Bridges? Why are they headless? What point is made by not showing their heads?

3. From her body language, how would you describe the attitude of the little girl? What is special about her looks?

4. Does the painting support, oppose, or remain neutral to desegregation? What evidence can you cite from the painting itself to support your answer?

5. Depending on your answer to the previous question, what apt title can you think of for this painting?

● WRITING ASSIGNMENT

Write an essay in which you analyze the effects on society of segregated public schools. Do not be afraid to take a stand on the issue. Ask yourself what segregation did to blacks and other minorities and what advantages are offered by public schools that encourage ethnic variety.

Elderly woman in a wheelchair, maneuvering her way at the airport.

© Ian Shaw/Alamy

● STUDYING THE IMAGE

1. When the elderly woman portrayed above reaches airport security, how much of a threat will she pose to the safety of other passengers? How much time should the agents spend on checking her baggage or person?

2. Since time often equals money, which passengers at airport security checkpoints should have the closest scrutiny? Describe them in general terms.

3. Because fear of terrorism has become part of our national mood since 9/11, which characteristic or trait among passengers at airports is worth observing closely—race, behavior, age, clothing, or something else?

4. How do you feel about the security regulations now in effect at U.S. airports? Are they worth the taxes spent on them or are they pointless and ineffective?

● WRITING ASSIGNMENT

Write an essay in which you suggest ways to improve the time spent at airport security checkpoints on passengers before they board their planes. You might research how other countries combat the threat of terrorist acts at their airports or border entries. If you believe that our security measures are excellent, then write an essay arguing for their retention.

Ron Krisel/Getty Images

● STUDYING THE IMAGE

1. The tragedy of the September 11, 2001, along with other terrorist suicide bombings committed by Middle Eastern men, have made many U.S. citizens fearful of any male who looks Arabic. How can this fear lead to racism?

2. If a particular race of people are associated with a campaign of terrorism, why is it racism if the authorities targeted those people for special scrutiny? What can the authorities do?

3. What facial traits might make this male suspect? When does this suspiciousness pass the boundary of common sense and become racist?

4. If you looked Middle Eastern, what steps would you take to allay the fears of the public that you might be a terrorist?

● WRITING ASSIGNMENT

Write an essay exploring the racial prejudices—subtle or blatant—that exist among you, members of your family, and your friends. If you feel you have no prejudices, write how you have been able to avoid these feelings.

THE STATUS OF WOMEN

Susan B. Anthony (1820–1906)

Harriet Tubman (1820–1913)

Eleanor Roosevelt (1884–1962)

Rosa Parks (1913–2005)

● STUDYING THE IMAGES

1. Susan B. Anthony was a leader in the women's suffrage movement. How has the right to vote changed the status of women in the United States?

2. Harriet Tubman was a runaway slave who led more than 300 slaves to freedom during the American Civil War. How much did the abolitionist movement help the civil rights cause?

3. Eleanor Roosevelt, the wife of U.S. President Franklin Delano Roosevelt, was a social activist. Should a first lady remain in the background while her husband is in office or involve herself in her favorite causes?

4. Rosa Parks inspired the black civil rights movement by refusing to give up her seat to a white man on a bus in 1955, as was the law in Alabama. How much courage did this take? Was the result worth the rebellion?

● WRITING ASSIGNMENT

Do the necessary research, then write an essay on female leaders who through their exemplary performance have opened leadership doors to others of their gender.

© Gallo Images/CORBIS

● STUDYING THE IMAGE

1. In which part of the world do you think this photo was taken? What clues to the woman's origin does the image provide?

2. Where do you think the woman is headed? What might she be carrying in the basket on her head?

3. What does the picture suggest about the lifestyle of this woman?

4. How does this woman measure up to your expectations of femininity? Explain your answer.

● WRITING ASSIGNMENT

Write an essay proposing what we in the United States can do to promote better working conditions among the women in third-world countries. Consider such organizations as the United Nations, the Red Cross, and certain international religious institutions.

Barbara Davidson/Dallas Morning News/CORBIS

● STUDYING THE IMAGE

1. What is your reaction to seeing these women dressed in burkhas?

2. In what country might they live? For what reason do you think they are wearing burkhas? (If you are not sure, do an Internet search of the word *burkha*.)

3. If you could see the expressions on the women's faces, what emotions would they reveal? Joy or sadness? Determination or humility?

4. How would you deal with a government that forces you to wear clothing that totally hides your body?

● WRITING ASSIGNMENT

Write a letter to one of the women in the photo, telling her just how you feel about the way she is forced to hide her identity whenever she appears in public.

● STUDYING THE IMAGE

1. Under what circumstances do you think it appropriate for a woman to take her baby to work with her? How long do you think the mother should be allowed to do that? At what point would she need to find a caregiver for the baby?

2. How would you have reacted if the parent taking a baby to work had been a father? Why is that more, or less, appropriate?

3. What do this woman's looks tell you about her work? What kind of job do you think she has?

4. What alternative plan can women who must work use to assure good care for their children?

● WRITING ASSIGNMENT

Write an essay either defending or attacking the idea of women taking their children to work with them. Try to see the issue from both the employer's and the worker's point of view.

HOMELESSNESS

Viviane Moos/CORBIS

● STUDYING THE IMAGE

1. What title would you give this photo if it were to appear on a city poster?
2. What are some contrasts between the beggar and the passersby? How would you describe the expression on the face of the first woman passing by?
3. In what geographic areas do you think this scene is typical? What are the conditions that lead to such a scene? Who is responsible?
4. What is the gender of the homeless beggar? How does knowing that affect your response to the picture?

● WRITING ASSIGNMENT

Nearly all of us have either passed, or had casual encounters with, homeless people. Write an essay describing the homeless person and saying how he or she made you feel.

Japanese mother carrying her daughter through the rubble of their home after a gigantic tsunami hit Japan on April 5, 2011.

Epa/Dennis M. Sabangan/Landov

● STUDYING THE IMAGE

1. What is the dominant impression of this warlike scene of devastation? Express it in one declarative sentence.

2. Do any details in the picture reveal the young mother's reaction to what she sees? Describe them and imagine what the mother may be saying to herself.

3. Should people made homeless by a catastrophic act of nature be regarded with greater sympathy than those who are homeless due to economic conditions? Give reasons for your answer.

4. How do you feel about our government's helping the victims of other nations who have been rendered homeless by a natural disaster? Do you feel any obligation to reach out to people beyond our national borders? Explain your rationale on this question.

● WRITING ASSIGNMENT

Write an essay about the "new homelessness" caused by major natural disasters. Compare and contrast the plight of these homeless people with the plight of war refugees and the truly poor living on handouts or government welfare programs. In either case, state when and how society should step in to help.

● STUDYING THE IMAGE

1. How can a sympathetic bystander tell whether this family is really in financial distress or simply trying to make some easy money?

2. What economic or social problems can actually cause a family to become destitute and unable to cope?

3. How do you feel about the child in the picture? Why would some authorities interpret the child's presence as a form of abuse?

4. Which details in the picture reveal that the family is not completely deprived? What arguments can you give to urge someone to help this family? What arguments can you give that this is probably a hoax?

● WRITING ASSIGNMENT

Write an essay in which you propose a way other than legislation to assure that no family in our country is forced to sit outdoors and beg for food to survive. Consider the backing of personal charities, churches, community clubs, and the like. If you do not believe in helping the poor, then explain your position.

THE NEW TECHNOLOGY

Michael Blann/Getty Images

● STUDYING THE IMAGE

1. From the details revealed in this picture, what kind of event is being photo-graphed? List the details you singled out.

2. Do you own a cell phone? Why or why not?

3. In your view what is the greatest service rendered by cell phones? What, if any, are its disadvantages?

4. Assuming you own a cell phone, what adjustments would you have to make if you suddenly lost it. Would these adjustments be detrimental or beneficial?

5. What pleasant or unpleasant experience have you had as a result of using your cell phone?

● WRITING ASSIGNMENT

Write an essay in which you contrast the good with the bad aspects of cell phones in our society. Use specific examples to shore up your case.

Handout/MCT

President Obama's Facebook page.

● STUDYING THE IMAGE

1. Most Facebook participants place an action photo of themselves on their home pages, but Barack Obama's White House page shows the President in a dignified portrait. How would a snapshot of the President playing golf or basketball or playing with his daughters affect his image as President? Would it be more or less effective than a somber portrait? Explain yourself.

2. If you could be a Facebook "friend" with anyone living, whom would you choose? Why?

3. What problem, if any, does having a multitude of friends on Facebook present? How can you avoid this problem?

4. What aspects of Facebook do you enjoy most? Describe some appropriate examples. How many people have you befriended on Facebook? Have you made new intimate friendships through this social network?

5. How can social networking be used to improve global conditions? Cite one specific possibility.

● WRITING ASSIGNMENT

After researching the subject, write an essay on how social networking became part of the Spring Revolution in Egypt (in 2011). If you use outside sources to support your writing, be sure to cite references.

"I sold his unlisted phone number to telemarketers."

● STUDYING THE IMAGE

1. What is the ironic humor involved in this cartoon? What is the meaning of the speaker's confession? Explain it to yourself.

2. What importance does the technology of telemarketing bring to the satire of the cartoon?

3. What is your personal reaction to today's telemarketing to raise funds or to sell products? How do you think most people feel about this strategy?

4. What remedy could be used to diminish the intrusion of telemarketing on the privacy of individuals?

5. Under which circumstances would you consider telemarketing a useful and appropriate tool?

● WRITING ASSIGNMENT

Write a letter of complaint to some imaginary company that has bothered you with repeated automated phone calls, asking for money in support of their cause. Try to keep the tone of your essay civil, yet firm.

Patterns of Development

Chances are good that you have already heard of the rhetorical patterns or perhaps even practiced them in another class. Part Two of this book is devoted to teaching all eight rhetorical patterns as well as argumentation.

Behind the rhetorical patterns in composition is this simple idea: To write about a subject, you must first have thought about it, and this systematic thinking can be translated into an idealized pattern for writing. For example, you might choose to tell a story about your subject (narration); to describe it (description); to say how it happened (process analysis); to give examples of it (illustration and exemplification); to define it (definition); to compare it to something else (comparison and contrast); to break it down into its constituent parts (division and classification); or to list its known causes or effects (causal analysis). Superimposing one of these eight abstract modes or patterns on your subject will make it easier to write about.

Each of these rhetorical patterns is a composite of specific writing and organizing techniques that can be isolated and taught. All narrations are alike, whether they tell a story about aliens from Mars or about facing up to a bully. All descriptions draw on common organizing and focusing techniques, no matter what they describe. If you are writing a comparison and contrast, for example, you know that you must alternate between the compared items and that you must insert suitable transitions so your reader can follow this movement. If you are defining, you know that there are specific techniques to be used in a definition. Knowing that a subject is to be approached a certain way also endows a writer's purpose with a refreshing narrowness, for what is especially bedeviling to the writer is not necessarily the complexity of a subject, but the infinity of possible approaches suggested by the blank sheet of paper.

The advice that instructors often give beginning writers is to "Narrow your subject." Writing by rhetorical patterns allows you to limit and narrow your approach to a subject. When you say, "I'm going to divide and classify this subject," you have an abstract pattern in mind that you can follow. When you say, "I'm going to analyze cause," you also have an abstract pattern to follow. In either case, you are not left dangling between "What shall I say?" and "How shall I say it?" You know how to say it in the abstract. What's left is the application of the ideal pattern to your particular subject.

Here is an example—the subject of "guilt" as developed in the eight most widely used rhetorical patterns. Notice how the writer's focus shifts with the use of each new pattern.

Patterns of Development for the Subject "Guilt"

1. Narration

I was seven years old when I first became aware of the terrible power of guilt. For piling our toys into the toy box, Mother had rewarded my brother and me with five shiny pennies each. If I had had ten pennies instead of just five, I could have bought a gingerbread man with raisin eyes and sugar-frosted hair. The image danced in my head all day, until, finally, I crept into my brother's room and stole his five pennies. The next morning, as my brother and I were dressing to go to school, I hid all ten pennies in the pocket of my coat, cramming one of my father's handkerchiefs on top of them. As my brother and I lined up in front of Mother to be kissed goodbye, she looked at my bulging pocket with amazement. "What on earth do you have in your pocket?" she asked. "It's nothing," I said as offhandedly as I could. "It's nothing at all." Bewildered, but too busy to investigate any further, Mother kissed me good-bye. I ran out the door and down our gravel path as fast as my feet could carry me. But the farther from home I got, the more miserable I became. The shiny pennies in my pocket felt oppressively like one-ton boulders. And I was haunted by the idea that I had become a thief. Forgotten was the gingerbread man, for whose sake I had stolen my brother's pennies. Finally, unable to bear my horrible feeling of guilt, I ran back home to blurt out my crime to my mother.

2. Description

Never before had Pedro experienced such a depth of despair and such a sense of isolation. He began to avoid those nearest to him, returning their friendly greetings with rough and indifferent replies. Often he sat in his room staring vacantly into space with hollow eyes. His hands were cold and clammy most of the time, yet his forehead burned hot with a mysterious fever. Terrible nightmares haunted his sleep, causing him to rise out of bed in the middle of the night, overcome with terror. When strangers at the store asked him a simple question such as "Where is the thread?" or "Have you any molasses?" he would read silent accusations in their eyes and his hands would tremble. He had become a man tormented by guilt.

3. Process Analysis

Do you know the most effective way to handle a friend turned a debtor? Make the person feel guilty. Let us say that you lent your friend Tom $500 to buy a motorcycle, but he refuses to repay the loan. Your first step is to place him in a category of bogus moral superiority. Say, "Tom, you have always been a person of honor. Why do you refuse to pay what you owe me?" If that doesn't work, your second step is to take the behavior personally, indicating that it is causing you emotional pain. Say, "I can't tell you how disappointed I am that you are treating me worse than a total stranger. You would pay back your bank, your credit cards, but you ignore me, your best friend, who needs the money." Unless your present debtor and former friend is a sociopath, he will feel bad about hurting you. Finally, you can threaten to cut off the relationship, making the threat look as if it were the debtor's doing. Say, "Look, Tom, unless I get the money you owe me within a week, I will take your refusal to repay me as a sign that you don't care any more about our friendship." With that, you have really turned up the guilt barometer. Indeed, inducing guilt can be a powerful tool in the process of debt collection.

4. Illustration/Exemplification

Seneca once said, "Every guilty person is his own hangman." The truth of this observation can be illustrated by the lives of countless villains. One such is Macbeth, from Shakespeare's tragedy of the same name. At the instigation of his wife, Macbeth kills the king of Scotland and usurps his throne—an act of treachery for which Macbeth and his wife suffer torments of guilt. Lady Macbeth develops an obsession that her hands are stained with blood, and she wanders somnambulistically through the castle trying vainly to cleanse them. Before he murders the king, Macbeth hallucinates a dagger floating in the air. Later, after his assassins murder Banquo, Macbeth is tormented by hallucinations of Banquo's ghost. Eventually, Lady Macbeth commits suicide. Macbeth is killed during a rebellion of his noblemen, which is brought about—in the main—by the excesses to which his guilt has driven him.

5. Definition

Guilt is the remorse that comes from an awareness of having done something wrong. The origin of guilt is psychological. From childhood, we have all been conditioned by family and society to act within defined standards of reasonableness and decency. Gradually, over a period of years, these standards are internalized and modified to become the core of what is called "conscience." When we do something that violates these internalized standards, we feel guilty. If we have been brought up in a religious environment, we feel an added measure of guilt when we break what we think is a divine commandment.

Whenever we don't play according to our internalized rules, we feel miserable, and this misery is what guilt is all about.

6. Comparison and Contrast

Although the two words may seem to share some connotations, *guilt* is not a synonym for *blame*. Guilt must be felt; blame must be assessed. *Guilt* implies self-reproach that comes from an internal consciousness of wrong. *Blame* hints at fault that has been externally assessed. A man may suffer guilt yet be entirely exonerated of blame; conversely, he may be blamed and yet feel no guilt. In short, while guilt is a feeling, blame is a judgment—and that is the chief distinction between the two.

7. Division and Classification

The Bible identifies three kinds of guilt: guilt of the unpardonable sin, redeemable guilt, and guilt of innocence. First, the guilt of the unpardonable sin belongs to any being who has become so steeped in evil that a change for good is no longer possible. Lucifer is said to have committed this sin by which he cut himself off eternally from Yahweh, the source of all good. Second, redeemable guilt is guilt that can be erased because it belongs to one whose heart is not incorrigibly corrupt, but which has weakened temporarily under the pressure of temptation. King David, for instance, murdered Uriah in order to marry Bathsheba, Uriah's wife. But despite this sin, David was a noble king with a thirst for righteousness; he was redeemable. Finally, the guilt of innocence is the guilt that Jesus bore when he decided to be crucified for the collective wrong of mankind even though he was, of all men, most innocent. In other words, Jesus died as if he were guilty, when in fact his character was free from any trace of evil.

8. Causal Analysis

Guilt is caused by the failure of the will. The human mind, according to Freudian theory, is delicately balanced between the drive for instant gratification that comes from the id, and the desire for regulation and postponement that originates in the superego, which is sometimes identified with what we call the conscience. The function of the will is to mediate between these two desires. When the individual succumbs to temptation, the forces of the id have triumphed over the repression of the superego. But the superego fights back by tormenting the self with regret—in short, by evoking feelings of guilt. The stricter the superego, or conscience, the harsher the toll in guilt and the greater the person suffers. Whoever allows the will to fail must therefore pay for the gratification of the libido's urges in the coin of guilt.

These eight rhetorical modes allow us to teach idealized writing forms and techniques. You will not always use them, and you will most likely use them less and less consciously as your writing skills mature. But, in the beginning, you will find it easier to approach a writing assignment from the viewpoint of a specific mode rather than to invent a wholly original form for every essay.

8

Narration

What Narration Does

To narrate means to tell a story. It does not necessarily have to be a made-up story. Narration, in fact, is a relating of events in some climactic sequence. Whether the events you relate are imaginary or real, the narrative technique is more or less the same. On page 230, the paragraph on guilt in item 1 is an example of narration.

If there is a rhetorical mode that can be said to be inborn in some people, it is narration. Most of us think we can tell a good story, and almost all of us have tried our hand at storytelling.

Granted, our stories may have been oral and told on the front porch to family and friends, but a story and the techniques for telling one orally or in writing are essentially the same.

When to Use Narration

The most widespread use of narration occurs in fiction, whether in the short story or novel. Narration is also used in essays, minutes of business meetings, reports of scientific experiments, news releases, and case histories. Brief narratives, called anecdotes, are often used to effectively enliven or illustrate a point. Use narration whenever you need to relate an experience or present information in dramatic or purposeful sequence.

How to Write a Narrative

Narratives differ in content, length, and point, but the techniques they all use are remarkably similar. To write an engaging narrative, you need to do the following:

Have a Point The point of a story is what gives it movement—a beginning, a middle, and an end. If your story has no point, it will also seem to have no movement, to go nowhere, to become bogged down and stagnant. Good storytellers always begin with a point in mind. They want to show how absentminded Uncle Mickey has become; they wish to prove that "haste makes waste." From this beginning, the story should proceed without pause or slip. Sometimes a storyteller will even begin by revealing the point of the story, an admission that is often helpful to both writer and reader. A classic example of a story that begins by revealing its point is George Orwell's "Shooting an Elephant:"

> One day something happened which in a roundabout way was enlightening. It was a tiny incident in itself, but it gave me a better glimpse than I had had before of the real nature of imperialism—the real motives for which despotic governments act.

This introduction tells us what to expect. As we read on, we expect Orwell to deliver what he has advertised.

Have a point and stick to it—that age-old advice often given by writing teachers definitely applies to narration.

Pace the Story   Fiction tells lies about time—it has to. Real time is not always action-packed, does not always carry us to the dizzying brink or make us feel the throb of life. In fact, time is usually humdrum and dull in real life. But no reader wants a story to trudge through uneventful hours. What the reader wants is for the dull and humdrum to disappear in the puff of a sentence, and for the focus of the story always to be on time—that is, eventful and exciting. The technique of doing this is known as pacing.

All storytellers pace their materials to focus only on eventful periods and to ignore all inconsequential stretches in between. In the following example, taken from a story entitled "We're Poor," an entire season disappears in a single paragraph:

> I didn't go back to school that fall. My mother said it was because I was sick. I did have a cold the week that school opened; I had been playing in the gutters and had got my feet wet, because there were holes in my shoes . . . As long as I had to stay in the house anyway, they were all right. I stayed cooped up in the house, without any companionship . . .

In "We're Poor," the author, Floyd Dell, learns from a Christmas experience that his family is poor. The story consequently spends a good deal of time and attention on that climactic Christmas Eve during which the narrator makes this discovery, but the inconsequential months of the preceding fall are quickly dismissed in a paragraph.

Tell the Story from a Consistent Point of View   The point of view of a story is the angle from which it is told. This angle can be personal and intimate, referring to the narrator with the pronoun "I," or it can be from an omniscient point of view. In this view, the narrator is like a video camera sweeping over the scene and pausing briefly to focus on selected characters—describing how they look, what they say, and how they feel. Often this omniscient observer will select one central character, setting the person in relief so that he or she will catch the reader's intense and undivided attention. In any case, the writer must always stay in character when telling a story and must always remain consistent to the viewpoint from which he or she is telling it.

Here is an example of the omniscient point of view in a narrative. Telling the story of a troubled teacher-student relationship as an omniscient narrator, Joyce Carol Oates moves skillfully from character to character as if seeing everything clearly and truthfully. About the main female character, the narrator observes:

> Sister Irene was a tall, deft woman in her early thirties. What one could see of her face made a striking impression—serious, hard gray eyes, a long slender nose, a face waxen with thought. Seen at the right time, from the right angle, she was almost handsome. In her past teaching positions she had drawn a little upon the fact of her being young and brilliant and also a nun, but she was beginning to grow out of that.

A little further into the story, the narrator moves from Sister Irene to the male lead character, a student, seeing him just as clearly as she sees Sister Irene:

> About two weeks after the semester began, Sister Irene noticed a new student in her class. He was slight and fair-haired, and his face was blank, but not blank by accident, blank on purpose, suppressed and restricted into a dumbness that looked hysterical.

The story continues to develop both characters, the teacher and the student. Although Sister Irene is the central consciousness of the story, Allen Weinstein, the student, becomes a crucial part of the total narrative conflict—with the author recording faithfully all he does, says, and feels, just as she also records the comings and goings of Sister Irene. In fact, in this story, the narrator records even the actions and words of minor characters, which makes her a typical omniscient narrator.

Now consider the following excerpt from a vivid childhood memory by Beryl Markham in "Praise God for the Blood of the Bull":

> I lean for a moment on my spear peering outward at what is nothing, and then turn toward my thorn tree.
>
> "Are you here, Lakwani?" Arap Maina's voice is cool as water on shaded rocks.
>
> "I am here, Maina." He is tall and naked and very dark beside me. His *shuka* is tied around his left forearm to allow his body freedom to run.
>
> "You are alone, and you have suffered, my child."
>
> "I am all right, Maina, but I fear for Buller. I think he may die."
>
> Arap Maina kneels on the earth and runs his hand over Buller's body.
>
> *"He has been seriously and perhaps mortally wounded, Lakwani, but do not permit your mind to be too obsessed with any imaginary deficiencies or self-recriminations on your part. I conjecture that your lance has rescued him from a certain death, and God will recompense you for that . . ."*

If the final paragraph sounds bizarre to you in the context of the excerpt, it should. We have altered the dialogue (and added italics to clearly distinguish it from Markham's words) to dramatize what we mean by a lapse in consistency. In the final paragraph, Maina suddenly and inexplicably shifts from the simple speech of a native African to the pompous, long-winded speech of a British magistrate. A character in a narrative must always speak more or less the same way throughout and cannot lurch from one style of talk to another, as we have made Maina do. Make your characters consistent and your narrative will seem believable.

Insert Appropriate Details   Details are indispensable to narrative writing and can make the difference between boredom and delight in a reader. No one can teach you the art of including captivating details, but common sense tells us that you are more likely to include the right details if you write your narratives about what you truly know. Here, for example, in Beryl Markham's description of a warthog, we get the feeling that the writer has had personal experience with the animal:

> I know animals more gallant than the African warthog, but none more courageous. He is the peasant of the plains—the drab and dowdy digger in the earth. He is the uncomely but intrepid defender of family, home, and bourgeois convention, and he will fight anything of any size that intrudes upon his smug existence. Even his weapons are plebeian—curved tusks, sharp, deadly, but not beautiful, used inelegantly for rooting as well as for fighting.

If you cannot write about what you know, the next best thing is to know about what you write. The advice to always research your subject before writing about it cannot be given too strongly. Even veteran fiction writers do not simply plunge into their narratives without doing the spadework necessary to make their scenes authentic. Although personal experience is probably the best basis for a narrative, adequate and detailed research can be every bit as good.

Warming Up to Write a Narrative

1. **Choose one of the most interesting people whom you know well and sketch out a conflict you have had with him or her.** List the events that led up to the conflict and also indicate how it was resolved. Before actually narrating the conflict, delete from your list all items that would slow down your narrative with tedious or irrelevant material. Next, jot down the theme of your narrative—that is, the point it made or the lesson you learned about life and human relationships.

2. **Try to recall five moments in your life that somehow defined who you are.** It could be the time you lost an important contest, stood up to a bully, or first realized the importance of parents. List each moment as it occurs to you. Now, select from the list the moment that could best be turned into a good narration. Don't forget to write down how the moment defined who you are today.

3. **What is the most exciting and unusual experience that you've ever had?** Try to recall it with a richness of detail. Jot down on a notepad, without paying any attention to sequence, all the incidents and events that made up the experience. Write down everything that you remember about it. Later, after thinking about your list, take the out-of-sequence memories and try to assemble them in some climactic order. If this is not the way you usually work, how did this method of recalling an experience and writing about it work for you?

EXAMPLES

Shooting an Elephant

GEORGE ORWELL

Rhetorical Thumbnail

Purpose: to explain the dilemma of the colonial English

Audience: educated reader

Language: standard English

Strategy: uses an example of the rogue elephant to dramatize the absurdity of the colonial English's position in a foreign country

---

George Orwell (1903–1950) was the pseudonym of Eric Arthur Blair. Born in India and educated at Eton, he served with the imperial police in Burma and fought on the republican side in the Spanish civil war. Orwell published two influential novels, *Animal Farm* (1945) and *1984* (1949). He is widely admired for the crisp, lucid prose style of his essays.

To illustrate the plight of the Colonial English overseas, Orwell narrates a situation where, against his better judgment, he was practically forced to shoot an elephant.

● ● ●

1   In Moulmein, in Lower Burma, I was hated by large numbers of people—the only time in my life that I have been important enough for this to happen to me. I was sub-divisional police officer of the town, and in an aimless, petty kind of way anti-European feeling was very bitter. No one had the guts to raise a riot, but if a European woman went through the bazaars alone somebody would probably spit betel juice over her dress. As a police officer I was an obvious target and was baited whenever it seemed safe to do so. When a nimble Burman

tripped me up on the football field and the referee (another Burman) looked the other way, the crowd yelled with hideous laughter. This happened more than once. In the end the sneering yellow faces of young men that met me everywhere, the insults hooted after me when I was at a safe distance, got badly on my nerves. The young Buddhist priests were the worst of all. There were several thousand of them in the town and none of them seemed to have anything to do except stand on the street corners and jeer at Europeans.

2   All this was perplexing and upsetting. For at that time I had already made up my mind that imperialism was an evil thing and the sooner I chucked up my job and got out of it the better. Theoretically—and secretly, of course—I was all for the Burmese and all against their oppressors, the British. As for the job I was doing, I hated it more bitterly than I can perhaps make clear. In a job like that you see the dirty work of Empire at close quarters. The wretched prisoners huddling in the stinking cages of the lock-ups, the grey, cowed faces of the long-term convicts, the scarred buttocks of the men who had been flogged with bamboos—all these oppressed me with an intolerable sense of guilt. But I could get nothing into perspective. I was young and ill-educated and I had had to think out my problems in the utter silence that is imposed on every Englishman in the East. I did not even know that the British Empire is dying, still less did I know that it is a great deal better than the younger empires that are going to supplant it. All I knew was that I was stuck between my hatred of the empire I served and my rage against the evil-spirited little beasts who tried to make my job impossible. With one part of my mind I thought of the British Raj as an unbreakable tyranny, as something clamped down, in *saecula saeculorum*,[1] upon the will of prostrate peoples; with another part I thought that the greatest joy in the world would be to drive a bayonet into a Buddhist priest's guts. Feelings like these are the normal by-products of imperialism; ask any Anglo-Indian official, if you can catch him off duty.

3   One day something happened which in a roundabout way was enlightening. It was a tiny incident in itself, but it gave me a better glimpse than I had had before of the real nature of imperialism—the real motives for which despotic governments act. Early one morning the sub-inspector at a police station at the other end of the town rang me up on the phone and said that an elephant was ravaging the bazaar. Would I please come and do something about it? I did not know what I could do, but I wanted to see what was happening and I got onto a pony and started out. I took my rifle, an old .44 Winchester and much too small to kill an elephant, but I thought the noise might be useful *in terrorem*.[2] Various Burmans stopped me on the way and told me about the elephant's doings. It was not, of course, a wild elephant, but a tame one which had gone "must." It had been chained up, as tame elephants always are when their attack of "must" is due, but on the previous night it had broken its chain and escaped. Its mahout, the only person who could manage it when it was in that state, had set out in pursuit, but had taken the wrong direction and was

---

[1]Latin expression meaning *forever and ever*
[2]Latin expression meaning *as a warning.*

now twelve hours' journey away, and in the morning the elephant had suddenly reappeared in the town. The Burmese population had no weapons and were quite helpless against it. It had already destroyed somebody's bamboo hut, killed a cow and raided some fruit-stalls and devoured the stock; also it had met the municipal rubbish van and, when the driver jumped out and took to his heels, had turned the van over and inflicted violences upon it.

4   The Burmese sub-inspector and some Indian constables were waiting for me in the quarter where the elephant had been seen. It was a very poor quarter, a labyrinth of squalid bamboo huts, thatched with palm-leaf, winding all over a steep hillside. I remember that it was a cloudy, stuffy morning at the beginning of the rains. We began questioning the people as to where the elephant had gone and, as usual, failed to get any definite information. That is invariably the case in the East; a story always sounds clear enough at a distance, but the nearer you get to the scene of events the vaguer it becomes. Some of the people said that the elephant had gone in one direction, some said that he had gone in another, some professed not even to have heard of any elephant. I had almost made up my mind that the whole story was a pack of lies, when we heard yells a little distance away. There was a loud, scandalized cry of "Go away, child! Go away this instant!" and an old woman with a switch in her hand came round the corner of a hut, violently shooing away a crowd of naked children. Some more women followed, clicking their tongues and exclaiming; evidently there was something that the children ought not to have seen. I rounded the hut and saw a man's dead body sprawling in the mud. He was an Indian, a black Dravidian coolie, almost naked, and he could not have been dead many minutes. The people said that the elephant had come suddenly upon him round the corner of the hut, caught him with its trunk, put its foot on his back and ground him into the earth. This was the rainy season and the ground was soft, and his face had scored a trench a foot deep and a couple of yards long. He was lying on his belly with arms crucified and head sharply twisted to one side. His face was coated with mud, the eyes wide open, the teeth bared and grinning with an expression of unendurable agony. (Never tell me, by the way, that the dead look peaceful. Most of the corpses I have seen looked devilish.) The friction of the great beast's foot had stripped the skin from his back as neatly as one skins a rabbit. As soon as I saw the dead man I sent an orderly to a friend's house nearby to borrow an elephant rifle. I had already sent back the pony, not wanting it to go mad with fright and throw me if it smelt the elephant.

5   The orderly came back in a few minutes with a rifle and five cartridges, and meanwhile some Burmans had arrived and told us that the elephant was in the paddy fields below, only a few hundred yards away. As I started forward practically the whole population of the quarter flocked out of the houses and followed me. They had seen the rifle and were all shouting excitedly that I was going to shoot the elephant. They had not shown much interest in the elephant when he was merely ravaging their homes, but it was different now that he was going to be shot. It was a bit of fun to them, as it would be to an English crowd; besides they wanted the meat. It made me vaguely uneasy. I had no intention of shooting the elephant—I had merely sent for the rifle to defend

myself if necessary—and it is always unnerving to have a crowd following you. I marched down the hill, looking and feeling a fool, with the rifle over my shoulder and an ever-growing army of people jostling at my heels. At the bottom, when you got away from the huts, there was a metalled road and beyond that a miry waste of paddy fields a thousand yards across, not yet ploughed but soggy from the first rains and dotted with coarse grass. The elephant was standing eight yards from the road, his left side towards us. He took not the slightest notice of the crowd's approach. He was tearing up bunches of grass, beating them against his knees to clean them and stuffing them into his mouth.

6   I had halted on the road. As soon as I saw the elephant I knew with perfect certainty that I ought not to shoot him. It is a serious matter to shoot a working elephant—it is comparable to destroying a huge and costly piece of machinery—and obviously one ought not to do it if it can possibly be avoided. And at that distance, peacefully eating, the elephant looked no more dangerous than a cow. I thought then and I think now that his attack of "must" was already passing off; in which case he would merely wander harmlessly about until the mahout came back and caught him. Moreover, I did not in the least want to shoot him. I decided that I would watch him for a little while to make sure that he did not turn savage again, and then go home.

7   But at that moment I glanced round at the crowd that had followed me. It was an immense crowd, two thousand at the least and growing every minute. It blocked the road for a long distance on either side. I looked at the sea of yellow faces above the garish clothes—faces all happy and excited over this bit of fun, all certain that the elephant was going to be shot. They were watching me as they would watch a conjurer about to perform a trick. They did not like me, but with the magical rifle in my hands I was momentarily worth watching. And suddenly I realized that I should have to shoot the elephant after all. The people expected it of me and I had got to do it; I could feel their two thousand wills pressing me forward, irresistibly. And it was at this moment, as I stood there with the rifle in my hands, that I first grasped the hollowness, the futility of the white man's dominion in the East. Here was I, the white man with his gun, standing in front of the unarmed native crowd—seemingly the leading actor of the piece; but in reality I was only an absurd puppet pushed to and fro by the will of those yellow faces behind. I perceived in this moment that when the white man turns tyrant it is his own freedom that he destroys. He becomes a sort of hollow, posing dummy, the conventionalized figure of a sahib. For it is the condition of his rule that he shall spend his life in trying to impress the "natives," and so in every crisis he has got to do what the "natives" expect of him. He wears a mask, and his face grows to fit it. I had got to shoot the elephant. I had committed myself to doing it when I sent for the rifle. A sahib has got to act like a sahib; he has got to appear resolute, to know his own mind and do definite things. To come all that way, rifle in hand, with two thousand people marching at my heels, and then to trail feebly away, having done nothing—no, that was impossible. The crowd would laugh at me. And my whole life, every white man's life in the East, was one long struggle not to be laughed at.

8   But I did not want to shoot the elephant. I watched him beating his bunch of grass against his knees, with that preoccupied grandmotherly air that

elephants have. It seemed to me that it would be murder to shoot him. At that age I was not squeamish about killing animals, but I had never shot an elephant and never wanted to. (Somehow it always seems worse to kill a large animal.) Besides, there was the beast's owner to be considered. Alive, the elephant was worth at least a hundred pounds; dead, he would only be worth the value of his tusks, five pounds, possibly. But I had got to act quickly. I turned to some experienced-looking Burmans who had been there when we arrived, and asked them how the elephant had been behaving. They all said the same thing: he took no notice of you if you left him alone, but he might charge if you went too close to him.

9   It was perfectly clear to me what I ought to do. I ought to walk up to within, say, twenty-five yards of the elephant and test his behavior. If he charged, I could shoot; if he took no notice of me, it would be safe to leave him until the mahout came back. But also I knew that I was going to do no such thing. I was a poor shot with a rifle and the ground was soft mud into which one would sink at every step. If the elephant charged and I missed him, I should have about as much chance as a toad under a steam-roller. But even then I was not thinking particularly of my own skin, only of the watchful yellow faces behind. For at that moment, with the crowd watching me, I was not afraid in the ordinary sense, as I would have been if I had been alone. A white man mustn't be frightened in front of "natives"; and so, in general, he isn't frightened. The sole thought in my mind was that if anything went wrong those two thousand Burmans would see me pursued, caught, trampled on and reduced to a grinning corpse like that Indian up the hill. And if that happened it was quite probable that some of them would laugh. That would never do. There was only one alternative. I shoved the cartridges into the magazine and lay down on the road to get a better aim.

10   The crowd grew very still, and a deep, low, happy sigh, as of people who see the theatre curtain go up at last, breathed from innumerable throats. They were going to have their bit of fun after all. The rifle was a beautiful German thing with cross-hair sights. I did not then know that in shooting an elephant one would shoot to cut an imaginary bar running from ear-hole to ear-hole. I ought, therefore, as the elephant was sideway on, to have aimed straight at his ear-hole; actually I aimed several inches in front of this, thinking the brain would be further forward.

11   When I pulled the trigger I did not hear the bang or feel the kick—one never does when a shot goes home—but I heard the devilish roar of glee that went up from the crowd. In that instant, in too short a time, one would have thought, even for the bullet to get there, a mysterious, terrible change had come over the elephant. He neither stirred nor fell, but every line of his body had altered. He looked suddenly stricken, shrunken, immensely old, as though the frightful impact of the bullet had paralyzed him without knocking him down. At last, after what seemed a long time—it might have been five seconds, I dare say he sagged flabbily to his knees. His mouth slobbered. An enormous senility seemed to have settled upon him. One could have imagined him thousands of years old. I fired again into the same spot. At the second shot he did not collapse but climbed with desperate slowness to his feet and stood weakly

upright, with legs sagging and head drooping. I fired a third time. That was the shot that did for him. You could see the agony of it jolt his whole body and knock the last remnant of strength from his legs. But in falling he seemed for a moment to rise, for as his hind legs collapsed beneath him he seemed to tower upward like a huge rock toppling, his trunk reaching skywards like a tree. He trumpeted, for the first and only time. And then down he came, his belly towards me, with a crash that seemed to shake the ground even where I lay.

12   I got up. The Burmans were already racing past me across the mud. It was obvious that the elephant would never rise again, but he was not dead. He was breathing very rhythmically with long rattling gasps, his great mound of a side painfully rising and falling. His mouth was wide open—I could see far down into caverns of pale pink throat. I waited for a long time for him to die, but his breathing did not weaken. Finally I fired my two remaining shots into the spot where I thought his heart must be. The thick blood welled out of him like red velvet, but still he did not die. His body did not even jerk when the shots hit him, the tortured breathing continued without a pause. He was dying, very slowly and in great agony, but in some world remote from me where not even a bullet could damage him further. I felt that I had got to put an end to that dreadful noise. It seemed dreadful to see the great beast lying there, powerless to move and yet powerless to die, and not even to be able to finish him. I sent back for my small rifle and poured shot after shot into his heart and down his throat. They seemed to make no impression. The tortured gasps continued as steadily as the ticking of a clock.

13   In the end I could not stand it any longer and went away. I heard later that it took him half an hour to die. Burmans were bringing dahs and baskets even before I left, and I was told they had stripped his body almost to the bones by the afternoon.

14   Afterwards, of course, there were endless discussions about the shooting of the elephant. The owner was furious, but he was only an Indian and could do nothing. Besides, legally I had done the right thing, for a mad elephant has to be killed, like a mad dog, if its owner fails to control it. Among the Europeans opinion was divided. The older men said I was right, the younger men said it was a damn shame to shoot an elephant for killing a coolie, because an elephant was worth more than any damn Coringhee coolie. And afterwards I was very glad that the coolie had been killed; it put me legally in the right and it gave me a sufficient pretext for shooting the elephant. I often wondered whether any of the others grasped that I had done it solely to avoid looking a fool.

● Vocabulary

supplant (2)	labyrinth (4)	conventionalized (7)
prostrate (2)	squalid (4)	resolute (7)
despotic (3)	garish (7)	pretext (14)

● The Facts

1. Which class of Burmese did Orwell despise most of all?
2. What would likely happen to a white woman who went through the bazaars alone?
3. What is Orwell's opinion of the younger empires that were going to supplant the British Empire?
4. What is invariably the case with stories set in the East?
5. According to Orwell, what is a condition of white rule over the empire?

● The Strategies

1. Orwell writes: "They had not shown much interest in the elephant when he was merely ravaging their homes, but it was different now that he was going to be shot." What tone is he using here?
2. Why does Orwell use Latin phrases? What purpose do they have in the story?
3. The story is told in two tenses: the past and the present. What effect does this have on its telling?
4. Orwell encloses some remarks in parentheses in paragraphs 4 and 8. Why are these remarks set off in this way?
5. What analogy does Orwell use in paragraph 10 to describe his feelings about the crowd gathered to see him kill the elephant? Is this an appropriate analogy? Explain.

● The Issues

1. What is the value of a role and of role-playing in the relationships of everyday life?
2. What are the obvious disadvantages of role-playing?
3. How would you characterize Orwell's attitude toward the empire he serves?
4. How do you think the author might have behaved, and what do you think he might have done, if other Europeans had been with him when he met the elephant?
5. What circumstances of today's life might similarly make someone, say, a student, feel impelled to behave in a way contrary to his or her better judgment?

● Suggestions for Writing

1. Analyze and discuss "Shooting an Elephant" as a story about the abstract versus the concrete, the general versus the particular.
2. Write an essay entitled "I Wore a Mask, and My Face Grew to Fit It." Tell how circumstances forced you into playing a part you secretly hated.

My Name Is Margaret

MAYA ANGELOU

> ### Rhetorical Thumbnail
>
> **Purpose:** to portray what life was like in the southern racist society
>
> **Audience:**   general educated reader
>
> **Language:**   Southern English, especially in the dialogue
>
> **Strategy:**   sketches an example of how the prejudice of the day suffocated everyone in the stereotypes of race

Maya Angelou (b. 1928) is novelist, poet, playwright, actress, composer, and singer. Her varied accomplishments have thrown her into the public limelight, where she is greatly admired as a speaker and reader of her own works. She is best known for her single-minded devotion to the cause of tolerance. Many of her novels recount incidents in which her characters must fight ardently to maintain their identity in a world of prejudice. Among her best-known works are *I Know Why the Caged Bird Sings* (1970), from which the selection that follows is taken, *Gather Together in My Name* (1974), *Singin' and Swingin' and Gettin' Merry Like Christmas* (1976), *Heart of a Woman* (1981), and *All God's Children Need Traveling Shoes* (1986). Angelou has also written volumes of poetry, including *Oh Pray My Wings Are Gonna Fit Me Well* (1975) and *I Shall Not Be Moved* (1990). She has become a role model for aspiring female writers of various minority backgrounds.

A black author, admired for her stories dealing with affronts to a black person's pride and sense of dignity, tells of an incident in which a white woman attempts to change the name of the author, who was then working for her.

• • •

1   Recently a white woman from Texas, who would quickly describe herself as a liberal, asked me about my hometown. When I told her that in Stamps my grandmother had owned the only Negro general merchandise store since the turn of the century, she exclaimed, "Why, you were a debutante." Ridiculous and even ludicrous. But Negro girls in small Southern towns, whether poverty-stricken or just munching along on a few of life's necessities, were given as extensive and irrelevant preparations for adulthood as rich white girls shown in magazines. Admittedly the training was not the same. While white girls learned to waltz and sit gracefully with a tea cup balanced on their knees, we were lagging behind, learning the mid-Victorian values with very little money to indulge them. (Come and see Edna Lomax spending the money she made picking cotton on five balls of ecru tatting thread. Her fingers are bound to snag

the work and she'll have to repeat the stitches time and time again. But she knows that when she buys the thread.)

2   We were required to embroider and I had trunkfuls of colorful dishtowels, pillowcases, runners and handkerchiefs to my credit. I mastered the art of crocheting and tatting, and there was a lifetime's supply of dainty doilies that would never be used in sacheted dresser drawers. It went without saying that all girls could iron and wash, but the finer touches around the home, like setting a table with real silver, baking roasts and cooking vegetables without meat, had to be learned elsewhere. Usually at the source of those habits. During my tenth year, a white woman's kitchen became my finishing school.

3   Mrs. Viola Cullinan was a plump woman who lived in a three-bedroom house somewhere behind the post office. She was singularly unattractive until she smiled, and then the lines around her eyes and mouth which made her look perpetually dirty disappeared, and her face looked like the mask of an impish elf. She usually rested her smile until late afternoon when her women friends dropped in and Miss Glory, the cook, served them cold drinks on the closed-in porch.

4   The exactness of her house was inhuman. This glass went here and only here. That cup had its place and it was an act of impudent rebellion to place it anywhere else. At twelve o'clock the table was set. At 12:15 Mrs. Cullinan sat down to dinner (whether her husband had arrived or not). At 12:16 Miss Glory brought out the food.

5   It took me a week to learn the difference between a salad plate, a bread plate and a dessert plate.

6   Mrs. Cullinan kept up the tradition of her wealthy parents. She was from Virginia. Miss Glory, who was a descendant of slaves that had worked for the Cullinans, told me her history. She had married beneath her (according to Miss Glory). Her husband's family hadn't had their money very long and what they had "didn't 'mount to much."

7   As ugly as she was, I thought privately, she was lucky to get a husband above or beneath her station. But Miss Glory wouldn't let me say a thing against her mistress. She was very patient with me, however, over the housework. She explained the dishware, silverware and servants' bells. The large round bowl in which soup was served wasn't a soup bowl, it was a tureen. There were goblets, sherbet glasses, ice-cream glasses, wine glasses, green glass coffee cups with matching saucers, and water glasses. I had a glass to drink from, and it sat with Miss Glory's on a separate shelf from the others. *Soup spoons, gravy boat, butter knives, salad forks* and *carving platter* were additions to my vocabulary and in fact almost represented a new language. I was fascinated with the novelty, with the fluttering Mrs. Cullinan and her Alice-in-Wonderland house.

8   Her husband remains, in my memory, undefined. I lumped him with all the other white men that I had ever seen and tried not to see.

9   On our way home one evening, Miss Glory told me that Mrs. Cullinan couldn't have children. She said that she was too delicate-boned. It was hard to imagine bones at all under those layers of fat. Miss Glory went on to say that the doctor had taken out all her lady organs. I reasoned that a pig's organs

included the lungs, heart and liver, so if Mrs. Cullinan was walking around without those essentials, it explained why she drank alcohol out of unmarked bottles. She was keeping herself embalmed.

10   When I spoke to Bailey about it, he agreed that I was right, but he also informed me that Mr. Cullinan had two daughters by a colored lady and that I knew them very well. He added that the girls were the spitting image of their father. I was unable to remember what he looked like, although I had just left him a few hours before, but I thought of the Coleman girls. They were very light-skinned and certainly didn't look very much like their mother (no one ever mentioned Mr. Coleman).

11   My pity for Mrs. Cullinan preceded me the next morning like the Cheshire cat's smile. Those girls, who could have been her daughters, were beautiful. They didn't have to straighten their hair. Even when they were caught in the rain, their braids still hung down straight like tamed snakes. Their mouths were pouty little cupid's bows. Mrs. Cullinan didn't know what she missed. Or maybe she did. Poor Mrs. Cullinan.

12   For weeks after, I arrived early, left late and tried very hard to make up for her barrenness. If she had had her own children, she wouldn't have had to ask me to run a thousand errands from her back door to the back door of her friends. Poor old Mrs. Cullinan.

13   Then one evening Miss Glory told me to serve the ladies on the porch. After I set the tray down and turned toward the kitchen, one of the women asked, "What's your name, girl?" It was the speckled-faced one. Mrs. Cullinan said, "She doesn't talk much. Her name's Margaret."

14   "Is she dumb?"

15   "No. As I understand it, she can talk when she wants to but she's usually quiet as a little mouse. Aren't you, Margaret?"

16   I smiled at her. Poor thing. No organs and couldn't even pronounce my name correctly.

17   "She's a sweet little thing, though."

18   "Well, that may be, but the name's too long. I'd never bother myself. I'd call her Mary if I was you."

19   I fumed into the kitchen. That horrible woman would never have the chance to call me Mary because if I was starving I'd never work for her. I decided I wouldn't pee on her if her heart was on fire. Giggles drifted in off the porch and into Miss Glory's pots. I wondered what they could be laughing about.

20   White folks were so strange. Could they be talking about me? Everybody knew that they stuck together better than the Negroes did. It was possible that Mrs. Cullinan had friends in St. Louis who heard about a girl from Stamps being in court and wrote to tell her. Maybe she knew about Mr. Freeman.

21   My lunch was in my mouth a second time and I went outside and relieved myself on the bed of four-o'clocks. Miss Glory thought I might be coming down with something and told me to go on home, that Momma would give me some herb tea, and she'd explain to her mistress.

22   I realized how foolish I was being before I reached the pond. Of course Mrs. Cullinan didn't know. Otherwise she wouldn't have given me two nice dresses

that Momma cut down, and she certainly wouldn't have called me a "sweet little thing." My stomach felt fine, and I didn't mention anything to Momma.

23   That evening I decided to write a poem on being white, fat, old and without children. It was going to be a tragic ballad. I would have to watch her carefully to capture the essence of her loneliness and pain.

24   The very next day, she called me by the wrong name. Miss Glory and I were washing up the lunch dishes when Mrs. Cullinan came to the doorway. "Mary?"

25   Miss Glory asked, "Who?"

26   Mrs. Cullinan, sagging a little, knew and I knew. "I want Mary to go down to Mrs. Randall's and take her some soup. She's not been feeling well for a few days."

27   Miss Glory's face was a wonder to see. "You mean Margaret, ma'am. Her name's Margaret."

28   "That's too long. She's Mary from now on. Heat that soup from last night and put it in the china tureen and, Mary, I want you to carry it carefully."

29   Every person I knew had a hellish horror of being "called out of his name." It was a dangerous practice to call a Negro anything that could be loosely construed as insulting because of the centuries of their having been called *niggers, jigs, dinges, blackbirds, crows, boots* and *spooks.*

30   Miss Glory had a fleeting second of feeling sorry for me. Then as she handed me the hot tureen she said, "Don't mind, don't pay that no mind. Sticks and stones may break your bones, but words . . . You know, I been working for her for twenty years."

31   She held the back door open for me. "Twenty years. I wasn't much older than you. My name used to be Hallelujah. That's what Ma named me, but my mistress give me 'Glory,' and it stuck. I likes it better too."

32   I was in the little path that ran behind the houses when Miss Glory shouted, "It's shorter too."

33   For a few seconds it was a tossup over whether I would laugh (imagine being named Hallelujah) or cry (imagine letting some white woman rename you for her convenience). My anger saved me from either outburst. I had to quit the job, but the problem was going to be how to do it. Momma wouldn't allow me to quit for just any reason.

34   "She's a peach. That woman is a real peach." Mrs. Randall's maid was talking as she took the soup from me, and I wondered what her name used to be and what she answered to now.

35   For a week I looked into Mrs. Cullinan's face as she called me Mary. She ignored my coming late and leaving early. Miss Glory was a little annoyed because I had begun to leave egg yolk on the dishes and wasn't putting much heart in polishing the silver. I hoped that she would complain to our boss, but she didn't.

36   Then Bailey solved my dilemma. He had me describe the contents of the cupboard and the particular plates she liked best. Her favorite piece was a casserole shaped like a fish and the green glass coffee cups. I kept his instructions in mind, so on the next day when Miss Glory was hanging out clothes and I had again been told to serve the old biddies on the porch, I dropped the empty serving tray. When I heard Mrs. Cullinan scream, "Mary!" I picked up the casserole and two of the green glass cups in readiness. As she rounded the kitchen door I let them fall on the tiled floor.

37   I could never absolutely describe to Bailey what happened next, because each time I got to the part where she fell on the floor and screwed up her ugly face to cry, we burst out laughing. She actually wobbled around on the floor and picked up shards of the cups and cried, "Oh, Momma. Oh, dear Gawd. It's Momma's china from Virginia. Oh, Momma, I sorry."

38   Miss Glory came running in from the yard and the women from the porch crowded around. Miss Glory was almost as broken up as her mistress. "You mean to say she broke our Virginia dishes? What we gone do?"

39   Miss Cullinan cried louder, "That clumsy nigger. Clumsy little black nigger."

40   Old speckled-face leaned down and asked, "Who did it, Viola? Was it Mary? Who did it?"

41   Everything was happening so fast I can't remember whether her action preceded her words, but I know that Mrs. Cullinan said, "Her name's Margaret, goddamn it, her name's Margaret." And she threw a wedge of the broken plate at me. It could have been the hysteria which put her aim off, but the flying crockery caught Miss Glory right over the ear and she started screaming.

42   I left the front door wide open so all the neighbors could hear.

43   Mrs. Cullinan was right about one thing. My name wasn't Mary.

"My Name Is Margaret," copyright © 1969 and renewed 1997 by Maya Angelou, from I KNOW WHY THE CAGED BIRD SINGS by Maya Angelou. Used by permission of Random House, Inc.

● Vocabulary

debutante (1)	sacheted (2)	ballad (23)
ludicrous (1)	impudent (4)	shards (37)
tatting (2)	barrenness (12)	crockery (41)

● The Facts

1. In their preparations for adulthood, what did both white girls and black girls have in common?
2. Where did black girls learn to set the table and cook?
3. What kind of housekeeper was Mrs. Viola Cullinan? How does the narrator view her habits?
4. Why does the narrator feel pity for Mrs. Cullinan?
5. Why did the narrator get furious at Mrs. Cullinan? What did the narrator do to vent her anger?

● The Strategies

1. From whose point of view is this story told? How does the point of view affect the narration? How is the narration paced?
2. The narrator calls Mrs. Cullinan's house an "Alice-in-Wonderland house." What kind of image does this label conjure up? Where else in the story does the narrator use an image from Lewis Carroll's *Adventures of Alice in Wonderland*? To what purpose?

3. Although the tale about Margaret's name is essentially a serious matter, there are nevertheless some humorous elements in the narrative. What humorous incidents can you point out? Refer to specific passages.

4. What examples of figurative language does the narrator use in paragraph 11? How effective are they?

5. Why does the narrator never explain who Bailey and Mr. Freeman are? From the context of the story, who do you think they are?

The Issues

1. The narrator is extremely sensitive about her name. Why is this so? How do you feel about your own name? Does it bother you when someone mispronounces or misspells it?

2. The narrator leaves the ending wide open. What do you think will happen to Margaret following this incident?

3. What does Margaret's decision to write a poem about Mrs. Cullinan indicate?

4. What is the relationship between Miss Glory and Mrs. Cullinan?

5. Describe Miss Glory. Do you think Margaret will ever be like her?

6. What do you think of Miss Glory's attempt to calm down Margaret after Mrs. Cullinan called her "Mary" from the doorway? (See paragraphs 30–32.) How does her reaction differ from Bailey's? Which reaction seems more appropriate to you?

Suggestions for Writing

1. Narrate an incident in which you reacted to someone who treated you with arrogance or meanness. Make your narrative come to life by using dialogue and vivid details.

2. Narrate an incident from your youth that taught you a lesson in tolerance concerning race, religion, sex, social status, or some other aspect of society. Pace the narration properly and use vivid details.

Shame

DICK GREGORY

Rhetorical Thumbnail

Purpose: to inform about his early life

Audience: general reader

Language: simple language, particularly the dialogue, of a child

Strategy: recreates from the "I" point of view the recollected experience of being shamed in school

Dick Gregory (b. 1932) is a political activist, comedian, and writer. He attended Southern Illinois University, where he was named Outstanding Athlete in 1953.

Gregory has been much admired for his interest in social issues such as world famine and for his outstanding ability as a standup comedian. In 1966, he ran for Mayor of Chicago, and in 1968, he was the presidential candidate of the Freedom and Peace Party. Gregory has written several books, including *From the Back of the Bus* (1962), *What's Happening?* (1965), *The Shadow That Scares Me* (1968), *Dick Gregory's Bible Tales* (1974), and his autobiography, *Up from Nigger* (1976). Gregory was one of the first black comedians to break the "color barrier" and perform for white audiences. His popularity is based on his ability to satirize race relations without being derogatory.

Even if you have never felt the poverty described by the narrator in the story that follows, you can probably remember someone from your childhood or adolescence who somehow represented all the romance and beauty for which you longed. Ponder the details that make the narrator's experience so heartbreaking.

• • •

1   I never learned hate at home, or shame. I had to go to school for that. I was about seven years old when I got my first big lesson. I was in love with a little girl named Helene Tucker, a light-complected little girl with pigtails and nice manners. She was always clean and she was smart in school. I think I went to school mostly to look at her. I brushed my hair and even got me a little old handkerchief. It was a lady's handkerchief, but I didn't want Helene to see me wipe my nose on my hand. The pipes were frozen again, there was no water in the house, but I washed my socks and shirt every night. I'd get a pot, and go over to Mr. Ben's grocery store, and stick my pot down into his soda machine. Scoop out some chopped ice. By evening the ice melted to water for washing. I got sick a lot that winter because the fire would go out at night before the clothes were dry. In the morning I'd put them on, wet or dry, because they were the only clothes I had.

2   Everybody's got a Helene Tucker, a symbol of everything you want. I loved her for her goodness, her cleanliness, her popularity. She'd walk down my street and my brothers and sisters would yell, "Here comes Helene," and I'd rub my tennis sneakers on the back of my pants and wish my hair wasn't so nappy and the white folks' shirt fit me better. I'd run out on the street. If I knew my place and didn't come too close, she'd wink at me and say hello. That was a good feeling. Sometimes I'd follow her all the way home, and shovel the snow off her walk and try to make friends with her Momma and her aunts. I'd drop money on her stoop late at night on my way back from shining shoes in the taverns. And she had a Daddy, and he had a good job. He was a paper hanger.

3   I guess I would have gotten over Helene by summertime, but something happened in that classroom that made her face hang in front of me for the next twenty-two years. When I played the drums in high school it was for Helene and when I broke track records in college it was for Helene and when I started standing behind microphones and heard applause I wished Helene could hear it, too. It wasn't until I was twenty-nine years old and married and making money that I really got her out of my system. Helene was sitting in that classroom when I learned to be ashamed of myself.

4   It was on a Thursday. I was sitting in the back of the room, in a seat with a chalk circle drawn around it. The idiot's seat, the troublemaker's seat.

5   The teacher thought I was stupid. Couldn't spell, couldn't read, couldn't do arithmetic. Just stupid. Teachers were never interested in finding out that you couldn't concentrate because you were so hungry, because you hadn't had any breakfast. All you could think about was noontime, would it ever come? Maybe you could sneak into the cloakroom and steal a bit of some kid's lunch out of a coat pocket. A bit of something. Paste. You can't really make a meal out of paste, or put it on bread for a sandwich, but sometimes I'd scoop a few spoonfuls out of the paste jar in the back of the room. Pregnant people get strange tastes. I was pregnant with poverty. Pregnant with dirt and pregnant with smells that made people turn away, pregnant with cold and pregnant with shoes that were never bought for me, pregnant with five other people in my bed and no Daddy in the next room, and pregnant with hunger. Paste doesn't taste too bad when you're hungry.

6   The teacher thought I was a troublemaker. All she saw from the front of the room was a little black boy who squirmed in his idiot's seat and made noises and poked the kids around him. I guess she couldn't see a kid who made noises because he wanted someone to know he was there.

7   It was on a Thursday, the day before the Negro payday. The eagle always flew on Friday. The teacher was asking each student how much his father would give to the Community Chest. On Friday night, each kid would get the money from his father, and on Monday he would bring it to the school. I decided I was going to buy me a Daddy right then. I had money in my pocket from shining shoes and selling papers and whatever Helene Tucker pledged for her Daddy I was going to top it. And I'd hand the money right in. I wasn't going to wait until Monday to buy me a Daddy.

8   I was shaking, scared to death. The teacher opened her book and started calling our names alphabetically.

9   "Helene Tucker?"

10   "My Daddy said he'd give two dollars and fifty cents."

11   "That's very nice, Helene. Very, very nice indeed."

12   That made me feel pretty good. It wouldn't take too much to top that. I had almost three dollars in dimes and quarters in my pocket. I stuck my hand in my pocket and held onto the money, waiting for her to call my name. But the teacher closed her book after she called everybody else in the class.

13   I stood up and raised my hand.

14   "What is it now?"

15   "You forgot me."

16   She turned toward the blackboard. "I don't have time to be playing with you, Richard."

17   "My Daddy said he'd . . ."

18   "Sit down, Richard, you're disturbing the class."

19   "My Daddy said he'd give . . . fifteen dollars."

20   She turned around and looked mad. "We are collecting this money for you and your kind, Richard Gregory. If your Daddy can give fifteen dollars you have no business being on relief."

21   "I got it right now, I got it right now, my Daddy gave it to me to turn in today, my Daddy said . . ."

22   "And furthermore," she said, looking right at me, her nostrils getting big and her lips getting thin and her eyes opening wide, "we know you don't have a Daddy."

23   Helene Tucker turned around, her eyes full of tears. She felt sorry for me. Then I couldn't see her too well because I was crying, too.

24   "Sit down, Richard."

25   And I always thought the teacher kind of liked me. She always picked me to wash the blackboard on Friday, after school. That was a big thrill, it made me feel important. If I didn't wash it, come Monday the school might not function right.

26   "Where are you going, Richard?"

27   I walked out of school that day, and for a long time I didn't go back very often. There was shame there.

28   Now there was shame everywhere. It seemed like the whole world had been inside that classroom, everyone had heard what the teacher had said, everyone had turned around and felt sorry for me. There was shame in going to the Worthy Boys Annual Christmas Dinner for you and your kind, because everybody knew what a worthy boy was. Why couldn't they just call it the Boys Annual Dinner, why'd they have to give it a name? There was shame in wearing the brown and orange and white plaid mackinaw the welfare gave to 3,000 boys. Why'd it have to be the same for everybody so when you walked down the street the people could see you were on relief? It was a nice warm mackinaw and it had a hood, and my Momma beat me and called me a little rat when she found out I stuffed it in the bottom of a pail full of garbage way over on Cottage Street. There was shame in running over to Mister Ben's at the end of the day and asking for his rotten peaches, there was shame in asking Mrs. Simmons for a spoonful of sugar, there was shame in running out to meet the relief truck. I hated that truck, full of food for you and your kind. I ran into the house and hid when it came. And then I started to sneak through alleys, to take the long way home so people going into White's Eat Shop wouldn't see me. Yeah, the whole world heard the teacher that day, we all know you don't have a Daddy.

● Vocabulary

mackinaw (28)

● The Facts

1. Where did the narrator learn shame?

2. What did the narrator do for Helene Tucker? How important was she in his life?

3. According to the narrator, why could he not do well in school? What did the teachers think?

4. What event at school caused shame to control the narrator's life for a long time? Summarize what happened.

5. What did the author dislike about the Worthy Boys Annual Christmas Dinner?

● The Strategies

1. The narration begins in paragraph 3, following two paragraphs of commentary about Helene Tucker, a girl on whom the narrator had a crush. What is the purpose of the preliminary paragraphs?

2. What dominant impression is always in the background of the narration? Why?

3. Beginning with paragraph 9, the narrator adds conversation to the narration. What is the effect of this technique?

4. What is the main theme (lesson about life) revealed in this story? Is it implied or stated?

5. In paragraph 5, what is the purpose of repeating the word "pregnant"? What does the author mean?

● The Issues

1. Do you agree with the narrator's comment that "everybody's got a Helene Tucker"? What does Helene Tucker symbolize? Give an example of a Helene Tucker from your own experience.

2. The teacher thought the narrator was a troublemaker. Was he really, or was there another reason for drawing attention to himself?

3. Why did the teacher humiliate the narrator when he announced that his father would donate fifteen dollars? Do you think the teacher should have handled the situation differently? If so, how should she have reacted?

4. The narrator states that he thought the teacher liked him because she always picked him to clean the blackboard on Friday. Why do you think she picked him?

5. Did the narrator do the right thing by not going back to the school often after the shame incident? What kept him away? Do you empathize or do you think the narrator was oversensitive?

● Suggestions for Writing

1. Write about an incident in which you or someone you love experienced shame. Use the techniques of pacing, using vivid details and making a point.

2. Write an essay in which you examine the psychological effects of poverty on children in elementary school.

On Black Fathering

CORNEL WEST

Rhetorical Thumbnail

Purpose: to eulogize his father

Audience: immediate audience: mourners at a funeral service

Language: elevated language, even occasionally biblical

Strategy: explains in great detail what the father meant to the family

Cornel West (b. 1953) is an influential writer on race, religion, and social problems. After several years of serving on the Harvard faculty as Professor of Religion and Afro-American studies, he recently joined the faculty at Princeton. His *Race Matters* (1993) was received with excitement and initiated a national dialogue about race issues, a dialogue that continued during the 2008 U.S. presidential campaign and beyond. The essay below was reprinted from *Faith of our Fathers* (1996) by Andre C. Willis.

More than anything else, this essay summarizes the stormy history of American blacks as they fought discrimination, poverty, and abuse within a society where white people often blocked them from fulfilling their economic, intellectual, and social potential.

• • •

1   One of the most difficult tasks to accomplish in American society is to be a solid, caring, and loving black father. To be a good black father, first you have to negotiate all of the absurd attacks and assaults on your humanity and on your capacity and status as a human being. Second, you have to provide materially and economically, as well as nurture psychologically, personally, and existentially. All of this requires a deep level of maturity. By maturity I mean a solid understanding of who one is as a person, and a sense of sacrifice and courage. For black men to reach that level of maturity and understanding is almost miraculous given the dehumanizing context for black men, and yet millions and millions have done it. It is a tribute to fulfill the highest standards of fatherhood. When I think of my own particular case, I think of my father, my grandfather, and his father, because what they were able to do was to sustain some sense of dignity and sacrifice even as they dealt with all the arrows that were coming at them on every level in American society.

2   Let's consider the economic level. In America, generally speaking, patriarchal definitions of men in relation to the economic front mean you have a job and provide for your family. Many black men did not (and do not) make enough money to provide for their families adequately because of their exclusion from jobs with a living wage. They then oftentimes tended, and tend, to

accent certain patriarchal identities (e.g., predatory or abusive behavior) in lieu of the fact that they could not perform the traditional patriarchal roles in American society.

3   Then on the home front, where black men had and have, oftentimes, wives who were and are subject to such white supremacist abuse, either at the white home where these sisters work(ed) or as a service worker in other parts of white society, most black men had to deal with the kinds of scars and bruises that come from knowing that you were supposed to protect your woman, as it were, which is also part of the patriarchal identity in America—a man ought to be able to protect his woman but could not protect her from the vicious abuse. Many black men also recognized that there was a relation between their not being able to get a job given the discrimination and segregation on the one hand and the tremendous power wielded by those white men who were often condoning the abuse of their own wives.

4   How children perceive their father is another interesting component of the dynamic that black fathers have to negotiate. How are black fathers able to convey to their children some affirmative sense of self, some sense of reality—given what is happening to these men on the economic front, given what many of them know is happening to their wives outside of the house, and given the perception by their own children that they are unable to fulfill the expected patriarchal role? In the tradition of the black father, the best ones—I think my grandfather and dad are good examples—came up with ways of negotiating a balance so that they would recognize that exclusion from the economic sphere was real, and recognize that possible abuse of their wives was real, and also recognize that they had to sustain a connection with their kids in which their kids could see the best in them despite the limited and dehumanizing circumstances under which they functioned.

5   My mother happened to be a woman who was not abused in the fashion described above. I remember one incident when a white policeman disrespected my mother. Dad went at him verbally and, in the eyes of the police, ended up violating the law. At that point he just drew a line in the sand that said, "You're going too far." I thank God that a number of incidents like that didn't happen, or he would have ended up in jail forever—like so many other brothers who just do not allow certain levels of disrespect of their mother, wife, sister, or daughter. As a man, what I was able to see in Dad was his ability to transform his own pain with a sense of laughter, and a sense of empathy, and a sense of compassion for others. This was a real act of moral genius Dad accomplished, and I think that it is part of the best of a tradition of moral genius. Unfortunately, large numbers of black men do not reach that level because the rage and the anger are just too deep; they just burn them out and consume their soul. Fortunately, on the other hand, you do have many black men that achieve this level and some that go beyond it.

6   In my own case as a father, I certainly tried to emulate and imitate Dad's very ingenious ways of negotiating the balances between what was happening on these different fronts, but because of the sacrifices he and Mom made, I had access to opportunities that he did not. When my son Cliff was born, I was

convinced that I wanted to try to do for him what Dad had done for me. But it was not to be—there was no way that I could be the father to my son that my dad was to me. Part of it was that my circumstances were very different. Another part was simply that I was not the man that my father was. My brother is actually the shining example of building on the rich legacy of my dad as a father much more than I am, because he gives everything—right across the board. He is there—whatever the circumstance—has spent time with the kids; he is always there in the same way that Dad was there for us. I'll always try to be a rich footnote to my brother, yet as a father I have certainly not been the person that he was. The effort has been there, the endeavor too, but the circumstances (as well as my not being as deep a person as he or my father) have not enabled me to measure up. On the other hand, my son Cliff turned out to be a decent and fascinating person—and he is still in process, of course.

7   The bottom line for my dad was always love, and he was a deeply Christian man—his favorite song was "I Will Trust in the Lord." He had a profound trust. His trust was much more profound than mine in some ways, even though I work at it. He had a deep love, and that's the thing I've tried to build on with Cliff. My hope and my inclination are that Cliff feels this love, but certainly it takes more than love to nurture and father a son or a daughter.

8   The most important things for black fathers to try to do are to give of themselves, to try to exemplify in their own behavior what they want to see in their sons and daughters, and, most important, to spend time with and give attention to their children. This is a big challenge, yet it is critical as we move into the twenty-first century.

9   The most difficult task of my life was to give the eulogy for my father. Everything else pales in the face of this challenge. Hence what Dad means to me—like my family, Cliff and Elleni—constitutes who and what I am and will be.

Eulogy

10   Clifton Lincoln West, Jr. What a man. What an individual. What a person. What a servant. We gather here, this afternoon in this sacred place and this consecrated space to say good-bye. To bid farewell to a good man, a great Christian who lived a grand and loving life. When I think of my father, I cannot but think of what he said to that reporter from the *Sacramento Bee* when they asked him, "What is it about you and what is it about your family—do you have a secret?" Dad said, "No, we live by Grace—in addition to that, me and his mother, we try to *be there*." I shall never forget that my father was not simply a man of quiet dignity, steadfast integrity, and high intelligence, but fundamentally and quintessentially he was a man of love, and love means being there for others. That's why when I think of Dad I recall that precious moment in the fifteenth chapter of John in the eleventh and twelfth verse: "These things have I given unto you that my joy might remain in you, and that your joy might be full. This is my commandment that ye love one another as I have loved you."

11   In the midst of Dad's sophistication and refinement he was always for real. He was someone who was down-to-earth because he took this commandment

seriously, and it meant he had to cut against the grain in a world in which he was going to endure lovingly and with compassion. Isn't that what the very core of the gospel is about? The thirteenth chapter of I Corinthians—that great litany of love that Dr. King talked about—deals with it. Dad used to read it all the time. I will never forget when he took me to college in Cambridge, the first time I ever flew on an airplane (it cost about ninety-five dollars then). Dad told me, "Corn, we're praying for you, and always remember: 'Though I speak with the tongues of men and of angels and have not love, I become as a sounding brass or a tinkling cymbal. And though I have the gift of prophecy, and understand all mysteries, and all knowledge; and though I have all faith, so that I could remove mountains, and have not love. I am nothing.' "

12   As we stand here on these stormy banks of Jordan and watch Dad's ship go by, may I remind each and every one of you that we come from a loving family, a courageous people of African descent, and a rich Christian tradition. We have seen situations in which history has pushed our backs against the wall, and life has knocked us to our knees. In the face of despair and degradation sometimes we know that all we can do is sing a song, or crack a smile, or say a prayer. Yet we refuse to allow grief and misery to have the last word.

13   Dad was a man of love, and if I was to adopt his perspective at this very moment, he would say, "Corn, don't push me in the limelight, keep your mother in mind, don't focus on me, keep the family in mind—I'm just a servant passing through." That's the kind of father I had.

14   But he didn't come to it by himself, you see. He was part of a family, he was part of a people, he was part of a tradition that went all the way back to gutbucket Jim Crow Louisiana, September 7, 1928. He was not supposed to make it, you see. Nobody would have believed that Clifton Lincoln West, Jr., the third child of C. L. West and Lovey West, would have been able to aspire to the heights that he did. No one would have predicted or projected that he would make it through the first three months in Louisiana—Cliff was not supposed to make that trip, you know. He was born the year before the stock market crashed. His family stayed three months in Louisiana, and Grandfather and Grandmother, with three young children in a snowstorm, journeyed on a train to Tulsa, Oklahoma. You all know what Tulsa, Oklahoma, was like. It was seven years after the major riot in this country in which over three hundred folks—black folks—were killed and Greenwood, Archer and Pine—that GAP corner—the Wall Street of black America was all burned out. But Grandmama had something else in mind, and the Lord did too.

15   Dad went on to Paul Laurence Dunbar Elementary School—to give you an idea of what side of town they were living on—and George Washington Carver Junior High School, and Booker T. Washington High School. It was there that he got to choose the idea of pulling from the best of the world but remaining not of the world. I like that about Dad. He wasn't so excessively pious or so excessively rigid that he became naive and got caught up in narrow doctrines and creeds and thought he was better than anybody else. That's not the kind of man he was. No. His faith was grounded in a love because he knew that he had fallen short of the glory of God. He knew he had inadequacies and short-

comings, but he was going to struggle anyhow; he was going to keep keeping on anyhow.

16   After high school he went on to the military for three years. He could have easily given his life for this country. When he returned to Tulsa, Oklahoma, he was refused admission at the University of Tulsa, and then went on to that grand institution, Fisk University, where he met that indescribably wonderful, beautiful, lovable honor student from Orange, Texas—Irene Bias. I'll never forget when we were at Fisk together, he described the place right outside, Jubilee Hall where they met. I said, "Dad, that's a special place," and he said, "Yes, that meeting was the beginning of the peak of my life." As their love began to grow and multiply the army grabbed him back again for eighteen months, but in the years to come they had young Clifton, my brother, to whom I'm just a footnote; myself, of course; and Cynthia and Cheryl. We moved from Oklahoma through Topeka, Kansas, on our way to 8008 48th Avenue, Glen Elder. Yes, how proud we were driving up in that bright orange Mercury. We were at the cutting edge of residential breakdown in Sacramento, but along the way, for almost a decade, Dad, and the men of Glen Elder—Mr. Peters, Mr. Pool, Mr. Powell, Mr. Reed—these were black men who cared and who worked together. These overworked yet noble men built the little league diamond by themselves, and then they organized the league into ten teams—minor and major leagues for the neighborhood. They provided a means by which character and integrity could be shaped among the young brothers. Then every Sunday, onto Shiloh—"can't wait for the next sermon of Reverend Willie P. Cooke, just hope that he didn't go too long"—but we knew that the Lord was working in him. Dad would always tell us, "You know how blessed I am, how blessed we are. Never think that we've come as far as we have on our own."

17   When we were in trouble, there was Mr. Fields, Mrs. Ray, and Mrs. Harris— there were hundreds of folks who made a difference. You all remember when Dad went to the hospital when he was thirty-one years old and the doctors had given up on him. There was a great sadness on Forty-eighth Avenue because he had left Mom with four little children. Granddad—the Reverend C. L. West, left his church for months to come and be with Mom—Grandmom came as well—and Dad was in the hospital in Oakland. They had given up on him; the medical profession had reached its conclusion and said they could do nothing.

18   And we said, "We know the power. Let Him step in." We knew that Reverend Cook hadn't been preaching that "Jesus is a rock in a weary land, and water in dry places, and food when you are hungry, and a mind regulator and a heart fixer" for nothing. And we came to Calvary in prayer.

19   Can you imagine how different our lives would have been if we had lost Dad then, in 1961, rather than 1994? Even in the midst of our fear we rejoice. It would have been a different world for each and every one of us, especially the children. Dad kept going after his recovery. He worked at McClellan Air Force Base—steadily missed some of those promotions he should have got, but he stayed convinced that he was going to teach people right no matter what, even given his own situation.

20   That's another thing I loved about him. People always ask me, "West, why do you still talk about love? It's played out. Why when you talk about blackness is it always linked to white brothers and sisters and yellow brothers and sisters and red brothers and sisters and brown brothers and sisters?" And I tell them about John 15:11–12. I tell them that I dedicated my life a long time ago to the same Jesus that Dad dedicated his life to, to the same Jesus that Reverend C. L. West dedicated his life, to the same Jesus that my grandfather on my mother's side and my grandmother on my mother's side dedicated their lives to, but, more important, I saw in the concrete with Dad and Mom, a love that transcends skin pigmentation. I saw it on the ground. Dad taught us that even as you keep track of the injustice, you don't lose track of the humanity. That's what love and being there are all about. Dad made it a priority and preference to be there for us. He made a choice. It meant that he would live a life of interruptions because those who are fundamentally committed to being there are going to be continually interrupted—your own agenda, your own project, are going to be interfered with. Dad was always open to that kind of interruption. He was able to translate a kind of unpredictable interruption into a supportive intervention in somebody else's life. More important, Dad realized that a being-there kind of love meant that you had to have follow up and follow through. One could not just show up—one has to follow up and follow through. This is the most difficult aspect of it. Love is inseparable from pain and hurt and sadness and sorrow and disappointment, but Dad knew that you had to have follow up and follow through. He knew that you had to struggle in the midst of that pain and that hurt—you had to have just not simply the high moments of love, but the funk of love, the stink and the stench of love. In all of his relationships Dad embodied precisely that struggle with the high moments of love and the low moments of love. He knew that the cross was not just about smiles and that it was not just about celebration—it was about sadness, stench, and funk. That is what the blood was about, not Kool-aid but blood. That's how inseparable scars, bruises, and wounds are from joy, affirmation, and wholeness: If you were serious about love, if you were serious about being there for people you were going to be there in the midst of any situation, any circumstances, any condition. Dad realized that God being there for us in any situation and circumstances meant that if he was going to be Godlike, he had to be there in any situation for us. I've been alive now for forty years, and on Thursday I'll be forty-one years old, and *not once has my mother or father disappointed me.* They have always been there. That is a blessing, and I do not deserve it. It's a blessing, and I am thankful for it.

21   So as we bid farewell to Dad, I want you all to know that I am looking forward to a family reunion. I am looking forward to union together on the other side of the Jordan. I am looking forward to seeing Dad in a place where the wicked will cease their troubling and the weary shall be at rest. I tell you when I get there, I'm going down Revelation Boulevard to the corner of John Street, right around the corner from Mark's place. But I want to go to Nahum's place. I don't want to be in Jeremiah's house, it would be too crowded. I don't even want to be down on Peter Street, too many people there—I want some quiet time. I want

to sit down with C. L. West, I want to sit down with Nick Bias, and I want to sit down with Aunt Juanita, and I want to sit down with Aunt Tiny. And I want to sit down with Dad! I want to let them know that we did the best that we could to keep alive the best of the legacy of love that they left to us. And when we come together, we will come together in a way in which there will be no more tears, no more heartache, no more heartbreak, no more sadness and sorrow, no more agony and anguish. We shall sit at the feet of the Lord and be blessed, and our souls will look back and wonder how we got over, how we got over.

● Vocabulary

existentially (1)	component (4)	integrity (10)
dehumanizing (1)	dynamic (4)	quintessentially (10)
patriarchal (2)	emulate (6)	litany (11)
accent (2)	ingenious (6)	degradation (12)
predatory (2)	exemplify (8)	gutbucket (14)
supremacist (3)	constitutes (9)	Jim Crow (14)
condoning (3)	consecrated (10)	pigmentation (20)

● The Facts

1. What, according to the author, makes it difficult for black men to develop the kind of image that their children can admire and imitate? Is this circumstance limited to black communities? Explain your answer.

2. What were the historical circumstances into which the author's father was born in Louisiana on September 7, 1928?

3. What forces came to the rescue whenever the West family was in trouble? Give some specific examples.

4. What role does the Bible play in the West family's moral code? Be specific in your answer.

5. Why was the author's mother not abused by her husband as were so many other black women of the time?

● The Strategies

1. Into what two parts is West's essay divided? Which purpose does each part serve? How does each part relate to the other?

2. In paragraph 6, the author uses redundant language when he writes, "I certainly tried to *emulate* and *imitate* . . ." Where else in the essay does he use redundancies? Point out at least to two other passages. What, if anything, does this redundant language add to the tone of the essay? Read the examples aloud to check their effect.

3. What is the purpose of the image used in the opening sentence of paragraph 11? To whom is the sentence addressed? What is your reaction to the image?

4. In paragraph 14, what does the allusion to "gutbucket Jim Crow" mean? Does this allusion continue to have an impact today?

5. How does the author end his eulogy? Is the ending appropriate for the theme of hardship and courage depicted throughout the eulogy? Why do you think the author mentions his desire to visit the prophet Nahum's place rather than that of Jeremiah?

● The Issues

1. Has the issue of race been solved since the 1990s, when West published his ideas on racism? Indicate where racism stands in our country today. What has been achieved and what, if anything, still needs to be accomplished?

2. What part do sorrow, despair, poverty, and struggling to survive play in black history and society? Support your answer with specific examples you can think of.

3. In paragraph 9, the author reveals that delivering his father's eulogy was one of the most difficult tasks of his life. What do you think he feared? Was his fear justified? Why or why not?

4. What role did religion play in the West family's life? Was it life-sustaining or detrimental? When was it especially prominent? What is your reaction to their faith?

5. The final paragraph is a description of how Christians find comfort in dealing with a loved one's death. They imagine what it will be like to meet the loved one in heaven, a place of everlasting happiness. What comfort do you think atheists conjure up when a loved one dies? What sort of eternity might they imagine?

● Suggestions for Writing

1. Write an essay in which you explain the most important trait your father has passed on to you. Use examples to clarify this trait.

2. Write an essay either attacking or defending the author's view that lack of self-esteem stands in the way of being a good father. Use evidence to support your view.

Those Winter Sundays

ROBERT HAYDEN

Robert Hayden (1913–1980) was born in Detroit, attended the University of Michigan, and taught at Fisk University. His *A Ballad of Remembrance* was awarded a prize at the 1966 World Festival of Negro Arts held in Dakar, Senegal.

The following poem recounts a childhood memory.

● ● ●

Sundays too my father got up early
and put his clothes on in the blueblack cold,
then with cracked hands that ached
from labor in the weekday weather made
5   banked fires blaze. No one ever thanked him.
I'd wake and hear the cold splintering, breaking.
When the rooms were warm, he'd call,
and slowly I would rise and dress,
fearing the chronic angers of that house,
10   Speaking indifferently to him,
who had driven out the cold
and polished my good shoes as well.
What did I know, what did I know
of love's austere and lonely offices?

"Those Winter Sundays." Copyright © 1966 by Robert Hayden, from COLLECTED POEMS OF ROBERT HAYDEN by Robert Hayden, edited by Frederick Glaysher. Used by permission of Liveright Publishing Company.

● Vocabulary

banked (5)   chronic (9)   austere (14)

● The Facts

1. What did the narrator's father do on Sundays?
2. How did the narrator react to his father in the morning?
3. How would you characterize the narrator's attitude as he looks back on this time with his father?

● The Strategies

1. In what poetic form is this narration framed? (Hint: Count the number of lines.)
2. The author writes about his father: "No one ever thanked him." Why do you think he chose to put it this way? Why not simply say "I never thanked him"?
3. The poet writes: "I'd wake and hear the cold splintering, breaking." What kind of figure of speech is this?
4. Examine the sentences in the poem. How many are there? What is the technique of running a sentence across several lines without an endstop or break?

● The Issues

1. What kind of work do you suppose the speaker's father did? How can his probable occupation be deduced from the poem?
2. What are "love's austere and lonely offices"? What other examples can you give of them?

● Suggestions for Writing

1. Write an analysis of this poem.
2. Write an essay in which you use Hayden's poem as a starting point for an essay about how a caring parent contributes to a child's sense of security.

ISSUE FOR CRITICAL THINKING AND DEBATE: TERRORISM

The September 11, 2001, suicide bombing of the World Trade Center in New York and the Pentagon in Washington D.C. was, to most of the horrified Western world, an act of unspeakable wickedness and evil. To some in the Islamic world, it was a deed of heroic martyrdom done in the name of God and one that guaranteed heaven to the self-sacrificing souls responsible for it. After the attack, as the rescuers sifted through the physical rubble, and the talking heads on television combed through the shreds of whys and whats, the irreconcilable divide between the terrorists and us became sharply clear. While we mourned for the victims and prayed for their families, elsewhere in the world some people rejoiced at our sorrow. Even now, when we think about the murderers' cold-bloodedness, their diabolical planning, and their fanatical sacrifice, many of us cannot comprehend the depth of the hate that drove them to invest so much time and energy into slaughtering so many innocents.

Why do they hate us so? We're used to being admired—our material wealth and lifestyle the envy of the world. Our history has repeatedly shown us to be a generous people, donating billions of dollars to help less-fortunate nations in the grip of war, famine, pestilence, or economic ruin. When we have won wars, we have always tried to help our former enemies rebuild rather than occupy their territories. Yet there are millions of people—some Islamic, some not—who hate us with such passion that they are willing, even eager, to sacrifice themselves in murderous and indiscriminate attacks aimed at our destruction. Al-Qaeda, the terrorist organization headed by Osama bin Laden until his assassination in 2011, even now reportedly continues to train assassins and saboteurs, all willing to blow themselves up in an attempt to hurt us. What stuns most Americans is that these people believe that their terroristic attacks are the will of God. Few of us associate God with mass slaughter; even fewer can comprehend the belief that the rewards of paradise will be lavished on such murderers.

The two female writers whose experiences we highlight here both reveal an intimate association with Islam. The first, Krista Bremer, an American journalist who married a Libyan-born Muslim, has written many articles exploring her relationship with a man whose culture is completely different from hers. After traveling to North Africa and meeting her husband's tribal people, she returned to the United States to write with respect and compassion about the profound differences as well as the surprising common ground between the two worlds she wanted to span. While her husband, Ismail Suayah, was reared in an impoverished fishing village on the coast of Libya by illiterate but devout Muslims, Bremer was brought up on the sunny beaches of Southern California in privileged circumstances by parents who had rejected organized religion. But she fell in love with a devout Muslim, whom she calls her soul mate. When Bremer fell in love, she accepted the challenge of a bicultural relationship involving joys as well as difficulties. In the essay that follows, Bremer writes about her husband's observance of Ramadan and how it challenged her desire to be tolerant.

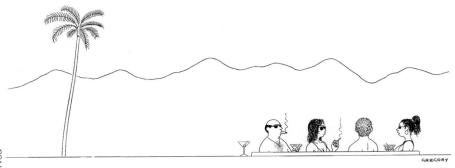

"I think that if these Islamic fundamentalists got to know us they'd like us."

The second writer was once married to Osama bin Laden's half brother, Yeslam, and saw firsthand how women are maltreated in the Islamic world. Her outlook is a bleak one, for she believes that change of any kind in the attitude of Islamic societies is unlikely. Divorced from Yeslam, an international businessman said to be worth hundreds of millions of Swiss francs due to his connections with Saudi Arabia and the bin Ladens, she now resides in Switzerland, trying to find peace in the West.

The student writer, a male studying to be a nurse, concentrates on the dynamics of fear used by all terrorists. His concern is the damage done to the American psyche when it is forced to survive in an atmosphere where any minute of any day, some religious zealot, working for a terrorist organization or in response to some inexplicable hate-filled voice inside his twisted mind, will cause another catastrophic explosion that will claim vast numbers of innocent lives.

We're not used to people trying to kill us. To many Americans, that kind of despicable plotting is a fact of life abroad, not life at home. With the horror of 9/11 etched forever in our memories, many of us remain jumpy, for we now know that there are people out there who hate us more than they love life.

What we should do about them is the fundamental question.

My Accidental Jihad

KRISTA BREMER

Krista Bremer (b. 1970) is an American journalist and assistant publisher of *The Sun,* a magazine specializing in personal essays, memoirs, politics, and true stories. Her work has appeared in several national and international periodicals, including *O: The Oprah Magazine, The Sun, Utne, The Sunday Times* (London), *Aquila Asia (Indonesia), CNN,* and *MSN.* Many of her personal essays explore the difficult challenge of her marriage to a devout Muslim while her beloved country is engaged in a war with two Muslim nations, Afghanistan and Iraq. Bremer wants to continue writing materials that will help her own family and readers to respect both Muslim and Western values. Bremer's writing has won her a Rona Jaffe Foundation Writers' Award, a Pushcart Prize, and a North Carolina Arts Fellowship. She is currently working on her memoir.

The author believes that at their core, all intimate relationships are bicultural because they involve two people who must observe life through each other's lens. Both partners speak different languages, have different rituals, and base their world views on different experiences. As you read Bremer's observations about Ramadan (the month-long Muslim ritual of fasting), try to imagine what it would be like to believe in some tradition totally foreign to you. What rituals do you observe that might require tolerance on the part of a stranger? Think about ways to develop tolerance toward others' convictions.

• • •

1   Early one morning in September, when our house is pitch-dark and the entire family is still asleep, my husband, Ismail, sits upright at the first sound of his alarm, dresses quickly, and leaves our bedroom. Later, after I've woken up and made my way downstairs for a cup of coffee, I find him standing at the counter, stuffing the last of his breakfast into his mouth, his eye on the clock as if he were competing in a pie-eating contest at the fair. The minute hand clicks forward, and, on cue, Ismail drops the food he's holding. I'm momentarily confused. My husband and I usually sit down together over our first cup of coffee, and he rarely eats breakfast. Then I realize: Ramadan has begun.

2   For the next month, nothing will touch my husband's mouth between sunup and sundown: Not food. Not water. Not my lips. A chart posted on our refrigerator tells him the precise minute when his fast must begin and end each day. I will find him in front of this chart again this evening, staring at his watch, waiting for it to tell him he may eat.

3   Ramadan is the ninth month of the lunar calendar, the month during which the Koran was revealed to the Prophet Mohammed through the angel Gabriel. Each year, more than one billion Muslims observe Ramadan by fasting from dawn to dusk. In addition to avoiding food and drink during daylight hours, Muslims are expected to refrain from all other indulgences: sexual relations, gossip, evil thoughts—even looking at "corrupt" images on television, in magazines, or on the Internet. Ramadan is a month of purification, during which Muslims are called upon to make peace with enemies, strengthen ties with family and friends, cleanse themselves of impurities, and refocus their lives on God. It's like a month-long spiritual tuneup.

4   My husband found fasting easier when he lived in Libya, surrounded by fellow Muslims. Everyone's life changes there during the fast: people work less (at least, those who work outside the home), take long naps during the day, and feast with family and friends late into the night. Now, with a corporate job and an American wife who works full time, my husband has a totally different experience of Ramadan. He spends most of his waking hours at work, just as he does every other month of the year. He still picks up our son from day care and shares cooking and cleaning responsibilities at home. Having no Muslim

friends in our Southern college town, he breaks his fast alone, standing at our kitchen counter. Here in the United States, Ramadan feels more like an extreme sport than a spiritual practice. Secretly I've come to think of it as "Ramathon."

5   I try to be supportive of Ismail's fast, but it's hard. The rules seem unnecessarily harsh to me, an American raised in the seventies by parents who challenged the status quo. The humility required to submit to such a grueling, seemingly illogical exercise is not in my blood. In my family, we don't submit. We question the rules. We debate. And we do things our own way. I resent the fact that Ismail's life is being micromanaged by the chart in the kitchen. Would Allah really hold it against him if he finished his last bite of toast, even if the clock says it's a minute past sunrise? The no-water rule seems especially cruel to me, and I find the prohibition against kissing a little melodramatic. I'm tempted to argue with Ismail that the rules are outdated, but he has a billion Muslims in his corner, whereas I have yet to find another disgruntled American wife who feels qualified to rewrite one of the five pillars of Islam.

6   People say that for a relationship to work, a couple needs to have a shared passion. My husband and I do have one: food. Years ago, when we first met, we shared other passions, such as travel, long runs on wooded trails, live music, and poetry readings. But now that we have two small kids, those indulgences have fallen by the wayside one by one. No matter how busy our lives get, however, we have to eat. On days when it seems we have nothing in common, when I struggle to recall what brought us together in the first place, one good meal can remind me. Ismail is an amazing cook. I remember in great detail the meal he prepared for me the first night we spent together: the walnuts simmering slowly in the thick, sweet blood-red pomegranate sauce; the chicken that slipped delicately away from the bone, like silk falling from skin. The next morning the scent of coriander ground into strong coffee filled his small apartment as he served me olives and fresh bread for breakfast.

7   Our love heated up like a sauce on the stove, our lives slowly blending together, the flavors becoming increasingly subtle and complex. I'd watch him prepare a bunch of cilantro on the counter, carefully separating the stalks with patient attention, gently plucking each leaf from its stem. He could toast pine nuts in a pan while carrying on a conversation with me and not burn a single one, magically rescuing them from the heat just as they turned the perfect shade of brown. Using his buttery fingertips, he would separate paper-thin sheets of phyllo dough without tearing any. He always served me first and studied my expression closely as I took a bite, his face lighting up in response to my pleasure. When he took his first taste, his eyes closed halfway, and a low moan of pleasure escaped from his mouth. There in the kitchen, all the evidence was before me: he was patient, attentive, thorough, economical, generous, creative, and sensual. I was ready to bear his children.

8   But when my husband fasts, our relationship becomes a bland, lukewarm concoction that I find difficult to swallow. I'm not proud of this fact. After all, he isn't the only one in our house with a spiritual practice: I stumble out of bed in the dark most mornings and meditate in the corner of our room with my back to him, trying to find that bottomless truth beyond words. Once in

a great while, I'll drag him to church on Sunday. Whenever I suggest we say grace at the table, he reaches willingly for my hand, and words of gratitude flow easily from him. He has never criticized my practices, even when they are wildly inconsistent or contradictory. But Ramadan is not ten minutes of meditation or an hour-long sermon; it's an entire month of deprivation. Ismail's God is the old-fashioned kind, omnipresent and stern, uncompromising with his demands. During Ramadan this God expects him to pray on time, five times a day—and to squeeze in additional prayers of forgiveness as often as he can. My God would never be so demanding. My God is a flamboyant and fickle friend with a biting wit who likes a good party. My God is transgendered and tolerant to a fault; he/she shows up unexpectedly during peak moments, when life feels glorious and synchronous, then disappears for long stretches of time.

9   But Ramadan leaves little room for dramatic flair. There is no chorus of voices or public celebration—just a quiet and steady submission to Allah in the privacy of one's home. For some Muslims who live in the West, the holiday becomes even more private, since their friends and colleagues are often not even aware of their fast.

10   During the early days of Ramadan, Ismail deals with his hunger by planning his next meal and puttering around the kitchen. In the last half-hour before the sun sets, he rearranges the food in our refrigerator or wipes down our already-clean counters. At night in bed, as I drift off to sleep, he reviews each ingredient in the baklava he intends to make the following evening. "Do you think I should replace the walnuts with pistachios?" he whispers. In the middle of the workday, when I call his cell phone, I hear the beeping of a cash register in the background. He is wandering the aisles of our local grocery store. "I needed to get out of the office," he says matter-of-factly, as if all men escaped to the grocery store during lunch.

11   The last hours before he breaks his fast are the most difficult and volatile time of day for him. Coincidentally, they are the same hours at which I return home from work. I open the door and find him collapsed on the couch, pale and exhausted, our children running in circles around the room. Ismail is irritable, and his thoughts trail off in midsentence. I dread seeing him in this state. I count on my husband to speak coherently, to smile on a regular basis, and to enjoy our children. This humorless person on my couch is no fun. Every few days I ask (with what I hope sounds like innocent curiosity) what he's learned from his fast so far. I know this is an unfair question. How would I feel if he poked his head into our bedroom while I was meditating and asked, *How's it going? Emptied your mind yet?*

12   One balmy Saturday in the middle of Ramadan, we go to hear an outdoor lecture by a Sufi Muslim teacher who is visiting from California. The teacher sits cross-legged under a tree on a colorful pillow while the sun streams down on him through a canopy of leaves. After a long silence, he sweeps his arms in front of him, a beatific expression on his face, and reminds us to notice the beauty that surrounds us. "If you don't," he says, "you're not fasting—you're just going hungry."

13   I take a sidelong glance at Ismail. He is looking very hungry to me these days. I guess I imagined that during his fast a new radiance would emanate from him. I imagined him moving more slowly, but also more lovingly. I imagined a Middle Eastern Gandhi, sitting with our children in the garden when I got home from work. In short, I imagined that his spiritual practice would look more . . . well, *spiritual.* I didn't imagine the long silences between us or how much his exhaustion would irritate me. I didn't imagine him leaping out of bed in a panic, having slept through his alarm, and running downstairs to swallow chunks of bread and gulp coffee before the sun came up. I didn't imagine his terse replies to my attempts to start a conversation, or his impatience with our children.

14   I thought I understood the rules of Ramadan: the timetable on the refrigerator, the five daily prayers. But I didn't understand that the real practice is addressing a toddler's temper tantrum or a wife's hostile silence when you haven't eaten or drunk anything in ten hours. I was like the children of Israel in the Bible, who once complained that, despite their dutiful fasting, God still wasn't answering their prayers. The children of Israel had it all wrong: God doesn't count calories. The fast itself only sets the stage. God is interested in our behavior and intentions while we are hungry. Through his prophet Isaiah, God gave the children of Israel a piece of his mind:

15   Behold, in the day of your fast you seek your own pleasure, and oppress all your workers. Behold, you fast only to quarrel and to fight and to hit with a wicked fist. Fasting like yours this day will not make your voice to be heard on high. (Isaiah 58:3–4)

16   Ismail tells me that in the Middle East, Ramadan is a time of extremes: There are loving gatherings among family and friends at night, and a tremendous public outpouring of charity and generosity to those in need. At the same time, the daytime streets become more dangerous, filled with nicotine and caffeine addicts in withdrawal. People stumble through the morning without their green or black tea, drunk so dark and thick with sugar that it leaves permanent stains even on young people's teeth. Desperate smokers who light up in public risk being ridiculed or even attacked by strangers. The streets reverberate with angry shouts and car horns, and traffic conflicts occasionally escalate into physical violence.

17   Our home, too, becomes more volatile during Ramadan. Ismail's temper is short; my patience with him runs thin. I accuse him of being grumpy. He accuses me of being unsupportive. I tell him he is failing at Ramadan, as if it were some sort of exam. I didn't ask for this spiritual test, I tell him. As if I could pick and choose which parts of him to take into my life. As if he were served up to me on a plate, and I could primly push aside what I didn't care for—his temper, his doubt, his self-pity—and keep demanding more of his delicious tenderness.

18   And then there is my husband's unmistakable Ramadan scent. Normally I love the way he smells: the faint scent of soap and laundry detergent mixed with the warm muskiness of his skin. But after a few days of fasting, Ismail begins to smell *different.* Mostly it's his breath. The odor is subtle but distinct and persists no matter how many times he brushes or uses mouthwash. When I get close to him, it's the first thing I notice. I do a Google search for "Ramadan and

halitosis" and learn that this is a common side effect of fasting—so common that the Prophet Mohammed himself even had something to say about it: "The smell of the fasting person's breath is sweeter to Allah than that of musk." Allah may delight in this smell, but I don't. I no longer rest my head on Ismail's chest when we lie in bed at night. I begin to avoid eye contact and increase the distance between us when we speak. I no longer kiss him on impulse in the evening. I sleep with my back to him, resentful of this odor, which hangs like an invisible barrier between us.

19   The purpose of fasting during Ramadan is not simply to suffer hunger, thirst, or desire, but to bring oneself closer to *taqwa:* a state of sincerity, discipline, generosity, and surrender to Allah; the sum total of all Muslim teachings. When, in a moment of frustration, I grumble to my husband about his bad breath, he responds in the spirit of taqwa: He listens sympathetically and then apologizes and promises to keep his distance. He offers to sleep on the couch if that would make me more comfortable. He says he wishes I had told him earlier so he could have spared me any discomfort. His humility catches me off guard and makes my resentment absurd.

20   This month of Ramadan has revealed to me the limits of my compassion. I recall a conversation I had with Ismail in the aftermath of September 11, 2001, when the word *jihad* often appeared in news stories about Muslim extremists who were hellbent on destroying the United States. According to Ismail, the Prophet Mohammed taught that the greatest jihad, or struggle, of our lives is not the one that takes place on a battlefield, but the one that takes place within our hearts—the struggle to increase self-discipline and become a better person. This month of Ramadan has thrown me into my own accidental jihad, forcing me to wrestle with my intolerance and self-absorption. And I have been losing ground in this battle, forgetting my husband's intentions and focusing instead on the petty ways I am inconvenienced by his practice.

21   Ramadan is meant to break our rigid habits of overindulgence, the ones that slip into our lives as charming guests and then refuse to leave, taking up more and more space and stealing our attention away from God. And it's not just the big habits, the ones that grab us by the throat—alcohol, coffee, cigarettes—but the little ones that take us gently by the hand and lead us stealthily away from the truth. I begin to notice my own compulsions, the small and socially acceptable ones that colonize my day: The way I depend on regular exercise to bolster my mood. The number of times I check my e-mail. The impulse to watch a movie with my husband after our children are in bed, rather than let the silence envelop us both. And the words: all the words in books, in magazines, on the computer; words to distract me from the mundane truth of the moment. I begin to notice how much of my thinking revolves around what I will consume next.

22   I am plump with my husband's love, overfed by his kindness, yet I still treat our marriage like an all-you-can-eat buffet, returning to him over and over again to fill my plate, as if our vows guaranteed me unlimited nourishment. During Ramadan, when he turns inward and has less to offer me, I feel indignant. I want to make a scene. I want to speak to whoever is in charge, to demand what I think was promised me when I entered this marriage. But now

I wonder: Is love an endless feast, or is it what people manage to serve each other when their cupboards are bare?

23   In the evening, just before sundown, Ismail arranges three dates on a small plate and pours a tall glass of water, just as the Koran instructs him to do, just as the Prophet Mohammed himself did long ago. Then he sits down next to me at the kitchen counter while I thumb through cookbooks, wondering what to make for dinner. He waits dutifully while the phone rings, while our daughter practices scales on the piano, while our son sends a box of Legos crashing onto our wood floor. Then, at the moment the sun sets, he lifts a date to his mouth and closes his eyes.

Reprinted with permission from Krista Bremer.

● Vocabulary

lunar (3)   indulgences (3)   sensual (7)
purification (3)   micromanaged (5)   volatile (11)

● The Facts

1. When is Ramadan celebrated? What does it represent? How is it observed?

2. Why did the author's husband find it easier to honor Ramadan in Libya than in the United States? Do you agree with her assumption? Why or why not?

3. What are the "Five Pillars of Islam"? If you don't already know them, do some research and list them numerically. If you had to list the most important pillars of your religious or ethical system, what would they be?

4. According to the author, what shared passion has contributed to the success of her bicultural marriage? How does the husband solidify this passion?

5. In what condition does the author find her husband when she returns from work during Ramadan? What does his condition elicit in her?

● The Strategies

1. What is the relationship between the title of the essay and its content? Interpret the title and explain what it means to you. Do you consider the title captivating? If you can suggest a better title, do so.

2. What is the importance of paragraph 3? Would the essay be just as clear to the average reader if the paragraph had been left out? Explain your answer.

3. What contrast is drawn between paragraph 7 and 8? Which writing technique contributes to the vividness of the paragraphs? How convincing are the author's statements? Do you think her feelings are justified in both paragraphs? Explain your answer.

4. What aspect of Ramadan does the author emphasize in paragraphs 10 and 11? How does she portray the reality that accompanies intensified fasting and praying? What is her view of these rituals?

5. How does the author conclude her essay? Is the question the author asks her husband fair or unfair? Do you think she really uses an innocent tone when she asks her question? What is her purpose in asking the question?

● The Issues

1. After reviewing this essay and pondering the author's words, how would you describe her general attitude toward Ramadan? What is your reaction to the author's description of Ramadan? Expanding the discussion, how tolerant should we be toward the religious stance of devoted Muslims?

2. Do you agree or disagree with the author that some of the prohibitions of Ramadan are outdated? How do you think a good Muslim would defend such a prohibition as kissing or watching TV? What is the premise on which such prohibitions are based? What is your opinion of the premise?

3. So far, the marriage between the author and her husband seems to be working. They have two children, for whom they have provided an enriched and happy environment. What elements, as seen in the essay, are responsible for the harmony existing in the marriage? What might destroy the harmony at some future time?

4. The essay ends somewhat abruptly. How do you explain the sudden stop? Is it justified? Why or why not?

5. This essay is the perfect backdrop for a discussion about the importance of similar religious beliefs in a marriage. How important is it for a husband and wife to share the same views about God, the conflict between good and evil, what happens after we die, and other religious issues? Make a case for or against the idea similar religious beliefs shared by married couples is necessary to a harmonious relationship.

● Suggestions for Writing

1. Using the Internet and other sources to shore up your views, write an essay in which you either defend or challenge the following statement: "The Muslim culture is so different from that of most citizens in the United States that we consistently misread the intentions and long-range goals of faithful Muslims."

2. Write an essay in which you praise those aspects of the Muslim faith that, if followed sincerely, would create a noble, peaceful, caring society. Or, choosing those aspects of the Muslim faith that you find impossible to support, write an essay arguing why they are unacceptable as spiritual guidelines. Begin with a clear thesis which you support with strong evidence.

"Postscript" to My Life in Saudi Arabia

CARMEN BIN LADEN

Carmen bin Laden (b. 1955) was the sister-in-law of Osama bin Laden, who was the world's most wanted terrorist until U.S. Navy SEALs captured and killed him in 2011. Born in Switzerland to a Swiss father and Persian mother, she received international attention when she published her autobiography *Inside the Kingdom*, in which she tells how she fell in love with the rich Yeslam bin Laden, leaving her life in Geneva, Switzerland, to live among the bin Ladens in Jeddah, Saudi

Arabia. She traces her growing resentment toward what she considers one of the world's most powerful, secretive, and repressive countries. In order to save her daughters from the fate of other Arabic women, she eventually divorced Yeslam and moved back to Geneva, where she lives with her daughters. Both she and her husband were educated in the United States, a country Carmen loves and admires. The book was originally written for Europeans in French, German, Dutch, Italian, and Spanish.

The essay that follows was written years after Carmen bin Laden experienced her life as a member of the bin Laden family; however, the memories never faded, and she was determined that her own three daughters would live in a free country. For a full account of a wealthy woman's life in a fundamentalist Muslim world, read Carmen bin Laden's shocking autobiography Inside the Kingdom (2005).

• • •

1   Three and a half years have gone by since the tragic and dreadful events of September 11, 2001, when so many innocent lives were lost.* For the victims' families and loved ones the acute sense of loss and pain continues. My heart goes out to them and I only hope that in some way the passing of time can alleviate their suffering.

2   My daughters live with a daily reminder of that day, for their name has become synonymous with it. Even if one day they marry, their presence will

Lynsey Addario/CORBIS

● Many Muslim women are forced to live under suffocating anonymity.

*Editor's note: Over a decade has gone by.

always provoke an echo of hushed whispers and raised eyebrows. If you're born a Bin Ladin, you'll always be a Bin Ladin**—I doubt the stigma will ever go away. Wafah, Najia, and Noor have been raised with the taste of freedom—with the ability to live, to function, and to make decisions for themselves, believing that their willpower and actions will guide their successes or failures. As free Western women they should be able to be the masters of their own destiny, and yet, after years of struggle to obtain their freedom, my girls are trapped in the prison of their name.

3   In my daily life and my travels with my girls since 9/11, I have witnessed this often. Strolling down Fifth Avenue in Manhattan, Noor, now 17, stopped me, suddenly taken aback. "Mom, what would all these people think of me if they knew my name?" she asked. I realized that she will ask herself that question all her life. The difficulty—the challenge—that my children now face is enormous, making me wonder if they will ever be able to use their intellectual and artistic gifts to pursue their goals and dreams. My wish is that people will understand their burden, and judge them solely on the basis of their talents and abilities.

4   With *Inside the Kingdom*, I had hoped to lighten that burden. I had hoped that by being honest about our story and our struggle to gain freedom I could erase any suspicions about where our loyalties lie. And indeed, as we meet people in America who have read my book, or seen me in interviews, we find ourselves overwhelmed by their warmth and generosity, their genuine understanding and fellowship, and their ability to go beyond the obstacle of our name. Even just blocks away from the awful physical reminder of the attacks on the Manhattan landscape, it seems that the people we meet truly welcome us. Knowing the greatness of America and the fairness of its people—their willingness to question facts, their ability to perceive and respect individuals, their empathy and warmth—I can say that I am not surprised. I had always known, deep down, that people from the "land of the free" would understand our inextricable dilemma. But I am moved by my daughters' surprise, and I take this opportunity to say that we will always be immensely grateful for this understanding.

5   So many people have come up to me in the street to tell me how brave I have been and how much they admire me. I find myself completely at a loss to respond. I don't see myself as brave. I am a woman who carried out my duty and responsibility as a mother. I defended my children, and I defended our principles, our love of freedom. True courage belongs to women like those who set up clandestine classrooms in Afghanistan so they could teach little girls to read and write in spite of the very real danger that the Taliban authorities would find them and have them whipped and imprisoned, or worse. That is my standard of courage.

6   *Inside the Kingdom* was also my explanation, to my daughters and to the world, of what I perceived in my years of living in Saudi Arabia. I expected questions, even criticisms, about those views. I never imagined that my personal

---

**Editor's note: "bin Laden" and "bin Ladin" are both correct spellings of the name.

story, and my long struggle to keep my daughters, would give rise to such interest and so many questions. Not a week passes by without my receiving kind letters of sympathy and understanding, all of them moving, and each of them touching my heart. One lady wrote to me, "You made me cry, you made me laugh, and above all, you made me think." I could not have dreamed of a more valuable prize. This flood of warmth has reinforced my respect for the American spirit. I also received letters that echoed my sad experience. I have always been aware of the situation of mothers, less fortunate than I, whose children are trapped in Saudi Arabia, and wondered how I could help. Now I have decided to create an association, to join our forces and to bring their plight to the attention of the general public.

7   After years of living with the constant, chilling fear that I might lose my children, I won the most important personal battle: legal custody. And now I am determined not to be dismissed like a repudiated Saudi wife. The divorce procedure in Geneva courts, which has lasted for more than ten years, has been characterized by misleading statements and outright lies. With the habitual Saudi disdain for judicial systems other than their own, officials of the Bin Laden Organization have refused to appear before the Swiss court. In Yeslam's long effort to hide the vast extent of his wealth, legal requests for evidence from the Saudi Arabian authorities were returned unanswered, or with misleading information. So I found myself obliged to begin a private investigation into the holdings of my husband and the Bin Laden family.

8   The six-year-long investigation that I undertook led me to the discovery of more than a hundred companies, many of them offshore. Since 9/11, some of those companies have been closed down. In response to the many unanswered questions and the gravity of the subject matter, I am currently working on a book that will throw unprecedented new light on the secret business of the Bin Laden empire.

9   Generally, as I reflect on my years in Saudi Arabia and my current life in Europe, it seems to me that we are experiencing a clash of cultures between our Western ideals and the values and growing might of Islamic fundamentalism. Fundamentalists have always existed. Thirty years ago, the places they come from started to accumulate the potent wealth of petrodollars. Silently, unnoticed by the West, they began distributing their riches through charities, Koranic schools, mosques, and religious institutions, and their power to influence others began to swell. In 1975 only one country's legal system was based on the Islamic Sharia religious code***: Saudi Arabia. Since then, Iran, Sudan and other countries have adopted Sharia too, and most Muslim countries around the world face insistent demands from powerful—often Saudi-funded—fundamentalist groups, that they, too, establish this harsh, medieval code.

***Editor's note: The Sharia is the body of Islamic law that involves strict rules, such as banning alcohol, fasting during Ramadan, praying daily, and minimizing the education of women and their access to the work force.

10 The fundamentalists' efforts to impose their values on others are not limited to Muslim countries. I see the signs everywhere. Perhaps because of my background, I am more sensitive to them, or more vigilant. In Canada, I am told, Islamic tribunals in cities such as Toronto seek to regulate divorce, custody, and inheritance issues in the Muslim community—and this is tolerated, under the Arbitration Act of the province of Ontario. This troubles me.

11 In France, some public swimming pools have instituted women-only hours. Throughout Europe, Islamic authorities influence Muslim children to go to school in veils. Girls are deprived of the pleasure of sports, hindered by their veils and cumbersome clothing, and they submit to the strictest form of Islam without speaking out or questioning anything. I find this intolerable. On November 2, 2004, a fanatical fundamentalist assassinated the Dutch filmmaker Theo van Gogh as he strolled through the streets of Amsterdam because he had photographed verses from the Koran printed on women's bodies. I can understand that those images might have shocked some people, but Van Gogh paid with his life for exercising his right to free speech in a democracy. That frightens me.

12 I frequently find myself in situations that illuminate the unbridgeable gulf between our societies. A few months ago, I was a guest speaker at the Oxford Union debating society. After dinner, the cook asked to speak with me. I listened as he told me that I was giving the West a false picture of Islam. He said he had lived in Britain for years, and had become British. He was a practicing Muslim, and he was steeped in both cultures. So I asked him if a practicing Muslim could dissociate the Sharia religious law from his faith in Islam. "Absolutely not," he replied. "Those are the laws of God."

13 So, I asked, "In today's world, we should cut off the hands of thieves?"

14 "That is God's law," he replied, "and it is a deterrent."

15 He had just made my point for me, and I told him so. He had lived for many years in England and he was British, but his archaic, brutal concept of justice and law ran much deeper than that. I knew better than to argue with him; there was no way I could reconcile the complete incompatibility—the clash of thought—that lay between us.

16 This is a small example of a larger issue, and one that is growing in importance. For years, the West didn't see it coming, but now, surely, we must, for it involves our society too. It has become impossible for fundamentalist Muslims to separate the Sharia code from their religious beliefs. For them it simply cannot be done, for the Sharia is an indissociable part of their religion. Any alternative point of view is unacceptable for these zealots, which is why democracy as we know it in the West may not be able to exist in the Muslim world. A fundamentalist cannot allow the ideas that he sees as his religious law to be subjected to scrutiny and debate.

17 In the West, our laws can be reviewed and changed to adapt to our modern world. An unjust and outdated law is questioned. It is noticed, resented, and fought about, sometimes bitterly. Ours is not a perfect society, but it has the strength and flexibility to examine itself and change. We look forward and we seek to improve our laws and our society. To Islamic fundamentalists, Sharia

law is immutable. All society must be guided by the way the original community of Muslims in the seventh century lived and thought. Therefore everyone looks backward.

18   What I saw in Saudi Arabia was a culture that refused to evolve. After the tragedy of 9/11, Americans began to ask why they should be so hated. I think the issue goes deeper than Osama Bin Laden's hatred of America. I think he has a larger plan: to propagate what he and many others like him see as the "pure" form of Islam, and to establish it in the Muslim world and beyond, wherever he can.

19   Think of this: There are 1.2 billion Muslims in the world. Not all of them, by any means, are fanatics, and I do not mean to suggest that they are. But even assuming only ten percent of Muslims follow the strongest, most conservative precepts of Islam, that is 120 million people. Of that number, surely no more than ten percent are extremists. But that means 12 million people have been ideologically conditioned to impose their conservative conception of Islam on others. And perhaps ten percent of those extremists are so fanatical that they are prepared to die for their beliefs (because dying for them will earn them eternal paradise). This means that scattered all over the world, a shadow army more than one million people strong is primed to attack Western values and Western culture.

20   The de facto spearhead of this shadow army is my former brother-in-law, Osama Bin Laden. To those who long to obey his every whim, Osama is a hero; to the less zealous, he remains a charismatic figure of a good Muslim.

21   Certain of his popularity among the faithful, Osama Bin Laden had the arrogance to release a video four days before the U.S. presidential election. He confirmed that he had masterminded the 9/11 attacks, and blamed his barbaric action on American policy. He even had the nerve to advise Americans on "the best way to avoid another tragedy." He compared the American government to "a crocodile attacking a helpless child" and threatened to "bleed America." I was outraged. He dared to offend the victims' families by calling the attack that he instigated a "tragedy." But if he considered it tragic, then why did he do it? He admitted that he had ordered the violence, then acted as if it were someone else's fault—the fault of the victim. He never questioned the rightness of what he did, and showed no remorse for the people he murdered. I could only shake with rage.

22   Osama Bin Laden's attacks are not limited to America. On the morning of March 11, 2004, four bombs exploded on three crowded commuter trains in Spain's capital city of Madrid. At least 173 people were killed, and more than 400 were wounded. This horrible, heartless attack on innocent people heading to work bore the sign of Osama Bin Laden's twisted thinking. Like the others who share his views, he will stop at nothing.

23   Today the fundamentalists are more convinced than ever that they hold the real truth of Islam, and that it is their duty to show their fellow Muslims the true path. I say this with regret: I am convinced that their position won't change any time soon. I have also come to believe that you cannot change a country from the outside. The change must come from within.

24   Will Saudi women, for example, ever *want* the freedoms that Western women fought so hard to get? To overturn the laws in Saudi Arabia that deny women certain basic human rights, the women there would have to want freedom. They would have to fight for it. But in my years living among them, I saw no desire in Saudi Arabian women to change their situation.

25   In the twenty-first century, women everywhere should have the freedom to choose how they live their lives. In Saudi Arabia, it seems to me, most women would recoil at the idea of giving their daughters our kind of freedom. They would not want them to learn openness, equality, freedom of thought, or anything that might lead them to question their culture. Most Saudi women don't see the restrictions imposed on them as a repression of their personality. Many of them actually choose to remain under the guardianship of men, because they see it as protection. They embrace it, and they perpetuate it. They don't see the bars of the cages they are making for themselves and their children.

26   In Saudi Arabia, the deep-rooted and basic tenets of society are never questioned, for anything that is fundamental to Saudi society is based on religion, and religion cannot be doubted. Even the liberal, dissident Saudis—and there are some, both male and female—oppose only details. They demand only practical and convenient changes, such as the right to drive a car. They criticize aspects of the al-Saud regime: that it is corrupt, bloated, parasitical, unworthy in some way. But the real problems in Saudi Arabia go so much deeper. No government arising in that country today would be able to forgo the deep beliefs of Wahabi Islam.

27   We are thus at an impasse: our world, and theirs. They cannot change, and we must not. We should not allow them to use our tolerance to impose their intolerance on us. Today fundamentalists have the power to affect us in places they were previously unable to reach. They can strike us wherever they please. And I fear that this will continue, now and for as long as the powerful families of the oil kingdoms continue to feel it is either their moral duty or just politically useful for them to spend hundreds of millions of dollars to spread their beliefs.

28   As a young woman, I was naïvely confident that freedom would come soon to Saudi Arabia. Now I am no longer so sure. Because of my struggle for my daughters. I have thought so much about life in Saudi Arabia, about what I know of the characteristics of that society. And I ask myself of the hardest question: How can we overcome such a violent clash of cultures?

From INSIDE THE KINGDOM by Carmen Bin Ladin. Copyright © 2004 by Carmen Bin Ladin. By permission of Grand Central Publishing.

● Vocabulary

synonymous (2)	repudiated (7)	dissociate (12)
provoke (2)	disdain (7)	deterrent (14)
stigma (2)	gravity (8)	archaic (15)
fellowship (4)	unprecedented (8)	reconcile (15)
inextricable (4)	vigilant (10)	indissociable (16)
dilemma (4)	tribunals (10)	zealots (16)
clandestine (5)	illuminate (12)	scrutiny (16)

immutable (17)   spearhead (20)   perpetuate (25)
propagate (18)   charismatic (20)   tenets (26)
primed (19)   recoil (25)   parasitical (26)
de facto (20)

● The Facts

1. What fear concerning her daughters' name plagued the writer and drove her to write a book about life in Saudi Arabia? Do you believe the fear is warranted? Give reasons for your answer.

2. What standard of bravery does the author use to label a woman "brave"? Does she consider herself brave when measured by that standard? Why or why not?

3. According to Carmen bin Laden, what is the most important personal battle she won? Why do you think this battle was so important? What similar battles do divorced couples face in the United States? Cite examples of the problems confronted.

4. According to the author, what circumstance supported the Muslim fundamentalists in their urge to spread the conservative Muslim religion to all parts of the world?

5. According to the author, what was Osama bin Laden's ultimate plan? What is your answer to this plan?

● The Strategies

1. What does the title "Postscript" mean with respect to the author's autobiographical work titled *Inside the Kingdom: My Life in Saudi Arabia*? What is the opposite of a "Postscript"?

2. What is the topic sentence of paragraph 10? How does the author support it? What rhetorical mode does she use? How effective is she?

3. What is the purpose of citing the author's experience at the Oxford Union debating society? How does this experience relate to the author's overall thesis?

4. What is the purpose of quoting population statistics in paragraph 19? Do these statistics add useful substance or useless clutter to the essay? Give reasons for your answer.

5. What paradox does the author use in paragraph 21? How effective is it? What does it do to the image of Osama bin Laden? What does being Osama bin Laden's sister-in-law do to the author's argument? Does it help or detract?

● The Issues

1. What are the beliefs that aggravate the clash of ideas between Muslim fundamentalism and Western liberalism as described by Carmen bin Laden? What concerns you most about this clash?

2. What is your view of the Muslim punishment code based on "an eye for an eye and a tooth for a tooth"? Do you think it would be effective to cut off the hands of thieves or to kill women caught in adultery? How does the American punishment code differ from that of fundamentalist Islam?

3. What is unhealthy about a country like Saudi Arabia that refuses to evolve? What does the author like about the Western system of laws as opposed to Saudi Arabia's system? Do you agree or disagree with her view? Give reasons for your answer.

4. In paragraph 19, the author indicates that right now a "shadow army" of more than one million people stands ready and eager to attack Western values and culture. Who are the soldiers in this "shadow army"? Do you believe this army exists? If it does, how can we resist it? If it does not, then how should we answer the author's claim?

5. According to the author, what is the only way to change a society that has been led astray in its definition of truth? Do you agree with the author? If so, what test should your fellow students use for finding truth, and how would you go about changing the direction of society? If you do not believe in the author's view of the only way change can occur, then state what stratagem you think might work.

● Suggestions for Writing

1. Write a letter to Carmen bin Laden in which you thank her for her candid insights into the world of fundamentalist Islam. Of course, you will not send this letter, but it could stimulate your reflections on inflexible societies and heighten your awareness of how important it is to live in a free society.

2. Write an essay in which you describe certain features of our society that might appall people from more conservative cultures. Consider the violence and sexual explicitness of our films, the total lack of taste in some of the lyrics of our music and its thudding sounds, and the crass materialism we exhibit in the cars we drive and the money we spend on ourselves. You might even compare the veiled look of the Saudi Arabian young women with the clothes that allow Western girls to bare just about every inch of their bodies.

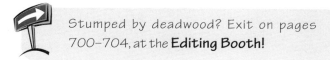

Stumped by deadwood? Exit on pages 700–704, at the **Editing Booth!**

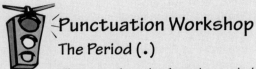

Punctuation Workshop
The Period (.)

These are the rules for using periods:

1. Put a period at the end of a sentence:

WRONG: We made a dash for the bus we almost missed it. (This is a run-on sentence.)

RIGHT: We made a dash for the bus. We almost missed it.

WRONG: I never knew my grandfather, he died when I was three years old. (This is called a comma splice.)

RIGHT: I never knew my grandfather. He died when I was three years old.

2. Put a period after most abbreviations:

Mr.	A.D.	Dr.	Wed.	sq. ft.
Ms.	etc.	Jan.	P.M.	lbs.

EXCEPTIONS: mph, FM, TV, VCR, NBC, NATO, IRS, DMV

Dictionaries sometimes give you an option: U.S.A. or USA. When in doubt, consult your dictionary or instructor.

Student Corner

Jeffrey Metherell
University of Idaho

Terrorism: America in Fear

On December 7, 1941, the U.S. naval base in Pearl Harbor was brutally and successfully attacked by the Japanese Imperial Navy. That this assault occurred while negotiations were still taking place between Japan and the U.S. and, even more ironic, that a formal declaration of war did not reach the U.S. until the next day, prompted a huge American outcry. It also elicited a harsh statement from President Franklin Roosevelt, in which he predicted that December 7 would be "a date that will live in infamy." And so it has. "Remember Pearl Harbor" became the rallying cry, and the attack became synonymous with all that is cowardly and underhanded. But then, the calendar reached September 11, 2001, and the events of that awful day eclipsed the events of December 7, 1941. Suddenly, treachery had a new anniversary, and 9/11 is now the date that lives in infamy!

There are some eerie similarities between the two attacks. Obviously, both were devastating shocks to the U.S. Both occurred on American soil (greatly adding to the jolt factor). Beyond the material damage (battleships lost and buildings destroyed) the death tolls were approximately the same—2,402 at Pearl Harbor and 2,977 innocent victims from the 9/11 attack. Both attacks promptly plunged our country into war. The aftermath of both attacks included a barrage of hate crimes, ethnic stereotyping, and racial persecution. And although it can be argued that in both events the primary damage inflicted was widespread fear, this is where a distinction can be made. Whereas following Pearl Harbor, we Americans knew who the enemy was, what it looked like, and, for the most part, where it resided, we can make none of these assumptions following 9/11. And that is why in the years after December 7, 1941, we were "America at war," whereas since 9/11, we have become "America in fear."

No fear is stronger or deeper than fear of the unknown. We fight a faceless and nameless enemy, who could literally be living and working in our neighborhood. It could be a group of zealous students enrolled at the local community college; it could be one disgruntled loner who has converted to Islam; or it could even be a bus driver whose soft-spoken ways fool everyone. Terrorists do not jump out of dark alleys, wearing Jihad turbans or gang masks. There are no parades of enemy soldiers with smartly pressed uniforms and unfurled banners marching in unison while showcasing their numbers and weaponry. There is no Geneva Convention or rules of engagement or any form of chivalry. Furthermore, we are not fighting against a "bully" country that has an unquenchable thirst for power, territory, or conquests. Instead, we are fighting against an ideology—a religious fervor that derives from the maniacal twisting and creative interpretation of an ancient document. Herein we find another similarity between the kamikaze pilots of WWII and the suicide bombers of Al Qaeda. Nothing struck more fear to the souls of U.S. naval men than a kamikaze pilot's willingness to explode his plane on the deck of a ship, sacrificing himself for his emperor, who was commonly believed to be a god, descendant from the sun goddess Amaterasu. The kamikaze pilots were proud to be martyrs for the "holy" emperor of Japan, just as the members of Al Qaeda are proud to be martyrs for the glorious cause of obliterating "the infidels" who disgrace Allah and his prophet. The kamikaze pilots were driven by the heroism of dying for their godlike emperor, but the Muslim terrorists had an additional motivation—the reward at death of immediately entering the gates of Paradise to live with the 72 pure and erotic virgins who would be their companions throughout eternity. The unrelenting passion with which both the kamikaze pilots and the Muslim terrorists acted highlights the extremism which martyrdom can embrace— with one added chilling difference: The terrorism since 9/11 does not limit itself to targeting purely military assets and personnel. In fact, civilians are usually the target as fear is ultimately and primarily the objective.

It has been 70 years since the attack on Pearl Harbor. That time segment basically constitutes a generation. December 7, 1941, is mostly a historical memory—conjuring up little visceral reaction. It's been more than a decade since 9/11, and the same can certainly not be said about that date. The horror of that infamous day still pervades our thoughts, and the pallor of fear still envelopes our country. We are America in fear.

How I Write

By personality, I tend to be a "scribble-outside-of-the-lines" type of individual. Now this doesn't mean that I necessarily denounce all rules and regulations. But, I do recognize that my forte is creativity as opposed to order. How does this apply to my writing? Well, let's just say that it's a question of focus. If I focus primarily on the methodology of writing something, I find myself feeling rather hedged in and constricted. I am much more effective if I let the creative juices percolate and apply the rules at some point later. My older sister, who teaches elementary school, tells me that she encourages young students, when they write, to start out with a "sloppy copy." I find this suggestion to be as useful as the one that dark chocolate is actually good for you. I needed to hear the latter only once! I live by the "sloppy copy" (in fact, usually more than one). Generally speaking, if the creative juices aren't flowing, then neither is the ink. In sum, I break the classic rules of writing in a blatant and unapologetic fashion. I encourage creative thinking on the subject; then I transfer those thoughts to paper, and begin sewing it all together—making sure to observe the aforementioned methodology. It's backward. But, it works for me.

How I Wrote This Essay

I must admit that I wasn't immediately captured with this subject. I mean, what could I really add to the mountains of writing that already exist on terrorism? For me, then, it was important to somehow come up with a fresh thought. I'm not one who is usually as stimulated by historical facts as I am by human emotions. Once I began to focus on the unique phenomenon of fear that terrorism has engendered, writing on the subject became easier. I'm not sure from where the comparison between Pearl Harbor and 9/11 came, but the more I thought about it, the more I liked that direction. I followed my own quirky methodology (as described in the above paragraph). Specifically, my "sloppy copy" was the next step in the process. I followed it by knitting out the randomness and applying those blasted rules.

My Writing Tip

I realize that I run the risk of sounding like Dr. Phil, but my strongest advice is, "Be yourself!" In other words, if you are by nature a creative, "scribble-out-of-the-lines" kind of person, then be that person even when you write.

Don't let the rules of writing and proper methodology keep you from writing!

Use the rules to help shape what you write or to transform it from random to orderly and logical.

● CHAPTER WRITING ASSIGNMENTS

1. Write an essay in which you narrate an incident that proves one of the following:
   a. People are often bigoted.
   b. Having good neighbors is important.
   c. Pets are often astoundingly loyal.
   d. Difficulties can be stepping stones to success.

● WRITING ASSIGNMENTS FOR A SPECIFIC AUDIENCE

1. Write a diary entry, listing chronologically the major events of your day. Treat your diary as a confidential, intimate friend to whom you can trust your innermost feelings.
2. Write to your parents, narrating an incident that happened recently and somehow impacted you're attitude toward other people.

● IMAGE GALLERY WRITING ASSIGNMENT

Visit pages IG-1–IG-3 of our image gallery and study all three images dealing with terrorism. Then choose the image that most appeals to you. Answer the questions and do the writing assignment.

Pointer from a Pro

BE CONCISE

A college class was told they had to write a short story in as few words as possible. The instructions were that the story had to contain the following three items:

1. Religion
2. Sexuality
3. Mystery

Below is the one A+ short story in the class.

"Good God, I'm pregnant! I wonder who did it."

—from <Popcorntom@aol.com>
(Retrieved Nov. 20, 2010)

We could not resist including this pointer because its humorous hyperbole draws immediate attention to brevity and terseness.

9

Description

What Description Does

A description is a word picture. It is the writer's attempt to capture with words the essence and flavor of a scene, person, or thing. No matter what you have heard to the contrary, a sharply drawn description can be every bit as moving as a picture. Focus and concentration contribute more to a vivid description than either the size of the writer's vocabulary or the heedless splattering of adjectives on a page. Here is an example of what we mean. The author Charles Reade, in this excerpt from *The Cloister and the Hearth*, is describing a medieval inn partly through the eyes, but mainly through the nose, of a weary traveler:

> In one corner was a travelling family, a large one; thence flowed into the common stock the peculiar sickly smell of neglected brats. Garlic filled up the interstices of the air. And all this with closed window, and intense heat of the central furnace, and the breath of at least forty persons.
>
> They had just supped.
>
> Now Gerard, like most artists, had sensitive organs, and the potent effluvia struck dismay into him. But the rain lashed him outside, and the light and the fire tempted him in.
>
> He could not force his way all at once through the palpable perfumes, but he returned to the light again and again like a singed moth. At last he discovered that the various smells did not entirely mix, no fiend being there to stir them around. Odor of family predominated in two corners; stewed rustic reigned supreme in the center; and garlic in the noisy group by the window. He found, too, by hasty analysis, that of these the garlic described the smallest aerial orbit, and the scent of reeking rustic darted farthest—a flavor as if ancient goats, or the fathers of all foxes, had been drawn through a river, and were here dried by Nebuchadnezzar.

The predominant characteristic of this vivid description is its focus. Instead of trying to give us a sweeping view of the dingy inn, the writer zooms in on how bad it smells. The stink of the inn is the dominant impression of this description, and the writer's every word, image, and metaphor aim only to serve up this stench to our nostrils.

When to Use Description

Next to narration, description is probably the most widely used of all the rhetorical modes. In letters, journal entries, reports, and memos, we describe places we have visited, people we have met, and adventures that we have had. Over the course of any given week, it is likely that we have painted a word picture, if not in writing, then certainly in speech.

How to Write a Description

There are some well-known techniques of description that all writers use. We recommend that you practice them in your own writing.

Focus on a Dominant Impression Vivid descriptions invariably focus on a single, dominant impression and unremittingly deliver it. Nothing distracts from the dominant impression; every word and image is devoted to rendering it keener and sharper. By dominant impression, we mean a feature of the scene that is characteristic of it. Not all scenes have strikingly characteristic features, and writers must often absorb the atmosphere of a place before they can sum it up in a dominant impression. Some scenes, however, will give off a dominant impression that leaps out at you. For example, a freeway at rush hour is anything but a scene of placidity; usually it is a tangled skein of cars jockeying for position or trying to nose from one lane into another. To describe a freeway scene at rush hour, you should word your dominant impression to take in the antics of the drivers, the fumes of the cars, the background grind and roar of traffic. You might write, as your dominant impression, "The San Diego Freeway at rush hour is a bedlam of traffic noise, choking fumes, and aggressive drivers." Then you would support that dominant impression with specific images and details.

Here is a description of the Spanish night that uses this technique:

> The Spanish night is so deep and pompous as quite to browbeat the noisier light of day. The buildings, which always look clear-cut and newly built, become, against the dark stress of evening, brilliantly crisp and more brittle than glass. A long line of white buildings will tower up to threaten you with its proud, wave-like bulwarks. At every corner, behind the dark trees that are deep, still areas of water, there will rise up another of those strutting waves out of the depth. In its turn it will draw up, holding itself to full height before it launches a leonine assault on your puny presence. Then it will hold itself back from you before the superior strength of the next glittering wave that you meet, as you walk through the brittle moonlight. In this way the slowest progress through a town will be running the gauntlet of a whole pack of hungry shadows.
>
> —Sacheverell Sitwell, *Southern Baroque Art*

The paragraph vividly captures the sights and sensations associated with *nightfall* over a Spanish town. At its core is a single, overwhelming impression of night "so deep and pompous as quite to browbeat the noisier light of day." All of the details in the paragraph support this dominant impression.

The dominant impression of your description should be the heart of the person, place, or scene you are attempting to describe. If you are describing an elderly aunt who is dull, use her dullness as your dominant impression. If you are writing a description of a Christmas shopping scene, word your dominant impression to show the frazzled and weary shoppers, the harried salesclerks, the dazzling Christmas lights.

However, you should not account for every speck in the scene you are describing in your dominant impression. For example, among the streaming throngs in the department store at Christmas, there are bound to be a few souls who are calm and composed and seemingly immune to the shopping frenzy. Because these lucky few are not at all representative of the overall scene, you should leave them out lest they water down the description. Similarly, if your sister is mainly a bundle of nerves, that is how you should paint her on the page, even if you have glimpsed her in rare moments of serenity.

Use Images in Your Descriptions Most of us know the basics of imagery, especially the simile and the metaphor. We know that the simile is an image based on an explicit comparison. For example, in *The King of the Birds*, Flannery O'Connor describes the crest of a peabiddy with this simile: "This looks at first like a bug's antennae and later like the head feathers of an Indian." We also know that the metaphor is an image based on an indirect comparison with no obvious linking word such as "as" or "like" used to cement it. For example, in *Once More to the Lake*, E. B. White uses metaphors to describe a thunderstorm: "Then the kettle drum, then the snare, then the bass drum and cymbals, then crackling light against the dark, and the gods grinning and licking their chops in the hills." This is how a thunderstorm seems to the writer—it makes noises like many drums and flashes wicked lights against the hills that look like gods licking their chops. Even though the writer omits the "like" that might have made the comparison explicit, we still get the picture.

In addition to these basic images, which every writer occasionally uses, there are some hard-won lessons about descriptive imagery that can be imparted. The first is this: Vivid images do not miraculously drip off the pen but are usually the result of the writer reworking the material repeatedly. If nothing original or fresh occurs to you after you've sat at your desk for a scant few minutes trying to write a description, all it means is that you did not sit long enough or work hard enough. Reread what you have written. Try to picture in your mind the person, place, or thing you are struggling to describe. Cut a word here; replace another there; persistently scratch away at what you have written and you'll soon be astonished at how much better it gets.

The second lesson about writing vivid images is summed up in the adage "Less is more." Overdoing a descriptive passage is not only possible, it is very likely. If you are unhappy with a description you have written, instead of stuffing it with more adjectives, try taking some out. Here is an example of a bloated and overdone description, from *Delina Delaney* by Amanda McKittrick Ros. The speaker is trying his utmost to describe his feelings as he says goodbye to his sweetheart:

I am just in time to hear the toll of a parting bell strike its heavy weight of appalling softness against the weakest fibers of a heart of love, arousing and tickling its dormant action, thrusting the dart of evident separation deeper into its tubes of tenderness, and fanning the flame, already inextinguishable, into volumes of blaze.

This is wretched stuff, of course. One can see the writer huffing and puffing at the pen as she tries desperately to infuse her hero's words with passion. She fails awfully from too much effort.

Appeal to All of Your Reader's Senses Most of us are so unabashedly visual that we are tempted to deliver only looks in our descriptions. There is usually much more to a scene than its looks; you could also write about how it sounds, smells, or feels. The best descriptions draw on all kinds of images and appeal to as many senses as are appropriate. Here is an example from Elspeth Huxley's *The Flame Trees of Thika*. The writer is describing a World War I troop train as it leaves an African station at night carrying soldiers to the front:

> The men began to sing the jingle then that was so popular then—"Marching to Tabora"; and the shouts and cheers, the whistles, the hissing and chugging of the engine, filled the station as a kettle fills with steam. Everything seemed to bubble over; men waved from windows; Dick gave a hunting cry; the red hair of Pioneer Mary flared under a lamp; the guard jumped into his moving van; and we watched the rear light of the last coach vanish, and heard the chugging die away. A plume of sparks, a long coil of dancing fireflies, spread across the black ancient shoulder of the crater Menegai; and gradually the vast digesting dark of Africa swallowed up all traces of that audacious grub, the hurrying train.

This description is a mixture of appeals to our senses of sight and hearing. The men sing and cheer, and the engine chugs and hisses. We see Pioneer Mary's red hair and the sparks from the train's engine. We are regaled with a clever simile, "filled the station as a kettle fills with steam," and treated to a riveting image, "the vast digesting dark of Africa swallowed up all traces of that audacious grub, the hurrying train." Did the author really just sit down and calmly mine this rich descriptive vein without effort? We do not know, but most likely not. If her experience is at all typical, she hit this mother lode of imagery only after persistent and labored digging.

Warming Up to Write a Description

1. Train yourself to be observant. Withdraw to your room or some other familiar place with a notepad and pencil or your laptop and place yourself at an angle where you have a sweeping view. Jot down or type the details of what the place looks like. After you have absorbed the details, formulate a dominant impression of the place and write it down or type it on your laptop.

An example might be, "My room always makes me feel cozy because it is filled with mementos from my childhood." Or, "The Hometown Buffet, a restaurant five blocks away from where I live, is a spot where one can breathe in all kinds of smells, hear all kinds of noises, and observe all kinds of people." Next, write only those details that support the dominant impression.

2. Drive through your town or neighborhood, focusing on eyesores that you think the local authorities should correct. Examples might be a huge refuse bin sitting outside a popular coffee house, withered flowers in a planter at the side of a real estate office, or broken-down cars and car parts littering someone's front yard. Take notes that describe the eyesore with sensory details of sight, sound, smell, and touch.

3. Rewrite these undescriptive and dull sentences to make them vivid. Use figurative language whenever possible.
    a. The convalescent hospital smelled unappetizing.
    b. His face bore many signs indicating his old age.
    c. The protesters were quite loud and active.
    d. The snow falling on the creek is lovely.
    As an added exercise, complete the following sentences to make them vividly descriptive:
    e. The squirrels chased each other up and down the trees as if . . .
    f. Jasmine's eyes were so deeply green, they looked like . . .
    g. The suitcase fell off the rack of our car and crashed on the highway, causing . . .
    h. A cold wind blew from the north, shaking up the trees and bending their trunks back and forth so that from a distance the aspen grove looked like . . .

EXAMPLES

The Libido for the Ugly

H. L. MENCKEN

Rhetorical Thumbnail

Purpose: to describe the repellent ugliness of an area surrounding Pittsburgh

Audience: magazine readers

Language: oratorical English

Strategy: takes the perspective of a passenger on a train travelling through the Pittsburgh countryside

Henry Louis Mencken (1880–1956) was an editor, author, and critic. He began his journalism career at the *Baltimore Morning Herald* and later became editor of the *Baltimore Evening Herald*. From 1906 until his death, he was on the staff of the *Baltimore Sun* (or *Evening Sun*). In 1924, with George Jean Nathan, Mencken founded the *American Mercury* and served as its editor from 1925 to 1933. Mencken's writing was chiefly devoted to lambasting the smug, conventional attitudes of the middle class. Among his numerous works is *The American Language*, a monumental study of the American idiom, first published in 1919.

Few writers have such an eye for colorful detail as the incomparable Mencken, at his best when he's railing against physical ugliness *or storming against a tradition he dislikes. In the essay that follows, Mencken turns his literary wrath against the ugliness of the industrial heartland of America in the 1920s.*

● ● ●

1   On a Winter day some years ago, coming out of Pittsburgh on one of the expresses of the Pennsylvania Railroad, I rolled eastward for an hour through the coal and steel towns of Westmoreland county. It was familiar ground; boy and man, I had been through it often before. But somehow I had never quite sensed its appalling desolation. Here was the very heart of industrial America, the center of its most lucrative and characteristic activity, the boast and pride of the richest and grandest nation ever seen on earth—and here was a scene so dreadfully hideous, so intolerably bleak and forlorn that it reduced the whole aspiration of man to a macabre and depressing joke. Here was wealth beyond computation, almost beyond imagination—and here were human habitations so abominable that they would have disgraced a race of alley cats.

2   I am not speaking of mere filth. One expects steel towns to be dirty. What I allude to is the unbroken and agonizing ugliness, the sheer revolting monstrousness, of every house in sight. From East Liberty to Greensburg, a distance of twenty-five miles, there was not one in sight from the train that did not insult and lacerate the eye. Some were so bad, and they were among the most pretentious—churches, stores, warehouses, and the like—that they were downright startling; one blinked before them as one blinks before a man with his face shot away. A few linger in memory, horrible even there: a crazy little church just west of Jeannette, set like a dormer-window on the side of a bare, leprous hill; the headquarters of the Veterans of Foreign Wars at another forlorn town; a steel stadium like a huge rat-trap somewhere further down the line. But most of all I recall the general effect—of hideousness without a break. There was not a single decent house within eye-range from the Pittsburgh suburbs to the Greensburg yards. There was not one that was not misshapen, and there was not one that was not shabby.

3   The country itself is not uncomely, despite the grime of the endless mills. It is, in form, a narrow river valley, with deep gullies running up into the hills. It is thickly settled, but not noticeably overcrowded. There is still plenty of room for building, even in the larger towns, and there are very few solid blocks. Nearly every house, big and little, has space on all four sides. Obviously, if there were architects of any professional sense or dignity in the region, they would have

perfected a chalet to hug the hillsides—a chalet with a high-pitched roof, to throw off the heavy winter snows, but still essentially a low and clinging building, wider than it was tall. But what have they done? They have taken as their model a brick set on end. This they have converted into a thing of dingy clapboards, with a narrow, low-pitched roof. And the whole they have set upon thin, preposterous brick piers. By the hundreds and thousands these abominable houses cover the bare hillsides, like gravestones in some gigantic and decaying cemetery. On their deep sides they are three, four and even five stories high; on their low sides they bury themselves swinishly in the mud. Not a fifth of them are perpendicular. They lean this way and that, hanging on to their bases precariously. And one and all they are streaked in grime, with dead and eczematous patches of paint peeping through the streaks.

4   Now and then there is a house of brick. But what brick! When it is new it is the color of a fried egg. When it has taken on the patina of the mills it is the color of an egg long past all hope or caring. Was it necessary to adopt that shocking color? No more than it was necessary to set all of the houses on end. Red brick, even in a steel town, ages with some dignity. Let it become downright black, and it is still sightly, especially if its trimmings are of white stone, with soot in the depths and the high spots washed by the rain. But in Westmoreland they prefer that uremic yellow, and so they have the most loathsome towns and villages ever seen by mortal eye.

5   I award this championship only after laborious research and incessant prayer. I have seen, I believe, all of the most unlovely towns of the world; they are all to be found in the United States. I have seen the mill towns of decomposing New England and the desert towns of Utah, Arizona and Texas. I am familiar with the back streets of Newark, Brooklyn and Chicago, and have made scientific explorations to Camden, N.J., and Newport News, Va. Safe in a Pullman, I have whirled through the gloomy, God-forsaken villages of Iowa and Kansas, and the malarious tide-water hamlets of Georgia. I have been to Bridgeport, Conn., and to Los Angeles. But nowhere on this earth, at home or abroad, have I seen anything to compare to the villages that huddle along the line of the Pennsylvania from the Pittsburgh yards to Greensburg. They are incomparable in color, and they are incomparable in design. It is as if some titanic and aberrant genius, uncompromisingly inimical to man, had devoted all the ingenuity of Hell to the making of them. They show grotesqueries of ugliness that, in retrospect, become almost diabolical. One cannot imagine mere human beings concocting such dreadful things, and one can scarcely imagine human beings bearing life in them.

6   Are they so frightful because the valley is full of foreigners—dull, insensate brutes, with no love of beauty in them? Then why didn't these foreigners set up similar abominations in the countries that they came from? You will, in fact, find nothing of the sort in Europe—save perhaps in the more putrid parts of England. There is scarcely an ugly village on the whole Continent. The peasants, however poor, somehow manage to make themselves graceful and charming habitations, even in Spain. But in the American village and small town the pull is always toward ugliness, and in that Westmoreland valley it has been yielded to with an eagerness bordering upon passion. It is incredible that mere ignorance should have achieved such masterpieces of horror.

7   On certain levels of the American race, indeed, there seems to be a positive libido for the ugly, as on other and less Christian levels there is a libido for the beautiful. It is impossible to put down the wallpaper that defaces the average American home of the lower middle class to mere inadvertence, or to the obscene humor of the manufacturers. Such ghastly designs, it must be obvious, give a genuine delight to a certain type of mind. They meet, in some unfathomable way, its obscure and unintelligible demands. They caress it as "The Palms" caresses it, or the art of the movie, or jazz. The taste for them is as enigmatical and yet as common as the taste for dogmatic theology and the poetry of Edgar A. Guest.

8   Thus I suspect (though confessedly without knowing) that the vast majority of the honest folk of Westmoreland county, and especially the 100% Americans among them, actually admire the houses they live in, and are proud of them. For the same money they could get vastly better ones, but they prefer what they have got. Certainly there was no pressure upon the Veterans of Foreign Wars to choose the dreadful edifice that bears their banner, for there are plenty of vacant buildings along the track-side, and some of them are appreciably better. They might, indeed, have built a better one of their own. But they chose that clapboarded horror with their eyes open, and having chosen it, they let it mellow into its present shocking depravity. They like it as it is: beside it, the Parthenon would no doubt offend them. In precisely the same way the authors of the rat-trap stadium that I have mentioned made a deliberate choice. After painfully designing and erecting it, they made it perfect in their own sight by putting a completely impossible pent-house, painted a staring yellow, on top of it. The effect is that of a fat woman with a black eye. It is that of a Presbyterian grinning. But they like it.

9   Here is something that the psychologists have so far neglected: the love of ugliness for its own sake, the lust to make the world intolerable. Its habitat is the United States. Out of the melting pot emerges a race which hates beauty as it hates truth. The etiology of this madness deserves a great deal more study than it has got. There must be causes behind it; it arises and flourishes in obedience to biological laws, and not as a mere act of God. What, precisely, are the terms of those laws? And why do they run stronger in America than elsewhere? Let some honest Privat Dozent in pathological sociology apply himself to the problem.

● Vocabulary

lucrative (1)	uremic (4)	inadvertence (7)
aspiration (1)	malarious (5)	enigmatical (7)
macabre (1)	aberrant (5)	dogmatic (7)
lacerate (2)	inimical (5)	Parthenon (8)
dormer-window (2)	grotesqueries (5)	etiology (9)
clapboards (3)	insensate (6)	Privat Dozent (9)
eczematous (3)	libido (7)	pathological (9)
patina (4)		

● The Facts

1. What area of the country does this essay describe?
2. What is the principal occupation of the region?
3. Mencken not only criticizes the architecture of the region, he also suggests an alternative. What sort of architecture does he think is suited to this region?
4. On what does Mencken blame the ugliness he describes?
5. What are Mencken's views of the villages in Europe? In his view, how do they compare with American towns?

● The Strategies

1. A good description focuses on and develops a dominant impression. Examine the second paragraph. What is the dominant impression here?
2. Examine the third paragraph. What dominant impression does Mencken focus on in his description of the buildings?
3. With what aspect of the ugliness does paragraph 4 deal?
4. "I have seen, I believe, all of the most unlovely towns of the world; they are all to be found in the United States." Why does he say *unlovely* rather than *ugly*? Which is more effective? Why?
5. "And one and all they are streaked in grime, with dead and eczematous patches of paint peeping through the streaks." What comparison is implied in this metaphor?

● The Issues

1. One of the most vigilant civic groups in the United States today is the environmentalists—men and women determined to preserve historical buildings, wilderness areas, seacoasts, and public parks. What importance do you attribute to the efforts of these people? What do you think would happen if they no longer cared?
2. Mencken seems to feel that although architectural ugliness on any scale is lamentable, it is especially insulting when the edifice is pretentious. Do you agree with Mencken's view? Why or why not?
3. What stretch of highway in the United States is charmingly beautiful and stands in total contrast to Mencken's description of the houses in Westmoreland County? Describe this stretch in detail, focusing on architectural characteristics.
4. Do you agree with Mencken that Americans are psychologically obsessed with ugliness? If you agree, try to find reasons for this obsession. If you disagree, prove that Mencken is wrong by citing instances in which typical Americans have promoted beauty and good taste.
5. If you were to oversee a development of beautiful homes, what aesthetic requirements would you insist on? Describe the development in concrete terms.

● **Suggestions for Writing**

1. Write an essay describing the town or city where you live.

2. Write an analysis of Mencken's diction in this essay, paying particular attention to his use of adjectives.

Hell

JAMES JOYCE

> ### Rhetorical Thumbnail
>
> **Purpose:** to describe hell in the most vivid and concrete terms imaginable
>
> **Audience:** educated novel readers
>
> **Language:** standard English
>
> **Strategy:** uses biblical and other theological references to paint a graphic word picture of hell

James Joyce (1882–1941) is considered by many to be among the most significant novelists of the twentieth century. He was born in Dublin, Ireland, and educated at University College, Dublin. Joyce, a writer who pushed language to its outer limit of comprehensibility, wrote poetry, short stories, and novels. His major novels include *A Portrait of the Artist as a Young Man* (1916), *Ulysses* (written between 1914 and 1921 and published in the United States in 1933), and *Finnegan's Wake* (1939).

Joyce, in this selection from A Portrait of the Artist as a Young Man, *shows us the wreathing fires of hell and persuades us to smell its stench of brimstone and sin. The description that follows is so graphic, so detailed, and so filled with such shuddering imagery, that we almost believe that someone has returned from this dreadful place to tell the tale.*

● ● ●

1   Hell is a strait and dark and foulsmelling prison, an abode of demons and lost souls, filled with fire and smoke. The straitness of this prisonhouse is expressly designed by God to punish those who refused to be bound by His laws. In earthly prisons the poor captive has at least some liberty of movement, were it only within the four walls of his cell or in the gloomy yard of his prison. Not so in hell. There, by reason of the great number of the damned, the prisoners are heaped together in their awful prison, the walls of which are said to be four thousand miles thick: and the damned are so utterly bound and helpless that, as a blessed saint, saint Anselm, writes in his book on similitudes, they are not even able to remove from the eye a worm that gnaws it.

2   —They lie in exterior darkness. For, remember, the fire of hell gives forth no light. As, at the command of God, the fire of the Babylonian furnace lost its heat but not its light so, at the command of God, the fire of hell, while retaining the intensity of its heat, burns eternally in darkness. It is a never-ending storm of darkness, dark flames and dark smoke of burning brimstone, amid which the bodies are heaped one upon another without even a glimpse of air. Of all the plagues with which the land of the Pharaohs was smitten one plague alone, that of darkness, was called horrible. What name, then, shall we give to the darkness of hell which is to last not for three days alone but for all eternity?

3   —The horror of this strait and dark prison is increased by its awful stench. All the filth of the world, all the offal and scum of the world, we are told, shall run there as to a vast reeking sewer when the terrible conflagration of the last day has purged the world. The brimstone too which burns there in such prodigious quantity fills all hell with its intolerable stench; and the bodies of the damned themselves exhale such a pestilential odour that as saint Bonaventure says, one of them alone would suffice to infect the whole world. The very air of this world, that pure element, becomes foul and unbreathable when it has been long enclosed. Consider then what must be the foulness of the air of hell. Imagine some foul and putrid corpse that has lain rotting and decomposing in the grave, a jellylike mass of liquid corruption. Imagine such a corpse a prey to flames, devoured by the fire of burning brimstone and giving off dense choking fumes of nauseous loathsome decomposition. And then imagine this sickening stench, multiplied a millionfold and a millionfold again from the millions upon millions of fetid carcasses massed together in the reeking darkness, a huge and rotting human fungus. Imagine all this and you will have some idea of the horror of the stench of hell.

4   —But this stench is not, horrible though it is, the greatest physical torment to which the damned are subjected. The torment of fire is the greatest torment to which the tyrant has ever subjected his fellow creatures. Place your finger for a moment in the flame of a candle and you will feel the pain of fire. But our earthly fire was created by God for the benefit of man, to maintain in him the spark of life and to help him in the useful arts, whereas the fire of hell is of another quality and was created by God to torture and punish the unrepentant sinner. Our earthly fire also consumes more or less rapidly according as the object which it attacks is more or less combustible so that human ingenuity has even succeeded in inventing chemical preparations to check or frustrate its action. But the sulphurous brimstone which burns in hell is a substance which is specially designed to burn forever and for ever with unspeakable fury. Moreover our earthly fire destroys at the same time as it burns so that the more intense it is the shorter is its duration: but the fire of hell has this property that it preserves that which it burns and though it rages with incredible intensity it rages for ever.

5   —Our earthly fire again, no matter how fierce or widespread it may be, is always of a limited extent: but the lake of fire in hell is boundless, shoreless and bottomless. It is on record that the devil himself, when asked the question by a certain soldier, was obliged to confess that if a whole mountain were thrown into the burning ocean of hell it would be burned up in an instant like

a piece of wax. And this terrible fire will not afflict the bodies of the damned only from without but each lost soul will be a hell unto itself, the boundless fire raging in its very vitals. O, how terrible is the lot of those wretched beings! The blood seethes and boils in the veins, the brains are boiling in the skull, the heart in the breast glowing and bursting, the bowels a redhot mass of burning pulp, the tender eyes flaming like molten balls.

6   And yet what I have said as to the strength and quality and boundlessness of this fire is as nothing when compared to its intensity, an intensity which it has as being the instrument chosen by divine design for the punishment of soul and body alike. It is a fire which proceeds directly from the ire of God, working not of its own activity but as an instrument of divine vengeance. As the waters of baptism cleanse the soul with the body so do the fires of punishment torture the spirit with the flesh. Every sense of the flesh is tortured and every faculty of the soul therewith: the eyes with impenetrable utter darkness, the nose with noisome odours, the ears with yells and howls and execrations, the taste with foul matter, leprous corruption, nameless suffocating filth, the touch with redhot goads and spikes, with cruel tongues of flame. And through the several torments of the senses the immortal soul is tortured eternally in its very essence amid the leagues upon leagues of glowing fires kindled in the abyss by the offended majesty of the Omnipotent God and fanned into everlasting and ever increasing fury by the breath of the anger of the Godhead.

7   Consider finally that the torment of this infernal prison is increased by the company of the damned themselves. Evil company on earth is so noxious that even the plants, as if by instinct, withdraw from the company of whatsoever is deadly or hurtful to them. In hell all laws are overturned: there is no thought of family or country, of ties, of relationships. The damned howl and scream at one another, their torture and rage intensified by the presence of beings tortured and raging like themselves. All sense of humanity is forgotten. The yells of the suffering sinners fill the remotest corners of the vast abyss. The mouths of the damned are full of blasphemies against God and of hatred for their fellow sufferers and of curses against those souls which were their accomplices in sin. In olden times it was the custom to punish the parricide, the man who had raised his murderous hand against his father, by casting him into the depths of the sea in a sack in which were placed a cock, a monkey and a serpent. The intention of those lawgivers who framed such a law, which seems cruel in our times, was to punish the criminal by the company of hateful and hurtful beasts. But what is the fury of those dumb beasts compared with the fury of execration which bursts from the parched lips and aching throats of the damned in hell when they behold in their companions in misery those who aided and abetted them in sin, those whose words sowed the first seeds of evil thinking and evil living in their minds, those whose immodest suggestions led them on to sin, those whose eyes tempted and allured them from the path of virtue. They turn upon those accomplices and upbraid them and curse them. But they are helpless and hopeless: it is too late now for repentance.

Vocabulary

strait (1)
similitudes (1)
offal (3)
conflagration (3)

prodigious (3)
pestilential (3)
fetid (3)
noisome (6)

execrations (6)
parricide (7)
allured (7)
upbraid (7)

The Facts

1. How thick are the walls of hell?
2. What peculiar characteristics does the fire of hell have?
3. What is the greatest physical torment that the damned of hell suffer?
4. What is the source of the fire in hell?
5. How were parricides punished in olden times?

The Strategies

1. Examine carefully this description of hell. What is its overall structure? How are its paragraphs deployed?
2. Examine paragraph 4. How is it developed? What is its purpose?
3. What is the purpose of mentioning the "earthly prisons" in paragraph 1?
4. Examine paragraph 5. How is this paragraph structured? What technique does the writer use to make his description so vivid?
5. In the novel *A Portrait of the Artist as a Young Man*, the preacher delivers this description of hell in a sermon. Identify at least one technique that the preacher uses to involve his listeners in the description.

The Issues

1. For the most part, modern minds have rejected the medieval view of a physical hell, where the damned suffer such tortures as heat, cold, foul smell, laceration, and persecution from demons. What, if anything, has replaced this notion of hell?
2. In your view, why do many people believe in paradise and hell? What disadvantage or advantage does the lack of belief in these places provide?
3. What effect do you think this sermon on hell might have on young boys listening to it? What is your opinion of the technique used?
4. Is torture as a means of punishment ever justified in a civilized society? Why or why not?
5. A portion of Dante's hell was reserved for those who encouraged others to sin. Where in this excerpt does Joyce express a similar idea? Why do both Dante and Joyce call down a harsh judgment on those who aid and abet evil?

Suggestions for Writing

1. Write an essay on hell as it is described here, arguing for or against a belief in its existence.
2. Write a brief description of heaven following the example of this selection.

A Worn Path

EUDORA WELTY

Rhetorical Thumbnail

Purpose: to create a word picture of a grandmother's devotion to her grandson

Audience: educated readers

Language: standard English and Southern Creole

Strategy: portrays in almost poetic terms the journey of a woman named Phoenix, whose heroic purpose for making it is not revealed until the end

---

Eudora Welty (1909–2001) is an American novelist and short-story writer whose tales about eccentric but charming characters from small Mississippi towns have won her a large audience. The best known of her stories have been collected in *A Curtain of Green* (1941), *The Wide Net* (1943), and *The Golden Apples* (1949). Among her novels are *Delta Wedding* (1946), *The Ponder Heart* (1954), and *The Optimist's Daughter* (1972). In 1983, she delivered the William E. Massey Sr. Lectures in American Civilization at Harvard, which were published as *One Writer's Beginnings* (1984).

In this story, a woman, undaunted by age and hardships, presses on toward her goal—to get the medicine her sick grandchild must have in order to survive.

• • •

1   It was December—a bright frozen day in the early morning. Far out in the country there was an old Negro woman with her head tied in a red rag, coming along a path through the pinewoods. Her name was Phoenix Jackson. She was very old and small and she walked slowly in the dark pine shadows, moving a little from side to side in her steps, with the balanced heaviness and lightness of a pendulum in a grandfather clock. She carried a thin, small cane made from an umbrella, and with this she kept tagging the frozen earth in front of her. This made a grave and persistent noise in the still air, that seemed meditative, like the chirping of a solitary little bird.

2   She wore a dark striped dress reaching down to her shoetops, and an equally long apron of bleached sugar sacks, with a full pocket; all neat and tidy, but every time she took a step she might have fallen over her shoelaces, which dragged from her unlaced shoes. She looked straight ahead. Her eyes were blue with age. Her skin had a pattern all its own of numberless branching wrinkles and as though a whole little tree stood in the middle of her forehead, but a golden color ran underneath, and the two knobs of her cheeks were illuminated by a yellow burning under the dark. Under the red rag her hair came down on her neck in the frailest of ringlets, still black, and with an odor like copper.

3   Now and then there was a quivering in the thicket. Old Phoenix said, "Out of my way, all you foxes, owls, beetles, jack rabbits, coons, and wild animals! . . . Keep out from under these feet, little bobwhites . . . Keep the big wild hogs out of my path. Don't let none of those come running my direction. I got a long way." Under her small black-freckled hand her cane, limber as a buggy whip, would switch at the brush as if to rouse up any hiding things.

4   On she went. The woods were deep and still. The sun made the pine needles almost too bright to look at, up where the wind rocked. The cones dropped as light as feathers. Down in the hollow was the mourning dove—it was not too late for him.

5   The path ran up a hill. "Seem like there is chains about my feet, time I get this far," she said, in the voice of argument old people keep to use with themselves. "Something always take a hold on this hill—pleads I should stay."

6   After she got to the top she turned and gave a full, severe look behind where she had come. "Up through pines," she said at length. "Now down through oaks."

7   Her eyes opened their widest and she started down gently. But before she got to the bottom of the hill a bush caught her dress.

8   Her fingers were busy and intent, but her skirts were full and long, so that before she could pull them free in one place they were caught in another. It was not possible to allow the dress to tear. "I in the thorny bush," she said. "Thorns, you doing your appointed work. Never want to let folks past—no sir. Old eyes thought you was a pretty little green bush."

9   Finally, trembling all over, she stood free, and after a moment dared to stoop for her cane.

10   "Sun so high!" she cried, leaning back and looking, while the thick tears went over her eyes. "The time getting all gone here."

11   At the foot of this hill was a place where a log was laid across the creek.

12   "Now comes the trial," said Phoenix.

13   Putting her right foot out, she mounted the log and shut her eyes. Lifting her skirt, leveling her cane fiercely before her, like a festival figure in some parade, she began to march across. Then she opened her eyes and she was safe on the other side.

14   "I wasn't as old as I thought," she said.

15   But she sat down to rest. She spread her skirts on the bank around her and folded her hands over her knees. Up above her was a tree in a pearly cloud of mistletoe. She did not dare to close her eyes, and when a little boy brought her a little plate with a slice of marble-cake on it she spoke to him. "That would be acceptable," she said. But when she went to take it there was just her own hand in the air.

16   So she left that tree, and had to go through a barbed-wire fence. There she had to creep and crawl, spreading her knees and stretching her fingers like a baby trying to climb the steps. But she talked loudly to herself: she could not let her dress be torn now, so late in the day, and she could not pay for having her arm or her leg sawed off if she got caught fast where she was.

17   At last she was safe through the fence and risen up out in the clearing. Big dead trees, like black men with one arm, were standing in the purple stalks of the withered cotton field. There sat a buzzard.

18   "Who you watching?"

19   In the furrow she made her way along.

20   "Glad this not the season for bulls," she said, looking sideways, "and the good Lord made his snakes to curl up and sleep in the winter. A pleasure I don't see no two-headed snake coming around that tree, where it come once. It took a while to get by him, back in the summer."

21   She passed through the old cotton and went into a field of dead corn. It whispered and shook, and was taller than her head. "Through the maze now," she said, for there was no path.

22   Then there was something tall, black, and skinny there, moving before her.

23   At first she took it for a man. It could have been a man dancing in the field. But she stood still and listened, and it did not make a sound. It was as silent as a ghost.

24   "Ghost," she said sharply, "who be you the ghost of? For I have heard of nary death close by."

25   But there was no answer, only the ragged dancing in the wind.

26   She shut her eyes, reached out her hand, and touched a sleeve. She found a coat and inside that an emptiness, cold as ice.

27   "You scarecrow," she said. Her face lighted. "I ought to be shut up for good," she said with laughter. "My senses is gone. I too old. I the oldest people I ever know. Dance, old scarecrow," she said, "while I dancing with you."

28   She kicked her foot over the furrow, and with mouth drawn down shook her head once or twice in a little strutting way. Some husks blew down and whirled in streamers about her skirts.

29   Then she went on, parting her way from side to side with the cane, through the whispering field. At last she came to the end, to a wagon track, where the silver grass blew between the red ruts. The quail were walking around like pullets, seeming all dainty and unseen.

30   "Walk pretty," she said. "This is the easy place. This is the easy going."

31   She followed the track, swaying through the quiet bare fields, through the little strings of trees silver in their dead leaves, past cabins silver from weather, with the doors and windows boarded shut, all like old women under a spell sitting there. "I walking in their sleep," she said, nodding her head vigorously.

32   In a ravine she went where a spring was silently flowing through a hollow log. Old Phoenix bent and drank. "Sweetgum makes the water sweet," she said, and drank more. "Nobody know who made this well, for it was here when I was born."

33   The track crossed a swampy part where the moss hung as white as lace from every limb. "Sleep on, alligators, and blow your bubbles." Then the track went into the road.

34   Deep, deep the road went down between the high green-colored banks. Overhead the live-oaks met, and it was as dark as a cave.

35   A black dog with a lolling tongue came up out of the weeds by the ditch. She was meditating, and not ready, and when he came at her she only hit him a little with her cane. Over she went in the ditch, like a little puff of milkweed.

36   Down there, her senses drifted away. A dream visited her, and she reached her hand up, but nothing reached down and gave her a pull. So she lay there and presently went to talking. "Old woman," she said to herself, "that black dog come up out of the weeds to stall you off, and now there he sitting on his fine tail, smiling at you."

37   A white man finally came along and found her—a hunter, a young man, with his dog on a chain.

38   "Well, Granny!" he laughed. "What are you doing there?"

39   "Lying on my back like a June-bug waiting to be turned over, mister," she said, reaching up her hand.

40   He lifted her up, gave her a swing in the air, and set her down, "Anything broken, Granny?"

41   "No sir, them old dead weeds is springy enough," said Phoenix, when she had got her breath. "I thank you for your trouble."

42   "Where do you live, Granny?" he asked, while the two dogs were growling at each other.

43   "Away back yonder, sir, behind the ridge. You can't even see it from here."

44   "On your way home?"

45   "No sir, I going to town."

46   "Why, that's too far! That's as far as I walk when I come out myself, and I get something for my trouble." He patted the stuffed bag he carried, and there hung down a little closed claw. It was one of the bobwhites, with its beak hooked bitterly to show it was dead. "Now you go on home, Granny!"

47   "I bound to go to town, mister," said Phoenix. "The time come around."

48   He gave another laugh, filling the whole landscape. "I know you colored people! Wouldn't miss going to town to see Santa Claus!"

49   But something held Old Phoenix very still. The deep lines in her face went into a fierce and different radiation. Without warning she had seen with her own eyes a flashing nickel fall out of the man's pocket on to the ground.

50   "How old are you, Granny?" he was saying.

51   "There is no telling, mister," she said, "no telling."

52   Then she gave a little cry and clapped her hands, and said, "Git on away from here, dog! Look! Look at that dog!" She laughed as if in admiration. "He ain't scared of nobody. He a big black dog." She whispered, "Sick him!"

53   "Watch me get rid of that cur," said the man. "Sick him, Pete! Sick him!"

54   Phoenix heard the dogs fighting and heard the man running and throwing sticks. She even heard a gunshot. But she was slowly bending forward by that time, further and further forward, the lids stretched down over her eyes, as if she were doing this in her sleep. Her chin was lowered almost to her knees. The yellow palm of her hand came out from the fold of her apron. Her fingers slid down and along the ground under the piece of money with the grace and care they would have in lifting an egg from under a sitting hen. Then she slowly

straightened up, she stood erect, and the nickel was in her apron pocket. A bird flew by. Her lips moved. "God watching me the whole time. I come to stealing."

55   The man came back, and his own dog panted about them. "Well, I scared him off that time," he said, and then he laughed and lifted his gun and pointed it at Phoenix.

56   She stood straight and faced him.

57   "Doesn't the gun scare you?" he said, still pointing it.

58   "No sir, I seen plenty go off closer by, in my day, and for less than what I done," she said, holding utterly still.

59   He smiled, and shouldered the gun. "Well, Granny," he said, "you must be a hundred years old, and scared of nothing. I'd give you a dime if I had any money with me. But you take my advice and stay home, and nothing will happen to you."

60   "I bound to go on my way, mister," said Phoenix. She inclined her head in the red rag. Then they went in different directions, but she could hear the gun shooting again and again over the hill.

61   She walked on. The shadows hung from the oak trees to the road like curtains. Then she smelled wood-smoke, and smelled the river, and she saw a steeple and the cabins on their steep steps. Dozens of little black children whirled around her. There ahead was Natchez shining. Bells were ringing. She walked on.

62   In the paved city it was Christmas time. There were red and green electric lights strung and crisscrossed everywhere, and all turned on in the day time. Old Phoenix would have been lost if she had not distrusted her eyesight and depended on her feet to know where to take her.

63   She paused quietly on the sidewalk, where people were passing by. A lady came along in the crowd, carrying an armful of red-, green-, and silver-wrapped presents; she gave off perfume like the red roses in hot summer, and Phoenix stopped her.

64   "Please, missy, will you lace up my shoe?" She held up her foot.

65   "What do you want, Grandma?"

66   "See my shoe," said Phoenix. "Do all right for out in the country, but wouldn't look right to go in a big building."

67   "Stand still then, Grandma," said the lady. She put her packages down carefully on the sidewalk beside her and laced and tied both shoes tightly.

68   "Can't lace 'em with a cane," said Phoenix. "Thank you, missy. I doesn't mind asking a nice lady to tie up my shoes when I gets out on the street."

69   Moving slowly and from side to side, she went into the stone building and into a tower of steps, where she walked up and around and around until her feet knew to stop.

70   She entered a door, and there she saw nailed up on the wall the document that had been stamped with the gold seal and framed in the gold frame which matched the dream that was hung up in her head.

71   "Here I be," she said. There was a fixed and ceremonial stiffness over her body.

72   "A charity case, I suppose," said an attendant who sat at the desk before her.

73   But Phoenix only looked above her head. There was sweat on her face; the wrinkles shone like a bright net.

74   "Speak, up, Grandma," the woman said. "What's your name? We must have your history, you know. Have you been here before? What seems to be the trouble with you?"

75   Old Phoenix only gave a twitch to her face as if a fly were bothering her.

76   "Are you deaf?" cried the attendant.

77   But then the nurse came in.

78   "Oh, that's just old Aunt Phoenix," she said. "She doesn't come for her-self—she has a little grandson. She makes these trips just as regular as clock-work. She lives away back off the Old Natchez Trace." She bent down. "Well, Aunt Phoenix, why don't you just take a seat? We won't keep you standing after your long trip." She pointed.

79   The old woman sat down, bolt upright in the chair.

80   "Now, how is the boy?" asked the nurse.

81   Old Phoenix did not speak.

82   "I said, how is the boy?"

83   But Phoenix only waited and stared straight ahead, her face very solemn and withdrawn into rigidity.

84   "Is his throat any better?" asked the nurse. "Aunt Phoenix, don't you hear me? Is your grandson's throat any better since the last time you came for the medicine?"

85   With her hand on her knees, the old woman waited, silent, erect and mo-tionless, just as if she were in armor.

86   "You mustn't take up our time this way, Aunt Phoenix," the nurse said. "Tell us quickly about your grandson, and get it over. He isn't dead, is he?"

87   At last there came a flicker and then a flame of comprehension across her face, and she spoke.

88   "My grandson. It was my memory had left me. There I sat and forgot why I made my long trip."

89   "Forgot?" The nurse frowned. "After you came so far?"

Then Phoenix was like an old woman begging a dignified forgiveness for waking up frightened in the night. "I never did go to school—I was too old at the Surrender," she said in a soft voice. "I'm an old woman without an educa-tion. It was my memory fail me. My little grandson, he is just the same, and I forgot it in the coming."

90   "Throat never heals, does it?" said the nurse, speaking in a loud, sure voice to Old Phoenix. By now she had a card with something written on it, a little list. "Yes. Swallowed lye. When was it—January—two—three years ago—"

91   Phoenix spoke unasked now. "No, missy, he not dead, he just the same. Every little while his throat begin to close up again, and he not able to swallow. He not get his breath. He not able to help himself. So the time come around, and I go on another trip for the soothing medicine."

92   "All right. The doctor said as long as you came to get it you could have it," said the nurse. "But it's an obstinate case."

93   "My little grandson, he sit up there in the house all wrapped up, waiting by himself," Phoenix went on. "We is the only two left in the world. He suffer

and it don't seem to put him back at all. He got a sweet look. He going to last. He wear a little patch quilt and peep out, holding his mouth open like a little bird. I remembers so plain now. I not going to forget him again, no, the whole enduring time. I could tell him from all the others in creation."

94   "All right." The nurse was trying to hush her now. She brought her a bottle of medicine. "Charity," she said, making a check mark in a book.

95   Old Phoenix held the bottle close to her eyes and then carefully put it into her pocket.

96   "I thank you," she said.

97   "It's Christmas time, Grandma," said the attendant. "Could I give you a few pennies out of my purse?"

98   "Five pennies is a nickel," said Phoenix stiffly.

99   "Here's a nickel," said the attendant.

100   Phoenix rose carefully and held out her hand. She received the nickel and then fished the other nickel out of her pocket and laid it beside the new one. She stared at her palm closely, with her head on one side.

101   Then she gave a tap with her cane on the floor.

102   "This is what come to me to do," she said. "I going to the store and buy my child a little windmill they sells, made out of paper. He going to find it hard to believe there such a thing in the world. I'll march myself back where he waiting, holding it straight up in this hand."

103   She lifted her free hand, gave a little nod, turned round, and walked out of the doctor's office. Then her slow step began on the stairs, going down.

● Vocabulary

meditative (1)	maze (21)	sweetgum (32)
illuminated (2)	nary (24)	lolling (35)
bobwhites (3)	strutting (28)	radiation (49)
limber (3)	husks (28)	ceremonial (71)
appointed (8)	pullets (29)	lye (90)
furrow (19)		

● The Facts

1. In paragraph 1, to what piece of antique furniture is Phoenix Jackson's walk compared? What characteristic is Welty trying to get across? Later on in the narrative, where is the same piece of furniture alluded to again? Why?

2. What is the purpose of the old woman's journey?

3. Essentially this is the story of a courageous woman. What part of the trip is especially difficult for her? How does she manage this obstacle?

4. What details indicate that Phoenix Jackson is slightly senile and therefore not always in touch with reality?

5. What excuse does the old woman offer for not remembering what errand she is on?

The Strategies

1. What is the plot structure of the story? What is the conflict in the plot? When is the conflict resolved?

2. Analyze Phoenix's language. What is conveyed through her speech?

3. Point out some instances of humor. What kind of humor is used?

4. During what decade would you judge this story to have taken place? What clues to your answer are given in the story?

5. In paragraph 85, we read: "With her hand on her knees, the old woman waited, silent, erect and motionless, just as if she were in armor." What meaning do you attribute to this passage?

The Issues

1. In Egyptian mythology, the phoenix was a bird of great splendor that consumed itself by fire every 500 years and rose renewed from its own ashes. In what way is Phoenix Jackson like this bird?

2. The narrative abounds in descriptive passages. What is the dominant impression in paragraph 2? Are any details included that do not support this impression? What other descriptive passages can you identify?

3. Why does Phoenix keep talking to herself? What do her monologues add to the total portrait of her?

4. What is the meaning of the episode in which Phoenix steals the nickel? Does the act offend our sense of honesty? Explain your answer.

5. What significance can you attribute to the fact that the journey takes place at Christmas time?

6. Phoenix Jackson's journey is in the literary tradition of the mythological quest. What aspects of the story place it in that tradition?

Suggestions for Writing

1. Using your imagination, describe Phoenix's journey home. Make your scenes descriptive by providing details that support a dominant impression.

2. Write an essay in which you describe a loving relationship between a grandparent and a grandchild or between a person and a pet.

Pigeon Woman

MAY SWENSON

May Swenson (1913–1989) poet, playwright, and lecturer, was born in Logan, Utah, and educated at Utah State University. She resided in and near New York City until her death. She published a number of collections of poetry including her last volume, *In Other Words* (1987).

The meaning of "Pigeon Woman" emerges from the irony contained in a strange old lady's fantasy.

* * *

Slate, or dirty-marble-colored,
or rusty-iron-colored, the pigeons
on the flagstones in front of the
Public Library make a sharp lake

5   into which the pigeon woman wades
at exactly 1:30. She wears a
plastic pink raincoat with a round
collar (looking like a little

girl, so gay) and flat gym shoes,
10   her hair square-cut, orange.
Wide-apart feet carefully enter
the spinning, crooning waves

(as if she'd just learned how
to walk, each step conscious,
15   an accomplishment); blue knots in the
calves of her bare legs (uglied marble),

age in angled cords of jaw
and neck, her pimento-colored hair,
hanging in thin tassels, is gray
20   around a balding crown.

The day-old bread drops down
from her veined hand dipping out
of a paper sack. Choppy, shadowy ripples
the pigeons strike around her legs.

25   Sack empty, she squats and seems to rinse
her hands in them—the rainy greens and
oily purples of their necks. Almost
they let her wet her thirsty fingertips—

but drain away in an untouchable tide.
30   A make-believe trade

she has come to, in her lostness
or illness or age—to treat the motley

city pigeons at 1:30 every day, in all
weathers. It is for them she colors
35   her own feathers. Ruddy-footed
on the lime-stained paving,

purling to meet her when she comes,
they are a lake of love. Retreating
from her hands as soon as empty,
40   they are the flints of love.

Vocabulary

crooning (12)   motley (32)   flints (40)
pimento (18)   purling (37)

The Facts

1. What is the dominant impression conveyed by this "pigeon woman"? In terms of her looks, what role could she play in a fairy tale?
2. As the poem develops, how do our feelings change about the woman?
3. Describe the fantasy that gives purpose to the woman's life.
4. What is the meaning of the final stanza?
5. Is this woman an impossible figment of the poet's imagination or does she represent a kind of reality? Comment.

The Strategies

1. How does the level of language used contribute to the description of the woman?
2. How do you explain the image of the pigeons as a lake?
3. What are the "blue knots in the calves of her bare legs"? Comment on the effectiveness of this image.
4. What is the meaning of the metaphor "her own feathers" in the next-to-last stanza?
5. Interpret the metaphor "the flints of love" in the final line.

The Issues

1. Various public as well as private agencies have been concerned with the plight of the poor, especially women who have been labeled "bag ladies," "crazy drifters," or "old female transients." What suggestions do you have for dealing with this alienated group of our population? Are we doing enough, or should we do more?
2. What is it that keeps this woman from giving up on life? What do you consider the driving force that keeps most people who lead desperate lives from committing suicide?
3. The woman in the poem chooses to feed a flock of pigeons. What other activities could give meaning to such a person's life?
4. How would you describe the male counterpart of the pigeon woman? Include the details of his appearance.
5. What measures do you suggest for reducing the number of street vagrants in our major cities?

Suggestions for Writing

1. Write an essay comparing the pigeon woman with Phoenix Jackson from the previous story.
2. Imagine the loneliness that comes from being old and alone. Describe this loneliness in terms of specific, concrete details.

ISSUE FOR CRITICAL THINKING AND DEBATE: SELF-IMAGE

Everywhere we look, we see people who are enormously obese. We also see men and women who look as if they were advertising for a circus—with spiked green hair, tattoos up and down their bodies, and piercings that disfigure their noses, ears, and lips. In other words, certain segments of our society seem so obsessed with their looks that they draw attention to themselves by looking bizarre. A totally different group worship at the shrine of glamour as portrayed by their idols in popular magazines and on the cinema or television screen. You can observe them sweating away on exercise machines, dieting on tofu, or paying out their hard-earned money to hire a trainer who will show them exactly how to build up their abs and shoulders. In fact, we are told that average Americans are exposed to 1,500 ads every day and spend dozens of hours per week watching television commercials that promise to transform them into male or female icons of an adulating public. Well, you might think that the media would try to reflect the average look when selling products, but not so. The majority of women models are much thinner and sleeker than the average woman in our cities or suburbs. Similarly, the men are more muscular and well-toned than the men we see walking the aisles of the supermarket or shopping malls.

Since the media glorifies these exotic images and exhibits them on electronic screens, on paper, and on billboards everywhere, young people grow up thinking that if they don't look according to these models, they must be losers. Advertisements create enormous anxiety about weight and body contours in adolescents, who are already insecure about their place in society. Some college graduates have actually postponed looking for jobs until they could achieve the "right weight" or "good muscle tone." This mass mirage sells huge amounts of products, but it also creates low self-esteem and severe depression.

Changing one's look has become a multi-billion-dollar business. In the last decade, huge companies have been built on the new psychology of first impressions that places a higher premium on physical attractiveness than on talent or personality. "Extreme makeover" programs that pool the resources of various plastic surgeons, cosmetic dentists, and personal trainers to transform ugly ducklings into sleek swans proliferate on television. This endless parade of comely flesh would give any alien observer watching from afar the mistaken impression that most Americans are attractive and physically fit instead of chronically overweight and sick. One is tempted to wonder if all of this pressure to live up to a certain standard of beauty does not lead to self-destruction rather than self-improvement.

The discussion that follows brings to the table a commonsense approach to the problem of physical appearance and self-image. First is a survey and an essay by Cindy Maynard, a dietician who teaches young people to accept their bodies and to focus on achieving a healthy lifestyle rather than on attempting to imitate the ideal body images of popular film stars. Second is an article by a PhD and pioneer in brain/mind research, Jill Ammon-Wexler. In straightforward and concise language she insists that a good self-image is the foundation of success in life, and she shows you how to overhaul your self-image if you are not who you want to be. Third is a student essay from a psychology major explaining the reasons why young people go for piercings and tattoos.

Nothing is definitively resolved here, nor would one expect it to be. How we see ourselves is even a more complex phenomenon than how others see us. In the end the only solution may come from that old adage: Be yourself—whether you're fat, thin, in between, or truly an out-and-out hunk or hottie.

"No, your eyes are perfect, but fake glasses would sure make you look smarter."

Body Image

CINDY MAYNARD

Cindy Maynard is a health and medical writer and a registered dietitian living in San Diego. She often writes for *Current Health* magazine, a weekly publication. Her advice on body image has helped many young people to escape the trap of seeing themselves as physically unattractive or even repulsive.

According to the author, "body image dissatisfaction is so epidemic in our society that it's almost considered normal." Teenagers, whose self-confidence is already battered by the constant drumbeat of advertisements touting the ideal body, are especially sensitive to the charge of being fat. The essay that follows opens with a questionnaire that tests

*the reader's body image I.Q. and then offers helpful tips on how to view the body in a
healthy way.*

• • •

Body Image Questionnaire: How Do You Measure Up?

1 When you look in the mirror, what do you see? When you walk past a shop window and catch a glimpse of your body, what do you notice first? Are you proud of
what you see, or do you think, "I'm too short, I'm too fat, If only I were thinner or
more muscular"? Most people answer negatively. Take the following quiz and see
how your Body Image I.Q. measures up. Check the most appropriate answer:

1. Have you avoided sports or working out because you didn't want to be
   seen in gym clothes? Yes _____ No _____

2. Does eating even a small amount of food make you feel fat?
   Yes _____ No _____

3. Do you worry or obsess about your body not being small, thin or good
   enough? Yes _____ No _____

4. Are you concerned your body is not muscular or strong enough?
   Yes _____ No _____

5. Do you avoid wearing certain clothes because they make you feel fat?
   Yes _____ No _____

6. Do you feel badly about yourself because you don't like your body?
   Yes _____ No _____

7. Have you ever disliked your body? Yes _____ No _____

8. Do you want to change something about your body?
   Yes _____ No _____

9. Do you compare yourself to others and "come up short"?
   Yes _____ No _____

2 If you answered "Yes" to three or more questions, you may have a negative body image.

Mirror, Mirror

3 Girls are overly concerned about weight and body shape. They strive for the
"perfect" body and judge themselves by their looks, appearance, and above all
thinness. But boys don't escape either. They are concerned with the size and
strength of their body. There has been a shift in the male body image. Boys live
in a culture that showcases males as glamorous "macho" figures who have to
be "tough," build muscles and sculpt their bodies—if they want to fit in. They
think they have to be a "real" man, but many admit being confused as to what
that means or what's expected of them. This confusion can make it harder than
ever to feel good about themselves.

4 Some sports can contribute to a negative body image. The need to make
weight for a sport like wrestling or boxing can cause disordered eating. But

© Lon C. Diehl / Photo Edit

● Since weight-loss pills and regimens are a multi-million-dollar business, can they be trusted?

other boys say sports make them feel better about themselves. Jon, a 15-year-old, states, "Guys are in competition, especially in the weight room. They say, 'I can bench 215 lbs.' and the other guy says, 'Well, I can bench 230 lbs.' If you're stronger, you're better." Daniel, age 16, shares, "Guys are into having the perfect body. But if you feel good about your body, you automatically feel good about yourself."

5   Most of our cues about what we should look like come from the media, our parents, and our peers. This constant obsession with weight, the size of our bodies, and longing for a different shape or size can be painful.

6   Where do these negative perceptions come from? Here are just a few of the factors contributing to negative perceptions and obsessions about our bodies.

Mission Impossible

7 The media play a big part. Surrounded by thin models and TV stars, teenage girls are taught to achieve an impossible goal. As a result, many teenage girls intensely dislike their bodies and can tell you down to the minutest detail what's wrong with them. Most teens watch an average of 22 hours of TV a week and are deluged with images of fat-free bodies in the pages of health, fashion, and teen magazines. The "standard" is impossible to achieve. A female should look like, and have the same dimensions as Barbie, and a male should look like Arnold Schwarzenegger. Buff *Baywatch* lifeguards, the well-toned abs of any cast member of *Melrose Place* or *Friends*, and music-video queens don't help.

8 Take a look at the ten most popular magazines on the newspaper racks. The women and men on the covers represent about .03 percent of the population. The other 99.97% don't have a chance to compete, much less measure up. Don't forget it's a career with these people. They're pros. Many have had major body make-overs and have a full-time personal trainer. Most ads are reproduced, airbrushed, or changed by computer. Body parts can be changed at will.

9 The images of men and women in ads today do not promote self-esteem or positive self image. They're intended to sell products. In the U.S. billions of dollars are spent by consumers who pursue the perfect body. The message "thin is in" is sold thousands of times a day through TV, movies, magazines, billboards, newspapers and songs. Advertising conveys the message "You're not O.K. Here's what you need to do to fix what's wrong." Girls and boys believe it and react to it. In a 1997 Body Image Survey, both girls and boys reported that "very thin or muscular models" made them feel insecure about themselves.

10 Western society places a high value upon appearance. Self-worth is enhanced for those who are judged attractive. Those who are deemed unattractive can feel at a disadvantage. The message from the media, fashion, and our peers can create a longing—a longing to win the approval of our culture and fit in at any cost. And that can be disastrous to our self-esteem.

11 Parents can give mixed messages, too, especially if they're constantly dieting or have body or food issues of their own. How we perceive and internalize these childhood messages about our bodies determines our ability to build self-esteem and confidence in our appearance.

12 The diet/fitness craze is mind-boggling. It's not just dieting, it's diet foods and diet commercials. Everybody's counting fat grams. Listen to the conversation in the lunch room, locker room, or on the bus to school. The talk centers around dieting, fat thighs, or tight "abs" and how many pounds can be lost with the latest diet. This kind of intense focus on food and fat can lead to abnormal eating habits or disordered eating, a precursor to eating disorders, which is taking it to the extreme.

13 Awareness of eating disorders got a big boost in 1995 when Princess Di began talking openly about her struggles with bulimia. Actress Tracy Gold, still struggling with her eating disorder, continues to help others by discussing her eating disorder with the media. Recently many organizations have initiated an effort to expand awareness of eating disorders and promote a positive body image and self-esteem.

Body Image, Body Love

14   Why is a positive body image so important? Psychologists and counselors agree that a negative body image is directly related to self-esteem. The more negative the perception of our bodies, the more negative we feel about ourselves.

15   Being a teenager is a time of major change. Besides the obvious changes in size and shape, teens are faced with how they feel about themselves. Body image and self-esteem are two important ways to help promote a positive image.

16   When most people think about body image they think about aspects of physical appearance, attractiveness, and beauty. But body image is much more. It is the mental picture a person has of his/her body as well as their thoughts, feelings, judgments, sensations, awareness, and behavior. Body image is developed through interactions with people and the social world. It's our mental picture of ourselves; it's what allows us to become ourselves.

17   Body image influences behavior, self-esteem, and our psyche. When we feel bad about our body, our satisfaction and mood plummet. If we are constantly trying to push, reshape, or remake our bodies, our sense of self becomes unhealthy. We lose confidence in our abilities. It's not uncommon for people who think poorly of their bodies to have problems in other areas of their lives, including sexuality, careers, and relationships.

18   A healthy body image occurs when a person's feelings about his/her body are positive, confident and self-caring. This image is necessary to care for the body, find outlets for self-expression, develop confidence in your physical abilities, and feel comfortable with who you are.

19   Self-esteem is a personal evaluation of your worth as a person. It measures how much you respect yourself:

     physically (how happy you are with the way you look)
     intellectually (how well you feel you can accomplish your goals)
     emotionally (how much you feel loved)
     morally (how you think of yourself as a person)

20   How you see yourself affects every part of your life. High self-esteem makes for a happier life. It allows you to be your own person and not have others define you.

21   Self-esteem, self-confidence, and self-respect are all related. Self-esteem is also defined as the judgments people make about themselves and is affected by self-confidence and respect. Self-confidence is believing in our ability to take action and meet our goals. Self-respect is the degree to which we believe we deserve to be happy, have rewarding relationships, and stand up for our rights and values. All these factors affect whether or not we will have a healthy body image.

22   To begin to achieve healthy images of ourselves and our bodies is a challenge. Here are some things you can do to start feeling better about your body and yourself.

Making Peace with Your Body and Self

23   When you look in the mirror, make yourself find at least one good point for every demerit you give. Become aware of your positives.

24   Decide which of the cultural pressures—glamour, fitness, thinness, media, peer group—prevent you from feeling good about yourself. How about not buying fashion magazines which promote unrealistic body images?

25   Exercise gets high marks when it comes to breeding positive body feelings. It makes us feel better about our appearance, and improves our health and mood.

26   Emphasize your assets. You have many. Give yourself credit for positive qualities. If there are some things you want to change, remember self-discovery is a lifelong process.

27   Make friends with the person you see in the mirror. Say, "I like what I see. I like me." Do it until you believe it.

28   Question ads. Instead of saying, "What's wrong with me?" say, "What's wrong with this ad?" Write the company. Set your own standards instead of letting the media set them for you.

29   Ditch dieting and bail on the scale. These are two great ways to develop a healthy relationship with your body and weight.

30   Challenge size-bigotry and fight size discrimination whenever you can. Don't speak of yourself or others with phrases like "fat slob," "pig out," or "thunder thighs."

31   Be an example to others by taking people seriously for what they say, feel, and do rather than how they look.

32   Accept the fact that your body's changing. In teen years, your body is a work in progress. Don't let every new inch or curve throw you off the deep end.

33   You know you are successful when you look at your image in the mirror and instead of asking, "What's wrong with me?" you can say, "There's nothing really wrong with me." And little by little you'll find you can stop disliking your body. When Clister Smith, age 15, was asked how we can like our bodies better, he said, "Quit worrying about what others think of you. If you want to change your body, do it for yourself and not for anyone else."

34   This is the starting point. It is from this new way of looking at a problem that we can begin to feel better about ourselves. Make this the time to accept the natural dimensions of your body instead of drastically trying to change them. You can't exchange your body for a new one. So the best thing is to find peace with the one you have. Your body is where you're going to be living the rest of your life. Isn't it about time you made it home?

● Vocabulary

cues (5)	internalize (11)	initiated (13)
obsession (5)	precursor (12)	plummet (17)
perceptions (6)	bulimia (13)	dimensions (34)
airbrushed (8)		

● The Facts

1. What is the purpose of the questionnaire preceding the rest of the essay? Do you consider it useful? Give reasons for your answer.

2. How do boys and girls differ in their views of their bodies? What do both views have in common?

3. From what source do most of us receive our cues about the way we should appear to others? In your opinion, are these cues valid or are there other, more important, sources of validation? Explain your answer.

4. Why, according to Maynard, don't the ads in today's magazines promote a good self-image in their readers? Do you agree with Maynard's view? Why or why not?

5. According to Maynard, which of the steps in making peace with your body receives "high marks"? Why is this so?

● The Strategies

1. What about the author's writing style strikes you? Is it embroidered and complex or simple and straightforward? Consider the length of paragraphs and the sentence structure.

2. Many of the paragraphs consist of one or two declarative sentences that are not developed the way more sophisticated works develop a topic sentence. What advantage do these staccato statements have? What is your reaction to the style of this essay?

3. Where do you think the author got her idea for the heading "Mirror, Mirror" at the start of the essay? How effective is this heading? What other heading can you suggest?

4. What purpose does the question in paragraph 6 serve? Is the question ever answered in the essay? If so, how? If not, why not?

5. Why does the author keep using the personal pronoun "you" in writing this essay? Would a less personal approach be more effective?

● The Issues

1. Do you agree with the author that certain sport requirements can cause boys to suffer from a poor self-image? What is your feeling about today's emphasis on weight lifting, jogging, and training on gym equipment?

2. Why does the author use the title "Mission Impossible" in her third segment? What is the impossible mission to which she refers? Do you agree with her? Give reasons for your answer.

3. How does the author view diets and diet foods? State your own view about how dieting fits into your lifestyle.

4. Who was Princess Di, and how did she help the cause of eating disorders? What was the contribution of Tracy Gold? What do both of these women have in common?

5. Of the many tips offered under the heading "Making Peace with Your Body and Self," which do you consider the most helpful? Do you agree with the author that following all of the tips is only a beginning? Support your answers with reasons.

● Suggestions for Writing

1. Looking at yourself in the mirror, find those outer and inner qualities you like best about yourself. Then write an essay titled "The Person I See When I Look

in the Mirror." Do not allow negative thoughts to influence your description. This essay is supposed to present you at your best.

2. Write an essay describing a piece of TV advertising that you do not consider a threat to your self-image. Indicate clearly why this ad does not make you feel inferior or abnormal.

Acquiring Your Self-Image

JILL AMMON-WEXLER

Jill Ammon-Wexler, or "Dr. Jill" as she is known to her public, is a PhD in psychology, a pioneer brain/mind researcher, and veteran advisor to the Pentagon, a presidential commission, top executives, executive teams, entrepreneurs, and numerous well-known personalities. She was one of the first scientists to introduce brainwave training to the executive world and is the creator of the web's first complete mental workout ezone, the Quantum Brain Gym at www.quantumbraingym.com. Dr. Jill is the author of numerous books, including her bestseller, *Zap Your Life: Feel the Power* (2007). Her articles often focus on the power of belief in yourself and on how to enhance brain power. Dr. Jill currently resides in Idaho, where she enjoys nature and her cats.

One of Dr. Jill's favorite quotations is as follows: "The greatest personal power you have is the power to choose your own thoughts." Keep this comment in mind as you follow the author's admonitions on how to build a self-image that can be one of your most important assets. Consider how your brain is the most valuable tool in your attempt to be successful. We suggest that as you read, you make some notes about habits you may have developed that will either help or stand in the way of developing a good self-image.

• • •

1   If I asked you to describe yourself, what self-image would you paint? Another way to put it is this: Who do you believe you are?

2   Your self-image is just what the term says—an image consisting of the mosaic of ideas you hold about your own self. In short—how you view your capabilities and skills, your body, your mind, and your personal potential.

3   But while almost everyone agrees that it's important to have a good self-image, very few people seem to know how to acquire one—or even how they got the self-image they now have.

The History of Your Self-Image

4   You began to form your self-image and your sense of worth as a very young child. As you interacted with the important people in your life, you received messages from them about your self.

5   Over the years these messages collected in your impressionable subconscious mind, and created what has become your self-image.

6   Then belief moved in, setting those messages into mental cement. The result is that today you believe that you actually are your subconscious collection of other people's impressions of you.

7   This process continues to this day—and acts to reinforce what you already believe about your self.

8   Think about that for a moment.

9   The interesting thing about beliefs is that they are usually not open to question or reason. We just automatically believe them to be true.

10   So, if you believe you lack self-confidence, are a poor public speaker, do not know how to lead others, will never be successful, or do not have the ability to create a really good relationship, and so on—guess what. You will defend that belief even to yourself.

11   This occurs because the intense emotional component attached to a belief automatically causes your brain to resist any attempt to question it with reason.

12   And in the meantime your subconscious mind, which has a photographic memory of every event that went into the making of your self-concept beliefs, will make sure your actions reflect any limiting beliefs.

How to Overhaul Your Self-Image

13   Your self-image determines what you will (and will not) achieve in your life. So if you are not who you want to be, or are not living the life you want to live, the place to start is with an overhaul of your self-image.

14   Anything else will just create more of the same.

15   After over 30 years in the field of psychology, there is one thing I can absolutely guarantee to you. That one thing is this: You are absolutely NOT who you think you are.

16   Your self-image does not mirror who you really are today. You are not that collection of painful or limiting memories.

17   You are not that kid who was always told to speak only when spoken to. You are not that little girl who fell a lot only because she needed corrective glasses. You are not stupid because you had more interest in drawing than reading and math.

18   You are none of those things. You are NOT your past history. So stop believing that old stuff—and stop acting as though it were true.

Here is a reminder of what you really are:

1. You Are Unique

19   There is literally no one else like you. No one else thinks as you do, has your ideas, or does things the way you do. No one else has your unique set of talents and abilities.

20   Your brain is as unique as your fingerprints. No one has your mind and memories. No one. You are not ordinary. Actually no one is.

21   Stand up and carry yourself with dignity, because this is your life. You and only you live in your skin—and it is your unique right to decide how to best do that.

2. Your Limits Are Not Real

22   It is today an accepted truth that we really do create our own reality. You have a choice to simply react to what is happening to and around you—or you can choose to respond.

23   There's a big difference between reacting and responding. Reacting is an automatic knee-jerk response to life—while responding involves a conscious choice.

24   You can respond to your desire for a better self-image by taking conscious action to replace those old beliefs. Simply begin to challenge those old beliefs about yourself. Drag them out of your dark subconscious mind out into the sunlight of conscious examination.

3. You Have Unlimited Personal Power

25   Here is something else I can guarantee: Most of those old limiting beliefs about your self will not hold up under conscious examination.

26   And once you begin to challenge this old stuff, you will discover that what you thought were your limits do not have validity in your current reality.

27   The greatest personal power you have is the power to choose your own thoughts. Read that sentence again.

28   The great Earl Nightingale* once said: "You become what you think."

29   The truth of this is so powerful it is almost overwhelming. You and you alone decide what you will think—and what you will believe your limits and potentials are.

30   And you and you alone will decide what to do with this awesome power.

31   The fact is this: You can recreate your self, and build and strengthen virtually any aspect of your being or area of your life. Just choose to consciously build your own beliefs and take action.

32   I have personally been down in the trenches too—and can guarantee the way out is simply a decision. Just do it. Stand up right now and roar like a lion.

"Acquiring Your Self-Image" by Dr. Jill Ammon-Wexler. Reprinted with permission.

● Vocabulary

mosaic (2)	photographic (12)	conscious (23)
impressionable (5)	overhaul (13)	validity (26)
subconscious (5)	corrective (17)	
component (11)	unique (17)	

● The Facts

1. What is your answer to the questions posed in the opening paragraph? List it on paper in one declarative sentence that begins with "I am . . ." and goes on to give a condensed version of who you think you are. How do you feel about

---

*Earl Nightingale (1921–1989) was an American motivational speaker and author of *Strangest Secret*, which sold millions of copies and was considered one of the great motivational books of all time.

doing this exercise? Was it helpful or a waste of time? Was it difficult or easy to accomplish? Give reasons for your answer.

2. According to the author, what determines your self-image? What elements over time created the artistic mosaic that is now you? If you agree with Wexler's definition, give an idea of how the process has worked in your life.

3. In paragraph 14, what guarantee does the author give you? How important is this guarantee to the process of overhauling your self-image? What is the first step you must take in the refurbishing act? If you were to advise a friend on how to accomplish it, what would you tell him or her?

4. According to the author, what makes each person elite and exciting rather than common and lackluster? What evidence can you bring to the discussion to support the author's view of each person as unique?

5. What happens when you consciously examine the limiting beliefs you have held about yourself? Do you agree with the author on this point? Why or why not?

● The Strategies

1. What about the composition of paragraphs in this essay immediately strikes the reader? To what kind of audience would this style appeal?

2. How does the author make the reader feel involved in the content being presented? Point to specific passages that prove your answer. What advantage does this approach have?

3. How does the author build toward the main point of her essay? Which idea does she explore in greatest depth? Explain your answer.

4. What figures of speech enrich Ammon-Wexler's essay? Choose two or three and explain how they are used to illuminate a certain idea.

5. Where in the essay does the author give direct commands? In your view, how effective are these commands? Are they helpful or do you think they might be too dictatorial? Explain your answer.

● The Issues

1. The thesis of this essay is based on the premise that the human brain is a depository of memories that create either a good self-image or a poor one. Is the premise solid or can it be challenged? Support your answer with facts from your experience or that of other people.

2. What is the implication of paragraph 13? Explain it by supplying an appropriate example.

3. By what authority can the author state (see paragraph 21) that "it is today an accepted truth that we really do create our own reality"? If you were to challenge or qualify this statement, how would you go about doing so?

4. One of the important lessons promulgated in the essay is the difference between *reacting* and *responding* to what is happening around you. Explain the difference in your own words and indicate which reaction is preferable.

5. The answer to the problem of having a poor self-image is succinctly proclaimed in the final paragraph of the essay. Is the answer too glib? Can one simply make a decision and then roar like a lion? Bringing the tools of critical thinking to the author's proposal, explain the meaning of the final paragraph and evaluate it.

● Suggestions for Writing

1. Write an essay in which you shore up the idea that the greatest personal power you have is the power to choose your thoughts.

2. In 500 words or less, defend or challenge the proposition that your brain is more important than your heart.

Stumped by ready-made phrases? Exit on page 702, at the **Editing Booth!**

Punctuation Workshop
The Comma (,)

1. **Put a comma before *and, but, for, or, nor, yet, so* when they connect two independent clauses:** He played the guitar, and his brother played the saxophone.

2. **Put a comma between more than two items in a series:** Isaac ordered a salami sandwich, a salad, and ice cream.

   > **TREAT AN ADDRESS OR DATE AS ITEMS IN A SERIES:** He was born March 5, 1951, in Stoneham, Massachusetts.
   > **OMIT COMMAS IF ONLY THE MONTH AND YEAR ARE USED IN A DATE:** The revolution began in May 1980.

3. **Use a comma after an introductory expression or an afterthought:** Well, that certainly was stressful.

4. **Use a comma after a dependent clause that begins a sentence:** Skating across the pond, she fell and broke her ankle.

5. **Put commas around the name of a person spoken to:** Be careful, Professor Gomez, not to slip.

6. **Put a comma around any expression that interrupts the flow of the sentence:** The poor, however, can't live only on food stamps.

7. **Put commas around material that is not essential to meaning:** Joseph Pendecost, who is a tile expert, will lecture on artistic kitchens.

   > **BUT IF THE CLAUSE IS ESSENTIAL TO MEANING, NO COMMAS ARE NEEDED:** The man who is a tile expert will lecture on artistic kitchens. (No other man will lecture except the tile expert.)

8. **Use commas to separate a speaker from dialogue:** "Forget him," the mother said.

9. **Use commas as necessary to prevent misreading:**

   > **Woman:** without her, man is nothing.
   > **Woman,** without her man, is nothing.

Shelley Taylor
State University of New York, Oswego
Body Modification—Think about It!

Not long ago I heard a rumor that Barbie, that icon of glamour and favorite doll of girls from several generations, is getting a butterfly tattoo for her 40th birthday—or is it her 45th? Well, no matter, she hasn't aged a day in her life. She has to keep up with the latest fashion statements. After all, her future and reputation are at stake.

Almost everywhere you look these days you can see people with some sort of body alterations. The vast majority of these alterations are body piercings and tattoos. On a walk through a school campus or a shopping mall, for instance, you are bound to see ears adorned by multiple earrings, jeweled drops cascading down eyebrows, and glittering nose studs. There are yin yang symbols etched on ankles, cartoon characters inked on arms, and roses and names of loved ones permanently stamped on wrists (some other pictures aren't quite as "nice.") These are just examples of things you can *see*; many other body parts, including tongues, belly buttons (well, I guess you *can* see those), and genitals, are routinely pierced, and tattoos can appear practically anywhere.

Actually, throughout history, people from various cultures have decorated their bodies with piercings and tattoos. In 1992, a 4,000-year-old body of a tattooed man was found in an Austrian glacier. From 4000 to 2000 B.C., Egyptians identified tattooing with fertility and nobility. Body piercing has been used as a symbol of royalty and courage, as well as other lauded attributes. In some societies, body piercing and tattoos have long been used in initiation rites and as socialization symbols.

Piercing is performed without anesthesia by either a spring-loaded ear-piercing gun or piercing needles, ranging in diameter from six to eighteen gauge. A tattoo is created by an electric needle, which injects colored pigment into small, deep holes made in the skin. Far too often, however, cruder and less-sanitary methods are used. Even under the best conditions, the process is painful. The discomfort of getting a tattoo has been compared to that of hair removal by electrolysis.

So, why is body alteration so popular? Why do people do this to themselves? The reason most often cited is that individuals feel a need to express themselves in a creative way. They want to tell the world "who they are" (or who they wish they were). The vast majority of body piercings and tattoos are performed on adolescents, many of whom consider what they wear and how they look to be as important as food and water. Modifying their bodies is their way of being non-traditional and "different."

Interestingly enough, however, being different is the last thing they really want to do. If their peers, especially those who comprise the "in crowd," are doing something, they feel that they need to do it, too. They want to share a common identity, to belong to the group, to fit in. The media plays a big role in all of this. Models, sports idols, members of their favorite music groups, all endorsed by magazines, television, and movies, show off their body piercings and tattoos proudly, as the latest and "coolest" thing.

Teens *do* strive to be different from their parents and anyone in the older generation. Body alterations are one way for them to say, "I'm growing up and making decisions on my own." This becomes, in a way, a rite of passage, declaring that they are changing and becoming mature. They are seeking their own place in society and a sense of empowerment. They are celebrating their growth toward and into adulthood.

Many would argue that changing their appearance is a relatively harmless way for adolescents to meet the need to search for their identities and to explore less traditional paths. After all, purple hair, hole-filled jeans, and sparkling navel jewels can hardly be compared with drugs and violence. Dress styles come and go, just as they have for centuries, and continue to make the world more interesting and less boring, if nothing else.

The very fact that fads pass so quickly, however, should give one pause when he or she is considering body alterations. While hair color and apparel can be changed easily, a piercing or a tattoo is a physical change that is harder to discard. Body piercing can be relatively temporary in the long run, unless certain types of infection or scarring occur, but its immediate implications can have far-reaching results. A tattoo, however, is permanent. It is not something a person can just take off and throw away when it is no longer in style or desirable. Obviously, this fact points out the utter foolishness of having the name of a boyfriend or girlfriend (or even a spouse) adorning some part of your body forever. What a way to complicate your future!

The question of appearance is an important one. Whether we like it or not, we cannot disregard how we are perceived by others. This factor makes a huge difference in our lives. It takes only ten to fifteen seconds for someone to create a first impression that can affect his or her life for years to come. Nowhere is this truer than in the job market. A prospective employer will take note of your appearance, before giving you a chance to answer a single question or tell about your qualifications. Tattoos and body piercings do not project the type of image that is valued in the conservative business community. Consequently, those who choose to have these body alterations will probably have fewer job opportunities than those who decide not to.

Health is a major issue that must be considered. There are potential health risks involved with the initial process of body piercing and tattooing. Take the tongue, for instance. Tongues swell to twice their normal size when first punctured. This often interferes with eating and effective breathing. Infections, blood clots, drooling, and damaged taste buds and nerves can also develop. Even broken teeth, choking, or impeded speech are possible. Other piercings can cause problems as well. Pierced navels take up to 12 months to heal and are painful, especially when irritated by waistbands. Nipple piercing may cause infection, an allergic reaction to the ring, or scarred milk ducts, which permanently interfere with breast-feeding. The cartilage in the upper ear heals slowly and may become infected. Piercing can cause permanent scarring and keloid formation. An allergic reaction to metal can result in contact dermatitis.

This is just the beginning. Even more serious side effects can occur. Piercing can be responsible for endocarditis, urethral rupture, and a serious infection of the penis foreskin that can result in disability or death. Piercings and tattoos present the risk of chronic infection, hepatitis B and C, tetanus, and theoretically HIV, especially when proper sterilization and safety procedures are not followed. Black henna tattoos can cause significant rashes and allergies, which can lead to kidney failure and even death. These are especially dangerous to young children.

This brings me to another point. It is illegal for commercial tattoo and body-piercing businesses to administer body modification to a person younger than eighteen years of age unless a parent or guardian signs a consent form. An unfortunate response to this law is the practice of "homemade" tattoos and piercings. Adolescents are getting these body alterations from friends or other amateurs who make their own tools with the use of pens, erasers, and paper clips and perform the procedures under unsanitary conditions. Very young children are being influenced to "be cool" like the older kids they look up to and want to emulate, often with tragic consequences. Not long ago, in an elementary school in Fort Worth, Texas, ten third-graders tried to give themselves tattoos using razor blades.

Literally, then, body modification can be a matter of life and death. This is true in another way, which some may not be aware of. As I alluded to before, this practice can represent symbols of group identity. This is often associated with gangs. Members of gangs apply tags or marks to show that they belong to their particular group. Middle-school students (grades five to eight) acquire most of these tags as a part of gang initiation. Specific color and clothing combinations and tattoos are examples of such tagging. Tattoos are usually applied by fellow gang members.

I worked for a short time in a detention facility for adjudicated youth, ages twelve to eighteen, who had each been convicted of at least one crime. As part of our training, we attended a seminar given by a law officer who had spent years studying gang operations and working with individual gang members. He informed us that graffiti, artwork, specific colors, styles of clothing, music, and dances were all part of the messages that gangs send to their own members and to those who belong to rival gangs.

They establish territory and warn other groups of violent repercussions if this territory is not respected. Even dance moves and hand signals have significant meaning. He told of a rock music performer who was murdered by the "Bloods" because he did the "Crip Walk" (or was it the other way around?) and made "disrespectful" signs with his fingers while on a public stage. Immediately I thought of the thousands of kids who are permanently marked with gang tattoos and the danger in which this places them. It is a known fact that prisoners with these tattoos are in fear for their lives while they are incarcerated with other criminals who have come out of rival gangs.

This fear of gang reprisal, along with the tendency of employers and law officials to associate tattoo markings with crime-related activities, has caused many to try to get their tattoos removed. Often these people are gang members who want out. Yet of the ten million Americans who have tattoos, almost half want their tattoos removed—for a variety of reasons. Clinics that offer tattoo removal are springing up everywhere, not only in the U.S., but in other countries as well, especially those in Central and South America. The demand is still more than can be accommodated at this time. Tattoo removal is expensive and is also a very long and painful process. Laser treatments cost thousands of dollars each and have been likened to hot bacon grease streaming down the skin. After multiple sessions, there is still a shadow on the skin while the laser-transmitted pigment enters the lymph system. Other methods of removal involve cutting the skin off with a scalpel or sanding the tattoo off with a wire brush. Many times, total success is not achieved.

So how do you decide what is right for you? Just be sure to consider everything very carefully. As you can see, there is a lot to think about. Take your time. Don't rush out and do something drastic without asking a lot of questions. Are you doing this for yourself or because you want to be like your friends? After all, it is your body. Are the benefits worth all of the risks involved? Are there career plans to consider? How do you think you will want to look in ten years or so? That reminds me—if you decide to go ahead with this, don't gain weight. A cute little frog tattooed onto a size-four stomach can look pretty scary after it has stretched and grown, twenty, thirty, or more pounds later.

Remember that this decision will most likely affect the rest of your life. That makes it extremely important, wouldn't you say? Whether you are a teenager, a young adult, or a middle-aged person who has always dreamed of doing something fun and outrageous, don't forget to look at all sides of this issue. It will be well worth the trouble. At the risk of being unoriginal, I would like to end with a quotation from one of those very wise anonymous writers for *The College Chalkboard* Web site: "Ponder before you pierce, and think before you ink." I couldn't have said it better myself.

How I Write

Before I actually begin writing, I do a lot of reflective thinking and organizing in my mind. I decide what information I am going to include and try to get a rough idea of the order and format I want to use. I usually sketch out an outline that I can follow. When actually writing the piece, I sit down at the computer and start typing, referring constantly to my outline. I edit and make changes as I go along until I am satisfied with the result. After I have finished, I read through my work several times to do further editing.

How I Wrote This Essay

While working on this piece, I used the Internet to look up a few sites and articles on my subject to get an idea about current research, others' opinions, etc. I searched my memory for incidents in my own experience and illustrations that were relevant to the issue. Finally, I synthesized and integrated all of this information to formulate my own thoughts, feelings, and insights.

My Writing Tips

- Start your writing with something that will capture the attention of your reader—such as an interesting story or illustration, an amazing fact, or a dynamic statement.
- Be imaginative, descriptive, and creative.
- Avoid using redundant words and phrases in your writing.
- Make sure that your grammar and spelling are correct and that your ideas are presented as clearly as possible.
- Be sincere. Always be present in your work. Anyone can write down a bunch of facts, but your own insights and personality can make the words come to life.
- Leave your reader with something to think about. (I personally think the introduction and conclusion are the crucial parts of an essay.)

CHAPTER WRITING ASSIGNMENTS

1. Write an essay in which you describe one of the following places:
   a. The most peaceful place you know
   b. The most disturbing place you have ever been to
   c. The most boring place you know

2. Write an essay describing a particularly vivid dream. Begin by thinking of and writing down a dominant impression for the scenes you saw in your dream. Using that dominant impression as your thesis, write a description that is supported by specific details.

WRITING ASSIGNMENTS FOR A SPECIFIC AUDIENCE

1. Write a diary entry, describing the major events of your day. Treat your diary as a confidential, intimate friend to whom you can trust your innermost feelings.

2. Write to a family member, describing to them your college living quarters, or a letter to a friend, describing your favorite spot on campus.

IMAGE GALLERY ASSIGNMENT

Visit pages IG-4–IG-6 of our image gallery and study all three pairs of images dealing with self-image. Then choose the image that most appeals to you. Answer the questions and do the writing assignment.

Pointer from a Pro

WRITE ABOUT THE FAMILIAR

I write about the things that disturb me, the things that won't let me alone, the things that are eating slowly into my brain at three in the morning, the things that unbalanced my world. Sometimes these are things I've seen. Sometimes they're only sentences, sometimes scenes, sometimes complete narratives. I carry these things around inside my head until I'm compelled to write them down to get rid of them. I sit down and begin.

—Roxana Robinson, "If You Invent the Story, You're the First to See How It Ends."
Writers on Writing.

The point is that when you feel passionate about your writing, your ideas will glisten; whereas when you feel indifferent, your writing will tend to be dreary like your attitude.

10

Process Analysis

What Process Analysis Does

An essay that gives instructions on how to do something or describes how something was done is developed by process analysis. Many best-sellers have been written in this mode, all bearing such telltale how-to titles as *How to Make a Million in Real Estate* or *How to Learn Spanish the Easy Way*. Historians such as Will Durant use process analysis to tell us how Spartan warriors were trained, how Christianity became the dominant religion of Western civilization, and how the Battle of Normandy was won. Like narration, process analysis presents information in chronological order, commonly in the form of instructions. Here, a student explains the process of cooking vegetables in a microwave oven:

> If you follow these seven easy steps, you will have the pleasure of eating vegetables cooked *al dente*, the way they are done in the finest restaurants where nouvelle cuisine is the rage:
>
> First, choose three vegetables that normally take approximately the same time to cook (for instance, carrots, broccoli, and summer squash). For aesthetic purposes it is a good idea to choose vegetables of different colors.
>
> Second, slice the vegetables into bite-size pieces or slices, depending on which is easier.
>
> Third, arrange the pieces in alternating circles on a ceramic quiche plate.
>
> Fourth, add butter, salt, and pepper to taste.
>
> Fifth, pour one-half cup of water over the vegetables.
>
> Sixth, place a piece of plastic wrap over the plate and seal the sides.
>
> Last, cook the vegetables in the microwave oven for four minutes on "high." The vegetables will be crisply delicious and ready to serve the most discriminating of palates. Best of all, the vitamins will be preserved.

Although process analysis is a simple rhetorical mode and is fairly straightforward to write, it is often done badly and with irksome consequences. Anyone who has ever struggled to understand an inept manual meant to explain some necessary but practical chore can attest to the importance of clear process writing.

When to Use Process Analysis

Although found in all kinds of writing, process explanations are common in science and technology, where they vary from instructions on how to perform a simple test for acidity to how to diagnose a high-risk pregnancy with ultrasound. Many of your classes will require you to write various process explanations: A political-science teacher may ask you to describe how a bill is passed in Congress; a geology teacher, how glaciers are formed; a botany teacher, how flowers are reproduced. Process explanations can range from a historical blow-by-blow account of Custer's Last Stand to an anthropological explanation of how ancient tribes buried their dead.

How to Write a Process Analysis

The first and most important step in writing a process essay is to select an appropriate subject. Decide whether your overall purpose is to give instructions or to inform. If you intend, say, to instruct readers in how to organize a volunteer team to nab graffiti writers or how to study for the SAT, your purpose is to give instructions. On the other hand, if you want to list the circumstances that led to the collapse of the dot-com companies in 2001 or the sequence of events that led to the resignation of President Richard Nixon, your purpose is to inform. In writing either kind of essay, you must know and be able to cite appropriate details.

State Your Purpose in a Clear Thesis The second step in writing your process essay is to begin with a thesis that plainly states your overall aim. "It is possible for you to acquire a competitive spirit" is an example of a thesis that leaves your reader in the dark and is singularly unhelpful to you, the writer. On the other hand, the thesis "You can acquire a competitive spirit by practicing five personality traits" establishes an agenda for the writer and tells the reader what to expect—a recital and description of the five traits. Similarly, "I want to inform you how juveniles are imprisoned," tells your reader practically nothing. Contrast it with this more helpful thesis: "Juveniles face four legal steps before they can be imprisoned."

A convenient and simple way to make the steps of your explanation stand out is to number them 1, 2, 3, etc. For example, in an explanation to a non-swimmer of *how* to become drownproof, the logical sequence of steps is as follows:

1. Take a deep breath.
2. Float vertically in the water.

3. Lift the arms to shoulder height and give scissor kicks while flapping the arms down in a winging motion.

4. Raise the head out of the water and exhale.

This sequence of steps is the only one that works, so your explanation must cover it accurately.

Organize the Sequence of Steps Logically Next, you should arrange the steps in the most logical order. Essays that cover simple how-to tasks, such as changing a tire or baking a cake are best organized chronologically. On the other hand, essays on broader topics, such as how to build self-esteem in a child, how to make a marriage work, or how Stalin rose to power, are best organized in order of importance.

Regardless of which arrangement you use, you should single out and explain each step clearly. It often helps to sketch out the steps exactly as they will occur in your chosen order. For example, let us say that your parents won a court case against a landlord for discriminating against them because of their ethnic origin. Using your familiarity with their case, combined with further research, you decide to write a paper on how to file an antidiscrimination housing suit. Here are your steps, outlined chronologically:

1. File the complaint with the local Fair Housing Council.

2. Explain your reasons for filing to the investigator who hears your complaint.

3. If the investigation uncovers evidence of discrimination, state or federal authorities will formally accuse the landlord of discrimination. (If your case has no merit, the matter will probably fizzle out here.)

4. Choose between appearing before an administrative hearing officer or hiring an attorney to file a lawsuit in civil court.

5. Either the case will be solved through a settlement or the state will impose a punitive fine to compensate for damages.

Once you have outlined these steps clearly, all you have to do is flesh out the essay with necessary facts and details.

Explain Everything The devil is said to be in the details, and that is clearly the case in process essays. Always assume that your reader is uninformed about your subject. Explain everything. Don't be vague, as maddeningly unhelpful manuals often are. If your essay is giving specific directions about how to do something, simply address the reader directly, as in a command: "Next, [you] fold the paper along the dotted line. . . . Then, [you] write your personal number in the upper left-hand corner," and so on.

It also helps to carefully signal the succession of described steps with words such as "first," "second," "next," "then," and "finally." Within each step, using words such as "before," "after," and "while" can help the reader keep track of the discussion. It might even be helpful to mention a previous step before going on to the next. For example, in a process essay about how juveniles are imprisoned, the first step might be for the police to bring the youth to a screening office. If so, you might introduce the second step this way, "If after the screening has taken place the case still cannot be informally resolved, the second step is to arrange a date for a court hearing."

As we said, process essays are usually straightforward and relatively simple to write. Most require no poetic or metaphoric language—a manual so written would drive consumers over the brink—and generally demand nothing more of a writer than a sensible grasp of facts and the ability to explain them in understandable sequence.

Warming Up to Write a Process Analysis

1. Choosing one of the following how-to processes, write down in chronological order or in order of importance the steps involved in completing the task. Do not omit a step.

   a. How to trim a Christmas tree

   b. How to intelligently read a newspaper

   c. How to make your college professors like you

   d. How to get ready for a long-distance bicycle race

   e. How to ask for a dinner date, or how to turn down a dinner date

2. Choosing one of the following how-it-happened processes, write down the major steps that led up to it.

   a. How a friend of yours got hooked on an illegal drug such as cocaine or ecstasy

   b. How a serious accident that involved you or a loved one occurred

   c. How Saddam Hussein was finally caught, detained, and executed

   d. The stages of AIDS

3. From each group, choose the best topic for a process essay.

   a. **1.** How to fly a commercial airplane

      2. How to wash a car

      3. How to write a novel

      4. How to speak Chinese

   b. **1.** How the world came into being

      2. How your great-grandfather became a millionaire

      3. The stages of international economic bankruptcy

      4. How the United Nations functions

EXAMPLES

My Strangled Speech

DAN SLATER

Rhetorical Thumbnail

Purpose: to list the steps involved in overcoming a serious stuttering problem and thereby inspire other stutterers to work on curing their problem

Audience: anyone who has suffered from stuttering, who knows someone with a stutter, or who is interested in the causes of stuttering

Language: formal English that includes some scientific terminology

Strategy: describes vividly what stuttering is and then describes methodically the steps taken by the author to overcome what he considers a personal humiliation and shame

Dan Slater (b. 1977) is a lawyer who has successfully combined a legal career with freelance writing. He graduated from Colgate University with a B. A. in international relations. During his university studies, he also studied abroad In Madrid and in London. Later he attended Brooklyn Law School and earned a J.D., which led to a position with Kay Scholer LLP as a litigation associate representing corporate and individual clients in commercial and Intellectual property matters. Since 2009, Slater has contributed numerous essays to prestigious periodicals, such as *The New York Times, The Washington Post, New York* magazine, *GQ* magazine, and *American Lawyer* magazine. The essay below was reprinted from *The Washington Post.*

This essay reveals in aching details the agony suffered by stutterers. From the time he was four years old, the author blocked on words, and even today, he does not feel completely free from the dreadful fear of stumbling on some hard consonant and turning himself into an object of ridicule in the eyes of his audience. As you read, try to identify with the stutterer's humiliation and his enormous battle with fear. Try to understand the origin of the impediment and follow the steps the author took throughout his life to correct this handicap so that he could express himself unhesitatingly and smoothly in public.

. . .

1   What that I remember most about my stutter is not the stupefying vocal paralysis, the pursed eyes, or the daily ordeal of gagging on my own speech, sounds ricocheting off the back of my teeth like pennies trying to escape a piggy bank.

Those were merely the mechanics of stuttering, the realities to which one who stutters adjusts his expectations of life. Rather, what was most pervasive about my stutter is the strange role it played in determining how I felt about others, about you.

2   My stutter became a barometer of how much confidence I felt in your presence. Did I perceive you as friendly, patient, kind? Or as brash and aggressive? How genuine was your smile? Did you admire my talents, or were you wary of my more unseemly traits? In this way I divided the world into two types of people: those around whom I stuttered and those around whom I might not.

3   The onset of my stutter occurred under typical circumstances: I was 4; I had a father who carried a stutter into adulthood; and, at the time, my parents were engaged in a bitter, protracted, Reagan-era divorce that seemed destined for mutually assured destruction.

4   My mother chronicled my speech problems in her diaries from the period. Sept. 26, 1981: "Daniel has been biting his fingernails for the past several weeks; along with stuttering up." July 8,1982: "After phone call (with his father) Danny stuttering quite a bit, blocking on words."

5   In fact, my father and I had different stutters. His was what speech therapists consider the more traditional kind, in which the first syllable of a word gets repeated. "Bus" might sound like "aba-aba-abus." Mine was a blockage, a less extreme version of what King George VI, portrayed by Colin Firth, must deal with in the new movie *The King's Speech*.

6   My vocal cords would strangle certain sounds. Hard consonants—K's, D's, hard C's, and hard G's—gave me hell. A year of speech therapy in childhood helped me develop a set of tools for defeating the impediment, or at least concealing it well enough to fool most of the people most of the time. Like many other stutterers, I evolved a verbal dexterity. Embarking on a sentence was like taking a handoff and running through the line of scrimmage:

7   I'd look five or 10 words upfield, and if I saw a mean word, such as "camping," I'd stiff-arm it and cut back hard in search of a less-resistant path, opting perhaps for something more literal: "I want to sleep in the woods this weekend."

8   But the strategies of substitution and circumlocution were never foolproof. The stuttering rat always lurks. When I was 14 years old, I wanted to ask a girl to the high school dance. Unfortunately, her name was Kim. I sweated it out for a few days, waiting for gumption to arrive. When I finally called Kim's house, her mother answered.

9   "Yeah hi, I was wondering if ahhh ... if ahhh...if..."

10   I needed to bust through that K. But all I could do was pant, breathless, as the K clung to the roof of my mouth like a cat in a tree.

11   I breathed deeply and said at once: "YeahhiIwaswonderingifKimwas there."

12   "Kim?" her mother said with a laugh. "Are you sure?"

13   Another deep breath: "Ohyeah I' msureKim."

14   When Kim took the phone, she told me her mom thought it was funny that I'd forgotten whom I'd called. I laughed along with them, of course, because

it was preferable to forget the name of a girl you liked than to be thought an idiot.

15   More than 3 million Americans stutter, about 1 percent of the population. Stuttering afflicts four times as many males as females. Five percent of preschool children stutter as a normal developmental trend and outgrow it without therapy. While no single cause has been identified, stuttering is thought to result from a combination of genetics (about 60 percent of those who stutter have a family member who stutters), neurophysiology, and family dynamics, such as a legacy of high achievement (and the persistent pressures to perform that typically accompany it).

16   Stuttering, like other enigmatic ailments, has a checkered past. Beginning more than 2,000 years ago, one ridiculous theory followed another. Aristotle, who may have stuttered, believed the stutterer's tongue was too thick and therefore '"too sluggish to keep pace with the imagination." Galen, the Greek doctor, claimed the stutterer's tongue was too wet; the Roman physician Celsus suggested gargling and massages to strengthen a weak tongue. Such quackery reached its logical climax in the 19th century, when Johann Friedrich Dieffenbach, the Prussian plastic surgeon, decided that people stuttered because their tongues were too unwieldy. In several cases he cut the organ down to size.

17   It wasn't until the early 20th century that serious steps were taken to understand and treat stuttering. Therapists tended to focus on the adolescent context in which stuttering evolves. Albert Murphy, a speech pathologist at Boston University, promoted a psychogenic theory, suggesting that the roots of stuttering "lie in disturbed interpersonal relationships and the stutterer's fractured self-image."

18   This theory is at the heart of *The King's Speech*. Screenwriter David Seidler, a stutterer, focused on the trust-building process through which an Australian speech therapist coaxes out of King George his earliest memories. In the breakthrough scene, the king recounts his childhood torments inflicted by his older brother, Edward, the sting of ridicule, and his mistreatment at the hands of the royal nanny.

19   The psychogenic theory can be a seductive one—My parents screwed me up!—but it has largely fallen out of fashion, replaced by physiological diagnoses that call for techniques such as breathing exercises and delayed auditory feedback, which uses hearing-aid-like devices that play the stutterer's speech back to him.

20   For a stutterer, every speech hang-up carves a little more confidence out of him, leaving behind an ever-deepening sinkhole of shame and self-hatred. A child who stutters might excel at science, be a good reader, throw a perfect spiral pass, or demonstrate loyal friendship. But in his mind he only stutters, and that is all that matters. Every stuttering incident intensifies that feedback loop of failure inside his head—"Everyone thinks I'm an idiot"—making the next speech attempt even more difficult.

21   Yet small victories—even one fluent sentence—can be equally emboldening, because the stutterer is a powerful believer. "I'll keep trying to speak," he thinks, "because tomorrow I might just be able to." The trick, for me, was

switching that internal soundtrack from "Oh no, here we go again" to "Breathe, relax, and let it ride."

22   When I was 8, my mother took me to a speech therapist. He was a big-hearted, supremely patient man with whom I spent many afternoons discussing my favorite things: football, movies, and my baseball card collection. He taught me the "air-flow" technique developed by Martin Schwartz, a professor at New York University Medical Center. Schwartz believed that stuttering is caused when the vocal cords clamp shut. To release them, the stutterer is instructed to sigh, inaudibly, just before speaking. Like a roller coaster, my speech therapist would tell me, the words get a free ride on the airflow.

23   After a year of therapy, I wasn't completely fluent, but I left with new confidence and a toolkit for dealing with my stutter. One of those tools entailed practicing fluency through imitation, whether quoting songs or spouting movie lines with my brother.

24   This was all about changing the feedback loop of failure: Psychologically, I could slide into a different character, no longer expecting to loathe the sound of my own voice. Physiologically, imitation provided new feedbacks to my breathing and voice mechanisms: a different pitch, a different articulation, and a different rate of speaking to which I could peg my own speech.

25   However, just as the word-switching technique was never foolproof, neither was imitation. When I was 16, the stuttering rat emerged again.

26   In a class about the legal system, I was assigned to be the prosecutor in a mock murder trial. I would have to write and deliver an opening statement. *A Few Good Men,* a movie about a military trial, had recently been released on video. I loved the way Kevin Bacon strutted before the jury, so self-assured and confident of his case against the defendants. So I practiced in his speaking style. I even wrote the last sentence of his monologue into my own statement.

27   The next morning, when I stepped to the podium, I tried to relax and breathe. But a straitjacket of stress shut me down; the muscles in my throat and chest choked off the air. Thanks to pure stubbornness, I persisted, blocking on every fifth word of a 500-word speech. By the time I reached the Kevin Bacon line—"These are the facts of the case and they are undisputed"—I couldn't move sentences with a dolly.

28   A couple of days later, the teacher stopped me in the hallway and said, "Dan, I had no idea. It was so courageous of you to try." She was a sweet woman, but it was the last thing I wanted to hear. The recognition of one's stutter can be as humiliating as the stutter itself. I'd been found out.

29   During college I ditched a couple of class presentations and made it through a couple of others. In law school I spoke fluently before groups on several occasions but declined an offer to be in the mock trial club. During six years in journalism, including a stint at *The Wall Street Journal,* I've found radio interviews to be much easier than videotaped segments.

30   I'm 33 now. I believe I'm mostly cured of my stutter. Yet when I recently visited a speech therapist in New York and spoke with him, he disagreed. He said that none of my speech during our meeting had indicated disfluency.

But when I confessed that I switch words several times per day and think quite often about my stutter, he said: "A lot of energy goes into hiding it, to hoping no one finds out. You're thinking about it a lot. We would not call this a mark of success." Think about it a lot? But of course.

31   For all the empathy that can make a good speech therapist effective, perhaps there's one thing a non-stutterer can never understand: If we go to therapy, we think about it. If we don't go to therapy, we think about it. It's always there. Either it defines us or we find ways of accommodating it, working toward a state of peaceful coexistence, pushing on with the Kims and the Katies.

"Stuttering, even if not as severe as in 'The King's Speech,' can be shameful" by Dan Slater appeared in THE WASHINGTON POST, December 20, 2010. Reprinted with permission from the author.

Vocabulary

stupefying (1)	dexterity (6)	inaudibly (22)
ricocheting (1)	circumlocution (8)	articulation (24)
pervasive (1)	enigmatic (16)	monologue (26)
protracted (3)	quackery (16)	disfluency (30)

The Facts

1. What, according to the author, was the most persistent aspect of his stuttering? Why is this puzzling? How do you explain this irony?

2. From the author's comments, what can one deduce about the typical circumstances under which stuttering starts? If this is the case, what behavior should parents avoid as they rear their children?

3. Which words were particularly conducive to stuttering? How did the author side-step these words? What do you think this technique required?

4. What important coping mechanism did Professor Martin Schwartz teach the author? Describe the technique in your own words. How effective do you consider this technique? What are its advantages?

5. On what basis did the speech therapist in New York (see paragraph 30) imply that the author was still not cured of his stutter? Do you agree with his implication? Was the therapist wise to offer his comments? Explain your answer.

The Strategies

1. How does the title of the essay connect with its content? Is the connection clear as the reader proceeds through the essay? Describe your reaction to the title.

2. What historical reference does the author use in paragraph 5? What does this reference contribute to the purpose of the essay? If you don't recognize the reference, look it up on the Internet.

3. What strategy does the author use to illumine the extreme anxiety felt by a stutterer trying to get a date with a girl? What advantage does this strategy have?

4. How many major steps were involved in the author's search for a cure to his stutter? List them In the order of their occurrence. In your opinion, which step was the most successful? What additional step, if any, can you suggest?

5. Paragraphs 15–19 provide an overview of the history of stuttering therapy, including some statistics. What, if anything does this information contribute to the essay? How helpful was it to your understanding of the author's impediment? Explain your answers.

● The Issues

1. What is the most important psychological insight provided by the author? What information can sensitive readers absorb and use in their relationships with people who have speech problems? Describe situations in which you felt unsure about how to handle a conversation with someone suffering from a speech impediment. Discuss some helpful ways to handle such a quandary.

2. According to the author, stuttering cannot be traced to a single cause but possibly to a combination of genetics, neurophysiology, and family dynamics. How would a cure be hastened if science could discover a single cause for this troublesome impediment? How serious do you consider stuttering as an impediment to a person's career? Explain your answer.

3. Do you agree with the author that the psychogenic theory of stuttering can be a seductive one? (See paragraph 19.) Make a case for or against this theory, based on your own experience or that of people you know.

4. What was wrong with the attitude of the teacher who spoke to the author after he had delivered his opening statement as the prosecutor in a mock murder trial? After all, she obviously revealed empathy and admiration. Analyze her comment in light of the author's reaction. What alternative response would you suggest?

5. What is the thesis of this essay? Where is it stated? What are the most striking ideas about stuttering you gained from this essay? State what help the essay provided in your future relationship with people who have speech impediments.

● Suggestions for Writing

1. After researching the Internet, write a report on today's prevalent opinions of expert speech therapists concerning the status of stuttering. Be sure to refer to valid and respected sources.

2. Using Slater's essay as a model, write an essay in which you mark out the steps you used to deal with some learning difficulty you faced in the past or are facing now.

Hunting Octopus in the Gilbert Islands

SIR ARTHUR GRIMBLE

Rhetorical Thumbnail

Purpose: amuse and entertain

Audience: readers and listeners of popular material

Language: standard English

Strategy: uses conversational English as befitting a radio broadcast

Sir Arthur Grimble (1888–1956) was a British colonial government official and writer. After receiving an education from Magdalene College at Cambridge, he joined the colonial service in the Pacific and was posted to the Gilbert and Ellice Islands, where he remained in various positions from 1914 until 1933. From 1933 to 1948, he worked as administrator and then governor of the Windward Islands, retiring from the colonial service in 1948. In retirement, Grimble developed a talent for narrating his island experiences on radio for the British Broadcasting Corporation. The result was a series of talks that became so popular that they were published under the title of *A Pattern of Islands* (1952), from which the following excerpt was taken.

Grimble relates an amusing story of watching two young boys hunting just off a reef in the Gilbert Islands. His curiosity about what the boys were doing got him into a predicament from which he could not escape without taking part in their sport. In the course of telling this riveting story, Grimble gives us a process explanation of how the Gilbertese hunt and kill octopus.

• • •

1 The Gilbertese happen to value certain parts of the octopus as food, and their method of fighting it is coolly based upon the one fact that its arms never change their grip. They hunt for it in pairs. One man acts as the bait, his partner as the killer. First, they swim eyes-under at low tide just off the reef, and search the crannies of the submarine cliff for sight of any tentacle that may flicker out for a catch. When they have placed their quarry, they land on the reef for the next stage. The human bait starts the real game. He dives and tempts the lurking brute by swimming a few strokes in front of its cranny, at first a little beyond striking range. Then he turns and makes straight for the cranny, to give himself into the embrace of those waiting arms. Sometimes nothing happens. The beast will not always respond to the lure. But usually it strikes.

2   The partner on the reef above stares down through the pellucid water, waiting for his moment. His teeth are his only weapon. His killing efficiency depends on his avoiding every one of those strangling arms. He must wait until

his partner's body has been drawn right up to the entrance of the cleft. The monster inside is groping then with its horny mouth against the victim's flesh, and sees nothing beyond it. That point is reached in a matter of no more than thirty seconds after the decoy has plunged. The killer dives, lays hold of his pinioned friend at arm's length, and jerks him away from the cleft; the octopus is torn from the anchorage of its proximal suckers, and clamps itself the more fiercely to its prey. In the same second, the human bait gives a kick which brings him, with quarry annexed, to the surface. He turns on his back, still holding his breath for better buoyancy, and this exposes the body of the beast for the kill. The killer closes in, grasps the evil head from behind, and wrenches it away from its meal. Turning the face up towards himself, he plunges his teeth between the bulging eyes, and bites down and in with all his strength. That is the end of it. It dies on the instant; the suckers release their hold; the arms fall away; the two fishers paddle with whoops of delighted laughter to the reef, where they string the catch to a pole before going to rout out the next one.

3   Any two boys of seventeen, any day of the week, will go out and get you half a dozen octopus like that for the mere fun of it. Here lies the whole point of this story. The hunt is, in the most literal sense, nothing but child's play to the Gilbertese.

4   As I was standing one day at the end of a jetty in Tarawa lagoon, I saw two boys from the near village shouldering a string of octopus slung on a pole between them. I started to wade out in their direction, but before I hailed them they had stopped, planted the carrying-pole upright in a fissure and, leaving it there, swum off the edge for a while with faces submerged evidently searching for something under water. I had been only a few months at Tarawa, and that was my first near view of an octopus hunt. I watched every stage of it from the dive of the human bait to the landing of the dead catch. When it was over, I went up to them. I could hardly believe that in those few seconds, with no more than a frivolous-looking splash or two on the surface, they could have found, caught and killed the creature they were now stringing up before my eyes. They explained the amusing simplicity of the thing.

5   "There's only one trick the decoy-man must never forget," they said, "and that's not difficult to remember. If he is not wearing the water-spectacles of the Men of Matang,[1] he must cover his eyes with a hand as he comes close to the *kika* (octopus), or the sucker might blind him." It appeared that the ultimate fate of the eyes was not the thing to worry about; the immediate point was that the sudden pain of a sucker clamping itself to an eyeball might cause the bait to expel his breath and inhale sea-water; that would spoil his buoyancy, and he would fail then to give his friend the best chance of a kill.

6   Then they began whispering together. I knew in a curdling flash what they were saying to each other. Before they turned to speak to me again, a horrified conviction was upon me. My damnable curiosity had led me into a trap from which there was no escape. They were going to propose that I should take a turn at being the bait myself, just to see how delightfully easy it was.

---

[1]"Men of Matang" is the Gilbertese phrase for white foreigners.

7   And that is what they did. It did not even occur to them that I might not leap at the offer. I was already known as a young Man of Matang who liked swimming, and fishing, and laughing with the villagers; I had just shown an interest in this particular form of hunting; naturally, I should enjoy the fun of it as much as they did. Without even waiting for my answer, they gleefully ducked off the edge of the reef to look for another octopus—a fine fat one— mine. Left standing there alone, I had another of those visions . . .

8   It was dusk in the village. The fishers were home, I saw the cooking-fires glowing orange-red between the brown lodges. There was laughter and shouted talk as the women prepared the evening meal. But the laughter was hard with scorn. "What?" they were saying, "Afraid of a kika? The young Man of Matang? Why, even the boys are not afraid of a kika!" A curtain went down and rose again on the Residency; the Old Man was talking: "A leader? You? The man who funked a schoolboy game? We don't leave your sort in charge of Districts." The scene flashed to my uncles: "Returned empty," they said. "We always knew you hadn't got it in you. Returned empty . . ."

9   Of course it was all overdrawn, but one fact was beyond doubt; the Gilbertese reserved all their most ribald humour for physical cowardice. No man gets himself passed for a leader anywhere by becoming the butt of that kind of wit. I decided I would rather face the octopus.

10   I was dressed in khaki slacks, canvas shoes and a short-sleeved singlet. I took off the shoes and made up my mind to shed the singlet if told to do so; but I was wildly determined to stick to my trousers throughout. Dead or alive, said a voice within me, an official minus his pants is a preposterous object, and I felt I could not face that extra horror. However, nobody asked me to remove anything.

11   I hope I did not look as yellow as I felt when I stood to take the plunge; I have never been so sick with funk before or since. "Remember, one hand for your eyes," said someone from a thousand miles off, and I dived.

12   I do not suppose it is really true that the eyes of an octopus shine in the dark; besides, it was clear daylight only six feet down in the limpid water; but I could have sworn the brute's eyes burned at me as I turned in towards his cranny. That dark glow—whatever may have been its origin—was the last thing I saw as I blacked out with my left hand and rose into his clutches. Then, I remember chiefly a dreadful sliminess with a herculean power behind it. Something whipped round my left forearm and the back of my neck, binding the two together. In the same flash, another something slapped itself high on my forehead, and I felt it crawling down inside the back of my singlet. My impulse was to tear at it with my right hand, but I felt the whole of that arm pinioned to my ribs. In most emergencies the mind works with crystal-clear impersonality. This was not even an emergency, for I knew myself perfectly safe. But my boyhood's nightmare was upon me. When I felt the swift constriction of those disgusting arms jerk my head and shoulders in towards the reef, my mind went blank of every thought save the beastliness of contact with that squat head. A mouth began to nuzzle below my throat, at the junction of the collar-bones. I forgot there was anyone to save me. Yet something still directed me to hold my breath.

13   I was awakened from my cowardly trance by a quick, strong pull on my shoulders, back from the cranny. The cables around me tightened painfully, but I knew I was adrift from the reef. I gave a kick, rose to the surface and turned on my back with the brute sticking out of my chest like a tumour. My mouth was smothered by some flabby moving horror. The suckers felt like hot rings pulling at my skin. It was only two seconds, I suppose, from then to the attack of my deliverer, but it seemed like a century of nausea.

14   My friend came up between me and the reef. He pounced, pulled, bit down, and the thing was over—for everyone but me. At the sudden relaxation of the tentacles, I let out a great breath, sank, and drew in the next under water. It took the united help of both boys to get me, coughing, heaving and pretending to join in their delighted laughter, back to the reef. I had to submit there to a kind of war-dance round me, in which the dead beast was slung whizzing past my head from one to the other. I had a chance to observe then that it was not by any stretch of fancy a giant, but just plain average. That took the bulge out of my budding self-esteem. I left hurriedly for the cover of the jetty, and was sick.

● Vocabulary

quarry (1)	pinioned (2)	herculean (12)
proximal (2)	ribald (9)	limpid (12)
pellucid (2)	singlet (10)	constriction (12)
annexed (2)	funk (11)	

● The Facts

1. What two roles in hunting octopus do the hunting partners separately play?
2. What weapon do the Gilbertese use to kill the octopus?
3. What danger does the decoy man face in the octopus hunt?
4. Why did the author consent to take part in the sport of octopus hunting?
5. After the hunt was over, what did the author do?

● The Strategies

1. What do you think is the most prominent feature of the style of this piece?
2. What can you infer about Grimble's attitude toward octopuses from the words he uses to describe them?
3. In describing the reaction (see, particularly, paragraph 8) that might follow his refusal to take part in the octopus hunt, what simple device does Grimble use to make the scene humorous?
4. In paragraph 13, Grimble writes that he was awakened from his "cowardly trance." What is your opinion of this characterization? What effect does it and other self-deprecatory remarks have on the tone of the story?
5. This process explanation of how the Gilbertese hunt octopus consists of two major parts. What are they, and how effective do you find them?

The Issues

1. In spite of the deprecating remarks Grimble makes about his lack of courage, what picture of him emerges from this tale?

2. How does the portrait that Grimble draws of the octopus match your own knowledge of that creature?

3. Had Grimble not been a colonial official assigned to the Gilbert Islands, what do you think his reaction would have been to the invitation from the boys to join the octopus hunt?

4. Based on this story, what can you infer about the Gilbertese and their culture?

5. Imagine yourself in Grimble's place. What would you have done when the Gilbertese boys invited you to take part in the octopus hunt?

Suggestions for Writing

1. Write a process essay depicting the steps involved in any sporting event you've experienced.

2. Write an essay showing how you got entangled in doing something you did not really want to do.

Hitler's Workday

WILLIAM SHIRER

Rhetorical Thumbnail

Purpose: to inform us about a typical workday in the life of Chancellor Adolf Hitler of Germany

Audience: originally written as a diary entry intended for limited consumption

Language: standard English

Strategy: provides specific details ranging from facts about the Chancellor's diet to whom he sees daily

William Shirer (1904–1993) was a journalist and critic from Florida who covered the Third Reich for CBS radio during the 1930s and 1940s. Between 1942 and 1948, he wrote a syndicated column for the *New York Herald-Tribune* and worked for the Mutual Broadcasting System before becoming a full-time writer. His monumental *The Rise and Fall of the Third Reich* (1960) won the National Book Award and became a controversial best-seller, with some critics accusing him of oversensationalizing his subject. Among his many other books are *Berlin Diary: The Journal of a Foreign Correspondent* (1941) and a two-volume memoir, *Twentieth-Century Journey* (1976 and 1984).

Taken from Berlin Diary, *this process excerpt, dated November 5, 1939, gives a step-by-step recounting of a typical workday in the life of Nazi dictator Adolf Hitler. Shirer was then a correspondent for CBS and relied on information provided by unnamed informants.*

• • •

Berlin, *November 5*

1   CBS wants me to broadcast a picture of Hitler at work during war-time. I've been inquiring around among my spies. They say: He rises early, eats his first breakfast at seven A.M. This consists usually of either a glass of milk or fruit juice and two or three rolls, on which he spreads marmalade liberally. Like most Germans, he eats a second breakfast, this one at nine A.M. It's like the first except that he also eats a little fruit. He begins his working day by wading into state papers (a job he detests, since he hates detail work) and discussing the day's program with his adjutants, chiefly S. A. Leader Wilhelm Brückner and especially with his deputy, Rudolf Hess, who was once his private secretary and is one of the few men he trusts with his innermost thoughts. During the forenoon he usually receives the chiefs of the three armed services, listens to their reports and dictates decisions. With Göring he talks about not only air force matters but general economic problems, or rather results, since he's not interested in details or even theories on this subject.

2   Hitler eats a simple lunch, usually a vegetable stew or a vegetable omelet. He is of course a vegetarian, teetotaler, and non-smoker. He usually invites a small circle to lunch, three or four adjutants, Hess, Dr. Diettrich, his press chief, and sometimes Göring. A one-percent beer, brewed specially for him, is served at this meal, or sometimes a drink made out of kraut called "Herve," flavoured with a little Mosel wine.

3   After lunch he returns to his study and work. More state papers, more conferences, often with his Foreign Minister, occasionally with a returned German ambassador, invariably with some party chieftain such as Dr. Ley or Max Amann, his old top sergeant of the World War and now head of the lucrative Nazi publishing house Eher Verlag, which gets out the *Völkische Beobachter* and in which Hitler is a stockholder. Late in the afternoon Hitler takes a stroll in the gardens back of the Chancellery, continuing his talk during the walk with whoever had an appointment at the time. Hitler is a fiend for films, and on evenings when no important conferences are on or he is not overrunning a country, he spends a couple of hours seeing the latest movies in his private cinema room at the Chancellery. News-reels are a great favourite with him, and in the last weeks he has seen all those taken in the Polish war, including hundreds of thousands of feet which were filmed for the army archives and will never be seen by the public. He likes American films and many never publicly exhibited in Germany are shown him. A few years ago he insisted on having *It Happened One Night* run several times. Though he is supposed to have a passion for Wagnerian opera, he almost never attends the Opera here in Berlin. He likes the Metropol, which puts on tolerable musical comedies with emphasis on pretty dancing girls. Recently he had one of the girls who struck his fancy to tea. But only to tea. In the evening, too, he likes to have in Dr. Todt, an imaginative engineer who built the

great Autobahn network of two-lane motor roads and later the fortifications of the Westwall. Hitler, rushing to compensate what he thinks is an artistic side that was frustrated by non-recognition in his youthful days in Vienna, has a passion for architects' models and will spend hours fingering them with Dr. Todt. Lately, they say, he has even taken to designing new uniforms. Hitler stays up late, and sleeps badly, which I fear is the world's misfortune.

● Vocabulary

teetotaler (2)   lucrative (3)

● The Facts

1. What time does Hitler eat his breakfast?
2. How many breakfasts does Hitler eat?
3. With whom does Hitler usually eat lunch? What is he likely to have for lunch?
4. What kind of entertainment is Hitler particularly fond of?
5. What particular movie did Hitler run several times a few years ago?

● The Strategies

1. What logical method of organization does Shirer use in recounting Hitler's workday?
2. In writing a process essay, a writer will often use some common words and phrases to indicate steps in the process. What are some of these words and phrases that Shirer uses?
3. Shirer was a lifelong journalist. What characteristic of this piece reveals his journalistic training?
4. In paragraph 3, Shirer writes that when Hitler is "not overrunning a country" he likes to watch movies. How would you characterize the tone of that observation?
5. In paragraph 2, Shirer says of Hitler that he is "of course a vegetarian, teetotaler, and non-smoker." What do you think Shirer implies by writing "of course"?

● The Issues

1. Shirer says that he has been inquiring among his spies. How would you characterize the kind of information his spies uncovered?
2. Based on this entry, what can you infer about Shirer's personal attitude toward Hitler?
3. What do you think of the ethics of the request made to Shirer—to find out the personal details of a world leader's daily life?
4. Shirer says that "Hitler stays up late, and sleeps badly." Why do you think he fears this as "the world's misfortune"?
5. What picture of Hitler and his work habits emerges from this journal entry? Why are we still fascinated by any information about Adolf Hitler?

● Suggestions for Writing

1. Write a journal entry that chronicles in step-by-step sequence how you spend a typical day.
2. Write a process essay showing the steps involved in keeping a journal.

In the Emergency Room

WILLA CARROLL

Willa Carroll (b. 1973) is primarily a dance teacher living in New York City. She specializes in an exercise method called "pilates," which is an innovative work-out connecting the mind with the body. She has also written poems, including the one reprinted below from *Tin House,* a magazine whose stated goal is "to widen the circle of literary magazine readers and to make extinct the preciousness and staid nature of journals past."

The poem below is organized in the logical process of steps an emergency room physician would use to treat an injury. Each step triggers reflections by the patient, making for a complex layering of insights and memories.

● ● ●

>   *I'm going to inspect the injury.*
>   He removes my homemade tourniquet, a pink scarf
>   wrapped around a washcloth. So bright in here,
>   the doctors robed up, scrubbed down,
> 5 heroes in gloves.
>   *First I'll irrigate the wound.*
>   Fields of corn in late August, rows of green
>   alternating with rows of dirt. Water from the hose
>   tasted like green rubber and metal spigot.
> 10 We sang in school choir about Sam Patch,
>   who jumped Niagara falls, only to be swallowed
>   in the gray froth of the lesser Genesee.
>   *The crowd stood round and held its breath,*
>   *As Sam plunged downward to his death,*
> 15 *O Sammy, O what a fate*
>   *for Sammy.*
>   *Now I'll apply the disinfectant.*
>   A picnic blanket is left behind in the moonlight,
>   like a shed wedding dress.
> 20 This clearing, flanked with trees, spiked with goldenrod,
>   is where you ask, *Will you?* I lie, saying *Yes.*
>   Overhead the stars go slow, taking their time to arrive.
>   The insects move fast underneath me, assessing my body.

They have so many names, and we have so little time
25 to get acquainted.
    I'm injecting the first shot of anesthesia.
    Pain is perfect. Total. One-pointed. No maybes.
    The doctor is skilled, but *you,* your touch is wrong,
    always has been, your hands articulate as bread loaves,
30 knocking my glasses as you bumble through the motion
    of stroking my hair.
    It's almost over, this is the last shot.
    Winter has come, the first snowfall half kills everything.
    I'm numb as cotton, kissing a rubber mouth, swimming
35 inside a Ziploc bag.
    I'm now tying the sutures.
    Such delicate work. The red gash is disappearing
    like a girl folding her legs,
    or velvet curtains closing on a stage.
40 My mother is a great seamstress. I refuse
    to even do buttons.
    Last knot.
    A scar is a seal on an inner glowing.
    We grew tomatoes in the front yard. Left too long
45 on the vine, they would split open from their own ripeness.
    I'd pick these first, before their juices expired,
    opening them where they'd opened themselves. Sprinkling salt,
    eating fat slices with my hands, the flesh still warm
    from the sun.

Willa Carroll, "In the Emergency Room" originally appeared in TIN HOUSE magazine, Issue #33. Reprinted by permission.

Vocabulary

tourniquet (2)	disinfectant (17)	anesthesia (26)
irrigate (6)	spiked (20)	
flanked (20)	assessing (23)	

The Facts

1. What is the process described in this poem? How many steps does the speaker list in the process?

2. Who is the speaker of the poem? What role does that person play? What does the italicized dialogue mean?

3. As the doctor irrigates the wound, what does the patient remember?

4. What other memories arise to distract the speaker (and the reader) from the task of taking care of the wound?

5. What is difficult about trying to assess the facts of this poem? How can you be sure of the correctness of your interpretation?

The Strategies

1. Which passages of the poem are connected to its title?
2. What contrast does the poet establish between the lines in italics and the lines in regular print?
3. What are some of the striking images used throughout the poem? What do these images contribute to the poem? Comment on at least two images.
4. What stanzaic form does the poem use? What does the form tell us about the poem?
5. How does the last line of each stanza function? What is its purpose?

The Issues

1. Poems are often highly charged moments recollected in tranquility. Sometimes they are symbolic. What moment is the poet describing? Does it in anyway seem symbolic to you?
2. What is your interpretation of the reference to doctors as "heroes in gloves"?
3. What is the meaning of the sentence "Pain is perfect" in Stanza 4?
4. What importance is given to the anesthesia involved? Explain your answer.
5. The speaker's imagination keeps drifting to a marriage proposal and its consequences. What details of the poem indicate that the love relationship had problems? On what note does the poem end?

Suggestions for Writing

1. Write an essay in which you recreate the process of getting hurt and being cured. Use the same step-by-step method seen in Carroll's poem.
2. Remembering a time when someone deeply hurt your feelings, write a process essay on the steps necessary to get over a serious heartache.

ISSUE FOR CRITICAL THINKING AND DEBATE: AGEISM

The painting *My Parents*, by Henry Koerner, symbolically sums up the issue of ageism in its portrayal of two elderly people deep in a woods. Lost in thought, the man is walking on a separate path away from the woman, who sits near a tree and stares down the narrow trail that unwinds and ominously ends ahead of her. The painting—actually a portrait of Koerner's parents who were exterminated by the Nazis—reminds us that aging also brings infirmity and befuddlement, which intensify the separations that occur naturally at the end of life. Koerner wrote that he spent many days walking with his parents peacefully through the woods of Vienna before World War II and that the painting was meant to commemorate that experience. Yet, in this portrayal, the painting is unrepresentative of growing old today because many of our elderly spend their last days not in an idyllic woodland, but in a grimy apartment or a cheap room.

The essayists in this section address ageism from quite different perspectives. As the title of Malcolm Cowley's essay reminds us, he was past eighty when he wrote the book from which this excerpt comes, and he finds philosophical consolations in growing old. He is not embittered, but a stoical, observant elder. Food tastes wonderful when you are old, he tells us; napping drowsily in the sun is blissful. On the other hand, the view from Ann Morrison requires no philosophical consolation or stoicism. In her essay, she radiates admiration and enthusiasm for French women, who seem to grow old with inevitable grace. Rather than have women waste time railing against the pressures of growing old, Morrison suggests that they pamper their skin and keep their bodies healthy in order to develop an inner beauty that radiates to their entire look. Perhaps we should listen when she insists that to age gracefully, we must feel good about ourselves. It is mind over makeup. The student essay is a lucid attempt by a Yale student to persuade her readers to stand up against policies that victimize the elderly in our society.

Ageism, unlike other issues, will ultimately and personally affect every reader of this book who achieves life expectancy. It is an issue that is progressively becoming not only more common, but more pressing. Unprecedented numbers of Baby Boomers are aging, making America inevitably older and grayer. According to the 2000 census, 37.7 million Americans were between the ages of 45 and 54. The median age (about half the population) in 1820

Curtis Galleries, Minneapolis, MN

● *My Parents, Henry Koerner*
Is old age really a walk in the park?

was 16.7 years; by 1980, it had jumped to 30; in the 1990 census, it was 32.9 years. In the 2000 census it was 35.3 years, the highest it has ever been.

If you die young or in your middle years, you will escape the consequences of ageism. Otherwise, ageism will surely and eventually affect your life. Indeed, how you treat the elderly today when you are young might well foreshadow how the young will treat you when you yourself are numbered among the elderly.

The View from Eighty

MALCOLM COWLEY

Malcolm Cowley (1898–1989), American critic and poet, was born in Belsano, Pennsylvania, and educated at Harvard. After World War I, Cowley lived abroad for many years among the so-called "lost generation" of writers, eventually writing about them in *Exile's Return* (1934) and *Second Flowering* (1973). He was the literary editor of *The New Republic* from 1930 to 1940 and numbers among his published works *A Dry Season* (poems, 1942), *Blue Juanita: Collected Poems* (1964), and *The View from Eighty* (1981), from which this excerpt was taken.

• • •

1   Even before he or she is 80, the aging person may undergo another identity crisis like that of adolescence. Perhaps there had also been a middle-aged crisis, the male or the female menopause, but for the rest of adult life he had taken himself for granted, with his capabilities and failings. Now, when he looks in the mirror, he asks himself, "Is this really me?"—or he avoids the mirror out of distress at what it reveals, those bags and wrinkles. In his new makeup he is called upon to play a new role in a play that must be improvised. André Gide, that long-lived man of letters, wrote in his journal, "My heart has remained so young that I have the continual feeling of playing a part, the part of the 70-year-old that I certainly am; and the infirmities and weaknesses that remind me of my age act like a prompter, reminding me of my lines when I tend to stray. Then, like the good actor I want to be, I go back into my role, and I pride myself on playing it well."

2   In his new role the old person will find that he is tempted by new vices, that he receives new compensations (not so widely known), and that he may possibly achieve new virtues. Chief among these is the heroic or merely obstinate refusal to surrender in the face of time. One admires the ships that go down with all flags flying and the captain on the bridge.

3   Among the vices of age are avarice, untidiness, and vanity, which last takes the form of a craving to be loved or simply admired. Avarice is the worst of those three. Why do so many old persons, men and women alike, insist on hoarding money when they have no prospect of using it and even when they have no heirs? They eat the cheapest food, buy no clothes, and live in a single room when they could afford better lodging. It may be that they regard money

as a form of power; there is a comfort in watching it accumulate while other powers are dwindling away. How often we read of an old person found dead in a hovel, on a mattress partly stuffed with bankbooks and stock certificates! The bankbook syndrome, we call it in our family, which has never succumbed.

4   Untidiness we call the Langley Collyer syndrome. To explain, Langley Collyer was a former concert pianist who lived alone with his 70-year-old brother in a brownstone house on upper Fifth Avenue. The once fashionable neighborhood had become part of Harlem. Homer, the brother, had been an admiralty lawyer, but was now blind and partly paralyzed; Langley played for him and fed him on buns and oranges, which he thought would restore Homer's sight. He never threw away a daily paper because Homer, he said, might want to read them all. He saved other things as well and the house became filled with rubbish from roof to basement. The halls were lined on both sides with bundled newspapers, leaving narrow passageways in which Langley had devised booby traps to catch intruders.

5   On March 21, 1947, some unnamed person telephoned the police to report that there was a dead body in the Collyer house. The police broke down the front door and found the hall impassable, then they hoisted a ladder to a second-story window. Behind it Homer was lying on the floor in a bathrobe; he had starved to death. Langley had disappeared. After some delay, the police broke into the basement, chopped a hole in the roof, and began throwing junk out of the house, top and bottom. It was 18 days before they found Langley's body, gnawed by rats. Caught in one of his own booby traps, he had died in a hallway just outside Homer's door. By that time the police had collected, and the Department of Sanitation had hauled away, 120 tons of rubbish, including besides the newspapers, 14 grand pianos and the parts of a dismantled Model T Ford.

6   Why do so many old people accumulate junk, not on the scale of Langley Collyer, but still in a dismaying fashion? Their tables are piled high with it, their bureau drawers are stuffed with it, their closet rods bend with the weight of clothes not worn for years. I suppose that the piling up is partly from lethargy and partly from the feeling that everything once useful, including their own bodies, should be preserved. Others, though not so many, have such a fear of becoming Langley Collyers that they strive to be painfully neat. Every tool they own is in its place, though it will never be used again; every scrap of paper is filed away in alphabetical order. At last their immoderate neatness becomes another vice of age, if a milder one.

7   The vanity of older people is an easier weakness to explain, and to condone. With less to look forward to, they yearn for recognition of what they have been: the reigning beauty, the athlete, the soldier, the scholar. It is the beauties who have the hardest time. A portrait of themselves at twenty hangs on the wall, and they try to resemble it by making an extravagant use of creams, powders, and dyes. Being young at heart, they think they are merely revealing their essential persons. The athletes find shelves for their silver trophies, which are polished once a year. Perhaps a letter sweater lies wrapped in a bureau drawer. I remember one evening when a no-longer athlete had guests for dinner and tried to find his sweater. "Oh, that old thing," his wife said. "The moths got into it and I threw it away." The athlete sulked and his guests went home early.

8   Often the yearning to be recognized appears in conversation as an innocent boast. Thus, a distinguished physician, retired at 94, remarks casually that a disease was named after him. A former judge bursts into chuckles as he repeats bright things that he said on the bench. Aging scholars complain in letters (or one of them does), "As I approach 70 I'm becoming avid of honors, and such things—medals, honorary degrees, etc.—are only passed around among academics on a *quid pro quo* basis (one hood capping another)." Or they say querulously, "Bill Underwood has ten honorary doctorates and I have only three. Why didn't they elect me to . . .?" and they mention the name of some learned society. That search for honors is a harmless passion, though it may lead to jealousies and deformations of character, as with Robert Frost in his later years. Still, honors cost little. Why shouldn't the very old have more than their share of them?

9   To be admired and praised, especially by the young, is an autumnal pleasure enjoyed by the lucky ones (who are not always the most deserving). "What is more charming," Cicero observes in his famous essay *De Senectute*, "than old age surrounded by the enthusiasm of youth! . . . Attentions which seem trivial and conventional are marks of honor—the morning call, being sought after, precedence, having people rise for you, being escorted to and from the forum. . . . What pleasures of the body can be compared to the prerogatives of influence?" But there are also pleasures of the body, or the mind, that are enjoyed by a greater number of older persons.

10   Those pleasures include some that younger people find hard to appreciate. One of them is simply sitting still, like a snake on a sunwarmed stone, with a delicious feeling of indolence that was seldom attained in earlier years. A leaf flutters down; a cloud moves by inches across the horizon. At such moments the older person, completely relaxed, has become a part of nature—and a living part, with blood coursing through his veins. The future does not exist for him. He thinks, if he thinks at all, that life for younger persons is still a battle royal of each against each, but that now he has nothing more to win or lose. He is not so much above as outside the battle, as if he had assumed the uniform of some neutral country, perhaps Liechtenstein or Andorra. From a distance he notes that some of the combatants, men or women, are jostling ahead—but why do they fight so hard when the most they can hope for is a longer obituary? He can watch the scrounging and gouging, he can hear the shouts of exultation, the moans of the gravely wounded, and meanwhile he feels secure; nobody will attack him from ambush.

11   Age has other physical compensations besides the nirvana of dozing in the sun. A few of the simplest needs become a pleasure to satisfy. When an old woman in a nursing home was asked what she really liked to do, she answered in one word: "Eat." She might have been speaking for many of her fellows. Meals in a nursing home, however badly cooked, serve as climactic moments of the day. The physical essence of the pensioners is being renewed at an appointed hour; now they can go back to meditating or to watching TV while looking forward to the next meal. They can also look forward to sleep, which has become a definite pleasure, not the mere interruption it once had been.

12   Here I am thinking of old persons under nursing care. Others ferociously guard their independence, and some of them suffer less than one might expect from being lonely and impoverished. They can be rejoiced by visits and meetings, but they

also have company inside their heads. Some of them are busiest when their hands are still. What passes through the minds of many is a stream of persons, images, phrases, and familiar tunes. For some that stream has continued since childhood, but now it is deeper; it is their present and their past combined. At times they conduct silent dialogues with a vanished friend, and these are less tiring—often more rewarding—than spoken conversations. If inner resources are lacking, old persons living alone may seek comfort and a kind of companionship in the bottle. I should judge from the gossip of various neighborhoods that the outer suburbs from Boston to San Diego are full of secretly alcoholic widows. One of those widows, an old friend, was moved from her apartment into a retirement home. She left behind her a closet in which the floor was covered wall to wall with whiskey bottles. "Oh, those empty bottles!" she explained. "They were left by a former tenant."

13   Not whiskey or cooking sherry but simply giving up is the greatest temptation of age. It is something different from a stoical acceptance of infirmities, which is something to be admired. At 63, when he first recognized that his powers were failing, Emerson wrote one of his best poems, "Terminus":

> It is time to be old,
> To take in sail: The god of bounds,
> Who sets to seas a shore,
> Came to me in his fatal rounds,
> And said: "No more!
> No farther shoot
> Thy broad ambitious branches, and thy root.
> Fancy departs: no more invent;
> Contract thy firmament
> To compass of a tent."

14   Emerson lived in good health to the age of 79. Within his narrowed firmament, he continued working until his memory failed; then he consented to having younger editors and collaborators. The givers-up see no reason for working. Sometimes they lie in bed all day when moving about would still be possible, if difficult. I had a friend, a distinguished poet, who surrendered in that fashion. The doctors tried to stir him to action, but he refused to leave his room. Another friend, once a successful artist, stopped painting when his eyes began to fail. His doctor made the mistake of telling him that he suffered from a fatal disease. He then lost interest in everything except the splendid Rolls-Royce, acquired in his prosperous days, that stood in the garage. Daily he wiped the dust from its hood. He couldn't drive it on the road any longer, but he used to sit in the driver's seat, start the motor, then back the Rolls out of the garage and drive it in again, back twenty feet and forward twenty feet; that was his only distraction.

15   I haven't the right to blame those who surrender, not being able to put myself inside their minds or bodies. Often they must have compelling reasons, physical or moral. Not only do they suffer from a variety of ailments, but also they are made to feel that they no longer have a function in the community. Their families and neighbors don't ask them for advice, don't really listen when they speak, don't call on them for efforts. One notes that there are not a few recoveries from apparent senility when that situation changes. If it doesn't change, old persons

may decide that efforts are useless. I sympathize with their problems, but the men and women I envy are those who accept old age as a series of challenges.

16   For such persons, every new infirmity is an enemy to be outwitted, an obstacle to be overcome by force of will. They enjoy each little victory over themselves, and sometimes they win a major success. Renoir was one of them. He continued painting, and magnificently, for years after he was crippled by arthritis; the brush had to be strapped to his arm. "You don't need your hand to paint," he said. Goya was another of the unvanquished. At 72 he retired as an official painter of the Spanish court and decided to work only for himself. His later years were those of the famous "black paintings" in which he let his imagination run (and also of the lithographs, then a new technique). At 78 he escaped a reign of terror in Spain by fleeing to Bordeaux. He was deaf and his eyes were failing; in order to work he had to wear several pairs of spectacles, one over another, and then use a magnifying glass; but he was producing splendid work in a totally new style. At 80 he drew an ancient man propped on two sticks, with a mass of white hair and beard hiding his face and with the inscription "I am still learning."

17   Giovanni Papini said when he was nearly blind, "I prefer martyrdom to imbecility." After writing sixty books, including his famous *Life of Christ*, he was at work on two huge projects when he was stricken with a form of muscular atrophy. He lost the use of his left leg, then of his fingers, so that he couldn't hold a pen. The two big books, though never to be finished, moved forward slowly by dictation; that in itself was a triumph. Toward the end, when his voice had become incomprehensible, he spelled out a word, tapping on the table to indicate letters of the alphabet. One hopes never to be faced with the need for such heroic measures.

18   "Eighty years old!" the great Catholic poet Paul Claudel wrote in his journal. "No eyes left, no ears, no teeth, no legs, no wind! And when all is said and done, how astonishingly well one does without them!"

● Vocabulary

improvised (1)	lethargy (6)	indolence (10)
infirmities (1)	condone (7)	exultation (10)
avarice (3)	querulously (8)	climactic (11)
succumbed (3)	deformations (8)	nirvana (11)
immoderate (6)	prerogatives (9)	

● The Facts

1. What kind of crisis does the aging person undergo?
2. What are the virtues of old age? What are its main vices?
3. What is the Langley Collyer syndrome? Why do old people suffer so often from it? What part does society's treatment of the elderly play in this syndrome?
4. Why are some old people so vain?
5. What pleasures do the old revel in?

The Strategies

1. Aside from examples that illustrate what it is like to be old, what kind of supporting detail does Cowley use? What does its use add to the essay?

2. What is the function of the question in paragraph 6?

3. Old people, says Cowley, suffer chronically from avarice, untidiness, and vanity. He gives extended examples of the second and third of these, but not of the first. How does he support his view that the old are often avaricious? What rhetorical logic lies behind this omission of examples?

4. What extended analogy does Cowley use to describe how the young appear to the old? How effective is this analogy?

5. In this excerpt, Cowley gives anecdotes about aging in others, rather than in himself. Do you think this a better tactic than focusing on his own experiences? Why or why not?

The Issues

1. Has Cowley overlooked any vices or virtues associated with old age? Make a written list of the characteristics of old age you wish to avoid and then a second list of characteristics you wish to develop.

2. What is your answer to the question posed in paragraph 3: "Why do so many old persons, men and women alike, insist on hoarding money when they have no prospect of using it and even when they have no heirs?" Do you agree with Cowley's suggestion that perhaps they regard money as a form of power, or are there other reasons for the avarice?

3. What about old age do you fear most? What do you plan to do in order to alleviate your fear?

4. In "Rabbi Ben Ezra," the famous Victorian poet Robert Browning wrote these lines:

> Grow old along with me!
> The best is yet to be,
> The last of life, for which the first was made:
> Our times are in His hand Who saith, "A whole I planned,
> Youth shows but half, trust God: see all, nor be afraid."

What parallels do you see in this excerpt and in Cowley's essay?

5. What kind of person do you imagine yourself to be at age 80? Describe in detail what kinds of clothes you will wear, how you will spend your time, and what philosophy will guide your existence.

Suggestions for Writing

1. Some sociologists have suggested that because women generally outlive men, marriage laws should be relaxed to allow the elderly to practice polygamy (wherein a man has more than one wife or mate) as a way of reducing the number of lonely widows. Express your views on this issue in an essay in which you use examples to support your thesis.

2. Write an essay giving examples of the way age has affected an elderly friend or relative.

"I don't know, Harry. This has the ring of authenticity."

Aging Gracefully, the French Way

ANN M. MORRISON

Ann M. Morrison (b. 1952) is founder and president of the New Leaders Institute, a consulting and research firm in Delmar, California. She is also a senior fellow at the Center for Creative Leadership, an international nonprofit organization focusing on diverse facets of leadership training and development. In 1977, she graduated with a Master's degree in psychology from Bucknell University. As a result of her deep interest in women's careers, Morrison became the co-editor of two books: *Breaking the Glass Ceiling: Can Women Reach the Top of America's Corporations?* (1994) and *The New Leaders: Leadership Diversity in America* (1996). The essay below originally appeared in *The New York Times*.

As you study Morrison's essay, you may note with surprise that the author—whose work has largely focused on trying to remove the barriers that keep women from competing with

men in top positions of the workforce—is also keenly interested in keeping women look-
ing noticeably female, not male. She is particularly impressed with the way French women
tackle the aging process by slowing it down and paying attention to their bodies.

● ● ●

1   I OFTEN see an elderly woman in my Paris neighborhood waltzing down the
street to her own imagined music, flashing a slightly demented smile at everyone she passes. Anywhere else, I would cross the street to avoid her. But she
always wears a matching, if slightly kooky, outfit—like the red print skirt, loose
cardigan and scarlet cloche hat she wore one day this spring—has great posture and is beautifully made up.

2   She clearly loves being herself. And she makes me think that in France,
women might forget everything else as they age—but never their sense
of style.

3   If there is a secret to aging well, Frenchwomen must know it. At least
that's what Americans think. We look at actresses like Juliette Binoche, 46,
or politicians like Segolene Royal, 56, or superstars like Catherine Deneuve,
66, and figure that they must have special insights into the "maturation"
process.

4   And even the average Frenchwoman—say, shopping along the Rue du
Faubourg St.-Honore or enjoying a leisurely lunch on the Left Bank, or strolling through the Luxembourg Gardens—seems to defy the notion that, as one
grows older, you either have to disguise that process with Botox, eye-lifts, lip
plumpers and all sorts of procedures that convey a desperate "youthful" look,
or else just give up altogether and let the ravages of time take their toll.

5   But do these women really have the answers when it comes to the aging
process?

6   Women on both sides of the Atlantic realize that the keys to aging well are
obvious, but challenging if you have bad genes, spend too much time in the sun
or smoke a lot. But while American women, like me at least, approach personal
care with practical efficiency, the Frenchwomen I know regard the pampering
of the skin, hair and body as an enjoyable, gratifying ritual.

7   Looking attractive, at any age, is just what Frenchwomen do, especially
the urban ones. For Parisiennes, maintaining their image is as natural as tying
a perfect scarf or wearing stilettos on cobblestone streets. Beauty is a tradition
handed down from generation to generation. "My grandmother always told me,
'Never neglect yourself, not even in the tiniest details,'" my friend Francoise
Augier said, with a sweeping head-to-toe gesture. The French actress Leslie
Caron, still Gigi-like at 79, told me her mother's favorite saying: "Women's skin
is too fair to go bare."

8   Not that French adolescents are any more likely than their American counterparts to heed their mothers' advice. My neighborhood esthetician, Martine, is
concerned that so many of her young clients (age 12 and up) go outdoors without sunscreen. Maybe she shouldn't worry. A survey by the market research
company Mintel found that 33 percent of French girls between 15 and 19 are
already using anti-aging or anti-wrinkle creams.

9   Though Frenchmen are clearly interested—they shamelessly ogle women on the street—beauty is a female topic. When, over dinner, I asked a grandmother of three how she managed to stay beautiful, she deflected my question, saying, "I never discuss these things in front of my husband."

10   The No. 1 response to my informal survey of Frenchwomen about the years of magical aging is not gaining weight. Ever. If a Frenchwoman happens to see an additional kilogram or two on her bathroom scale, she will do whatever is necessary to force the needle back where it belongs. "I keep my weight steady, no ups and downs," Ms. Caron said. "I avoid all excess." She claims to eat all kinds of food in small—her friends say minuscule—portions, and she doesn't drink alcohol. It's not so much that "French Women Don't Get Fat," as the title of Mireille Guiliano's best seller had it. Rather, Frenchwomen won't get fat.

11   Not that they exercise. When my husband and I arrived in Paris and asked our personal banker—everyone has one—for a gym recommendation, her response was: "Why? Gyms are a form of torture." It seems the only acceptable way to burn calories is to walk.

12   If Frenchwomen don't walk enough to stay en forme, there is always a pill, a lotion, a machine or a treatment to do the trick. Pharmacies have counters full of diet and figure-improving remedies. One cream promises "accelerated reduction in the areas resistant to diet" (hips, thighs and buttocks). Capsules assure a flatter stomach in four weeks. A poster recently plastered all over Paris Metro stations advertises a tiny Slendertone "Electronic Muscle Stimulation" belt that claims to provide, in a single session, the equivalent of 120 abdominal crunches. (It's available in the United States, too.)

13   Frenchwomen also recommend facials, massages and spa "cures" in their campaign against wrinkles, cellulite and saggy bottoms, bellies and breasts. One spa favorite is thalassotherapy, the seawater-based treatment that originated in France. It involves water jets, seaweed wraps, mud baths and sea-fog inhalation, meant to improve circulation, promote sleep, tone muscles and reduce cellulite. Some women are resourceful enough—or have legitimate medical reasons, like arthritis—to get doctors' prescriptions for weeks at their favorite spa. That means government health insurance covers much of the bill.

14   As for makeup, Frenchwomen of almost every age (except those teenagers) regard less as best. Heavy foundation has a tendency to emphasize wrinkles and pores, and most women avoid it in favor of a bit of blush. Those who do use foundation make sure that it blends with the skin, often by applying it just after moisturizing. The idea is to look as natural as possible: a little color on the eyelids, mascara, maybe a bit of eyeliner and lip gloss.

15   Of course, it's easy to look natural if your skin is great. And that may be where the French secrets really are. According to a 2008 Mintel report, Frenchwomen spend about $2.2 billion a year on facial skin care—as much as Spanish, German and British women put together. If you happen to use the bathroom in a French home—something that is not considered polite, by the way—you might see a line of skin care products rivaling a shelf at Duane Reade.

16   There will be day creams (with sunscreen), night creams (without it), re-pulping creams, serums, moisturizers, cleansers, toners and salves for anything from orange-peel skin to varicose veins. But you might not find much soap. Ms. Caron says she doesn't use it on her face or her body (except for "certain places"). Madame Figaro magazine recently quoted the French actress and TV presenter Lea Drucker as saying, "The day I stopped using soap, my life changed." Post-transformation, she uses a hydrating cream.

17   As in America, some women in France turn to dermatologists for their skin care, and their visits are likely to be covered by health insurance. Even the generous French system does not pay for Botox, collagen or hyaluronan injections, nor for "lifting" and most other cosmetic surgery.

18   That doesn't stop Frenchwomen from having "something done."

19   The objective of plastic surgery in France, according to Dr. Michel Soussaline, a Paris surgeon with more than 30 years of experience, is "to keep the natural beauty and charm of each individual woman, not to fit some current ideal of beauty." After all, trends change. In the United States, he says, women who spend a lot of money on face-lifts want to show off their investments. (Maybe that explains the pumped-up lips and smooth cheeks that the American actress Ellen Barkin, 56, recently displayed on the Cannes red carpet.)

20   By contrast, Frenchwomen prefer results that look as natural as possible. (Cannes photos of Isabelle Huppert, 57, show elegant, un-enhanced aging.) In France, I have only one friend who has confessed to having had surgery, a discreet operation to firm up a sagging chin and flabby neck. She is thrilled with the result: no one notices.

21   Hair rituals come in two kinds: getting rid of the unwanted stuff on legs and underarms (older women tend to prefer depilatories), and making the most of what's on top of the head. That means a good cut every three to four weeks, and a reasonably natural color. A plethora of beauty salons (50 of them in my arrondissement) and mostly low prices (as little as 18 euros, or about $22, for a cut, shampoo and blow-dry) make frequent hair maintenance easy. Frenchwomen use conditioners and other post-shampoo treatments, followed by a cold-water rinse. "It helps the circulation," said a friend.

22   Of course, the whole idea that Frenchwomen age better than Americans is debatable. Obesity rates are rising in France, though they are still far lower than in the United States. And not every movie star or politician remains ageless. The midcentury sex symbol Brigitte Bardot, now 75, is gray, wrinkly and overweight. Martine Aubry, the chubby head of the French Socialist Party and almost 60, is not known for her sense of style. And when I asked Katie Breen, a Frenchwoman who is a former editor at Marie Claire magazine, to name a woman who had aged particularly well, her answer was decidedly un-French: Meryl Streep.

23   For Frenchwomen, aging seems to be a matter of mind over makeup. If women feel good about themselves, right down to their La Perla 100-euro panties, they look good, too. Francoise Sagan once wrote, "There is a certain age when a woman must be beautiful to be loved, and then there comes a time

when she must be loved to be beautiful." And many Frenchwomen seem to be well loved as they get older—by their tight-knit families, their friends and, perhaps most importantly, themselves. Case in point: my loony neighbor—completely coordinated, perfectly made up, thoroughly French.

Vocabulary

demented (1)	stilettos (7)	cellulite (13)
ravages (4)	esthetician (8)	dermatologists (17)
gratifying (6)	deflected (9)	plethora (21)

The Facts

1. According to paragraph 4, in what areas of Paris do the women seem to negate the American temptation to have Botox injections, liposuction, lip plumpers, or other drastic cosmetic procedures in order to defy old age? Why do you think the author chose these particular neighborhoods? If you are unfamiliar with them, check a city map of Paris on the Internet.

2. According to Morrison, what is the basis of the Parisienne's aging gracefully? What difference exists between the advice given to Judith Ortiz Cofer by her mother (see pp. 377–378) and that given to Francoise Augier by her grandmother?

3. What is the major goal of the average French woman as she ages compared with the major goal of the average American woman? Do you agree with the author's distinction? Give reasons for your answer.

4. When the author did a survey of French women and their desire to keep looking attractive as they aged, what did she find to be the crux issue? Do you agree or disagree with this view? If you agree, state why; if you disagree, state what you consider the central requirement of remaining attractive while aging.

5. In paragraph 14, we are told that French women of all ages consider "less" makeup as "best." In other words, they opt for moderation. What is your response to the moderation standard? Notice that the author excludes French teenagers from this Golden Rule approach. Studying the Image Gallery on p. IG-4, and paying particular attention to the young man in plaid pants and the young girl in a revealing dress, what do you think is the motivation of these teenagers as far as their looks are concerned? What is the motivation of most teenagers? Consider such factors as individuality, making a social impact, and feeling insecure or even outcast.

The Strategies

1. What is the author's thesis? Where is it first stated? What is the purpose of the opening paragraph? How is the final paragraph connected to the opening?

2. What are some vivid images that increase the pleasure of reading this essay? Select two or three and explain their effectiveness.

3. How does Morrison organize her essay? Does she seem to follow a written outline or does her essay develop organically—one major idea leading to another? Try to trace the progress of her essay.

4. What is the "case in point" being made by the author? See the final paragraph. Why do you think Morrison chose to end her essay with this statement?

5. Paragraphs 8 and 11 both begin with sentence fragments. Why are professional writers often excused from following hard-core grammatical rules? Why is such laxity usually not allowed in student writing?

● The Issues

1. How important is it for women to grow old gracefully? Is physical appearance as important as inner beauty? Would you rather have a grandmother who looks like Marilyn Monroe, but treats people with haughty disdain, or one who looks like Grandma Moses but sends out rays of cheer everywhere she appears? Or, is there some ideal compromise you envision? Offer your honest, unbridled opinion on this matter.

2. What is your opinion of women or men who opt for cosmetic surgery? When is this kind of procedure appropriate and when is it irrational or even stupid? Provide specific examples of appropriate as well as inappropriate cosmetic surgeries.

3. Would you vote for legislation, similar to that of certain governments in Europe, that would pay for spa treatments that are supposed to cure arthritis, improve circulation, promote sleep, tone muscles, and reduce cellulite? Why or why not? In your view what is the government's responsibility toward the health of its aging citizenry? On what principle do you base your judgment?

4. From your observation of various cultures, which one do you think promotes the aging of women best? Are you convinced that pampering the skin, hair, and body helps women to age gracefully, or is it just "an enjoyable, gratifying ritual" (see paragraph 6)? Try to analyze what has caused some women you know to age more gracefully than others. Could women in general learn from the lifestyles of these women? If so, explain how.

5. What advice regarding aging would you give a teenager interested in the process? Begin with the highest priority and descend to the lowest. Cite any wisdom you have accrued from people who have aged gracefully.

● Suggestions for Writing

1. Write an essay taking the stand that a good self-image is the most important requirement of being attractive to other people.

2. After researching the Internet on the subject of aging, write a paper about how to age gracefully. Analyze and synthesize several appropriate ideas or quotations from experts.

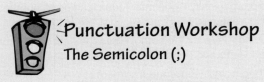

Punctuation Workshop
The Semicolon (;)

1. **Put a semicolon between two closely related independent clauses not joined by *and, but, for, or, nor, yet, so:***

   The bakery was closed on Sunday; we settled for crackers.

   Oatmeal contains antioxidants; it is good for the heart.

   The scout lifted his binoculars; a yellow object was floating in the water.

   Some grapes are seedless; others are not.

2. **Put a semicolon in front of *however, therefore, nevertheless, then,* and *therefore* when these adverbial conjunctions connect two independent clauses:**

   I love email; however, I don't want just anyone to have access to my email address.

   Most people have bad habits they constantly try to break; therefore, psychologists keep getting new patients.

   The gate gave a tired squeak; then, it suddenly flew open.

Notice that a semicolon precedes the adverbial conjunction, but a comma follows it. Actually, you can write acceptably without ever using semicolons because a period can always be used instead.

3. **Use semicolons to separate items in a series already separated by commas:**

   Her garden consists of flowers, common and exotic; vegetables, native as well as imported; and species of herbs found nowhere else on the island.

Student Corner

Kimberly Caitlin Wheeler
Yale University
Final Draft: Aging

There is a general perception in our society that once you reach middle age, you are "Over the hill and going down." As people get older, their value, unlike that of wine, is perceived to decrease. Thus the elderly are "worthless" members of society: They contribute nothing, but take much. This prejudice against the elderly and even the middle aged, ageism, is a big problem in our youth-oriented culture. Ageism does not end with mere perceptions, but also begets action. There are problems with age discrimination both in the entertainment industry and the workplace, but neither problem can be solved without a change in attitude towards the elderly.

Ageism is extremely noticeable within the entertainment industry. Most television programs and movies cater to the younger members of society. The shows portray young characters who are usually facing age-specific problems, such as starting a career or raising a family. Those who have reached retirement and have raised their families are often ignored or are peripheral characters. There are virtually no shows that sympathetically portray the interests of the elderly. One consequence of this is that people begin to perceive the elderly through the eyes of the media—as valueless members of society.

The entertainment industry has some economic justifications in producing only shows geared towards a younger audience. Research has shown that the 18-to-44 age group has more spending money than members of older age groups. Older age groups are actually wealthier, but they are less likely to spend money frivolously. They are not as receptive to advertisements and product trends. Because members of the 18-to-44 age group are more likely to spend their money, advertisers who pay for television shows want shows that members of this age group are watching, and support "younger" shows. Likewise, film studios, eager to make box office money, tend to produce shows designed for a more youthful audience.

Age discrimination also appears in the workplace. Employers are often unwilling to hire or keep workers that have reached a certain age. They perceive these workers as incompetent and lacking ambition. For example, the European Union recently implemented a policy of not hiring workers over the age of 35. This policy is unjustified. For most jobs, mature employees bring added skill and experience that can actually improve their performance. The one exception to this rule is in the area of technological advances. In today's workplace, where computers are an essential means of performing tasks, and the Internet forms the hub of office communication, those trained in a less technological age may find themselves at a disadvantage. In a survey done by Great Britain's Motorola Company, 22% of people ages 16 to 24 had had no Internet training, compared to 78% of people over the age of 65. Those over 65 were also less enthusiastic about technology or comfortable using high-tech equipment or online services. Thus many older workers lack skills that are essential in a high-tech work environment. This often offsets their advantages of experience and dedication.

Solutions to the problems that create age discrimination do exist, but before they can be implemented, it is necessary to overcome the prejudice against older people in this country. The general perception of the elderly as worthless and burdensome members of the society needs to change. Older people should be valued for their knowledge, experience, and successes. Once the attitude has changed, it is possible to affect the solutions for the entertainment industry and the workplace. If older people are perceived as valued customers and quality shows are created for them, they are more likely to watch them and spend their money. Likewise, if mature workers were trained in the use of advanced technology, this skill would add to their other resources of experience and knowledge. Life doesn't have to go downhill at age 40; it should become a time to reap the rewards of previous successes, a time to enjoy maturity.

How I Write

When I first get a topic, I like to take a few days and think about it. I may do some preliminary research, but what I usually do is just think, and jot down any ideas that come to me. This is a technique known to some as "procrastination," but it really is useful. When I have thought for a few days, I do some research to find facts and figures to support my ideas, or to derive ideas. I usually go to the library for books or periodicals. For a contemporary topic such as this, I like to turn to the Internet. Once I get books, I skim them for discussions of my topic, then take notes at my computer. I print out these notes, then sit down, away from the computer with a pencil, my notes, and a notebook, and plan my paper. My first step is to come up with a rough outline—usually two or three points to talk about. I then read through my material and find information that directly relates to the points that I may use in my paper later. I cut out my notes, divide them into piles that relate to each point, then tape them together in the order I want to use them. Once this is accomplished, I can begin writing the paper.

I always write the paper from scratch at the computer, because I type more quickly than I write and it is easier to make changes later. I like to listen to music while I write for several reasons. I usually listen to classical music, which is supposed to boost your IQ and focus. Music also helps when you're writing in a crowded dorm room. With headphones on, it is easier to block out the distracting conversations of my roommates. I also use earplugs sometimes. When I am typing and my fingers or brain cramp up, I take a short break and literally run around the room. Or I get a drink of water or have a short conversation with someone. When I return to writing, my brain is refreshed and ready to go. After I've finished writing, I look at the paper. If it is too short, I look for things I could explain more fully; and if it is too long, I look for things to cut. Then I print the paper out to proofread for obvious errors. At this point, I like to put it down for a while and do something else. Then I can come back to it and see what really needs to be revised and changed. Sometimes it is a few sentences, and sometimes it is the entire focus of the paper. After revising, I spell check and proofread again before printing it out and turning it in. Then I stop thinking about it until I get it back from the professor.

How I Wrote This Essay

For this paper, because I was writing at home, I used a slightly different approach. Because this topic was such a contemporary one, I turned first to the Internet for research. I typed "ageism" into several different search engines, then browsed the pages offered to see what looked interesting or relevant. I printed out the pages that appeared to be most useful, then sat down on the couch with my pencil, my notebook, and my Web pages. I came up with main points, found some statistics to use in my paper, then began writing. I stopped a few times in the middle—for dinner, and to check my email—but I eventually finished it. Then I printed it out to proofread. I marked my revisions, then went back to the computer and changed them.

My Writing Tip

Always write your body paragraphs first. I often don't know exactly what my thesis is until I'm done with the paper, so I always write an introduction and conclusion last. This also makes it easier to begin to write—usually the most difficult thing about writing a paper!

● CHAPTER WRITING ASSIGNMENTS

Write a process analysis about one of the following topics:

1. How to cook your favorite dish
2. How you celebrate a favorite holiday
3. How you reconciled two friends who were not speaking to each other
4. How you study for a big test

● WRITING ASSIGNMENTS FOR A SPECIFIC AUDIENCE

1. Describe to your parents your typical workday so that they will not feel that you are wasting too much time.
2. Explain to an audience of business executives how the English education you are currently receiving will make you a better employee.

● IMAGE GALLERY WRITING ASSIGNMENT

Visit pages IG-7–IG-9 of our image gallery and study all three images dealing with ageism. Then choose the image that most appeals to you. Answer the questions and do the writing assignment.

Pointer from a Pro

BE SINCERE

> I hold that man as hateful
> As the gates of hell
> Who says one thing, while another in his heart
> Lies hidden well
>
> —Homer (ca. 850 B.C.)

Trying to be on paper something you are not in real life will hamper you as a writer. Granted, sincerity is difficult to prove because we can't see into the hearts and minds of others; yet, phonies usually reveal themselves in their exaggerations or contradictions. If you want to write well, you should continually ask yourself, "Do I really mean that? Or am I just saying it to look good?"

11

Illustration/Exemplification

What Illustration/Exemplification Does

To *illustrate* means to give examples that clarify what you are trying to say. Short or long, illustrations are especially useful for embodying abstract ideas or sharpening ambiguous generalizations. They might consist of one item or a list of items that exemplify something, as in this paragraph, which illustrates what the author means by the "Discipline of Nature or of Reality":

> A child, in growing up, may meet and learn from three different kinds of discipline. The first and most important is what we might call the Discipline of Nature or of Reality. When he is trying to do something real, if he does the wrong thing or doesn't do the right one, he doesn't get the result he wants. If he doesn't pile one block right on top of another, or tries to build on a slanting surface, his tower falls down. If he hits the wrong key, he hears the wrong note. If he doesn't hit the nail squarely on the head, it bends, and he has to pull it out and start with another. If he doesn't measure properly when he is trying to build, it won't open, close, fit, stand up, fly, float, whistle, or do whatever he wants it to do. If he closes his eyes when he swings, he misses the ball. A child meets this kind of discipline every time he tries to do something, which is why it is so important in school to give children more chances to do things, instead of just reading or listening to someone talk (or pretending to) . . .
>
> —John Holt, *Kinds of Discipline*

On the other hand, an illustration might consist of one extended example rather than a list. Here is an example:

> Even the shrewdest of men cannot always judge what is useful and what is not. There never was a man so ingeniously practical as Thomas Alva Edison, surely the greatest inventor who ever lived, and we can take him as our example.

In 1896 he patented his first invention. It was a device to record votes mechanically. By using it, congressmen could press a button and all their votes would be instantly recorded and totaled. There was no question but that the invention worked; it remained only to sell it. A congressman whom Edison consulted, however, told him, with mingled amusement and horror, that there wasn't a chance of the invention's being accepted, however unfailingly it might work.

A slow vote, it seemed, was sometimes a political necessity. Some congressmen might have their opinions changed in the course of a slow vote where a quick vote might, in a moment of emotion, commit Congress to something undesirable.

Edison, chagrined, learned his lesson. After that, he decided never to invent anything unless he was sure that it would be needed and wanted and not merely because it worked.

—Isaac Asimov, *Of What Use?*

When to Use Illustration

The illustration is typically used to support an assertion or point. On every page, in almost every paragraph, writers who wish to communicate their meaning must back up their assertions with appropriate examples. It is not enough to generalize that such and such is the case, as you might do in a casual chat. To make your assertions believable, you must back them up with specific instances. Illustration is often practiced in combination with other modes of development, such as definition, description, classification, causal analysis, and so forth. In the following paragraph, for instance, two examples are used to define "romantic recognition":

Romantic recognition. Two examples will do. When we were flying from Erivan, the capital of Armenia, to Sukhum, on the Black Sea, a Soviet scientist, who spoke English, tapped me on the shoulder and then pointed to a fearsome rock face, an immeasurable slab bound in the iron of eternal winter. "That," he announced, "is where Prometheus was chained." And then all my secret terror—for a journey among the mountains of the Caucasus in a Russian plane is to my unheroic soul an ordeal—gave way for a moment to wonder and delight, as if an illuminated fountain had shot up in the dark. And then, years earlier, in the autumn of 1914, when we were on a route march in Surrey, I happened to be keeping step with the company commander, an intelligent Regular lent to us for a month or two. We were passing a little old woman who was watching us from an open carriage, drawn up near the entrance to a mansion. "Do you know who that is?" the captain asked; and of course I didn't. "It's the Empress Eugenie," he told me; and young and loutish as I was in those days, nevertheless there flared about me then, most delightfully, all the splendor and idiocy of the Second Empire, and I knew that we, every man Jack of us, were in history, and knew it once and for all.

—J. B. Priestly, *Romantic Recognition*

Here, an illustration is used to help describe the humility of John Masefield, the English poet:

> This quality of his can best be illustrated by his behavior that night. When the time came for him to read his poems, he would not stand up in any position of pre-eminence but sheltered himself behind the sofa, in the shade of an old lamp, and from there he delivered passages from "The Everlasting Mercy," "Dauber," "The Tragedy of Nan," and "Pompey the Great." He talked, too, melodiously, and with the ghost of a question mark after each of his sentences as though he were saying, "Is that right? Who am I to lay down the law?" And when it was all over, and we began to discuss what he had said, all talking at the top of our voices, very superficially, no doubt, but certainly with a great deal of enthusiasm, it was with a sudden shock that I realized that Masefield had retired into his shell, and was sitting on the floor, almost in the dark, reading a volume of poems by a young and quite unknown writer.
>
> —Beverley Nichols, *Twenty-Five*

Illustration is especially effective as support for a persuasive argument. For example, the bland assertion that animal experimentation is necessary to the advancement of science will persuade more forcefully when coupled with an example of how an infant's life was saved by a surgical procedure learned in practice on laboratory animals.

An illustration can also be visual: a picture, chart, map, line drawing, graph, or spreadsheet. Such visual illustrations are used widely in scientific and technical writing.

How to Use Illustration

1. **An illustration must be real and specific.** It must not consist simply of a restatement of what you've already said. Here is an example of a paragraph whose "illustration" is merely a rewording of a preceding statement:

> Before being sold to the American colonies, many slaves had acquired a knowledge of Wolof and Mandingo, the creolized English that had come into use along the Guinea coast as a trade language. For example, many slaves were conversant in both of these languages.

Although the writer uses "for example," what follows is not an authentic illustration but only further commentary. Here is an improvement:

> Before being sold to the American colonies, many slaves had acquired a knowledge of Wolof and Mandingo, the creolized English that had come into use along the Guinea coast as a trade language. For example, when a runaway slave who could speak no English was arrested in Pennsylvania in 1731, his white interrogators had no difficulty in finding another Wolof-speaking slave to act as an interpreter.

The illustration now supports the assertion that many slaves came to America already knowing creolized English.

2. **An illustration should be clearly introduced and contextually linked to the point it is intended to support.** If you reread the preceding paragraphs in this section, you will notice that the writers generally use some introductory phrases such as "take him as our example," "two examples will do," or "for example." Such phrases are needed when the context of the paragraph does not alert the reader that an illustration is to follow. On the other hand, if it is clear from the context that an illustration is to follow, no introductory phrase is necessary:

> While viruses and bacteria cause most of the common diseases suffered by people who live in the developed world, protozoa are the major cause of disease in undeveloped tropical zones. Of these diseases, the most widespread are malaria, amoebic dysentery, and African sleeping sickness.

The first sentence makes it plain that malaria, amoebic dysentery, and African sleeping sickness are examples of diseases caused by protozoa in the tropical zones.

Beware, however, of plunging too abruptly into an illustration:

> The idea that art does not exist among the lower animals is a primitive notion. The bower birds of Australia decorate their bowers with shells, colored glass, and shining objects. Some paint their walls with fruit pulp, wet powdered charcoal, or paste of chewed-up grass mixed with saliva. One kind of bower bird even makes a paintbrush from a wad of bark to apply the paint.

Notice how this passage is improved with a transition:

> The idea that art does not exist among the lower animals is a primitive notion. A perfect illustration of art in the animal kingdom is the art of the amazing bower birds of Australia. These birds decorate their bowers with shells, colored glass, and shining objects. Some paint their walls with fruit pulp, wet powdered charcoal, or paste of chewed-up grass mixed with saliva. One kind of bower bird even makes a paintbrush from a wad of bark to apply the paint.

Some illustrations need to be followed by commentary that interprets them for the reader. Here is an example:

> In 1796 Edward Jenner observed that people who came down with cowpox were protected against the far more serious infection of smallpox; therefore, he decided to infect people with cowpox to keep them

from getting smallpox. In 1881 Louis Pasteur accidentally left a culture of chicken cholera out on a shelf. Two weeks later, having returned from a vacation, he injected the culture into some laboratory animals and found to his surprise that the animals, instead of getting cholera, had become immune to the disease. These two experiences illustrate the beginnings of genetic engineering, a science that is now on the verge of splicing out from a virulent microbe the genes that cause disease. Millions of seriously ill people hope to be cured from deadly viruses through the miracles of genetic engineering.

The last two sentences of the paragraph interpret by telling us that the examples cited were illustrations of early genetic engineering. Whether you should use an introductory phrase or a concluding phrase, or simply embed your illustration within the context of the paragraph, is mainly a matter of common sense. Use phrases to introduce your illustrations only if they are necessary. In every case, you should ask yourself whether you have made your point clearly enough to be instantly understood. If the answer is no, then you should add whatever sentence or phrase is necessary to complete your illustration.

3. **An illustration should always be relevant to the point you are making.** If it is not, you should leave it out. Again, much of this judgment is a matter of common sense. But sometimes we get paragraphs that read like this:

> My stepfather is a stodgy person. For example, he contributes money every year to the Audubon fund. He serves as an usher in church and is a Scoutmaster for my half-brother's troop. He is active in a club that devotes its time to restoring old buildings in our town.

Not being instances of "stodginess," the examples given do not support the writer's assertion. It is better to avoid illustrations entirely than to cite irrelevant ones that do not support your point.

Warming Up to Write an Illustration

1. Following are five different theses that could well be developed through examples. Sketch out three examples for two theses of your choice. Be sure that each example supports the thesis.

   a. If you shop wisely, you can save large amounts of money.

   b. My mom and dad hear and see things differently.

   c. Sometimes imperfections are beautiful.

   d. Not being covered by medical insurance can be disastrous.

   e. My boyfriend (or girlfriend or spouse) always thinks of romantic things to do.

2. Answer the following questions by listing an example that clarifies the answer to the question.

   a. What makes a snowy landscape beautiful?

   b. What are some typical elements of authority against which teenagers rebel?

   c. Why do most people admire firefighters?

   d. What makes our national parks so valuable?

   e. What are the worst aspects of homelessness?

3. Provide an appropriate example to illustrate each of the following facts.

   a. Being a dentist requires ultimate patience.

   b. The President of the United States is not always a role model.

   c. Email is one of the great inventions of the last decade.

   d. Modern medicine has created miracle cures.

   e. Saying good-bye can be heart wrenching.

EXAMPLES

The Myth of the Latin Woman: I Just Met a Girl Named Maria

JUDITH ORTIZ COFER

Rhetorical Thumbnail

Purpose: to demonstrate the painful effects of thoughtless stereotyping

Audience: educated readers with a curiosity about people

Language: standard English with a few Spanish expressions thrown in to highlight the author's background

Strategy: uses vivid examples to point out the foolishness of seeing people in terms of ethnic types rather than as individual Americans

Judith Ortiz Cofer (b. 1952) is an American poet and novelist whose writings form a bridge between her childhood in tropical Puerto Rico and her adult life in New Jersey. As a result of this twofold background, Cofer never felt fully grounded in either the Latino or the mainstream U.S. culture. In Puerto Rico she was accused of sounding like a *gringa* whereas in New Jersey she was teased about her "Spanish accent." This constant feeling of being wrenched by two cultures has added strains of sensitivity to Cofer's stories about a *Latina* overcoming her sense of alienation. In the process, she has become an inspiration to other young women who have faced the challenge of feeling like outcasts in society. Cofer is the author of a novel *The Line of the Sun* (1989); a collection of essays and poetry, *Silent Dancing* (1990); and two books of poetry, *Terms of Survival* (1987) and *Reaching for the Mainland* (1987). Among her most recent works is *A Love Story Beginning in Spanish: Poems* (2005). The essay below is taken from her collection *The Latin Deli: Prose and Poetry* (1993).

Because every social snub has its standards of beauty, behavior, and achievement, it does not take much for newcomers to feel unwelcome or ostracized when they have been stereotyped as foreigners. Children, of course, are the most vulnerable victims of social snubbing. If they are overweight, handicapped, or slow in learning, they can quickly become the victims of bullies, who delight in tormenting the alien or weak. As you read this essay, try to think what it would be like if you were transposed to a place whose language you did not speak and whose traditions you did not observe. Use your imagination to formulate a plan that would help build up your self confidence and resolve to triumph in a hostile milieu.

· · ·

1   On a bus trip to London from Oxford University where I was earning some graduate credits one summer, a young man, obviously fresh from a pub, spotted me and as if struck by inspiration went down on his knees in the aisle. With both hands over his heart he broke into an Irish tenor's rendition of "Maria" from *West Side Story.* My politely amused fellow passengers gave his lovely voice the round of gentle applause it deserved. Though I was not quite as amused, I managed my version of an English smile: no show of teeth, no extreme contortions of the facial muscles—I was at this time of my life practicing reserve and cool. Oh, that British control, how I coveted it. But "Maria" had followed me to London, reminding me of a prime fact of my life: you can leave the island, master the English language, and travel as far as you can, but if you are a Latina, especially one like me who so obviously belongs to Rita Moreno's gene pool, the island travels with you.

2   This is sometimes a very good thing—it may win you that extra minute of someone's attention. But with some people, the same things can make *you* an island—not a tropical paradise but an Alcatraz, a place nobody wants to visit. As a Puerto Rican girl living in the United States and wanting like most children to "belong," I resented the stereotype that my Hispanic appearance called forth from many people I met.

3   Growing up in a large urban center in New Jersey during the 1960s, I suffered from what I think of as "cultural schizophrenia." Our life was designed by my parents as a microcosm of their *casas* on the island. We spoke in Spanish, ate Puerto Rican food bought at the *bodega,* and practiced strict Catholicism at a church that allotted us a one-hour slot each week for mass, performed in Spanish by a Chinese priest trained as a missionary for Latin America.

4   As a girl I was kept under strict surveillance by my parents, since my virtue and modesty were, by their cultural equation, the same as their honor. As a

teenager I was lectured constantly on how to behave as a proper *senorita*. But it was a conflicting message I received, since the Puerto Rican mothers also encouraged their daughters to look and act like women and to dress in clothes our Anglo friends and their mothers found too "mature" and flashy. The difference was, and is, cultural; yet I often felt humiliated when I appeared at an American friend's party wearing a dress more suitable to a semi-formal than to a playroom birthday celebration. At Puerto Rican festivities, neither the music nor the colors we wore could be too loud.

5   I remember Career Day in our high school, when teachers told us to come dressed as if for a job interview. It quickly became obvious that to the Puerto Rican girls "dressing up" meant wearing their mother's ornate jewelry and clothing, more appropriate (by mainstream standards) for the company Christmas party than as daily office attire. That morning I had agonized in front of my closet, trying to figure out what a "career girl" would wear. I knew how to dress for school (at the Catholic school I attended, we all wore uniforms), I knew how to dress for Sunday mass, and I knew what dresses to wear for parties at my relatives' homes. Though I do not recall the precise details of my Career Day outfit, it must have been a composite of these choices. But I remember a comment my friend (an Italian American) made in later years that coalesced my impressions of that day. She said that at the business school she was attending, the Puerto Rican girls always stood out for wearing "everything at once." She meant, of course, too much jewelry, too many accessories. On that day at school we were simply made the negative models by the nuns, who were themselves not credible fashion experts to any of us. But it was painfully obvious to me that to the others, in their tailored skirts and silk blouses, we must have seemed "hopeless" and "vulgar." Though I now know that most adolescents feel out of step much of the time, I also know that for the Puerto Rican girls of my generation that sense was intensified. The way our teachers and classmates looked at us that day in school was just a taste of the cultural clash that awaited us in the real world, where prospective employers and men on the street would often misinterpret our tight skirts and jingling bracelets as a "come-on."

6   Mixed cultural signals have perpetuated certain stereotypes—for example, that of the Hispanic woman as the "hot tamale" or sexual firebrand. It is a one-dimensional view that the media have found easy to promote. In their special vocabulary, advertisers have designated "sizzling" and "smoldering" as the adjectives of choice for describing not only the foods but also the women of Latin America. From conversations in my house I recall hearing about the harassment that Puerto Rican women endured in factories where the "boss-men" talked to them as if sexual innuendo was all they understood, and worse, often gave them the choice of submitting to their advances or being fired.

7   It is custom, however, not chromosomes, that leads us to choose scarlet over pale pink. As young girls, it was our mothers who influenced our decisions about clothes and colors—mothers who had grown up on a tropical island where the natural environment was a riot of primary colors, where showing your skin was one way to keep cool as well as to look sexy. Most important of

all, on the island, women perhaps felt freer to dress and move more provocatively since, in most cases, they were protected by the traditions, mores, and laws of a Spanish/Catholic system of morality and machismo whose main rule was: *You may look at my sister, but if you touch her I will kill you.* The extended family and church structure could provide a young woman with a circle of safety in her small pueblo on the island; if a man "wronged" a girl, everyone would close in to save her family honor.

8   My mother has told me about dressing in her best party clothes on Saturday nights and going to the town's plaza to promenade with her girlfriends in front of the boys they liked. The males were thus given an opportunity to admire the women and to express their admiration in the form of *piropos:* erotically charged street poems they composed on the spot. (I have myself been subjected to a few *piropos* while visiting the island, and they can be outrageous, although custom dictates that they must never cross into obscenity.) This ritual, as I understand it, also entails a show of studied indifference on the woman's part; if she is "decent," she must not acknowledge the man's impassioned words. So I do understand how things can be lost in translation. When a Puerto Rican girl dressed in her idea of what is attractive meets a man from the mainstream culture who has been trained to react to certain types of clothing as a sexual signal, a clash is likely to take place. I remember the boy who took me to my first formal dance leaning over to plant a sloppy, over-eager kiss painfully on my mouth; when I didn't respond with sufficient passion, he remarked resentfully: "I thought you Latin girls were supposed to mature early," as if I were expected to *ripen* like a fruit or vegetable, not just grow into womanhood like other girls.

9   It is surprising to my professional friends that even today some people, including those who should know better, still put others "in their place." It happened to me most recently during a stay at a classy metropolitan hotel favored by young professional couples for weddings. Late one evening after the theater, as I walked toward my room with a colleague (a woman with whom I was coordinating an arts program), a middle-aged man in a tuxedo, with a young girl in satin and lace on his arm, stepped directly into our path. With his champagne glass extended toward me, he exclaimed "Evita!"

10   Our way blocked, my companion and I listened as the man half-recited, half-bellowed "Don't Cry for Me, Argentina." When he finished, the young girl said: "How about a round of applause for my daddy?" We complied, hoping this would bring the silly spectacle to a close. I was becoming aware that our little group was attracting the attention of the other guests. "Daddy" must have perceived this too, and he once more barred the way as we tried to walk past him. He began to shout-sing a ditty to the tune of "La Bamba"—except the lyrics were about a girl named Maria whose exploits rhymed with her name and gonorrhea. The girl kept saying "Oh, Daddy" and looking at me with pleading eyes. She wanted me to laugh along with the others. My companion and I stood silently waiting for the man to end his offensive song. When he finished, I looked not at him but at his daughter. I advised her calmly never to ask her

father what he had done in the army. Then I walked between them and to my room. My friend complimented me on my cool handling of the situation, but I confessed that I had really wanted to push the jerk into the swimming pool. This same man—probably a corporate executive, well-educated, even worldly by most standards—would not have been likely to regale an Anglo woman with a dirty song in public. He might have checked his impulse by assuming that she could be somebody's wife or mother, or at least *somebody* who might take offense. But, to him, I was just an Evita or a Maria: merely a character in his cartoon-populated universe.

11   Another facet of the myth of the Latin woman in the United States is the menial, the domestic—Maria the housemaid or countergirl. It's true that work as domestics, as waitresses, and in factories is all that's available to women with little English and few skills. But the myth of the Hispanic menial—the funny maid, mispronouncing words and cooking up a spicy storm in a shiny California kitchen—has been perpetuated by the media in the same way that "Mammy" from *Gone with the Wind* became America's idea of the black woman for generations. Since I do not wear my diplomas around my neck for all to see, I have on occasion been sent to that "kitchen" where some think I obviously belong.

12   One incident has stayed with me, though I recognize it as a minor offense. My first public poetry reading took place in Miami, at a restaurant where a luncheon was being held before the event. I was nervous and excited as I walked in with notebook in hand. An older woman motioned me to her table, and thinking (foolish me) that she wanted me to autograph a copy of my newly published slender volume of verse, I went over. She ordered a cup of coffee from me, assuming that I was the waitress. (Easy enough to mistake my poems for menus, I suppose.) I know it wasn't an intentional act of cruelty. Yet of all the good things that happened later, I remember that scene most clearly, because it reminded me of what I had to overcome before anyone would take me seriously. In retrospect I understand that my anger gave my reading fire. In fact, I have almost always taken any doubt in my abilities as a challenge, the result most often being the satisfaction of winning a convert, of seeing the cold, appraising eyes warm to my words, the body language change, the smile that indicates I have opened some avenue for communication. So that day as I read, I looked directly at that woman. Her lowered eyes told me she was embarrassed at her faux pas, and when I willed her to look up at me, she graciously allowed me to punish her with my full attention. We shook hands at the end of the reading and I never saw her again. She has probably forgotten the entire incident, but maybe not.

13   Yet I am one of the lucky ones. There are thousands of Latinas without the privilege of an education or the entrees into society that I have. For them life is a constant struggle against the misconceptions perpetuated by the myth of the Latina. My goal is to try to replace the old stereotypes with a much more interesting set of realities. Every time I give a reading, I hope the stories I tell, the dreams and fears I examine in my work, can achieve some universal truth

that will get my audience past the particulars of my skin color, my accent, or my clothes.

14   I once wrote a poem in which I called all Latinas "God's brown daughters." This poem is really a prayer of sorts, offered upward, but also, through the human-to-human channel of art, outward. It is a prayer for communication and for respect. In it, Latin women pray "in Spanish to an Anglo God/with a Jewish heritage," and they are "fervently hoping/that if not omnipotent,/at least He be bilingual."

Judith Ortiz Cofer: "The Myth of the Latin Woman: I Just Met a Girl Named Maria" from *The Latin Deli: Prose and Poetry.* © 1993 by Judith Ortiz Cofer. Reprinted by permission of The University of Georgia Press.

● Vocabulary

microcosm (3)	coalesced (5)	facet (11)
surveillance (4)	innuendo (6)	faux pas (12)
composite (5)	chromosomes (7)	

● The Facts

1. What is the meaning of "myth" as used in the title of this essay? What other term might be appropriate? Where did the word originate? What connotations surround it?

2. When the author tried to imitate the British people, what traits did she practice on the bus ride from Oxford to London? What is your reaction to her version of the English smile?

3. Why did the author agonize over what to wear on Career Day at her high school? What would you wear for Career Day if it were held this week? Describe your clothing and accessories in detail. What is the general look you would want to achieve?

4. Why did Puerto Rican girls wear bright colors and clothing that left bear skin showing? What kept Puerto Rican boys from disrespectful behavior toward girls who dressed provocatively?

5. What happened at the author's first public poetry reading to highlight the problem of stereotyping Latinas? Think of a similar example you have witnessed.

● The Strategies

1. The author could have written an essay in which she defined *stereotype* and then eloquently attacked people who hurt others by treating them as if they were carbon copies of their cultural kind. She could have limited herself to abstract logic and persuasion, but instead, the author simply offers several concrete examples of when she was treated as a typical Latina and not as the talented individual she is. What advantage, if any, does the author's approach have? What is your reaction to her personal story?

2. What is the schizophrenia experienced early on by the author? Explain it in your own words. Do you think young people from mainstream cultures could experience a similar kind of schizophrenia? Support your claim.

3. What is the grammatical antecedent of "This" at the beginning of paragraph 2? How is this indefinite pronoun clarified? Do you consider the strategy effective? Explain your answer.

4. What is your judgment of the middle-aged man who sang "Don't Cry for Me, Argentina," followed by some shouted song with obscene lyrics? If you had been in the narrator's place, how would you have handled the situation? What seemed to be the main motivation of the narrator's approach?

5. Why does the author save the anecdote about the menial, the domestic until the last? Evaluate how this strategy supports the thesis of the essay.

The Issues

1. According to the author, if you look like Rita Moreno, "the island travels with you" (see paragraph 1). What is the significance of this observation? Are there gene pools other than the Hispanic one that tend to define people in our country? Give examples of how the gene pool works—for good or bad.

2. Do you agree with the author that mothers can send conflicting messages to their daughters? If so, what are some of these messages you have personally observed in the environment in which you grew up? What were the consequences? Give specific examples.

3. In the essay, little is said of the father's influence. What influence, if any, do fathers have in forming the image of girls in our society? Describe the effect of that influence as you have experienced or observed it at close hand.

4. In many ways, most immigrants feel alienated from their new homeland. Why is this so? What could our society do to make the transition from one culture to the other easier for immigrants? Suggest specific programs or attitudes.

5. Building on the author's intimation in paragraph 2 that moving to a new cultural environment can be "a very good thing," what are some examples of the good that can accrue to immigrants who have moved to a new country? Consider such matters as being bilingual; understanding various attitudes toward religion, etiquette, or the opposite sex; not being afraid to travel; and being open to many wide-ranging traditions rather than just those revered in our country.

Suggestions for Writing

1. Write an essay in which you imagine yourself a student transported to a country such as France, Russia, China, or Mexico to live. Using your imagination and common sense, cite some vivid examples of the difficulties you might encounter and how you would resolve them.

2. Write an essay about some famous American—male or female—who was brought up in a foreign country but became an admired U.S. citizen. Examples to consider are Alexander Hamilton, Albert Einstein, Father Edward Flanagan, Felix Frankfurter, Mikhail Baryshnikov, Vladimir Nabakov, Kahil Gibran, Sammy Sosa, Hakeem Olajuwan, Mary Antin, Gloria Estefan, Madeleine Albright, and Ruby Keeler. Check the Internet for other suitable candidates.

Clever Animals

LEWIS THOMAS

Rhetorical Thumbnail

Purpose: to convey to the reader the same fascination with animal behavior experienced by the author

Audience: any reader interested in animal behavior

Language: a clarity of style that engages any educated reader

Strategy: to support by specific examples the author's thesis that "there is no end to the surprises that an animal can think up in the presence of an investigator"

Lewis Thomas (1913–1993) was one of the few physicians of his day to bridge the gap between science and literature. Born in New York and a graduate of Harvard Medical School, he spent most of his illustrious career as a researcher and administrator. Throughout his work, he was associated with numerous prestigious institutions, including Yale University Medical School and the Memorial Sloan-Kettering Cancer Center, where he served as president. He contributed important knowledge to cancer research and to immunology. In 1971, while Thomas was chairman of the Department of Pathology at Yale Medical School, he was asked by the editor of the *New England Journal* to write a monthly essay, a request he fulfilled. These essays were so well received that in 1974, twenty-nine of his essays were published in a volume titled *The Lives of a Cell.* His writing style and voice were so compelling and popular with readers that other essays followed. Famous writers like Joyce Carol Oates praised his "effortless, beautiful style." Other books by Thomas include *The Medusa and the Snail* (1979), *The Youngest Science: Notes of a Medicine-Watcher* (1983), *Late Night Thoughts on Listening to Mahler's Ninth Symphony* (1983) *Could I Ask You Something?* (1985), *Et Cetera Et Cetera: Notes of a Word Watcher* (1990), and *The Fragile Species* (1992). Today, long after his death in 1993, Thomas continues to be recognized as a serious writer of prose that combines insights into science, especially microbiology and immunology, with philosophical reflections about the connection between humans and nature.

In the essay that follows, reprinted from Late Night Thoughts on Listening to Mahler's Ninth Symphony, *you will detect the author's famous witty and graceful style as he provides various examples of peculiar animal behavior that has completely baffled scientific researchers. As you read, try to conjure up memories of when you observed certain animals who seemed smarter than the human beings around them. Jot down the details that made your observation exciting.*

• • •

1   Scientists who work on animal behavior are occupationally obliged to live chancier lives than most of their colleagues, always at risk of being fooled by the animals they are studying or, worse, fooling themselves. Whether their experiments involve domesticated laboratory animals or wild creatures in the field, there is no end to the surprises that an animal can think up in the presence of an investigator. Sometimes it seems as if animals are genetically programmed to puzzle human beings, especially psychologists.

2   The risks are especially high when the scientist is engaged in training the animal to do something or other and must bank his professional reputation on the integrity of his experimental subject. The most famous case in point is that of Clever Hans, the turn-of-the-century German horse now immortalized in the lexicon of behavioral science by the technical term, the "Clever Hans Error." The horse, owned and trained by Herr von Osten, could not only solve complex arithmetical problems, but even read the instructions on a blackboard and tap out infallibly, with one hoof, the right answer. What is more, he could perform the same computations when total strangers posed questions to him, with his trainer nowhere nearby. For several years Clever Hans was studied intensively by groups of puzzled scientists and taken seriously as a horse with something very like a human brain, quite possibly even better than human. But finally in 1911, it was discovered by Professor O. Pfungst that Hans was not really doing arithmetic at all; he was simply observing the behavior of the human experimenter. Subtle, unconscious gestures—nods of the head, the holding of breath, the cessation of nodding when the correct count was reached—were accurately read by the horse as cues to stop tapping.

3   Whenever I read about that phenomenon, usually recounted as the exposure of a sort of unconscious fraud on the part of either the experimenter or the horse or both, I wish Clever Hans would be given more credit than he generally gets. To be sure, the horse couldn't really do arithmetic, but the record shows that he was considerably better at observing human beings and interpreting their behavior than humans are at comprehending horses or, for that matter, other humans.

4   Cats are a standing rebuke to behavioral scientists wanting to know how the minds of animals work. The mind of a cat is an inscrutable mystery, beyond human reach, the least human of all creatures and at the same time, as any cat owner will attest, the most intelligent. In 1979, a paper was published in *Science* by B. R. Moore and S. Stuttard entitled "Dr. Guthrie and Felis domes-ticus or: tripping over the cat," a wonderful account of the kind of scientific mischief native to this species. Thirty-five years ago, E. R. Guthrie and G. P. Horton described an experiment in which cats were placed in a glass-fronted puzzle box and trained to find their way out by jostling a slender vertical rod at the front of the box, thereby causing a door to open. What interested these investigators was not so much that the cats could learn to bump into the vertical rod, but that before doing so each animal performed a long ritual of highly stereotyped movements, rubbing their heads and backs against the front of the box, turning in circles, and finally touching the rod. The experiment has ranked as something of a classic in experimental psychology, even raising in some minds the notion of a ceremony of superstition on the part of

cats: before the rod will open the door, it is necessary to go through a magical sequence of motions.

5   Moore and Stuttard repeated the Guthrie experiment, observed the same complex "learning" behavior, but then discovered that it occurred only when a human being was visible to the cat. If no one was in the room with the box, the cat did nothing but take naps. The sight of a human being was all that was needed to launch the animal on the series of sinuous movements, rod or no rod. door or no door. It was not a learned pattern of behavior, it was a cat greeting a person.

6   The French investigator R. Chauvin was once engaged in a field study of the boundaries of ant colonies and enlisted the help of some enthusiastic physicists equipped with radioactive compounds and Geiger counters. The ants of one anthill were labeled and then tracked to learn whether they entered the territory of a neighboring hill. In the middle of the work the physicists suddenly began leaping like ballet dancers, terminating the experiment, while hundreds of ants from both colonies swarmed over their shoes and up inside their pants. To Chauvin's ethological eye it looked like purposeful behavior on both sides.

7   Bees are filled with astonishments, confounding anyone who studies them, producing volumes of anecdotes. A lady of our acquaintance visited her sister, who raised honeybees in northern California. They left their car on a side road, suited up in protective gear, and walked across the fields to have a look at the hives. For reasons unknown, the bees were in a furious mood that afternoon, attacking in platoons, settling on them from all sides. Let us walk away slowly, advised the beekeeper sister, they'll give it up sooner or later. They walked until bee-free, then circled the fields and went back to the car, and found the bees there, waiting for them.

8   There is a new bee anecdote for everyone to wonder about. It was reported from Brazil that male bees of the plant-pollinating euglossine species are addicted to DDT. Houses that had been sprayed for mosquito control in the Amazonas region were promptly invaded by thousands of bees that gathered on the walls, collected the DDT in pouches on their hind legs, and flew off with it. Most of the houses were virtually stripped of DDT during the summer months, and the residents in the area complained bitterly of the noise. There is as yet no explanation for this behavior. They are not harmed by the substance; while a honeybee is quickly killed by as little as six micrograms of DDT, these bees can cart away two thousand micrograms without being discommoded. Possibly the euglossine bees like the taste of DDT or its smell, or maybe they are determined to protect other insect cousins. Nothing about bees, or other animals, seems beyond imagining.

● Vocabulary

genetically (1)	phenomenon (3)	ethological (6)
infallibly (2)	rebuke (4)	confounding (7)
cessation (2)	sinuous (5)	discommoded (8)

● The Facts

1. Why do scientists working on animals lead chancier lives than other scientists? Why are psychologists particularly vulnerable? Defend, challenge, or qualify the author's comment.

2. Who was "Clever Hans"? What did he contribute to the study of behavioral science?

3. How does the author rank cats in the realm of behavioral science? Where do they stand when judged by the same standards as human beings? Discuss why you think cats are either adored or hated by people. How do you personally respond to cats?

4. What was R. Chauvin's reaction to the ant experiment? How would you interpret the ants' behavior?

5. Why, according to the essay, are bees worth studying? What has been your experience with bees? Which of the two possible reasons proposed for why the euglossine bees carted away the DDT seems more plausible? Explain your answer.

● The Strategies

1. What is the thesis of the essay and where is it first stated? How does the placement of the thesis help guide the reader?

2. What pattern of paragraph development dominates the essay? In what way does this pattern help to support the author's thesis?

3. How would you describe the author's tone? Provide an example or two from the essay to support your description.

4. Has the essay increased your sense of wonder as you contemplate animals and their connection to human beings? Do you think the examples Thomas provided were effective? Explain your reaction. Think of some personal examples you might share with the class.

5. Did Thomas' conclusion seem satisfying? Did he provide enough examples or do you wish he had given several more? Support your answer with reasons.

● The Issues

1. What is your view of scientists who do research on animals? Do you believe that the government should legislate limits to how animals are used in clinical research? What about the kind of research Thomas describes? Is it different since it does not appear to involve cruelty to animals. To bolster your opinion, use the critical thinking skills you have developed so far.

2. Thomas suggests that cats are a constant rebuke to behavioral scientists. What is his reason for this opinion? Defend, challenge, or qualify his view.

3. What elements turn Thomas' essay into more than just pleasant and endearing anecdotes about animals, but into a more serious scientific study? What, if anything of importance, have you learned? Would you quote Thomas as an authority in behavioral science? Why or why not?

4. If you compare the writing in this essay with the writing of articles published in journals such as *American Psychologist, Contemporary Psychology, Behavioral Neuroscience, Journal of Personality and Social Psychology, or Journal of Experimental Psychology,* you will notice that the styles of writing are quite different one from the other. What do you think accounts for the difference? Is the difference necessary? Explain your answer.

5. What is the most amazing encounter you have ever had with an animal? How did this encounter affect your attitude about the essential intelligence of animals and their connection to human beings?

● Suggestions for Writing

1. If you or someone you know has a pet that seems able to perform amazing feats, describe this ability by providing appropriate examples to demonstrate your point.

2. After doing some research on the subject, describe some historical or mythological animal that revealed human or even superhuman characteristics. Describe the animal and provide a vivid account of the animal's ability. Consider, for example, Pegasus in Greek mythology or the real Swiss Saint Bernard rescue dogs.

"Mirror, Mirror, on the Wall . . ."

JOHN LEO

Rhetorical Thumbnail

Purpose: to acquaint us with standards of beauty

Audience: educated magazine readers

Language: informal journalistic English

Strategy: to establish through the use of examples from history that beauty is a relative concept

John Leo (b. 1935), associate editor of *Time,* was born in Hoboken, New Jersey, and educated at the University of Toronto. He has been associated with *Commonweal, The New York Times,* the *Village Voice,* and more recently as editor and columnist for *U.S. News and World Report.*

In the following brief essay from Time, *Leo discusses and gives examples of the relativity of beauty. He amuses us with examples that show how the standards of beauty have changed over the years.*

● ● ●

1   The poet may insist that beauty is in the eye of the beholder; the historian might argue that societies create the image of female perfection that they want. There has always been plenty of evidence to support both views. Martin Luther thought long, beautiful hair was essential. Edmund Burke recommended delicate, fragile women. Goethe insisted on "the proper breadth of the pelvis and the necessary fullness of the breasts." Hottentot men look for sharply projecting buttocks. Rubens favored a full posterior, and Papuans require a big nose. The Mangaians of Polynesia care nothing of fat or thin and never seem to notice face, breasts or buttocks. To the tribesmen, the only standard of sexiness is well-shaped female genitals.

2   An anthropologized world now knows that notions of what is most attractive do vary with each age and culture. One era's flower is another's frump. Primitive man, understandably concerned with fertility, idealized ample women. One of the earliest surviving sculptures, the Stone Age Venus of Willendorf, depicts a squat woman whose vital statistics—in inches—would amount to 96–89–96. This adipose standard stubbornly recurs in later eras. A 14th-century treatise on beauty calls for "narrow shoulders, small breasts, large belly, broad hips, fat thighs, short legs and a small head." Some Oriental cultures today are turned on by what Simone de Beauvoir calls the "unnecessary, gratuitous blooming" of wrap-around fat.

3   The Greeks were so concerned with working out precise proportions for beauty that the sculptor Praxiteles insisted that the female navel be exactly midway between the breasts and genitals. The dark-haired Greeks considered fair-haired women exotic, perhaps the start of the notion that blondes have more fun. They also offered early evidence of the rewards that go to magnificent mammaries. When Phryne, Praxiteles' famous model and mistress, was on trial for treason, the orator defending her pulled aside her veil, baring her legendary breasts. The awed judges acquitted her on the spot.

4   Romans favored more independent, articulate women than the Greeks. Still, there were limits. Juvenal complains of ladies who "discourse on poets and poetry, comparing Vergil with Homer . . . Wives shouldn't read all the classics—there ought to be some things women don't understand."

5   In ancient Egypt, women spent hours primping: fixing hair, applying lipstick, eye shadow and fingernail polish, grinding away body and genital hair with pumice stones. It worked: Nefertiti could make the cover of *Vogue* any month she wanted. For Cleopatra, the most famous bombshell of the ancient world, eroticism was plain hard work. Not a natural beauty, she labored diligently to learn coquettishness and flattery and reportedly polished her amatory techniques by practicing on slaves.

6   If Cleopatra had to work so hard at being desirable, can the average woman do less? Apparently not. In the long history of images of beauty, one staple is the male tendency to spot new flaws in women, and the female tendency to work and suffer to remedy them. In the Middle Ages, large women rubbed themselves with cow dung dissolved in wine. When whiter skin was demanded, women applied leeches to take the red out. Breasts have been strapped down,

cantilevered up, pushed together or apart, oiled and siliconed and, in 16th-century Venice, fitted with wool or hair padding for a sexy "duck breast" look, curving from bodice to groin. In the long run, argues feminist Elizabeth Gould Davis, flat-chested women are evolutionary losers. Says she: "The female of the species owes her modern mammary magnificence to male sexual preference."

7   Still, a well-endowed woman can suddenly find herself out of favor when cultural winds change. The flapper era in America is one example. So is Europe's Romantic Age, which favored the wan, cadaverous look. In the 1820s, women sometimes drank vinegar or stayed up all night to look pale and interesting. Fragility was all. Wrote Keats: "God! she is like a milkwhite lamb that bleats / For man's protection."

8   Victorians took this ideal of the shy, clinging vine, decorously desexed it, and assigned it to the wife. According to one well-known Victorian doctor, it was a "vile aspersion" to suggest that women were capable of sexual impulses. Inevitably that straitlaced era controlled women's shapes by severe compression of the waistline, without accenting breasts or hips.

9   Those womanly curves reasserted themselves at the turn of the century. During the hourglass craze, Lillie Langtry seemed perfection incarnate at 38–18–38. Since then, the ideal woman in Western culture has gradually slimmed down. Psyche, the White Rock girl,[1] was 5 ft. 4 in. tall and weighed in at a hippy 140 lbs. when she first appeared on beverage bottles in 1893. Now, sans cellulite, she is 4 in. taller and 22 lbs. lighter.

10   In psychological terms, the current slim-hipped look amounts to a rebellion against male domination: waist-trimming corsets are associated with male control of the female body, and narrow hips with a reluctance to bear children. Says Madge Garland, a former editor of *British Vogue*: "The natural shape of the female body has not been revealed and free as it is today for 1,500 years." W. H. Auden once complained that for most of Western history, the sexy beautiful women have seemed "fictionalized," set apart from real life. In the age of the natural look, a beauty now has to seem as though she just strolled in from the beach at Malibu. Like Cheryl Tiegs.

● Vocabulary

frump (2)	coquettishness (5)	cellulite (9)
adipose (2)	cantilevered (6)	incarnate (9)
gratuitous (2)	aspersion (8)	
amatory (5)	decorously (8)	

● The Facts

1. What kinds of women did primitive man idealize?
2. What was the Greeks' standard of beauty?

---

[1]Psyche has been the emblem of White Rock–brand soft drinks and mixes since the nineteenth century.—ED.

3. According to feminist Elizabeth Gould Davis, to what do women owe their "modern mammary magnificence"?

4. What kind of feminine beauty was favored during Europe's Romantic Age?

5. What does the modern, slim-hipped look signify in psychological terms?

The Strategies

1. What notion do most of the examples in this essay support? Where is this notion stated?

2. Much of the detail about beauty is given not in full-blown examples, but in sketchy references to the opinions of famous people. What are such references called?

3. In paragraph 3, what does the anecdote about Phryne exemplify?

4. The author quotes Goethe, Simone de Beauvoir, Juvenal, Elizabeth Gould Davis, John Keats, Madge Garland, and W. H. Auden. What effect does all this opinion sampling have on the tone of the essay?

5. In paragraph 6, the author writes: "In the long history of images of beauty, one staple is the male tendency to spot new flaws in women, and the female tendency to work and suffer to remedy them." How does the author proceed to support and document this view?

The Issues

1. Paragraph 2 alludes to an "anthropologized world." How would you define this world? What significance lies in this label?

2. What, for you, constitutes a beautiful female? A beautiful male? Refer to specific examples from history, from the current scene, or from your personal encounters.

3. How do you feel about the present emphasis on an athletic female body? Is it justified, or does it diminish some other innately feminine characteristic? Give reasons for your answer.

4. Even if you agree with the poet that beauty is in the eye of the beholder, argue that true beauty must follow certain standards. Suggest what these standards might be when applied to, say, a painting or a sculpture.

5. In paragraph 8, the author describes the typical Victorian wife as a woman who must never be perceived as having sexual impulses. How does the typical Victorian wife compare with the women we observe in the movies or on TV today? Give examples to support your view.

Suggestions for Writing

1. Write an essay that specifies your idea of human beauty. Give convincing examples to illustrate your point.

2. Write an essay in which you argue that human beauty is in the eye of the beholder.

ISSUE FOR CRITICAL THINKING AND DEBATE: DRUGS AND SOCIETY

Ours is a society awash in a transcontinental tidal surge of drugs. We awake to the kick of caffeine, soothe our nerves with tobacco, ease our tension headaches with aspirin, wind down the day with alcohol, and swallow an antihistamine to help us sleep—all perfectly legal, respectable, and even expected.

But there is a dark side to this epidemic of drug use. Over 400,000 of us perish annually from the effects of tobacco. Some 23 million of us regularly take illegal drugs, ranging from marijuana to cocaine to heroin. A causal relationship exists between drug addiction and criminal wrongdoing. Here are some current statistics to ponder: According to the U.S. Department of Justice (Bureau of Justice Statistics), currently 600,000 people in the United States are addicted to heroin, a considerable increase since the notorious drug era of the 1980s. The annual number of Marijuana initiates has reached 2.3 million. Methamphetamine use is increasing and so are the so-called "club drugs" such as Ketamine, Quaaludes, Xanax, MDMa, and LSD, used by glamorous young adults who become models for ordinary youngsters to imitate.

One of the most alarming trends is the use of illegal tobacco and alcohol among youth. Children who use these substances increase their chances of lifelong dependency problems and catastrophic health crises. Every day, 3,000 children begin smoking cigarettes regularly. As a result, one third of these youngsters will have their lives shortened. The Substance Abuse and Mental Health Services Administration has declared that half of all high school students use illicit drugs by the time they graduate. What do these statistics portend about the future? Here is the grim forecast: 1. Maternal drug abuse will contribute to birth defects. 2. Chronic drug abuse will lead to sexually transmitted diseases. 3. Underage use of tobacco and alcohol will lead to premature deaths. 4. Drug use will add to the burdens of the work place by decreasing productivity.

Then there are the nightmares faced by our correctional facilities. The largest percentage of arrests (75.1%) are for drug-related causes. Drug offenders continue to crowd our nation's jails and prisons. The increase in drug offenders accounts for nearly three-fourths of the growth in federal prison inmates. Drug trafficking is also on the increase, generating violent crimes that have been well documented in newspaper headlines exposing the terror inflicted by drug cartels from Mexico, Columbia, and Guatemala. Unfortunately, illegal drugs remain readily available--often through gangs like the Crips, Bloods, and Dominican or Jamaican "posses." In sum, the problem has not disappeared, but is spreading.

The political response to the spreading tide of illegal drugs has been predictable: Conservatives urge heightened efforts at the interdiction of illegal drugs, mandatory drug testing, stiffer prison terms for pushers, and a crackdown on recreational users. Liberals and libertarians advocate an agenda of education and rehabilitation and, probably the most controversial measure of all, the legalization of drug use.

To begin the discussion, we present an article excerpted from *Time* magazine and written by their senior writer, Michael D. Lemonick, about the dangers of addiction and the difficulty addicts face when they try to fight the uncontrollable craving for whatever opens the floodgates to their pleasure center.

Making the case for legalization, and doing so in his usual caustic style, is the novelist and writer Gore Vidal. His argument is not new, but it is refreshingly presented. Prohibition increases the allure of drugs, argues Vidal, and it is only because our society is so devoted to the concepts of sin and punishment that we reject out of hand this simple solution.

England and a few other European countries have experimented with the legalization of drugs, and with some success, but no society as complex and variegated as ours has ever attempted to legalize drugs on such a vast scale as would be involved if the liberals were to win this argument. The consequences of legalization might ultimately be anyone's guess. Given the strong moral strain that permeates American political thinking, however, we think Vidal is right, and that unless drug abuse becomes incalculably worse than it is today, legalization will likely remain a topic for academic debate rather than be adopted as national policy by any present or future administration.

© David Turnley/CORBIS

● When is therapy the proper help for addiction?

From the pages of

How We Get Addicted

MICHAEL D. LEMONICK

Michael D. Lemonick is the senior writer at Climate Central, a nonpartisan organization whose mission is to communicate climate science to the public. Prior to joining Climate Central, he was a science writer at *Time* magazine in New York and before that, he was a senior editor at *Discover* magazine. After graduating from Harvard with a degree in economics, he studied journalism at Columbia University. His passion for science led him to write numerous articles about diverse topics, such as ocean exploration, astrophysics, Biblical archaeology, brain research, and Egyptology. His first love, however, has remained astronomy, as revealed by the books he has written. Among his best-known titles are these: *The Light at the Edge of the Universe* (1993), *Other Worlds* (1999), *Echo of Big Bang* (2005), and *The Georgian Star* (2009), an account of how William and Caroline Herschel revolutionized our understanding of the cosmos. Lemonick lives in New Jersey with his wife, the photographer Eileen Hohmuth-Lemonick, and daughter Hannah.

● ● ●

1   I was driving up the Massachusetts Turnpike one evening last February when I knocked over a bottle of water. I grabbed for it, swerved inadvertently—and a few seconds later found myself blinking into the flashlight beam of a state trooper. "How much have you had to drink tonight, sir?" he demanded. Before I could help myself, I blurted out an answer that was surely a new one to him. "I haven't had a drink," I said indignantly, "since 1981."

2   It was both perfectly true and very pertinent to the trip I was making. By the time I reached my late 20s, I'd poured down as much alcohol as normal people consume in a lifetime and plenty of drugs—mostly pot—as well. I was, by any reasonable measure, an active alcoholic. Fortunately, with a lot of help, I was able to stop. And now I was on my way to McLean Hospital in Belmont, Mass., to have my brain scanned in a functional magnetic-resonance imager (fMRI). The idea was to see what the inside of my head looked like after more than a quarter-century on the wagon.

3   Back when I stopped drinking, such an experiment would have been unimaginable. At the time, the medical establishment had come to accept the idea that alcoholism was a disease rather than a moral failing; the American Medical Association (AMA) had said so in 1950. But while it had all the hallmarks of other diseases, including specific symptoms and a predictable course, leading to disability or even death, alcoholism was different. Its physical basis was a complete mystery—and since nobody forced alcoholics to drink, it was still seen, no matter what the AMA said, as somehow voluntary. Treatment

consisted mostly of talk therapy, maybe some vitamins and usually a strong recommendation to join Alcoholics Anonymous. Although it's a totally nonprofessional organization, founded in 1935 by an ex-drunk and an active drinker, AA has managed to get millions of people off the bottle, using group support and a program of accumulated folk wisdom.

4   While AA is astonishingly effective for some people, it doesn't work for everyone; studies suggest it succeeds about 20% of the time, and other forms of treatment, including various types of behavioral therapy, do no better. The rate is much the same with drug addiction, which experts see as the same disorder triggered by a different chemical. "The sad part is that if you look at where addiction treatment was 10 years ago, it hasn't gotten much better," says Dr. Martin Paulus, a professor of psychiatry at the University of California at San Diego. "You have a better chance to do well after many types of cancer than you have of recovering from methamphetamine dependence."

5   That could all be about to change. During those same 10 years, researchers have made extraordinary progress in understanding the physical basis of addiction. They know now, for example, that the 20% success rate can shoot up to 40% if treatment is ongoing (very much the AA model, which is most effective when members continue to attend meetings long after their last drink). Armed with an array of increasingly sophisticated technology, including fMRIs and PET scans, investigators have begun to figure out exactly what goes wrong in the brain of an addict--which neurotransmitting chemicals are out of balance and what regions of the brain are affected. They are developing a more detailed understanding of how deeply and completely addiction can affect the brain, by hijacking memory-making processes and by exploiting emotions. Using that knowledge, they've begun to design new drugs that are showing promise in cutting off the craving that drives an addict irresistibly toward relapse--the greatest risk facing even the most dedicated abstainer.

6   "Addictions," says Joseph Frascella, director of the division of clinical neuroscience at the National Institute on Drug Abuse (NIDA), "are repetitive behaviors in the face of negative consequences, the desire to continue something you know is bad for you."

7   Addiction is such a harmful behavior, in fact, that evolution should have long ago weeded it out of the population: if it's hard to drive safely under the influence, imagine trying to run from a saber-toothed tiger or catch a squirrel for lunch. And yet, says Dr. Nora Volkow, director of NIDA and a pioneer in the use of imaging to understand addiction, "the use of drugs has been recorded since the beginning of civilization. Humans in my view will always want to experiment with things to make them feel good."

8   That's because drugs of abuse co-opt the very brain functions that allowed our distant ancestors to survive in a hostile world. Our minds are programmed to pay extra attention to what neurologists call salience—that is, special relevance. Threats, for example, are highly salient, which is why we instinctively try to get away from them. But so are food and sex because they help the individual and the species survive. Drugs of abuse capitalize on this ready-made programming. When exposed to drugs, our memory systems, reward circuits, decision-making skills and conditioning kick in—salience in overdrive—to

create an all consuming pattern of uncontrollable craving. "Some people have a genetic predisposition to addiction," says Volkow. "But because it involves these basic brain functions, everyone will become an addict if sufficiently exposed to drugs or alcohol."

9   That can go for nonchemical addictions as well. Behaviors, from gambling to shopping to sex, may start out as habits but slide into addictions. Sometimes there might be a behavior-specific root of the problem. Volkow's research group, for example, has shown that pathologically obese people who are compulsive eaters exhibit hyperactivity in the areas of the brain that process food stimuli—including the mouth, lips and tongue. For them, activating these regions is like opening the floodgates to the pleasure center. Almost anything deeply enjoyable can turn into an addiction, though.

10   Of course, not everyone becomes an addict. That's because we have other, more analytical regions that can evaluate consequences and override mere pleasure seeking. Brain imaging is showing exactly how that happens. Paulus, for example, looked at methamphetamine addicts enrolled in a VA hospital's intensive four-week rehabilitation program. Those who were more likely to relapse in the first year after completing the program were also less able to complete tasks involving cognitive skills and less able to adjust to new rules quickly. This suggested that those patients might also be less adept at using analytical areas of the brain while performing decision-making tasks. Sure enough, brain scans showed that there were reduced levels of activation in the prefrontal cortex, where rational thought can override impulsive behavior. It's impossible to say if the drugs might have damaged these abilities in the relapsers—an effect rather than a cause of the chemical abuse—but the fact that the cognitive deficit existed in only some of the meth users suggests that there was something innate that was unique to them. To his surprise, Paulus found that 80% to 90% of the time, he could accurately predict who would relapse within a year simply by examining the scans.

11   Another area of focus for researchers involves the brain's reward system, powered largely by the neurotransmitter dopamine. Investigators are looking specifically at the family of dopamine receptors that populate nerve cells and bind to the compound. The hope is that if you can dampen the effect of the brain chemical that carries the pleasurable signal, you can loosen the drug's hold.

12   One particular group of dopamine receptors, for example, called D3, seems to multiply in the presence of cocaine, methamphetamine and nicotine, making it possible for more of the drug to enter and activate nerve cells. "Receptor density is thought to be an amplifier," says Frank Vocci, director of pharmacotherapies at NIDA. "[Chemically] blocking D3 interrupts an awful lot of the drugs' effects. It is probably the hottest target in modulating the reward system."

13   But just as there are two ways to stop a speeding car—by easing off the gas or hitting the brake pedal—there are two different possibilities for muting addiction. If dopamine receptors are the gas, the brain's own inhibitory systems act as the brakes. In addicts, this natural damping circuit, called GABA

(gamma-aminobutyric acid), appears to be faulty. Without a proper chemical check on excitatory messages set off by drugs, the brain never appreciates that it's been satiated.

14   As it turns out, vigabatrin, an antiepilepsy treatment that is marketed in 60 countries (but not yet in the U.S.), is an effective GABA booster. In epileptics, vigabatrin suppresses overactivated motor neurons that cause muscles to contract and go into spasm. Hoping that enhancing GABA in the brains of addicts could help them control their drug cravings, two biotech companies in the U.S., Ovation Pharmaceuticals and Catalyst Pharmaceuticals, are studying the drug's effect on methamphetamine and cocaine use. So far, in animals, vigabatrin prevents the breakdown of GABA so that more of the inhibitory compound can be stored in whole form in nerve cells. That way, more of it could be released when those cells are activated by a hit from a drug. Says Vocci, optimistically: "If it works, it will probably work on all addictions."

15   Another fundamental target for addiction treatments is the stress network. Animal studies have long shown that stress can increase the desire for drugs. In rats trained to self-administer a substance, stressors such as a new environment, an unfamiliar cage mate or a change in daily routine push the animals to depend on the substance even more.

16   Among higher creatures like us, stress can also alter the way the brain thinks, particularly the way it contemplates the consequences of actions. Recall the last time you found yourself in a stressful situation—when you were scared, nervous or threatened. Your brain tuned out everything besides whatever it was that was frightening you—the familiar fight-or-flight mode. "The part of the prefrontal cortex that is involved in deliberative cognition is shut down by stress," says Vocci. "It's supposed to be, but it's even more inhibited in substance abusers." A less responsive prefrontal cortex sets up addicts to be more impulsive as well.

17   Hormones—of the male-female kind—may play a role in how people become addicted as well. Studies have shown, for instance, that women may be more vulnerable to cravings for nicotine during the latter part of the menstrual cycle, when the egg emerges from the follicle and the hormones progesterone and estrogen are released. "The reward systems of the brain have different sensitivities at different points in the cycle," notes Volkow. "There is way greater craving during the later phase."

18   That led researchers to wonder about other biological differences in the way men and women become addicted and, significantly, respond to treatments. Alcohol dependence is one very promising area. For years, researchers had documented the way female alcoholics tend to progress more rapidly to alcoholism than men. This telescoping effect, they now know, has a lot to do with the way women metabolize alcohol. Females are endowed with less alcohol dehydrogenase—the first enzyme in the stomach lining that starts to break down the ethanol in liquor—and less total body water than men. Together with estrogen, these factors have a net concentrating effect on the alcohol in the blood, giving women a more intense hit with each drink. The pleasure from that extreme high may be enough for some women to feel satisfied and therefore

drink less. For others, the intense intoxication is so enjoyable that they try to duplicate the experience over and over.

19   But it's the brain, not the gut, that continues to get most of the attention, and one of the biggest reasons is technology. It was in 1985 that Volkow first began using PET scans to record trademark characteristics in the brains and nerve cells of chronic drug abusers, including blood flow, dopamine levels and glucose metabolism--a measure of how much energy is being used and where (and therefore a stand-in for figuring out which cells are at work). After the subjects had been abstinent a year, Volkow rescanned their brains and found that they had begun to return to their predrug state. Good news, certainly, but only as far as it goes.

20   "The changes induced by addiction do not just involve one system," says Volkow. "There are some areas in which the changes persist even after two years." One area of delayed rebound involves learning. Somehow in methamphetamine abusers, the ability to learn some new things remained affected after 14 months of abstinence. "Does treatment push the brain back to normal," asks NIDA's Frascella, "or does it push it back in different ways?"

21   If the kind of damage that lingers in an addict's learning abilities also hangs on in behavioral areas, this could explain why rehabilitation programs that rely on cognitive therapy—teaching new ways to think about the need for a substance and the consequences of using it—may not always be effective, especially in the first weeks and months after getting clean. "Therapy is a learning process," notes Vocci. "We are trying to get [addicts] to change cognition and behavior at a time when they are least able to do so."

22   One important discovery: evidence is building to support the 90-day rehabilitation model, which was stumbled upon by AA (new members are advised to attend a meeting a day for the first 90 days) and is the duration of a typical stint in a drug-treatment program. It turns out that this is just about how long it takes for the brain to reset itself and shake off the immediate influence of a drug. Researchers at Yale University have documented what they call the sleeper effect--a gradual re-engaging of proper decision making and analytical functions in the brain's prefrontal cortex--after an addict has abstained for at least 90 days.

23   This work has led to research on cognitive enhancers, or compounds that may amplify connections in the prefrontal cortex to speed up the natural reversal. Such enhancement would give the higher regions of the brain a fighting chance against the amygdala, a more basal region that plays a role in priming the dopamine-reward system when certain cues suggest imminent pleasure—anything from the sight of white powder that looks like cocaine to spending time with friends you used to drink with. It's that conditioned reflex—identical to the one that caused Ivan Pavlov's famed dog to salivate at the ringing of a bell after it learned to associate the sound with food—that unleashes a craving. And it's that phenomenon that was the purpose of my brain scans at McLean, one of the world's premier centers for addiction research.

24   In my heyday, I would often drink even when I knew it was a terrible idea—and the urge was hardest to resist when I was with my drinking buddies, hearing the clink of glasses and bottles, seeing others imbibe and smelling the

aroma of wine or beer. The researchers at McLean have invented a machine that wafts such odors directly into the nostrils of a subject undergoing an fMRI scan in order to see how the brain reacts. The reward circuitry in the brain of a newly recovering alcoholic should light up like a Christmas tree when stimulated by one of these alluring smells.

25   I chose dark beer, my absolute favorite, from their impressive stock. But I haven't gotten high for more than a quarter-century; it was an open question whether I would react that way. So after an interview with a staff psychiatrist to make sure I would be able to handle it if I experienced a craving, I was fitted with a tube that carried beer aroma from a vaporizer into my nose. I was then slid into the machine to inhale that still familiar odor while the fMRI did its work.

26   Even if the smells triggered a strong desire to drink, I had long since learned ways to talk myself out of it—or find someone to help me do so. Like the 90-day drying-out period that turns out to parallel the brain's recovery cycle, such a strategy is in line with other new theories of addiction. Scientists say extinguishing urges is not a matter of getting the feelings to fade but of helping the addict learn a new form of conditioning, one that allows the brain's cognitive power to shout down the amygdala and other lower regions. "What has to happen for that cue to extinguish is not for the amygdala to become weaker but for the frontal cortex to become stronger," says Vocci.

27   While such relearning has not been studied formally in humans, Vocci believes it will work, on the basis of studies involving, of all things, phobias. It turns out that phobias and drugs exploit the same struggle between high and low circuits in the brain. People placed in a virtual-reality glass elevator and treated with the antibiotic D-cycloserine were better able to overcome their fear of heights than those without benefit of the drug. Says Vocci: "I never thought we would have drugs that affect cognition in such a specific way."

28   Such surprises have even allowed experts to speculate whether addiction can ever be cured. That notion goes firmly against current beliefs. A rehabilitated addict is always in recovery because cured suggests that resuming drinking or smoking or shooting up is a safe possibility—whose downside could be devastating. But there are hints that a cure might not in principle be impossible. A recent study showed that tobacco smokers who suffered a stroke that damaged the insula (a region of the brain involved in emotional, gut-instinct perceptions) no longer felt a desire for nicotine.

29   That's exciting, but because the insula is so critical to other brain functions—perceiving danger, anticipating threats—damaging this area isn't something you would ever want to do intentionally. With so many of the brain's systems entangled with one another, it could prove impossible to adjust just one without throwing the others into imbalance.

30   Nevertheless, says Volkow, "addiction is a medical condition. We have to recognize that medications can reverse the pathology of the disease. We have to force ourselves to think about a cure because if we don't, it will never happen." Still, she is quick to admit that just contemplating new ideas doesn't make them so. The brain functions that addiction commandeers may simply be so complex that sufferers, as 12-step recovery programs have emphasized for

decades, never lose their vulnerability to their drug of choice, no matter how healthy their brains might eventually look.

31   I'm probably a case in point. My brain barely lit up in response to the smell of beer inside the fMRI at McLean. "This is actually valuable information for you as an individual," said Scott Lukas, director of the hospital's behavioral psychopharmacology research laboratory and a professor at Harvard Medical School who ran the tests. "It means that your brain's sensitivity to beer cues has long passed."

32   That's in keeping with my real-world experience; if someone has a beer at dinner, I don't feel a compulsion to leap across the table and grab it or even to order one for myself. Does that mean I'm cured? Maybe. But it may also mean simply that it would take a much stronger trigger for me to fall prey to addiction again—like, for example, downing a glass of beer. But the last thing I intend to do is put it to the test. I've seen too many others try it—with horrifying results.

● Vocabulary

inadvertently (1)   exploiting (5)   imaging (7)
pertinent (2)   abstainer (5)   co-opt (8)

● The Facts

1. Why is the author able to bring a special kind of authority to the subject of addiction? How soon is the reader aware of this authority?

2. What was the purpose of the author's trip up the Massachusetts Turnpike? Why do you think the author never reveals the results of his trip? Do you wish he had? Explain your answer.

3. Back in the 1980s how was alcoholism defined? How had it been defined in the past? What difference does the definition make?

4. What major problem exists in categorizing alcoholism as a disease? What, if anything, is being done about solving this problem?

5. What, according to the essay, is at the heart of all addictions? Explain the answer in your own words.

● The Strategies

1. How does the title of the essay relate to its content? Is the relationship clear? What questions, if any, remained in your mind after reading to the end of the essay?

2. What technique does the author use to captivate your attention right from the start of his essay? What other technique might also work well?

3. What is the purpose of the opening line of paragraph 5? How important is it in relationship to what the author has written so far? What feeling should it elicit from the reader?

4. How does Lemonick keep his essay from becoming a sordid tale about the self-destructive paths followed by addicts? How convincing is his approach? Would you have preferred more emotion or sentiment? Why or why not?

5. What is the purpose of the final paragraph? Evaluate this conclusion. What critical thinking does it require?

● The Issues

1. What is the difference between an "active alcoholic" (see paragraph 2) and any other kind of alcoholic? Explain the difference by using appropriate examples.

2. How does Joseph Frascella define addiction? Do you agree with his definition? What other definition explains the term? How important is it to know what addiction means? Give reasons for your answer.

3. What is the author's train of thought when he explains the irony that the evolutionary process has not been able to weed out addicts? Catalog the process leading to his conclusion. Do you agree? Explain your response.

4. What role does salience play in the process of addiction? Try to explain it in your own words. How reliable do you consider the role of salience as connected with addiction? What evidence does the author offer for the reliability of this term?

5. Most of us have had some experience—directly or indirectly—with addiction. From what you understand about addiction, how serious a problem do you consider it in today's society? What do you think can be done to improve or solve this social predicament? Offer some concrete steps.

● Suggestions for Writing

1. Write an essay either defending or arguing against the proposal that drug addicts be sent to rehabilitation centers rather than to prison or jail. Begin with a clear thesis and support your points with evidence from valid experience or expert testimony.

2. Write an essay in which you describe and explain the damage alcohol or drugs have inflicted on our culture. Conclude with an appeal for help to cure the problem.

Drugs

GORE VIDAL

Gore Vidal (b. 1925), is a writer of novels, plays, short stories, book reviews, and essays. A few of his major novels include *The City and the Pillar* (1948), *Julian* (1964), *Myra Breckenridge* (1968), *1876* (1976), *Burr* (1980), *Creation* (1981), and *Lincoln* (1984).

• • •

1   It is possible to stop most drug addiction in the United States within a very short time. Simply make all drugs available and sell them at cost. Label each drug with a precise description of what effect—good and bad—the drug will have on the taker. This will require heroic honesty. Don't say that marijuana is addictive or dangerous when it is neither, as millions of people know—unlike "speed," which kills most unpleasantly, or heroin, which is addictive and difficult to kick.

2   For the record, I have tried—once—almost every drug and liked none, disproving the popular Fu Manchu theory that a single whiff of opium will enslave the mind. Nevertheless many drugs are bad for certain people to take and they should be told why in a sensible way.

3   Along with exhortation and warning, it might be good for our citizens to recall (or learn for the first time) that the United States was the creation of men who believed that each man has the right to do what he wants with his own life as long as he does not interfere with his neighbor's pursuit of happiness (that his neighbor's idea of happiness is persecuting others does confuse matters a bit).

4   This is a startling notion to the current generation of Americans. They reflect a system of public education which has made the Bill of Rights, literally, unacceptable to a majority of high school graduates (see the annual Purdue reports) who now form the "silent majority"—a phrase which that underestimated wit Richard Nixon took from Homer who used it to describe the dead.

5   Now one can hear the warning rumble begin: if everyone is allowed to take drugs everyone will and the GNP will decrease, the Commies will stop us from making everyone free, and we shall end up a race of Zombies, passively murmuring "groovie" to one another. Alarming thought. Yet it seems most unlikely that any reasonably sane person will become a drug addict if he knows in advance what addiction is going to be like.

6   Is everyone reasonably sane? No. Some people will always become drug addicts just as some people will always become alcoholics, and it is just too bad. Every man, however, has the power (and should have the legal right) to kill himself if he chooses. But since most men don't, they won't be mainliners either. Nevertheless, forbidding people things they like or think they might enjoy only makes them want those things all the more. This psychological insight is, for some mysterious reason, perennially denied our governors.

7   It is a lucky thing for the American moralist that our country has always existed in a kind of time-vacuum: we have no public memory of anything that happened before last Tuesday. No one in Washington today recalls what happened during the years alcohol was forbidden to the people by a Congress that thought it had a divine mission to stamp out Demon Rum—launching, in the process, the greatest crime wave in the country's history, causing thousands of deaths from bad alcohol, and creating a general (and persisting) contempt among the citizenry for the laws of the United States.

8   The same thing is happening today. But the government has learned nothing from past attempts at prohibition, not to mention repression.

9   Last year when the supply of Mexican marijuana was slightly curtailed by the Feds, the pushers got the kids hooked on heroin and deaths increased dramatically, particularly in New York. Whose fault? Evil men like the Mafiosi? Permissive Dr. Spock? Wild-eyed Dr. Leary? No.

10   The Government of the United States was responsible for those deaths. The bureaucratic machine has a vested interest in playing cops and robbers. Both the Bureau of Narcotics and the Mafia want strong laws against the sale and use of drugs because if drugs are sold at cost there would be no money in it for anyone.

11   If there was no money in it for the Mafia, there would be no friendly playground pushers, and addicts would not commit crimes to pay for the next fix. Finally, if there was no money in it, the Bureau of Narcotics would wither away, something they are not about to do without a struggle.

12   Will anything sensible be done? Of course not. The American people are as devoted to the idea of sin and its punishment as they are to making money—and fighting drugs is nearly as big a business as pushing them. Since the combination of sin and money is irresistible (particularly to the professional politician), the situation will only grow worse.

● Vocabulary

exhortation (3)   perennially (6)   repression (8)

● The Facts

1. What specific proposal does Vidal make for selling drugs?
2. According to Vidal, to whom is the Bill of Rights unacceptable?
3. What lesson about repression does Vidal say the government has largely forgotten?
4. Which two groups, according to Vidal, have a vested interest in prolonging the ban against drugs?
5. What dismal prophecy does Vidal make at the conclusion of his argument? How has his prophecy stood the test of time?

● The Strategies

1. Vidal opens his argument with a blunt declaration of his position and without any softening up of the opposition with statistics or background material. What do you think the reaction to this opening would be if this were an essay written by a student? Why?
2. Vidal admits to having used almost every drug and having liked none. How does this frank admission affect his argument?
3. What one word in paragraph 5 dates this essay as from another era?
4. What is the rhetorical purpose of paragraphs 5 and 6?
5. Aside from its blunt tone, what characteristic of this essay would make it unsuitable as a student submission in a writing class?

The Issues

1. What do you think is the likely effect of a governmental attitude that says all drugs are bad for you?

2. What do you think would happen if all drugs were legalized?

3. Vidal says that "forbidding people things they like or think they might enjoy only makes them want those things all the more." Do you think this a truth or a cliché? Why?

4. If the government of the United States sprays marijuana crops with a herbicide that then poisons an unknowing user, who is morally responsible?

5. Do you agree with Vidal that the American people are hooked on the idea of sin and punishment? Why or why not?

Suggestions for Writing

1. Write an essay relating any encounter you have had with, or have heard some-one else tell about, drugs.

2. Write an essay in which you use critical thinking skills to attack or defend Vidal's opinions concerning the legalization of drugs.

Ed Kashi/CORBIS

Will one wrong choice easily ruin a life?

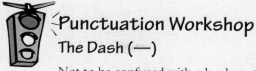

Punctuation Workshop
The Dash (—)

Not to be confused with a hyphen, the dash is a flexible punctuation mark.

1. **Use a dash to announce an abrupt break or change in thought:**

    All of us need redemption—or is it acceptance?

    Light reveals the world to us—a world often tarnished.

    Let me tell you about kayaking—no, I mean canoeing.

2. **Use a dash to set off parenthetical elements you want to emphasize.**

    The new Pope—with the help of the Vatican—repeatedly emphasizes religious liberty.

    Strong personal feelings—love, admiration, fear—are often easier to admit in a letter rather than face to face.

3. **Use a dash to emphasize a list.**

    Tortured, undecided, fearful—my father embodied all of these character traits.

    Do not overuse dashes as easy substitutes for commas, periods, or other punctuation marks.

Linda Kunze
Glendale Community College
Drug Use: The Continuing Epidemic

Brakes squeal as the late-model Mercury Sable speeds down the street. Onlookers stare in amazement while the driver recklessly maneuvers in and out of traffic. Suddenly, the car jumps the curb and slams head on into a power pole. Moments later, police arrive to find the young female driver dead behind the steering wheel. In her hand she clutches the six-tenths of a gram of rock cocaine she had just purchased.

No, this scenario is not the opening scene from the latest big-screen action adventure. Sadly, it is a true story and just another example of the death and destruction caused by the continued popularity and use of illicit drugs. The National Institute of Drug Addiction reports that drug users function at 67 percent of their capacity and have three times as many accidents as those who do not use drugs. With some 6 million Americans using cocaine and over 20 million regularly using marijuana, the problem is widespread and pervasive (*Drugs,* August 8, 2003).

Drug use is far from new. It has been a major problem in America for decades. According to Linda Villarosa, author of *Body & Soul,* heroin and cocaine (two powerfully addictive drugs) were first introduced to consumers back at the turn of the century as ingredients in many over-the-counter medical remedies and soft drinks. In time, when the addictive properties of these narcotics were discovered, heroin, cocaine, and many other harmful drugs were outlawed, but this action came far too late. The overpowering problem of drug abuse and addiction had already begun to spread across America.

Today, almost every adult American is aware of the dangers involved with the use of illegal substances. However, this knowledge has not stopped the rapid increase of drug abuse in this nation. According to the Substance Abuse and Mental Health Services Administration (SAMHSA), an estimated 90.8 million adults 18 or older have used marijuana at least once in their lifetimes. Some 2.1 million persons age 12 or older have used ecstasy at least one time over the past year. Of this number, some 50.3 percent also used between two and four other illegal drugs (U.S. Department of Health and Human Services, June 16, 2005). Drug dependency and addiction are becoming far too common in this country, and it is so tempting to close our eyes and turn our backs to the drug epidemic and just wish it away.

Unfortunately, denying the problems caused by the ever-growing use and abuse of narcotics will not save anyone from the torments of drug abuse and addiction. Although there are no easy answers to this age-old problem, early education seems to be the only truly effective weapon the nation has against this equal-opportunity destroyer known as drug abuse.

For education to be an effective deterrent to drug abuse, it must begin as early as grade school, because according to Schools Without Drugs, a recent pamphlet published by the United States Department of Education, "One out of every six 13-year-olds has used marijuana (at least once) and fifty-four percent of high school seniors have tried some type of illicit drug by the time they are ready to graduate." Children must be taught the dangers of drug abuse and strategies to avoid the use of these substances, prior to junior and senior high school where availability and peer pressure make drug use all too acceptable and easy to fall for.

The news is not all bad, however. In fact, in 2004 drug use declined significantly among eighth-graders from 9.7 percent to 8.4 percent. What makes this statistic heartening is that the decline was across-the-board for all drugs. While abuse will not go away overnight, the numbers show that if we persevere in our attempts at the elimination of illegal drugs, sooner or later we will achieve some positive effects. With this in mind, we must continue to educate everyone, young and old, on the evils of illegal drugs and remain persistent in the fight against their use. We all deserve a drug-free future.

References

Drugs in the workplace. (2003, August 8). Retrieved June 21, 2005, from Florida State University College of Business website: http://www.cob.fsu.edu/jmi/articles/drugs.asp

U.S. Department of Health and Human Services, Substance Abuse and Mental Health Services Administration. (2005, June 16). *Substance abuse and mental health statistics.* Retrieved June 21, 2005, from http://www.drugabusestatistics.samhsa.gov

How I Write

I always sit down and brainstorm—usually alone—before I write anything. In other words, I mull over ideas to see how they might work. I have never been gifted in the art of formal outlines, but I do jot down any idea that can be developed successfully. I like to work at home, with country music playing in the background.

How I Wrote This Essay

I located as many sources on drug abuse as time permitted. I then narrowed my sources down to the amount needed. I wrote one draft and put it away for a week. After the week was up, I reread my paper, changing what I didn't like and improving what I did like. The introduction is always the hardest for me to write. Everything else flows from there.

My Writing Tip

Write what you know and develop your own style. Always give yourself enough time to do the assignment well, because a shoddy assignment leads only to embarrassment.

CHAPTER WRITING ASSIGNMENTS

1. Write an essay in which you provide illustrations from history, physics, biology, psychology, or literature to prove one of the following maxims:
   a. "Every man is the architect of his own fortune." (Seneca)
   b. "The injury of prodigality leads to this, that he who will not economize will have to agonize." (Confucius)
   c. "The foundation of every state is the education of its youth." (Diogenes)
   d. "The pull of gravity exerts far more influence than one might think." (Anonymous)
   e. "Satire is the guerrilla weapon of political warfare." (Horace Greeley)

2. Choose one of the following terms and write an essay giving examples of it.
   a. romance
   b. tyranny
   c. education
   d. humility
   e. prejudice
   f. law

WRITING ASSIGNMENTS FOR A SPECIFIC AUDIENCE

1. Addressing yourself to a group of eighth graders, write an essay about avoiding drugs, using examples from your own experience, that of acquaintances and friends, or of experts.

2. Give examples to back up this statement: "Freedom usually comes at a high price."

IMAGE GALLERY WRITING ASSIGNMENT

Visit pages IG-10–IG-12 of our image gallery and study all three images dealing with drugs. Then choose the image that most appeals to you. Answer the questions and do the writing assignment.

BE CLEAR

First clarity; then, clarity; and last, clarity.

—Anatole France

(When he was asked what he considered the most important ingredient of good writing)

Poetry and metaphysics may contain clusters of mystery or obscurity, but most important ideas can be expressed in clear language. Clarity in writing is like fresh air. Lack of clarity is like dense smoke. Which would you rather breathe?

12

Definition

What Definition Does

Definition means spelling out exactly what a word or phrase means. Articles, essays, and entire books have been written for the sole purpose of defining some abstract or disputed word, term, or phrase. Here is an example of a paragraph that defines *plot*.

> Let us define a plot. We have defined a story as a narrative of events arranged in their time-sequence. A plot is also a narrative of events, the emphasis falling on causality. "The king died and then the queen died," is a story. "The king died, and then the queen died of grief," is a plot. The time sequence is preserved, but the sense of causality overshadows it. Or again: "The queen died, no one knew why, until it was discovered that it was through grief at the death of the king." This is a plot with a mystery in it, a form capable of high development. It suspends the time sequence, it moves as far away from the story as its limitations will allow. Consider the death of the queen. If it is a story we say, "and then?" If it is a plot we ask, "why?" That is the fundamental difference between these two aspects of the novel. A plot cannot be told to a gaping audience of cavemen or to a tyrannical sultan or to their modern descendant the movie-public. They can only be kept awake by "and then-and then." They can only supply curiosity. But a plot demands intelligence and memory also.
>
> —E. M. Forster, "Aspects of the Novel"

In the preceding paragraph, the author not only defines *plot*, he distinguishes it from *story*. When he is done, we get a sense not only of what a plot is, but of what it is not.

When to Use Definition

What do words and phrases mean? Especially for abstract words and phrases, the answer is not always simple. It would be easy enough to explain to a Martian what the word *pencil* means because, as a last resort, we can produce one and wave it under the creature's antennas. But how do we explain the meaning of *love* to this alien? Or the meaning of *human rights?* Or even the meaning of *sovereignty?* None of these words overlays an object or thing to which we can point. Each is an idea or concept and, therefore, definable only by experience or words. The problem is that it is difficult, if not impossible, to find two people who have had such an identical experience with *love* or *human rights* or *sovereignty* that they will instantly agree on a common meaning. This is where words rush in to fill the gap.

Definitions are especially useful, then, if your essay hinges on one of these disputed abstractions. If you were writing an essay on *love,* for example, you could not take it for granted that your reader knows what you mean by that word. You would have to define it. You would have to write your definition in such a way as to make it instantly clear to your particular audience.

How to Use Definition

1. **Begin your definition by saying what the term means.** The traditional method is to first place the term in a general class and then show how it differs from others found there. Known as a *lexical definition,* this is the method of defining used by dictionaries. Here is an example:

   A *library* is a repository for artistic and literary materials.

   Repository is identified as the general class to which *library* belongs, but a specialization in artistic and literary materials distinguishes it from other repositories.

   Here are some more examples of lexical definitions:

   A *motor scooter* is a two-wheeled vehicle with small wheels and a low-powered gasoline engine geared to the rear wheel.

   An *oligarchy* is government by the few, especially a small group of people, such as one family.

   Education is the process of systematic instruction in order to impart *knowledge* or skill.

   Mercy is the kind and compassionate treatment of an offender.

   This is a useful and preliminary way of saying what a term means. First show where the term belongs, then distinguish it from others in that same class. Consciously and unconsciously, we practice this method of defining every day.

2. **Expand your definition, if necessary, with an etymological analysis of the term.** The *etymology* of a word is an explanation of its roots, of what it originally meant, and is often useful in shedding light on how the current meaning of a word evolved. Here is an example of an etymological analysis that helps us to understand the meaning of the word *bible:*

   In the derivation of our word *Bible* lies its definition. It comes from the Greek word *biblion,*[1] which in its plural *biblia* signifies "little books."

---

[1]*Biblos* was the name given to the inner bark of the papyrus, and the word *biblion* meant a papyrus roll, upon which the Bible was originally copied.

The Bible is actually a collection of little books, of every sort and description, written over a long period of time, the very earliest dating, in part at least, as far back as 1200 B.C. or perhaps even earlier; the latest as late as A.D. 150. In its rich and manifold nature it might be called a *library* of Hebrew literature; in its slow production over a period of many centuries it might be termed a survey of that literature to be understood as we understand a *survey* of English literature, in which we become familiar with types of English prose and poetry from Anglo-Saxon times to our own.

—Mary Ellen Chase, "What Is the Bible?"

3. **Clarify your definition by stating what the word is not or does not mean.** For instance, the meaning of *mythology* can be clarified by the statement that it is not merely "a story filled with lies." Likewise, *liberty* can be clarified by showing that it does not simply mean "doing anything one wants at any time." In the following paragraph, the term *empirical medicine* is partially defined by what it is not:

By the practice of empirical medicine we mean that conclusions are reached as a result of experience and observation. Diagnoses are made and cures are found as a result of practical experience. Empirical medicine is not the practice of medicine based on scientific theories or knowledge but on what works. Because of its disregard for scientific knowledge, empirical medicine is often considered charlatanry by academicians.

In essays, the overriding aim of a defining paragraph is usually to clarify the meaning of a certain term. Occasionally, however, the technical or dictionary meaning of a word or phrase may not be what the writer is trying to convey. Indeed, some definitions may be philosophical or poetic, as in the following example:

Home is where you hang your hat. Or home is where you spent your childhood, the good years when waking every morning was an excitement, when the round of the day could always produce something to fill your mind, tear your emotions, excite your wonder or awe or delight. Is home that, or is it the place where the people you love live, or the place where you have buried your dead, or the place where you want to be buried yourself? Or is it the place where you come in your last desperation to shoot yourself, choosing the garage or the barn or the woodshed in order not to mess up the house, but coming back anyway to the last sanctuary where you can kill yourself in peace?

—Wallace Stegner, *The Big Rock Candy Mountain*

4. **Expand your definition with examples.** A well-chosen example can add volumes of clarity to your meaning. In the following paragraph, the author tells us what she thinks the word *manhood* means in America:

> America has defined the roles to which each individual should subscribe. It has defined "manhood" in terms of its own interests and "femininity" likewise. An individual who has a good job, makes a lot of money and drives a Cadillac is a real man, and conversely, an individual who is lacking in these "qualities" is less of a man. The advertising media in this country continuously inform the American male of his need for indispensable signs of his virility—the brand of cigarettes that cowboys prefer, the whiskey that has a masculine tang or the label of the jock strap that athletes wear.
>
> —Frances M. Beal, "Double Jeopardy: To Be Black and Female"

Whether you agree with this definition, you can at least grasp the author's meaning from her examples.

5. **To define a complex term properly, you may need to practice a combination of techniques: You may have to cite examples, analyze etymology, and/or provide a lexical definition.** Here is a paragraph in which the writer uses all three devices to define *idiopathic diseases:*

<table>
<tr><td>*examples*</td><td rowspan="3">We have a roster of diseases which medicine calls "idiopathic," meaning that we do not know what causes them. The list is much shorter than it used to be; a century ago, common infections like typhus fever, tuberculosis, and meningitis were classed as idiopathic illnesses. Originally, when it first came into the language of medicine, the term had a different, highly theoretical meaning. It was assumed that most human diseases were intrinsic, due to inbuilt failures of one sort or another, things gone wrong with various internal humors. The word "idiopathic" was intended to mean, literally, a disease having its own origin, a primary disease without any external cause. The list of such disorders has become progressively shorter as medical science has advanced, especially within this century, and the meaning of the term has lost its doctrinal flavor; we use "idiopathic" now to indicate simply that the cause of one particular disease is unknown. Very likely, before we are finished with medical science, and with luck, we will have found that all varieties of disease are the result of one or another sort of meddling, and there will be no more idiopathic illness.</td></tr>
<tr><td>*etymology*</td></tr>
<tr><td>*lexical definition*</td></tr>
</table>

> —Lewis Thomas, *The Medusa and the Snail*

Remember that your definition is incomplete if it leaves gaps in the meaning of a term or fails to clearly answer the question, "What does this mean?" Keep that question in mind when you write a definition and do your utmost to answer it until your meaning is unmistakably clear to your reader.

As you write your defining essays, beware of the most common student error—*the circular definition*. To say that "taxation is the act of imposing taxes" is repetitious. Better to say "Taxation is the principle of levying fees to support basic government services." Provide examples and details until you have answered the question "What is it?"

Warming Up to Write a Definition

1. Getting together with three or four of your classmates, sit down and discuss the best definition for each of the following terms. If needed, you may use a dictionary. Once you have agreed on the best definition, write it on a sheet of paper, using only one sentence. Refine the written definition until it could serve as a thesis statement for an essay.

   a. kleptomania

   b. astrology

   c. insanity

   d. terrorism

   e. deportation

2. In the following paragraph, the word *renaissance* needs to be defined for readers who are not familiar with it. Define the term by using at least three other words in the passage that explain what the word means. Write down your definition so that it could be used as the thesis of an essay about any community experiencing what Harlem is going through.

   > Harlem, a community in northern Manhattan that hit bottom in the 1980s when poverty, neglected housing and drug-related crime took their toll, is enjoying a lively second *renaissance*. Some Harlemites dismiss the resurgence as little more than a real estate boom, because the neighborhood's magnificent 19th-century townhouses are being snapped up at a rapid rate. You'll also hear that the cultural scene doesn't compare with the Harlem's first flowering, in the 1920s, which was animated by extraordinary creativity in politics, the arts and especially the written word. But if it's true there are no stand-ins today for fiery W. E. B. DuBois, gentle Langston Hughes, or patrician Duke Ellington, the second renaissance is still taking shape . . . Highbrow, mainstream, pop, hiphop, avant-garde— Harlem's cultural and artistic revival is evident on nearly every block.

   —From Peter Hellman, "Coming Up Harlem," *Smithsonian,* November 2002

3. In the blanks provided, check those definitions that are *not* correct; then provide the correct definitions.

   a. _____ *Charismatic* means disgusting.

   b. _____ *Desolation* means a feeling of despair.

   c. _____ A *skeptic* is one who is gullible.

d. _____ *Suburban* means out in the country.

e. _____ A *turret* is a tower or steeple.

f. _____ To *pay homage* means to ridicule.

g. _____ A *residue* is an evil citizen.

h. _____ *Genetic* means inherited.

i. _____ To *scrutinize* means to study or pore over.

j. _____ *Sovereignty* means debauchery.

4. Rewrite the following definitions to delete the circular meaning.

   a. A *terrorist* is simply a person who tries to terrorize others.

   b. *Prostitution* is the work done by prostitutes.

   c. *Liberty* means to be free like a bird.

   d. *Patriotism* is the act of being patriotic.

   e. Having *popular* appeal means that one appeals to the public.

EXAMPLES

Of Altruism, Heroism, and Nature's Gifts in the Face of Terror

NATALIE ANGIER

Rhetorical Thumbnail

Purpose: to inform

Audience: educated readers

Language: standard English

Strategy: cites evidence from research and theoretical speculation to define the role of altruism and heroism in genetics

Natalie Angier (b. 1958), a contributing writer on the staff of *The New York Times,* is a Pulitzer Prize–winning journalist. She has published several books, including the following: *Natural Obsessions: Striving to Unlock the Deepest Secrets of the Cancer Cell* (1989), *The Beauty of the Beastly: New Views on the Nature of Life* (1995), and *Woman: An Intimate Geography* (1999). The essay reprinted below is from the *New York Times*, September 18, 2001.

The author tackles the topic of how, and why, human beings perform heroic deeds that require much self-sacrifice.

• • •

1   The only support for a definition of *altruism* that the author cites is testimonial evidence. Yet the testimonies are so skillfully woven into theoretical discussions that they never seem intrusive or weak or out-of-place.

2   For the wordless, formless, expectant citizens of tomorrow, here are some postcards of all that matters today:

> Minutes after terrorists slam jet planes into the towers of the World Trade Center, streams of harrowed humanity crowd the emergency stairwells, heading in two directions. While terrified employees scramble down, toward exit doors and survival, hundreds of New York firefighters, each laden with seventy to one hundred pounds of lifesaving gear, charge upward, never to be seen again.

3   As the last of four hijacked planes advances toward an unknown but surely populated destination, passengers huddle together and plot resistance against their captors, an act that may explain why the plane fails to reach its target, crashing instead into an empty field outside Pittsburgh.

4   Hearing of the tragedy whose dimensions cannot be charted or absorbed, tens of thousands of people across the nation storm their local hospitals and blood banks, begging for the chance to give blood, something of themselves to the hearts of the wounded—and the heart of us all—beating against the void.

5   Altruism and heroism. If not for these twin radiant badges of our humanity, there would be no us, and we know it. And so, when their vile opposite threatened to choke us into submission last Tuesday, we rallied them in quantities so great we surprised even ourselves.

6   Nothing and nobody can fully explain the source of the emotional genius that has been everywhere on display. Politicians have cast it as evidence of the indomitable spirit of a rock-solid America; pastors have given credit to a more celestial source. And while biologists in no way claim to have discovered the key to human nobility they do have their own spin on the subject. The altruistic impulse, they say, is a nondenominational gift, the birthright and defining characteristic of the human species.

7   As they see it, the roots of altruistic behavior far predate Homo sapiens, and that is why it seems to flow forth so readily once tapped. Recent studies that model group dynamics suggest that a spirit of cooperation will arise in nature under a wide variety of circumstances.

8   "There's a general trend in evolutionary biology toward recognizing that very often the best way to compete is to cooperate," said Dr. Barbara Smuts, a professor of anthropology at the University of Michigan, who has published papers on the evolution of altruism. "And that, to me, is a source of some solace and comfort."

9   Moreover, most biologists concur that the human capacity for language and memory allows altruistic behavior—the desire to give, and to sacrifice for the sake of others—to flourish in measure far beyond the cooperative spirit seen in other species.

10   With language, they say, people can learn of individuals they have never met and feel compassion for their suffering, and honor and even emulate their heroic deeds. They can also warn one another of any selfish cheaters or malign tricksters lurking in their midst.

11   "In a large crowd, we know who the good guys are, and we can talk about, and ostracize, the bad ones," said Dr. Craig Packer, a processor of ecology and evolution at the University of Minnesota. "People are very concerned about their reputation, and that, too, can inspire us to be good."

12   Oh, better than good.

"There's a grandness in the human species that is so striking, and so profoundly different from what we see in other animals," he added. "We are an amalgamation of families working together. This is what civilization is derived from."

13   At the same time, said biologists, the very conditions that encourage heroics and selflessness can be the source of profound barbarism as well. "Moral behavior is often a within-group phenomenon," said Dr. David Sloan Wilson, a professor of biology at the State University of New York at Binghamton. "Altruism is practiced within your group and often turned off toward members of other groups."

14   The desire to understand the nature of altruism has occupied evolutionary thinkers since Charles Darwin, who was fascinated by the apparent existence of altruism among social insects. In ant and bee colonies, sterile female workers labor ceaselessly for their queen, and will even die for her when the nest is threatened. How could such seeming selflessness evolve, when it is exactly those individuals that are behaving altruistically that fail to breed and thereby pass their selfless genes along?

15   By a similar token human soldiers who go to war often are at the beginning of their reproductive potential, and many are killed before getting the chance to have children. Why don't the stay-at-homes simply outbreed the do-gooders and thus bury the altruistic impulse along with the casualties of combat?

16   The question of altruism was at least partly solved when the British evolutionary theorist William Hamilton formulated the idea of inclusive fitness: The notion that individuals can enhance their reproductive success not merely by having young of their own, but by caring for their genetic relatives as well. Among social bees and ants, it turns out, the sister workers are more closely related to one another than parents normally are to their offspring; thus it behooves the workers to care more about current and potential sisters than to fret over their sterile selves.

17   The concept of inclusive fitness explains many brave acts observed in nature. Dr. Richard Wrangham, a primatologist at Harvard, cites the example of the red colobus monkey. When they are being hunted by chimpanzees, the male monkeys are "amazingly brave." Dr. Wrangham said, "As the biggest and strongest members of their group, they undoubtedly could escape quicker than the other." Instead, the males jump to the front, confronting the chimpanzee hunters while the mothers and offspring jump to safety. Often, the much bigger chimpanzees pull the colobus soldiers off by their tails and slam them to their deaths.

18   Their courageousness can be explained by the fact that colobus monkeys live in multimale multifemale groups in which the males are almost always related. So in protecting the young monkeys, the adult males are defending their kin.

19   Yet, as biologists are learning, there is more to cooperation and generosity than an investment in one's nepotistic patch of DNA. Lately, they have accrued evidence that something like group selection encourages the evolution of traits beneficial to a group, even when members of the group are not related.

20   In computer simulation studies, Dr. Smuts and her colleagues modeled two types of group-living agents that would behave like herbivores: one that would selfishly consume all the food in a given patch before moving on, and another than would consume resources modestly rather than greedily, thus allowing local plant food to regenerate.

21   Researchers had assumed that cooperators could collaborate with genetically unrelated cooperators only if they had the cognitive capacity to know goodness when they saw it.

22   But the data suggested otherwise. "These models showed that under a wide range of simulated environmental conditions you could get selection for prudent, cooperative behavior," Dr. Smuts said, even in the absence of cognition or kinship. "If you happened by chance to get good guys together, they remained together because they created a mutually beneficial environment."

23   This sort of win-win principle, she said, could explain all sorts of symbiotic arrangements, even among different species—like the tendency of baboons and impalas to associate together because they use each other's warning calls.

24   Add to this basic mechanistic selection for cooperation the human capacity to recognize and reward behaviors that strengthen the group—the tribe, the state, the church, the platoon—and selflessness thrives and multiplies. So, too, does the need for group identity. Classic so-called minimal group experiments have shown that when people are gathered together and assigned membership in arbitrary groups, called, say, the Greens and the Reds, before long the members begin expressing amity for their fellow Greens or Reds and animosity toward those of the wrong "color."

25   "Ancestral life frequently consisted of intergroup conflict," Dr. Wilson of SUNY said. "It's part of our mental heritage."

26   Yet he does not see conflict as inevitable. "It's been shown pretty well that where people place the boundary between us and them is extremely flexible and strategic," he said. "It's possible to widen the moral circle, and I'm optimistic enough to believe it can be done on a worldwide scale."

27   Ultimately, though, scientists acknowledge that the evolutionary framework for self-sacrificing acts is overlaid by individual choice. And it is there, when individual firefighters or office workers or airplane passengers choose the altruistic path that science gives way to wonder.

28   Dr. James J. Moore, a professor of anthropology at the University of California at San Diego, said he had studied many species, including many different primates, "We're the nicest species I know," he said. "To see those guys risking their lives, climbing over rubble on the chance of finding one person alive, well, you wouldn't find baboons doing that." That horrors of last week

notwithstanding, he said, "the overall picture to come out about human nature is wonderful."

29   "For every 50 people making bomb threats now to mosques," he said, "there are 500,000 people around the world behaving just the way we hoped they would, with empathy and expressions of grief. We are amazingly civilized."

30   True, death-defying acts of heroism may be the province of the few. For the rest of us, simple humanity will do.

● Vocabulary

altruism (title)	solace (8)	nepotistic (20)
harrowed (2)	emulate (10)	accrued (20)
indomitable (6)	malign (10)	simulation (21)
celestial (6)	ostracize (11)	herbivores (21)
nobility (6)	amalgamation (13)	cognitive (22)
nondenominational (6)	derived (13)	symbiotic (24)
Homo sapiens (7)	inclusive (17)	primates (29)

● The Facts

1. How does the author define *altruism?* Where does she state her definition?
2. What image does the author superimpose on the three scenes described in paragraphs 2, 3, and 4? Why do you suppose she used this image?
3. What source have politicians credited for the heroic actions during the World Trade Center tragedies? How does their source differ from that credited by the clergy?
4. What example from the chimpanzee world does the author use to prove that altruism predates the existence of *Homo sapiens?* What term does she use for the kind of altruism shown to other members of the group rather than just to close relatives?
5. What three human characteristics make the altruism of human beings so much more astounding than that of animals? Which of the three do you consider the most important? Give reasons for your answer.

● The Strategies

1. What voice does the author use in her opening paragraph? To whom is it addressed?
2. How does the author gain scholarly authority in her essay? Were you convinced by her opinions and statements? Explain your answer.
3. What is the effect of paragraph 12? Why was it not deleted since it is brief and not developed?
4. What does paragraph 17 contribute to the puzzle of altruism or heroism?
5. What is the function of the word *ultimately* in paragraph 28?

The Issues

1. As you recollect the tragedy of September 11, 2001, what picture stands out most clearly and emphatically in your mind? What does the picture say about our society?

2. What does the author mean when she indicates that without altruism and heroism, humanity as we know it would not exist? Do you agree with this opinion? Would you qualify it in any way? Explain your answer.

3. Which of the scenes described at the start of Angier's essay impressed you most? Give reasons for your answer. Have students suggest what they might have done, had they been part of the scene.

4. Why are language and memory important to human altruism and heroism? What other features of being human contribute to the development of selflessness and the desire to protect others?

5. Do you agree with Dr. Moore's assessment that "we're the nicest species" known? What is your general judgment concerning the goodness or evil of human beings?

Suggestions for Writing

1. Write an essay in which you define *heroism* by illustrating your definition with a selfless, courageous act you witnessed or read about.

2. On the Internet, research the concept of *altruism* and write a paper in which you turn the results of your research into a thesis, which you then develop into a 500-word essay. Cite at least two or three valid sources that you integrate smoothly into your text.

Entropy

K.C. COLE

Rhetorical Thumbnail

Purpose: to define and clarify *entropy* so that the average reader can understand the concept

Audience: readers who have time to ponder and enjoy well-written newspaper columns

Language: standard English, written in the kind of casual voice that creates intimacy between writer and audience

Strategy: to define entropy so that readers will not lose hope when they observe the disorder catapulting around them, but will realize that human energy, applied at the right time and place, can prevent the descent into chaos or inertia

K.C. Cole is a writer covering physical science for the *Los Angeles Times*, where she also writes the column "Mind Over Matter." Cole spent her early childhood in Rio de Janeiro and grew up in Port Washington, New York, and Shaker Heights, Ohio. After graduating from Barnard College with a degree in political science, she worked for Radio Free Europe as an editor and subsequently lived in the former Czechoslovakia, the Soviet Union, and Hungary. An article she wrote for *New York Times Magazine* about the Soviet Union's invasion of Czechoslovakia was so well received, that she instantly became famous as a news reporter. While working as a writer and editor at the *Saturday Review* in San Francisco, she became intrigued with Frank Oppenheimer's Exploratorium science museum and started writing about science. Cole is the author of numerous national best sellers. Among her works are the following: *What Only a Mother Can Tell You About Having a Baby (1982), Between the Lines* (1984), *The Universe and the Teacup: The Mathematics of Truth and Beauty* (1999), *and First You Build a Cloud: Reflections on Physics as a Way of Life* (1999). The selection below was first published as a "Hers" column in the *New York Times*.

Reading Cole's essay should make you feel grateful for a writer who can explain physics in simple and clear language. While entropy can be made to seem incomprehensible, Cole uses details and examples from ordinary life to describe the concept so that the reader realizes that entropy is nothing more than the normal decay and disintegration we observe all around us—something each of us must confront, explore, and work out.

• • •

1   It was about two months ago when I realized that entropy was getting the better of me. On the same day my car broke down (again), my refrigerator conked out and I learned that I needed root-canal work in my right rear tooth. The windows in the bedroom were still leaking every time it rained and my son's baby sitter was still failing to show up every time I really needed her. My hair was turning gray and my typewriter was wearing out. The house needed paint and I needed glasses. My son's sneakers were developing holes and I was developing a deep sense of futility.

2   After all, what was the point of spending half of Saturday at the Latundromat if the clothes were dirty all over again the following Friday?

3   Disorder, alas, is the natural order of things in the universe. There is even a precise measure of the amount of disorder, called entropy. Unlike almost every other physical property (motion, gravity, energy), entropy does not work both ways. It can only increase. Once it's created it can never be destroyed. The road to disorder is a one-way street.

4   Because of its unnerving irreversibility, entropy has been called the arrow of time. We all understand this instinctively. Children's rooms, left on their own, tend to get messy, not neat. Wood rots, metal rusts, people wrinkle and

flowers wither. Even mountains wear down; even the nuclei of atoms decay. In the city we see entropy in the rundown subways and worn-out sidewalks and torn-down buildings, in the increasing disorder of our lives. We know, without asking, what is old. If we were suddenly to see the paint jump back on an old building, we would know that something was wrong. If we saw an egg unscramble itself and jump back into its shell, we would laugh in the same way we laugh at a movie run backward.

5   Entropy is no laughing matter, however, because with every increase in entropy energy is wasted and opportunity is lost. Water flowing down a mountainside can be made to do some useful work on its way. But once all the water is at the same level it can work no more. That is entropy. When my refrigerator was working, it kept all the cold air ordered in one part of the kitchen and warmer air in another. Once it broke down the warm and cold mixed into a lukewarm mess that allowed my butter to melt, my milk to rot and my frozen vegetables to decay.

6   Of course the energy is not really lost, but it has diffused and dissipated into a chaotic caldron of randomness that can do us no possible good. Entropy is chaos. It is loss of purpose.

7   People are often upset by the entropy they seem to sec in the haphazardness of their own lives. Buffeted about like so many molecules in my tepid kitchen, they feel that they have lost their sense of direction, that they are wasting youth and opportunity at every turn. It is easy to see entropy in marriages, when the partners are too preoccupied to patch small things up, almost guaranteeing that they will fall apart. There is much entropy in the state of our country, in the relationships between nations—lost opportunities to stop the avalanche of disorders that seems ready to swallow us all.

8   Entropy is not inevitable everywhere, however. Crystals and snowflakes and galaxies are islands of incredibly ordered beauty in the midst of random events. If it was not for exceptions to entropy, the sky would be black and we would be able to see where the stars spend their days; it is only because air molecules in the atmosphere cluster in ordered groups that the sky is blue.

9   The most profound exception to entropy is the creation of life. A seed soaks up some soil and some carbon and some sunshine and some water and arranges it into a rose. A seed in the womb takes some oxygen and pizza and milk and transforms it into a baby.

10   The catch is that it takes a lot of energy to produce a baby. It also takes energy to make a tree. The road to disorder is all downhill but the road to creation takes work. Though combating entropy is possible, it also has its price. That's why it seems so hard to get ourselves together, so easy to let ourselves fall apart.

11   Worse, creating order in one corner of the universe always creates more disorder somewhere else. We create ordered energy from oil and coal at the price of the entropy of smog.

12   I recently took up playing the flute again after an absence of several months. As the uneven vibrations screeched through the house, my son covered his ears and said, "Mom, what's wrong with your flute?" Nothing was wrong with my flute, of course. It was my ability to play it that had atrophied, or entropied, as the case may be. The only way to stop that process was to practice every day, and sure enough my tone improved, though only at the price of constant work. Like anything else, abilities deteriorate when we stop applying our energies to them.

13   That's why entropy is depressing. It seems as if just breaking even is an uphill fight. There's a good reason that this should be so. The mechanics of entropy are a matter of chance. Take any ice-cold air molecule milling around my kitchen. The chances that it will wander in the direction of my refrigerator at any point are exactly 50-50. The chances that it will wander away from my refrigerator are also 50-50. But take billions of warm and cold molecules mixed together, and the chances that all the cold ones will wander toward the refrigerator and all the warm ones will wander away from it are virtually nil.

14   Entropy wins not because order is impossible but because there are always so many more paths toward disorder than toward, order. There are so many more different ways to do a sloppy job than a good one, so many more ways to make a mess than to clean it up. The obstacles and accidents in our lives almost guarantee that constant collisions will bounce us on to random paths, get us off the track. Disorder is the path of least resistance, the easy but not the inevitable road.

15   Like so many others, I am distressed by the entropy I see around me today. I am afraid of the randomness of international events, of the lack of common purpose in the world; I am terrified that it will lead into the ultimate entropy of nuclear war. I am upset that I could not in the city where I live send my child to a public school; that people are unemployed and inflation is out of control; that tensions between sexes and races seem to be increasing again; that relationships everywhere seem to be falling apart.

16   Social institutions—like atoms and stars—decay if energy is not added to keep them ordered. Friendships and families and economies all fall apart unless we constantly make an effort to keep them working and well oiled. And far too few people, it seems to me, are willing to contribute consistently to those efforts.

17   Of course, the more complex things are, the harder it is. If there were only a dozen or so air molecules in my kitchen, it would be likely—if I waited a year or so—that at some point the six coldest ones would congregate inside the freezer. But the more actors in the equation—the more players in the game—the less likely it is that their paths will coincide in an orderly way. The more pieces in the puzzle, the harder it is to put back together once order is disturbed. "Irreversibility," said a physicist, "is the price we pay for complexity."

"Entropy" by K. C. Cole is reprinted with permission from the author.

Vocabulary

futility (1)	diffused (6)	buffeted (7)
unnerving (4)	dissipated (6)	tepid (7)
irreversibility (4)	caldron (6)	atrophied (12)
nuclei (4)	randomness (6)	molecule (13)

The Facts

1. What details give us a clue to the time in which the essay was written? Is the time necessary to the main point of the essay? Cite reasons for your answer.

2. Where in the essay is the term *entropy* first defined? What rules pertaining to a proper definition does the author observe? Does the definition clarify the term for you? If it does not, what is it lacking? What better definition can you provide?

3. According to the author, just about everything in our universe is subject to entropy, but what are some exceptions? What noticeable characteristic do these exceptions reveal? Provide some examples from your own experience.

4. Where in your immediate sphere do you most clearly see the workings of entropy? What, if any, steps have you taken to prevent the entropy from descending into total chaos? What foreign countries seem most vulnerable to entropy? Explain your choices.

5. According to the author, why does entropy have a winning edge in the race between disorder and order? Do you agree or disagree with the author's assessment? Give an example from your own experience to support your answer.

The Strategies

1. Why do you think the author titled his essay "entropy" instead of a more common title like "Disorder?" How does Cole capture the reader's interest with such a scientific concept as *entropy?*

2. What is the thesis of the essay and where is it stated? What does the thesis accomplish for the reader? What problem does the thesis solve?

3. What purpose does the opening sentence of paragraph 5 serve? What would happen to the essay if this sentence were deleted? Try to substitute a sentence of your own and see what happens to the flow of the essay.

4. At which point in the essay does the author focus on what really concerns her the most about the concept of entropy? Is the timing of the focus justified strategically? Explain your answer.

5. What three metaphors does the author use in the final paragraph of her essay? What do they have in common? What point do they stress?

● The Issues

1. What ideas contained in this essay really disturbed you or made you think about the order versus disorder around you? Point to two or three passages from the essay and explain your reaction to them.

2. Do you agree or disagree with the author's view (see paragraph 14) that entropy wins because there are so many more paths toward disorder than toward order? Cite examples from your own experience to support or challenge her argument.

3. As you analyze your life style, which kind of person do you tend to be—orderly or disorderly? How has your sense of order affected the way you see yourself? What changes, if any, would you like to make in the way you deal with the order or chaos around you?

4. What relationship exists between entropy and energy? Make a case for what would happen to our society if entropy were to win over energy? Cite an example to clarify your view.

5. From the list of social institutions mentioned in paragraph 16, which one do you consider crucial to the fabric of society? How do you propose to use energy to save it from chaos? Be specific in your prescription.

● Suggestions for Writing

1. Choosing one of the following terms whose definition depends on who is using it, write what you think it means. Use several appropriate examples and try to persuade your reader that your definition is the correct one:

   a. feminine

   b. pornography

   c. progressive

   d. racist

   e. tolerance

2. Cole claims that "abilities deteriorate when we stop applying our energies to them." Write an essay in which you use this concept as your thesis and try to persuade your reader that it is true. Use statistics, specific examples, quotations, or any other means that will support your thesis.

In Praise of the Humble Comma

PICO IYER

> ## Rhetorical Thumbnail
>
> **Purpose:** discuss comma usage in modern writing
>
> **Audience:** educated readers
>
> **Language:** standard English
>
> **Strategy:** uses a multitude of examples to emphasize the role and meaning of punctuation

Pico Iyer is a freelance writer and contributing editorial writer for *Time*. He has also written numerous books about exotic places and countries, among them *The Lady and the Monk: Four Seasons in Kyoto* (1992), *Falling off the Map: Some Lonely Places of the World* (1994), *Cuba and the Light* (1996), and *Global Soul: Jet Lag, Shopping Malls, and the Search for Home* (2000).

This essay appeared as the featured essay on the back page of Time *(June 13, 1988). Its purpose is to define punctuation in general and the comma specifically. Iyer suggests that punctuation marks are highly underrated because they give writing elegance as well as clarity, often keeping it from becoming a jumble of words strung across a page.*

●　●　●

1   The gods, they say, give breath, and they take it away. But the same could be said—could it not?—of the humble comma. Add it to the present clause, and, all of a sudden, the mind is, quite literally, given pause to think; take it out if you wish or forget it and the mind is deprived of a resting place. Yet still the comma gets no respect. It seems just a slip of a thing, a pedant's tick, a blip on the edge of our consciousness, a kind of printer's smudge almost. Small, we claim, is beautiful (especially in the age of the microchip). Yet what is so often used, and so rarely recalled, as the comma—unless it be breath itself?

2   Punctuation, one is taught, has a point: to keep up law and order. Punctuation marks are the road signs placed along the highway of our communication—to control speeds, provide directions and prevent head-on collisions. A period has the unblinking finality of a red light; the comma is a flashing yellow light that asks us only to slow down; and the semicolon is a stop sign that tells us to ease gradually to a halt, before gradually starting up again. By establishing the relations between words, punctuation establishes the relations between the people using words. That may be one reason why schoolteachers exalt it and lovers defy it ("We love each other and belong to each other let's don't ever hurt each other Nicole let's don't ever hurt each other," wrote Gary Gilmore to his girlfriend). A comma, he must have known, "separates inseparables," in the clinching words of H. W. Fowler, King of English Usage.

3   Punctuation, then, is a civic prop, a pillar that holds society upright. (A run-on sentence, its phrases piling up without division, is as unsightly as a sink piled high with dirty dishes.) Small wonder, then, that punctuation was one of the first proprieties of the Victorian age, the age of the corset, that the modernists threw off: the sexual revolution might be said to have begun when Joyce's Molly Bloom spilled out all her private thoughts in 36 pages of unbridled, almost unperioded and officially censored prose; and another rebellion was surely marked when E. E. Cummings first felt free to commit "God" to the lower case.

4   Punctuation thus becomes the signature of cultures. The hot-blooded Spaniard seems to be revealed in the passion and urgency of his doubled exclamation points and question marks ("¡Caramba! ¿Quién sabe?"), while the impassive Chinese traditionally added to his so-called inscrutability by omitting directions from his ideograms. The anarchy and commotion of the '60s were given voice in the exploding exclamation marks, riotous capital letters and Day-Glo italics of Tom Wolfe's spray-paint prose; and in Communist societies, where the State is absolute, the dignity—and divinity—of capital letters is reserved for Ministries, Sub-Committees and Secretariats.

5   Yet punctuation is something more than a culture's birthmark; it scores the music in our minds, gets our thoughts moving to the rhythm of our hearts. Punctuation is the notation in the sheet music of our words, telling us when to rest, or when to raise our voices; it acknowledges that the meaning of our discourse, as of any symphonic composition, lies not in the units but in the pauses, the pacing and the phrasing. Punctuation is the way one bats one's eyes, lowers one's voice or blushes demurely. Punctuation adjusts the tone and color and volume till the feeling comes into perfect focus: not disgust exactly, but distaste; not lust, or like, but love.

6   Punctuation, in short, gives us the human voice, and all the meanings that lie between the words. "You aren't young, are you?" loses its innocence when it loses the question mark. Every child knows the menace of a dropped apostrophe (the parent's "Don't do that" shifting into the more slowly enunciated "Do not do that"), and every believer, the ignominy of having his faith reduced to "faith." Add an exclamation point to "To be or not to be . . ." and the gloomy Dane has all the resolve he needs; add a comma, and the noble sobriety of "God save the Queen" becomes a cry of desperation bordering on double sacrilege.

7   Sometimes, of course, our markings may be simply a matter of aesthetics. Popping in a comma can be like slipping on the necklace that gives an outfit quiet elegance, or like catching the sound of running water that complements, as it completes, the silence of a Japanese landscape. When V. S. Naipaul, in his latest novel, writes, "He was a middle-aged man, with glasses," the first comma can seem a little precious. Yet it gives the description a spin, as well as a subtlety, that it otherwise lacks, and it shows that the glasses are not part of the middle-agedness, but something else.

8   Thus all these tiny scratches give us breadth and heft and depth. A world that has only periods is a world without inflections. It is a world without shade. It has a music without sharps and flats. It is a martial music. It has a jack-boot rhythm. Words cannot bend and curve. A comma, by comparison, catches the gentle drift of the mind in thought, turning in on itself and back on itself,

reversing, redoubling and returning along the course of its own sweet river music; while the semicolon brings clauses and thoughts together with all the silent discretion of a hostess arranging guests around her dinner table.

9   Punctuation, then, is a matter of care. Care for words, yes, but also, and more important, for what the words imply. Only a lover notices the small things: the way the afternoon light catches the nape of a neck, or how a strand of hair slips out from behind an ear, or the way a finger curls around a cup. And no one scans a letter so closely as a lover, searching for its small print, straining to hear its nuances, its gasps, its sighs and hesitations, poring over the secret messages that lie in every cadence. The difference between "Jane (whom I adore)" and "Jane, whom I adore," and the difference between them both and "Jane—whom I adore—" marks all the distance between ecstasy and heartache. "No iron can pierce the heart with such force as a period put at just the right place," in Isaac Babel's lovely words; a comma can let us hear a voice break, or a heart. Punctuation, in fact, is a labor of love. Which brings us back, in a way, to gods.

● Vocabulary

pedant's (1)	enunciated (6)	inflections (8)
proprieties (3)	ignominy (6)	martial (8)
inscrutability (4)	aesthetics (7)	nuances (9)
ideograms (4)	heft (8)	

● The Facts

1. Which of Iyer's many definitions best explains *punctuation*? Which seems most helpful, and which least? Give reasons for your answers.
2. The author never gives a formal definition of the comma. What reason can you offer for this omission?
3. What does the author mean when he suggests that punctuation is the "signature of cultures"?
4. In the author's view, how is punctuation related to music?
5. According to the author, what would writing be like if it were deprived of the comma?

● The Strategies

1. Why does the author entitle his essay "In Praise of the Humble Comma" when most of the essay deals with punctuation in general?
2. What is the author's style in this essay? How effective do you consider it?
3. What is the author's tone when he uses the word "humble" in connection with the comma?
4. What technique does the author use in closing his essay? How effective is it?
5. How does the author establish coherence between paragraphs 5 and 6?

The Issues

1. If punctuation is indeed "the signature of cultures," then how would you describe the kind of signature our culture uses? What kind of culture is behind this signature?

2. In your own writing, which punctuation mark gives you the most trouble? Which do you find the most helpful? Give reasons for your answers.

3. Review paragraph 3. What is your reaction to the author's view that our modern age has thrown off the Victorian restrictions of punctuation? If the author's view is true, has our new freedom improved writing? Why or why not?

4. How important is it for students to learn how to write with care? Support your answer with reasons.

5. What examples can you provide to support Isaac Babel's opinion that "[n]o iron can pierce the heart with such force as a period put at just the right place"? Use your imagination to create appropriate sentences.

Suggestions for Writing

1. Write an essay in which you create your own definition of *punctuation*.

2. Write an essay in which you either support or challenge the author's view that punctuation is a matter of care for what words imply.

3. Write an essay in which you assign responsibility for teaching punctuation to the proper educational institution.

Kitsch

GILBERT HIGHET

Rhetorical Thumbnail

Purpose: to amuse and entertain

Audience: educated readers

Language: standard English with a douse of irony, hyperbole, and satire

Strategy: to explain the concept of kitsch without sounding like an insufferable snob

Gilbert Highet (1906–1978) was born in Glasgow, Scotland, educated at the University of Glasgow and at Oxford, and became an American citizen in 1951. A classicist, Highet was known for his scholarly and critical writing, including *The Classical Tradition* (1949) and *The Anatomy of Satire* (1962).

You probably have had some experience with "kitsch" even if you do not know what the word means. You may have friends or relatives whose furniture, curios, or even favorite books are clearly kitschy. Gilbert Highet draws mainly on literary examples to define kitsch; but, as you shall see, the concept applies to nearly all matters of bad taste.

• • •

1   If you have ever passed an hour wandering through an antique shop (not looking for anything exactly, but simply looking), you must have noticed how your taste gradually grows numb, and then—if you stay—becomes perverted. You begin to see unsuspected charm in those hideous pictures of plump girls fondling pigeons, you develop a psychopathic desire for spinning wheels and cobblers' benches, you are apt to pay out good money for a bronze statuette of Otto von Bismarck, with a metal hand inside a metal frock coat and metal pouches under his metallic eyes. As soon as you take the things home, you realize that they are revolting. And yet they have a sort of horrible authority; you don't like them; you know how awful they are; but it is a tremendous effort to drop them in the garbage, where they belong.

2   To walk along a whole street of antique shops—that is an experience which shakes the very soul. Here is a window full of bulbous Chinese deities; here is another littered with Zulu assagais, Indian canoe paddles, and horse pistols which won't fire; the next shopfront is stuffed with gaudy Italian majolica vases, and the next, even worse, with Austrian pottery—tiny ladies and gentlemen sitting on lace cushions and wearing lace ruffles, with every frill, every wrinkle and reticulation translated into porcelain: pink; stiff; but fortunately not unbreakable. The nineteenth century produced an appalling amount of junky art like this, and sometimes I imagine that clandestine underground factories are continuing to pour it out like illicit drugs.

3   There is a name for such stuff in the trade, a word apparently of Russian origin, *kitsch*[1]: it means vulgar showoff, and it is applied to anything that took a lot of trouble to make and is quite hideous.

4   It is paradoxical stuff, kitsch: It is obviously bad: so bad that you can scarcely understand how any human being would spend days and weeks making it, and how anybody else would buy it and take it home and keep it and dust it and leave it to her heirs. It is terribly ingenious, and terribly ugly, and utterly useless; and yet it has one of the qualities of good art—which is that, once seen, it is not easily forgotten. Of course it is found in all the arts: think of Milan Cathedral, or the statues in Westminster Abbey, or Liszt's settings of Schubert songs. There is a lot of it in the United States—for instance, the architecture of Miami, Florida, and Forest Lawn Cemetery in Los Angeles. Many of Hollywood's most ambitious historical films are superb kitsch. Most Tin Pan Alley love songs are perfect 100 per cent kitsch.

5   There is kitsch in the world of books also. I collect it. It is horrible, but I enjoy it.

---

[1]The Russian verb *keetcheetsya* means "to be haughty and puffed up."

6   The gem of my collection is the work of the Irish novelist Mrs. Amanda McKittrick Ros, whose masterpiece, *Delina Delaney,* was published about 1900. It is a stirringly romantic tale, telling how Delina, a fisherman's daughter from Erin Cottage, was beloved by Lord Gifford, the heir of Columbia Castle, and—after many trials and even imprisonment—married him. The story is dramatic, not to say impossible; but it is almost lost to view under the luxuriant style. Here, for example, is a sentence in which Mrs. Ros explains that her heroine used to earn extra cash by doing needlework:

> She tried hard to assist in keeping herself a stranger to her poor old father's slight income by the use of the finest production of steel, whose blunt edge eyed the reely covering with marked greed, and offered its sharp dart to faultless fabrics of flaxen fineness.

7   Revolting, but distinctive: what Mr. Polly called "rockockyo" in manner.

For the baroque vein, here is Lord Gifford saying goodbye to his sweetheart:

> My darling virgin! my queen! my Delina! I am just in time to hear the toll of a parting bell strike its heavy weight of appalling softness against the weakest fibers of a heart of love, arousing and tickling its dormant action, thrusting the dart of evident separation deeper into its tubes of tenderness, and fanning the flame, already unextinguishable, into volumes of blaze.

8   Mrs. Ros had a remarkable command of rhetoric, and could coin an unforgettable phrase. She described her hero's black eyes as "glittering jet revolvers." When he became ill, she said he fell "into a state of lofty fever"—doubtless because commoners have high fever, but lords have lofty fever. And her reflections on the moral degeneracy of society have rarely been equaled, in power and penetration:

> Days of humanity, whither hast thou fled? When bows of compulsion, smiles for the deceitful, handshakes for the dogmatic, and welcome for the tool of power live under your objectionable, unambitious beat, not daring to be checked by the tongue of candour because the selfish world refuses to dispense with her rotten policies. The legacy of your forefathers, which involved equity, charity, reason, and godliness, is beyond the reach of their frivolous, mushroom offspringódeceit, injustice, malice and unkindnessóand is not likely to be codiciled with traits of harmony so long as these degrading vices of mock ambition fester the human heart.

9   Perhaps one reason I enjoy this stuff is because it so closely resembles a typical undergraduate translation of one of Cicero's finest perorations: sound and fury, signifying nothing. I regret only that I have never seen Mrs. Ros's poetry. One volume was called *Poems of Puncture* and another *Bayonets of*

Bastard Sheen: alas, jewels now almost unprocurable. But at least I know the opening of her lyric written on first visiting St. Paul's Cathedral:

> Holy Moses, take a look,
> Brain and brawn in every nook!

10   Such genius is indestructible. Soon, soon now, some earnest researcher will be writing a Ph.D. thesis on Mrs. Amanda McKittrick Ros, and thus (as she herself might put it) conferring upon her dewy brow the laurels of concrete immortality.

11   Next to Mrs. Ros in my collection of kitsch is the work of the Scottish poet William McGonagall. This genius was born in 1830, but did not find his vocation until 1877. Poor and inadequate poets pullulate in every tongue, but (as the *Times Literary Supplement* observes) McGonagall "is the only truly memorable bad poet in our language." In his command of platitude and his disregard of melody, he was the true heir of William Wordsworth as a descriptive poet.

12   In one way his talents, or at least his aspirations, exceeded those of Wordsworth. He was at his best in describing events he had never witnessed, such as train disasters, shipwrecks, and sanguinary battles, and in picturing magnificent scenery he had never beheld except with the eye of the imagination. Here is his unforgettable Arctic landscape:

> Greenland's icy mountains are fascinating and grand,
> And wondrously created by the Almighty's command;
> And the works of the Almighty there's few can understand:
> Who knows but it might be a part of Fairyland?
>
> Because there are churches of ice, and houses glittering like glass,
> And for scenic grandeur there's nothing can it surpass,
> Besides there's monuments and spires, also ruins,
> Which serve for a safe retreat from the wild bruins.
>
> The icy mountains they're higher than a brig's topmast,
> And the stranger in amazement stands aghast
> As he beholds the water flowing off the melted ice
> Adown the mountain sides, that he cries out, Oh! how nice!

13   McGonagall also had a strong dramatic sense. He loved to tell of agonizing adventures, more drastic perhaps but not less moving than that related in Wordsworth's "Vaudracour and Julia." The happy ending of one of his "Gothic" ballads is surely unforgettable:

> So thus ends the story of Hanchen, a heroine brave,
> That tried hard her master's gold to save,
> And for her bravery she got married to the miller's eldest son,
> And Hanchen on her marriage night cried Heaven's will be done.

14   These scanty selections do not do justice to McGonagall's ingenuity as a rhymester. His sound effects show unusual talent. Most poets would be baffled by the problem of producing rhymes for the proper names General Graham and Osman Digna, but McGonagall gets them into a single stanza, with dazzling effect:

> Ye sons of Great Britain, I think no shame
> To write in praise of brave General Graham!
> Whose name will be handed down to posterity without any
>   stigma,
> Because, at the battle of El-Tab, he defeated Osman Digna.

15   One of McGonagall's most intense personal experiences was his visit to New York. Financially, it was not a success. In one of his vivid autobiographical sketches, he says, "I tried occasionally to get an engagement from theatrical proprietors and music-hall proprietors, but alas! 'twas all in vain, for they all told me they didn't encourage rivalry." However, he was deeply impressed by the architecture of Manhattan. In eloquent verses he expressed what many others have felt, although without adequate words to voice their emotion:

> Oh! Mighty City of New York, you are wonderful to behold,
> Your buildings that magnificent, the truth be it told;
> They were the only thing that seemed to arrest my eye,
> Because many of them are thirteen stories high.
>
> And the tops of the houses are all flat,
> And in the warm weather the people gather to chat;
> Besides on the house-tops they dry their clothes,
> And also many people all night on the house-tops repose.

16   Yet McGonagall felt himself a stranger in the United States. And here again his close kinship with Wordsworth appears. The Poet Laureate, in a powerful sonnet written at Calais, once reproached the English Channel for delaying his return by one of those too frequent storms in which (reckless tyrant!) it will indulge itself:

> Why cast ye back upon the Gallic shore,
> Ye furious waves! a patriotic Son
> Of England?

17   In the same vein McGonagall sings with rapture of his return to his "ain countree":

> And with regard to New York, and the sights I did see,
> One street in Dundee is more worth to me,
> And, believe me, the morning I sailed from New York,
> For bonnie Dundee—my heart it felt as light as a cork.

18   Indeed, New York is a challenging subject for ambitious poets. Here, from the same shelf, is a delicious poem on the same theme, by Ezra Pound:

> My City, my beloved
> Thou art a maid with no breasts
> Thou art slender as a silver reed.
> Listen to me, attend me!
> And I will breathe into thee a soul,
> And thou shalt live for ever.

19   The essence of this kind of trash is incongruity. The kitsch writer is always sincere. He really means to say something important. He feels he has a lofty spiritual message to bring to an unawakened world, or else he has had a powerful experience which he must communicate to the public. But either his message turns out to be a majestic platitude, or else he chooses the wrong form in which to convey it—or, most delightful of all, there is a fundamental discrepancy between the writer and his subject, as when Ezra Pound, born in Idaho, addresses the largest city in the world as a maid with no breasts, and enjoins it to achieve inspiration and immortality by listening to him. This is like climbing Mount Everest in order to carve a head of Mickey Mouse in the east face.

20   Bad love poetry, bad religious poetry, bad mystical prose, bad novels both autobiographical and historical—one can form a superb collection of kitsch simply by reading with a lively and awakened eye. College songs bristle with it. The works of Father Divine[2] are full of it—all the more delightful because in him it is usually incomprehensible. One of the Indian mystics, Sri Ramakrishna, charmed connoisseurs by describing the Indian scriptures (in a phrase which almost sets itself to kitsch-music) as fried in the butter of knowledge and steeped in the honey of love.

21   Bad funeral poetry is a rich mine of the stuff. Here, for example, is the opening of a jolly little lament, "The Funeral" by Stephen Spender, apparently written during his pink period:

> Death is another milestone on their way,
> With laughter on their lips and with winds blowing round
> Them
> They record simply
> How this one excelled all others in making driving belts.

22   Observe the change from humanism to communism. Spender simply took Browning's "Grammarian's Funeral," threw away the humor and the marching rhythm, and substituted wind and the Stakhanovist[3] speed-up. Such also is a delicious couplet from Archibald MacLeish's elegy on the late Harry Crosby:

> He walks with Ernest in the streets in Saragossa
> They are drunk their mouths are hard they saw qué cosa.

23   From an earlier romantic period, here is a splendid specimen. Coleridge attempted to express the profound truth that men and animals are neighbors in

---

[2]A black evangelist of New York.—ED.

[3]Alexei Stakhanov, a Russian miner who devised a worker incentive system.—ED.

a hard world; but he made the fundamental mistake of putting it into a monologue address to a donkey:

> Poor Ass! Thy master should have learnt to show
> Pity—best taught by fellowship of Woe!
> Innocent foal! thou poor despised forlorn!
> I hail thee brother. . . .

24   Once you get the taste for this kind of thing it is possible to find pleasure in hundreds of experiences which you might otherwise have thought either anesthetic or tedious: bad translations, abstract painting, grand opera . . . Dr. Johnson, with his strong sense of humor, had a fancy for kitsch, and used to repeat a poem in celebration of the marriage of the Duke of Leeds, composed by "an inferiour domestick . . . in such homely rhimes as he could make":

> When the Duke of Leeds shall married be
> To a fine young lady of high quality,
> How happy will that gentlewoman be
> In his Grace of Leed's good company.
> She shall have all that's fine and fair,
> And the best of silk and sattin shall wear;
> And ride in a coach to take the air,
> And have a house in St. James's Square.

25   Folk poetry is full of such jewels. Here is the epitaph on an old gentleman from Vermont who died in a sawmill accident:

> How shocking to the human mind
> The log did him to powder grind.
> God did command his soul away
> His summings we must all obey.

26   Kitsch is well known in drama, although (except for motion pictures) it does not usually last long. One palmary instance was a play extolling the virtues of the Boy Scout movement, called *Young England*. It ran for a matter of years during the 1930s, to audiences almost wholly composed of kitsch-fanciers, who eventually came to know the text quite as well as the unfortunate actors. I can still remember the opening of one magnificent episode.

> Scene: a woodland glade. Enter the hero, a Scoutmaster, riding a bicycle, and followed by the youthful members of his troop. They pile bicycles in silence. Then the Scoutmaster raises his finger, and says (accompanied fortissimo by most of the members of the audience):

> Fresh water must be our first consideration.

27   In the decorative arts kitsch flourishes, and is particularly widespread in sculpture. One of my favorite pieces of bad art is a statue in Rockefeller Center, New York. It is supposed to represent Atlas, the Titan condemned to carry the

sky on his shoulders. That is an ideal of somber, massive tragedy: greatness and suffering combined as in Hercules or Prometheus. But this version displays Atlas as a powerful moron, with a tiny little head, rather like the panfried young men who appear in the health magazines. Instead of supporting the heavens, he is lifting a spherical metal balloon: it is transparent, and quite empty; yet he is balancing insecurely on one foot like a furniture mover walking upstairs with a beach ball; and he is scowling like a mad baboon. If he ever gets the thing up, he will drop it; or else heave it onto a Fifth Avenue bus. It is a supremely ridiculous statue, and delights me every time I see it.

28   Perhaps you think this is a depraved taste. But really it is an extension of experience. At one end, Homer. At the other, Amanda McKittrick Ros. At one end, Hamlet. At the other, McGonagall, who is best praised in his own inimitable words:

> The poetry is moral and sublime
> And in my opinion nothing could be more fine.
> True genius there does shine so bright
> Like unto the stars of night.

Copyright © 1934 by Gilbert Highet, renewed. Reprinted by permission of Curtis Brown, Ltd.

● Vocabulary

psychopathic (1)	ingenious (4)	mystical (20)
frock coat (1)	luxuriant (6)	incomprehensible (20)
bulbous (2)	perorations (9)	connoisseurs (20)
Zulu (2)	unprocurable (9)	anesthetic (24)
assagais (2)	pullulate (11)	palmary (26)
majolica (2)	platitude (11)	extolling (26)
reticulation (2)	sanguinary (12)	fortissimo (26)
appalling (2)	rapture (17)	spherical (27)
illicit (2)	incongruity (19)	depraved (28)
paradoxical (4)	enjoins (19)	inimitable (28)

● The Facts

1. Where in his essay does Highet give a succinct definition of *kitsch*? After reading the essay, how would you explain this term to a friend who has never heard it?

2. What examples of kitsch does Highet provide? Name the three that impressed you most. Give reasons for your choice.

3. What metaphor does Mrs. Ros use to describe her hero's black eyes? Provide a metaphor or simile that would not be kitsch.

4. What characteristics of William McGonagall's poetry make it kitsch? Give a brief critique of two or three excerpts reprinted by Highet.

5. What is the essence of kitsch, according to the author? In what paragraph is this essence revealed?

● The Strategies

1. What is the predominant tone of the essay? Supply appropriate examples of this tone.

2. Point out some examples of striking figurative language in the essay. Are they serious or humorous?

3. What mode of development does Highet use more than any other? How does this method help his definition?

4. In the final paragraph, what is the irony of using McGonagall's own words to praise him?

● The Issues

1. Can you think of some well-known examples of kitsch in the United States besides those cited by Highet? What makes them kitsch?

2. Highet admits that certain kitsch items delight him. Explain how a person of taste might feel such delight.

3. How do you explain the overwhelming popularity of kitsch?

4. Popular lyrics are always a good source of kitsch. What lines from one of today's well-known songs can you quote as an example of kitsch? Do you still like the song even though it is kitsch? Give reasons for your answer.

5. Following are excerpts from two love poems (A and B). Which of them might be considered kitsch? Why?

A.

> The time was long and long ago,
> And we were young, my dear;
> The place stands fair in memory's glow,
> But it is far from here.
> The springtimes fade, the summers come,
> Autumn is here once more;
> The voice of ecstasy is dumb,
> The world goes forth to war.
> But though the flowers and birds were dead,
> And all the hours we knew,
> And though a hundred years had fled,
> I'd still come back to you.

B.

> Ah, love, let us be true
> To one another! for the world, which seems
> To lie before us like a land of dreams,
> So various, so beautiful, so new,
> Hath really neither joy, nor love, nor light,

Nor certitude, nor peace, nor help for pain;
And we are here as on a darkling plain
Swept with confused alarms of struggle and flight,
Where ignorant armies clash by night.

● Suggestions for Writing

1. Using Gilbert Highet's definition of *kitsch*, choose one area of popular taste today and show how it fits the definition.

2. Write a paragraph in which you compare or contrast the meaning of *camp* with that of *kitsch*.

Ars Poetica

ARCHIBALD MACLEISH

Archibald MacLeish (1892–1982), poet and playwright, was born in Glencoe, Illinois, and educated at Yale University. Trained as a lawyer, MacLeish served as librarian of Congress and as an adviser to President Franklin D. Roosevelt. A recurrent theme in his poetry was his deep apprehension about the rise of fascism. MacLeish won a Pulitzer Prize for a poetry collection, *Conquistador* (1932), and another for his play *J. B.* (1958).

In this famous poem, MacLeish proposes a succinct definition of poetry. The poem comes from a collection of poems spanning the years 1917 to 1982.

● ● ●

1   A poem should be palpable and mute
As a globed fruit,

Dumb
As old medallions to the thumb,

5   Silent as the sleeve-worn stone
Of casement ledges where the moss has grown—

A poem should be wordless
As the flight of birds.

A poem should be motionless in time
10   As the moon climbs,

Leaving, as the moon releases
Twig by twig the night-entangled trees,

Leaving, as the moon behind the winter leaves,
Memory by memory the mind—

15 A poem should be motionless in time
    As the moon climbs.

    A poem should be equal to:
    Not true

    For all the history of grief
20 An empty doorway and a maple leaf.

    For love
    The leaning grasses and two lights above the sea—

    A poem should not mean
    But be.

● Vocabulary

palpable (1)   medallions (4)   casement (6)

● The Facts

1. The translation of the poem's Latin title is "The Art of Poetry." Why is the title in Latin? How does the title relate to the poem?
2. Where does MacLeish give an explicit definition of poetry? How does he convey to the reader what poetry is?
3. In lines 17 and 18, what does MacLeish mean by the words "equal to: / Not true"?
4. The final stanza contains MacLeish's summarized view of poetry. What is your interpretation of the stanza?

● The Strategies

1. "Ars Poetica" is developed through a series of paradoxes. Analyze and interpret each.
2. MacLeish suggests that all the history of grief could be summarized by "an empty doorway and a maple leaf." Do you consider this an appropriate image? Can you suggest another equally appropriate image?
3. What image does MacLeish suggest for love? Do you find this image appropriate? Explain.
4. What synonyms for *mute* does the poet use? Cite them all.
5. What is the significance of repeating the fifth stanza in the eighth stanza?

● The Issues

1. What are some other definitions of *poetry*? What is your own definition? How does it compare to or contrast with MacLeish's definition?

2. How do you interpret MacLeish's statement that "A poem should be equal to: / Not true"? Provide an example to clarify this statement.

3. What does the author mean when he writes in stanza 4 that "A poem should be wordless / As the flight of birds"? How does this statement relate to Highet's notion of kitsch? (See Highet's essay on pp. 428–435.)

4. Find a short poem that, in your view, perfectly exemplifies MacLeish's view that a poem should "not mean / But be." Do you like this poem? Why or why not?

● Suggestions for Writing

1. Consult a collection of the works of Wordsworth, Coleridge, Keats, or Shelley, for a definition of poetry. Contrast that definition with the one in "Ars Poetica." State which definition you like best and why.

2. Write a paragraph in which you give a definition of *love,* and support that definition with appropriate images. Then write another paragraph in which you do the same thing for *hate.*

ISSUE FOR CRITICAL THINKING AND DEBATE: IMMIGRATION

Some years ago we took an airplane trip from Atlanta to Zürich, Switzerland, aboard a Swissair jet. During the long crossing, we felt sorry for the poor pilot. The flight attendants spoke to each other in Swiss dialect. Every time he made an announcement, he had to repeat it in English, French, German, and Swiss German. For most of the eight-hour flight, the pilot quite sensibly remained mute. But his behavior brought to mind one predicted effect of immigration that Americans fear the most—the tendency of new arrivals to settle in communities where they can speak their mother tongue rather than learn English. Miami, and much of Florida, has virtually become a bilingual land, with Spanish as the primary language. California and Texas are in a similar predicament. Countries whose people are polyglot rather than sharing one common language have a tendency to develop profound divisions and differences based on linguistic groupings. One has only to think of Québec and the deep antagonisms that exist between French and English-speaking Canadians. The lack of a common language is one reason the European Union is faltering in its attempt to unite that deeply divided continent.

When it comes to immigrants and immigration, Americans are truly a deeply conflicted people. The vast majority of us are the descendants of immigrants, some with fathers and mothers who came here from other countries, others with foreign great ancestors. It is a rare American whose origin one or two or three generations back does not lie abroad. One of this book's authors, for example, is a Jamaican immigrant who became a naturalized American citizen many years ago. The other was born to American parents living abroad and grew up speaking French within her immediate family, coming to the United States to attend college as a teenager. The wife of the male author is the granddaughter of a Polish immigrant who spoke mainly Polish and, even at the end of her life, only badly fractured English. The wife's own mother speaks both Polish and English; the wife herself speaks only English, and has some regrets about not learning her grandmother's language. In this evolution of language, the family is almost stereotypical, with the experience being repeated throughout millions of American households.

Is immigration good for America? The answer you get depends on whom you ask. In 2004, National Public Radio, collaborating with Harvard's Kennedy School of Government and the Kaiser Family Foundation, undertook a survey of 1,100 native Americans and nearly 800 immigrants and found deep divisions in the opinion of those polled, with 37 percent saying that immigration should be kept the same, 41 percent that it should be decreased, and only 18 percent saying that it should be increased. Those Americans who had direct contact with some immigrant group were, as a whole, less negative about immigrants. Among the strongest fears of the native population was that immigrants would displace Americans from jobs. Another fear was that America would be changed by the influx of immigrants. Since 9/11, many Americans have expressed the fear that terrorists might exist among immigrants not screened carefully. Yet even the most rabid opponent of immigration has to admit that immigrants do much of the dirty work in our communities, such as digging ditches, cleaning houses, sweeping streets, picking fruit, and other kinds of manual labor that natives do not like to do.

Immigrants bring blessings to America, not the least of which is a variegated cuisine and a unique outlook. What would American cuisine be like without French crème brulee, Italian pizza, Chinese chow mein, Greek gyros, Middle Eastern falafel, or Mexican enchiladas? The infusion of cultural richness into the melting pot is the primary contribution of successive waves of immigrants. There are other benefits as well, one of which is pointed out by writer Eduardo Porter. Immigrants, many of whom are on shaky legal footing, contribute billions of dollars to Social Security, yet they draw no benefits. Without them, Social Security would be in even worse shape than presently reported. As for the charge often made that the country is being overrun by immigrant groups, writer Bill Bryson points out a fact often overlooked: that the vast continent of America is really underpopulated and with far fewer immigrants than European countries such as France and England. It really is an oddity that so many of us, the children and grandchildren of immigrants, would take such a negative attitude toward what is, in effect, a nearly universal common background of immigration roots.

Aside from their contributions of crafts and foods, immigrants bring to the table a fresh perspective of wonderment to the grand experiment that is America. They do not whine as natives are likely to, for they are not used to the manifold opportunities in business and education and to the social advancement that are available to the hardworking newcomer and that many natives take for granted. This, of all the immigrant's endowments, is probably the greatest and the least appreciated of all gifts: namely, the gift of fresh eyes to see anew for us and to remind us that no matter what our difficulties or passing worries might be, all in all we have it pretty good.

"Liberals!"

Illegal Immigrants
Are Bolstering Social Security with Billions

EDUARDO PORTER

Eduardo Porter is a journalist and prolific contributor to the business section of *The New York Times,* writing dozens of articles each year. He has covered subjects ranging from the effect of oil demand on the U.S. trade deficit to an essay on why Monaco is a country. The essay below was published in the *Times* on April 5, 2005.

• • •

1   STOCKTON, Calif.—Since illegally crossing the Mexican border into the United States six years ago, Angel Martínez has done backbreaking work, harvesting asparagus, pruning grapevines and picking the ripe fruit. More recently, he has also washed trucks, often working as much as 70 hours a week, earning $8.50 to $12.75 an hour.

2   Not surprisingly, Mr. Martínez, 28, has not given much thought to Social Security's long-term financial problems. But Mr. Martínez—who comes from the state of Oaxaca in southern Mexico and hiked for two days through the desert to enter the United States near Tecate, some 20 miles east of Tijuana— contributes more than most Americans to the solvency of the nation's public retirement system.

3   Last year, Mr. Martínez paid about $2,000 toward Social Security and $450 for Medicare through payroll taxes withheld from his wages. Yet unlike most Americans, who will receive some form of a public pension in retirement and

will be eligible for Medicare as soon as they turn 65, Mr. Martínez is not entitled to benefits.

4   He belongs to a big club. As the debate over Social Security heats up, the estimated seven million or so illegal immigrant workers in the United States are now providing the system with a subsidy of as much as $7 billion a year.

5   While it has been evident for years that illegal immigrants pay a variety of taxes, the extent of their contributions to Social Security is striking: the money added up to about 10 percent of last year's surplus—the difference between what the system currently receives in payroll taxes and what it doles out in pension benefits. Moreover, the money paid by illegal workers and their employers is factored into all the Social Security Administration's projections.

6   Illegal immigration, Marcelo Suárez-Orozco, co-director of immigration studies at New York University, noted sardonically, could provide "the fastest way to shore up the long-term finances of Social Security."

7   It is impossible to know exactly how many illegal immigrant workers pay taxes. But according to specialists, most of them do. Since 1986, when the Immigration Reform and Control Act set penalties for employers who knowingly hire illegal immigrants, most such workers have been forced to buy fake IDs to get a job.

8   Currently available for about $150 on street corners in just about any immigrant neighborhood in California, a typical fake ID package includes a green card and a Social Security card. It provides cover for employers, who, if asked, can plausibly assert that they believe all their workers are legal. It also means that workers must be paid by the book—with payroll tax deductions.

9   IRCA, as the immigration act is known, did little to deter employers from hiring illegal immigrants or to discourage them from working. But for Social Security's finances, it was a great piece of legislation.

10   Starting in the late 1980s, the Social Security Administration received a flood of W-2 earnings reports with incorrect—sometimes simply fictitious—Social Security numbers. It stashed them in what it calls the "earnings suspense file" in the hope that someday it would figure out whom they belonged to.

11   The file has been mushrooming ever since: $189 billion worth of wages ended up recorded in the suspense file over the 1990s, two and a half times the amount of the 1980s.

12   In the current decade, the file is growing, on average, by more than $50 billion a year, generating $6 billion to $7 billion in Social Security tax revenue and about $1.5 billion in Medicare taxes.

13   In 2002 alone, the last year with figures released by the Social Security Administration, nine million W-2s with incorrect Social Security numbers landed in the suspense file, accounting for $56 billion in earnings, or about 1.5 percent of total reported wages.

14   Social Security officials do not know what fraction of the suspense file corresponds to the earnings of illegal immigrants. But they suspect that the portion is significant.

15   "Our assumption is that about three-quarters of other-than-legal immigrants pay payroll taxes," said Stephen C. Goss, Social Security's chief actuary, using the agency's term for illegal immigration.

Vocabulary

solvency (2)	factored (5)	plausibly (8)
subsidy (4)	sardonically (6)	deter (9)
doles (5)	shore up (6)	fictitious (10)

The Facts

1. How accurate are the figures reported concerning illegal entries into the United States?

2. How did Angel Martínez find his way to the United States? Do you think his journey is typical of that of other illegal immigrants?

3. How much money did Martínez contribute in 2004? What is ironic about his contribution? Did this figure surprise you? Explain your answer.

4. What amazing fact about how much money illegal immigrants pay toward Social Security is brought to light in this essay? Does this fact change your views on illegal immigration?

5. What is the IRCA? What was its intent? What has been the unforeseen result?

The Strategies

1. Where does the author place the thesis of his essay? What advantage does this placement have?

2. How does the author grab the reader's attention while introducing his subject? What is your reaction to his technique?

3. According to the author, what is happening while "the debate over Social Security heats up"? Who is participating in this debate? Where do you stand on the issue?

4. What is the importance of the reference to Marcelo Suárez-Orozco in paragraph 6?

5. What is the role of statistics in this essay? Do they help or hinder? Support your opinion with examples from the essay.

The Issues

1. Did Porter's essay in any way change your opinion about illegal immigrants? What was your opinion before reading the essay, and what is it now?

2. Porter describes the backbreaking work of harvesting asparagus, pruning grapevines, picking the ripe fruit, and washing trucks performed by Angel Martínez. What other kinds of work have you watched illegal immigrants perform? Has any of this work been rewarded with high wages? What sort of work do they typically carry out?

3. Why is it that illegal immigrants contribute so heftily to Social Security and Medicare? Should the situation be changed? If so, how? If not, why not?

4. What is the government doing with all of the phony Social Security numbers they discover because of the fake IDs purchased by illegal immigrants? How can this situation be corrected? Suggest some corrective measures.

5. Why has the term "other than legal immigrants" (OTLI) evolved? What is your reaction to this term? What better term, if any, can you suggest?

● Suggestions for Writing

1. Write an essay in which you describe how you feel about the many immigrant workers who help grow our food and keep our cities clean. Begin with a vivid description of their tasks and then explain how you feel about these workers. Ask yourself these questions: Do I show enough respect for these immigrants? Do I think they should receive appropriate medical and social benefits? Support your view with documentary evidence—by quoting an expert on the subject of immigrant workers.

2. Write a vivid portrait of an acquaintance or loved one who has spent his or her life doing physical labor. Make sure that your portrait reflects how you feel about this person. For instance, if Aunt Julia cleans houses as a living, indicate how she does her job and what kind of person she is.

© Jeff Greenberg/Photo Edit

● Why are pride and belonging such a powerful part of the swearing-in ceremony for immigrants who receive U.S. citizenship?

Wide-open Spaces

BILL BRYSON

Bill Bryson (b. 1952) was born in Des Moines, Iowa, but spent twenty years in England, working as a journalist for *The Independent* and *The Times*. He moved to the United States in 1995 and returned to England in 2003. He continues to delight audiences with books that are not only perceptive but also hilariously funny. Among his bestsellers are the following: *African Diary* (2002), *A Short History of Nearly Everything* (2003), *A Walk in the Woods* (1998), and *I'm a Stranger Here Myself* (1999), from which the essay below was excerpted. The writer is American-born and reared but at heart an Englishman. After a stay of twenty years in England, he returned to America with a point of view informed by an English perspective. As you read this essay, try to keep an open mind and to remember that the author has a reputation for a snide sense of humor.

• • •

1   Here are a couple of things to bear in mind as you go through life: Daniel Boone was an idiot, and it's not worth trying to go to Maine for the day from Hanover, New Hampshire. Allow me to explain.

2   I was fooling around with a globe the other evening and was mildly astounded to discover that here in Hanover I am much closer to our old house in Yorkshire than I am to many other parts of the United States. Indeed, from where I sit to Attu, the westernmost of Alaska's Aleutian Islands, is almost four thousand miles. Put another way, a person in London is closer to Johannesburg than I am to the outermost tip of my own country.

3   Of course, you could argue that Alaska is not a fair comparison because there is so much non-U.S. territory between here and there. But even if you confine yourself to the mainland United States, the distances are imposing, to say the least. From my house to Los Angeles is about the same as from London to Lagos. We are, in a word, talking big scale here.

4   Here is another arresting fact to do with scale. In the past twenty years (a period in which, let the record show, I was doing my breeding elsewhere), the population of the United States increased by almost exactly the equivalent of Great Britain's. I find that quite amazing, not least because I don't know where all these new people are.

5   A remarkable thing about America, if you have been living for a long time in a crowded little place like the United Kingdom, is how very big and very empty so much of it is. Consider this: Montana, Wyoming, and North and South Dakota have an area twice the size of France but a population less than that of south London. Alaska is bigger still and has even fewer people. Even my own adopted state of New Hampshire, in the relatively crowded Northeast, is 85 percent forest, and most of the rest is lakes. You can drive for very long periods in New Hampshire and never see anything but trees and mountains—not a house or a hamlet or even, quite often, another car.

6   I am constantly caught by this. Not long ago, I had a couple of friends over from England and we decided to take a drive over to the lakes of western Maine. It had the makings of a nice day out. All we had to do was cross New Hampshire—which is, after all, the fourth tiniest state in America—and go a little way over the state line into our lovely, moose-strewn neighbor to the east. I figured it would take about two hours—two and a half tops.

7   Well, of course you have anticipated the punchline. Six hours later we pulled up exhausted at the shore of Rangeley Lake, took two pictures, looked at each other, and wordlessly got back in the car and drove home. This sort of thing happens all the time.

8   The curious thing is that a very great many Americans don't seem to see it this way. They think the country is way too crowded. Moves are constantly afoot to restrict access to national parks and wilderness areas on the grounds that they are dangerously overrun. Parts of them *are* unquestionably crowded, but that is only because 98 percent of visitors arrive by car, and 98 percent of those venture no more than a couple of hundred feet from their metallic wombs. Elsewhere, however, you can have whole mountains to yourself, even in the most popular parks on the busiest days. Yet I may soon find myself barred from hiking in many wilderness areas unless I had the foresight to book a visit weeks beforehand, because of perceived overcrowding.

9   Even more ominously, there is a growing belief that the best way of dealing with this supposed crisis is by expelling most of those not born here. There is an organization whose name escapes me (it may be "Dangerously Small-Minded Reactionaries for a Better America") that periodically runs earnest, carefully reasoned ads in the *New York Times, Atlantic Monthly*, and other important and influential publications, calling for an end to immigration because, as one of its ads explains, it "is devastating our environment and the quality of our lives." Elsewhere it adds, "Primarily because of immigration we are rushing at breakneck speed toward an environmental and economic disaster." Oh, give me a break, please.

10   You could, I suppose, make an economic or even cultural case for cutting back on immigration, but not on the grounds that the country is running out of room. Anti-immigration arguments conveniently overlook the fact that America already expels a million immigrants a year and that those who are here mostly do jobs that are too dirty, low-paying, or unsatisfying for the rest of us to do. Getting rid of immigrants is not suddenly going to open employment opportunities for those born here; all it's going to do is leave a lot of dishes unwashed, a lot of beds unmade, and a lot of fruit unpicked. Still less is it going to miraculously create a lot more breathing space for the rest of us.

11   America already has one of the lowest proportions of immigrants in the developed world. Just 6 percent of people in the United States are foreign born, compared with, for instance, 8 percent in Britain and 11 percent in France. America may or may not be heading for an environmental and economic disaster, but if so it certainly isn't because six people in every hundred were born somewhere else.

12   There aren't many human acts more foolishly simplistic or misguided, or more likely to lead to careless evil, than blaming general problems on small minorities, yet that seems to be quite a respectable impulse where immigration is concerned these days. Two years ago, Californians voted overwhelmingly for Proposition 187, which would deny health and education services to illegal immigrants. Almost immediately upon passage of the proposition, Governor Pete Wilson ordered the state health authorities to stop providing prenatal care to any woman who could not prove that she was here legally. Now please correct me by all means, but does it not seem just a trifle harsh—a trifle barbaric even—to imperil the well-being of an unborn child because of the actions of its parents?

13   No less astounding in its way, the federal government recently began removing basic rights and entitlements even from legal immigrants. We are in effect saying to them: "Thank you for your years of faithful service to our economy, but things are a little tough at the moment, so we aren't prepared to help you. Besides, you have a funny accent."

14   I'm not arguing for unlimited immigration, you understand, just a sense of proportion in how we treat those who are here already. The fact is, America is one of the least crowded countries on earth, with an average of just 68 people per square mile, compared with 256 in France and over 600 in Britain. Altogether, only 2 percent of the United States is classified as "built up."

15   Of course, Americans have always tended to see these things in a different way. Daniel Boone famously is supposed to have looked out his cabin window one day, seen a wisp of smoke rising from a homesteader's dwelling on a distant mountain, and announced his intention to move on, complaining bitterly that the neighborhood was getting too crowded.

16   Which is why I say Daniel Boone was an idiot. I just hate to see the rest of my country going the same way.

From I'M A STRANGER HERE MYSELF by Bill Bryson, copyright © 1999 by Bill Bryson. Used by permission of Broadway Books, a division of Random House, Inc.

● Vocabulary

arresting (4)	ominously (9)	barbaric (12)
punchline (7)	periodically (9)	imperil (12)
venture (8)	prenatal (12)	entitlements (13)

● The Facts

1. What major fact does Bryson try to bring out in his essay? Is this a disputable fact? Explain your answer.

2. According to the author, how rapidly has the population of the United States grown? What comparison does the author make?

3. What impression do people from European countries get when they visit the United States?

4. According to the author, most Americans disagree with his view. What is their perception?

5. From Bryson's point of view, what causes the most beautiful wilderness areas to be overcrowded? What statistic does the author cite to support his declaration?

● The Strategies

1. Early in the essay, the author calls Daniel Boone an "idiot." What dangerous ground is he treading on when he uses such a demeaning label? Who is Daniel Boone? How do you feel about his being called an "idiot"?

2. What strategy is the author using when he mentions an organization that may be called "Dangerously Small-Minded Reactionaries for a Better America"?

3. How does the author underscore the fact that the United States has one of the lowest proportions of immigrants in the developed world? Do you consider his strategy effective? Give reasons for your answer.

4. At what point in the essay does the author shift from writing about the geography of the United States to the problem of immigration? What good reason is there for not attacking the immigration issue earlier?

5. What is the tone of the quotation used by the author in paragraph 13? What is your response to this paragraph?

● The Issues

1. For the author, an American who spent twenty years in England, what is the "remarkable thing" about America? Do you, too, find it remarkable? Explain your answer.

2. The author dislikes the thought that someday he may have to make a reservation in order to hike in a certain wilderness area. To him this would be a ridiculous requirement considering how most mountainous areas remain free of human visitors. How do you feel about forest rangers who require a reservation for hiking along certain trails? What logical reason can you suggest for such a requirement?

3. According to the author, what is the only result that will come from expelling all the immigrants who work in our country? Do you agree with Bryson on this point? Explain yourself.

4. How strongly does the author feel about blaming our general problems on the minorities in our country? What is your reaction?

5. Is the author for or against unlimited immigration? What approach does he propose? Does his idea appeal to your sense of justice, or do you think the author goes overboard one way or another? Explain your view.

● Suggestions for Writing

1. Write a journal entry in which you dream about the most beautiful, pristine vacation spot in the United States. Then describe an ideal vacation there. Indicate whether you would want to be alone or have company during this retreat.

If your choice is to be alone, explain why you want seclusion. If your choice is to have company, then describe the company you would choose.

2. Bryson draws our attention to the absurdity of being paranoid about allowing foreigners into our country with its thousands of miles of open spaces. Write an essay in which you refute Bryson's view. Like Bryson, use some appropriate quotations and examples to shore up your case.

Stumped by ending an essay? Exit on pages 710–711, at the **Editing Booth!**

Punctuation Workshop
The Apostrophe (')

The apostrophe shows ownership, the omission in a contraction, and certain plurals.

1. Use an apostrophe + *s* to show ownership.

> Pete's baseball bat
>
> Someone's mistake
>
> This bicycle is Katie's. (A possessive can follow the word to which it belongs.)
>
> Venus's beauty
>
> For a plural that ends in *s*, omit an additional *s*.
>
> The Dodgers' baseball camp (rather than *Dodgers's*)

2. Use an apostrophe to show an omission in a contraction.

> don't (for *do not*)
>
> can't (for *cannot*)
>
> High school class of '52

CAUTION: Don't confuse the contraction *who's* with the pronoun *whose*.

3. Use the apostrophe to form certain plurals.

> He crossed all of his t's and dotted all of his i's.
>
> I love to read about the 1800s (*1800's* is sometimes acceptable).
>
> Her l's are written in bold strokes

 CAUTION: Do not use an apostrophe to form plural nouns that don't show ownership. (The lions were restless—not *lion's*. The Goldmans were out of town—not *Goldman's*.)

Dave Herman
Georgia State University
Immigrants in America

An immigrant is a person whose ancestral roots lie in another country. By that definition nearly all Americans are immigrants or the descendants of immigrants. Even the Native Americans, the so-called American Indians, are immigrants whose ancestors came to the new world via the Bering Straits, which geologists tell us was once connected to the North American continent by a land bridge. Ours, like it or not, is an immigrant society.

One disadvantage of this widespread immigrant influence is an attitude of snobbery that some American citizens have, depending on when their ancestors came to the United States. The most conspicuous example of this is an organization called Daughters of the American Revolution (DAR for short). To be a member of this snobbish group, you have to prove that one of your ancestors fought in the American Revolution. The guidelines for eligibility declare that membership is open to any woman who can prove "lineal, bloodline descent from an ancestor who aided in achieving American independence," adding that the applicant "must provide documentation for each statement of birth, marriage, and death" ("Become a Member").

The children of immigrants sometimes hold a condescending or embarrassed attitude toward their parents, especially if the parents have a strong foreign accent from a language other than English. Often the children make excuses for the way their parents mispronounce words or ignore grammar rules. Once the third generation emerges, the language of the first generation has usually been lost, with only nostalgic scraps of idioms and quaint sayings surviving.

In my own family, for example, my grandmother speaks Spanish, which is her native tongue, and so does my mother. An aunt or two understand a few words. But only my mother has mastered the language, probably because she has a good ear. The third

Herman   2

generation, of which I'm a member, speaks no Spanish. One cousin can understand a phrase here and there if the speaker enunciates clearly and slowly. But for the most part, the language is Greek to my generation. Because the cultural emphasis in those days was on instant adaptation to a new society, the children were encouraged to speak English everywhere, even at home. Those who fear that immigrants will introduce and cling to the mother tongue of their parents don't understand the tremendous pressure immigrants and their children are subjected to by American society. Even Miami, which has a majority Hispanic population and where Spanish seems to be the language of the majority, has a bilingual population that speaks both English and Spanish fluently.

I think immigration has been good for America. Wherever there is a brain drain going on in some foreign country of our world, it is likely that the brains leaving their homeland are flowing into America. My uncle, for example, went to school with a boy who later became an astrophysicist for NASA. This boy become so important to the space program that when he came back to the village where my father and he came from, he was in the company of two Secret Service agents as his personal bodyguards.

In my neighborhood are three families from what used to be Armenia. The children have all done well at the University. One is a neurosurgeon, one a gynecologist, and one a successful businessman. Several of the other children are still at the University pursuing advanced degrees. It is impossible to estimate in dollars alone what these three families have or will contribute to the society in which they were born because their parents had migrated to America.

We are a society of immigrants. And we're better off for it. The problems of adjustment to a new culture, or a new culture adjusting to the influx of immigrants, are minor compared to the richness and blessings that immigration bestows on America. There's a reason why the inscription of the base of the Statue of Liberty says,

Give me your tired, your poor,

Your huddled masses yearning to breathe free,

The wretched refuse of your teeming shore,

Send these, the homeless, tempest-tossed to me,

I lift my lamp beside the golden door!

Emma Lazarus, the poet who wrote this jingle, was no fool. She knew a good thing when she saw it.

Work Cited

"Become a Member: Eligibility." *National Society Daughters of the American Revolution*. DAR, 2005. Web. 7 July 2005.

How I Write

I write late at night or early in the morning. I cannot write during the day because my thoughts race too fast for writing. I have to be in a slower mode in order to write effectively. Mostly, I rewrite everything over two or three times just to make it smooth.

How I Wrote This Essay

I tried to personalize the topic by thinking of immigrants I knew who contributed some substance to America. I didn't want to just recite statistics, which tends to be boring anyway. Plus, by using examples within my reach, I thought that would make the essay easier to read and more interesting.

My Writing Tip

Go over your work again and again. Sometimes when you can't get something just right, an idea will occur to you if you keep going over the material. I know this sounds boring, but it's the technique that works for me.

● **CHAPTER WRITING ASSIGNMENTS**

1. In an essay, define *history*. Allow your definition to function as the essay's thesis.

2. Define yourself in an essay, and support your definition with evidence from your life. Here is how one student defined herself: "I am a consummate pessimist because I always expect the darkest of all possible outcomes."

3. Write a definition of *superstition* so that you leave no doubt in the reader's mind as to what the term means.

4. Choose one of the following terms and write an essay in which you first define the term as a dictionary would. Then give an extended definition, using the development most suitable for answering the question, "What is it?"

curiosity	mercurial
genetic	pratfall

● **WRITING ASSIGNMENTS FOR A SPECIFIC AUDIENCE**

1. Define the term *authority* for a seven-year-old child.

2. Write an essay defining *failure* to an audience of your peers.

● **IMAGE GALLERY WRITING ASSIGNMENT**

Visit pages IG-13–IG-15 of our image gallery and study all three images dealing with immigration. Then choose the image that most appeals to you. Answer the questions and do the writing assignment.

Pointer from a Pro

LET YOUR WRITING PERCOLATE

We're horrible judges of the comparative quality of our own work, particularly in the moment. What feels good and what feels bad when we're writing something, isn't always a good indicator of quality.

—Tycho Goren

Usually, if you place a night between writing and checking the product, you will see your writing with renewed clarity because while you were sleeping, your subconscious writer's mind was editing and revising.

13

Comparison/Contrast

What Comparison/Contrast Does

To *compare* is to point out how two things are similar; to *contrast* is to stress how they are dissimilar. To say that both John Calvin and Martin Luther were persecuted by the Catholic Church, opposed to conservative theology, and personally against materialistic self-indulgence is to make a comparison. A contrast between the two men, however, might stress that Luther wanted the Church to return to the primitive simplicity of the apostles, whereas Calvin heartily supported the advancement of capitalism. The following passage from a student essay draws a contrast, indicated by the use of the highlighted contrasting words and expressions, between Egyptian and Greek mythologies.

> A brief consideration of Egyptian mythology contrasted with the mythology of the Greeks is enough to convince us of the revolution in thought that must have taken place from one age to the other. The Egyptian gods had no resemblance to anything in the real world, whereas the Greek gods were fashioned after real Greek people. In Egypt the gods typically worshiped consisted of a towering colossus, so immobile and so distorted that no human could imagine it alive; or a woman with a cat's head, suggesting inflexible, inhuman cruelty; or a monstrous mysterious sphinx, aloof from anything we might consider human. The Egyptian artists' interpretations of the divine were horrid bestial shapes that combined men's heads with birds' bodies or portrayed lions with eagle wings—creatures that could inhabit only terrifying nightmares. The monstrosities of an invisible world were what the Egyptians worshiped. The Greek interpretation of divinity stands in opposition to this dark picture. The Greeks were preoccupied with the visible world. Unlike the Egyptians, they found their desires satisfied in what they could actually see around them. The ancient statues of Apollo, for instance, resemble

the strong young bodies of athletes contending in the Olympic games. Homer describes Hermes as if he were a splendid Greek citizen. Generally the Greek artists found their gods in the idealized beauty or intelligence of actual human counterparts. In direct contrast to the Egyptians, they had no wish to create some hideous fantasy that they then called God.

On the other hand, the following passage finds similarities between whales and human beings:

> Whales and human beings are like two nations of individuals who have certain characteristics in common. As mammals they both are warm-blooded, giving milk and breathing air. As social creatures they both have basic urges for privacy as well as for fraternization. As species bent on reproduction they both show similar patterns of aggression during courtship, the male trying to gain the female's attention and the female responding. Finally, as mystical beings they both are caught in the net of life and time, fellow prisoners of the splendor, travail, and secrets of earth.

Comparisons that take the form of extended analogies are frequently used to clarify abstract or complex ideas. One of the most famous examples of this use comes from the biblical accounts of Jesus's remarks:

> The kingdom of heaven is like unto a grain of mustard seed, which a man took and sowed in his field: which indeed is less than all seeds; but when it is grown, it is greater than the herbs, and becometh a tree, so that the birds of the heaven come and lodge in the branches thereof.
>
> —Matthew 13:31–32

By comparing the kingdom of heaven to a mustard seed, which would have been familiar to his agrarian listeners, Jesus explains the power and the influence that a life dedicated to God can exert.

When to Use Comparison/Contrast

The odds are that you will not get through college without having to write a comparison/contrast, either in an essay exam or in a research paper. An English exam may typically ask for a contrast between the tragic flaws of Oedipus and Othello. A sociology question may call for a comparison between the demands of the feminist and civil rights movements. You may be asked to catalogue the differences between substances of organic and inorganic chemistry, or you may be asked to write an essay contrasting the traits of apes in captivity with those of apes who live in the wild. Comparison/contrast questions, in fact, commonly arise in every imaginable discipline.

How to Use Comparison/Contrast

1. **Use logical bases of contrast.** Suppose you want to develop the key thought "My college experience is teaching me that good instructors are a different breed from bad ones." You must first decide on your bases for contrast. You must ask yourself in which areas of instruction you wish to contrast the activities of good teachers with bad teachers. The following three could be your choice: (1) time spent on lesson preparation; (2) willingness to tolerate dissent; (3) personal relationships with students. Having chosen your bases, write down the three areas under consideration on the left side of a sheet of paper and then create two columns (one for good instructors, the other for bad instructors) in which you will place comments, as follows:

	Good instructors	Bad instructors
1. Time spent on lesson preparation	Good instructors constantly revise lessons, including up-to-date reviews, newspaper clippings, research results, and other relevant material. They refer to more than one source work and give suggestions for further reading. Lectures and discussions are the result of clear objectives.	Bad instructors give the same lectures year in and year out, including the same dead jokes. They do nothing but spell out rudimentary facts, to be memorized verbatim for final tests. They often spend class time on dull workbook assignments. They show as many movies as possible, during which they nap.
2. Willingness to tolerate dissent	Good instructors welcome arguments as a way of bringing life into the classroom and of pointing out alternatives. Like Socrates, they believe the classroom dialectic is a valid teaching method.	Bad instructors see dissent or discussion as a threat to discipline and to their authority, so they avoid both. They feel safe only when they are parroting themselves or the textbook.
3. Personal relationships with students	Good instructors spend time beyond office hours listening to student questions or complaints. They willingly clarify difficult problems. They never embarrass or patronize students.	Bad instructors are usually too busy off campus to spend time in personal consultation with students. They make students who ask for special help feel inferior.

2. **Use either the alternating or block method of contrast.** Once you have made a preliminary sketch, you can develop it simply by adding a few transitional words and phrases, as has been done in the following passage (transitions are highlighted):

My college experience is teaching me that good instructors are a different breed from bad ones. In terms of time spent on lesson preparation, good instructors constantly revise their lessons, including such items as up-to-date reviews, newspaper clippings, research results, or any other relevant material. They refer to more than one source work and give suggestions for further reading. Their lectures and discussions are the obvious result of clear objectives. In contrast, bad instructors give the same lectures year in and year out, including the same dead jokes. Only the rudimentary facts are spelled out in class, to be memorized verbatim and regurgitated on final tests. They often spend classroom time on dull workbook assignments or, as often as possible, a movie, during which they take a nap.

Another big difference between good and bad instructors is in their willingness to tolerate dissent. Good instructors welcome arguments as a way of bringing life into the classroom and of pointing out alternatives. Like Socrates, they believe that the classroom dialectic is a valid learning method. Bad instructors, however, take the opposite tack. They see dissent or discussion as a threat to their discipline and to their authority, so they avoid both. They feel safe only when they are parroting themselves or their textbooks.

Good and bad instructors differ markedly in their relationship to students. Good instructors spend time beyond office hours listening to student questions or complaints. They willingly clarify difficult problems, and they never embarrass or patronize students. Bad instructors, on the contrary, are usually too busy off campus to spend time in personal consultation with students. They deliver their lectures and disappear. The student who asks for special help is made to feel inferior.

The preceding example demonstrates the *alternating* method of comparison/contrast. The paragraph is written to alternate back and forth from one side of an issue to the other. Another system—called the *block* method—uses separate paragraphs for each side of the issue, as illustrated in the following passage that contrasts two views of Jewish history:

On the one hand, the Diaspora Jews can say that this talk of a predestination drama is a lot of nonsense. What has happened is only an interesting constellation of accidental, impersonal events, which some people have distorted out of all proportions to reality. We were defeated in war, they could say, we lost our land, we were exiled, and now it is our turn to disappear, just as under similar circumstances the Sumerians, the

Hittites, the Babylonians, the Assyrians, the Persians—yes, even the Jews in the Kingdom of Israel—disappeared.

On the other hand, they can say that their ancestors could not have been pursuing a mere illusion for 2,000 years. They could say that if we are God's Chosen People as our forefathers affirmed, if we have been placed in an exile to accomplish a divine mission as our Prophets predicted, and since we did receive the Torah, then we must survive to fulfill our Covenant with God.

—Max I. Dimont, *The Indestructible Jews*

The alternating and block methods of comparison/contrast are further clarified in the following two outlines contrasting the Toyota Camry and the Volkswagen Jetta on the basis of cost, performance, and looks:

Alternating Outline

First paragraph I. Cost

A. Camry

B. Jetta

Second paragraph II. Performance

A. Camry

B. Jetta

Third paragraph III. Looks

A. Camry

B. Jetta

Block Outline

First paragraph I. Camry

A. Cost

B. Performance

C. Looks

Second paragraph II. Jetta

A. Cost

B. Performance

C. Looks

3. **Make sure that the items to be compared/contrasted belong to the same class.** Some common ground must exist between items in order for a comparison/contrast to be meaningful. For example, a comparison between a hummingbird and a cement mixer or between backgammon and Dutch Cleanser would be silly. On the other hand, some usefulness can be derived

from a comparison between the Chinese and Japanese languages or between golf and tennis—pairings that belong to common groups: Asian languages and sports, respectively. Moreover, the expression of the comparison/contrast must be grammatically accurate:

Wrong: Our telephone system is better than Russia.

Here, a telephone system is contrasted with all of Russia.

Right: Our telephone system is better than *that* of Russia.

or

Our telephone system is better than Russia's.

Wrong: Ed's income is less than his wife.

Here, Ed's income is contrasted with his wife.

Right: Ed's income is less than that of his wife.

or

Ed's income is less than his wife's.

4. **Deal with both sides of the question.** All comparisons and contrasts are concerned with two sides, and you must deal equally with both. Do not mention one side and assume that your reader will fill in the other side. If you are contrasting the summer weather in Death Valley with the summer weather at Donner Pass, you cannot say:

In Death Valley the heat is so intense that even lizards wilt.

and assume that your reader will fill in "but at Donner Pass the summers remain cool." You must draw the contrast fully, as in the following:

In Death Valley the heat is so intense that even lizards wilt, whereas at Donner Pass a cool breeze freshens even the hottest day.

5. **Use expressions indicating comparison/contrast.** Although comparison requires less back-and-forth movement than does contrast, you must nevertheless take both sides into account by stating exactly what traits they have in common. For instance, in pointing out that in some ways high schools are *like* prisons, you cannot restrict yourself to discussing the domineering principal, the snoopy truant officer, the pass required to leave campus, or the punitive grading system. You must mention both sides, indicating that the domineering principal in high school is like the stern warden in prison; that the snoopy truant officer who makes sure that students attend school has much *in common with the prison guards* who make sure that inmates stay in prison; that the pass required to leave campus is *similar* to the formal permission required to leave a locked ward; and that the punitive grading system of high schools is *like* the demerit system of prisons. These expressions

serve as signposts in your text, telling your reader how your different points relate.

The following expressions indicate comparison:

also	as well as
bears resemblance to both . . .	and in common with
in like manner	like
likewise	neither . . . nor
similar	too

The following expressions indicate contrast:

although this may be true	at the same time
but	for all that
however	in contrast to
in opposition to	nevertheless
on the contrary	on the one hand . . . on the other hand
otherwise	still
unlike	whereas
yet	

Contrast emphasizes the separate sides of an issue by pulling them apart as much as possible in order to clarify their differences. Comparison is less two-sided because it tries to draw together both sides of an issue in order to reveal what they have in common. In short, *contrasts diverge, comparisons converge.* Refer back to the contrast example on page 456, and note how Egyptian mythology and Greek mythology are placed far apart so that their ideological differences stand out. Note also how the underlined expressions indicating contrast clarify the shift from one side to the other.

Warming Up to Write a Comparison/Contrast

Comparing and contrasting are normal ways people think, so you should not have too much difficulty completing these exercises.

1. For the item on the left of each column, write three or four characteristics that describe the item; then write contrasting characteristics for the item at the right.

   Example:

   Teacher Smith
   Pleasant
   Always prepared
   Fascinating in his presentations

   Teacher Brown
   Grouchy
   Sometimes disorganized
   Usually boring

a. Historical romances   Myths

b. Tornadoes   Cyclones

c. Friend with bad ethics   Friend with good ethics

d. Working in a restaurant   Working in a hospital

e. Watching a movie on TV   Watching a movie in a theater

2. Write down three bases of contrast (not comparison) for each of the following subjects.

   a. Two close friends

   b. Two church services

   c. Two holidays

   d. Two sports teams (or persons)

   e. Two attitudes toward work

3. Write down at least three aspects in which each of the following pairs are similar.

   a. A farm and a garden

   b. A storm and a lover's quarrel

   c. An ant hill and city government

   d. Fishing and looking for a wife

   e. An eagle and a lion

EXAMPLES

Breast Cancer No. 2

MARGARET OVERTON

Rhetorical Thumbnail

Purpose: to tear away the mask of objective and impersonal science in order to reveal the true face of a medical doctor dealing with life and death

Audience: readers of popular periodical opinions

Language: standard English, laced with medical terms and expressions

Strategy: uses the objective point of view of the physician, but also creates a sad mood while describing the plight of a patient facing a malignant cancer that will surely claim her life

Margaret Overton is a physician practicing anesthesia in the Chicago area. Since completing a Master's of Fine Arts degree in writing at the Art Institute of Chicago, Overton has been at work on a memoir. Her ability to make readers understand the physician-patient relationship and to explain medical procedures in plain language is a gift to anyone reading her work.

In probing this essay, you need to reach beyond the external actions depicted, to what is taking place in the doctor's mind as she represses her emotions in order to focus on the demanding job of saving human life. Notice how her sense of duty conflicts with her compassion for the girl who is about to undergo chemo or some similar procedure to fight her deadly cancer. Detect the contrast between the doctor's determination to remain emotionally detached from her patient in order to do a good job, and her despair when she realizes the impossibility of saving this life. But another contrast also surfaces—the contrast between the controlling energy of the physician and the helpless weakness of the patient. Try to follow the thread of these intertwining differences.

• • •

1   It's 5 o'clock, and the long cases are over. There's just one more to go—the last of the day. One of my partners throws open the operating-room door and stands facing me with his mask down around his neck, his surgeon's gown backward and hanging open over dirty scrubs, his pants pulled low by double pagers at his waist.

2   "Want me to do your last case?" he asks.

3   I consider saying yes—my shoulders ache. I'm getting a cold, and I've been here since 6:30 a.m. "Nah, but thanks." I know the case will be short. Better to save up favors for when the kids are sick or have a basketball game.

4   Anyway it's a simple case. Pretty straightforward. Not even a general anesthetic but intravenous sedation for a central line insertion, probably for chemo or something. Young patient—a young woman—a surgeon I like, nurses I enjoy working with. Easy as can be, no more than an hour. I draw up drugs into fresh syringes. The surgeon will inject local anesthetic into her skin. I pick up the phone in the OR, call home and tell my older daughter I won't be too late tonight. She says she needs help with math homework.

5   In presurgery, where the patients wait with family members, I flip open my patient's chart to the nursing admission form. The patient's name is Onica M.; the diagnosis is breast cancer, recurrent. The hospital stamps her identification card on the right-hand corner of each page of her chart. The stamp shows her age as 039. This distinguishes her from patients named Onica M. with recurrent breast cancer who are, perhaps, 139? I, too, am 039.

6   Onica lies on a metal cart, dressed in the universal uniform of the patient—the hospital gown that snaps at the shoulders and ties in the back. She's covered by the usual institutional white sheet, over which the institutional white blanket has been placed to prevent the institutional chill. She's been stripped of her clothes, jewelry, nail polish and makeup; her distinguishing characteristics are now elemental—she's allowed to maintain her general build, hair color, facial features. Soon we'll cover her head with a disposable hat, and she'll look

almost like us—except of course for the ways in which terminal disease has transformed her. That's always the giveaway.

7   When I reach out to shake her hand, I notice she's tiny, thin, petite—a sprite of a person. Big-boned and tall, more like my father than my mother, I've always envied petite women, the way they constantly surprise you by being more than they seem. During adolescence I stared at my thighs and longed to be shorter, as short as most other girls, short enough to be normal. Now I no longer mind the height, but I still take note of what I'll never be.

8   Onica's skin is light tan and her hair light brown. She reaches out to grasp my hand with her small, bony one, holds it fiercely in hers, grips mine a moment longer than necessary. Her hand makes me think of a crunchy, Middle Eastern delicacy: the fig birds they deep-fry and eat whole. When she releases me, her arm remains outstretched, suspended, floating in space, as if she isn't sure she should have let go. We smile at each other, or rather, I do; she doesn't smile so much as grin. Onica is cute, a pixie, a pert, perky woman who might have been a member of the pompon squad in high school, like Annette Sullivan or Sherry Kopinsky. Someone everyone liked. Dimples crease her cheeks when she grins. I shake hands with her father, who sits quietly beside her, staring at nothing, looking prosperous but lost, ineffably sad.

9   He kisses Onica's check, then we leave him in presurgery and wheel Onica back to the operating room, where I attach the monitors—ECG electrodes, blood-pressure cuff, pulse oximeter. I start giving her drugs. Lidocaine, then fentanyl, then midazolam. I plug in the propofol infusion, set the pump to her body weight and a low dose. I can judge the effects of the medication more easily if she's talking, so while the drugs are starting to work, I ask her questions. I pay attention to the pace and cadence of her answers, wait for the speech to gradually slur. Everyone's tolerance is different, so I titrate the drugs to the desired effect.

10   "Are you married?" I ask, holding her arm above the IV site, rubbing gently to take the sting out of the medicine.

11   "Oh, yeah," she answers, her voice bright with enthusiasm, "and I've got two kids, a boy and a girl."

12   "How old are they?"

13   "My son is 11, and my daughter's 9."

14   "So they're what—in third and fifth?"

15   "Third and sixth," she answers, her words slightly thick, coming a little bit slower. "They're two and a half years apart, but three years in school." I look down and smile behind my facemask. Once again I see that grin—a quick twitch of tense facial muscles. Onica uses her dimples wisely, I think. She uses them to hide her fear, perhaps, or anger or sadness. In truth I don't know what she hides. I can't even imagine, so I slide another milligram of midazolam into her IV.

16   "What sports do they play?"

17   "Douglas, my son, well, Douglas... likes... soccer..."
     Her eyes drift shut, and I nod to Maylie, the circulating nurse. She can begin the prep.

18   Maylie brings the prep stand close to the OR table. She folds the cotton blanket down to Onica's waist, refastens the safety belt on top of it. She

removes the hospital gown, unsnapping it at the shoulders and turning it down to the waist. Despite the noise of the monitors, I hear Maylie's gasp. On Onica's chest, in place of breasts, which I knew she didn't have, sit two raw, lumpy, ulcerative masses. Scarred, puckered, with purple draining from angry red, these things disfigure her small body and silently scream cancer. I turn away, pull down my mask, and take a deep breath. Mercifully, amazingly, there is no odor. After a moment I look back and meet Maylie's tired eyes. Our gazes are drawn back against our wills to Onica.

19   "What...?" Our scrub nurse, Paula, stops speaking, looks at me.

20   I shake my head. Though her eyes are closed, our patient is technically awake.

21   Gish, the general surgeon, enters the OR with hands raised and dripping. Paula hands him a towel, and as he dries his hands, he walks toward me and leans close.

22   "She had a TRAM flap breast reconstruction elsewhere," he whispers, "then a recurrence of her cancer. She got irradiated, and the flap broke down. That's all scar tissue and cancer." He backs away and looks straight at me. "Nice, huh?"

23   I sit down at the head of the OR table, touch Onica on the shoulder. "How you doing?" I ask. "You okay?"

24   She murmurs an assent, and once again, a slight grin appears and disappears. Her eyes remain shut. I stand up to affix the drapes, give Onica an additional bolus of propofol before Gish injects the local anesthetic into her skin. I whisper, "You'll feel a little sting now, as the numbing medicine goes in."

25   She barely flinches with the needle stick. I sit back down to continue my charting, observing Onica frequently to make sure she stays sleepy and unaware throughout the procedure. I listen to the rhythmic pattern of the monitors, the buzz of the electrocautery unit, while another part of me hurtles through space, through time, forward blindly, without any understanding of how movement occurs, entangled in the flawed harness of the helping profession. Though there are many layers to this job, the horror is a small part, a part that can be ignored, if you know how, that is, if you're good at it. I am a professional trained to function within an official, circumscribed vocabulary. The words I need—right now—to describe this exact moment don't exist within that lexicon.

26   Here's the thing. I absorb horror only in snippets, in quotas, one at a time, day after day. I preserve their essences, tell myself I will attend to them later, after the homework—perhaps I even mean it— but then another patient comes along. There's another job to do, another mess to slog through, and fatigue sets in; life sets in, and I don't do it. Not right, anyway. Not well enough. Part of this is self-protection. The other part, I've come to understand, is that compassion ultimately fails. How else can it be? I take care of patients when I am tired and alert and proud of my children and angry with my husband and upset because the radiator pipe broke and flooded my kitchen and when I am worried about the dog's rash. I have, after all, a job to do. I cannot permit immobilization. But on certain days with certain patients—she is 039, like me—I cannot help but see the whole of it.

27   I look back down at Onica, at the half-grin she wears even in repose. I remember the first TRAM flap I saw, and the anger comes rushing back to me. I've hated that plastic surgeon ever since. Does anger assuage survivor guilt? Perhaps my feelings are political, leftovers from a feminist upbringing. Who but a man would be clever enough to imagine transforming womanhood in the first place—relocating abdominal muscles upward to recreate breast tissue while performing a concomitant tummy tuck? Massive surgery, long hours of blood loss and anesthesia, undoubtedly sold on the premise that one surgery fixes you right up—good as new, better even. Then the cancer recurs—of course it does—in our patient, this young mother of two who will not see her children grow up but will watch them as they watch her suffer and die a slow death with little or no dignity.

28   In the recovery room, Onica is awake again and cheerful. I stand at her bedside and say nothing, just fiddle with the wires connecting her to the monitors. I ask mundane questions: what her husband does, where she grew up. I do not ask the questions I want to ask: Do you have a family history? What asshole plastic surgeon talked you into this abomination? How do you discuss the cancer with your kids? I do not ask, though I know she would tell me. It would be so easy to plunder her medical history. Onica M., with the grin for others, would tell me all her secrets, answer the questions I have no right to ask. But I don't ask. Someday perhaps I'll learn a language in which compassion does not fail or intrude or strip a sick woman of her strength or self-protection, a language in which compassion thrives, despite this gilded vocabulary. Maybe someday I will learn that language; I do not know it now.

29   My pager goes off yet again. Both daughters now need help with their math homework. Still I sit beside Onica until she leaves the recovery room to go back to her father, her family, her life and the end of her 39th year.

"Breast Cancer No. 2" by Margaret Overton appeared in CREATIVE NONFICTION, Issue 20: Clarity. Reprinted with permission from Dr. Margaret Overton.

● Vocabulary

intravenous (4)	pixie (8)	quotas (26)
sedation (4)	ineffably (8)	essences (26)
insertion (4)	cadence (9)	slog (26)
syringes (4)	titrate (9)	assuage (27)
recurrent (5)	bolus (24)	concomitant (27)
elemental (6)	snippets (26)	mundane (28)
sprite (7)		

● The Facts

1. In paragraph 4, the author calls the surgical case for which she will administer the anesthetic "simple." What does she mean by this label? After reading further, do you agree that the case is simple? Explain your answer.

2. What physical contrast exists between the narrator and the patient? How does this difference affect the meaning of the essay? What reaction does the difference elicit from you?

3. Why does paragraph 9 contain so many technical facts? Do they add or detract from the flow of the narrative? Support your answer with a logical explanation.

4. Where in the essay is the patient's diagnosis fully explained? Who gives the explanation? Although the explanation is brief, what can the reader extract from it? Share your reactions to the explanation.

5. What limitations does the author express in paragraph 26? What is it that she plans "to attend to" later? Do you think she ever will? Is she justified or not in the "excuses" she makes? Explain your answers.

● The Strategies

1. What is the thesis of the essay? Since it is not expressed in one clear sentence in the opening paragraph or elsewhere in the essay, but is rather inferred from several key comments made by the author throughout the essay, what are these key comments? Paragraphs 25–27 are of particular relevance. If you were to supply a one-sentence thesis, what would it be? Write it on a piece of paper and share it with the class.

2. What is the purpose of paragraph 18? How did you react to the details revealed in this paragraph?

3. The author uses several figures of speech throughout the essay. Which two or three do you consider the most powerful? Point them out and explain their force.

4. What is the author's attitude toward the reconstruction performed by some plastic surgeon? How is this attitude conveyed? Using the critical thinking skills you have acquired, respond to the author's view.

5. Do you think the ending of the essay wraps up the author's main point and leaves the reader satisfied? Do you wish she had been more conclusive and positive? Give reasons for your evaluation.

● The Issues

1. Much of the essay deals with the problem of guilt experienced by the doctor, who can't spend enough time with her needy patient because mundane duties demand her attention. What comfort or suggestion would you offer parents, teachers, ministers, doctors, nurses, or other caregivers to allay their guilt about feeling neglectful?

2. Do you think it is credible that Onica engages in a cheerful and friendly conversation with her anesthesiologist when Onica is so seriously ill? What keeps her from breaking down and weeping with fear? Try to think of the human condition as it is described in the essay.

3. How does paragraph 36 reveal some strong private thoughts that fill the author and trouble her. Why do you think Onica's particular case affected the author so deeply?

4. What does the author mean when she says, "Though there are many layers to this job, the horror is a small part, a part that can be ignored, if you know how, that is, if you're good at it"? Does this comment ring true, considering the job described? Explain your answer.

5. How is the final sentence of paragraph 25 connected with the final sentence of paragraph 28? How are both of these sentences related to the questions the author did not ask Onica (paragraph 28)? What is your reaction to the questions she would have liked to ask but did not?

● Suggestions for Writing

1. After researching on the Internet the topic of "breast reconstruction," write an essay in which you indicate whether or not reconstructive surgery is now a safe risk.

2. Write an essay in which you explore this passage, taken from Overton's essay: "Someday perhaps I'll learn a language in which compassion does not fail or intrude or strip a sick woman of her strength or self-protection, a language in which compassion thrives, despite the gilded vocabulary."

Diogenes and Alexander

GILBERT HIGHET

Rhetorical Thumbnail

Purpose: to re-create a historical meeting between two epic personalities

Audience: anyone with an interest in history

Language: standard English

Strategy: to re-create the immediacy of the moment, the essay uses the omniscient viewpoint and the historical present

---

Gilbert Highet (1906–1978) was born in Glasgow, Scotland, educated at the University of Glasgow and at Oxford, and became an American citizen in 1951. A classicist, Highet was known for his scholarly and critical writing, including *The Classical Tradition* (1949) and *The Anatomy of Satire* (1962).

This essay describes a meeting between two sharply contrasting personalities in Greek history—the Greek Cynic philosopher Diogenes (c. 412–323 BC) and Alexander the Great (356–323 BC), King of Macedonia. Highet shows that although the two men occupied strikingly different positions in Greek society, they shared at least one quality that made them unique among the people of their time.

● ● ●

1 Lying on the bare earth, shoeless, bearded, half-naked, he looked like a beggar or a lunatic. He was one, but not the other. He had opened his eyes with the sun at dawn, scratched, done his business like a dog at the roadside, washed at the

public fountain, begged a piece of breakfast bread and a few olives, eaten them squatting on the ground, and washed them down with a few handfuls of water scooped from the spring. (Long ago he had owned a rough wooden cup, but he threw it away when he saw a boy drinking out of his hollowed hands.) Having no work to go to and no family to provide for, he was free. As the market place filled up with shoppers and merchants and gossipers and sharpers and slaves and foreigners, he had strolled through it for an hour or two. Everybody knew him, or knew of him. They would throw sharp questions at him and get sharper answers. Sometimes they threw jeers, and got jibes; sometimes bits of food, and got scant thanks; sometimes a mischievous pebble, and got a shower of stones and abuse. They were not quite sure whether he was mad or not. He knew they were mad, each in a different way; they amused him. Now he was back at his home.

2   It was not a house, not even a squatter's hut. He thought everybody lived far too elaborately, expensively, anxiously. What good is a house? No one needs privacy; natural acts are not shameful; we all do the same things, and need not hide them. No one needs beds and chairs and such furniture: the animals live healthy lives and sleep on the ground. All we require, since nature did not dress us properly, is one garment to keep us warm, and some shelter from rain and wind. So he had one blanket—to dress him in the daytime and cover him at night—and he slept in a cask. His name was Diogenes. He was the founder of the creed called Cynicism (the word means "doggishness"); he spent much of his life in the rich, lazy, corrupt Greek city of Corinth, mocking and satirizing its people, and occasionally converting one of them.

3   His home was not a barrel made of wood: too expensive. It was a storage jar made of earthenware, something like a modern fuel tank—no doubt discarded because a break had made it useless. He was not the first to inhabit such a thing: the refugees driven into Athens by the Spartan invasion had been forced to sleep in casks. But he was the first who ever did so by choice, out of principle.

4   Diogenes was not a degenerate or a maniac. He was a philosopher who wrote plays and poems and essays expounding his doctrine; he talked to those who cared to listen; he had pupils who admired him. But he taught chiefly by example. All should live naturally, he said, for what is natural is normal and cannot possibly be evil or shameful. Live without conventions, which are artificial and false; escape complexities and superfluities and extravagances: only so can you live a free life. The rich man believes he possesses his big house with its many rooms and its elaborate furniture, his pictures and his expensive clothes, his horses and his servants and his bank accounts. He does not. He depends on them, he worries about them, he spends most of his life's energy looking after them; the thought of losing them makes him sick with anxiety. They possess him. He is their slave. In order to procure a quantity of false, perishable goods he has sold the only true, lasting good, his own independence.

5   There have been many men who grew tired of human society with its complications, and went away to live simply—on a small farm, in a quiet village, in a hermit's cave, or in the darkness of anonymity. Not so Diogenes. He was not a recluse, or a stylite, or a beatnik. He was a missionary. His life's aim was clear to him: it was "to restamp the currency." (He and his father had once

been convicted for counterfeiting, long before he turned to philosophy, and this phrase was Diogenes' bold, unembarrassed joke on the subject.) To restamp the currency: to take the clean metal of human life, to erase the old false conventional markings, and to imprint it with its true values.

6   The other great philosophers of the fourth century before Christ taught mainly their own private pupils. In the shady groves and cool sanctuaries of the Academy, Plato discoursed to a chosen few on the unreality of this contingent existence. Aristotle, among the books and instruments and specimens and archives and research-workers of his Lyceum, pursued investigations and gave lectures that were rightly named esoteric "for those within the walls." But for Diogenes, laboratory and specimens and lecture halls and pupils were all to be found in a crowd of ordinary people. Therefore he chose to live in Athens or in the rich city of Corinth, where travelers from all over the Mediterranean world constantly came and went. And, by design, he publicly behaved in such ways as to show people what real life was. He would constantly take up their spiritual coin, ring it on a stone, and laugh at its false superscription.

7   He thought most people were only half-alive, most men only half-men. At bright noonday he walked through the market place carrying a lighted lamp and inspecting the face of everyone he met. They asked him why. Diogenes answered, "I am trying to find a man."

8   To a gentleman whose servant was putting on his shoes for him, Diogenes said, "You won't be really happy until he wipes your nose for you: that will come after you lose the use of your hands."

9   Once there was a war scare so serious that it stirred even the lazy, profit happy Corinthians. They began to drill, clean their weapons, and rebuild their neglected fortifications. Diogenes took his old cask and began to roll it up and down, back and forward. "When you are all so busy," he said, "I felt I ought to do something!"

10   And so he lived—like a dog, some said, because he cared nothing for privacy and other human conventions, and because he showed his teeth and barked at those whom he disliked. Now he was lying in the sunlight, as contented as a dog on the warm ground, happier (he himself used to boast) than the Shah of Persia. Although he knew he was going to have an important visitor, he would not move.

11   The little square began to fill with people. Page boys elegantly dressed, spearmen speaking a rough foreign dialect, discreet secretaries, hard-browed officers, suave diplomats, they all gradually formed a circle centered on Diogenes. He looked them over, as a sober man looks at a crowd of tottering drunks, and shook his head. He knew who they were. They were the attendants of the conqueror of Greece, the servants of Alexander, the Macedonian king, who was visiting his newly subdued realm.

12   Only twenty, Alexander was far older and wiser than his years. Like all Macedonians he loved drinking, but he could usually handle it; and toward women he was nobly restrained and chivalrous. Like all Macedonians he loved fighting; he was a magnificent commander, but he was not merely a military automaton. He could think. At thirteen he had become a pupil of the greatest mind in Greece, Aristotle. No exact record of his schooling survives. It is clear,

though, that Aristotle took the passionate, half-barbarous boy and gave him the best of Greek culture. He taught Alexander poetry: the young prince slept with the *Iliad* under his pillow and longed to emulate Achilles, who brought the mighty power of Asia to ruin. He taught him philosophy, in particular the shapes and uses of political power: a few years later Alexander was to create a supranational empire that was not merely a power system but a vehicle for the exchange of Greek and Middle Eastern cultures.

13   Aristotle taught him the principles of scientific research: during his invasion of the Persian domains Alexander took with him a large corps of scientists, and shipped hundreds of zoological specimens back to Greece for study. Indeed, it was from Aristotle that Alexander learned to seek out everything strange which might be instructive. Jugglers and stunt artists and virtuosos of the absurd he dismissed with a shrug; but on reaching India he was to spend hours discussing the problems of life and death with naked Hindu mystics, and later to see one demonstrate Yoga self-command by burning himself impassively to death.

14   Now, Alexander was in Corinth to take command of the League of Greek States which, after conquering them, his father Philip had created as a disguise for the New Macedonian Order. He was welcomed and honored and flattered. He was the man of the hour, of the century: he was unanimously appointed commander-in-chief of a new expedition against old, rich, corrupt Asia. Nearly everyone crowded to Corinth in order to congratulate him, to seek employment with him, even simply to see him: soldiers and statesmen, artists and merchants, poets and philosophers. He received their compliments graciously. Only Diogenes, although he lived in Corinth, did not visit the new monarch. With that generosity which Aristotle had taught him was a quality of the truly magnanimous man, Alexander determined to call upon Diogenes. Surely Diogenes, the God-born, would acknowledge the conqueror's power by some gift of hoarded wisdom.

15   With his handsome face, his fiery glance, his strong supple body, his purple and gold cloak, and his air of destiny, he moved through the parting crowd, toward the Dog's kennel. When a king approaches, all rise in respect. Diogenes did not rise, he merely sat up on one elbow. When a monarch enters a precinct, all greet him with a bow or an acclamation. Diogenes said nothing.

16   There was a silence. Some years later Alexander speared his best friend to the wall, for objecting to the exaggerated honors paid to His Majesty; but now he was still young and civil. He spoke first, with a kindly greeting. Looking at the poor broken cask, the single ragged garment, and the rough figure lying on the ground, he said: "Is there anything I can do for you, Diogenes?"

17   "Yes," said the Dog, "Stand to one side. You're blocking the sunlight."

18   There was silence, not the ominous silence preceding a burst of fury, but a hush of amazement. Slowly, Alexander turned away. A titter broke out from the elegant Greeks, who were already beginning to make jokes about the Cur that looked at the King. The Macedonian officers, after deciding that Diogenes was not worth the trouble of kicking, were starting to guffaw and nudge one another. Alexander was still silent. To those nearest him he said quietly, "If I were not Alexander, I should be Diogenes." They took it as a paradox, designed to close the awkward little scene with a polite curtain line. But Alexander meant it. He understood Cynicism as the others could not. Later he took one

of Diogenes' pupils with him to India as a philosophical interpreter (it was he who spoke to the naked *addhus*). He was what Diogenes called himself, a cosmopolités, "citizen of the world." Like Diogenes, he admired the heroic figure of Hercules, the mighty conqueror who labors to help mankind while all others toil and sweat only for themselves. He knew that of all men then alive in the world only Alexander the conqueror and Diogenes the beggar were truly free.

Vocabulary

expounding (4)	discoursed (6)	suave (11)
conventions (4)	contingent (6)	supranational (12)
superfluities (4)	archives (6)	virtuosos (13)
stylite (5)	superscription (6)	

Professor Highet explains the meanings of several words used in the essay. How does he interpret the following?

Cynicism (2)	Diogenes (14)	cosmopolités (18)
esoteric (6)		

The Facts

1. What characteristics do Diogenes and Alexander share?
2. In what ways are Diogenes and Alexander different?
3. What is Diogenes's rationale for living so humbly?
4. According to Diogenes, the richer a man is, the more enslaved he becomes. How does he explain this statement?
5. How did the teaching method of Diogenes differ from that of Plato or Aristotle?
6. Paragraph 12 states that Alexander was far older and wiser than his twenty years. How is this maturity indicated?
7. According to the essay, Alexander "understood Cynicism as the others could not." What is Cynicism? Why did Alexander understand it better than others?

The Strategies

1. In what paragraph does the focus shift from Diogenes to Alexander?
2. Does Highet draw his contrast by alternating back and forth between Diogenes and Alexander, or does he first draw a full portrait of Diogenes and then a full portrait of Alexander? What does Highet's method require of the reader?
3. How do you explain the paradox "If I were not Alexander, I should be Diogenes" (paragraph 18)?
4. The opening paragraph contains a sentence characterized by balance and parallelism. What are the opening words of this sentence?
5. What is the literary term for the phrase "to restamp the currency"? What is the meaning?
6. What topic sentence covers paragraphs 7, 8, and 9? How is it developed?

● The Issues

1. Which of the two men—Alexander or Diogenes—had a better chance for leading a contented life? Give reasons for your answer.

2. Reread the essay "My Wood" by E. M. Forster, pages 185–187, then make a connection between Alexander's and Diogenes's lives and the essay. Ask yourself which of the two world figures most closely resembles the owner of the wood. Why?

3. Respond to paragraph 2: Do you agree with the idea that man should live naturally and that we have become far too elaborate? Give reasons for your answer.

4. How important are philosophy, poetry, and the principles of scientific investigation—all subjects taught to Alexander by Aristotle—to a modern curriculum? What other subjects, if any, would you add to a balanced curriculum?

5. Which would you prefer to be—a person of power or a person of influence? Be specific in describing yourself, later in life, as having achieved either of these characteristics. What job would you be holding? What kind of family life would you lead?

● Suggestions for Writing

1. Write an essay in which you state why you admire Alexander more than Diogenes, or vice versa. Base your essay on the portraits of the two men as drawn by Highet.

2. Choosing one of the pairs listed here, write an essay developed by contrast. Begin with a thesis that summarizes the contrast. Keep in mind the bases of your contrast.

   a. Jealousy/envy
   b. Thoreau/Gandhi
   c. Wisdom/knowledge
   d. Statesman/politician
   e. Old age/youth

Grant and Lee: A Study in Contrasts

BRUCE CATTON

Rhetorical Thumbnail

Purpose: to compare/contrast two principals in the Civil War

Audience: history buffs

Language: standard English

Strategy: heaps up details to draw this contrast

Bruce Catton (1899–1978) is regarded as one of the most outstanding Civil War historians of the twentieth century. His books include *Mr. Lincoln's Army* (1951), *Glory Road* (1952), *A Stillness at Appomattox* (1953, Pulitzer Prize), and *This Hallowed Ground* (1956).

The following essay contrasts two famous personalities in American Civil War history: Ulysses S. Grant (1822–1885), commander in chief of the Union army and, later, eighteenth president of the United States (1869–1877), and his principal foe in the Civil War, Robert E. Lee (1807–1870), general in chief of the Confederate armies, who surrendered his forces to Grant in April of 1865. The essay illustrates the development of a comparison/contrast between paragraphs, rather than within a paragraph.

• • •

1   When Ulysses S. Grant and Robert E. Lee met in the parlor of a modest house at Appomattox Court House, Virginia, on April 9, 1865, to work out the terms for the surrender of Lee's Army of Northern Virginia, a great chapter in American life came to a close, and a great new chapter began.

2   These men were bringing the Civil War to its virtual finish. To be sure, other armies had yet to surrender, and for a few days the fugitive Confederate government would struggle desperately and vainly, trying to find some way to go on living now that its chief support was gone. But in effect it was all over when Grant and Lee signed the papers. And the little room where they wrote out the terms was the scene of one of the poignant, dramatic contrasts in American history.

3   They were two strong men, these oddly different generals, and they represented the strengths of two conflicting currents that, through them, had come into final collision.

4   Back of Robert E. Lee was the notion that the old aristocratic concept might somehow survive and be dominant in American life.

5   Lee was tidewater Virginia, and in his background were family, culture, and tradition . . . the age of chivalry transplanted to a New World which was making its own legends and its own myths. He embodied a way of life that had come down through the age of knighthood and the English country squire. America was a land that was beginning all over again, dedicated to nothing much more complicated than the rather hazy belief that all men had equal rights and should have an equal chance in the world. In such a land Lee stood for the feeling that it was somehow of advantage to human society to have a pronounced inequality in the social structure. There should be a leisure class, backed by ownership of land; in turn, society itself should be keyed to the land as the chief source of wealth and influence. It would bring forth (according to this ideal) a class of men with a strong sense of obligation to the community; men who lived not to gain advantage for themselves, but to meet the solemn obligations which had been laid on them by the very fact that they were privileged. From them the country would get its leadership; to them it could look for the higher values—of thought, of conduct, of personal deportment—to give it strength and virtue.

6   Lee embodied the noblest elements of this aristocratic ideal. Through him, the landed nobility justified itself. For four years, the Southern states had fought a desperate war to uphold the ideals for which Lee stood. In the end, it almost seemed as if the Confederacy fought for Lee; as if he himself was the Confederacy . . . the best thing that the way of life for which the Confederacy stood could ever have to offer. He had passed into legend before Appomattox. Thousands of tired, underfed, poorly clothed Confederate soldiers, long since past the simple enthusiasm of the early days of the struggle, somehow considered Lee the symbol of everything for which they had been willing to die. But they could not quite put this feeling into words. If the Lost Cause, sanctified by so much heroism and so many deaths, had a living justification, its justification was General Lee.

7   Grant, the son of a tanner on the Western frontier, was everything Lee was not. He had come up the hard way and embodied nothing in particular except the eternal toughness and sinewy fiber of the men who grew up beyond the mountains. He was one of a body of men who owed reverence and obeisance to no one, who were self-reliant to a fault, who cared hardly anything for the past but who had a sharp eye for the future.

8   These frontier men were the precise opposites of the tidewater aristocrats. Back of them, in the great surge that had taken people over the Alleghenies and into the opening Western country, there was a deep, implicit dissatisfaction with a past that had settled into grooves. They stood for democracy, not from any reasoned conclusion about the proper ordering of human society, but simply because they had grown up in the middle of democracy and knew how it worked. Their society might have privileges, but they would be privileges each man had won for himself. Forms and patterns meant nothing. No man was born to anything, except perhaps to a chance to show how far he could rise. Life was competition.

9   Yet along with this feeling had come a deep sense of belonging to a national community. The Westerner who developed a farm, opened a shop, or set up in business as a trader, could hope to prosper only as his own community prospered—and his community ran from the Atlantic to the Pacific and from Canada down to Mexico. If the land was settled, with towns and highways and accessible markets, he could better himself. He saw his fate in terms of the nation's own destiny. As its horizons expanded, so did his. He had, in other words, an acute dollars-and-cents stake in the continued growth and development of his country.

10   And that, perhaps, is where the contrast between Grant and Lee becomes most striking. The Virginia aristocrat, inevitably, saw himself in relation to his own region. He lived in a static society which could endure almost anything except change. Instinctively, his first loyalty would go to the locality in which that society existed. He would fight to the limit of endurance to defend it, because in defending it he was defending everything that gave his own life its deepest meaning.

11   The Westerner, on the other hand, would fight with an equal tenacity for the broader concept of society. He fought so because everything he lived by was tied to growth, expansion, and a constantly widening horizon. What he lived by would survive or fall with the nation itself. He could not possibly stand by unmoved in the face of an attempt to destroy the Union. He would combat it with everything he had, because he could only see it as an effort to cut the ground out from under his feet.

12   So Grant and Lee were in complete contrast, representing two diametrically opposed elements in American life. Grant was the modern man emerging; beyond him, ready to come on the stage, was the great age of steel and machinery, of crowded cities and a restless, burgeoning vitality. Lee might have ridden down from the old age of chivalry, lance in hand, silken banner fluttering over his head. Each man was the perfect champion of his cause, drawing both his strengths and his weaknesses from the people he led.

13   Yet it was not all contrast, after all. Different as they were—in background, in personality, in underlying aspiration—these two great soldiers had much in common. Under everything else, they were marvelous fighters. Furthermore, their fighting qualities were really very much alike.

14   Each man had, to begin with, the great virtue of utter tenacity and fidelity. Grant fought his way down the Mississippi Valley in spite of acute personal discouragement and profound military handicaps. Lee hung on in the trenches at Petersburg after hope itself had died. In each man there was an indomitable quality . . . the born fighter's refusal to give up as long as he can still remain on his feet and lift his two fists.

15   Daring and resourcefulness they had, too; the ability to think faster and move faster than the enemy. These were the qualities which gave Lee the dazzling campaigns of Second Manassas and Chancellorsville and won Vicksburg for Grant.

16   Lastly, and perhaps greatest of all, there was the ability, at the end, to turn quickly from war to peace once the fighting was over. Out of the way these two men behaved at Appomattox came the possibility of a peace of reconciliation. It was a possibility not wholly realized, in the years to come, but which did, in the end, help the two sections to become one nation again . . . after a war whose bitterness might have seemed to make such a reunion wholly impossible. No part of either man's life became him more than the part he played in their brief meeting in the McLean house at Appomattox. Their behavior there put all succeeding generations of Americans in their debt. Two great Americans, Grant and Lee—very different, yet under everything very much alike. Their encounter at Appomattox was one of the great moments of American history.

● Vocabulary

poignant (2)	sanctified (6)	diametrically (12)
deportment (5)	obeisance (7)	burgeoning (12)
embodied (6)	tenacity (11)	

● The Facts

1. What was Lee's background? What ideal did he represent?
2. What was Grant's background? What did he represent?
3. What was Grant's view of the past? What was his attitude toward society and democracy?

4. What was the most striking contrast between Grant and Lee?

5. Catton writes that the behavior of Grant and Lee at Appomattox "put all succeeding generations of Americans in their debt" (paragraph 16). Why?

● The Strategies

1. Although the article is entitled "Grant and Lee: A Study in Contrasts," Catton begins by examining what Lee represented. Why? What logic is there to his order?

2. What function does paragraph 4 serve? Why is this one sentence set off in a separate paragraph?

3. What common contrast phrase does paragraph 11 use?

4. In paragraph 8, the author writes: "These frontier men were the precise opposites of the tidewater aristocrats." What do these types have to do with a contrast between Grant and Lee?

5. What function does paragraph 8 serve?

● The Issues

1. Does an aristocracy still survive in our multicultural United States? If you believe it has survived, describe what and where it is. If you believe it has vanished, then describe what has taken its place.

2. Which kind of citizen do you admire most—the aristocrat or the frontiersman? Which do you believe is needed most for the betterment of our society today? Give reasons for your answers.

3. The aristocrat believes in form and tradition. How important are these ideas, in your view? With which traditions would you be willing to part? Which would you want to keep?

4. What two women from history present an interesting contrast in two cultures? Describe both women and their contrasting cultures.

5. Which U.S. president, besides Ulysses S. Grant, is known for his support of economic growth and expansion? Do you favor continued growth and expansion, or are there other values you cherish more?

● Suggestions for Writing

1. Examine and analyze the organization of the contrast in this essay. In what various respects are Grant and Lee contrasted? How does Catton order and structure his contrast?

2. Discuss the idea that a society can benefit from the presence of a privileged class. Or, conversely, take the position that a society can benefit from the presence of an underprivileged class.

Baba and Me

KHALED HOSSEINI

> ## Rhetorical Thumbnail
>
> **Purpose:** to entertain
>
> **Audience:** general interest readers
>
> **Language:** standard English
>
> **Strategy:** lavish use of crisp details in painting this word portrait of the writer's father

Khaled Hosseini (b. 1965) became an international sensation with the publication of his first novel, *The Kite Runner* (2003), from which this reading comes. Although the author contends that the novel is pure fiction, the reader cannot help but wonder if Hosseini's youth, lived in Afghanistan, did not imprint itself on this story. Hosseini was born in Kabul, Afghanistan, the oldest of five children. His mother taught Farsi and history at a large girls' high school in Kabul. In 1976, Hosseini's family was relocated to Paris, France, where his father was assigned a diplomatic post in the Afghan embassy. The assignment would have returned the Hosseini family to Afghanistan in 1980, but by then the country had already witnessed the bloody communist coup and the Soviet invasion. Thus, the Hosseini family asked for and was granted political asylum in the United States, where Khaled Hosseini eventually graduated from the U.C. San Diego School of Medicine. He has been in practice as an internist since 1996. His second novel, *A Thousand Splendid Suns* (2007) also deals with Afghanistan and has received high literary praise. Now Hosseini's reading audience eagerly anticipates his next novel.

As you read the narrator's comparison of his father and himself, you might reflect on your own father to see how you were influenced by him, what kind of image he left on your consciousness and in what vital ways he shaped your character.

● ● ●

1   Lore has it my father once wrestled a black bear in Baluchistan with his bare hands. If the story had been about anyone else, it would have been dismissed as *laaf,* that Afghan tendency to exaggerate—sadly, almost a national affliction; if someone bragged that his son was a doctor, chances were the kid had once passed a biology test in high school. But no one ever doubted the veracity of any story about Baba. And if they did, well, Baba did have those three parallel scars coursing a jagged path down his back. I have imagined Baba's wrestling match countless times, even dreamed about it. And in those dreams, I can never tell Baba from the bear.

2   It was Rahim Khan who first referred to him as what eventually became Baba's famous nickname, *Toophan agha,* or "Mr. Hurricane." It was an apt

enough nickname. My father was a force of nature, a towering Pashtun speci-men with a thick beard, a wayward crop of curly brown hair as unruly as the man himself, hands that looked capable of uprooting a willow tree, and a black glare that would "drop the devil to his knees begging for mercy," as Rahim Khan used to say. At parties, when all six-foot-five of him thundered into the room, attention shifted to him like sunflowers turning to the sun.

3   Baba was impossible to ignore, even in his sleep. I used to bury cotton wisps in my ears, pull the blanket over my head, and still the sounds of Baba's snoring—so much like a growling truck engine—penetrated the walls. And my room was across the hall from Baba's bedroom. How my mother ever managed to sleep in the same room as him is a mystery to me. It's on the long list of things I would have asked my mother if I had ever met her.

4   In the late 1960s, when I was five or six, Baba decided to build an orphan-age. I heard the story through Rahim Kahn. He told me Baba had drawn the blueprints himself despite the fact that he'd had no architectural experience at all. Skeptics had urged him to stop his foolishness and hire an architect. Of course, Baba refused, and everyone shook their heads in dismay at his obsti-nate ways. Then Baba succeeded and everyone shook their heads in awe at his triumphant ways. Baba paid for the construction of the two-story orphanage, just off the main strip of Jadeh Maywand south of the Kabul river, with his own money. Rahim Kahn told me Baba had personally funded the entire project, paying for the engineers, electricians, plumbers, and laborers, not to mention the city officials whose "mustaches needed oiling."

5   It took three years to build the orphanage. I was eight by then. I remember the day before the orphanage opened, Baba took me to Ghargha Lake, a few miles north of Kabul. He asked me to fetch Hassan too, but I lied and told him Hassan had the runs. I wanted Baba all to myself. And besides, one time at Ghargha Lake, Hassan and I were skimming stones and Hassan made his stone skip eight times. The most I managed was five. Baba was there, watching, and he patted Hassan on the back. Even put his arm around his shoulder.

6   We sat at a picnic table on the banks of the lake, just Baba and me, eating boiled eggs with *kofta* sandwiches—meatballs and pickles wrapped in *naan*. The water was a deep blue and sunlight glittered on its looking glass-clear sur-face. On Fridays, the lake was bustling with families out for a day in the sun. But it was mid-week and there was only Baba and me, us and a couple of long-haired, bearded tourists—"hippies," I'd heard them called. They were sitting on the dock, feet dangling in the water, fishing poles in hand. I asked Baba why they grew their hair long, but Baba grunted, didn't answer. He was preparing his speech for the next day, flipping through a havoc of handwritten pages, making notes here and there with a pencil. I bit into my egg and asked Baba if it was true what a boy in school had told me, that if you ate a piece of eggshell, you'd have to pee it out. Baba grunted again.

7   I took a bite of my sandwich. One of the yellow-haired tourists laughed and slapped the other one on the back. In the distance, across the lake, a truck lumbered around a corner on the hill. Sunlight twinkled in its side-view mirror.

8   "I think I have *saratan*," I said. Cancer. Baba lifted his head from the pages flapping in the breeze. Told me I could get the soda myself, all I had to do was look in the trunk of the car.

9   Outside the orphanage, the next day, they ran out of chairs. A lot of people had to stand to watch the opening ceremony. It was a windy day, and I sat behind Baba on the little podium just outside the main entrance of the new building. Baba was wearing a green suit and a caracul hat. Midway through the speech, the wind knocked his hat off and everyone laughed. He motioned to me to hold his hat for him and I was glad to, because then everyone would see that he was *my* father, *my* Baba. He turned back to the microphone and said he hoped the building was sturdier than his hat, and everyone laughed again. When Baba ended his speech, people stood up and cheered. They clapped for a long time. Afterward, people shook his hand. Some of them tousled my hair and shook my hand too. I was so proud of Baba, of us.

10   But despite Baba's successes, people were always doubting him. They told Baba that running a business wasn't in his blood and he should study law like his father. So Baba proved them all wrong by not only running his own business but becoming one of the richest merchants in Kabul. Baba and Rahim Khan built a wildly successful carpet-exporting business, two pharmacies, and a restaurant.

11   When people scoffed that Baba would never marry well—after all, he was not of royal blood—he wedded my mother, Sofia Akrami, a highly educated woman universally regarded as one of Kabul's most respected, beautiful, and virtuous ladies. And not only did she teach classic Farsi literature at the university, she was a descendant of the royal family, a fact that my father playfully rubbed in the skeptics' faces by referring to her as "my princess."

12   With me as the glaring exception, my father molded the world around him to his liking. The problem, of course, was that Baba saw the world in black and white. And he got to decide what was black and what was white. You can't love a person who lives that way without fearing him too. Maybe even hating him a little.

13   When I was in fifth grade, we had a mullah who taught us about Islam. His name was Mullah Fatiullah Khan, a short, stubby man with a face full of acne scars and a gruff voice. He lectured us about the virtues of *zakat* and the duty of *hadj*, he taught us the intricacies of performing the five daily *namaz* prayers, and made us memorize verses from the Koran—and though he never translated the words for us, he did stress, sometimes with the help of a stripped willow branch; that we had to pronounce the Arabic words correctly so God would hear us better. He told us one day that Islam considered drinking a terrible sin; those who drank would answer for their sin on the day of *Qiyamat*, Judgment Day. In those days, drinking was fairly common in Kabul. No one gave you a public lashing for it, but those Afghans who did drink did so in private, out of respect. People bought their scotch as "medicine" in brown paper bags from selected "pharmacies." They would leave with the bag tucked out of sight, sometimes drawing furtive, disapproving glances from those who knew about the store's reputation for such transactions.

14   We were upstairs in Baba's study, the smoking room, when I told him what Mullah Fatiullah Khan had taught us in class. Baba was pouring himself a whiskey from the bar he had built in the corner of the room. He listened, nodded, took a sip from his drink. Then he lowered himself into the leather sofa, put down his drink, and propped me up on his lap. I felt as if I were sitting on a pair of tree trunks. He took a deep breath and exhaled through his nose, the air hissing through his mustache for what seemed an eternity. I couldn't decide whether I wanted to hug him or leap from his lap in mortal fear.

15   "I see you've confused what you're learning in school with actual education," he said in his thick voice.

16   "But if what he said is true then does it make you a sinner, Baba?"

17   "Hmm." Baba crushed an ice cube between his teeth. "Do you want to know what your father thinks about sin?"

18   "Yes."

19   "Then I'll tell you," Baba said, "but first understand this and understand it now, Amir: You'll never learn anything of value from those bearded idiots."

20   "You mean Mullah Fatiullah Khan?"

21   Baba gestured with his glass. The ice clinked. "I mean all of them. Piss on the beards of all those self-righteous monkeys."

22   I began to giggle. The image of Baba pissing on the beard of any monkey, self-righteous or otherwise, was too much.

23   "They do nothing but thumb their prayer beads and recite a book written in a tongue they don't even understand." He took a sip. "God help us all if Afghanistan ever falls into their hands."

24   "But Mullah Fatiullah Khan seems nice," I managed between bursts of tittering.

25   "So did Genghis Khan," Baba said. "But enough about that. You asked about sin and I want to tell you. Are you listening?"

26   "Yes," I said, pressing my lips together. But a chortle escaped through my nose and made a snorting sound. That got me giggling again.

27   Baba's stony eyes bore into mine and, just like that, I wasn't laughing anymore. "I mean to speak to you man to man. Do you think you can handle that for once?"

28   "Yes, Baba jan," I muttered, marveling, not for the first time, at how badly Baba could sting me with so few words. We'd had a fleeting good moment—it wasn't often Baba talked to me, let alone on his lap—and I'd been a fool to waste it.

29   "Good," Baba said, but his eyes wondered. "Now, no matter what the mullah teaches, there is only one sin, only one. And that is theft. Every other sin is a variation of theft. Do you understand that?"

30   "No, Baba jan," I said, desperately wishing I did. I didn't want to disappoint him again.

31   Baba heaved a sigh of impatience. That stung too, because he was not an impatient man. I remembered all the times he didn't come home until after dark, all the times I ate dinner alone I'd ask Ali where Baba was, when he was coming home, though I knew full well he was at the construction site,

overlooking this, supervising that. Didn't that take patience? I already hated all the kids he was building the orphanage for; sometimes I wished they'd all died along with their parents.

32   "When you kill a man, you steal a life," Baba said. "You steal his wife's right to a husband, rob his children of a father. When you tell a lie, you steal someone's right to the truth. When you cheat, you steal the right to fairness. Do you see?"

33   I did. When Baba was six, a thief walked into my grandfather's house in the middle of the night. My grandfather, a respected judge, confronted him, but the thief stabbed him in the throat, killing him instantly—and robbing Baba of a father. The townspeople caught the killer just before noon the next day; he turned out to be a wanderer from the Kunduz region. They hanged him from the branch of an oak tree with still two hours to go before afternoon prayer. It was Rahim Khan, not Baba, who had told me that story. I was always learning things about Baba from other people.

34   "There is no act more wretched than stealing, Amir," Baba said. "A man who takes what's not his to take, be it a life or a loaf of *naan* . . . I spit on such a man. And if I ever cross paths with him, God help him. Do you understand?"

35   I found the idea of Baba clobbering a thief both exhilarating and terribly frightening. "Yes, Baba."

36   "If there's a God out there, then I would hope he has more important things to attend to than my drinking scotch or eating pork. Now, hop down. All this talk about sin has made me thirsty again."

37   I watched him fill his glass at the bar and wondered how much time would pass before we talked again the way we just had. Because the truth of it was, I always felt like Baba hated me a little. And why not? After all, I *had* killed his beloved wife, his beautiful princess, hadn't I? The least I could have done was to have had the decency to have turned out a little more like him. But I hadn't turned out like him. Not at all.

38   In school, we used to play a game called *Sherjangi*, or "Battle of the Poems." The Farsi teacher moderated it and it went something like this: You recited a verse from a poem and your opponent had sixty seconds to reply with a verse that began with the same letter that ended yours. Everyone in my class wanted me on their team, because by the time I was eleven, I could recite dozens of verses from Khayyám, Háfez, or Rumi's famous *Masnawi*. One time, I took on the whole class and won. I told Baba about it later that night, but he just nodded, muttered, "Good."

39   That was how I escaped my father's aloofness, in my dead mother's books. That and Hassan, of course. I read everything, Rumi, Háfez, Saadi, Victor Hugo, Jules Verne, Mark Twain, Ian Fleming. When I had finished my mother's books—not the boring history ones, I was never much into those, but the novels, the epics—I started spending my allowance on books. I bought one a week from the bookstore near Cinema Park, and stored them in cardboard boxes when I ran out of shelf room.

40   Of course, marrying a poet was one thing, but fathering a son who preferred burying his face in poetry books to hunting . . . well, that wasn't how

Baba had envisioned it, I suppose. Real men didn't read poetry—and God forbid they should ever write it! Real men—real boys—played soccer just as Baba had when he had been young. Now *that* was something to be passionate about. In 1970, Baba took a break from the construction of the orphanage and flew to Tehran for a month to watch the World Cup games on television, since at the time Afghanistan didn't have TVs yet. He signed me up for soccer teams to stir the same passion in me. But I was pathetic, a blundering liability to my own team, always in the way of an opportune pass or unwittingly blocking an open lane. I shambled about the field on scraggy legs, squalled for passes that never came my way. And the harder I tried, waving my arms over my head frantically and screeching, "I'm open! I'm open!" the more I went ignored. But Baba wouldn't give up. When it became abundantly clear that I hadn't inherited a shred of his athletic talents, he settled for trying to turn me into a passionate spectator. Certainly I could manage that, couldn't I? I faked interest for as long as possible. I cheered with him when Kabul's team scored against Kandahar and yelped insults at the referee when he called a penalty against our team. But Baba sensed my lack of genuine interest and resigned himself to the bleak fact that his son was never going to either play or watch soccer.

41   I remember one time Baba took me to the yearly *Buzkashi* tournament that took place on the first day of spring, New Year's Day. Buzkashi was, and still is, Afghanistan's national passion. A *chapandaz*, a highly skilled horseman usually patronized by rich aficionados, has to snatch a goat or cattle carcass from the midst of a melee, carry that carcass with him around the stadium at full gallop, and drop it in a scoring circle while a team of other *chapandaz* chases him and does everything in its power—kick, claw, whip, punch—to snatch the carcass from him. That day, the crowd roared with excitement as the horsemen on the field bellowed their battle cries and jostled for the carcass in a cloud of dust. The earth trembled with the clatter of hooves. We watched from the upper bleachers as riders pounded past us at full gallop, yipping and yelling, foam flying from their horses' mouths.

42   At one point Baba pointed to someone. "Amir, do you see that man sitting up there with those other men around him?"

43   I did.

44   "That's Henry Kissinger."

45   "Oh," I said. I didn't know who Henry Kissinger was, and I might have asked. But at the moment, I watched with horror as one of the *chapandaz* fell off his saddle and was trampled under a score of hooves. His body was tossed and hurled in the stampede like a rag doll, finally rolling to a stop when the melee moved on. He twitched once and lay motionless, his legs bent at unnatural angles, a pool of his blood soaking through the sand.

46   I began to cry.

47   I cried all the way back home. I remember how Baba's hands clenched around the steering wheel. Clenched and unclenched. Mostly, I will never forget Baba's valiant efforts to conceal the disgusted look on his face as he drove in silence.

48   Later that night, I was passing by my father's study when I overheard him speaking to Rahim Khan. I pressed my ear to the closed door.

49   "—grateful that he's healthy," Rahim Khan was saying.

50   "I know, I know. But he's always buried in those books or shuffling around the house like he's lost in some dream."

51   "And?"

52   "I wasn't like that." Baba sounded frustrated, almost angry.

53   Rahim Khan laughed. "Children aren't coloring books. You don't get to fill them with your favorite colors."

54   "I'm telling you," Baba said, "I wasn't like that at all, and neither were any of the kids I grew up with."

55   "You know, sometimes you are the most self-centered man I know," Rahim Khan said. He was the only person I knew who could get away with saying something like that to Baba.

56   "It has nothing to do with that."

57   "Nay?"

58   "Nay."

59   "Then what?"

60   I heard the leather of Baba's seat creaking as he shifted on it. I closed my eyes, pressed my ear even harder against the door, wanting to hear, not wanting to hear. "Sometimes I look out this window and I see him playing on the street with the neighborhood boys. I see how they push him around, take his toys from him, give him a shove here, a whack there. And, you know, he never fights back. Never. He just . . . drops his head and . . ."

61   "So he's not violent," Rahim Khan said.

62   "That's not what I mean, Rahim, and you know it," Baba shot back. "There is something missing in that boy."

63   "Yes, a mean streak."

64   "Self-defense has nothing to do with meanness. You know what always happens when the neighborhood boys tease him? Hassan steps in and fends them off. I've seen it with my own eyes. And when they come home, I say to him, 'How did Hassan get that scrape on his face?' And he says, 'He fell down.' I'm telling you, Rahim, there is something missing in that boy."

65   "You just need to let him find his way," Rahim Khan said.

66   "And where is he headed?" Baba said. "A boy who won't stand up for himself becomes a man who can't stand up to anything."

67   "As usual you're oversimplifying."

68   "I don't think so."

69   "You're angry because you're afraid he'll never take over the business for you."

70   "Now who's oversimplifying?" Baba said. "look, I know there's a fondness between you and him and I'm happy about that. Envious, but happy. I mean that. He needs someone who . . . understands him, because God knows I don't. But something about Amir troubles me in a way that I can't express. It's like . . ." I could see him searching, reaching for the right words. He lowered his voice, but I heard him anyway. "If I hadn't seen the doctor pull him out of my wife with my own eyes, I'd never believe he's my son."

71   The next morning, as he was preparing my breakfast, Hassan asked if something was bothering me. I snapped at him, told him to mind his own business.

72   Rahim Khan had been wrong about the mean streak thing.

"Chapter 3," from THE KITE RUNNER by Khaled Hosseini, copyright © 2003 by Khaled Hosseini. Used by permission of Riverhead Books, an imprint of Penguin Group (USA) Inc. and Doubleday Canada.

● Vocabulary

lore (1)	mullah (13)	opportune (40)
penetrated (3)	intricacies (13)	shambled (40)
skeptics (4)	furtive (13)	squalled (40)
obstinate (4)	mortal (14)	aficionados (41)
lumbered (7)	chortle (26)	bellowed (41)
caracul (9)	exhilarating (35)	melee (45)
virtuous (11)	moderated (38)	valiant (47)

● The Facts

1. What is the lore circulating about the narrator's father? What does this lore establish immediately? Do you believe it? Of what other famous story does it remind you?

2. What happened to the narrator's mother? What bearing does this fact have on the relationship between son and father?

3. What characteristics, in addition to being athletic and physically powerful, describe Baba? What is Amir's reaction to his father?

4. According to Baba, what is the most hideous sin in life? What standard does Baba use to evaluate this sin? Do you agree with him? What do you consider the worst sin on earth?

5. What excuse for drinking, despite the Koran's admonition against it, does Baba give? To what extent do you agree with Baba?

6. To whom does Baba confide his feelings about Amir? How do you know that Amir knows how his father feels about his lack of athletic ability? How typical is Baba's attitude toward his son? What is the source of Amir's love of poetry and books?

7. Why is Baba so frustrated about Amir's approach to life? Does this frustration seem justified? Explain your answer.

● The Strategies

1. Which paragraph best describes Baba's sense of obligation and selfless generosity to his country? Who explains to Amir how outstanding his father is? Is this an accurate source to describe Baba's reputation?

2. What is the meaning of the figure of speech "mustaches needed oiling"?

3. What does the reference to "hippies" contribute to the narration? What reference later on makes the same contribution?

4. Why are paragraphs 52 through 56 so short?

5. What figures of speech are found throughout the essay? Point out two that captured your attention. What do these figures of speech add to the essay?

● The Issues

1. What is the essential theme of this narration? What is the story about? Try to formulate the theme in one sentence.

2. How do you know that Baba is a passionate patriot? Point to specific places in the story that reveal his concern for civic duties.

3. How does Baba's orphanage affect Amir's relationship with his father? What are some specific results?

4. Why is Baba so passionate about the sin of stealing? What is revealed in the narrative that gives a clue to his passion?

5. What is Baba's opinion of the mullahs, who eventually formed the Taliban in Afghanistan? What about them is particularly disgusting to Baba? Do you think he was justified in his attitude?

● Suggestions for Writing

1. Write an essay in which you contrast a son and his father who are thoroughly different from each other. Begin your contrast by stating the overall difference, such as, "Ben's father is determined to control his entire family and does not allow Ben to make any major decisions on his own." Then establish the bases of the contrast, considering such aspects as looks, hobbies, educational level, attitude toward money, and capacity for affection.

2. Write an essay in which you contrast yourself with one of your closest friends. Be sure to state an overall contrast and to choose three or four bases of contrast. Use vivid details that will increase the appeal of your essay.

ISSUE FOR CRITICAL THINKING AND DEBATE: ONLINE DATING

People in bygone eras would never have imagined that one day young men and women would have their romantic liaisons arranged by some electronic machine. Back in those days polite society organized formal coming-out dances where young women could meet proper young men and eventually find an appropriate beau to marry. The matriarchs of the neighborhood made sure that only the best gentlemen in the area had access to the well-bred ladies of the manor. Much bowing, scraping, and card proffering took place before parents would begin the process of evaluating any young man who might send a flirtatious smile toward one of their daughters. Today, the search for love and marriage partners takes place through the computer. People hungry for a date sign up with one of the popular computer dating services, such as eHarmony.com, Match.com, Perfect-match.com, Chemistry.com, or Spark.com. After filling out the required papers and paying a fee, they can start emailing the right match. Research by several universities, including Stanford, indicates clearly that online dating is becoming a growing business and an acceptable way to find a wife or husband. Friends, families, churches, and community functions are still common places where young people meet and connect, but the Internet is rapidly displacing these venues across the social spectrum. Just read the blogs or tweets about popular Internet dating services, and you will realize that a huge tidal wave of romantic activity is taking place in cyber space. Lonely widows, busy executives, frustrated youth, and even neglected housewives are filling out profiles and selling themselves to some prospective date. Not long ago, we heard a divorced mother of two teenagers lament that every man she met was either a rogue or a dolt. "I would love to meet a soul mate or even just a good friend, but the men available are culturally deprived and can't carry on a decent conversation. Who wants to sit at a bar and listen to someone whine like a child because so-and-so signed up with such-and-such a league, or watch everyone suddenly roar and scream when Big Bob makes a touch down? I'd rather stay home and read a good book." Men can be disillusioned as well. "I love politics," said one male law student, "but I'm a liberal and can't stand to have my date condemn universal healthcare as if it would ultimately usher in an age of Stalinist Communism." The aim of computer dating is to keep mismatches to a minimum by making sure that all profiles submitted clarify important issues, such as religious commitments, cultural tastes, and educational levels. Accompanying photographs are supposed to give the viewer a correct idea of the potential date's looks (although so far a major complaint is that too many profiles are dishonest or enhanced to make the applicant look more attractive than reality merits).

Online dating magazines suggest that over 120,000 marriages—many of them happy—take place each year as the direct result of meeting online. The forecast is that this number will continue to grow without serious impediment. With that new lens reflecting our future, we might do well to pay attention to what pundits and new-age yentas are saying. In our debate section, we present three essays that tackle the issue from different points of view. The first essay is an article written by psychologist and researcher Robert Epstein for *Scientific American*. Epstein carefully analyzes the pitfalls as well as advantages of computer dating. According to him, the hype is huge and the findings somewhat disturbing; yet, he predicts a bright future for this social practice. The second essay is a warning, based on personal experience, to use the Internet only for meeting a potential date, but not for deciding on a soul mate because suitable online dating is impossible since computers cannot detect the chemistry needed to fall in love. The student essay reflects the opinion of a female freshman at a small private college in Washington State. She views computer dating with fear, preferring to stick with the old-fashioned way of meeting prospective dates—in classes or at college-sponsored events. We suggest that the subject of online dating is worth some serious debate pro and con since statistics point out that the practice is not going away any time soon.

The Truth about Online Dating

ROBERT EPSTEIN

Robert Epstein (b. 1953) is an author, editor, researcher, and professor. He received a PhD in Psychology from Harvard University, where he studied with the famous B. F. Skinner. His editing skills led him to become editor of *Psychology Today* and then contributing editor for *Scientific American Mind.* He is the founder and director emeritus of the Cambridge Center for Behavioral Studies in Massachusetts. Epstein has hosted a number of psychology-related radio programs that stress adolescence, artificial intelligence, creativity, mental health, and relationship skills. Epstein is a prolific writer, with over 200 articles to his credit and numerous books, among them *Pure Fitness: Body Meets Mind* (1996), *Self-Help Without the Hype* (1997), *Irrelativity* (1997), and *Teen 1.0: Saving Our Children and Families from the Torment of Adolescence* (2010). The essay below was reprinted from *Scientific American.*

The best way to read this essay is with an open mind because despite all of the negative public ranting about online dating, many couples have met through this service and have found happiness with each other. Conversely, some catastrophic combinations have resulted from online dating. Perhaps some of Epstein's critical insights may encourage you to see through all the hype put out by online dating services to the reality of what online dating can offer in the way of good as well as bad. While you may find some aspects disturbing, you may also decide that a computer yenta may have many advantages over some pushy human being. As you read, ask yourself these questions: (1) Under what circumstances is online dating appropriate? (2) How should a prospective date present himself or herself in the profile requested? (3) What is the safest way to become intimate?

• • •

1   About two years ago I arranged to meet for coffee with a woman I had corresponded with online. I arrived early and sat at a table in a conspicuous spot. After a few minutes, a woman came to my table, sat down and said with big smile, "Hi, I'm Chris!" But Chris was not the woman in the online photos. This wasn't a question of an age discrepancy or a new hairdo. She was a completely different woman. Chris was in marketing, you see, and to her it was simply a good strategy to post photographs that would draw in as many "customers" as possible. I never said a word about the photos. I just enjoyed our conversation and the refreshments. A few weeks later I noticed that Chris had replaced the photos with those of yet *another* woman.

2   In the U.S. alone, tens of millions of people are trying to find dates or spouses online every day. How accurate are the ads they find? And just how successful is online dating compared with conventional dating? These and other questions have recently stimulated a small explosion of studies by social scientists. The research is quickly revealing many surprising things about the new world of online dating, and some of the findings could be of great value to the millions who now look to the Internet to find love.

Deception at Light Speed

3   Experiences such as the one I had with Chris are multiplying by the thousands: some people online lie quite drastically about their age, marital or parental status, appearance, income or profession. There are even Web sites, such as www.DontDateHimGirl.com, where people go to gripe, and a few lawsuits have been filed against online services by disgruntled suitors. Just how bad is deception in online dating?

4   To put this issue in context, bear in mind that deception has always played at least a small role in courting. One could even argue that deception is a *necessary* part of wooing a potential partner ("Yes, I *love* sports!") and even of forming successful long-term relationships ("No, that dress doesn't make you look fat at all!").

5   But cyberspace introduces a host of new possibilities. Survey research conducted by media researcher Jeana Frost of Boston University and the

Massachusetts Institute of Technology suggests that about 20 percent of online daters admit to deception. If you ask them how many other people are lying, however—an interviewing tactic that probably gets closer to the truth-that number jumps to 90 percent.

6   Because self-reported data can be unreliable, especially those from people asked to confess bad things about themselves, several researchers have sought objective ways to quantify online deception. For example, psychologist Jeffrey Hancock of Cornell University and communications professor Nicole Ellison of Michigan State University bring people into a lab, where they measure height and weight and then check the numbers against those in their online profiles. The preliminary data suggest that, on average, online profiles shave off about five pounds and add perhaps an inch in height. According to Ellison, although deception is "fairly common, the lies are of a very small magnitude." On the other hand, she says that the shorter and heavier people are, the bigger the lies.

7   In another attempt to collect objective data on deception, economists Guenter Hitsch and Ali Hortacsu of the University of Chicago and psychologist Dan Ariely of M.I.T. compared the heights and weights of online daters with the same statistics obtained from national census data. Like Hancock and Ellison, they found that online height is exaggerated by only an inch or so for both men and women but that women appear to understate their weight more and more as they get older: by five pounds when they are in their 20s, 17 pounds in their 30s and 19 pounds in their 40s.

8   For men, the major areas of deception are educational level, income, height, age and marital status; at least 13 percent of online male suitors are thought to be married. For women, the major areas of deception are weight, physical appearance and age. All of the relevant research shows the importance of physical appearance for both sexes, and online daters interpret the absence of photos negatively. According to one recent survey, men's profiles without photos draw one fourth the response of those with photos, and women's profiles without photos draw only one sixth the response of those with photos.

9   If you are a Garrison Keillor fan, you have probably heard about the fictional Lake Wobegon on National Public Radio, where "all the women are strong, all the men are good-looking, and all the children are above average." In the online dating community, similar rules apply: in one study, only 1 percent of online daters listed their appearance as "less than average."

Rationale for Falsehoods

10   Why so much inaccuracy? One theory, formulated in the late 1980s and early 1990s by Sara Kiesler and her colleagues at Carnegie Mellon University, suggests that by its very nature "computer-medialed communication" is disinhibiting, causing people to say just about anything they feel like saying. Because people typically use screen names rather than real ones, their ramblings are anonymous and hence not subject to social norms. There are also no physical cues or consequences—no visible communication gestures, raised eyebrows,

grimaces, and so on—to keep people's behavior in check. As a result, online daters tend to construct what Ellison and her colleagues Jennifer Gibbs of Rutgers University and Rebecca Heino of Georgetown University call an "ideal self" rather than a real one. A study published recently by Ellison and her colleagues even suggests that online daters often regret it when they do tell the truth, feeling that too much honesty, especially about negative attributes, creates a bad impression.

11   There are also straightforward, practical reasons for lying. One recent study showed that men claiming incomes exceeding $250,000 got 151 percent more replies than men claiming incomes less than $50,000, for example. Many women are quite open about listing much younger ages, often stating in the text of their profiles that they have listed a younger age to make sure they turn up in searches. (Because men often use age cutoffs in their searches, women who list ages above that cutoff will never be seen.)

12   My research assistant Rachel Greenberg and I have examined the age issue by plotting a histogram of the ages of 1,000 men and 1,000 women selected at random from the national database of Match.com, arguably now the largest of the online matchmaking services. We speculated that from age 29 on—the point at which people in our culture tend to become sensitive about growing older—we might see some distinctive patterns in the distribution of ages. For men, a small spike appeared in the distribution at 32 and a large one at 36. The number of men calling themselves 36 was dramatically higher than the average frequency of men between the ages of 37 and 41.

13   For women, we found three clear age spikes at 29, 35 and 44. The difference between the number of women claming to be 29 and the average frequency of women claiming to be between ages 30 and 34 was nearly eight times larger than we would expect by chance. Apparently women at certain ages are reluctant to reveal those ages—and certain numerical ages are especially appealing, presumably because our culture attaches less stigma to those ages.

Tests That Fail

14   I have been a researcher for about 30 years and a test designer for nearly half those years. When I see extravagant ads for online tests that promise to find people a soul mate, I find myself asking, "How on earth could such a test exist?"

15   The truth is, it doesn't.

16   For a psychometric evaluation to be taken seriously by scientists, the test itself needs to clear two hurdles. It needs to be shown to be reliable—which means, roughly, that you can count on it to produce stable results. And it needs to be shown to be a valid measure of what it is supposed to be measuring. With a test that matches people up, such validity would be established by showing that the resulting romantic pairings are actually successful.

17   Criteria for establishing test reliability are quite rigorous. Once relevant data are collected, the results are typically submitted to the scientific community for scrutiny. A peer-reviewed report (one vetted by other knowledgeable researchers in the field) is ultimately published in an academic journal.

18   Several online services are now built entirely around claims that they have powerful, effective, "scientific" matchmaking tests—most notably eHarmony.com, promoted by clinical psychologist Neil Warren; PerfectMatch.com, promoted by sociologist Pepper Schwartz of the University of Washington; and Chemistry.com (a recent spin-off of Match.com), promoted by anthropologist Helen Fisher of Rutgers. But not one of the tests they offer has ever been subjected to the type of outside scientific verification that I have described.

19   Why would a major company such as eHarmony, which claims to have 12 million members, *not* subject its "scientific, 29-dimension" test to a scientific validation process? In 2004 eHarmony personnel did present a paper at a national convention claiming that married couples who met through eHarmony were happier than couples who met by other means. Typically such a paper would then be submitted for possible publication in a peer-reviewed journal. But this paper has still not been published, possibly because of its obvious flaws—the most problematic being that the eHarmony couples in the study were newlyweds (married an average of six months), whereas the couples in the control group (who had met by other means) were way past the honeymoon period (married an average of 2.1 years). (eHarmony personnel, including its founder, Neil Warren, did not respond to requests to be interviewed for this article.)

20   In 2005, using eHarmony's own published statistics, a team of credible authorities—among them Philip Zimbardo, a former president of the American Psychological Association—concluded in an online white paper: "When eHarmony recommends someone as a compatible match, there is a 1 in 500 chance that you'll marry this person.... Given that eHarmony delivers about 1.5 matches a month, if you went on a date with all of them, it would take 346 dates and 19 years to reach [a] 50% chance of getting married." The team also made the sweeping observation that "there is no evidence that... scientific psychology is able to pair individuals who will enjoy happy, lasting marriages."

21   Think about how difficult this task is. Most online matching is done, for example, by pairing up people who are "similar" in various respects. But you do not need to look farther than your own family and friends to know that similarity is not always a good predictor of success in a relationship. Sometimes opposites really do attract. How could an online test possibly determine whether you should be paired with someone similar or with someone different, or with some magic mix?

22   And even if validated predictive tests eventually appeared online, how could such tests possibly predict how two people will feel when they finally meet—when that all-important "chemistry" comes into play? Oddly enough, eHarmony does not even ask people about their body type, even though research shows unequivocally that physical appearance is important to both men and women.

23   But the biggest problem with online testing is the "false negative problem." A test that determines in advance whom you might meet and whom you will *never* meet necessarily fails to allow certain people to meet who would adore each other. The good news, though, is that according to psychologist

Larry D. Rosen of California State University, Dominguez Hills, "In our studies only 30 percent of the people say they use [online tests] at all, and most of those people find them ridiculous."

High Hopes and Poor Odds

24   Advertising materials from the largest online dating services—Match, eHarmony, True.com and Yahoo! Personals—suggest that more than 50 million Americans are now using such services (assuming relatively little overlap in membership) and that satisfaction levels are high. But recent independent studies suggest that only 16 million Americans were using online dating services by late 2005 and that satisfaction levels were low. Based on a phone survey with more than 2,000 people, Jupiter Research reports that "barely one quarter of users reported being very satisfied or satisfied with online personals sites." Another extensive survey conducted by Pew Internet & American Life Projects suggests that 66 percent of Internet users think that online dating is a "dangerous activity."

25   According to Trish McDermott, a longtime spokesperson for Match and now an executive at Engage.com, the confusion over membership figures results from the fact that while a large company such as Match might advertise that it has 15 million members, less than a million are actually paying customers. The others have full profiles online—an important marketing draw—but cannot respond to e-mails. This is one of several reasons, according to McDermott, why many paying members get frustrated by a lack of response to their e-mails; the vast majority of people in the profiles simply cannot respond.

26   One of my greatest concerns about online dating has to do with what I call "the click problem." We already have a commitment problem in America, one of several reasons why roughly half of first marriages and about two thirds of second marriages here end in divorce. Online dating probably is making things worse.

27   No matter what Hollywood tells us, long-term relationships take patience, skill and effort. In cyberspace, unfortunately, the bar is so long and the action so quick that few people are willing to put up with even the slightest imperfection in a potential mate. If someone is the wrong height or wears the wrong shoes or makes the wrong kind of joke, he or she is often dismissed instantly. After all, it is a simple matter to go back and click, with tens of thousands of potential mates ready to fill the void.

Virtual Dating and More

28   These many problems notwithstanding, the future of online dating and matchmaking looks bright. Interest is growing rapidly, and intense competition will force rapid changes in the kinds of services that are offered. In 2001 online dating was a $40-million business; that figure is expected to break $600 million, with more than 800 businesses, both large and small, vying for every dollar.

29   The online dating model is already developing rapidly. Phase one—the Long Bar—is exemplified by companies such as Match, True and Yahoo! Personals. Phase two—the Long Test—is the bread and butter of companies like eHarmony and PerfectMatch. But phase three is already well under way.

30   Engage, for example, allows members to bring friends and family with them online, all of whom can prowl the profiles, checking people out and matching them up. Members can also rate the politeness of their dates, as well as the accuracy of the profiles. This is the new "community" approach to online matching—a naturalistic, social corrective for the deception that plagues cyberspace. The community approach is also evident in the sprawling new social networking sites such as Facebook, Friendster and MySpace; MySpace alone has more than 100 million members. Although the social networking sites appeal mainly to young users and are not strictly dating sites, they bring the community back into whatever dating is generated there. On mega dating sites such as eHarmony and Match, dating is done in complete social isolation, a matter of great concern to Ellison and other researchers in this area.

31   And the next step in online dating—"virtual dating"—is already being developed. Using special software developed by the M.I.T. Media Lab, researchers Frost, Ariely and Harvard University's Michael I. Norton recently reported that people who had had a chance to interact with each other (by computer only) on a virtual tour of a museum subsequently had more successful face-to-face meetings than people who had viewed only profiles. One major bonus: virtual dating takes care of the safety concerns that prevent many people from meeting in person.

32   Take this just a small step forward: people meeting and chatting in a romantic virtual cafe on the Champs-Élysées in Paris—seeing and hearing each other online as they interact in this beautiful setting. Andrew Fiore, a doctoral candidate at the University of California, Berkeley, who studies online dating, suggests that in a few years we will even be able to add physiological signs to the experience—the sound of your date's heartbeat, perhaps?

33   Add community-based matchmaking to enriched virtual dating, and we have turned the Internet into the greatest yenta the world has ever known.

● Vocabulary

discrepancy (1)	disinhibiting (10)	stigma (13)
media (5)	attributes (10)	psychometric (16)
mediated (10)	histogram (12)	mega (30)

● The Facts

1. Of the many statistics cited in this essay, which one had the strongest impact on you and caused you to reflect most seriously? Give specific reasons for your answer.

2. What is the difference between *reliable* and *valid* as discussed in paragraph 16? What requirement for proper measuring DON'T companies like eHarmony.com, PerfectMatch.com, and Chemistry.com fulfill? What is your reaction to the author's criticism of these company's testing results?

3. According to the author, what are the major reasons people lie when they seek dates online? What other possible reasons might exist for slanting the truth? What approach to truth do you think people should take when they fill out their profiles online?

4. What do you think of the recent development of virtual dating? How will it impact the success of online dating as a means toward permanent romance or marriage? What are its advantages or disadvantages?

5. What expertise does the author bring to the subject of online tests? What is his opinion of tests that promise to find people their soul mates? Do you agree or disagree with him? Explain yourself.

● The Strategies

1. What strategy does the author use to capture your attention at the start of the essay? Was he successful? Why do you think he used this strategy?

2. The title of the essay purports to tell "the truth about online dating." In your opinion, does the essay fulfill this promise? Either challenge the title, qualify it, or support it.

3. What difference do you see between the voice of this author and, say, the voice of the author who wrote "Baba and Me" (see pp. 479–486). Why are these two essays so different in style? Is the difference necessary? Explain your answer.

4. How do you explain the author's use of subtitles in his essay? Did you find them useful or did they merely chop up the essay? Give persuasive reasons for your answer.

5. The conclusion of the essay amounts to one brief sentence. Do you find it satisfyingly conclusive or do you think it is too abrupt? If you consider the ending too abrupt, what kind of ending would you put forward?

● The Issues

1. The author is concerned about the lying that goes on when people fill out profiles in preparation for dating online. What is your personal reaction to this kind of exaggeration or distortion? How can it be prevented? Should it be prevented?

2. Do you think it is possible to create a service that would be able to find a soul mate for people who desperately want one? Or do you agree with the author that this is impossible? Provide evidence for your opinion.

3. Is it possible that too much honesty on the part of online daters might create a bad impression unnecessarily? What standard would you embrace for how much one should reveal online?

4. Do you agree or disagree with the author that Hollywood has a bad influence on long-term relationships? Dispute or support his view by citing personal or expert testimony and other appropriate evidence.

5. Why do you think thousands of people today are turning to online dating? What aspects, if any, of modern society are driving them to seek soul mates through a machine rather than through other people? What is your opinion of this trend?

● Suggestions for Writing

1. Write an essay in which you compare and contrast the benefits of online dating with those of conventional dating. Your thesis should indicate which system you prefer, and your essay should provide evidence to support your preference.

2. Write a profile biography intended to be placed online to attract a soul mate. Use humor if you wish, but be discreet about revealing any of the baggage that might be lurking in your background.

Computer Dating

Evaluating Internet Dating

TIM DAUGHTRY

Tim Daughtry wrote this informal essay for *Helium*, an online knowledge co-operative that encourages varied opinions on any subject of interest to its members. He wrote it as a favor to other fellow online daters who might be expecting more than is possible from their online dating experience. If you don't want to be a dating loser online, then you need to understand the limits of what any dating service can do for you.

Loved and relied upon by throngs of naïve people to fulfill their dreams of romance and love, online dating services are multiplying because they pledge to fill up the empty psyches of lonely people—no matter who or where they are. Online dating services now cater to Christians, gays, single moms, classical movie lovers, and any other special interest group. No one needs to feel left out. If you are eager to meet your soul mate, hop aboard the online train that will chug along to your destination heart throb. But wait, warning signs may signal a catastrophe ahead, so pay attention to Tim Daughtry's words because he writes from experience. Think about his words, and evaluate them critically.

• • •

1   Is online dating for losers? To answer this question, I may be breaking ranks with my fellow online daters. Moreover, I can't imagine that the many match-making websites out there will applaud my answer, but who else would be better to evaluate online dating than a loser?

2   Like most people, I am keen on the Internet. It's a good friend when no one else is around, and it's always available. Remindful of a vast library, it offers almost everything I would ever want to find. So I must admit that I was one of the first to enthusiastically hop aboard Internet's matchmaking train. I was not alone. There were and still are a multitude of single passengers on board, hoping to type their way to some special someone over the Internet rails.

3   I still think that for meeting a large group of what seem like people who are matched to you and possibly even interested in "meeting" you, the Internet is unmatched. But I purposely used that last word, "unmatched," to symbolize ironically where you will end up if you do anything more than use the Internet as a way to be exposed to more potential dating possibilities.

4   Before I tell you why the Internet is not the place to consummate your relationships, let me share with you why I decided to use the Internet for dating. When I felt lonely after my seventeen-year marriage had failed, the best advice anyone could give me was to take a yoga or cooking class, hang out in the grocery store late at night, or endure sundry other boring activities that no one really wants to do. By contrast, being able to actually communicate with a real person somewhere out there in our computer world sounded attractive and easy. After all, you didn't have to get dressed up nor even get out of your pajamas to make that initial contact. And you didn't need to worry if you didn't know how to write about yourself because most of the dating websites have

matchmakers who can create a scintillating "you" to use in presenting yourself to the other people out there who are pulling you up on their computer. All of a sudden you're getting far more activity than you ever had when frequenting bars, joining groups where people hung out, or waiting for your friends to set you up with a suitable date. Therefore, I admit that for exposure to people to get the dating ball rolling, the Internet is okay.

5   But that's where it should stop!

6   Unfortunately, we don't stop there, and that's why most of us using the Internet eventually become losers. No popular person would ever stoop to dating—if it can be called that—on the Internet. Picking a mate is one area where they would never let technology intrude. But too often those of us who have tried dating on the Internet have deluded ourselves into thinking that e-mailing someone is similar to dating. Nothing could be further from the truth. E-mail is a convenient tool only when we cannot talk to the person face-to-face. Need I remind you how you feel when someone in your office gets too comfortable with e-mailing you even though you're only two cubicles over from that person? Yet, we think that we can resort to this tool in order to find the most important person in our lives. When we losers find ourselves e-mailing our "date" more than two or three times, we are already making the mistake of starting to relate to that person electronically instead of in person. E-mailing someone is a very comfortable form of communication for the sender. On the receiving end the results may be quite mixed. What we need to keep in mind is this: The Internet is a convenient way of meeting several people whom we then can go on to call on the phone and meet in person. If online dating is to be used, it must be used minimally. The Internet might be a lot of things, but a matchmaker it is not.

6   What really happens when we type away to a person whom we really don't know and that individual types back? We are avoiding what we fear the most—rejection. Let me say that another way: We are postponing the chance that we might be rejected. And being the losers that we really are, we don't realize that our incessant typing to another person not only makes it easier for him or her to reject us, but almost makes rejection a certainty. If you hang with the person long enough through e-mail, one of you will say something regret-table. That's how e-mail sneaks up on you. You get comfortable with it. You forget that the other person is saving all of your e-mails. Then, one day you say something that puts a doubt in the other person's mind. And since you're not there in person to explain yourself, who knows how badly you are misin-terpreted? Many of us online daters have experienced what can happen at any moment with online dating—the e-mails stop. The person doesn't even do us the courtesy of telling us what we did wrong nor let us know that he or she is now cooling off and is actually no longer interested in us. The e-mails just stop, and the other person vanishes.

7   But that's okay—because now we have five new matches that technology has chosen for us, so it's easy to move on.

8   Do people who date online embellish who they are more than they would if they had met someone in the traditional way? Absolutely, wouldn't you? Why

in the world would people present themselves in a less than glamorous way when right at their fingertips they have an amazing tool that can make them look appealing? Don't get me wrong; I met eight dates with whom I started out on the Internet. They all looked just like their pictures. Their personalities were close to what they had revealed online. But what all of these eight people had in common was that they carried with them unresolved baggage from the past, and that information was not listed in their profile. Baggage is a reality. No one can escape it. It makes me laugh when I read someone's requirement that a mate show up with no baggage, because unless a person just landed here from another planet, all of us are either in a relationship, on the way out of one, or trying to recover from one. We carry baggage.

9   What about the matchmaking capabilities of technology? It seems to make sense that if we were honest about whom we are seeking and what we have to offer, a computer would be a great tool for finding a compatible person out there. That might be true if a relationship were nothing more than comparing our lives to another and seeing if our likes and dislikes were in sync. But a romantic relationship involves a little word called "chemistry," and so far the computer has not figured out what to do with chemical attraction. That's a shame since it just happens to be the single most important ingredient in a relationship. People often refer to cyber sex as if it were real; however, a computer cannot simulate sex nor can it notice chemical attraction when it's in the room. We're simply asking too much of our wonderful little computers.

10   So why do so many of us nowadays turn to the computer to date? Are we really losers? I can tell you why I turned to it. It was a way to have some kind of communication with someone of the opposite sex after the breakup of my marriage. I didn't want to meet anyone in person. I was really comfortable with a pen pal.

11   Online dating was a nonintrusive, comfortable way to meet people or at least make myself think I was meeting people. Actually meeting my online connections in person was like starting from scratch. And when there was no chemistry, the relationship went no place. But I knew I was a loser when in some of those cases, without verbalizing it to the other person, I rationalized, "Well if this doesn't work out, we can always go back to e-mailing one another." (Hmm)

12   The Internet, as I said at the outset, is a wonderful invention, and I personally love going there. But as capable as it is, I have come to realize that whenever machine meets man, the difference between us is apparent. Are we really losers if we dabble online and meet a few people? I think not, as long as we don't turn over the all-important part of our lives, referred to as "looking for our soul mates," to a machine that has no soul, no heart, and no radar to see if chemistry happens between us and someone we meet. After all, our computers couldn't care less if the general public calls us online daters "losers" because a computer cannot feel. It can only do what we tell it to do, and we haven't yet figured out how to tell it to have its radar up and running when that special person comes within our view. Only our hearts and our emotions are capable of detecting that bond.

13   So, keep using the Internet to meet people. E-mail them a couple of times and then meet them in person and turn off your computer. Don't keep e-mailing these mystery persons, confining your relationship with them to an online collection of letters sent back and forth. That's not a dating; that's having pen pal. You don't have to be a loser.

"Is Online Dating for Losers" by Tim Daughtry with permission from Helium, Inc.

● Vocabulary

consummate (4)	sundry (4)	embellish (9)
yoga (4)	incessant (7)	nonintrusive (12)

● The Facts

1. Why does the author think he is breaking ranks with other online daters? Give reasons why you agree or disagree with him on this point.

2. Why did the author start using the Internet as a dating service? Have you known other people who use it for that reason? What other reasons have caused people you know to date online? Are these reasons sound and logical? Support your answer.

3. How does the Internet guarantee that online daters will have increased exposure to possible dates?

4. According to the author, what are we really avoiding when we date online rather than person to person? Give your assessment of this view.

5. Why does the author think people often embellish their profiles online? How does he qualify his statement? Do you approve of online daters making themselves look better than they really are? Explain your answer.

● The Strategies

1. Where is the writer's argument summarized? What advantage, if any, does this placement have? State his thesis in one declarative statement.

2. In paragraph 3, how is the word "unmatched" used? What does this strategy add to the essay?

3. What kind of voice does the author use to communicate with his readers? What audience would he be most likely to influence? What kind of audience might ignore him?

4. When comparing Daughtry's essay with that of Robert Epstein, what difference in approach do you notice? Which essay do you find more informative? Which do you find more helpful as a guide to online dating?

5. Did the content of the essay fulfill the expectations you had when you read its title? Explain why it did or did not.

● The Issues

1. What is your response to the writer's suggestion that if you meet someone online, you should limit your online communication to two or three emails, and

then you should make an effort to meet the date in person? What might be some pitfalls of meeting as soon as possible? What suggestions do you have for a smooth transition from email to personal encounter? Discuss these with your classmates to see how they react.

2. For someone who feels, as the author does, that no reliable places exist where you can easily meet an appropriate date, what suggestion do you have beside the ones mentioned in paragraph 4? Think of places where the danger involved in meeting a total stranger is minimized.

3. For whom do you think online dating is more useful—males or females? Support your answer with real-life experiences and testimony.

4. Do you agree with the author that relating to a date electronically is a barrier to romance? Try to dispute this negative view of electronic communication by presenting evidence that email correspondence can lead to genuine and deep-rooted romance.

5. How important is the role played by fear of rejection in any attempt to date someone? Why are some people less worried about rejection than others? Explain the phenomenon in your own words.

● Suggestions for Writing

1. Answer one of the following questions by developing it into a persuasive essay:

   a. To be effective, what factors should an online dating service always provide?

   b. What sets apart a good online dating service from a bad one?

2. Write an essay exploring the importance or irrelevance of having prospective dates post a photo online?

Stumped by rhetorical questions? Exit on page 703, at the **Editing Booth!**

Punctuation Workshop
The Question Mark (?)

Put a question mark after a direct question, but not after an indirect question:

> **DIRECT:** What is keeping the catcher from reading the pitcher's signals?

> **INDIRECT:** We asked what was keeping the catcher from reading the pitcher's signals.

> **DIRECT:** Did you understand the insulting question, "Do you have a low I.Q.?"

(A question within a question contains only one question mark, inside the closing quotation mark.)

> **INDIRECT:** They were asked if they understood the insulting question.

A series of direct questions having the same subject can be treated as follows:

What on earth is little Freddy doing? Laughing? Crying? Screaming?

Sometimes a declarative sentence contains a direct question that requires a question mark:

He asked his neighbor, "Have you seen the raccoon?" (The question mark goes inside the quotation mark.)

 CAUTION: Do not write an indirect question as if it were a direct question:

> **WRONG:** He asked her would she join the team?

> **RIGHT:** He asked her if she would join the team.

Kindra M. Neuman
Walla Walla University, Washington
"OMGILY2!!" Online Dating Is at Your Own Risk

Today's world has varied drastically from what it was a century ago. Many aspects have changed, such as transportation, entertainment, communication, and style. Perhaps one of the most startling changes has taken place in the way modern couples date. In the past, couples dated as a result of being introduced by relatives or friends, enrolling in the same college class, or attending events of mutual interest. However, in the last decade dating trends have changed dramatically as more and more dating takes place on the Internet. Despite some people's objections, traditional courting has transformed itself into a lazy, risky, and impatient search for love.

Many reasons make online dating objectionable. One of these reasons is the simple truth that online dating is bogus. The online dating world is full of scams. When you use the computer as your advertising medium, it is not difficult to turn yourself into someone totally different from who you really are and sell yourself as this new person to some gullible victim. While of course you personally would never be that dishonest, there are plenty of people out there who are. Getting involved with online dating is often a straight path toward being painfully deceived. Magazine articles and blog sites reveal numerous cases where young girls meet what appears to be a wonderful guy online and then schedule to meet him, only to find out that he is not the handsome, fascinating, athletic young man he claimed to be in his resume, but rather he turns out to be a boring lout. Moreover, many young girls have found themselves in dangerous situations when they agreed to meet someone they believed they could trust. I live in the dormitory of a private college, where dating is safe, but my roommate and friends are constantly hearing about rape cases that occurred when a girl met a male online, and took the chance of meeting him in person. Meeting people online can be very dangerous. The computer screen you are staring at intently may not be a castle door, leading to your Prince Charming, but in fact may serve as a protective barrier from the vicious monster leering on the other side.

Online Dating magazine offers several good tips for avoiding risky online daters. First of all, it is important never to give away your address or any home information. This is one of the worst things you could do because a stalker can now follow you home. Second, if you insist on meeting an online date, use your own transportation and meet in a public place. If the situation were to take a dangerous turn, you would not want to be in a dark street with no traffic. Third, do not assume that your date is safe. Maintain a skeptical attitude. It is crucial that you stay in touch with the still small voice in your head. If you feel uncomfortable or wary, don't brush those feelings aside. A special tip for women is to pay your part of the expenses of the date. Often men will offer to pay, but expect sexual favors in return. What you thought was to be a friendly get-acquainted dinner turns out to be a skirmish for your body. Last but not least, always tell someone where you are going. That way, if you don't return on time, your contact can check on you and call the police if the situation warrants doing do. *Online Dating* magazine posts these tips because many unpleasant and even dangerous incidents have happened that could have been avoided if these simple rules had been followed.

In addition to being disappointing or unsafe, computer dating deprives you of the opportunity to get to know people in depth. You may waste a large amount of time in aimless and foggy Internet "chatting" when you could have realized after one regular date that you aren't interested in furthering your acquaintance with this person. Interacting with people in person builds social skills that help you judge a person's motives, interests, and lifestyle. Being face to face with people allows you to interpret their thoughts and ideas better than through electronic means because you can engage in follow-up questions that demand evidence for the beliefs they hold.

Blogs, tweets, texting, and emails may be cover ups for attitudes you wouldn't like if you knew about them. Also, conversing online makes it easy for you to act differently than the way you might act in person. You might discover yourself saying things over the computer that you might never say in person. Research indicates that most people present themselves online in a much better light than they do in reality. Fat people represent themselves as thinner than they are; non readers act as if they read constantly; and males (especially) act as if they were more successful and richer than they really are. It is easy to be someone you aren't when there is a computer screen separating you from the other end of the conversation.

Computer dating also takes a lot less effort, thus making it less special, than old-fashioned dating. Taking the time to go out with someone is far more meaningful than just sending someone a quick text or email. Spending time and effort on individuals shows that you care about them. Internet usage should be kept to a minimum when dealing with relationships. People were made to socialize with one another in flesh and blood—not merely in cyber space.

Online dating deprives you of one of the greatest joys in life— discovering a soul mate among the crowd of people in your milieu and getting to spend quality time with that person face to face. There is no equal to spending time one on one with another individual whom you know to be part of your world in order to truly get acquainted. In doing so, you experience genuine meaning and feeling as the relationship builds. Don't desperately chase down love by filling out eHarmony resumes to find a match. True love will find you.

How I Write

I use many different approaches to writing a paper. Occasionally I will grab a piece of scratch paper and write down some points I would like to cover. However, most of the time I just sit down at my desk and write the paper. Somehow I think the thoughts in my head and I am able to put them down on paper. I have been blessed with an opinionated attitude and rarely seem short of words. After I write my paper, I go through it to edit any grammar or punctuation issues that I see. Next I adjust any sentences that seem unclear or awkward. When I am done with my paper, I normally send it to my Dad and have him read it through. More often than not, he has a few pointers as far as grammar is concerned. I used to hate it when he would "grade" my papers, but since then I have come to appreciate his constructive criticism. While my strategy for writing may be different than yours, if works for me. And I am able to whip out a paper in a reasonable amount of time!

How I Wrote This Essay

I wrote this paper by making a list of reasons why online dating seemed objectionable. I wrote down my reasons, and then recruited a few additional reasons from a few of my friends. After that, I plopped myself down in front of my computer and started writing—and I kept writing until I had transferred all of my ideas to paper. The next step was to reread what I had written and to adjust anything that needed editing. Next, I emailed the essay to my parents. I enjoy sending my writing pieces to my parents because not only do they have constructive criticism, but they also make me feel more confident about my papers. A little applause here and there is a nice boost to my self-esteem. After getting the thumbs up from my Dad, I feel like it's safe to turn in my paper to the professor.

My Writing Tip

My tip to you is to embrace the opinions you have. Opinions are what make articles interesting. Discover your point of view and then get data to back up your stance. Also, find out what works best for you in order to complete your paper. If you feel the need to create a step-by-step outline, then go with that. Maybe you are a person who uses flash cards to keep track of your data before you begin. Or maybe you are like me and you can just sit down and write. Whatever may get you into the groove, use it! Once you know your pattern, you are set to go. After that the sky is the limit.

● CHAPTER WRITING ASSIGNMENTS

1. Write an essay in which you contrast one of the following pairs of concepts:
   a. Hearing–Listening
   b. Liberty–License
   c. Servant–Slave
   d. Democracy–Demagoguery
   e. Art–Craft
   f. Having an opinion–Being opinionated
   g. Talent–Ability
2. Using the Internet as your research tool, write a paper comparing the levels of job satisfaction in two different professions. Consider such matters as personal growth, financial benefits, future prospects, and relationships with colleagues. Be sure to synthesize outside sources as indicated in Chapter 2 and Chapter 3.

● WRITING ASSIGNMENTS FOR A SPECIFIC AUDIENCE

1. Write a letter to a younger brother or sister—or an imaginary one—contrasting college with high school. Be sure to choose appropriate bases for the contrast, such as academic rigor, social life, relationships with teachers, and independence.
2. With the help of some Internet research, write an essay in which you compare the satisfaction of customers using eHarmony.com with that of customers using Match.com as their online dating service. Be sure that you take a fair and balanced approach to the comparison.

● IMAGE GALLERY WRITING ASSIGNMENT

Visit pages IG-16–IG-18 of our image gallery and study the images dealing with online dating. Then choose the image that most appeals to you. Answer the questions and do the writing assignment.

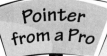

CONQUER WRITER'S BLOCK

> *People have writer's block not because they can't write, but because they despair of writing eloquently.*
>
> —Anna Quindlen

College students are especially vulnerable to this kind of sudden mental paralysis when they face a deadline for an assignment. Here are three pieces of practical advice:

1. Quit dissing yourself; you aren't the idiot you think you are.
2. Trust yourself because your ideas count.
3. Clear your mind for a while—by taking a walk, listening to music, or chatting with another person.

Then go back and tackle your writing assignment with a new perspective. Start placing words—random words—on paper. Eventually your mind will unblock, and your writing will flow.

14

Division/Classification

What Division/Classification Does

To write a division/classification essay means to break down a subject into its constituent types. If you write a paragraph on the kinds of books in your library, the types of cars in your miniature-car collection, or the varieties of humor in Mark Twain's works, you are classifying. A prime purpose of division/classification is to discover the nature of a subject by a study of its parts and their relationships to the larger whole. For example, the following paragraph tries to explain and understand people by grouping them together into two primary categories:

> A simple experiment will distinguish two types of human nature. Gather a throng of people and pour them into a ferry-boat. By the time the boat has swung into the river you will find that a certain proportion have taken the trouble to climb upstairs in order to be out on deck and see what is to be seen as they cross over. The rest have settled indoors to think what they will do upon reaching the other side, or perhaps lose themselves in apathy or tobacco smoke. But leaving out those apathetic, or addicted to a single enjoyment, we may divide all the alert passengers on the boat into two classes: those who are interested in crossing the river, and those who are merely interested in getting across. And we may divide all the people on the earth, or all the moods of people, in the same way. Some of them are chiefly occupied with attaining ends, and some with receiving experiences. The distinction of the two will be more marked when we name the first kind practical, and the second poetic, for common knowledge recognizes that a person poetic or in a poetic mood is impractical, and a practical person is intolerant of poetry.
>
> —Max Eastman, *Poetic People*

Division and classification are common to the way we think. We divide and classify the plant and animal kingdoms into phyla, genera, families, and species; we divide the military into the Army, Navy, Air Force, Marines, and Coast Guard. We divide and classify people into kinds and types. When we ask, "What kind of person is he?" we are asking for information developed by division and classification. An assignment asking for an essay developed by division, therefore, is an exercise in this common mode of thinking.

When to Use Division/Classification

Division/classification is especially useful in analyzing big, complex subjects. All of us draw on categories—some accurate, some prejudicial—in our attempts to understand the world around us. We wonder what type of person a certain man or woman is, and when we think we know, we react accordingly. This is not necessarily bad, so long as we do not hold false categories about people that function as prejudices. We speculate on the experiences that happen to us and try to sort them into understandable types. We say that yesterday was that kind of day and that last year was that sort of year. We have theories about kinds of love, types of friends, varieties of personalities. Science, philosophy, and even the practical arts are largely based on classifications. Biology sorts animals and plants into genera and species; medicine organizes diseases into types; chemistry classifies substances; and literature classifies writing. The concept of types rescues us from the tyranny of uniqueness and spares us from having to individually study every event, object, person, or thing. Without categories that tell us that this is like that, experience would have no predictive value and we would be overwhelmed by the uniqueness of every butterfly, thunderstorm, or love affair.

How to Use Division/Classification

1. **All good writing is based on clear thinking, but division/classification most decidedly so.** To classify is to think and analyze, to see relationships between individual items where none are obvious. You are, in a sense, superimposing your mind's filing cabinet onto the world. To classify accurately, then, you must base your typing and sorting on a single principle. This means that your sorting must be done on the basis of one criterion or your scheme will be a muddle. A simple example would be if you were to classify sports by whether or not they involve physical contact and lumped tennis in with football. Obviously, tennis is a noncontact sport, and your sorting would be inaccurate. Likewise, if you were writing a paper on the works written by Samuel Johnson and came up with the following list:

   a. Johnson's poetry

   b. Johnson's prose

   c. Johnson's dictionary

   d. Boswell's Life of Johnson

your division/classification would also be false. Boswell's *Life of Johnson* is not by Johnson but about him and, therefore, does not belong in your list. In a more formal context, we see this error repeated in the following paragraph, whose division/classification is not based on a single principle:

> Mass production in American industry is made up of four distinct elements: division of labor, standardization through precision tooling, assembly line, and consumer public. First is the division of labor, which means that a complicated production process is broken down into specialized individual tasks that are performed by people or machines who concentrate on these tasks only. Second is the standardization of parts as a result of precision tooling. This means that each part can be produced by machines both for interchangeability and for assembly by semiskilled workers. Third is the assembly line, which is a method of moving the work from one person to another in a continual chain of progress until the item is completed. This is a way of moving the work to the person, instead of the person to the work. The last element is the consumer public. Without it mass production would be a futile endeavor, for it is the public that buys up all the mass-produced items as quickly as they roll off the assembly line.

Clearly, the division/classification is not based on a single principle. Division of labor, standardization through precision tooling, and the use of an assembly line may be part of the mass-production process, but the consumer public plainly is not. Only after production has been completed and an item is ready to be marketed does the consumer enter into the picture. As it stands, the paragraph has misrepresented the elements involved in mass production.

2. **Make your division/classification complete.** A complete division/classification is one that includes all the parts of the subject being divided. If you were to classify sports by whether they involve the use of a ball and left out soccer, your division/classification would be incomplete. If you omitted the short story from an essay classifying types of literature, you would likewise be guilty of this error. Similarly, if you were to divide the family of Equidae into its main categories, you would have to include the horse, the ass, and the zebra. Leave out any of these, and your division/classification would be incomplete.

3. **Avoid the overlapping of categories.** Here is an example of an overlapping division in the division/classification of literature according to genres:
   a. Poetry
   b. Short story
   c. Humor
   d. Drama
   e. Novel

   Humor is not a genre but a characteristic of poetry, a short story, a drama, or a novel. Therefore, it does not belong in this list.

Warming Up to Write a Division/Classification

1. Here's a good exercise to get your brain to think in terms of classification—that is, inventing categories into which to divide a subject and then placing items into each category. As quickly as possible, divide each of the following subjects into as many categories as seems sensible. Keep a list of the categories. If, after rereading your list, a category doesn't fit, delete it.

   a. Books

   b. Clothing

   c. Modern inventions

   d. Weather

   e. Computer games

   f. Pets

   g. Music

   h. Meals

2. In the following classifications, check the category that does not fit and write down the reasons why it should be excluded.

   a. Dreams

   _____1. sexual

   _____2. paralyzing

   _____3. imagining

   _____4. replaying the day

   b. Cars

   _____1. SUVs

   _____2. trucks

   _____3. sedans

   _____4. electric cars

   c. Family games

   _____1. card games

   _____2. ping pong

   _____3. domino games

   _____4. board games

   d. Houses in which to live

   _____1. sheds

   _____2. cottages

   _____3. mansions

   _____4. tract homes

e. Jobs

_____1. technical

_____2. waiter

_____3. professional

_____4. hard labor

3. Looking back at Exercise 1, choose one of the subjects you classified into categories; then pick one of the categories and place at least three items in it. For instance, if you classified meals into *hors d'oeuvres, main dishes, side dishes,* and *desserts,* you might choose "main dishes" as your category and then list the following items as belonging to it: meat, poultry, fish, and vegetarian substitute. Make sure that your items are appropriately related to the category.

EXAMPLES

Move Over, Teams

PAUL M. MUCHINSKY

Rhetorical Thumbnail

Purpose: to entertain

Audience: Industrial and Organizational psychology (I-O) students

Language: standard English

Strategy: parodies the field's affinity for sorting people and their habits into groups and categories

Paul M. Muchinsky is a psychology professor at the University of North Carolina, Greensboro. He was educated at Iowa State University, Kansas State University, and Purdue University, from which he received a PhD in Industrial Organizational Psychology. Dr. Muchinsky was a recipient of the Distinguished Teaching Award for outstanding contributions to Industrial and Organizational Psychology. In 2008, he was awarded the Honorary Doctor of Science degree from Gettysburg College. His *Psychology Applied to Work* (1981) is one of the leading textbooks in industrial psychology and is now in its 10th edition. The essay that follows first appeared in the January 2005 issue of the magazine of the Society for Industrial and Organizational Psychology, Inc.

This hilarious essay was published in 2005 in The Industrial Organizational Psychologist—*a magazine whose readership is hardly associated with humor. Keeping a straight face, the writer comes up with hilarious names that divide groups into some oddball categories.*

• • •

1   I am rarely wrong. But when I am wrong, I am really wrong. I couldn't have been more wrong about this "team" thing. I thought the team concept would be like a rain event (as my local TV meteorologist calls it): something that blows into town, does its thing, then leaves. No way. I am convinced that teams are here to stay. I-O psychology might as well bury the individual as an object of study and embrace our new love object, the collectivity.

2   I believe in the value of diversity. Not long ago I successfully passed a diversity training workshop. Diversity means differentness. If we are now doing the collective thing, at the very least let's dignify the whole affair by studying a diversity of collectivities, not just teams. Here are 10 other collectivities that deserve their place and space as objects of study by I-O psychologists.

3   1. Here's a group we don't know much about. Monks. If you run a key word search on monks, I bet you won't come up with much. That's primarily because the *Journal of Monk Behavior* is not in our computerized literature base. A group of monks is an *abomination*. I always thought an abomination was a bad thing, but not necessarily so. What if a particular group of monks had and needed no contact with the outside world? They selected their own members, did their own plumbing and electrical work, baked their own bread, raised their own crops, and so on. Do you think they would refer to themselves as a *total abomination?*

4   2. Here's a group you simply won't believe. Morons don't have their own group. Neither do imbeciles. But idiots do. Do you know what a bunch of idiots are called? A *thicket*. It's bad enough when you encounter one idiot at work, but can you imagine running into several of them?

5   Spouse: "Hi honey. Welcome home. How was your day at the office? Can I make you a drink?"

6   I-O: "What a day I had! I ran into these idiots. I don't know where they came from. They said black was white, up was down, and in was out. I nearly lost it."

7   Spouse: "These idiots, were they like, a group?"

8   I-O: "No."

9   Spouse: "A bunch?"

10   I-O: "No."

11   Spouse: "A bevy?"

12   I-O: "No."

13   Spouse: "A crew?"

14   I-O: "No."

15   Spouse: "A squad?"

16   I-O: "No."

17   Spouse: "A thicket?"

18   I-O: "Yeah, that's it. A thicket of idiots."

19   Spouse: "Would you like your drink now?"

20   I-O: "Yes, and please make it a double."

21   3. I'm not surprised this group has a name, but I was surprised to learn what it is. A group of lawyers is called a *huddle*. Maybe it's because at recess in a trial they always huddle up. I can't help but think of football when I think of a huddle of lawyers. Something like this. "Before entering the huddle, attorney

Schwartz looks over at the CEO for any last-second signals. Schwartz then calls the play. Attorneys Robinson and Davis will run interference for attorney Smith, who will deliver the motion to dismiss on the unsuspecting defense. All right, *habeas corpus* on two. Let's go."

22   4. Even philosophers have their own name. They are called a *ponder*. Maybe it's because philosophers like to ponder weighty issues. I bet this group knows how to party. I envision a meeting of the Southern Philosophical Association holding their annual meeting in Natchez, Mississippi. Out on the veranda are two veteran philosophers, Rhett and Beauregard. Amidst the honeysuckle and jasmine, they are sipping on mint juleps. They are observing clusters of their colleagues engaged in passionate conversations about such topics as the meaning of meaning. Just then the weather turns inclement. Rhett turns to his colleague and says, "Bo, I wonder if we should wander over yonder to take a gander at that ponder. They seem to be lost in their own thoughts. They appear not to realize it is starting to hail."

23   5. If any group has a perfect name, it is this group. A bunch of bureaucrats is called a *shuffle*. How many times have you been shuffled around when trying to get a straight answer from bureaucrats? Trying to get your driver's license renewed with the Department of Motor Vehicles would be a prime example. The clerk says, "If your birthday falls on an odd-numbered day in an even-numbered year, get in Line 1. However, if you were born in a year that was a leap year, ignore this direction. But if this year is a leap year, then reinstate that direction. If the last thing I told you is false, but the first thing I told you is true, should you believe me? Now, if your birthday falls on an even-numbered day in an odd-numbered year, get in Line 2. However . . . " Do the shuffle!

24   6. Here is one that just doesn't make much sense. Not only do I not understand why this group rates a name, but how did they get this name? A group of nudists is called a *hangout*. I can see a hangdown, but not a hangout.

25   7. Here's a tricky one. A bunch of car dealers is called a *lot*. You probably thought it is the cars themselves that are positioned on a lot. Well, it's also the people who sell them to you. A commercial: "So what do you like most about the sales department at Jayhawk Chrysler, Dodge, Mitsubishi Motors?" Satisfied customer: "Their attentiveness to customer needs. They have lots of lots on their lots."

26   8. Not to be outdone, car mechanics also have their own name. A bunch of car mechanics is called a clutch. Not a brake, or an accelerator, but a *clutch*. Maybe this group got itself named after what it works on much of the day. Remember when we were 15 and were taking driving lessons? Some grizzled old driving instructor was trying to teach us how to brake, steer, accelerate, and use the clutch, all at the same time. By now we must have realized, looking back, that this poor slob must have drawn the short straw in getting this work assignment. Just about any work assignment involving cars, including changing the oil, has got to be better than teaching 15-year-olds how to drive one. Remember when the car started to stall, and the driving instructor screamed, "Release the clutch!"? Maybe he really wasn't yelling at us. Maybe he was wishing aloud for someone to lay off the car mechanics about whom he was envious.

27   9. A group of widows is called an *ambush*. I can see something like this: A heavy manufacturing company is under a lot of pressure to produce orders.

The HR director is sympathetic to the need for further production, but he is also concerned about the welfare of the workforce. The HR director addresses the production supervisors. "Fellows, I know you have to meet your production schedules, but I'm telling you that you are pushing your men too hard. They're coming to me complaining about being overworked, stressed-out, and on the verge of collapse. I'm telling you that you gotta ease up a bit. If you don't, you're just setting this company up for an ambush."

28   10. This group has a rather predictable name. A group of mathematicians is called a *number*. I think they could have been more original than that, but who am I to judge? Suppose there is a national association of mathematicians, organized by state associations of mathematicians, each being a number. But there is dissent among some of the groups of mathematicians. At the national conference, the president intones the danger of splinter groups within the association. "I understand some of our numbers are up while other numbers are down, yet other numbers are difficult to interpret. I only hope when we add all the numbers together, their sum total will achieve unity for our association." What if one particular number was repeatedly successful in winning raffles and contests. Would we call it a "lucky number?" You could have fun with this one.

29   My point is simple. We can't pick and choose which collectivities we will study. As I-O psychologists, our tent should be inclusive and we should welcome any and all parties. That means we give equal and fair treatment to abominations, thickets, huddles, ponders, shuffles, hangouts, lots, clutches, ambushes, and numbers, as well as teams. We will not exhibit bias or preferential treatment toward any one group over any other. I can't wait to read the first meta-analysis on clutchwork.

30   I feel it is only fair that if I-O psychology is now in the business of studying collectivities, we should have our own name. The mathematicians have theirs, the philosophers have theirs, but I-O psychologists have none. The bird kingdom has many collective nouns for its respective members. The most linguistically evocative collective noun refers to a group of larks. Larks are beautiful, graceful, and agile creatures, who collectively are called an *exaltation*. I-O psychologists are also beautiful, graceful, and agile. I decree that we shall, from here on out, refer to ourselves as an exultation of I-O psychologists. The most beautiful of all the beautiful I-O psychologists are those who serve on the Executive Committee of SIOP. They shall now be known as the Executive Exultation. What a euphonious name. I propose the members of the Executive Exultation shall have their ID badges at our national conference adorned with long flowing streamers to indicate their special status. Embossed on the streamers will be the outline of a lark. That's the least we can do to honor the larks. After all, we stole their name.

31   I understand SIOP is considering changing its name. Some people want to jettison the old industrial prefix. That only solves half the problem. If we are now going to be studying collectivities and not individuals, our name should reflect what we are. SIOP should change its name to SOS: The Society for Organizational Sociologists.

● Vocabulary

meteorologist (1)	shuffle (23)	dissent (28)
collectivity (1)	nudists (24)	raffles (28)
diversity (2)	grizzled (26)	linguistically (30)
abomination (3)	ambush (27)	evocative (30)
ponder (22)	HR (Human Resources) (27)	exultation (30)
inclement (22)	predictable (28)	euphonious (30)

● The Facts

1. How factual is this essay? Is this an essay that will teach you the major "facts" about the groups the author categorizes? Explain your answers.

2. How many teams does the author categorize, and in what paragraph does he list them all?

3. What does the opening paragraph indicate about the author? What aspect of his profession had he misjudged?

4. The author begins his classification with the category of monks. Why do you suppose he placed them at the head of his list?

5. What is the name he suggests for the group of psychologists who want to study collectivities? What connotations go along with this name?

● The Strategies

1. What is the purpose of Muchinsky's overall strategy? In other words, what purpose is served by his language, his examples, and his categories? What reaction does he expect from his readers?

2. What rhetorical mode does the author use? How does the mode suit the purpose of this essay?

3. Why is the essay so humorous? Point out what you think is the most humorous passage and state why it made you laugh.

4. Why are paragraphs 7 through 20 so short? Explain the reason.

5. What humorous ploy does the author use in describing the nudists in paragraph 24? Is the humor in good taste, or might some readers be offended?

● The Issues

1. If a serious message is contained within this humorous essay, what might it be? Does the essay support a serious message? Why or why not?

2. What is the author's definition of an *idiot*? How effective is this definition in terms of the average reader? Do you have a better or different definition? If so, what is it? How does the term "thicket" fit this group?

3. How does the author's description of the philosopher category fit the popular impression of philosophers? How does the author connect the name for the group to the subject matter with which they deal? How does the author maintain a humorous stance? Is the humor gentle or vitriolic? Explain your answer.

4. Why do you think the author calls a group of widows an *ambush*? What popular view is he exploiting? What better name can you suggest?

5. The final paragraph may be confusing to most readers, who may not understand its context, but what is the main point that is clearly understandable?

● Suggestions for Writing

1. Using Muchinsky's formula for classification, try to think of other groups that deserve to be classified under a heading you humorously supply. If you can't think of any human groups, see if you can come up with groups of animals or objects.

2. Choosing one of Muchinsky's groups, divide it into appropriate subcategories. You may be either humorous or serious. For example, you might choose the category of bureaucrats and subdivide them as follows: (1) educators, (2) church officials, (3) politicians, and (4) accountants. The point is to create a classification.

Thinking as a Hobby

WILLIAM GOLDING

> ## Rhetorical Thumbnail
>
> **Purpose:** to entertain/enlighten
>
> **Audience:** anyone who is an educated reader
>
> **Language:** academic English with a light touch
>
> **Strategy:** uses common objects in the headmaster's office to represent forms of thinking

English novelist William Golding (1911–1993) was educated at Oxford. Golding once described his hobbies as "thinking, classical Greek, sailing, and archaeology." His works include *The Pyramid* (1964), *The Scorpion God* (1971), and *Paper Work* (1984), but he is best known for his novel *Lord of the Flies* (1954). In 1983, Golding won the Nobel Prize for Literature.

Division and classification are often creative thinking exercises in which the essayist looks for patterns and relationships that are not immediately obvious. In this essay, for example, William Golding concludes that there are three grades of thinking, which he explains with examples and anecdotes. Are there really only three grades of thinking? That is beside the point. The essayist is not a scientific researcher, but an expresser and shaper of opinion. As a professional writer, Golding takes liberties with his classification and does here what any essayist should do: He makes us think.

● ● ●

1   While I was still a boy, I came to the conclusion that there were three grades of thinking; and since I was later to claim thinking as my hobby, I came to an even stranger conclusion—namely, that I myself could not think at all.

2   I must have been an unsatisfactory child for grownups to deal with. I remember how incomprehensible they appeared to me at first, but not, of course, how I appeared to them. It was the headmaster of my grammar school who first brought the subject of thinking before me—though neither in the way, nor with the result he intended. He had some statuettes in his study. They stood on a high cupboard behind his desk. One was a lady wearing nothing but a bath towel. She seemed frozen in an eternal panic lest the bath towel slip down any farther, and since she had no arms, she was in an unfortunate position to pull the towel up again. Next to her, crouched the statuette of a leopard, ready to spring down at the top drawer of a filing cabinet labeled A–AH. My innocence interpreted this as the victim's last, despairing cry. Beyond the leopard was a naked, muscular gentleman, who sat, looking down, with his chin on his fist and his elbow on his knee. He seemed utterly miserable.

3   Some time later, I learned about these statuettes. The headmaster had placed them where they would face delinquent children, because they symbolized to him the whole of life. The naked lady was the *Venus of Milo*. She was Love. She was not worried about the towel. She was just busy being beautiful. The leopard was Nature, and he was being natural. The naked, muscular gentleman was not miserable. He was Rodin's *Thinker*, an image of pure thought. It is easy to buy small plaster models of what you think life is like.

4   I had better explain that I was a frequent visitor to the headmaster's study, because of the latest thing I had done or left undone. As we now say, I was not integrated. I was, if anything, disintegrated; and I was puzzled. Grownups never made sense. Whenever I found myself in a penal position before the headmaster's desk, with the statuettes glimmering whitely above him, I would sink my head, clasp my hands behind my back and writhe one shoe over the other.

5   The headmaster would look opaquely at me through flashing spectacles. "What are we going to do with you?"

6   Well, what *were* they going to do with me? I would writhe my shoe some more and stare down at the worn rug.

7   "Look up, boy! Can't you look up?"

8   Then I would look up at the cupboard, where the naked lady was frozen in her panic and the muscular gentleman contemplated the hindquarters of the leopard in endless gloom. I had nothing to say to the headmaster. His spectacles caught the light so that you could see nothing human behind them. There was no possibility of communication.

9   "Don't you ever think at all?"

10 No, I didn't think, wasn't thinking, couldn't think—I was simply waiting in anguish for the interview to stop.

11 "Then you'd better learn—hadn't you?"

12 On one occasion the headmaster leaped to his feet, reached up and plonked Rodin's masterpiece on the desk before me.

13   "That's what a man looks like when he's really thinking."

14   I surveyed the gentleman without interest or comprehension.

15   "Go back to your class."

16   Clearly there was something missing in me. Nature had endowed the rest of the human race with a sixth sense and left me out. This must be so, I mused, on my way back to the class, since whether I had broken a window, or failed to remember Boyle's Law, or been late for school, my teachers produced me one, adult answer: "Why can't you think?"

17   As I saw the case, I had broken the window because I had tried to hit Jack Arney with a cricket ball and missed him; I could not remember Boyle's Law because I had never bothered to learn it; and I was late for school because I preferred looking over the bridge into the river. In fact, I was wicked. Were my teachers, perhaps, so good that they could not understand the depths of my depravity? Were they clear, untormented people who could direct their every action by this mysterious business of thinking? The whole thing was incomprehensible. In my earlier years, I found even the statuette of the *Thinker* confusing. I did not believe any of my teachers were naked, ever. Like someone born deaf, but bitterly determined to find out about sound, I watched my teachers to find out about thought.

18   There was Mr. Houghton. He was always telling me to think. With a modest satisfaction, he would tell me that he had thought a bit himself. Then why did he spend so much time drinking? Or was there more sense in drinking than there appeared to be? But if not, and if drinking were in fact ruinous to health—and Mr. Houghton was ruined, there was no doubt about that—why was he always talking about the clean life and the virtues of fresh air? He would spread his arms wide with the action of a man who habitually spent his time striding along mountain ridges.

19   "Open air does me good, boys—I know it!"

20   Sometimes, exalted by his own oratory, he would leap from his desk and hustle us outside into a hideous wind.

21   "Now, boys! Deep breaths! Feel it right down inside you—huge draughts of God's good air!"

22   He would stand before us, rejoicing in his perfect health, an open-air man. He would put his hands on his waist and take a tremendous breath. You could hear the wind, trapped in the cavern of his chest and struggling with all the unnatural impediments. His body would reel with shock and his ruined face go white at the unaccustomed visitation. He would stagger back to his desk and collapse there, useless for the rest of the morning.

23   Mr. Houghton was given to high-minded monologues about the good life, sexless and full of duty. Yet in the middle of one of these monologues, if a girl passed the window, tapping along on her neat little feet, he would interrupt his discourse, his neck would turn of itself and he would watch her out of sight. In this instance, he seemed to me ruled not by thought but by an invisible and irresistible spring in his nape.

24   His neck was an object of great interest to me. Normally it bulged a bit over his collar. But Mr. Houghton had fought in the First World War alongside

both Americans and French, and had come—by who knows what illogic?—to a settled detestation of both countries. If either country happened to be prominent in current affairs, no argument could make Mr. Houghton think well of it. He would bang the desk, his neck would bulge still further and go red. "You can say what you like," he would cry, "but I've thought about this—and I know what I think!"

25   Mr. Houghton thought with his neck.

26   There was Miss Parsons. She assured us that her dearest wish was our welfare, but I knew even then, with the mysterious clairvoyance of childhood, that what she wanted most was the husband she never got. There was Mr. Hands—and so on.

27   I have dealt at length with my teachers because this was my introduction to the nature of what is commonly called thought. Through them I discovered that thought is often full of unconscious prejudice, ignorance and hypocrisy. It will lecture on disinterested purity while its neck is being remorselessly twisted toward a skirt. Technically, it is about as proficient as most businessmen's golf, as honest as most politicians' intentions, or—to come near my own preoccupation—as coherent as most books that get written. It is what I came to call grade-three thinking, though more properly, it is feeling, rather than thought.

28   True, often there is a kind of innocence in prejudices, but in those days I viewed grade-three thinking with an intolerant contempt and an incautious mockery. I delighted to confront a pious lady who hated the Germans with the proposition that we should love our enemies. She taught me a great truth in dealing with grade-three thinkers; because of her, I no longer dismiss lightly a mental process which for nine-tenths of the population is the nearest they will ever get to thought. They have immense solidarity. We had better respect them, for we are outnumbered and surrounded. A crowd of grade-three thinkers, all shouting the same thing, all warming their hands at the fire of their own prejudices, will not thank you for pointing out the contradictions in their beliefs. Man is a gregarious animal, and enjoys agreement as cows will graze all the same way on the side of a hill.

29   Grade-two thinking is the detection of contradictions. I reached grade two when I trapped the poor, pious lady. Grade-two thinkers do not stampede easily, though often they fall into the other fault and lag behind. Grade-two thinking is a withdrawal, with eyes and ears open. It became my hobby and brought satisfaction and loneliness in either hand. For grade-two thinking destroys without having the power to create. It set me watching the crowds cheering His Majesty the King and asking myself what all the fuss was about, without giving me anything positive to put in the place of that heady patriotism. But there were compensations. To hear people justify their habit of hunting foxes and tearing them to pieces by claiming that the foxes like it. To hear our Prime Minister talk about the great benefit we conferred on India by jailing people like Pandit Nehru and Gandhi. To hear American politicians talk about peace in one sentence and refuse to join the League of Nations in the next. Yes, there were moments of delight.

30   But I was growing toward adolescence and had to admit that Mr. Houghton was not the only one with an irresistible spring in his neck. I, too, felt the

compulsive hand of nature and began to find that pointing out contradiction could be costly as well as fun. There was Ruth, for example, a serious and attractive girl. I was an atheist at the time. Grade-two thinking is a menace to religion and knocks down sects like Skittles. I put myself in a position to be converted by her with an hypocrisy worthy of grade three. She was a Methodist—or at least, her parents were, and Ruth had to follow suit. But, alas, instead of relying on the Holy Spirit to convert me, Ruth was foolish enough to open her pretty mouth in argument. She claimed that the Bible (King James Version) was literally inspired. I countered by saying that the Catholics believed in the literal inspiration of Saint Jerome's Vulgate, and the two books were different. Argument flagged.

31   At last she remarked that there were an awful lot of Methodists, and they couldn't be wrong, could they—not all those millions? That was too easy, said I restively (for the nearer you were to Ruth, the nicer she was to be near to) since there were more Roman Catholics than Methodists anyway; and they couldn't be wrong, could they—not all those hundreds of millions? An awful flicker of doubt appeared in her eyes. I slid my arm round her waist and murmured breathlessly that if we were counting heads, the Buddhists were the boys for my money. But Ruth had really wanted to do me good, because I was so nice. She fled. The combination of my arm and those countless Buddhists was too much for her.

32   That night her father visited my father and left, red-cheeked and indignant. I was given the third degree to find out what had happened. It was lucky we were both of us only fourteen. I lost Ruth and gained an undeserved reputation as a potential libertine.

33   So grade-two thinking could be dangerous. It was in this knowledge, at the age of fifteen, that I remember making a comment from the heights of grade two, on the limitations of grade three. One evening I found myself alone in the school hall, preparing it for a party. The door of the headmaster's study was open. I went in. The headmaster had ceased to thump Rodin's *Thinker* down on the desk as an example to the young. Perhaps he had not found any more candidates, but the statuettes were still there, glimmering and gathering dust on top of the cupboard. I stood on a chair and rearranged them. I stood Venus in her bath towel on the filing cabinet, so that now the top drawer caught its breath in a gasp of sexy excitement. "A-ah!" The portentous *Thinker* I placed on the edge of the cupboard so that he looked down at the bath towel and waited for it to slip.

34   Grade-two thinking, though it filled life with fun and excitement, did not make for content. To find out the deficiencies of our elders bolsters the young ego but does not make for personal security. I found that grade two was not only the power to point out contradictions. It took the swimmer some distance from the shore and left him there, out of his depth. I decided that Pontius Pilate was a typical grade-two thinker. "What is truth?" he said, a very common grade-two thought, but one that is used always as the end of an argument instead of the beginning. There is a still higher grade of thought which says, "What is truth?" and sets out to find it.

35   But these grade-one thinkers were few and far between. They did not visit my grammar school in the flesh though they were there in books. I aspired to them, partly because I was ambitious and partly because I now saw my hobby as an unsatisfactory thing if it went no further. If you set out to climb a mountain, however high you climb, you have failed if you cannot reach the top.

36   I did meet an undeniably grade-one thinker in my first year at Oxford. I was looking over a small bridge in Magdalen Deer Park, and a tiny mustached and hatted figure came and stood by my side. He was a German who had just fled from the Nazis to Oxford as a temporary refuge. His name was Einstein.

37   But Professor Einstein knew no English at that time and I knew only two words of German. I beamed at him, trying wordlessly to convey by my bearing all the affection and respect that the English felt for him. It is possible—and I have to make the admission—that I felt here were two grade-one thinkers standing side by side; yet I doubt if my face conveyed more than a formless awe. I would have given my Greek and Latin and French and a good slice of my English for enough German to communicate. But we were divided; he was as inscrutable as my headmaster. For perhaps five minutes we stood together on the bridge, undeniable grade-one thinker and breathless aspirant. With true greatness, Professor Einstein realized that any contact was better than none. He pointed to a trout wavering in midstream.

38   He spoke: "Fisch."

39   My brain reeled. Here I was, mingling with the great, and yet helpless as the veriest grade-three thinker. Desperately I sought for some sign by which I might convey that I, too, revered pure reason. I nodded vehemently. In a brilliant flash I used up half of my German vocabulary. "*Fisch. Ja. Ja.*"

40   For perhaps another five minutes we stood side by side. Then Professor Einstein, his whole figure still conveying good will and amiability, drifted away out of sight.

41   I, too, would be a grade-one thinker. I was irreverent at the best of times. Political and religious systems, social customs, loyalties and traditions, they all came tumbling down like so many rotten apples off a tree. This was a fine hobby and a sensible substitute for cricket, since you could play it all the year round. I came up in the end with what must always remain the justification for grade-one thinking, its sign, seal and charter. I devised a coherent system for living. It was a moral system, which was wholly logical. Of course, as I readily admitted, conversion of the world to my way of thinking might be difficult, since my system did away with a number of trifles, such as big business, centralized government, armies, marriage . . .

42   It was Ruth all over again. I had some very good friends who stood by me, and still do. But my acquaintances vanished, taking the girls with them. Young women seemed oddly contented with the world as it was. They valued the meaningless ceremony with a ring. Young men, while willing to concede the chaining sordidness of marriage, were hesitant about abandoning the organizations which they hoped would give them a career. A young man on the first rung of the Royal Navy, while perfectly agreeable to doing away with big business and marriage, got as red-necked as Mr. Houghton when I proposed a world without any battleships in it.

43   Had the game gone too far? Was it a game any longer? In those prewar days, I stood to lose a great deal, for the sake of a hobby.

44   Now you are expecting me to describe how I saw the folly of my ways and came back to the warm nest, where prejudices are so often called loyalties, where pointless actions are hallowed into custom by repetition, where we are content to say we think when all we do is feel.

45   But you would be wrong. I dropped my hobby and turned professional.

46   If I were to go back to the headmaster's study and find the dusty statuettes still there, I would arrange them differently. I would dust Venus and put her aside, for I have come to love her and know her for the fair thing she is. But I would put the *Thinker*, sunk in his desperate thought, where there were shadows before him—and at his back, I would put the leopard, crouched and ready to spring.

© copyright William Golding Limited.

● Vocabulary

statuettes (2)	detestation (24)	flagged (30)
integrated (4)	clairvoyance (26)	restively (31)
penal (4)	disinterested (27)	libertine (32)
opaquely (5)	proficient (27)	inscrutable (37)
ruinous (18)	proposition (28)	veriest (39)
draughts (21)	solidarity (28)	revered (39)
impediments (22)	Skittles (30)	amiability (40)
monologues (23)		

● The Facts

1. Into what three types does Golding divide all thinking? Describe each type in your own words. Is there a value judgment implied in the division?

2. Why does Golding take up so much time describing some of his grade-school teachers? How are they related to the purpose of the essay?

3. Why is it so difficult to find grade-one thinkers? Describe someone whom you consider a grade-one thinker.

4. How do you interpret Golding's last two paragraphs? Has the author reverted to grade-three or grade-two thinking, or is he still a grade-one thinker? Comment.

5. What does the encounter between Golding and Albert Einstein indicate?

● The Strategies

1. In paragraph 2, the author describes three statuettes on a cupboard behind the headmaster's desk. In what paragraph is each of the statuettes explained? Why is the explanation necessary?

2. Much of the article reflects a young boy's point of view. How is this point of view achieved? Point to some specific passages.

3. Paragraphs 24, 25, and 27 refer to the word *neck* repeatedly. What has the neck come to symbolize in this context?

4. What is the analogy used in paragraph 28 to describe grade-three thinkers? Is the analogy effective? Explain.

5. What is Golding's purpose in alluding to the jailing of Nehru and Gandhi, and to the Americans' refusal to join the League of Nations?

● The Issues

1. To be a grade-one thinker, must one do away with big business, centralized government, armies, marriages, and so on? How could one be a grade-one thinker without wanting to destroy these?

2. Golding seems to indicate that his teachers were conformists, hypocrites, or men of prejudice. What kinds of thinkers do you remember your grade-school teachers to have been? Give examples of their thinking.

3. What groups in our society reveal typical grade-three thinking? Give reasons for your choices.

4. What, if anything, is important about grade-two thinking? Does one need to be a grade-two thinker before going on to grade one?

5. How does nature assist or resist grade-one thinking?

● Suggestions for Writing

1. Write an essay in which you answer the question "Does a college education help to eliminate prejudice and hypocrisy?" Support your answer with examples from your own experience.

2. Write an essay in which you divide your acquaintances into types according to the kinds of behavior they project. Be sure that your categories are mutually exclusive and that they take in as many of your acquaintances as possible.

Kinds of Discipline

JOHN HOLT

Rhetorical Thumbnail

Purpose: to inform

Audience: education students

Language: academic English

Strategy: to divide discipline into three primary types

John Holt (1923–1985), education theorist, was born in New York. He taught at Harvard University and the University of California, Berkeley. His works include

How Children Fail (1964), *How Children Learn* (1967), *Freedom and Beyond* (1972), from which this selection was taken, *Escape from Childhood* (1974), *Instead of Education* (1976), and *Teach Your Own* (1981).

Because discipline is an ambiguous and often misunderstood word, the author attempts to give it a clearer meaning by focusing on three specific kinds of discipline.

• • •

1   A child, in growing up, may meet and learn from three different kinds of disciplines. The first and most important is what we might call the Discipline of Nature or of Reality. When he is trying to do something real, if he does the wrong thing or doesn't do the right one, he doesn't get the result he wants. If he doesn't pile one block right on top of another, or tries to build on a slanting surface, his tower falls down. If he hits the wrong key, he hears the wrong note. If he doesn't hit the nail squarely on the head, it bends, and he has to pull it out and start with another. If he doesn't measure properly what he is trying to build, it won't open, close, fit, stand up, fly, float, whistle, or do whatever he wants it to do. If he closes his eyes when he swings, he doesn't hit the ball. A child meets this kind of discipline every time he tries to do something, which is why it is so important in school to give children more chances to do things, instead of just reading or listening to someone talk (or pretending to). This discipline is a great teacher. The learner never has to wait long for his answer; it usually comes quickly, often instantly. Also it is clear, and very often points toward the needed correction; from what happened he can not only see that what he did was wrong, but also why, and what he needs to do instead. Finally, and most important, the giver of the answer, call it Nature, is impersonal, impartial, and indifferent. She does not give opinions, or make judgments; she cannot be wheedled, bullied, or fooled; she does not get angry or disappointed; she does not praise or blame; she does not remember past failures or hold grudges; with her one always gets a fresh start, this time is the one that counts.

2   The next discipline we might call the Discipline of Culture, of Society, of What People Really Do. Man is a social, a cultural animal. Children sense around them this culture, this network of agreements, customs, habits, and rules binding the adults together. They want to understand it and be a part of it. They watch very carefully what people around them are doing and want to do the same. They want to do right, unless they become convinced they can't do right. Thus children rarely misbehave seriously in church, but sit as quietly as they can. The example of all those grownups is contagious. Some mysterious ritual is going on, and children, who like rituals, want to be part of it. In the same way, the little children that I see at concerts or operas, though they may fidget a little, or perhaps take a nap now and then, rarely make any disturbance. With all those grownups sitting there, neither moving nor talking, it is the most natural thing in the world to imitate them. Children who live among adults who are habitually courteous to each other, and to them, will soon learn to be courteous. Children who live surrounded by people who speak a certain

way will speak that way, however much we may try to tell them that speaking that way is bad or wrong.

3   The third discipline is the one most people mean when they speak of discipline—the Discipline of Superior Force, of sergeant to private, of "you do what I tell you or I'll make you wish you had." There is bound to be some of this in a child's life. Living as we do surrounded by things that can hurt children, or that children can hurt, we cannot avoid it. We can't afford to let a small child find out from experience the danger of playing in a busy street, or of fooling with the pots on the top of a stove, or of eating up the pills in the medicine cabinet. So, along with other precautions, we say to him, "Don't play in the street, or touch things on the stove, or go into the medicine cabinet, or I'll punish you." Between him and the danger too great for him to imagine we put a lesser danger, but one he can imagine and maybe therefore wants to avoid. He can have no idea of what it would be like to be hit by a car, but he can imagine being shouted at, or spanked, or sent to his room. He avoids these substitutes for the greater danger until he can understand it and avoid it for its own sake. But we ought to use this discipline only when it is necessary to protect the life, health, safety, or well-being of people or other living creatures, or to prevent destruction of things that people care about. We ought not to assume too long, as we usually do, that a child cannot understand the real nature of the danger from which we want to protect him. The sooner he avoids the danger, not to escape our punishment, but as a matter of good sense, the better. He can learn that faster than we think. In Mexico, for example, where people drive their cars with a good deal of spirit, I saw many children no older than five or four walking unattended on the streets. They understood about cars, they knew what to do. A child whose life is full of the threat and fear of punishment is locked into babyhood. There is no way for him to grow up, to learn to take responsibility for his life and acts. Most important of all, we should not assume that having to yield to the threat of our superior force is good for the child's character. It is never good for anyone's character. To bow to superior force makes us feel impotent and cowardly for not having had the strength or courage to resist. Worse, it makes us resentful and vengeful. We can hardly wait to make someone pay for our humiliation, yield to us as we were once made to yield. No, if we cannot always avoid using the Discipline of Superior Force, we should at least use it as seldom as we can.

4   There are places where all three disciplines overlap. Any very demanding human activity combines in it the disciplines of Superior Force, of Culture, and of Nature. The novice will be told, "Do it this way, never mind asking why, just do it that way, that is the way we always do it." But it probably is just the way they always do it, and usually for the very good reason that it is a way that has been found to work. Think, for example, of ballet training. The student in a class is told to do this exercise, or that; to stand so; to do this or that with his head, arms, shoulders, abdomen, hips, legs, feet. He is constantly corrected. There is no argument. But behind these seemingly autocratic demands by the teacher lie many decades of custom and tradition, and behind that, the necessities of dancing itself. You cannot make the moves of classical ballet unless over many years you have acquired, and renewed every day, the needed strength and suppleness in scores of muscles and joints. Nor can you do the difficult motions, making

them look easy, unless you have learned hundreds of easier ones first. Dance teachers may not always agree on all the details of teaching these strengths and skills. But no novice could learn them all by himself. You could not go for a night or two to watch the ballet and then, without any other knowledge at all, teach yourself how to do it. In the same way, you would be unlikely to learn any complicated and difficult human activity without drawing heavily on the experience of those who know it better. But the point is that the authority of these experts or teachers stems from, grows out of their greater competence and experience, the fact that what they do works, not the fact that they happen to be the teacher and as such have the power to kick a student out of the class. And the further point is that children are always and everywhere attracted to that competence, and ready and eager to submit themselves to a discipline that grows out of it. We hear constantly that children will never do anything unless compelled to by bribes or threats. But in their private lives, or in extracurricular activities in school, in sports, music, drama, art, running a newspaper, and so on, they often submit themselves willingly and wholeheartedly to very intense disciplines, simply because they want to learn to do a given thing well. Our Little-Napoleon football coaches, of whom we have too many and hear far too much, blind us to the fact that millions of children work hard every year getting better at sports and games without coaches barking and yelling at them.

● Vocabulary

wheedled (1)   impotent (3)   autocratic (4)
ritual (2)

● The Facts

1. What principle or basis of division does Holt use?
2. How does Holt clarify for the reader what he means by "Discipline of Nature or of Reality"? Is this method of clarification effective? Why?
3. What are the advantages of learning from nature or reality?
4. According to the author, when should the discipline of superior force be used? Do you agree?
5. At the end of his essay, Holt identifies the most successful motivation for discipline. What is it?

● The Strategies

1. In the last sentence of paragraph 1, the author uses the feminine pronouns *she* and *her* in referring to nature. What is his purpose?
2. What transitional guideposts does the author use to gain coherence and organization?
3. What is the effect of labeling certain football coaches "Little Napoleons"?

● The Issues

1. What additional examples can you supply of the ways in which children submit to the discipline of culture or society?

2. What tips can you provide for someone who has no discipline in studying college courses? What method has worked best for you?

3. Holt warns adults that the use of superior force in order to punish children is never good for the children's characters (see paragraph 3) and should therefore be used as little as possible. What, in your opinion, is the result of never using this superior force in the training of children? Give examples to support your point.

4. Our society is witnessing the self-destruction of many young people through chemical abuse of one kind or another. How is this abuse tied to Holt's idea of discipline?

5. How important is discipline in your life? Do you choose friends who are strongly disciplined, or do you prefer those who are more "laid back"? Give reasons for your answers.

● Suggestions for Writing

1. Write an essay in which you divide discipline according to the kinds of effects it produces: for example, discipline that results in strong study habits.

2. Develop the following topic sentence into a three-paragraph essay: "To be successful, a person must have three kinds of discipline: of the intellect, of the emotions, and of the body." Use Holt's essay as a model for your organization.

The Idols

FRANCIS BACON

Rhetorical Thumbnail

Purpose: to inform

Audience: educated reader

Language: **sixteenth-century English**, as used by educated society in Francis Bacon's day

Strategy: exposes idols (false beliefs) by grouping them into four types

Francis Bacon (1561–1626) was born in London and educated at Trinity College, Cambridge, and Gray's Inn. Bacon is generally credited with applying the inductive method of logic to scientific investigation. His essays, which are notable for their aphoristic style, are his best-known works.

This excerpt comes from Novum Organum *(1620), possibly Bacon's most famous work. Bacon was struggling against the traditions of medieval scholasticism, which assumed a given and unchangeable set of premises from which, by deductive logic, one could infer truths about the world. Our way of thinking today, especially in science, is just the opposite, thanks in part to Bacon. We begin not with givens but with questions. We proceed by gathering data and using induction to draw conclusions. (See the discussion of logic in Chapter 16.) This method of thinking does not completely safeguard us from Bacon's Idols, but it does help keep them at bay.*

• • •

1   The *Idols* and false notions which have already preoccupied the human understanding, and are deeply rooted in it, not only so beset men's minds, that they become difficult to access, but even when access is obtained, will again meet and trouble us in the instauration of the sciences, unless mankind, when forewarned, guard themselves with all possible care against them.

2   Four species of *Idols* beset the human mind: to which (for distinction's sake) we have assigned names: calling the first *Idols of the Tribe;* the second *Idols of the Den;* the third *Idols of the Market;* the fourth *Idols of the Theater.*

3   The formation of notions and axioms on the foundations of true induction, is the only fitting remedy, by which we can ward off and expel these *Idols.* It is however of great service to point them out. For the doctrine of *Idols* bears the same relation to the interpretation of nature, as that of the confutation of sophisms does to common logic.

4   The *Idols of the Tribe* are inherent in human nature, and the very tribe or race of man. For man's sense is falsely asserted to be the standard of things. On the contrary, all the perceptions, both of the senses and the mind, bear reference to man, and not to the universe, and the human mind resembles those uneven mirrors, which impart their own properties to different objects, from which rays are emitted, and distort and disfigure them.

5   The *Idols of the Den* are those of each individual. For every body (in addition to the errors common to the race of man) has his own individual den or cavern, which intercepts and corrupts the light of nature; either from his own peculiar and singular disposition, or from his education and intercourse with others, or from his reading, and the authority acquired by those whom he reverences and admires, or from a different impression produced on the mind, as it happens to be preoccupied and predisposed, or equable and tranquil, and the like: so that the spirit of man (according to its several dispositions) is variable, confused, and as it were actuated by chance; and Heraclitus[1] said well that men search for knowledge in lesser worlds and not in the greater or common world.

6   There are also *Idols* formed by the reciprocal intercourse and society of man with man, which we call *Idols of the Market,* from the commerce and association of men with each other. For men converse by means of language; but words are formed at the will of the generality; and there arises from a bad and

---

[1]Greek philosopher of the sixth century BC—ED.

unapt formation of words a wonderful obstruction to the mind. Nor can the definitions and explanations, with which learned men are wont to guard and protect themselves in some instances, afford a complete remedy: words still manifestly force the understanding, throw everything into confusion, and lead mankind into vain and innumerable controversies and fallacies.

7   Lastly there are *Idols* which have crept into men's minds from the various dogmas of peculiar systems of philosophy, and also from the perverted rules of demonstration, and these we denominate *Idols of the Theater.* For we regard all the systems of philosophy hitherto received or imagined, as so many plays brought out and performed, creating fictitious and theatrical worlds. Nor do we speak only of the present systems, or of the philosophy and sects of the ancients, since numerous other plays of a similar nature can be still composed and made to agree with each other, the causes of the most opposite errors being generally the same. Nor, again, do we allude merely to the general systems, but also to many elements and axioms of sciences, which have become inveterate by tradition, implicit credence and neglect. We must, however, discuss each species of *Idols* more fully and distinctly in order to guard the human understanding against them.

● Vocabulary

beset (1)	inherent (4)	sects (7)
instauration (1)	equable (5)	dogmas (7)
confutation (3)	predisposed (5)	denominate (7)
axioms (3)	reciprocal (6)	implicit (7)
induction (3)	wont (6)	inveterate (7)
sophism (3)	credence (7)	

● The Facts

1. Exactly what is being divided in this essay? Why does Bacon use the term *idols?*
2. Using your own words, describe each idol in the order listed by Bacon. Supply an example for each from your own experience.
3. According to Bacon, what is the remedy for all these idols? How will this remedy work?

● The Strategies

1. What connection is there between Bacon's thought and his style?
2. Point out specific words or phrases to show that Bacon's style is archaic.
3. What method of thinking does Bacon use to conclude that idols preoccupy the human understanding? Trace his use of the method in the essay.
4. What is the analogy used to illustrate the last idol? Explain how this analogy helps clarify the idol.

● The Issues

1. Compare Bacon's division with some more contemporary ideas on the same subject. Is his essay still valid, or is it out of date? Give reasons for your answer.

2. What specific examples can you cite to illuminate Bacon's "idols of the tribe"?

3. How dangerous to present society are "idols of the market"? Give reasons for your opinion.

4. What examples can you cite from your own upbringing to indicate that you have bowed to "idols of the den"?

5. In your view, what ideas marketed publicly today are dangerous but highly seductive—especially for the naïve?

● Suggestions for Writing

1. Write an essay in which you divide your bad habits into three or four categories. Make sure that these categories are mutually exclusive and that they include the entire range of your bad habits.

2. Write a brief report on Francis Bacon's major contributions to society. In the report, organize these contributions into separate divisions.

English 101

BART EDELMAN

Bart Edelman (b. 1951) is a contemporary American poet who spent his childhood in Teaneck, New Jersey, the subject of many of his poems. Today he lives in southern California, and he gives poetry readings across the United States. He has been the recipient of numerous grants and fellowships to study literature in India, Egypt, Nigeria, and Poland. He is currently a professor of English at Glendale College in California. His poetry collections include *Crossing the Hackensack* (1993), *Under Damaris' Dress* (1996), *The Alphabet of Love* (1999), *The Gentle Man* (2001), and *The Last Mojito* (2005).

● ● ●

This poem conjures up familiar memories in anyone who has taken freshman composition and remembers the opening session when students are introduced to the requirements and goals of the course. The poet uses concrete language to convey vivid portraits of three kinds of students in class on opening day. As an organizing principle, division/classification is typically used in prose, but every now and again will also be found embedded in a poem.

> They appear—
> Always—
> That first day,
> Astray;

5 Some wait to fall,
Others to rise:
Here rests the tired boy,
The hour long,
He drops his brain
10 Upon the desk
And thinks he'd be better off dead,
Five worlds away
From Frost and Twain . . .
(He'll have no part of 101).
15 A fair-haired girl in knots
Twists her braids so tight
They make her ache;
She takes good notes,
Does what she's told,
20 If asked a quote
She knows it cold . . .
(But could a smile unclench those lips?)
Then the hand,
One resolute voice
25 Speaks through the bell
And the great stampede—
Engaged in speculation
We turn wheat to notion,
Sifting through each tiny grain . . .
30 (The composition now complete).

Reprinted with permission from Bart Edelman.

● Vocabulary

astray (4)   resolute (24)   stampede (26)

● The Facts

1. Where does the action of the poem take place? How do you know?
2. Who are "They" in the first line? Why are they described as "astray"?
3. What is meant by "He drops his brain/Upon the desk" in lines 9 and 10? Explain the figure of speech.
4. What kind of student is described in lines 15–22? Describe the student in your own words.
5. What is the meaning of the phrase "One resolute voice/Speaks through the bell"?

● The Strategies

1. In what sense is this poem a classification? What is being classified? How many items belong to the classification? List them.

2. After listing the first two students as a boy and a girl, why does the poet then refer to a "hand" and "voice" as the third student?

3. Why do you suppose the author chose the title "English 101" rather than, say, "Math 220" or "Economics 300"?

4. What comparison does the poet draw in lines 23–30? What other simile might be used? Use your poetic imagination to find one.

● The Issues

1. What is the theme (thesis) of this poem? State it in one sentence.

2. According to the poem, wherein lies a teacher's greatest classroom challenge?

3. If you were a teacher, which student would bother you more—the boy or the girl? Give reasons for your answer.

4. What is your opinion on the basic importance of freshman composition? Should it be a requirement? Why or why not?

5. In line 13, the poet refers to Frost and Twain. How are these two literary figures related to the theme of the poem?

● Suggestions for Writing

1. Write an essay in which you classify the various kinds of teachers who have taught you. For your bases of classification, consider such aspects as ability to communicate, personality, values, and attitude toward the subject matter.

2. Using Edelman's poem as a springboard, choose three or four friends who are representative types to classify your most intimate friends. Try to make each type come to life by using vivid details in describing him or her.

ISSUE FOR CRITICAL THINKING AND DEBATE: RACISM

Even to the casual observer, racism in America remains a festering problem. Its toxic influence ranges from blatant discrimination in the housing market, where minorities are deliberately steered to specific neighborhoods, to subtle hiring practices wherein deserving employees are denied promotions because of skin color. Blacks live shorter lives than whites, earn less money, and make up over half of U.S. murder victims (94 percent of whom are killed by other blacks). Compared to whites, blacks are also imprisoned more often and are more likely to be executed.

To remedy the inequality between whites and blacks, the U.S. Congress passed the Civil Rights Act of 1964 and set in place laws promoting affirmative action. The effect of this measure was to narrow the educational gap between blacks and whites. Black children today outnumber both white and Hispanic children enrolled in center-based preprimary education. Still, it is sobering to think that nearly one-third of all black families and nearly one-half of all black children still live in poverty. The National Urban League estimated in 2005 that the equality index of blacks stood at 73 percent when measured against whites, little changed from 2004.

How this inequality is viewed today depends as much on the viewer's race as on any facts. Predictably, the explanations for the causes of the inequality are divided along liberal/conservative fault lines. Liberals blame white racism and its poisonous legacy, arguing that the remedy for racial inequality is more government intervention. Conservatives argue that the time has come for racially neutral laws, with no affirmative action boost for minorities. Neither side denies the historical effects of racism. But whereas conservatives assert that the past is past and opportunities are now equal, liberals insist that the damage done to black consciousness by past injustices cannot be so casually dismissed.

These two themes are implicit in the pieces we have chosen for this debate. The first is a wrenching chapter from a book, *Warriors Don't Cry*, by an African American woman who helped desegregate Central High School in Little Rock, Arkansas, in 1954. Because this woman dared to want an education equal to what white Americans regard as their birthright, she was hounded with obscene phone calls, pelted with rocks, threatened by mobs, and tormented by her fellow students. The second reading is by a remarkable set of black sisters—Sarah L. and A. Elizabeth Delany—who wrote their memoirs when both were over 100 years old. The student essay by Carrie Moore argues that academic environments are often rigged against African Americans as they compete with non African Americans to succeed in college. The artwork of the chapter also reflects the problem of racism. For instance, the cartoon reproduced here ridicules the idea that racism can be cured by a superficial approach to cultural diversity. The photo on page 541 emphasizes the choice we all make between love and hate.

The fact that in 2008 Barack Obama was elected as the first African American male to run for President of the United States was a dramatic step in leveling the racism landscape. Nevertheless, the turmoil caused by racism continues to be as unsettling as it is unsettled. The liberal/conservative argument over race boils

GREGORY

*"In the interest of cultural diversity, we've hired Jason,
here, who owns a number of hip-hop CDs."*

down to these questions: How much is the past really past? What can we do to ensure that the ugly legacy of racism won't continue to poison the efforts of those men and women who try to make race relations better?

Warriors Don't Cry

MELBA PATILLO BEALS

Melba Patillo Beals (b. 1941) earned a degree from San Francisco State and a graduate degree from Columbia. She has worked as a reporter for NBC. Today she works as a communications consultant and has written books on public relations and marketing. In 1957, she was one of nine students chosen to integrate Central High School in Little Rock, Arkansas, in the wake of the 1954 Supreme Court decision *Brown* v. *Board of Education of Topeka, Kansas,* which declared segregated schools illegal. This reading is the opening chapter from her memoir of that traumatic experience, *Warriors Don't Cry* (1994).

• • •

1   In 1957, while most teenage girls were listening to Buddy Holly's "Peggy Sue," watching Elvis gyrate, and collecting crinoline slips, I was escaping the hanging rope of a lynch mob, dodging lighted sticks of dynamite, and washing away burning acid sprayed into my eyes.

2   During my junior year in high school, I lived at the center of a violent civil rights conflict. In 1954, the Supreme Court had decreed an end to segregated schools. Arkansas Governor Orval Faubus and states' rights segregationists defied that ruling. President Eisenhower was compelled to confront Faubus—to use U.S. soldiers to force him to obey the law of the land. It was a historic confrontation that generated worldwide attention. At the center of the controversy were nine black children who wanted only to have the opportunity for a better education.

3   On our first day at Central High, Governor Faubus dispatched gun-toting Arkansas National Guard soldiers to prevent us from entering. Mother and I got separated from the others. The two of us narrowly escaped a rope-carrying lynch mob of men and women shouting that they'd kill us rather than see me go to school with their children.

4   Three weeks later, having won a federal court order, we black children maneuvered our way past an angry mob to enter the side door of Central High. But by eleven that morning, hundreds of people outside were running wild, crashing through police barriers to get us out of school. Some of the police sent to control the mob threw down their badges and joined the rampage. But a few other brave members of the Little Rock police force saved our lives by spiriting us past the mob to safety.

5   To uphold the law and protect lives, President Eisenhower sent soldiers of the 101st Airborne Division, the elite "Screaming Eagles"—Korean Warheroes.

6   On my third trip to Central High, I rode with the 101st in an army station wagon guarded by jeeps with turret guns mounted on their hoods and helicopters roaring overhead. With the protection of our 101st bodyguards, we black students walked through the front door of the school and completed a full day of classes.

7   But I quickly learned from those who opposed integration that the soldiers' presence meant a declaration of war. Segregationists mounted a brutal campaign against us, both inside and out of school.

8   My eight friends and I paid for the integration of Central High with our innocence. During those years when we desperately needed approval from our peers, we were victims of the most harsh rejection imaginable. The physical and psychological punishment we endured profoundly affected all our lives. It transformed us into warriors who dared not cry even when we suffered intolerable pain.

9   I became an instant adult, forced to take stock of what I believed and what I was willing to sacrifice to back up my beliefs. The experience endowed me with an indestructible faith in God.

10   I am proud to report that the Little Rock experience also gave us courage, strength, and hope. We nine grew up to become productive citizens, with special insights about how important it is to respect the value of every human life.

11   I am often asked, in view of the state of race relations today, if our effort was in vain. Would I integrate Central if I had it to do over again? My answer is yes, unequivocally yes. I take pride in the fact that, although the fight for equality must continue, our 1957 effort catapulted the civil rights movement forward a giant step and shifted the fight to a more dignified battlefield. For the first time in history, a President took a very bold step to defend civil rights—our civil rights.

12   Back then, I naïvely believed that if we could end segregation in the schools, all barriers of inequality would fall. If you had asked me in 1957 what I expected, I would have told you that by this time our struggle for human rights would have been won. Not so. But I am consoled by the words my grandmother spoke: "Even when the battle is long and the path is steep, a true warrior does not give up. If each one of us does not step forward to claim our rights, we are doomed to an eternal wait in hopes those who would usurp them will become benevolent. The Bible says, WATCH, FIGHT, and PRAY."

13   Although I am perplexed by the state of race relations in this country today, I am at the same time very hopeful because I have ample evidence that what Grandmother promised me is true. With time and love, God solves all our problems. When we returned to Central High School for our first reunion in 1987, many Little Rock residents, white and black, greeted the nine of us as heroines and heroes. Hometown white folk in the mall smiled and said hello and offered directions even when they did not recognize us from our newspaper photos.

14   During all the fancy ceremonies, some of Arkansas's highest officials and businessmen came from far and wide to welcome us. And perhaps the most astounding evidence that things have indeed changed for the better was the attitude of Governor Bill Clinton.

15   "Call me Bill," he said, extending his hand, looking me in the eye. "You'all come on up to the house and sit a while." He flashed that charming grin of his. A few minutes of conversation assured me that his warm invitation was genuine. He is, after all, a man my brother refers to as "good people," based on their working relationship over the years.

16   So my eight friends and I found ourselves hanging out at the governor's mansion, the one Faubus built. Governor Clinton sauntered about serving soft drinks and peanuts. He and his wife, Hillary, were the kind of host and hostess who could make me feel at home even in the place where Faubus had hatched his devilish strategies to get the nine of us out of Central High School by any means possible.

17   "You'all ought to think about coming on back home now. Things are different," Governor Clinton said. He had been eleven years old when Faubus waged his segregationist battle against us. He displayed genuine respect for our contribution to the civil rights struggle. That visit was to become an evening I shall always treasure. As Chelsea played the piano and Bill and Hillary talked to me as though we'd known each other always, I found myself thinking, "Oh, Mr. Faubus, if only you and your friends could see us now."

18   My grandmother India always said God had pointed a finger at our family, asking for just a bit more discipline, more praying, and more hard work because He had blessed us with good health and good brains. My mother was one of the first few blacks to integrate the University of Arkansas, graduating in 1954. Three years later, when Grandma discovered I would be one of the first blacks to attend Central High School, she said the nightmare that had surrounded my birth was proof positive that destiny had assigned me a special task.

19   First off, I was born on Pearl Harbor Day, December 7, 1941. Mother says while she was giving birth to me, there was a big uproar, with the announcement that the Japanese had bombed Pearl Harbor. She remembers how astonished she was, and yet her focus was necessarily on the task at hand. There was trouble with my delivery because Mom was tiny and I was nine pounds. The doctor used forceps to deliver me and injured my scalp. A few days later, I fell ill with a massive infection. Mother took me to the white hospital, which reluctantly treated the families of black men who worked on the railroad. A doctor operated to save my life by inserting a drainage system beneath my scalp.

20   Twenty-four hours later I wasn't getting better. Whenever Mother sought help, neither nurses nor doctors would take her seriously enough to examine me. Instead, they said, "Just give it time."

21   Two days after my operation, my temperature soared to 106 and I started convulsing. Mother sent for the minister to give me the last rites, and relatives were gathering to say farewell.

22   That evening, while Grandmother sat in my hospital room, rocking me back and forth as she hummed her favorite hymn, "On the Battlefield for My Lord," Mother paced the floor weeping aloud in her despair. A black janitor who was sweeping the hallway asked why she was crying. She explained that I was dying because the infection in my head had grown worse.

23   The man extended his sympathy. As he turned to walk away, dragging his broom behind him, he mumbled that he guessed the Epsom salts hadn't worked after all. Mother ran after him asking what he meant. He explained that a couple of days before, he had been cleaning the operating room as they finished up with my surgery. He had heard the doctor tell the white nurse to irrigate my head with Epsom salts and warm water every two or three hours or I wouldn't make it.

24   Mother shouted the words "Epsom salts and water" as she raced down the hall, desperately searching for a nurse. The woman was indignant, saying, yes, come to think of it, the doctor had said something about Epsom salts. "But we don't coddle niggers," she growled.

25   Mother didn't talk back to the nurse. She knew Daddy's job was at stake. Instead, she sent for Epsom salts and began the treatment right away. Within two days, I was remarkably better. The minister went home, and the sisters from the church abandoned their death watch, declaring they had witnessed a miracle.

26   So fifteen years later, when I was selected to integrate Central High, Grandmother said, "Now you see, that's the reason God spared your life. You're supposed to carry this banner for our people."

● Vocabulary

decreed (2)   usurp (12)   sauntered (16)
endowed (9)   benevolent (12)   convulsing (21)
unequivocally (11)

● The Facts

1. What president ordered in the troops to ensure the integration of the high school that the author attended?
2. What does the author admit she naïvely believed would happen if the segregation of schools could be ended?
3. Who was governor of Arkansas when the author returned to her former high school for her reunion?
4. What happened to the author when she was born?
5. Whose muttered remark resulted in the author's getting the treatment that saved her life?

● The Strategies

1. The author wrote her memoir some forty years after the actual event. What kinds of problems do you think she encountered in writing this piece so many years after it happened?
2. How would you characterize the person who is telling the story? How old do you think she is? What characteristics of her language help project her onto the page?

3. What technique does the writer use to grab our interest in the opening paragraph?

4. The author tells the story of how she almost died when she was a baby, but does so with little or no editorial comment. Why is this an effective technique?

5. In addition to the author's religious convictions, what does the story about her illness as a newborn dramatically illustrate?

● The Issues

1. What effect do you think living through such a traumatic experience is likely to have on someone? How does it seem to have affected the author?

2. The author says that she is perplexed by the state of race relations today. How do you feel about the relationship between the races in the United States today?

3. What do you regard as the most pressing issue in race relations today? What solution do you have for that issue?

4. The author says that the experience of desegregating Central High made her an "instant adult." What do you think she meant by that? What is an *instant adult*?

5. What, in your opinion, is necessary to end racism in the United States?

● Suggestions for Writing

1. Write an essay about a personal encounter you have had with prejudice.

2. Write an essay about any side of racism.

genevieve laplante/Getty Images

● Why do love and hate coexist in life's great controversy between good and evil?

Incidents with White People

SARAH L. AND A. ELIZABETH DELANY

Sarah (Sadie) L. Delany (1890–1999) and Dr. A. Elizabeth (Bessie) Delany (1891–1995) were African American centenarian sisters who found fame and fortune in 1993 with the publication of their co-authored memoirs *Having Our Say: The Delany Sisters' First 100 Years,* written in collaboration with Amy Hill Hearth. The book was on the *New York Times* bestseller list for two years and has been translated into seven languages. The Delany sisters left one million dollars to St. Augustine College, on whose campus they were born, lived, and were educated.

In this excerpt from Having Our Say, *Bessie tells of leaving home in 1911 at age twenty to teach school in Boardman, North Carolina, where she boarded with a couple, Mr. and Mrs. Atkinson. We learn of her reaction to the news that the* Titanic *had sunk (1912) and how she narrowly escaped being lynched in Georgia. As you read the essay, ask yourself how you would have reacted if you had been in Bessie's shoes during the encounter with the drunken white man.*

* * *

1   Mr. Atkinson was the ugliest man I ever saw, and not at all well educated, but he was an absolute gentleman. He never bothered me once. His first name was Spudge, which was short for Spudgeon, or so he told me. He said he was named after a Baptist preacher who was legendary in those parts, and he was just appalled that this little Episcopalian girl had never heard of him.

2   There was no Episcopal Church in Boardman, so I attended Baptist or Methodist services. They were poor and had no hymnals. The Methodists had the words to their hymns scratched out in the margins of old pieces of paper, like the Sears catalog.

3   The food we ate in Boardman was about the worst diet I have ever been on. I have always been a slim thing, but Honey, I got fat while I was there! When I came home at Christmas I weighed 153 pounds, and people came from everywhere to see this fat Bessie. But I lost that weight eventually, and never gained it back. Sadie says it was from eating all that fatback and collards and sweet potatoes in Boardman.

4   Those people didn't know the first thing about vitamins or minerals. They were so poor and ignorant. It was the same thing Sadie was running into as Jeanes Supervisor in Wake County. Mama was worried about me, and she would send me these little care packages. She would go to a store in Raleigh called the California Fruit Company, and buy some grapefruits and ship them to me.

5   Well, Mr. Spudge Atkinson had never seen a grapefruit before. He said, "Miss Delany, what is that ugly-looking piece of fruit?" Now, I gave him a piece and he just puckered up and spit it out and said it was the worst, most sour,

miserable thing he'd ever put in his mouth! And I said, "Mr. Atkinson, if you're just going to waste my grapefruit, then please give it back to me." And he gave me the rest back, gladly. He sure did think that Miss Delany from Raleigh was peculiar, sitting on his porch sucking down grapefruit.

6   Mr. Atkinson tended to be a rather dramatic man. One time he came into my classroom and said, "Oh, Miss Delany! Miss Delany!" And I said, "What's the matter, Mr. Atkinson?" And he fell to the ground and said, "It's terrible, it's just terrible!" And I said, "What's terrible?" And he said, "That ship they said could not sink, well, it's done sunk! And all those rich white people have gone down with it, in that icy water!"

7   I didn't say it out loud, but I remember thinking, Too bad the *Titanic* didn't take more rich white people down with it, to its watery grave! Especially some of the rebby boys around here! Now, isn't that awful of me? Isn't it vicious? You see why this child is worried about getting into Heaven? Sadie is just shocked by me sometimes. Sadie just says, "Live, and let live."

8   But in a way, I was a sweet child, too. You know, when I was in Boardman and got my first paycheck—$40 a month—I paid nine dollars for my room and board and sent the rest home to Papa immediately. No one had asked me to do that. It just seemed like the right thing to do.

9   Well, I got a letter back from Mama. She thanked me for the money but she told me not to send any more. She told me to save it for myself, or I'd never get to college.

10   I saved most of my money, but I will admit that I spent some on a silk dress, yes, sir! Papa wouldn't let me have a silk dress—I guess because it was so expensive but also kind of sexy. So, when I was in Boardman I ordered several yards of silk. I think it was blue, with a thin white stripe. And I made myself a dress. Skirts were going up, and you could see the ankle when you walked. And when the men would see a glimpse of ankle they would say, "Ooooohweeee!" Papa didn't like that at all. When Sadie and I would wear those dresses, he would just scowl at us!! Today women show everything. They're crazy. Trust me, you can get in enough trouble just with a little ankle showing.

11   Now, after two years in Boardman, it was time for me to move on to a new teaching assignment. The people didn't want to see me go, but I was ready for a new challenge. So in 1913 I went to Brunswick, Georgia, to teach at Saint Athanasius, an Episcopal school for colored children. I wanted to see the world!

12   Brunswick was a sophisticated place compared to Boardman. The faculty lived together in a dormitory, and that is how I met my lifelong friend, Elizabeth Gooch. "Gooch," as I always called her, was the oldest one of us, and I was the youngest, and so the principal assigned the two of us to room together. I guess he thought Gooch would be a good influence on me, but I think I was a good influence on Gooch!

13   I didn't like Gooch that much at first. She didn't treat me the way I would have liked to be treated. For instance, she took the bed away from the window, so that I'd get the draft at night. But after a while, Gooch and I became good

friends. Sometimes, we'd go to the beach and see the turtles come in from the sea to nest.

14   Now, Georgia was a mean place—meaner than North Carolina. You know that song about Georgia, that sentimental song? Well, they can have it! They can have the whole state as far as I'm concerned.

15   In Georgia, they never missed a chance to keep you down. If you were colored and you tried on a hat or a pair of shoes, Honey, you owned 'em. What a rebby state! To be fair, I can understand why they didn't want Negroes to try on hats without buying them: because in those days, Negroes would grease their hair. And the store couldn't sell the hat if it got grease on it. So, to be fair, I think that was OK.

16   But it was on my way to my job in Brunswick in 1913 that I came close to being lynched. You see, I had to change trains in Waycross, Georgia. I was sitting in the little colored waiting room at the station, and I took my hair down and was combing it. I was fixing myself up. I was going to my new job, and I wanted to look nice.

17   Well, there I was with my long hair down when this white man opened the door, to the colored waiting room. There was no one in there except me and two colored teachers from New York who were traveling with me to Brunswick. The white man stuck his head in and started, well, leering at me. He was drunk, and he smelled bad, and he started mumbling things. And I said, "Oh, why don't you shut up and go wait with your own kind in the white waiting room?"

18   What happened next was kind of like an explosion. He slammed the door and I could hear him shouting at the top of his lungs outside, "The nigger bitch insulted me! The nigger bitch insulted me!"

19   The two colored teachers traveling with me slipped out the back without a word and made a beeline for the woods. They hid in the woods! I guess I can't blame them. A colored porter came in to see what this was all about, and he whispered to me, "Good for you!" But then he ran out on me, too. He left me there by myself.

20   Well, I could see a crowd begin to gather on the platform, and I knew I was in big trouble. Papa always said, "If you see a crowd, you go the other way. Don't even hang around long enough to find out what it's about!" Now, this crowd was outside, gathering for me.

21   By now, there were dozens of white people in the crowd, and the white man kept yelling, "Nigger bitch insulted me!" I was just waiting for somebody to get a rope. Thousands of Negroes had been lynched for far less than what I had just done. But I just continued to sit on the bench, combing my hair, while that white man was a-carrying on! I realized that my best chance was to act like nothing was happening. You see, if you acted real scared, sometimes that spurred them on.

22   Two things saved me: That glorious, blessed train rounded the bend, breaking up the crowd and giving me my way to get on out of there. And it helped that the white man was drunk as a skunk, and that turned off some of the white people.

23   But I wasn't afraid to die! I know you ain't got to die but once, and it seemed as good a reason to die as any. I was ready. Lord, help me, I was ready.

24   You know what Sadie says? Sadie says I was a fool to provoke that white man. As if I provoked him! Honey, he provoked me! Sadie says she would have ignored him. I say, how do you ignore some drunk, smelly white man treating you like trash? She says, child, it's better to put up with it, and live to tell about it. She says at the very least I should have run off into the woods with those other two teachers. She says I am lucky to be alive. But I would rather die than back down, Honey.

Reprinted by permission of Kodansha America, Inc. Excerpted from HAVING OUR SAY: THE DELANY SISTERS' FIRST 100 YEARS by Sarah and A. Elizabeth Delany with Amy Hill Hearth published by Kodansha America, Inc. (1993)

● Vocabulary

appalled (1)	vicious (7)	lynched (16)
legendary (1)	sophisticated (12)	spurred (21)

● The Facts

1. Which of the three religions in Boardman—Methodist, Baptist, Episcopalian— had the poorest membership? How was the poverty revealed? Who do you think made up the membership of the churches mentioned by the narrator?

2. What kind of diet made Bessie gain weight? What do we find out about Bessie's family and its knowledge of healthy foods? What kinds of foods should be blamed today for making so many youngsters obese?

3. What was your reaction to Bessie's admission that she wished more rich white people had sunk with the *Titanic?*

4. What is the difference between Bessie's personality and that of the rest of her family? Which attitude do you admire most? Explain your answer.

5. According to Bessie, what saved her from being lynched? Do you think she really was in danger of being lynched? Give reasons for your answer.

● The Strategies

1. How does the author keep this story a dramatic monologue in which the speaker is telling her story to an unseen, trusted interviewer? Give examples of the author's technique.

2. The title of the story is "Incidents with White People." How do the incidents portray the white people? Is the portrait flattering or not? Support your answer with examples from the narration.

3. What is the reference to "that sentimental song about Georgia" that Bessie discredits? What is the title of the song? Why does Bessie dislike Georgia?

4. How does Bessie refer to black people in this narration? Is this how blacks refer to themselves today in most American locations, or do they use other terminologies? Cite examples.

5. How well does the narrator handle the scene with the white drunk? What strategies does she use to keep the reader interested in the scene?

● The Issues

1. How is Mr. Atkinson portrayed in the narrative? How does the narrator seem to feel about him? Does the portrayal seem realistic or fantastic? Give reasons for your answer.

2. What reputation did silk dresses have among the conscientious parents of black girls at the time of this story? What might the equivalent be today?

3. What is your view of the black teachers who slipped out the back without a word and made a beeline for the woods? What is your view of the black porter who said, "Good for you!" and then ran away? What kinds of people today are fearless and stand up to be counted? Give examples.

4. What is your reaction to the advice from Bessie's father—"If you see a crowd, you go the other way. Don't even hang around long enough to find out what it's about!"? Is this sound advice, even today?

5. Bessie felt that she would rather die than back down in front of this crowd of whites when she had been insulted. She also felt that she could not just ignore the white drunk. Do you think she was right? Would you be willing to lay your life on the line if you were in a similar situation? What issue would you be willing to die for?

● Suggestions for Writing

1. Write an essay in which you offer your opinion as to why blacks were treated the way they were at the time Bessie and Sadie lived in the South.

2. In an ideal world, how would ethnic, economic, religious, and gender differences be treated? Answer this question in an essay.

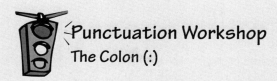

Punctuation Workshop
The Colon (:)

1. **Put a colon after a complete statement followed by a list or long quotation:**

   > These are the reading assignments for next week: Hawthorne's *Scarlet Letter,* two magazine articles about women today, and three books about feminism. This is what Stanley J. Randall said about perfection: "The closest to perfection a person ever comes is when he fills out an application form."

   Use a comma instead of a colon if the quotation is not introduced by a complete statement:

   > It was Thomas Jefferson who said, "One generation cannot bind another."

   Do not use a colon between a verb and its object or after *such as:*

   > **WRONG:** The contest winners were: Jerry Meyer, Ani Hossein, and Franco Sanchez.
   >
   > **RIGHT:** The contest winners were Jerry Meyer, Ani Hossein, and Franco Sanchez.
   >
   > **WRONG:** People no longer believe in evil spirits, such as: ghosts, witches, and devils.
   >
   > **RIGHT:** People no longer believe in evil spirits, such as ghosts, witches, and devils.

2. **Use a colon between figures that express time:**

   > Professor Stern entered the classroom at exactly 2:10 P.M.

3. **Use a colon between titles and subtitles:**

   > *The Golden Years: Telling the Truth about Aging*

4. **Use a colon after the salutation of a formal letter:**

   > Dear Mrs. Smith:

   The colon also appears in bibliographic data. (See the student paper on p. 779.)

Carrie Moore
Chamblee Charter High School
Color of Their Skin AND Content of Their Character

Martin Luther King, in his famous speech, declared that he hoped that his children would live in a nation where they "would not be judged by the color of their skin but by the content of their character." But would his opinion change if darker skin could actually be an advantage for college-bound students? Let us ponder this question.

With all of the opportunities for African Americans to obtain a college degree—National Achievement, affirmative action, minority scholarships—it appears to some observers that nonminority students are disadvantaged when it comes to attending college. All of these higher-educational prospects are supposedly "unfairly geared" so as to favor African Americans.

While it is true that a plethora of opportunities exist for African Americans and other minorities to successfully obtain a college degree, these recent gains can hardly be described as biased in favor of African Americans. One could argue that, yes, treatment of college-bound students is *unequal*, but given several circumstances, they are certainly not unjust. I am not arguing that these opportunities encompass some long overdue compensation for slavery. Nor am I arguing that African Americans are dumber than students of other races and therefore need lower standards in order to slide by in life.

As a middle-class National Achievement Semifinalist who technically did not have the PSAT score to qualify for National Merit (though I would like to point out that two African Americans qualified for both this school year), I feel obliged to present an argument regarding an environment rigged against African Americans.

The trouble begins at home. Studies have long shown that whatever influences infants and toddlers are exposed to as they develop affects their progress. For example, younger children have an easier time learning foreign languages or mastering a musical instrument than do adults. Moreover, talking to young children as though they were adults allows them to have better concepts of language and communication. Exposing children to different kinds of music stimulates brain function.

Since many African Americans are first-generation college students or are just now reaching the point where they are second- or third-generation college students (affirmative action began under President Johnson and has allowed the percentage of African Americans holding bachelor degrees to increase gradually over the years), it can be safely inferred that their initial development may not have been as progressive as that of students who have two parents who attended college. This is not to say that African-American parents have failed. They simply lack a fundamental part of education. After all, which parents, who have not earned a college degree, would consider reading Chaucer to their children or playing Mozart for them? Certainly not parents who never attended a college class and never had the faintest idea who Chaucer or Mozart was in the first place.

Consider also that if these parents do not have college degrees, they are probably breaking their backs to make even a small amount of money, meaning that they do not have the time to sit down with their children to discuss Greek philosophy, learn French, or read about the Spanish Civil War. In 2009, 14.3% of Americans were under the poverty line, 25.8% of whom were black, the highest percentage of any racial group (United States 14).

If it has been proven that a college degree can lead to a larger income over the years, it can be safely stated that there is a strong correlation between African Americans' place on the poverty line and their college graduation rate.

While these seemingly small nuances do not affect the overall "intellectual quotient" of first-generation college African-American students, they certainly do affect the results of standardized tests, such as the SAT. In 2009, the average SAT score for African Americans was 1276, the lowest of all racial groups (Marklein).

Even African-American students who are fortunate enough to be born to at least one parent who has a college degree are not *equal* to their white counterparts. If one opts out of attending a historically black college and university, then appreciation of African-American culture is severely limited. It is not so much that today's African Americans are told that they are inferior, though that is true in some cases, but they are certainly not told to celebrate their heritage. History is constantly taught as an appreciation of European and nonblack advancements, and, if there are mentions of achievements by minorities (such as the inventions of the traffic light and air-conditioning unit), then they are often fleeting references.

Moreover, when African-American achievement is discussed, it is usually referred to in terms of "firsts." Toni Morrison was the first African American to win the Nobel Prize in Literature. Hattie McDaniel was the first African American to win an Oscar in the category of Best Supporting Actress in 1940. Barack Obama was the first African American to hold the title of President of the United States. Not that these cannot be marked as advancements, but why can't we acknowledge what African Americans *do* first?

These are just a few of the conflicts that even African Americans who attend college face. True, African Americans can choose to immerse themselves in classes that focus on their culture, but let's face it: What kind of career can you have with a degree in African-American studies?

All of this is not to say that African Americans should be handed everything on a plate until the achievement gap finally closes. National statistics showing that only about 43% of African Americans graduate from college are enough to disprove that. There has to be a clear and comprehensive effort on the part of African-American students to earn a college degree that will make them competitive with other students applying for the best and most lucrative jobs in a variety of markets.

Programs such as National Achievement and minority scholarships with GPA cutoffs set out to reward African Americans and minority

Moore   4

students who try to meet them halfway. So yes, the current treatment of African Americans regarding college acceptances and scholarships is fair. Until an African American *can* slack off and get accepted to Harvard with a 2.75 GPA on legacy alone, these programs should stay in place.

Moore   5

Works Cited

Marklein, Mary Beth. "SAT Scores Show Disparities by Race, Gender, Family Income." *USATODAY.com.* USA TODAY, 26 Aug. 2009. Web. 18 May 2011.

United States. Census Bureau. *Income, Poverty, and Health Insurance Coverage in the United States: 2009.* By Carmen DeNavas-Walt, Bernadette D. Proctor, and Jessica C. Smith. Washington: GPO, 2010. Print.

How I Write

When I read a book, my eyes absorb the words on the pages while my imagination translates those words into vivid images, scenes, and details—an easy enough process. When I write, however, that once simple process takes place in a more complicated reverse. The detail will appear first—something as innocuous as an object in front of me or a piece of dialogue leftover from a previous conversation—and my mind will form a story, poem, or essay around it, adding flavor and color and pizzazz the way a chef jazzes up a simple dish before presenting it to others. Perhaps this is even the most fun part of writing—when your mind begins that initial work and you have not yet even realized that the idea you are pondering can become an essay or story or literary piece. It is only when you understand, "Hey! I can do something with this!" that the hard part arrives; you have to put pen to paper and work on converting that envisioned portrait to words that people who may or may not agree with you can understand. Therefore, when I write, I write quickly, using my computer, where the clacking of keys becomes almost hypnotic and I am forced to continue without thinking of losing that initial vision. Without that quick typing, an idea becomes stale and is easily discarded in favor of a fresher one. If I am lucky enough to make it through the first draft in a few sittings, I am no longer a writer but a reviser, molding and remolding until the piece resembles the initial dream that, hopefully, will be apparent to others.

How I Wrote This Essay

"Color of Their Skin AND Content of Their Character" was the result of a conversation that took place in my Advanced Placement Biology class a short time after the National Merit and National Achievement Finalists were announced. The National Merit Scholarship Corporation awarded scholarships worth $2,500 to students of all races who scored highly (around 215) on the PSAT. National Achievement is a subset of the NMSC. However, only African-American students were eligible to receive the scholarship funds. Because the African-American PSAT scores tended to be lower than those of other demographics, the average PSAT score required to receive the National Achievement Scholarship was around 180. With a 209 on the PSAT, I was awarded the National Achievement Scholarship and was very excited. However, a male Indian friend of mine who scored about the same as I did was irritated. "It's unfair that African Americans are awarded for mediocrity," he said. "Minority scholarships aren't helping minorities assimilate. They're babying them so that they don't have to work as hard. If America really wanted to achieve equality, it would give the opportunities to the best and brightest, regardless of race."

What followed this dialogue was a debate, with me pushing affirmative action and my friend arguing against it. Our forty-five-minute dispute did not end with the sound of the bell. Instead, I went home and researched the topic, resulting in this essay which was later published in the school newspaper.

My Writing Tip

Write for yourself, which essentially means write something you'd want to read. By writing something that interests you, you are immediately ensuring audience appeal. There is bound to be someone who will agree with you or find your work interesting simply because you represent a certain population or viewpoint. The work cannot fail. But when writers try to imitate someone else or write something simply because they believe it will be popular, the entire project becomes false.

● CHAPTER WRITING ASSIGNMENTS

1. In an essay, divide and classify one of the following subjects:
   a. Your friends
   b. Your relatives
   c. Things or activities that give you pleasure
   d. Classes you like to take
   e. Classes you don't like to take
2. Write an essay dividing and classifying the various techniques you have used over the years to make yourself a better writer.

● WRITING ASSIGNMENTS FOR A SPECIFIC AUDIENCE

1. Pretending that you're writing to a prospective employer, divide and classify your life into various stages leading up to the present.
2. Write a letter to anyone you admire, dividing and classifying into stages the changes you have undergone in your career ambitions since you were young.

● IMAGE GALLERY WRITING ASSIGNMENT

Visit pages IG-19–IG-22 of our image gallery and study all four images dealing with racism. Then choose the image that most appeals to you. Answer the questions and do the writing assignment.

USE DEFINITE, SPECIFIC, CONCRETE LANGUAGE

If those who have studied the art of writing are in accord on any one point, it is on this: the surest way to arouse and hold the attention of the reader is by being specific, definite, and concrete. The greatest writers—Homer, Dante, Shakespeare—are effective largely because they deal in particulars and report the details that matter. Their words call up pictures.

Note the difference between the examples on the left and those on the right:

A period of unfavorable weather set in.	It rained every day for a week.
He showed satisfaction as he took possession of his well-earned coin.	He grinned as he pocketed the reward.

—William Strunk, Jr., and E. B. White

15

Causal Analysis

What Causal Analysis Does

Causal analysis focuses specifically on explanations that show a connection between a situation and its cause or effect. It either answers the question "Why did this happen?" or "What will this do?" An answer to the first question will result in an explanation of cause; an answer to the second, a prediction of effect. An essay based on the controlling idea such as "The lack of tough antipollution laws is the cause of multiple illnesses, including cancer, in the United States" is *analyzing cause*. If the essay was based on the controlling idea that "A law to stiffen penalties against toxic polluters will clear our drinking water from cancer-causing chemicals," it would be *forecasting effect*.

As the diagram illustrates, cause points to past occurrences, whereas effect predicts future consequences.

cause ← situation → effect

Here, for example, is a causal analysis written to answer the question "Why are so many couples unable to discuss their marital problems?"

Barriers between husbands and wives are often caused by timidity. Many couples are embarrassed to discuss intimate problems, such as sexual maladjustment, personal hygiene, or religious beliefs. They prefer to let their discontent fester rather than confront it openly. A wife says, "I wouldn't hurt my husband by telling him that his dirty hands offend me." A husband says, "I dislike the way my wife compares me to her father in everything I do, from mowing the lawn to smoking my pipe, but I could never tell her so." Guilt feelings can reinforce this sort of timidity. If a wife or husband knows that a frank talk about sex, for instance, will uncover some past indiscretion, he or she will avoid the confrontation either out of personal guilt or fear of knowing about the other partner's past. The longer this silence is kept, the stronger and more destructive it becomes. Many a broken marriage can trace the break back to barriers in communication.

On the other hand, a slight shift in the approach to this topic leads naturally to a discussion of effect. An essay based on the question "What happens when two people no longer discuss their marital problems?" would now focus on the effect, rather than the cause, of no communication in a marriage:

> Barriers between husband and wife result in a tension-filled home. When marriage partners constantly overlook a problem or pretend it does not exist, they eventually become frustrated and angry. They develop feelings of isolation and rejection, as their unfulfilled yearnings become a gnawing hunger. Lacking communication, the marriage is left without an emotional safety valve to let off pent-up frustration. The ensuing strain increases as the angry partners take out hidden, unexpressed resentments on their children, using them as scapegoats for their own great void. In the beginning the tension may show itself only in minor misunderstandings or brief pout sessions, but as the barriers remain, these little hurts turn into large wounds. The husband may become belligerent toward the wife, belittling her in front of friends or ignoring her until she retreats in cold indignation. The wife may feel so rejected and worthless that she seeks another man to comfort her or to treat her with sensitivity. The tension grows. Soon the home has become a place of bitter hostility, where love and warmth are impossible.

When to Use Causal Analysis

Use causal analysis when you are trying to explain why something happened or to predict the likely results if an event does or does not occur. Throughout your college study you will probably be given many assignments that require writing in the causal analysis mode of development. A history paper might ask you to analyze the causes of the Louisiana Purchase in 1803; an astronomy exam, to explain the cause of the aurora borealis. In economics, you might be asked to predict what will happen to the American economy if oil prices surge. A psychology exam might require you to examine three results on the work of Carl Jung caused by his break with Sigmund Freud. Causal analysis is also commonly employed in argumentative papers written in all fields and disciplines.

How to Use Causal Analysis

Know the Differences among Necessary, Sufficient, and Contributory Cause   Three kinds of cause can create a given effect:

1. **A necessary cause is one that must be present for the effect to occur, but it alone cannot make the effect occur.** For instance, irrigation is necessary for a crop of good grapes, but irrigation alone will not cause a good crop. Enough sunshine, correct pruning, proper pesticides, and good soil are also required.

2. **A sufficient cause is one that can produce a given effect by itself.** For instance, an empty gasoline tank alone can keep a car from running, even though other problems such as a bad spark plug, a leaking hose, or ignition trouble may also be present.

3. **A contributory cause is one that might help produce an effect but cannot produce the effect by itself.** For instance, vitamin E may help a long-distance runner win a race but cannot by itself determine the performance of a runner who got a bad start, trained haphazardly, or is not properly conditioned. The runner may also win the race without the help of vitamin E.

Understanding the differences among these three causes will help you in your investigations of cause and effect and keep you from making dogmatic statements such as these:

> A vegetarian diet will prevent cancer.
>
> Acupuncture is the answer to anesthesiology problems in America.
>
> Violence on television is the cause of today's growing criminal violence.

Rather, you will soften your statements by inserting such phrases as "may be," "is a contributing factor," "is one of the reasons," or "is a major cause." A careful study of cause and effect teaches that few causes are sufficient; most are merely necessary or contributory.

Make Your Purpose Clear The excerpt from Henry Thoreau's book *Walden*, reprinted later in this chapter, opens with this clear statement: "I went to the woods because I wished to live deliberately, to front only the essential facts of life, and see if I could not learn what it had to teach, and not, when I came to die, discover that I had not lived." Thoreau then proceeds to explain the causes that led him to live in the woods. This sort of definiteness early in the piece adds a guiding focus to any explanation of cause.

Be Modest in Your Choice of Subject It is difficult enough to analyze the causes of simple effects without compounding your problem through the choice of a monstrously large subject. The student who tries to write an essay on the causes of war is already in deep trouble; such a complex phenomenon bristles with thousands of causes. Selecting a more manageable subject for causal analysis will make your task much easier.

Concentrate on Immediate Rather Than Remote Cause It is easy in analysis of cause to become entangled in the infinite. In a series of causations, the most likely cause is always the nearest. For example, take the case of a student—John Doe—who gets a poor grade on a test. Why? Probably because he failed to study. On the other hand, perhaps John failed to study because he thought he was doomed to fail anyway, and didn't see the point in exerting himself. Why? Probably because the instructor scared him with a lecture on how high her standards were and how hard it was to pass her class. Why did she do that? Probably because of pressure from the Regents, who accused her and her department of grading too easily. Why? The Regents, in turn, may have gotten tough because of an article critical of the department's standards that appeared in a newspaper and was written by a cub reporter who played loose with the facts. This story, in turn, was approved by an editor who had a toothache caused by a badly filled tooth. Yet, in spite of this chain of events, it is a stretch to claim that John Doe failed the test because of sloppy dentistry. Common sense must guide your thinking in this sort of analysis; but because infinity lies behind even the reason why someone purchases a popsicle, it is safer, as a rule of thumb, to stay with immediate cause and ignore the remote.

Don't Be Dogmatic about Cause   Institutions of learning rigorously demand that students analyze cause with caution and prudence. The reasoning is simple enough: Colleges and universities are quite determined to impress on their students the complexity of the world. It is advisable, therefore, that you be modest in your claims of causation. You can easily temper a dogmatic statement by interjecting qualifiers into your claims. Instead of writing:

> Violence in America is *caused* by violent television programs.

you could more prudently write:

> Violence in America is *influenced* by television programs.

If a student had written the following paragraph, it would no doubt have drawn the instructor's criticism:

> This brings me to the major cause of unhappiness, which is that most people in America act not on impulse but on some principle, and that principles upon which people act are usually based upon a false psychology and a false ethic. There is a general theory as to what makes for happiness and this theory is false. Life is conceived as a competitive struggle in which felicity consists in getting ahead of your neighbor. The joys which are not competitive are forgotten.

Yet this paragraph is from a Bertrand Russell article, "The Unhappy American Way," which readers have read with much sagacious head-nodding. Bertrand Russell was a Nobel laureate, a mathematician, and a noted philosopher when he wrote this. No doubt it is unfair, but his obvious accomplishments gain for him a temporary suspension of the rules against dogmatizing. Students, however, are not readily granted such license. We advise that, for the time being, anyway, you generalize about cause prudently.

Use Common Sense in Asserting Cause Most writers do not rigidly follow the principles of causal analysis except when they argue a technical question that must be explained according to the rules of logic. The following passage is an example of the free use of the principles of causal analysis:

> The association of love with adultery in much of medieval love poetry has two causes. The first lies in the organization of feudal society. Marriages, being matters of economic or social interest, had nothing whatever to do with erotic love. When a marriage alliance no longer suited the interests of the lord, he got rid of his lady with as much dispatch as he got rid of a horse. Consequently, a lady who might be nothing more than a commodious piece of property to her husband could be passionately desired by her vassal. The second cause lies in the attitude of the medieval Christian church, where the desire for erotic, romantic love was considered wicked and a result of Adam's sin in the Garden of Eden. The general impression left on the medieval mind by the church's official teachers was that all erotic pleasure was wicked. And this impression, in addition to the nature of feudal marriage, produced in the courtly poets the perverse desire to emphasize the very passion they were told to resist.

The student who wrote this paragraph does not demonstrate cause according to precise rules, but rather shows the commonsense result of her research into why medieval poetry emphasized adulterous love.

Warming Up to Write a Causal Analysis

Remember that causes look backward to the source of an event, whereas effects look forward to consequences. Here are some warm-up exercises that will help you focus on cause and effect.

1. List at least three causes for each of the following situations:
   a. Teenage smoking
   b. Recent increase in obesity
   c. Deadlock between executives and strong labor unions
   d. Children's feelings of guilt during a divorce
   e. Grownups not knowing how to use a computer
2. List at least three effects that result from the following situations:
   a. Loss of a parent while one is still young
   b. Having one's car stolen
   c. The fear of further terrorist attacks in the United States and other countries
   d. Listening to classical music
   e. Discovering a rat infestation in one's cellar

3. Write a thesis for each of the answers you gave to Exercise 1. Then pick the thesis that you think would lead to the best essay.

4. Write a thesis for each of the answers you gave to Exercise 2. Then pick the thesis that you think would lead to the best essay.

EXAMPLES

A Peaceful Woman Explains Why She Carries a Gun

LINDA M. HASSELSTROM

Rhetorical Thumbnail

Purpose: to justify why the author, a peace-loving woman, carries a gun

Audience: general reader, but especially women who feel vulnerable living alone

Language: standard English

Strategy: projects a reasonable persona while relating tense incidents from which gun ownership has rescued her

Linda M. Hasselstrom (b. 1943) is a writer and teacher who grew up in rural South Dakota. Her works include *Roadkill* (1984), a collection of her poetry, and *Land Circle* (1991), a collection of her essays.

Living alone on an isolated ranch may seem romantic to some who love nature or solitude, but it can be perilous to an unarmed woman. Embedded within the story line is the issue of who, if anyone, should have legal access to a gun.

• • •

1   I am a peace-loving woman. But several events in the past 10 years have convinced me I'm safer when I carry a pistol. This was a personal decision, but because handgun possession is a controversial subject, perhaps my reasoning will interest others.

2   I live in western South Dakota on a ranch 25 miles from the nearest town: for several years I spent winters alone here. As a free-lance writer, I travel alone a lot—more than 100,000 miles by car in the last four years. With women freer than ever before to travel alone, the odds of our encountering trouble seem to have risen. Distances are great, roads are deserted, and the terrain is often too exposed to offer hiding places.

3   A woman who travels alone is advised, usually by men, to protect herself by avoiding bars and other "dangerous situations," by approaching her car like an Indian scout, by locking doors and windows. But these precautions aren't always enough. I spent years following them and still found myself in dangerous situations. I began to resent the idea that just because I am female, I have to be extra careful.

4   A few years ago, with another woman, I camped for several weeks in the West. We discussed self-defense, but neither of us had taken a course in it. She was against firearms, and local police told us Mace was illegal. So we armed ourselves with spray cans of deodorant tucked into our sleeping bags. We never used our improvised Mace because we were lucky enough to camp beside people who came to our aid when men harassed us. But on one occasion we visited a national park where our assigned space was less than 15 feet from other campers. When we returned from a walk, we found our closest neighbors were two young men. As we gathered our cooking gear, they drank beer and loudly discussed what they would do to us after dark. Nearby campers, even families, ignored them: rangers strolled past, unconcerned. When we asked the rangers pointblank if they would protect us, one of them patted my shoulder and said, "Don't worry girls. They're just kidding." At dusk we drove out of the park and hid our camp in the woods a few miles away. The illegal spot was lovely, but our enjoyment of that park was ruined. I returned from the trip determined to reconsider the options available for protecting myself.

5   At that time, I lived alone on the ranch and taught night classes in town. Along a city street I often traveled, a woman had a flat tire, called for help on her CB radio, and got a rapist who left her beaten. She was afraid to call for help again and stayed in her car until morning. For that reason, as well as because CBs work best along line-of-sight, which wouldn't help much in the rolling hills where I live, I ruled out a CB.

6   As I drove home one night, a car followed me. It passed me on a narrow bridge while a passenger flashed a blinding spotlight in my face. I braked sharply. The car stopped, angled across the bridge, and four men jumped out. I realized the locked doors were useless if they broke the windows of my pickup. I started forward, hoping to knock their car aside so I could pass. Just then another car appeared, and the men hastily got back in their car. They continued to follow me, passing and repassing. I dared not go home because no one else was there. I passed no lighted houses. Finally they pulled over to the roadside, and I decided to use their tactic: fear. Speeding, the pickup horn blaring, I swerved as close to them as I dared as I roared past. It worked: they turned off the highway. But I was frightened and angry. Even in my vehicle I was too vulnerable.

7   Other incidents occurred over the years. One day I glanced out at a field below my house and saw a man with a shotgun walking toward a pond full of ducks. I drove down and explained that the land was posted. I politely asked him to leave. He stared at me, and the muzzle of the shotgun began to rise. In a moment of utter clarity I realized that I was alone on the ranch, and that he could shoot me and simply drive away. The moment passed: the man left.

8   One night, I returned home from teaching a class to find deep tire ruts in the wet ground of my yard, garbage in the driveway, and a large gas tank empty. A light shone in the house: I couldn't remember leaving it on. I was too embarrassed to drive to a neighboring ranch and wake someone up. An hour of cautious exploration convinced me the house was safe, but once inside, with the doors locked, I was still afraid. I kept thinking of how vulnerable I felt, prowling around my own house in the dark.

9   My first positive step was to take a kung fu class, which teaches evasive or protective action when someone enters your space without permission. I learned to move confidently, scanning for possible attackers. I learned how to assess danger and techniques for avoiding it without combat.

10   I also learned that one must practice several hours every day to be good at kung fu. By that time I had married George: when I practiced with him, I learned how close you must be to your attacker to use martial arts, and decided a 120-pound woman dare not let a six-foot, 220-pound attacker get that close unless she is very, very good at self-defense. I have since read articles by several women who were extremely well trained in the martial arts, but were raped and beaten anyway.

11   I thought back over the times in my life when I had been attacked or threatened and tried to be realistic about my own behavior, searching for anything that had allowed me to become a victim. Overall, I was convinced that I had not been at fault. I don't believe myself to be either paranoid or a risk-taker, but I wanted more protection.

12   With some reluctance I decided to try carrying a pistol. George had always carried one, despite his size and his training in martial arts. I practiced shooting until I was sure I could hit an attacker who moved close enough to endanger me. Then I bought a license from the county sheriff, making it legal for me to carry the gun concealed.

13   But I was not yet ready to defend myself. George taught me that the most important preparation was mental: convincing myself I could actually shoot a person. Few of us wish to hurt or kill another human being. But there is no point in having a gun; in fact, gun possession might increase your danger unless you know you can use it. I got in the habit of rehearsing, as I drove or walked, the precise conditions that would be required before I would shoot someone.

14   People who have not grown up with the idea that they are capable of protecting themselves—in other words, most women—might have to work hard to convince themselves of their ability, and of the necessity. Handgun ownership need not turn us into gunslingers, but it can be part of believing in, and relying on, ourselves for protection.

15   To be useful, a pistol has to be available. In my car, it's within instant reach. When I enter a deserted rest stop at night, it's in my purse, with my hand on the grip. When I walk from a dark parking lot into a motel, it's in my hand, under a coat. At home, it's on the headboard. In short, I take it with me almost everywhere I go alone.

16   Just carrying a pistol is not protection; avoidance is still the best approach to trouble. Subconsciously watching for signs of danger, I believe I've become

more alert. Handgun use, not unlike driving, becomes instinctive. Each time I've drawn my gun—I have never fired it at another human being—I've simply found it in my hand.

17   I was driving the half-mile to the highway mailbox one day when I saw a vehicle parked about midway down the road. Several men were standing in the ditch, relieving themselves. I have no objection to emergency urination, but I noticed they'd dumped several dozen beer cans in the road. Besides being ugly, cans can slash a cow's feet or stomach.

18   The men noticed me before they finished and made quite a performance out of zipping their trousers while walking toward me. All four of them gathered around my small foreign car, and one of them demanded what the hell I wanted.

18   "This is private land. I'd appreciate it if you'd pick up the beer cans."

20   "What beer cans?" said the belligerent one, putting both hands on the car door and leaning in my window. His face was inches from mine, and the beer fumes were strong. The others laughed. One tried the passenger door, locked; another put his foot on the hood and rocked the car. They circled, lightly thumping the roof, discussing my good fortune in meeting them and the benefits they were likely to bestow upon me. I felt very small and very trapped and they knew it.

21   "The ones you just threw out," I said politely.

22   "I don't see no beer cans. Why don't you get out here and show them to me, honey?" said the belligerent one, reaching for the handle inside my door.

23   "Right over there," I said, still being polite. "—there, and over there." I pointed with the pistol, which I'd slipped under my thigh. Within one minute the cans and the men were back in the car and headed down the road.

24   I believe this incident illustrates several important principles. The men were trespassing and knew it: their judgment may have been impaired by alcohol. Their response to the polite request of a woman alone was to use their size, numbers, and sex to inspire fear. The pistol was a response in the same language. Politeness didn't work: I couldn't match them in size or number. Out of the car, I'd have been more vulnerable. The pistol just changed the balance of power. It worked again recently when I was driving in a desolate part of Wyoming. A man played cat-and-mouse with me for 30 miles, ultimately trying to run me off the road. When his car passed mine with only two inches to spare, I showed him my pistol, and he disappeared.

25   When I got my pistol, I told my husband, revising the old Colt slogan, "God made men *and women*, but Sam Colt made them equal." Recently I have seen a gunmaker's ad with a similar sentiment. Perhaps this is an idea whose time has come, though the pacifist inside me will be saddened if the only way women can achieve equality is by carrying weapons.

26   We must treat a firearm's power with caution. "Power tends to corrupt, and absolute power corrupts absolutely," as a man (Lord Acton) once said. A pistol is not the only way to avoid being raped or murdered in today's world, but, intelligently wielded, it can shift the balance of power and provide a measure of safety.

● Vocabulary

improvised (4)	assess (9)	reluctance (12)
angled (6)	martial (10)	urination (17)
evasive (9)	paranoid (11)	trespassing (24)

● The Facts

1. How many times did the author actually use her pistol? In each case, what was the pistol's role? How do you feel about her use of a pistol?

2. Why is a woman who travels alone believed to be more vulnerable than a man who does the same? What other precautions besides avoiding bars, approaching her car carefully, and locking doors and windows can a woman traveling alone observe?

3. Why did the author have to go to town at night when she lived on a ranch out in the country? Could she have avoided the regular trips to town?

4. According to the author, why is the martial art of kung fu not an ideal deterrent to anyone with a criminal intent?

5. Why did the author buy a license from the county sheriff after she had practiced shooting and had purchased a gun? Do you think all gun owners should follow her example? Why or why not?

● The Strategies

1. Where is the thesis of the essay most clearly stated? Evaluate the merits of this particular position.

2. What rhetorical strategy does the author use to convince her readers that she did the appropriate thing by purchasing a pistol that she could easily hide from view? Were you convinced by her argument? Why or why not?

3. At what point in the essay does the author seem to be in the most danger? Explain your answer.

4. Which paragraphs of the essay constitute a fascinating drama with an exciting climax and a happy ending? What technique makes this passage so absorbing?

5. What is the purpose of the famous quotation by Lord Acton? In what context is this quotation usually used? Why does it fit the context of this essay as well?

● The Issues

1. How do you interpret the author's revision of the old Colt slogan, "God made men, but Sam Colt made them equal"? What do you think of the notion that carrying a gun is one way for women to achieve equality with men? Why does the author express sorrow at the thought that carrying weapons might be the only way women can achieve equality with men?

2. Do you believe the author was paranoid or an excessive risk taker? Did she in any way contribute to her own insecurity while living at the ranch? What, if anything, could she have done to better protect herself?

3. What are some useful ways in which women in general can learn to protect themselves when they are forced to be in an environment where they could be victims of criminals?

4. What is the most frightening encounter you have ever had? If you were a victim, how did you handle the situation?

5. What is your opinion of gun control? Support your opinion with logic and strong evidence.

● Suggestions for Writing

1. Write an essay in which you propose an effective solution for the crime of rape.

2. Using Hasselstrom's essay as a counterpoint, write an essay entitled *The Dangers of Carrying a Gun.*

Coming into Language

JIMMY SANTIAGO BACA

Rhetorical Thumbnail

Purpose: to depict the effect discovering literature had on the writer

Audience: educated reader

Language: standard English mixed up with some slang

Strategy: tells exactly what happened without blinking

Jimmy Santiago Baca (b. 1952) is one of several admired "Barrio" writers, so called because they emerged from the poverty and squalor of barrio life to portray their background with power and vividness. An ex-convict, Baca taught himself to read and write while in prison, eventually winning the American Book Award of 1988. Part Chicano and part Indian, he was abandoned by his parents when he was 2 and lived with his grandparents. By the time he was 5, his mother had been murdered by her second husband, his father had died of alcoholism, and Baca had lived in an orphanage, from which he escaped to survive on the streets. In time, he landed in prison on a drug charge (which he claimed was false) and was sent to maximum security and later placed in isolation because of his combative nature. Through an outside mentor, his writings gradually received international attention, and he was released from prison. Despite his tragic life, his writing—mostly poetry—dwells on rebirth rather than bitterness. Among his works are *Immigrants in Our Own Land* (1979), *Swords of Darkness* (1981), *What's Happening?* (1982), *Martin and Meditations on the South Valley* (1987), *Black Mesa Poems* (1989), and *Working in the Dark: Reflections of a Poet of the Barrio* (1990), from which the following essay is taken.

What follows is a horrifying yet heartwarming autobiographical account of the author's personal journey toward poetic birth. We are allowed an intimate glance into a man's scarred and demon-filled soul and we witness how he faces the horrors of prison life, including solitary confinement and the mental ward. We see and feel his torment and hellish despair, but we also watch his slow development as a writer as he is purged of crime and violence through an appreciation of the beauty of language.

• • •

1   On weekend graveyard shifts at St. Joseph's Hospital I worked the emergency room, mopping up pools of blood and carting plastic bags stuffed with arms, legs, and hands to the outdoor incinerator. I enjoyed the quiet, away from the screams of shotgunned, knifed, and mangled kids writhing on gurneys outside the operating rooms. Ambulance sirens shrieked and squad car lights reddened the cool nights, flashing against the hospital walls: gray–red, gray–red. On slow nights I would lock the door of the administration office, search the reference library for a book on female anatomy and, with my feet propped on the desk, leaf through the illustrations, smoking my cigarette. I was seventeen.

2   One night my eye was caught by a familiar-looking word on the spine of a book. The title was *450 Years of Chicano History in Pictures.* On the cover were black-and-white photos: Padre Hidalgo exhorting Mexican peasants to revolt against the Spanish dictators; Anglo vigilantes hanging two Mexicans from a tree; a young Mexican woman with rifle and ammunition belts crisscrossing her breast; César Chávez and field workers marching for fair wages; Chicano railroad workers laying creosote ties; Chicanas laboring at machines in textile factories; Chicanas picketing and hoisting boycott signs.

3   From the time I was seven, teachers had been punishing me for not knowing my lessons by making me stick my nose in a circle chalked on the blackboard. Ashamed of not understanding and fearful of asking questions, I dropped out of school in the ninth grade. At seventeen I still didn't know how to read, but those pictures confirmed my identity. I stole the book that night, stashing it for safety under the slop-sink until I got off work. Back at my boardinghouse, I showed the book to friends. All of us were amazed; this book told us we were alive. We, too, had defended ourselves with our fists against hostile Anglos, gasping for breath in fights with the policemen who outnumbered us. The book reflected back to us our struggle in a way that made us proud.

4   Most of my life I felt like a target in the cross hairs of a hunter's rifle. When strangers and outsiders questioned me I felt the hang-rope tighten around my neck and the trapdoor creak beneath my feet. There was nothing so humiliating as being unable to express myself, and my inarticulateness increased my sense of jeopardy, of being endangered. I felt intimidated and vulnerable, ridiculed and scorned. Behind a mask of humility, I seethed with mute rebellion.

5   Before I was eighteen, I was arrested on suspicion of murder after refusing to explain a deep cut on my forearm. With shocking speed I found myself handcuffed to a chain gang of inmates and bused to a holding facility to await trial. There I met men, prisoners, who read aloud to each other the works of Neruda, Paz, Sabines, Nemerov, and Hemingway. Never had I felt such freedom as in

that dormitory. Listening to the words of these writers, I felt that invisible threat from without lessen—my sense of teetering on a rotting plank over swamp water where famished alligators clapped their horny snouts for my blood. While I listened to the words of the poets, the alligators slumbered powerless in their lairs. Their language was the magic that could liberate me from myself, transform me into another person, transport me to other places far away.

6   And when they closed the books, these Chicanos, and went into their own Chicano language, they made barrio life come alive for me in the fullness of its vitality. I began to learn my own language, the bilingual words and phrases explaining to me my place in the universe. Every day I felt like the paper boy taking delivery of the latest news of the day.

7   Months later I was released, as I had suspected I would be. I had been guilty of nothing but shattering the windshield of my girlfriend's car in a fit of rage.

8   Two years passed. I was twenty now, and behind bars again. The federal marshals had failed to provide convincing evidence to extradite me to Arizona on a drug charge, but still I was being held. They had ninety days to prove I was guilty. The only evidence against me was that my girlfriend had been at the scene of the crime with my driver's license in her purse. They had to come up with something else. But there was nothing else. Eventually they negotiated a deal with the actual drug dealer, who took the stand against me. When the judge hit me with a million-dollar bail, I emptied my pockets on his booking desk: twenty-six cents.

9   One night in my third month in the county jail, I was mopping the floor in front of the booking desk. Some detectives had kneed an old drunk and hand-cuffed him to the booking bars. His shrill screams raked my nerves like a hack-saw on bone, the desperate protest of his dignity against their inhumanity. But the detectives just laughed as he tried to rise and kicked him to his knees. When they went to the bathroom to pee and the desk attendant walked to the file cabinet to pull the arrest record, I shot my arm through the bars, grabbed one of the attendant's university textbooks, and tucked it in my overalls. It was the only way I had of protesting.

10   It was late when I returned to my cell. Under my blanket I switched on a pen flashlight and opened the thick book at random, scanning the pages. I could hear the jailer making his rounds on the other tiers. The jangle of his keys and the sharp click of his boot heels intensified my solitude. Slowly I enunciated the words . . . p-o-n-d, ri-pple. It scared me that I had been reduced to this to find comfort. I always had thought reading a waste of time, that nothing could be gained by it. Only by action, by moving out into the world and confronting and challenging the obstacles, could one learn anything worth knowing.

11   Even as I tried to convince myself that I was merely curious, I became so absorbed in how the sounds created music in me and happiness, I forgot where I was. Memories began to quiver in me, glowing with a strange but familiar intimacy in which I found refuge. For a while, a deep sadness overcame me, as if I had chanced on a long-lost friend and mourned the years of separation. But soon the heartache of having missed so much of life, that had numbed me

since I was a child, gave way, as if a grave illness lifted itself from me and I was cured, innocently believing in the beauty of life again. I stumblingly repeated the author's name as I fell asleep, saying it over and over in the dark: Words-worth, Words-worth.

12   Before long my sister came to visit me, and I joked about taking her to a place called Kubla Khan and getting her a blind date with this *vato* named Coleridge who lived on the seacoast and was *malias* on morphine. When I asked her to make a trip into enemy territory to buy me a grammar book, she said she couldn't. Bookstores intimidated her, because she, too, could neither read nor write.

13   Days later, with a stub pencil I whittled sharp with my teeth, I propped a Red Chief notebook on my knees and wrote my first words. From that moment, a hunger for poetry possessed me.

14   Until then, I had felt as if I had been born into a raging ocean where I swam relentlessly, flailing my arms in hope of rescue, of reaching a shoreline I never sighted. Never solid ground beneath me, never a resting place. I had lived with only the desperate hope to stay afloat; that and nothing more.

15   But when at last I wrote my first words on the page, I felt an island rising beneath my feet like the back of a whale. As more and more words emerged, I could finally rest: I had a place to stand for the first time in my life. The island grew, with each page, into a continent inhabited by people I knew and mapped with the life I lived.

16   I wrote about it all—about people I had loved or hated, about the brutalities and ecstasies of my life. And, for the first time, the child in me who had witnessed and endured unspeakable terrors cried out not just in impotent despair, but with the power of language. Suddenly, through language, through writing, my grief and my joy could be shared with anyone who would listen. And I could do this all alone; I could do it anywhere. I was no longer a captive of demons eating away at me, no longer a victim of other people's mockery and loathing, that had made me clench my fist white with rage and grit my teeth to silence. Words now pleaded back with the bleak lucidity of hurt. They were wrong, those others, and now I could say it.

17   Through language I was free. I could respond, escape, indulge; embrace or reject earth or the cosmos. I was launched on an endless journey without boundaries or rules, in which I could salvage the floating fragments of my past, or be born anew in the spontaneous ignition of understanding some heretofore concealed aspect of myself. Each word steamed with the hot lava juices of my primordial making, and I crawled out of stanzas dripping with birth-blood, reborn and freed from the chaos of my life. The child in the dark room of my heart, that had never been able to find or reach the light switch, flicked it on now; and I found in the room a stranger, myself, who had waited so many years to speak again. My words struck in me lightning crackles of elation and thunderhead storms of grief.

18   When I had been in the county jail longer than anyone else, I was made a trustee. One morning, after a fist fight, I went to the unlocked and unoccupied office used for lawyer-client meetings, to think. The bare white room with its

fluorescent tube lighting seemed to expose and illuminate my dark and worthless life. And yet, for the first time, I had something to lose—my chance to read, to write; a way to live with dignity and meaning, that had opened for me when I stole that scuffed, second-hand book about the Romantic poets. In prison, the abscess had been lanced.

19   "I will never do any work in this prison system as long as I am not allowed to get my G.E.D." That's what I told the reclassification panel. The captain flicked off the tape recorder. He looked at me hard and said, "You'll never walk outta here alive. Oh, you'll work, put a copper penny on that, you'll work."

20   After that interview I was confined to deadlock maximum security in a subterranean dungeon, with ground-level chicken-wired windows painted gray. Twenty-three hours a day I was in that cell. I kept sane by borrowing books from the other cons on the tier. Then, just before Christmas, I received a letter from Harry, a charity house Samaritan who doled out hot soup to the homeless in Phoenix. He had picked my name from a list of cons who had no one to write to them. I wrote back asking for a grammar book, and a week later received one of Mary Baker Eddy's treatises on salvation and redemption, with Spanish and English on opposing pages. Pacing my cell all day and most of each night, I grappled with grammar until I was able to write a long true-romance confession for a con to send to his pen pal. He paid me with a pack of smokes. Soon I had a thriving barter business, exchanging my poems and letters for novels, commissary pencils, and writing tablets.

21   One day I tore two flaps from the cardboard box that held all my belongings and punctured holes along the edge of each flap and along the border of a ream of state-issue paper. After I had aligned them to form a spine, I threaded the holes with a shoestring, and sketched on the cover a hummingbird fluttering above a rose. This was my first journal.

22   Whole afternoons I wrote, unconscious of passing time or whether it was day or night. Sunbursts exploded from the lead tip of my pencil, words that grafted me into awareness of who I was; peeled back to a burning core of bleak terror, an embryo floating in the image of water, I cracked out of the shell wide-eyed and insane. Trees grew out of the palms of my hands, the threatening otherness of life dissolved, and I became one with the air and sky, the dirt and the iron and concrete. There was no longer any distinction between the other and I. Language made bridges of fire between me and everything I saw. I entered into the blade of grass, the basketball, the con's eye and child's soul.

23   At night I flew. I conversed with floating heads in my cell, and visited strange houses where lonely women brewed tea and rocked in wicker rocking chairs listening to sad Joni Mitchell songs.

24   Before long I was frayed like a rope carrying too much weight, that suddenly snaps. I quit talking. Bars, walls, steel bunk and floor bristled with millions of poem-making sparks. My face was no longer familiar to me. The only reality was the swirling cornucopia of images in my mind, the voices in the air. Mid-air a cactus blossom would appear, a snake-flame in blinding dance around it, stunning me like a guard's fist striking my neck from behind.

25   The prison administrators tried several tactics to get me to work. For six months, after the next monthly prison board review, they sent cons to my cell to hassle me. When the guard would open my cell door to let one of them in, I'd leap out and fight him—and get sent to thirty-day isolation. I did a lot of isolation time. But I honed my image-making talents in that sensory-deprived solitude. Finally they moved me to death row, and after that to "nut-run," the tier that housed the mentally disturbed.

26   As the months passed, I became more and more sluggish. My eyelids were heavy, I could no longer write or read. I slept all the time.

27   One day a guard took me out to the exercise field. For the first time in years I felt grass and earth under my feet. It was spring. The sun warmed my face as I sat on the bleachers watching the cons box and run, hit the handball, lift weights. Some of them stopped to ask how I was, but I found it impossible to utter a syllable. My tongue would not move, saliva drooled from the corners of my mouth. I had been so heavily medicated I could not summon the slightest gesture. Yet inside me a small voice cried out, I am fine! I am hurt now but I will come back! I am fine!

28   Back in my cell, for weeks I refused to eat. Styrofoam cups of urine and hot water were hurled at me. Other things happened. There were beatings, shock therapy, intimidation.

29   Later, I regained some clarity of mind. But there was a place in my heart where I had died. My life had compressed itself into an unbearable dread of be-ing. The strain had been too much. I had stepped over that line where a human being has lost more than he can bear, where the pain is too intense, and he knows he is changed forever. I was now capable of killing, coldly and without feeling. I was empty, as I have never, before or since, known emptiness. I had no connection to this life.

30   But then, the encroaching darkness that began to envelop me forced me to re-form and give birth to myself again in the chaos. I withdrew even deeper into the world of language, cleaving the diamonds of verbs and nouns, plung-ing into the brilliant light of poetry's regenerative mystery. Words gave off rings of white energy, radar signals from powers beyond me that infused me with truth. I believed what I wrote, because I wrote what was true. My words did not come from books or textual formulas, but from a deep faith in the voice of my heart.

31   I had been steeped in self-loathing and rejected by everyone and every-thing—society, family, cons, God and demons. But now I had become as the burning ember floating in darkness that descends on a dry leaf and sets flame to forests. The word was the ember and the forest was my life.

32   I was born a poet one noon, gazing at weeds and creosoted grass at the base of a telephone pole outside my grilled cell window. The words I wrote then sailed me out of myself, and I was transported and metamorphosed into the im-ages they made. From the dirty brown blades of grass came bolts of electrical light that jolted loose my old self; through the top of my head that self was re-leased and reshaped in the clump of scrawny grass. Through language I became the grass, speaking its language and feeling its green feelings and black root

sensations. Earth was my mother and I bathed in sunshine. Minuscule speckles of sunlight passed through my green skin and metabolized in my blood.

33   Writing bridged my divided life of prisoner and free man. I wrote of the emotional butchery of prisons, and of my acute gratitude for poetry. Where my blind doubt and spontaneous trust in life met, I discovered empathy and compassion. The power to express myself was a welcome storm rasping at tendril roots, flooding my soul's cracked dirt. Writing was water that cleansed the wound and fed the parched root of my heart.

34   I wrote to sublimate my rage, from a place where all hope is gone, from a madness of having been damaged too much, from a silence of killing rage. I wrote to avenge the betrayals of a lifetime, to purge the bitterness of injustice. I wrote with a deep groan of doom in my blood, bewildered and dumbstruck; from an indestructible love of life, to affirm breath and laughter and the abiding innocence of things. I wrote the way I wept, and danced, and made love.

Reprinted with permission from Jimmy Santiago Baca.

● Vocabulary

incinerator (1)	enunciated (10)	treatises (20)
inarticulateness (4)	primordial (17)	regenerative (30)
lairs (5)	subterranean (20)	creosoted (32)
extradite (8)	Samaritan (20)	metamorphosed (32)

● The Facts

1. Why did the author drop out of school in the ninth grade?
2. What reason does the author offer for his having been sent to prison on a murder charge?
3. Who are Wordsworth and Coleridge? How do they relate to the author?
4. What was the "island" on which the author finally could rest while he was in jail? (See paragraph 15.)
5. When a prison guard finally took the author out to the exercise field, why couldn't he talk or even make the slightest gesture?

● The Strategies

1. Who is the voice in this essay? What kind of person is revealed? How do you feel about him? What do you think are his reasons for writing the essay?
2. The author's experience is rendered in separate steps that could be called "the process of regeneration." What are the steps?
3. Where in this essay does the author reveal his poetic talent? Find specific examples of poetic utterances.
4. How does the author indicate the passage of time?
5. What do you think the author meant when he made the following statement: "Most of my life I felt like a target in the cross hairs of a hunter's rifle"? Explain this statement in your own words.

● The Issues

1. Which aspect of the author's artistic journey do you consider the climax of his experience as related in this essay? In other words, at which point does he recognize the possibilities inherent in language? Give reasons for your choice.

2. How can you explain the author's grasp of English grammar despite the fact that he was a school dropout?

3. How would you characterize the essence of Baca's life before he became a writer? How was it possible for him to become a writer?

4. What is your opinion of the punishment meted out by the author's teachers from the time he was 7 years old? What typical results does this kind of pedagogy produce?

5. Do you consider it a good idea to encourage prison inmates to develop their talents while in prison? Why or why not? If you believe the idea to have merit, what process would you suggest for assessing and promoting the prisoners' talents? If you believe the idea has no merit, indicate why.

● Suggestions for Writing

1. Language reached Baca in a way nothing else had. Write an essay that answers these questions: "Can every criminal be ëreached' on some level?" "Is there a good person inside even the most violent and apparently unrepentant criminal?"

2. Write an essay either attacking or defending our prison system in the way it helps inmates to improve themselves intellectually.

Bricklayer's Boy

ALFRED LUBRANO

Rhetorical Thumbnail

Purpose: to define and explore how a boy and his father were affected by the intrusion of class in their relationship

Audience: educated reader

Language: standard English with a journalistic slant

Strategy: is perfectly honest in describing how a son and his father became alienated from each other because of their respective jobs

Alfred Lubrano is a journalist on the staff of the *Philadelphia Inquirer.* He has written articles for numerous magazines, such as *Gentleman's Quarterly (GQ),* and he is a regular commentator on public radio. His book *Limbo: Blue-Collar Roots, White-Collar Dreams* (2003) identifies and describes an overlooked and little-understood cultural problem—the internal conflict of individuals raised in blue-collar homes but who work in white-collar jobs.

Imagine the possible gulf between a blue-collar father and a white-collar son. Not only is there a stark difference in what they do and earn, there are also unstated differences in the respect they are given and the way the world expects them to behave. Lubrano raises issues about class in America that many people find uncomfortable.

• • •

1   My father and I were college buddies back in the mid 1970s. While I was in class at Columbia, struggling with the esoterica du jour, he was on a bricklayer's scaffold not far up the street, working on a campus building.

2   Sometimes we'd hook up on the subway going home, he with his tools, I with my books. We didn't chat much about what went on during the day. My father wasn't interested in Dante, I wasn't up on arches. We'd share a *New York Post* and talk about the Mets.

3   My dad has built lots of places in New York City he can't get into: colleges, condos, office towers. He makes his living on the outside. Once the walls are up, a place takes on a different feel for him, as if he's not welcome anymore. It doesn't bother him, though. For my father, earning the dough that paid for my entrée into a fancy, bricked-in institution was satisfaction enough, a vicarious access.

4   We didn't know it then, but those days were the start of a branching off, a redefining of what it means to be a workingman in our family. Related by blood, we're separated by class, my father and I. Being the white-collar son of a blue-collar man means being the hinge on the door between two ways of life.

5   It's not so smooth jumping from Italian old-world style to U.S. yuppie in a single generation. Despite the myth of mobility in America, the true rule, experts say, is rags to rags, riches to riches. According to Bucknell University economist and author Charles Sackrey, maybe 10 percent climb from the working to the professional class. My father has had a tough time accepting my decision to become a mere newspaper reporter, a field that pays just a little more than construction does. He wonders why I haven't cashed in on that multi-brick education and taken on some lawyer-lucrative job. After bricklaying for thirty years, my father promised himself I'd never pile bricks and blocks into walls for a living. He figured an education—genielike and benevolent—would somehow rocket me into the consecrated trajectory of the upwardly mobile, and load some serious loot into my pockets. What he didn't count on was his eldest son breaking blue-collar rule No. 1: Make as much money as you can, to pay for as good a life as you can get.

6   He'd tell me about it when I was nineteen, my collar already fading to white. I was the college boy who handed him the wrong wrench on help-around-the-house Saturdays. "You better make a lot of money," my blue-collar handy dad wryly warned me as we huddled in front of a disassembled dishwasher I had neither the inclination nor the aptitude to fix. "You're gonna need to hire someone to hammer a nail into a wall for you."

7   In 1980, after college and graduate school, I was offered my first job, on a now-dead daily paper in Columbus, Ohio. I broke the news in the kitchen, where all the family business is discussed. My mother wept as if it were Vietnam. My father had a few questions: "Ohio? Where the hell is Ohio?"

8   I said it's somewhere west of New York City, that it was like Pennsylvania, only more so. I told him I wanted to write, and these were the only people who'd take me.

9   "Why can't you get a good job that pays something, like in advertising in the city, and write on the side?"

10   "Advertising is lying," I said, smug and sanctimonious, ever the unctuous undergraduate. "I wanna tell the truth."

11   "The truth?" the old man exploded, his face reddening as it does when he's up twenty stories in high wind. "What's truth?" I said it's real life, and writing about it would make me happy. "You're happy with your family," my father said, spilling blue-collar rule No. 2. "That's what makes you happy. After that, it all comes down to dollars and cents. What gives you comfort besides your family? Money, only money."

12   During the two weeks before I moved, he reminded me that newspaper journalism is a dying field, and I could do better. Then he pressed advertising again, though neither of us knew anything about it, except that you could work in Manhattan, the borough with the water-beading high gloss, the island polished clean by money. I couldn't explain myself, so I packed, unpopular and confused. No longer was I the good son who studied hard and fumbled endearingly with tools. I was hacking people off.

13   One night, though, my father brought home some heavy tape and that clear, plastic bubble stuff you pack your mother's second-string dishes in. "You probably couldn't do this right," my father said to me before he sealed the boxes and helped me take them to UPS. "This is what he wants," my father told my mother the day I left for Columbus in my grandfather's eleven-year-old gray Cadillac. "What are you gonna do?" After I said my good-byes, my father took me aside and pressed five $100 bills into my hands. "It's okay," he said over my weak protests. "Don't tell your mother."

14   When I broke the news about what the paper was paying me, my father suggested I get a part-time job to augment the income. "Maybe you could drive a cab." Once, after I was chewed out by the city editor for something trivial, I made the mistake of telling my father during a visit home. "They pay you nothin', and they push you around too much in that business," he told me, the rage building. "Next time, you gotta grab the guy by the throat and tell him he's a big jerk."

15   "Dad, I can't talk to the boss like that."

16   "Tell him. You get results that way. Never take any shit." A few years before, a guy didn't like the retaining wall my father and his partner had built. They tore it down and did it again, but the guy still bitched. My father's partner shoved the guy into the freshly laid bricks. "Pay me off," my father said, and he and his partner took the money and walked. Blue-collar guys have no patience

for office politics and corporate bile-swallowing. Just pay me off and I'm gone. Eventually, I moved on to a job in Cleveland, on a paper my father has heard of. I think he looks on it as a sign of progress, because he hasn't mentioned advertising for a while.

17   When he was my age, my father was already dug in with a trade, a wife, two sons and a house in a neighborhood in Brooklyn not far from where he was born. His workaday, family-centered life has been very much in step with his immigrant father's. I sublet what the real-estate people call a junior one-bedroom in a dormlike condo in a Cleveland suburb. Unmarried and unconnected in an insouciant, perpetual-student kind of way, I rent movies during the week and feed single women in restaurants on Saturday nights. My dad asks me about my dates, but he goes crazy over the word "woman." "A girl," he corrects. "You went out with a girl. Don't say ëwoman.' It sounds like you're takin' out your grandmother."

18   I've often believed blue-collaring is the more genuine of lives, in greater proximity to primordial manhood. My father is provider and protector, concerned only with the basics: food and home, love and progeny. He's also a generation closer to the heritage—a warmer spot nearer the fire that forged and defined us. Does heat dissipate and light fade further from the source? I live for my career, and frequently feel lost and codeless, devoid of the blue-collar rules my father grew up with. With no baby-boomer groomer to show me the way, I've been choreographing my own tentative shuffle across the wax-shined dance floor on the edge of the Great Middle Class, a different rhythm in a whole new ballroom.

19   I'm sure it's tough on my father, too, because I don't know much about bricklaying, either, except that it's hell on the body, a daily sacrifice. I idealized my dad as a kind of dawn-rising priest of labor, engaged in holy ritual. Up at five every day, my father has made a religion of responsibility. My younger brother, a Wall Street white-collar guy with the sense to make a decent salary, says he always felt safe when he heard Dad stir before him, as if Pop were taming the day for us. My father, fifty-five years old, but expected to put out as if he were three decades stronger, slips on machine-washable vestments of khaki cotton without waking my mother. He goes into the kitchen and turns on the radio to catch the temperature. Bricklayers have an occupational need to know the weather. And because I am my father's son, I can recite the five-day forecast at any given moment.

20   My father isn't crazy about this life. He wanted to be a singer and actor when he was young, but that was frivolous doodling to his Italian family, who expected money to be coming in, stoking the stove that kept hearth fires ablaze. Dreams simply were not energy-efficient. My dad learned a trade, as he was supposed to, and settled into a life of pre-scripted routing. He says he can't find the black-and-white publicity glossies he once had made.

21   Although I see my dad infrequently, my brother, who lives at home, is with the old man every day. Chris has a lot more blue-collar in him than I do, despite his management-level career; for a short time, he wanted to be a construction

worker, but my parents persuaded him to go to Columbia. Once in a while he'll bag a lunch and, in a nice wool suit, meet my father at a construction site and share sandwiches of egg salad and semolina bread.

22   It was Chris who helped my dad most when my father tried to change his life several months ago. My dad wanted a civil-service bricklayer foreman's job that wouldn't be so physically demanding. There was a written test that included essay questions about construction work. My father hadn't done anything like it in forty years. Why the hell they needed bricklayers to write essays I have no idea, but my father sweated it out. Every morning before sunrise, Chris would be ironing a shirt, bleary-eyed, and my father would sit at the kitchen table and read aloud his practice essays on how to wash down a wall, or how to build a tricky corner. Chris would suggest words and approaches.

23   It was so hard for my dad. He had to take a Stanley Kaplan-like prep course in a junior high school three nights a week after work for six weeks. At class time, the outside men would come in, twenty-five construction workers squeezing themselves into little desks. Tough blue-collar guys armed with No. 2 pencils leaning over and scratching out their practice essays, cement in their hair, tar on their pants, their work boots too big and clumsy to fit under the desks.

24   "Is this what finals felt like?" my father would ask me on the phone when I pitched in to help long-distance. "Were you always this nervous?" I told him yes. I told him writing's always difficult. He thanked Chris and me for the coaching, for putting him through school this time. My father thinks he did okay, but he's still awaiting the test results. In the meantime, he takes life the blue-collar way, one brick at a time.

25   When we see each other these days, my father still asks how the money is. Sometimes he reads my stories; usually he likes them, although he recently criticized one piece as being a bit sentimental: "Too schmaltzy," he said. Some psychologists say that the blue-white-collar gap between fathers and sons leads to alienation, but I tend to agree with Dr. Al Baraff, a clinical psychologist and director of the Men-Center in Washington, D.C. "The core of the relationship is based on emotional and hereditary traits," Baraff says. "Class [distinctions] just get added on. If it's a healthful relationship from when you're a kid, there's a respect back and forth that'll continue."

26   Nice of the doctor to explain, but I suppose I already knew that. Whatever is between my father and me, whatever keeps us talking and keeps us close, has nothing to do with work and economic class.

27   During one of my visits to Brooklyn not long ago, he and I were in the car, on our way to buy toiletries, one of my father's weekly routines. "You know, you're not as successful as you could be," he began, blue-collar blunt as usual. "You paid your dues in school. You deserve better restaurants, better clothes." Here we go, I thought, the same old stuff. I'm sure every family has five or six similar big issues that are replayed like well-worn videotapes. I wanted to fast-forward this thing when we stopped at a red light.

28   Just then my father turned to me, solemn and intense. His knees were aching and his back muscles were throbbing in clockable intervals that registered in his eyes. It was the end of a week of lifting fifty-pound blocks. "I envy you," he said quietly. "For a man to do something he likes and get paid for it—that's fantastic." He smiled at me before the light changed, and we drove on. To thank him for the understanding, I sprang for the deodorant and shampoo. For once, my father let me pay.

"Bricklayer's Boy" by Alfred Lubrano appeared in GQ MAGAZINE, 1989. Reprinted with permission from the author.

● Vocabulary

esoterica (1)	sanctimonious (10)	primordial (18)
vicarious (3)	unctuous (10)	progeny (18)
lucrative (5)	insouciant (17)	dissipate (18)
consecrated (5)	proximity (18)	choreographing (18)

● The Facts

1. What is the unfair irony about the work accomplished by the author's father?

2. What are the father's two rules about jobs? In what way did the author break these two rules? Do you think the author chose the right path? Explain your answer.

3. How does the father react to the news that his news reporter son was "chewed out" by his city editor? Is the father's reaction justified in your mind? Why or why not?

4. How would you evaluate bricklaying as a trade? What aspects of his father's blue-collar life does the son admire? If you think his admiration is warranted, explain why.

5. Where does the relationship between son and father stand at the end of the essay? What is your forecast for the future? Create some possible scenarios.

● The Strategies

1. This essay leans heavily on the rhetorical strategy of causal analysis. What cause and what effect are analyzed? What did you as a reader learn from this story?

2. One clear difference between the father and the son is language. How would you define this difference? How inevitable is it?

3. In developing the memories of his father, the author resorts to poetic images, such as in paragraph 19, where he describes his father as "a kind of dawn-rising priest of labor, engaged in holy ritual." How does such an image contrast with the reality of being a bricklayer? How can the image and reality be reconciled?

4. How does the essay explain the difference between a trade and a profession? In your opinion, which deserves more respect? Explain your answer.

5. What is the effect of the final paragraph? Express your personal reaction to it.

● The Issues

1. What is the thesis of this essay? State it in your own words as a single sentence.

2. What is your opinion of the view, often cited, that American mobility is a myth and that the true rule is "rags to rags, riches to riches"? Cite an example from your background or from history that denies the myth.

3. What feelings is the author depicting in paragraph 13? Do his feelings seem genuine or just a pose? Are these feelings typical of students leaving home for college?

4. How much does the author's old-style Italian family contribute to the misunderstanding of values between father and son? Would a story about a Chinese family have the same theme? In other words, do cultural factors affect father-son relationships? Explain your answer.

5. What advice would you give a son whose ambition to attend college is discouraged by his father as a waste of time? How can the son fulfill his desire to earn a college degree but still remain close to his father? Try to give specific advice.

● Suggestions for Writing

1. Write an analysis of the destructive effects caused by differences in lifestyle between some college students and their parents. Consider such matters as clothing, entertainment, music, hairstyle, and dating. Consider also the effect of religious or political differences.

2. Tell the story of some important lesson you learned from your father. Like Lubrano, use vivid details to enhance your account.

Why I Went to the Woods

HENRY DAVID THOREAU

Rhetorical Thumbnail

Purpose: to argue for a simple life

Audience: educated reader

Language: standard English

Strategy: makes a highly literary argument for a simpler life

Henry David Thoreau (1817–1862), essayist, lecturer, and moralist, was born in Concord, Massachusetts, and educated at Harvard University. He is regarded as one of the seminal influences on American thought and literature. His most famous work is *Walden* (1854), which grew out of the journal recording his solitary existence in a cabin beside Walden Pond, near Concord. His essay

"Civil Disobedience" (1849) has been enormously influential since it was first published and has affected the actions and thoughts of such men as Mahatma Gandhi and Martin Luther King, Jr.

In this excerpt from Walden, Thoreau explains why he went to the woods to live by himself. Unlike many of the writers in this section, Thoreau writes in a voice rich with metaphors, allusions, and images.

• • •

1   I went to the woods because I wished to live deliberately, to front only the essential facts of life, and see if I could not learn what it had to teach, and not, when I came to die, discover that I had not lived. I did not wish to live what was not life, living is so dear; nor did I wish to practice resignation, unless it was quite necessary. I wanted to live deep and suck out all the marrow of life, to live so sturdily and Spartanlike as to put to rout all that was not life, to cut a broad swath and shave close, to drive life into a corner, and reduce it to its lowest terms, and, if it proved to be mean, why then to get the whole and genuine meanness of it, and publish its meanness to the world; or if it were sublime, to know it by experience, and be able to give a true account of it in my next excursion. For most men, it appears to me, are in a strange uncertainty about it, whether it is of the devil or of God, and have somewhat hastily concluded that it is the chief end of man here to "glorify God and enjoy him forever."

2   Still we live meanly, like ants; though the fable tells us that we were long ago changed into men; like pygmies we fight with cranes; it is error upon error, and clout upon clout, and our best virtue has for its occasion a superfluous and evitable wretchedness. Our life is frittered away by detail. An honest man has hardly need to count more than his ten fingers, or in extreme cases he may add his ten toes, and lump the rest. Simplicity, simplicity, simplicity! I say, let your affairs be as two or three, and not a hundred or a thousand; instead of a million count half a dozen, and keep your accounts on your thumbnail. In the midst of this chopping sea of civilized life, such are the clouds and storms and quick sands and thousand-and-one items to be allowed for, that a man has to live, if he would not founder and go to the bottom and not make his port at all, by dead reckoning, and he must be a great calculator indeed who succeeds. Simplify, simplify. Instead of three meals a day, if it be necessary eat but one; instead of a hundred dishes, five; and reduce other things in proportion. Our life is like a German Confederacy, made up of petty states, with its boundary forever fluctuating, so that even a German cannot tell you how it is bounded at any moment. The nation itself, with all its so-called internal improvements, which, by the way are all external and superficial, is just such an unwieldy and overgrown establishment, cluttered with furniture and tripped up by its own traps, ruined by luxury and heedless expense, by want of calculation and a worthy aim, as the million households in the lands; and the only cure for it, as for them, is in a rigid economy, a stern and more than Spartan simplicity of life and elevation of purpose. It lives too fast. Men think that it is essential that the Nation have

commerce, and export ice, and talk through a telegraph, and ride thirty miles an hour, without a doubt, whether they do or not; but whether we should live like baboons or like men, is a little uncertain. If we do not get our sleepers, and forge rails, and devote days and nights to the work, but go to tinkering upon our lives to improve them, who will build railroads? And if railroads are not built, how shall we get to heaven in season? But if we stay at home and mind our business, who will want railroads? We do not ride on the railroad; it rides upon us. Did you ever think what those sleepers[1] are that underlie the railroad? Each one is a man, an Irishman, or a Yankee man. The rails are laid on them, and they are covered with sand, and the cars run smoothly over them. They are sound sleepers, I assure you. And every few years a new lot is laid down and run over; so that, if some have the pleasure of riding on a rail, others have the misfortune to be ridden upon. And when they run over a man that is walking in his sleep, a supernumerary sleeper in the wrong position, and wake him up, they suddenly stop the cars, and make a hue and cry about it, as if this were an exception. I am glad to know that it takes a gang of men for every five miles to keep the sleepers down and level in their beds as it is, for this is a sign that they may sometimes get up again.

3   Why should we live with such hurry and waste of life? We are determined to be starved before we are hungry. Men say that a stitch in time saves nine, and so they take a thousand stitches to-day to save nine to-morrow. As for work, we haven't any of any consequence. We have the Saint Vitus' dance, and cannot possibly keep our heads still. If I should only give a few pulls at the parish bell-rope, as for a fire, that is, without setting the bell, there is hardly a man on his farm in the outskirts of Concord, notwithstanding that press of engagements which was his excuse so many times this morning, nor a boy, nor a woman, I might almost say, but would forsake all and follow that sound, not mainly to save property from the flames, but, if we will confess the truth, much more to see it burn, since burn it must, and we, be it known, did not set it on fire,—or to see it put out, and have a hand in it, if that is done as handsomely; yes, even if it were the parish church itself. Hardly a man takes a half-hour's nap after dinner, but when he wakes he holds up his head and asks, "What's the news?" as if the rest of mankind had stood his sentinels. Some give directions to be waked every half-hour, doubtless for no other purpose; and then, to pay for it, they tell what they have dreamed. After a night's sleep the news is as indispensable as the breakfast. "Pray tell me anything new that has happened to a man anywhere on this globe,"—and he reads it over his coffee and rolls, that a man has had his eyes gouged out this morning on the Wachito River; never dreaming the while that he lives in the dark unfathomed mammoth cave of this world, and has but the rudiment of an eye himself.

4   For my part, I could easily do without the post-office. I think that there are very few important communications made through it. To speak critically, I never received more than one or two letters in my life—I wrote this some years ago—that were worth the postage. The penny-post is, commonly, an institution

---

[1]Cross ties; Thoreau is playing on the word.—ED

through which you seriously offer a man that penny for his thoughts which is so often safely offered in jest. And I am sure that I never read any memorable news in a newspaper. If we read of one man robbed, or murdered, or killed by accident, or one house burned, or one vessel wrecked, or one steamboat blown up, or one cow run over on the Western Railroad, or one mad dog killed, or one lot of grasshoppers in the winter,—we never need read of another. One is enough. If you are acquainted with the principle, what do you care for a myriad instances and applications? To a philosopher all news, as it is called, is gossip, and they who edit and read it are old women over their tea. Yet not a few are greedy after this gossip. There was such a rush, as I hear, the other day at one of the offices to learn the foreign news by the last arrival, that several large squares of plate glass belonging to the establishment were broken by the pressure,—news which I seriously think a ready wit might write a twelvemonth, or twelve years, beforehand with sufficient accuracy. As for Spain, for instance, if you know how to throw in Don Carlos and the Infanta, and Don Pedro and Seville and Granada, from time to time in the right proportions,—they may have changed the names a little since I saw the papers,—and serve up a bullfight when other entertainments fail, it will be true to the letter, and give us as good an idea of the exact state or ruin of things in Spain as the most succinct and lucid reports under this head in the newspapers: and as for England, almost the last significant scrap of news from that quarter was the revolution of 1649; and if you have learned the history of her crops for an average year, you never need attend to that thing again, unless your speculations are of a merely pecuniary character. If one may judge who rarely looks into the newspapers, nothing new does ever happen in foreign parts, a French revolution not excepted.

5   What news! how much more important to know what that is which was never old! "Kieou-he-yu (great dignitary of the state of Wei) sent a man to Khoung-tseu to know his news. Khoung-tseu caused the messenger to be seated near him, and questioned him in these terms: What is your master doing? The messenger answered with respect: My master desires to diminish the number of his faults, but he cannot come to the end of them. The messenger being gone, the philosopher remarked: What a worthy messenger! What a worthy messenger!" The preacher, instead of vexing the ears of drowsy farmers on their day of rest at the end of the week,—for Sunday is the fit conclusion of an ill-spent week, and not the fresh and brave beginning of a new one,—with this one other draggle-tail of a sermon, should shout with thundering voice, "Pause! Avast! Why so seeming fast, but deadly slow?"

6   Shams and delusions are esteemed for soundless truths, while reality is fabulous. If men would steadily observe realities only, and not allow themselves to be deluded, life, to compare it with such things as we know, would be like a fairy tale and the Arabian Nights' Entertainments. If we respected only what is inevitable and has a right to be, music and poetry would resound along the streets. When we are unhurried and wise, we perceive that only great and worthy things have any permanent and absolute existence, that petty fears and petty pleasures are but the shadow of the reality. This is always exhilarating and sublime. By closing the eyes and slumbering, and consenting to be

deceived by shows, men establish and confirm their daily life of routine and habit everywhere, which still is built on purely illusory foundations. Children, who play life, discern its true law and relations more clearly than men, who fail to live it worthily, but who think that they are wiser by experience, that is, by failure. I have read in a Hindoo book, that "there was a king's son, who, being expelled in infancy from his native city, was brought up by a forester, and, growing up to maturity in that state, imagined himself to belong to the barbarous race with which he lived. One of his father's ministers having discovered him, revealed to him what he was, and the misconception of his character was removed, and he knew himself to be a prince. So soul," continues the Hindoo philosopher, "from the circumstances in which it is placed, mistakes its own character, until the truth is revealed to it by some holy teacher, and then it knows itself to be Brahme." I perceive that we inhabitants of New England live this mean life that we do because our vision does not penetrate the surface of things. We think that that is which appears to be. If a man should walk through this town and see only the reality, where, think you, would the "Mill-dam" go to? If he should give us an account of the realities he beheld there, we should not recognize the place in his description. Look at the meetinghouse, or a court-house, or a jail, or a shop, or a dwelling-house, and say what that thing really is before a true gaze, and they would all go to pieces in your account of them. Men esteem truth remote, in the outskirts of the system, behind the farthest star, before Adam and after the last man. In eternity there is indeed something true and sublime. But all these times and places and occasions are now and here. God himself culminates in the present moment, and will never be more divine in the lapse of all the ages. And we are enabled to apprehend at all what is sublime and noble only by the perpetual instilling and drenching of the reality that surrounds us. The universe constantly and obediently answers to our conceptions; whether we travel fast or slow, the track is laid for us. Let us spend our lives in conceiving then. The poet or the artist never yet had so fair and noble a design but some of his posterity at least could accomplish it.

7   Let us spend one day as deliberately as Nature, and not be thrown off the track by every nutshell and mosquito's wing that falls on the rails. Let us rise early and fast, or breakfast, gently and without perturbation; let company come and let company go, let the bells ring and the children cry,—determined to make a day of it. Why should we knock under and go with the stream? Let us not be upset and overwhelmed in that terrible rapid and whirlpool called a dinner, situated in the meridian shallows. Weather this danger and you are safe, for the rest of the way is down hill. With unrelaxed nerves, with morning vigor, sail by it, looking another way, tied to the mast like Ulysses.[2]

8   If the engine whistles, let it whistle till it is hoarse for its pains. If the bell rings, why should we run? We will consider what kind of music they are

---

[2]tied . . . Ulysses: In Homer's *Odyssey,* Ulysses had himself tied to the mast of his boat so that he could listen, but not respond, to the irresistible songs of the sirens, who were believed to lure ships to their doom.—ED

like. Let us settle ourselves, and work and wedge our feet downward through the mud and slush of opinion, and prejudice, and tradition, and delusion, and appearance, that alluvion which covers the globe, through Paris and London, through New York and Boston and Concord, through Church and State, through poetry and philosophy and religion, till we come to a hard bottom and rocks in place, which we can call reality, and say, This is, and no mistake; and then begin, having a point d'appui,[3] below freshet and frost and fire, a place where you might found a wall or a state, or set a lamp-post safely, or perhaps a gauge, not a Nilometer, but a Realometer, that future ages might know how deep a freshet of shams and appearances had gathered from time to time. If you stand right fronting and face to face to a fact, you will see the sun glimmer on both its surfaces, as if it were a cimeter, and feel its sweet edge dividing you through the heart and marrow, and so you will happily conclude your mortal career. Be it life or death, we crave only reality. If we are really dying, let us hear the rattle in our throats and feel cold in the extremities; if we are alive, let us go about our business. Time is but the stream I go a-fishing in. I drink at it; but while I drink I see the sandy bottom and detect how shallow it is. Its thin current slides away, but eternity remains. I would drink deeper; fish in the sky, whose bottom is pebbly with stars. I cannot count one. I know not the first letter of the alphabet. I have always been regretting that I was not as wise as the day I was born. The intellect is a cleaver; it discerns and rifts its way into the secret of things. I do not wish to be any more busy with my hands than is necessary. My head is hands and feet. I feel all my best faculties concentrated on it. My instinct tells me that my head is an organ for burrowing, as some creatures use their snout and fore paws, and with it I would mine and burrow my way through these hills. I think that the richest vein is somewhere hereabouts; so by the divining-rod and thin rising vapors, I judge; and here I will begin to mine.

Vocabulary

superfluous (2)	succinct (4)	perturbation (7)
evitable (2)	pecuniary (4)	meridian (7)
supernumerary (2)	culminates (6)	alluvion (8)
rudiment (3)	posterity (6)	freshet (8)
myriad (4)		

The Facts

1. Why did Thoreau go to the woods? What, in his opinion, was wrong with the nation?

2. Thoreau writes: "We do not ride on the railroad; it rides upon us." What does he mean?

3. What is Thoreau's definition of "news"? What is his definition of "gossip"? According to Thoreau, how does news differ from gossip?

---

[3]point d'appui: point of stability.—ED

4. What does Thoreau mean when he says that the "universe constantly and obediently answers to our conceptions" (paragraph 6)? How, then, is truth possible?

5. Where, according to Thoreau, is truth to be found? What prevents us from finding it?

● The Strategies

1. Reread the final sentence of paragraph 1. What tone does Thoreau use?

2. Thoreau uses two anecdotes in this excerpt (paragraphs 5 and 6). What do these have in common? What do they indicate about the writer's philosophy?

3. "We have the Saint Vitus' dance, and cannot possibly keep our heads still" (paragraph 3). What figure of speech is this? Can you find other examples of this same figure of speech in the text? What effect do they have on Thoreau's writing?

4. "Our life is like a German Confederacy, made up of petty states, with its boundary forever fluctuating, so that even a German cannot tell you how it is bounded at any moment" (paragraph 2). What figure of speech is this? How does it differ from the example in the preceding question?

5. An allusion is a figure of speech in which some famous historical or literary figure or event is casually mentioned. Can you find an allusion in Thoreau's text? (*Hint:* Examine paragraph 7.) What effect does the allusion have on the writer's style?

● The Issues

1. Reread the essay *Diogenes and Alexander,* on pages 469–473. What views about society do Diogenes and Thoreau share? Do you agree with these views? Why or why not?

2. Thoreau witnessed the creation of the railroad and felt that it was an intrusion on life. In paragraph 2, he states, "We do not ride on the railroad; it rides upon us." What new industrial creation of your time might evoke a similar statement from some social commentator like Thoreau?

3. Do you agree with Thoreau that few important communications reach you through the post office? Why or why not?

4. In paragraph 6, Thoreau follows in Plato's footsteps when he tells us that only great and worthy things have absolute existence, but that petty things are a mere shadow of reality. Imagine yourself to be like Thoreau, living alone out in the woods. What would be essential to your life? What would seem petty? Give examples.

5. What memorable experience, if any, have you had of being alone in nature? How did this experience affect you? What did you learn from it?

Suggestions for Writing

1. Write an essay describing the clutter of petty affairs in your life. Suggest some ways of simplifying your affairs.

2. Pretend that you are Thoreau and that you have just been brought back to life and introduced to twentieth-century America. Write a diary putting down your first impressions.

Term Paper Suggestion

Thoreau was once sent to jail for refusing to pay his taxes. Research this episode and write about it.

The Storm

KATE CHOPIN

Rhetorical Thumbnail

Purpose: argue for a life of sexual freedom

Audience: educated reader

Language: use phonetic rendering of New Orleans Creole

Strategy: pictures a spontaneous sexual affair that hurts and harms no one

---

Kate O'Flaherty Chopin (1851–1904) was an American author of Creole-Irish descent, born in St. Louis. In 1870, she married a Louisiana businessman and lived with him in Natchitoches parish and New Orleans, where she acquired an intimate knowledge of Creole and Cajun life, on which she based most of her best stories. After her husband's death in 1883, she returned with their six children to St. Louis and began to write seriously. Her novel *The Awakening* (1899) caused a furor among readers because of its treatment of feminine sexuality that seemed to ignore the mores of the time. For the next sixty years, Chopin was virtually ignored. Today, her work is praised for its regional flavor and for its remarkable independence of mind and feeling. Among her works are two collections of short stories, *Bayou Folk* (1894) and *A Night in Acadie* (1897).

This story, "The Storm," makes light of an adulterous episode that takes place during a storm. Notice the parallels between the passion of the lovers and the ferocity of the storm as well as the serenity in both human and nature that follows afterwards. As you read this story, ask yourself if it seems to represent a particular feminist ideology toward sexuality.

● ● ●

I

1   The leaves were so still that even Bibi thought it was going to rain. Bobinôt, who was accustomed to converse on terms of perfect equality with his little son, called the child's attention to certain sombre clouds that were rolling with sinister intention from the west, accompanied by a sullen, threatening roar. They were at Friedheimer's store and decided to remain there till the storm had passed. They sat within the door on two empty kegs. Bibi was four years old and looked very wise.

2   "Mama'll be 'fraid, yes," he suggested with blinking eyes.

3   "She'll shut the house. Maybe she got Sylvie helpin' her this evenin'," Bobinôt responded reassuringly.

4   "No; she ent got Sylvie. Sylvie was helpin' her yistiday," piped Bibi.

5   Bobinôt arose and going across to the counter purchased a can of shrimps, of which Calixta was very fond. Then he returned to his perch on the keg and sat stolidly holding the can of shrimps while the storm burst. It shook the wooden store and seemed to be ripping great furrows in the distant field. Bibi laid his little hand on his father's knee and was not afraid.

II

6   Calixta, at home, felt no uneasiness for their safety. She sat at a side window sewing furiously on a sewing machine. She was greatly occupied and did not notice the approaching storm. But she felt very warm and often stopped to mop her face on which the perspiration gathered in beads. She unfastened her white sacque[1] at the throat. It began to grow dark, and suddenly realizing the situation she got up hurriedly and went about closing windows and doors.

7   Out on the small front gallery she had hung Bobinôt's Sunday clothes to air and she hastened out to gather them before the rain fell. As she stepped outside, Alcée Laballière rode in at the gate. She had not seen him very often since her marriage, and never alone. She stood there with Bobinôt's coat in her hands, and the big rain drops began to fall. Alcée rode his horse under the shelter of a side projection where the chickens had huddled and there were plows and a harrow piled up in the corner.

8   "May I come and wait on your gallery till the storm is over, Calixta?" he asked.

9   "Come 'long in, M'sieur Alcée."

10   His voice and her own startled her as if from a trance, and she seized Bobinôt's vest. Alcée, mounting to the porch, grabbed the trousers and snatched Bibi's braided jacket that was about to be carried away by a sudden gust of wind. He expressed an intention to remain outside, but it was soon apparent that he might as well have been out in the open: the water beat in upon the boards in driving sheets, and he went inside, closing the door after him. It was even necessary to put something beneath the door to keep the water out.

11   "My! what a rain! It's good two years since it rain' like that," exclaimed Calixta as she rolled up a piece of bagging and Alcée helped her to thrust it beneath the crack.

---

[1]work dress, house dress.—ED

12   She was a little fuller of figure than five years before when she married; but she had lost nothing of her vivacity. Her blue eyes still retained their melting quality; and her yellow hair, dishevelled by the wind and rain, kinked more stubbornly than ever about her ears and temples.

13   The rain beat upon the low, shingled roof with a force and clatter that threatened to break an entrance and deluge them there. They were in the dining room—the sitting room—the general utility room. Adjoining was her bed room, with Bibi's couch alongside her own. The door stood open, and the room with its white, monumental bed, its closed shutters, looked dim and mysterious.

14   Alcée flung himself into a rocker and Calixta nervously began to gather up from the floor the lengths of a cotton sheet which she had been sewing.

15   "If this keeps up, Dieu sait[2] if the levees goin' to stan' it!" she exclaimed.

16   "What have you got to do with the levees?"

17   "I got enough to do! An' there's Bobinôt with Bibi out in that storm—if he only didn' left Friedheimer's!"

18   "Let us hope, Calixta, that Bobinôt's got sense enough to come in out of a cyclone."

19   She went and stood at the window with a greatly disturbed look on her face. She wiped the frame that was clouded with moisture. It was stiflingly hot. Alcée got up and joined her at the window, looking over her shoulder. The rain was coming down in sheets obscuring the view of far-off cabins and enveloping the distant wood in a gray mist. The playing of the lightning was incessant. A bolt struck a tall chinaberry tree at the edge of the field. It filled all visible space with a blinding glare and the crash seemed to invade the very boards they stood upon.

20   Calixta put her hands to her eyes, and with a cry, staggered backward. Alcée's arm encircled her, and for an instant he drew her close and spasmodically to him.

21   "Bonté!"[3] she cried, releasing herself from his encircling arm and retreating from the window, "the house'll go next! If I only knew w'ere Bibi was!" She would not compose herself; she would not be seated. Alcée clasped her shoulders and looked into her face. The contact of her warm, palpitating body when he had unthinkingly drawn her into his arms, had aroused all the old-time infatuation and desire for her flesh.

22   "Calixta," he said, "don't be frightened. Nothing can happen. The house is too low to be struck, with so many tall trees standing about. There! aren't you going to be quiet? say, aren't you?" He pushed her hair back from her face that was warm and steaming. Her lips were as red and moist as pomegranate seed. Her white neck and a glimpse of her full, firm bosom disturbed him powerfully. As she glanced up at him the fear in her liquid blue eyes had given place to a drowsy gleam that unconsciously betrayed a sensuous desire. He looked down into her eyes and there was nothing for him to do but to gather her lips in a kiss. It reminded him of Assumption.

---

[2]French for "God knows."—ED
[3]French for "goodness."—ED

23   "Do you remember—in Assumption, Calixta?" he asked in a low voice broken by passion. Oh! she remembered; for in Assumption he had kissed her and kissed and kissed her; until his senses would well nigh fail, and to save her he would resort to a desperate flight. If she was not an immaculate dove in those days, she was still inviolate; a passionate creature whose very defenselessness had made her defense, against which his honor forbade him to prevail. Now—well, now—her lips seemed in a manner free to be tasted, as well as her round, white throat and her whiter breasts.

24   They did not heed the crashing torrents, and the roar of the elements made her laugh as she lay in his arms. She was a revelation in that dim, mysterious chamber; as white as the couch she lay upon. Her firm, elastic flesh that was knowing for the first time its birthright, was like a creamy lily that the sun invites to contribute its breath and perfume to the undying life of the world.

25   The generous abundance of her passion, without guile or trickery, was like a white flame which penetrated and found response in depths of his own sensuous nature that had never yet been reached.

26   When he touched her breasts they gave themselves up in quivering ecstasy, inviting his lips. Her mouth was a fountain of delight. And when he possessed her, they seemed to swoon together at the very borderland of life's mystery.

27   He stayed cushioned upon her, breathless, dazed, enervated, with his heart beating like a hammer upon her. With one hand she clasped his head, her lips lightly touching his forehead. The other hand stroked with a soothing rhythm his muscular shoulders.

28   The growl of the thunder was distant and passing away. The rain beat softly upon the shingles, inviting them to drowsiness and sleep. But they dared not yield.

29   The rain was over; and the sun was turning the glistening green world into a palace of gems. Calixta, on the gallery, watched Alcée ride away. He turned and smiled at her with a beaming face; and she lifted her pretty chin in the air and laughed aloud.

III

30   Bobinôt and Bibi, trudging home, stopped without at the cistern to make themselves presentable.

31   "My! Bibi, w'at will yo' mama say! You ought to be ashame'. You oughtn' put on those good pants. Look at 'em! An' that mud on yo' collar! How you got that mud on yo' collar, Bibi? I never saw such a boy!" Bibi was the picture of pathetic resignation. Bobinôt was the embodiment of serious solicitude as he strove to remove from his own person and his son's the signs of their tramp over heavy roads and through wet fields. He scraped the mud off Bibi's bare legs and feet with a stick and carefully removed all traces from his heavy brogans. Then, prepared for the worst—the meeting with an overscrupulous housewife, they entered cautiously at the back door.

32   Calixta was preparing supper. She had set the table and was dripping coffee at the hearth. She sprang up as they came in.

33   "Oh, Bobinôt! You back! My! but I was uneasy. W'ere you been during the rain? An' Bibi? he ain't wet? he ain't hurt?" She had clasped Bibi and was kissing him effusively. Bobinôt's explanations and apologies which he had been composing all along the way, died on his lips as Calixta felt him to see if he were dry, and seemed to express nothing but satisfaction at their safe return.

34   "I brought you some shrimps, Calixta," offered Bobinôt, hauling the can from his ample side pocket and laying it on the table.

35   "Shrimps! Oh, Bobinôt! you too good fo' anything!" and she gave him a smacking kiss on the cheek that resounded. "J'vous réponds,[4] we'll have a feas' to night! umph-umph!"

36   Bobinôt and Bibi began to relax and enjoy themselves, and when the three seated themselves at table they laughed much and so loud that anyone might have heard them as far away as Laballière's.

IV

37   Alcée Laballière wrote to his wife, Clarisse, that night. It was a loving letter, full of tender solicitude. He told her not to hurry back, but if she and the babies liked it at Biloxi, to stay a month longer. He was getting on nicely; and though he missed them, he was willing to bear the separation a while longer—realizing that their health and pleasure were the first things to be considered.

V

38   As for Clarisse, she was charmed upon receiving her husband's letter. She and the babies were doing well. The society was agreeable; many of her old friends and acquaintances were at the bay. And the first free breath since her marriage seemed to restore the pleasant liberty of her maiden days. Devoted as she was to her husband, their intimate conjugal life was something which she was more than willing to forego for a while.

39   So the storm passed and every one was happy.

● Vocabulary

sombre (1)	spasmodically (20)	cistern (30)
projection (7)	palpitating (21)	resignation (31)
harrow (7)	sensuous (22)	embodiment (31)
gallery (8)	immaculate (23)	solicitude (31)
deluge (13)	inviolate (23)	brogans (31)
monumental (13)	revelation (24)	effusively (33)
levees (16)	enervated (27)	conjugal (38)
incessant (19)		

---

[4]French for "I answer you."—ED.

● The Facts

1. What relationship exists between Calixta and Alcée? What do you infer from their past?
2. How does the storm contribute to the love tryst that takes place?
3. What caused the lovers to act so impetuously? Do you consider the cause valid and acceptable?
4. How do the lovers react to their mates after the love affair? Does the reaction seem plausible? Give reasons for your answer.
5. In paragraph 13, what is the significance of describing Calixta's bedroom as "dim and mysterious"? Explain the reference.

● The Strategies

1. What setting forms the backdrop for this story? What does the setting contribute?
2. What is the purpose of the Roman numerals dividing the story?
3. What kind of language does the author resort to in describing the passion of the two lovers? Point to specific examples.
4. What do you think of the title of this story? Is the story really about a storm? Explain your answer.
5. Where does the climax of the story take place? Explain your answer.

● The Issues

1. In your opinion, did the lovers handle the situation as morally as possible, given that they yielded to the temptation of the situation? If you disagree with their reactions, what should they have done?
2. The narrator tells us that Calixta's flesh "was knowing for the first time its birthright" (paragraph 24). What is meant by this statement? What similar comment is made about Alcée?
3. As indicated in the biographical headnote about Kate Chopin, the author's work was criticized for its "feminine sexuality." What do you think readers of her day thought about a story like "The Storm"? What is your view of Chopin's approach to sexuality as revealed in this story?
4. What kind of conjugal life do the couples described seem to share? What, if anything, is good about it?
5. What is the theme (main point) of the story? Express it in one sentence.

● Suggestions for Writing

1. Write an analysis of what happens when people lose control of their passions. Use examples to prove your point.
2. Write an essay offering your views about the causes of the widespread marital infidelity so common in our society today.

Design

ROBERT FROST

Robert Frost (1874–1963) was a lecturer, poet, and teacher. When he was 19 and working in a mill in Lawrence, Massachusetts, the *Independent* accepted and published "My Butterfly, an Elegy"—the poem that began Frost's career as one of America's great poets. Rugged New England farm life was the inspiration for many of his poems.

Like much of Frost's poetry, "Design" appears on the surface to be simple and plain, but a closer study reveals subtleties and depth. The speaker observes nature with a philosophic mind.

● ● ●

I found a dimpled spider, fat and white,
On a white heal-all, holding up a moth
Like a white piece of rigid satin cloth—
Assorted characters of death and blight
Mixed ready to begin the morning right,
Like the ingredients of a witches' broth—
A snow-drop spider, a flower like a froth,
And dead wings carried like a paper kite.

What had that flower to do with being white,
The wayside blue and innocent heal-all?
What brought the kindred spider to that height,
Then steered the white moth thither in the night?
What but design of darkness to appall?—
If design govern in a thing so small.

● Vocabulary

characters (4)   kindred (11)   appall (13)
blight (4)

● The Facts

1. The heal-all is a wildflower—usually blue or violet, but occasionally white—commonly found blooming along footpaths and roads. The name derives from the belief that this flower possessed healing qualities. As described in the first stanza, what do the spider, the heal-all, and the moth have in common?

2. Three questions are asked in the second stanza. How can these be condensed into one question? What answer is implied in the poem?

3. The "argument from design" was a well-known eighteenth-century argument for the existence of God. It proposed a broad view of history and the cosmos,

which revealed that some divine intelligence fashioned and then sustained existence. What twist does Frost give this argument?

4. Is the poem probing a sufficient, a necessary, or a contributory cause?

● The Strategies

1. What five examples of figurative language are used in the first stanza? Tell what effect each has.

2. In the second stanza, why does the poet use the adjective *kindred* in connection with the spider?

3. In the second stanza, what synonyms does the poet use to repeat the concept of design?

● The Issues

1. The question of whether our destinies are controlled by some higher intelligence concerns many thinking people. Why do you suppose human beings wrestle so often with this question?

2. How would you argue against Frost's theme? Use an example from nature to take the opposite viewpoint.

3. Judging from your experience, which of your intimate acquaintances are better able to cope with life—those with a strong belief in a God who controls human destiny, or those with the belief that existence is simply experience and that no God controls any aspect of the universe?

● Suggestions for Writing

1. Using an example from nature, write a brief essay showing how an incontrovertible harmony seems to regulate the activities of the world as a whole.

2. Write a brief essay in which you explain what in the poem causes you to like or dislike it.

ISSUE FOR CRITICAL THINKING AND DEBATE: THE STATUS OF WOMEN

Women in the United States are better off today than ever before. We can make that statement boldly on the evidence of statistics and from our own experience. In 1900, women could not vote, could not own property, and derived their legal status from whether they had husbands. Women, who did not win the right to vote until 1920, now vote in larger numbers than men. In a recent poll conducted by *USA Today,* 81 percent of the sampled women predicted the election of a woman president within the next twenty-five years.

Today, women work in as varied a range of occupations as men. Some are senators, CEOs, TV anchors, stockbrokers, and university presidents. Some have made financial fortunes while their husbands took care of the children. As Hillary Clinton proved in 2008, a woman can run for President of the United States with the support of eighty million voters. Only a few decades ago, when a woman's place was thought to be in the home and her job to care for her husband and family, such achievements would have been unthinkable.

In spite of these victories, the war for equality between men and women in the workplace and in society at large continues. One lingering bone of contention is the disparity between the salaries of men and the salaries of women for the same work. The 2005 U.S. census continued to reveal a great disparity between male

"It seems to me that ordination of women might brighten the place up a bit."

and female income among all races, with females earning an average of $28,000 contrasted with males earning $40,000. The 2000 census showed that for 1999, the median income of men was $35,922, in contrast to $26,292 for women. This inequality has persisted since record keeping began.

Anyone with even a scant knowledge of history would have to admit that the significant gains made in the status of woman were mainly won by the feminist movement. It is therefore a paradox that feminism has lost its appeal to many women of the upcoming generation. Daughters who today enjoy the benefits won by yesterday's militants regard feminism as their mother's movement, not theirs. In an ironic way, that attitude is a triumph for feminism, whose central aim has always been the empowerment of the individual to do, say, and think as he or she feels.

The change in the status of women, however, comes at a price. Women now face a world that no longer regards them as delicate and needing protection. If the *Titanic* disaster had happened in our era, the cry heard on deck would not be the chivalrous one that rang out in 1912 aboard the doomed ship, "Women and children first!" It would more likely be, "All persons for themselves!" For some conservative women, this has been too high a price to pay. For many other women, it's a bargain. The cartoon on page 593 addresses with gentle humor the problem of ordaining women to the priesthood or ministry. In a different tone, the cartoon on page 598 depicts an angry queen demanding power equal to that of the king.

Our essayists take predictably different tacks on the subject. Kate Gubata declares firmly that women should continue to work toward achieving total equality with men in every nook of life—from politics to economics. Rebecca E. Rubins believes that women have already achieved equality with men, making the feminist movement obsolete. The student essay, written by Paula Rewa of East Tennessee State University, argues that the word *woman* now mainly functions as an adjective—as in *woman* lawyer—but should be reclaimed as a noun. *Woman*—used as a noun—remains a woman, no matter how she dresses or what she does.

The New Feminism

KATE GUBATA

Kate Gubata writes a column for the Brown University student newspaper.

1   Jane is pro-choice. Jane loves chocolate. She backs candidates who strive to change the wages inequity that exists in this country. She likes boys who wear Abercrombie & Fitch. She wishes she looked a little more like Jennifer Lopez. She believes in human rights and equality for men and women.

2   Is she a feminist? Possibly. Is she a young woman in America? Without a doubt.

3   At a time when the term *feminism* often suggests the impression of the radical, almost militantly liberal rival of the male-dominated status quo, many young women are hesitant, if not outright opposed, to associate themselves with this exclusive group.

4   After all, that is feminism, right? Feminism defines my mother's generation. It represents at one extreme the assemblage of hairy-legged, men-hating conspirators to overthrow professional men's sports; on the softer side, feminists gather together to hold hands and listen to Helen Reddy. Why on earth would a young woman today deny herself the title of feminist?

5   One of the greatest barriers opposing the feminist movement today is the lack of interest of young women due to their misconceptions of the feminists' aims. Feminism is a progressive movement that seeks to bring about the change that will embed equality for men and women in all aspects of life, from the larger spheres of political, social and economic structure, to the ways in which men and women perceive each other throughout the course of common interaction. Feminism is not an abstract, ideological construct. It represents not an exclusive body of individual motivations but a movement that reaches everyone who believes in human rights.

6   How can we bridge the gap between feminist rhetoric and everyday life? How can feminists illuminate the aspects of the movement that affect the ways in which we on this campus live our lives?

7   Feminism is a movement of action. The goal of feminism today is to stimulate men and women to transform the aims of equality into reality. This is not an ideological mission. The causes of feminism are about action; as Brown students we can all become active participants. Choice, pay inequity, the recent passage of mifeprestone—"the abortion drug"—by the FDA, and the legal battles over homosexual marriage are some of the issues pertinent to feminists today. The various on-campus events intend to educate the Brown community as a whole and to promote a sense of unity among students who have an interest in these types of issues. The movements both on campus and in the local community to promote change are the mechanisms by which young people can use their ideas and energies to fuel united action.

8   Feminism does not have a feminist-checklist. Feminists embody the characteristics of free thought, openness to ideas, and the desire to pool resources with all people willing to work for equality. Feminism represents an inclusive, not exclusive assembly. The key to encompassing a wide range of interest is the resolution of the conflict many people sense between the abstract concepts of feminism and their personal emotions and ideas. A young woman who does not identify with her impression of the radical image of a feminist must not deny herself the opportunity to share her opinions and ideas with a group that is in fact more than willing to listen and learn. There is no dress code or behavior code for a feminist; the term *feminist* characterizes anyone who aspires to achieve equality and who believes in the power of the united fight for human rights.

9   What's the solution for Jane and others seeking the balance between the persona of the radical feminist ideology and feminism's role in the modern

lifestyle? Get involved. Keep an eye out for campus and community events that pertain to important feminist issues and goals. If a group interests you, dive in and make yourself heard; but leave your preconceptions at the door. Be prepared to find a diverse group of people who may share nothing but the will to achieve equality. Move over Helen Reddy; a new group of activists is ready to roar.

Kate Gubata, "The New Feminism," Brown Daily Herald, Oct. 26, 2000. Reprinted by permission of the author.

● Vocabulary

feminism (title)	ideological (5)	preconceptions (9)
militantly (3)	illuminate (6)	
assemblage (4)	persona (9)	

● The Facts

1. At the time of writing this essay, where is the author? What does her location bring to the essay?

2. According to the author, what is the goal of feminism today? What other goal(s), if any, do you consider important for women to pursue?

3. In paragraph 5 and again in paragraph 7, the author insists that feminism must not be an "ideological" movement. Why does the author shun ideology? What is more important to her than ideology? Do you agree with her? Explain your position.

4. According to the author, what issues should be of major concern to feminists today? Respond to each issue by evaluating its importance within the total social fabric of your environment.

5. What does the author mean when she writes that "Feminism does not have a feminist-checklist"? Do you think the movement *should* have a checklist? Explain your answer.

● The Strategies

1. In what paragraph does the author define feminism by stating what it is not? Is this a good technique to use when defining a term?

2. In what paragraph does the author associate feminism with a past generation? What effect does the association have? Offer your personal response.

3. What is the purpose of the question posed at the start of paragraph 9? Is the question ever answered? If yes, what is the answer; if no, why is no answer given?

4. Who is the "Jane" referred to at the beginning and at the end of the essay? Explain her function in the essay.

5. What is the author's tone in the final sentence of the essay? Explain why you think the author uses this tone to end her essay.

● The Issues

1. What does the term *feminist* conjure up in your mind? Do you react favorably or unfavorably to this term? Explain your answer.

2. In your view, what have women gained so far and what have they lost as a result of the feminist movement? Whom does the movement favor most? Whom does it favor least?

3. Do you agree with the author that one of the greatest barriers opposing the feminist movement today is the lack of interest on the part of young women? If the author is right, what do you think are the reasons for today's apathy on the part of young women? If you think the author is wrong, give reasons why you think so.

4. If a woman prefers to stay home and be a housewife once she is married, does she still have an obligation to get involved in feminist issues? Or should she focus more on matters of family values? Give reasons for your stand.

5. If you are a man, do you want your wife to have her own career, or would you prefer her to be a full-time homemaker? Explain your choice. If you are a woman, would you prefer to have a career or to be a full-time homemaker? Explain your choice. Consider also the possibility of combining a career with homemaking.

● Suggestions for Writing

1. Write an essay in which you define the term *feminism* as you understand it. Clarify your definition by using illustration, comparison/contrast, causal analysis, or any other rhetorical mode that helps you answer the question, "What is feminism?"

2. Re-read the question at the beginning of paragraph 9 to make sure you understand what is meant by feminist ideology and by the feminist's role in today's lifestyle. Then write an essay answering the question. Be sure to formulate a thesis that you support with appropriate evidence. For instance, you might write "The true feminist will support human rights while remaining nonmasculine in her manner." Or, if you really detest feminism, your thesis might read: "The feminist movement has done nothing but destroy family values, which are the foundation of a strong nation."

"Come on, now. It's my turn to hold the sceptre."

The Farce of Feminism

REBECCA E. RUBINS

Rebecca E. Rubins wrote this column for the *Harvard Crimson*.

1   Strolling through the Freshman Week Activities Fair, I was accosted by an energetic young woman from a women's issues group who asked me fiercely, "Do you support women?"—As I took my time answering, my interrogator laughingly remarked, "It'd be really sad if you didn't."

2   Although at the time I shrugged my shoulders and signed my name to the mailing list, the feeling of having been grouped into a general category against my will simply because of my sex haunted me. For the question being asked was not "Do I support women?"—which I certainly do—but "Do I support feminism?"—which I emphatically do not. Feminism is an outdated, misdirected ideology that perpetuates the very ills it condemns and harms women much more than it helps them.

3   Perhaps there was once a time when feminism was warranted, when its name was not synonymous with self-pitying whining but with active efforts

toward positive change. In the early 20th century, when women still had not gained the right to vote, the suffragettes showed remarkable dedication in bringing the system's inherent inequality to the forefront of public awareness.

4   In recent years, however, feminism in America has found itself hopelessly bereaved of a cause for which to fight. Women in this country are now on an entirely equal footing with men and are sometimes even given preferential treatment. Instead of focusing on areas of the world where women are truly being oppressed, where they cannot show their ankles on the street without fear of being shot and killed, feminists of today spend their time creating support groups for one another and debating the relative disadvantages faced by girls in science and math classrooms. Feminism keeps women from naturally asserting their equality to men in an environment which is now conducive to such equality.

5   Feminism also creates a double standard for men and women, thus promoting the societal ills it supposedly opposes. Feminists laud women-only discussion groups, dance teams and drama clubs, but when men try to create or maintain similar men-only groups, they are accused of discrimination. The feminist movement operates on the principle that past wrongs done to women can be remedied by preferential treatment now—that two wrongs will make a right. This reverse discrimination is not only unethical but also belies their alleged opposition to judgment or exclusion based on gender alone.

6   Finally, and most importantly, feminism accomplishes the exact opposite of what it intends. Instead of raising women's social status, it burdens them with a weighty sense of victimization that neither empowers them nor motivates men to view them as equals. Girls are not born feeling inferior to boys. Rather, it is their exposure to feminism that causes them to develop a slavelike mentality.

7   This is particularly evident in school, where the "feminist aspect" of every subject is now played up, thereby bringing social activism into the classroom where it only detracts from the learning process. English teachers ask students to apply feminist criticism to books with no semblance of a feminist outlook. History textbooks try to compensate for the fact that women were in the kitchen for most of recorded time by highlighting the life of one particular female or another regardless of how little she matters to history. Other programs, such as Take Your Daughter to Work Day, also impress upon young girls the notion that they are inherently inferior citizens who need rewritten history books and politically correct semi-holidays to raise them up to the level of their male peers who, incidentally, seem to do just fine without such support. In this way, the movement marginalizes women by reminding them constantly of their former subservient status and instilling in them at a very young age a dependency on the support of other women and on feminism to "survive" in a horribly male-dominated world.

8   If feminists were to take a step back and view the current situation of women in the country objectively, they might realize that women no longer need interest groups, support networks, activism and doctored curriculae—that they, in fact, are better off without feminists' supposed help. But that objective

view would leave feminists without a viable *raison d'etre*, and so they continue to ignore, for example, the possibility that the average female college student walking through an activities fair might support women but not support feminism, that she might instead consider feminism a threat to her own sense of self and empowerment.

9   Maybe feminists should start asking themselves the question, "Do we support women?" And maybe it's time someone said, "It's sad, but you don't."

● Vocabulary

farce (title)	preferential (4)	victimization (6)
accosted (1)	conducive (4)	marginalizes (7)
interrogator (1)	discrimination (5)	subservient (7)
ideology (2)	belies (5)	curriculae (curriculum) (8)
inherent (3)	alleged (5)	empowerment (8)

● The Facts

1. Why does the author entitle her essay "The Farce of Feminism"? Look up the word *farce* to make sure you understand its full meaning. In what way is the feminist movement a farce in the eyes of the author?

2. The author states that feminism promotes the very ills it condemns and thus harms women (see paragraph 2). To what ills is the author referring? Can you name other ills promoted by feminism?

3. According to the author, why do women no longer need feminism? Do you agree with her reasoning? Why or why not?

4. What is the difference between *feminine* and *feminism*? How important is it for the reader to be aware of the distinction?

5. What activities of feminism does the author particularly discredit? How do you feel about these activities? How important are they today? Evaluate them critically.

● The Strategies

1. What grabber does the author use to capture the reader's attention? How effective is it in keeping you interested in what follows?

2. Where does the author place her thesis? Why is it not in the opening or final paragraph? Is the placement effective? Explain your opinion.

3. How does the author make a transition from the past to the present as it concerns feminism? What is the purpose of such a transition? Where does it take place?

4. Paragraph 5 refers to a "double standard" created by feminism. What example does the author use to illustrate the double standard? In what other areas in politics or society do double standards occur? Provide some examples.

5. Why does the author return to the activities fair at the end of the essay? Is she being redundant or is there a good reason for the repeated reference? Explain your answer.

● The Issues

1. Do you agree that feminism has reached the point at which it perpetuates the very ills it condemns? If you agree, what are some of the ills that feminism perpetuates? Provide examples. If you believe that feminism must continue to fight for women's rights, what are these rights?

2. Do you think that women who have not had the advantage of a higher education and women with advanced degrees hold different attitudes toward feminism?

3. What is *reverse discrimination* as the author uses the term? What are some of the examples of reverse discrimination not mentioned in the essay? How can it be prevented?

4. Do you agree with the author that women today are better off without the help of feminism? What contribution might feminism still make to the cause of women?

5. What would your answer be to the question, "Do you support feminism?" What would your answer be to the question, "Do you support women?"

● Suggestions for Writing

1. Using the Internet as your research source, find out what contributions the suffragettes (see paragraph 3) made to the cause of feminism and write an essay using the information you uncovered.

2. Write an essay in which you contrast the position of Kate Gubata with that of Rebecca Rubins concerning feminism. Be sure to find some clear bases for the contrast. Review the *Road Map to Comparison/Contrast* in Chapter 13, page 456.

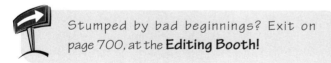

Stumped by bad beginnings? Exit on page 700, at the **Editing Booth!**

Punctuation Workshop
The Exclamation Point (!)

1. **Use the exclamation point after expressions of strong emotion, such as joy, surprise, disbelief, or anger:**

    Hooray! You beat the last record!

    Amazing! The snake is still alive.

    How dark the sky has suddenly become!

    Get out of my sight, you monster!

    "Stop that yelling immediately!" he shouted. (The comma or period that normally follows a direct quotation is omitted when the quotation has an exclamation point.)

2. **Use the exclamation point sparingly. Overuse will diminish its impact. Often a comma will suffice after a mild interjection, and a period will suffice after a mild exclamation or command:**

    Oh, now I see the difference in their attitude.

    How desperately he tried to please his mother.

    Please sit down and buckle your seat belt.

Paula Rewa

East Tennessee State University

"Woman" Is a Noun

From a local playground, a brave voice yells, "Are you a boy or a girl?" A cluster of children grin as they wait for my answer. They think they've caught me. "I'm a girl," I answer with a forced but friendly smile. I picture myself as they must see me . . . my stubble hair, my chunky black glasses and overloaded backpack. In my standard jeans and plain T-shirt, I'm not the collegiate Barbie they expect. I'm a curious blur as I walk past their games—an oddity.

In a restaurant, an older man at the bar asks me, "What are you, a man or a woman?" I wonder, if he thought I was a man, would he have asked? "I am a woman," I answer as he looks me over. I feel his eyes on me as I leave.

In the mirror, I ask myself, "Who am I?" I know the answer. I am a woman.

No matter what advances women have made in present-day society, we are still restricted by cultural expectations. If we choose to pursue a career, we become women in the workplace. If we have a family and a job, we become working mothers. We are women bankers, women lawyers, and women plumbers.

Today, it seems "woman" is used as an adjective. Defined positively, "woman" means feminine in appearance, even while wearing a suit. A woman person exists in a male world while retaining female qualities. Ideally, she is someone's wife. She is never taken for a "man."

Defined negatively, "woman" also means potentially bossy, overzealous, or emotionally driven (. . . the phrase "woman lawyer" makes more sense now, doesn't it?).

The adjective "woman" confers many, if not all, of these qualities. So where does this leave the woman person who does not fit? She is stripped of her womanhood. Her sexual orientation often is questioned.

It may be said that she is trying to be a man. Society pressures her to become the adjectival "woman."

The image of the working woman is simply a modern version of the homemaker dress of the fifties. The codes of womanly appearance dictate what is appropriate. It is acceptable for a woman to have short hair if she wears cosmetics. If she chooses not to wear cosmetics, she should have a naturally pretty face and wear feminine clothing. We may now have access to the world of business, but we are still put in our place as much as ever. Our suit jackets proclaim us as equals, while our skirts hint that we are really just women underneath.

Codes of appearance apply not only in corporate America but also in society in general. The look has changed, but we are still expected to conform. Today, women can wear anything that men wear. In fact, many popular stores carry only clothing that can be worn by both men and women. Yet the expectations persist: when a woman wears it, she must still look "woman."

Our culture must reclaim "woman" as a noun, and recognize that women remain women, regardless of what they wear or what they do. If they are accountants, call them accountants. To say "woman accountant" is unnecessary, and the implications of such a title are not appreciated. If a woman has short hair and prefers suits to skirts, do not assume that she wants to be a man. Instead, consider how secure she must be to feel comfortable without conforming to society's expectations.

Women must learn to cherish themselves without being slaves to femininity. Many women enjoy wearing dresses, and they should be applauded for their own expression of self. But dresses should not be mandatory, and neither should long hair, painted nails, or push-up bras. The true woman is the person inside, not the image she projects.

I have been asked many times if I am a man or a woman. Children ask out of curiosity, men ask with mockery. I answer without hesitation, because I know that "woman" is a noun. I may have very short hair. I may wear cosmetics only occasionally. But I am proud to be a woman, just as I am proud to be myself.

How I Write

When I sit down to write, the most important factor in my productivity is comfort. I do all my writing on a computer, but I don't sit directly in front of the screen, feet flat on the floor, and all that jazz. My high school typing teacher would probably be appalled to see me lounging on my couch with my keyboard on my knees, an extension cord reaching across the living room to my PC. I never have any music playing when I need to concentrate. I used to play my favorite artists as inspiration, but I tended to get carried away. As a result, the flavor of my writing was often influenced by the mood of the music.

I like to do all my writing on a computer, because it is much easier to revise over and over. I tend to revise as I write, and then over again several times as my essay develops. I find that this helps me maintain clarity and stay connected to what I'm writing. I find it frustrating to do first, second, and third drafts, because I feel I should wait for the next official "draft" to change something I don't like. In order to write effectively, it is essential that I give myself permission to change things any time I want. I do save different versions of my paper as it evolves, for reference and in case I decide I like something better the way it was. I also print out my paper several times, in order to make notes for necessary changes.

How I Wrote This Essay

When I get a new assignment or idea, I try to get something on paper immediately. Even if I don't end up using any of it, the writing gets my mind moving in a direction. It also solidifies the images and phrases that fly through my head when I'm excited about a new project.

For this essay, I was given the subject of "Women's Status: Gains or Losses?" I started by breaking down the subject. My first thought was "why not gains *and* losses?" Other questions followed, such as "What is our status?" "How are women perceived?" "What does 'woman' really mean?" I recorded these questions and others at the top of my paper, and kept them there for reference throughout the writing process.

The first time I sat down to work on this essay, I had so many thoughts swimming around in my head that the result was five different introductory paragraphs, all strung together with no connections. Instead of worrying about this, I set the essay aside for a few days and thought about what it was that I truly wanted to say. When I came back to my computer, my thoughts were much clearer, and I was able to mold what I had into a clear idea.

My Writing Tip

Above all, don't get frustrated when you start writing. I have my bouts with writer's block, but I try to keep writing: Write anything that pops into your head. Don't worry about if it's in the right place.

I tend to have three or four good sentences pushing along ahead of my cursor, just waiting for a good place for me to stick them in.

The trick is to keep going. Eventually, you'll hit on an idea, a sentence, or even a combination of words that say just what you want it to say, and the rest will flow from there.

Good luck!

● CHAPTER WRITING ASSIGNMENTS

1. Write a causal analysis for one of the following conditions:
   a. The poor writing habits of today's students
   b. The lack of popular financial support for museums, concerts, and other art forms
   c. The recent growth in prepared meals
   d. The need for prison reform
   e. The worldwide popularity of rock music
   f. The rise in child pornography
   g. The failure of the rapid transit system in most large cities
   h. The need to conserve our beaches
   i. Our tendency to buy throwaway items

2. In a written essay, analyze the causes behind the breakup of a relationship with which you are familiar.

● WRITING ASSIGNMENTS FOR A SPECIFIC AUDIENCE

1. Write a letter to a teacher you once had (but don't send it!) analyzing why you loved or hated his or her class.

2. Write an email to a group of your friends, proposing the formation of a book club that will encourage all of you to read more and better books. The letter should carefully analyze the needs that a book club would fulfill.

● IMAGE GALLERY WRITING ASSIGNMENT

Visit pages IG-23–IG-26 of our image gallery and study all of the images dealing with the status of women. Then choose the image that most appeals to you. Answer the questions and do the writing assignment.

Pointer from a Pro

SCRAP ADVERBS AND ADJECTIVES

Most adverbs and adjectives are not necessary. You will clutter your sentences and annoy the reader if you choose a verb or noun that has a precise meaning and then add an adverb or adjective that carries the same meaning. Don't tell us that the radio "blared loudly" or that someone "clenched his teeth tightly," because "to blare" is to be loud, and there is no other way to clench teeth than "tightly." . . . Most writers sow adjectives almost unconsciously into the soil of their prose to make it more lush and pretty. The sentences become longer and longer as they fill up with "stately elms" and "graceful boughs" and "frisky kittens" and "sleepy lagoons." This is adjective-by-habit, and it's a habit you should stop.

—William Zinsser

If you follow Zinsser's advice, you will be more succinct, which is an additional virtue in writing.

16

Argumentation and Persuasion

What Argumentation and Persuasion Do

Argumentation and persuasion are the fraternal twins of rhetoric. The difference between them is this: An argument appeals strictly by reason and logic; persuasion appeals by both logic and emotion. If you're pleading for more funding for diabetes research and you base your appeal primarily on numbers, you're making an argument. If you supplement the number crunching with testimony from diabetes sufferers who have been horribly affected by the disease, you're being persuasive. The forum in which the argument takes place will determine which tactic you should adopt. A formal paper for a philosophy class should be worded as an argument. An essay or article written for your student newspaper, depending on the topic, should be both logical and persuasive.

Argumentation, unlike the other modes of writing, is a term of rhetorical intent, not of form. It refers to any essay or speech whose aim is to sway or persuade a reader or listener. Because writers resort to many techniques and devices to achieve this aim, the argumentation essay tends to be a mixture of rhetorical forms; that is, you are likely to find the writer defining, describing, narrating, or even dividing during the course of the argument. The tone of the essay can vary from the savage sarcasm of Jonathan Swift's "A Modest Proposal" to the matter-of-fact tone of Gerry Garibaldi's "The Pregnancy Trap." The subject matter can include any topic from the nearly infinite spectrum of issues about which people argue.

When to Use Argumentation and Persuasion

Some people think that all writing is persuasive. Their reasoning is that even if you're describing a scene, what you're really doing is trying to persuade your reader to see through your eyes. If you are comparing two friends, you are hoping to convince your reader that your observations about them are true. Trace elements of the techniques of persuasion are no doubt present in other kinds of writing, but we formally apply the techniques of argumentation and persuasion when we're trying to bring someone around to our opinion or point of view. This may be in a debate or in an essay on a topic that requires you to advocate one side over another.

How to Use Argumentation and Persuasion

What elements are most likely to sway us in an argumentative essay—to make us change our minds and believe a writer's arguments? Research suggests some clues. First, there is our perception of the writer's credentials to hold an opinion on the subject. If we think the writer is competent and qualified on the subject—a medical doctor writing on a medical topic, for example—we are more likely to believe the advocated opinion. If you hold a particular qualification to write on the subject, then mentioning it will probably help. You do not have to blare out your credentials, but you can do it subtly. For example, in his essay on teenage pregnancies, Garibaldi tells us that he is an English teacher in an urban high school and that he became well acquainted with the problem of teenage pregnancies—a revelation that leaves us more likely to accept his views of them. If you are not an expert yourself, quoting an expert can certainly lend weight to your view.

Another element that inclines us to believe an argumentative essay is the quality of its reasoning. If the writer's logic is sound, if the facts and supporting details strike us as reasonable and strong, then we are likely to be swayed by the conclusions. Presenting your facts in all their sharpness while also making the links between the propositions of your argument instantly clear, will make it difficult for anyone to easily dismiss your conclusions.

Finally, arguments are persuasive if they appeal to our self-interests. We are more likely to believe an argument if we think there is something in it for us. This insight explains why arguers huff and puff to portray themselves and their views as if they agreed exactly with our self-interests, even if the correspondence is far-fetched. The underlying appeal of Jonathan Swift's ironic proposal, for instance, is to the self-interests of Irish citizens who Swift thinks would be better off in a unified Ireland free from British exploitation.

If your argument is not reasoned logically, it is unlikely to be effective. And if it is not backed with solid evidence, its claims will most likely arouse disbelief. When the issue at stake is a practical one, these two elements—logical reasoning and solid evidence—are basic requirements for any effective argument.

There are, in addition, some common strategies that writers use to make their arguments persuasive. Being persuasive involves more than being strictly logical; it takes in the whole range of writing skills—conciseness, clarity, and the ability to infuse a prose style with a distinctive personality. To write a persuasive argument, then, you should try to use the following techniques:

1. **Begin your argument at the point of contention.** This means that your initial paragraph should immediately focus on the issue being argued. Consider this opening from an argument by Henry Ford's grandson:

"We have room for but one language here, and that is the English language, for we intend to see that the crucible turns our people out as Americans and not as dwellers in a polyglot boarding house."

—Theodore Roosevelt

In the store windows of Los Angeles, gathering place of the world's aspiring peoples, the signs today ought to read, "English spoken here." Supermarket price tags are often written in Korean, restaurant menus in Chinese, employment-office signs in Spanish. In the new city of dreams, where gold can be earned if not found on the sidewalk, there are laborers and businessmen who have lived five, ten, 20 years in America without learning to speak English. English is not the common denominator for many of these new Americans. Disturbingly, some of them insist it need not be.

—William A. Henry III, *Against a Confusion of Tongues*

As you can see, the writing begins with a quotation from Theodore Roosevelt and a pointed paragraph that makes it immediately clear what he is arguing against: immigrants who refuse to learn English. He wastes no time in pointless preamble or beating around the bush.

Here are two openings from student essays arguing against offshore drilling. One begins with an ominous drift; the other gets immediately to the point.

Unfocused: I oppose offshore drilling for oil. But before I give my reasons for making this statement, I would like to review the various present sources of crude oil in our country. . . .

Focused: I oppose offshore drilling for oil because such a project could, in the name of energy, destroy thousands of square miles of our oceans and add to the already staggering amount of pollution on the earth . . .

Your opening sentence or sentences should underscore your stand as well as your preliminary reasoning.

2. **Draw your evidence from multiple sources.** This is a self-evident observation. If your argument is based on a single book or the testimony of one expert, it will be invariably weaker than if it draws support from many sources. Ideally, the direction and force of your research should lead you to different kinds and sources of evidence. However, student papers are often based on the writer's devotion to a single book or the point of view of one expert. This can be a crippling limitation, especially if your one book or one expert hold views that turn out to be wrong. The antidote for overreliance on a single source of evidence is to find a topic you're truly interested in.

3. **Pace your argument with some obvious movement.** Don't allow your argument to become clogged with a dreary recital of evidence or bogged down

with pointless hairsplitting. We suggest that you imagine the typical reader's reactions to any argumentative essay or speech:

Reader or Listener	*Your Response*
Ho hum!	Wake up the reader with a provocative introduction.
Why bring that up?	State your argument in clear, forceful language.
For instance?	Supply evidence and facts.
So what?	Restate the thesis, say what you expect the reader to do.

Responding to these four imagined reader/listener attitudes will give your argument a discernible movement.

4. **Begin your argument with an assumption that is either grounded in evidence or defensible.** You should not attempt to argue the unarguable or prove the unprovable. While the realm of the arguable is constantly expanding before an onslaught of mysticism and fantasy, many instructors would nevertheless find the following theses entirely unacceptable in an argumentative essay:

> Hell exists as a place of punishment for sinners to atone for wrongdoing committed on earth.
> The Great Depression of the 1930s was caused by a destructive astrological conjunction between the planets Venus and Mars.
> Cats and all manner of feline creatures are despicable, nauseating beasts.
> Arthur Conan Doyle, creator of Sherlock Holmes, was the greatest detective-story writer of all times.

All four propositions are based on personal belief and, therefore, unprovable in a strictly logical sense.

5. **Anticipate the opposition.** For instance, if you are arguing that a controversial cancer drug should be legalized, you must not only marshal evidence to show the effectiveness of the drug, you must also answer the arguments of those opposed to its legalization. You might, for instance, introduce these arguments this way:

> Opponents to the legalization of this drug claim that its use will prevent the cancer patient from using other remedies proven effective against cancer. This claim, however, misses the point.

Then get down to the point that has been missed.

A frequent tactic used in arguments is not only to sum up the opposition's viewpoint but also to point out any inconsistencies in it. Here is an example of this tactic from an argument in favor of using animals in medical research:

> Extremists within the animal-rights movement take the position that animals have rights equal to or greater than those of humans. It follows from this that even if humans might benefit from animal research, the cost to animals is too high. It is ironic that despite this moral position, the same organizations condone—and indeed sponsor—activities that appear to violate the basic rights of animals to live and reproduce. Each year 10,000,000 dogs are destroyed by public pounds, animal shelters and humane societies. Many of these programs are supported and even operated by animal-protectionist groups. Surely there is a strong contradiction when those who profess to believe in animal rights deny animals their right to life. A similar situation exists with regard to programs of pet sterilization, programs that deny animals the right to breed and to bear offspring and are sponsored in many cases by antivivisectionists and animal-rights groups. Evidently, animal-rights advocates sometimes recognize and subscribe to the position that animals do not have the same rights as humans. However, their public posture leaves little room for examining these subtleties or applying similar standards to animal research.
>
> —Frederick A. King, *Animals in Research: The Case for Experimentation*

Moral logic requires us to practice what we preach; if it can be shown that the opposition is more likely to preach than to practice, that is grounds for calling into question the sincerity of its views.

6. **Supplement your reasoning and evidence with an emotional appeal.** This tactic must, however, be used with discretion and caution—as we said, depending on the topic and the forum. Emotional appeal is no substitute for reasoned argument or solid evidence. However, used in supplementary doses, emotional appeal can be highly persuasive in dramatizing an outcome or condition in a way that evidence and facts alone cannot. Here is an example: A speaker is trying to persuade an audience to donate blood for the benefit of hemophiliacs. A hemophiliac himself, he spends the first half of his speech explaining factually what hemophilia is—reciting statistics about its incidence and discussing its symptoms. Then, to dramatize the awfulness of the disease, he resorts to an emotional appeal, using his own experience with the pain of hemophilia:

> Because medical science had not advanced far enough, and fresh blood was not given often enough, my memories of childhood and adolescence are memories of pain and heartbreak. I remember missing school for weeks and months at a stretch—of being very proud because I attended school once for four whole weeks without missing a single day. I remember the three long years when I couldn't even walk because repeated hemorrhages had twisted my ankles and knees to pretzel-like forms. I remember being pulled to school in a wagon while other boys rode their bikes, and being pushed to my table. I remember sitting in the dark empty

classroom by myself during recess while the others went out in the sun to run and play. And I remember the first terrible day at the big high school when I came on crutches and built-up shoes carrying my books in a sack around my neck.

But what I remember most of all is the pain. Medical authorities agree that a hemophilic joint hemorrhage is one of the most excruciating pains known to mankind.

To concentrate a large amount of blood into a small compact area causes a pressure that words can never hope to describe. And how well I remember the endless pounding, squeezing pain. When you seemingly drown in your own perspiration, when your teeth ache from incessant clenching, when your tongue floats in your mouth and bombs explode back of your eyeballs; when darkness and light fuse into one hue of gray; when day becomes night and night becomes day and time stands still—and all that matters is that ugly pain. The scars of pain are not easily erased.

—Ralph Zimmerman, *Mingled Blood*

The appeal is moving and effective and contributes to the persuasiveness of the speaker's plea.

7. **Avoid common logical fallacies.** A logical fallacy occurs when you draw a conclusion that is false or deceptive. Often an argument may seem to be moving in the right direction, but on closer inspection, it has veered off the reasonable course and ends in confusion. Here are the most common logical fallacies to avoid:

Ad hominem **(Latin for "to the man")** Here the writer mounts a personal attack on an individual rather than dealing with the argument under consideration. **Example:** "Senator X's proposal to cut inflation is nonsensical; however, that should not surprise us since the senator flunked economics in college."

Ad populum **(Latin for "to the public")** The writer appeals to feelings, passions, or prejudices shared by large segments of the population. **Example:** "The illegal immigrants crossing our borders will bring in gangs, dope, and vile beliefs or habits that will eventually ruin our country." This logical fallacy overlooks the valuable skills and labor provided by many of the illegal immigrants who have entered our country.

False analogy The writer mistakenly compares two situations that have some characteristics in common, treating them as if they were alike in all respects. **Example:** "Since we have legalized cigarettes, we should legalize marijuana, which does not cause lung cancer the way cigarettes do." The writer overlooks a major difference between the two drugs: Marijuana impairs a person's powers of perception and judgment, whereas cigarettes do not.

Begging the question An argument that "begs the question" is one that moves in circles rather than forward. **Example:** "I am against prostitution because it dehumanizes women by having them sell themselves." The writer is saying that prostitution is wrong because it involves women prostituting themselves.

Ignoring the question (also known as the "red herring") This logical fallacy involves shifting the focus of discussion to points that have nothing to do with the basic argument. **Example:** "We must not re-elect Congressman X because he does not believe in subsidizing our farmers during droughts. Moreover, the congressman wants to get rid of Christmas crèches in the lobbies of all City Halls. Do we really want an atheist to represent us in Congress?" Remember that the original argument was about farm subsidies, not religion.

Either-or reasoning Here the writer sees an issue in black or white, with no shades of gray in between. **Example:** "If the administration gets rid of our Music Appreciation and German classes in order to balance the college budget, we shall soon become a technological school rather than a well-balanced undergraduate college." Many colleges with good reputations have had to cut certain nonrequired courses during temporary budget crises.

Hasty generalization It is human to draw conclusions before adequately sampling a situation. But in writing an argument, it is important that your evidence be sufficient and representative. **Example:** "Embryonic stem cell research offers hope to millions of people suffering from diabetes, Parkinson's, and spinal injuries. In the next election, do not vote for those narrow-minded religious fanatics who oppose embryonic stem cell research." Not everyone who is opposed to stem cell research is a narrow-minded religious fanatic.

Non sequitur **(Latin for "it does not follow")** An argument based on a non sequitur has a faulty premise. **Example:** "All women who have dark skin and wear head scarves hate Americans and support any Jihad that will annihilate us. The counselor of our honor students, Miriam Hussein, has dark skin and always wears a head scarf; therefore, she is to be suspected of disloyalty to the United States." In this example, the major premise ("all women who have dark skin and wear head scarves hate Americans and support any Jihad that will annihilate us") is false; therefore, the conclusion will be false.

All of the logical fallacies mentioned above can crop up when writers do not use solid evidence to support their arguments but instead rely on flimsy hearsay, illogical connections, or improperly tested assumptions to force agreement on their readers.

Warming Up to Write an Argument

1. Write down at least three objections to each of the following propositions:

   a. Women should be drafted into the military.

   b. The United Nations should have its own army.

   c. The euro should now be used in every country of the world.

    d. Every official meeting of Congress should begin with prayer.

    e. "I am not responsible for saving the world."

2. For each of the following areas, list three topics you think you could develop into a persuasive argument:

    a. Something in your personal life you would like to change

    b. A social or political problem that needs solving

    c. An area of education you would like to see improved

3. Sketch out some ideas you would use to support the following quotations:

    a. "Opinions founded on prejudice are always sustained with the greatest violence."

        —Francis Jeffrey

    b. "The most tragic paradox of our time is to be found in the failure of nation-states to recognize the imperatives of internationalism."

        —Chief Justice Earl Warren

    c. "There is no greater lie than a truth misunderstood."

        —William James

    d. "The drive toward complex technical achievement offers a clue to why the U.S. is good at space gadgetry and bad at slum problems."

        —John Kenneth Galbraith

EXAMPLES

Why Don't We Complain?

WILLIAM F. BUCKLEY, JR.

Rhetorical Thumbnail

Purpose: to argue against passivity in the face of outrageously poor service

Audience: educated readers

Language: standard English with a snooty touch

Strategy: a variety of examples embedded in a narration

William F. Buckley, Jr. (1925–2008) was an American editor, writer, and television host. Born into a family of wealth and privilege, he was educated in England, France, the Millbrook School in New York, and Yale University. At the age of 25, he became a literary sensation with the publication of his book, *God and Man at Yale* (1950), a stinging indictment of what later would be called "political correctness." His magazine, the *National Review*, reflected his conservative views about politics and society; his television show, *Firing Line*, in which he debated liberals of the day, made him into an American icon during the Ronald Reagan presidency.

Buckley not only analyzes why we are allegedly not a complaining nation, but also he finds a positive side to griping and being more assertive. Today Buckley's essay—written before the days of blogging, tweeting, and open frustration—probably describes a less complaining America than we observe.

● ● ●

1   It was the very last coach and the only empty seat on the entire train, so there was no turning back. The problem was to breathe. Outside the temperature was below freezing. Inside the railroad car, the temperature must have been about 85 degrees. I took off my overcoat, and a few minutes later my jacket, and noticed that the car was flecked with the white shirts of passengers. I soon found my hand moving to loosen my tie. From one end of the car to the other, as we rattled through Westchester Country, we sweated; but we did not moan.

2   I watched the train conductor appear at the head of the car. "Tickets, all tickets, please!" In a more virile age, I thought, the passengers would seize the conductor and strap him down on a seat over the radiator to share the fate of his patrons. He shuffled down the aisle, picking up tickets, punching commutation cards. *No one addressed a word to him.* He approached my seat, and I drew a deep breath of resolution. "Conductor," I began with a considerable edge to my voice. . . . Instantly the doleful eyes of my seatmate turned tiredly from his newspaper to fix me with a resentful stare: what question could be so important as to justify my sibilant intrusion into his stupor? I was shaken by those eyes. I am incapable of making a discreet fuss, so I mumbled a question about what time were we due in Stamford (I didn't even ask whether it would be before or after dehydration could be expected to set in), got my reply, and went back to my newspaper and to wiping my brow.

3   The conductor had nonchalantly walked down the gauntlet of eighty sweating American freemen, and not one of them had asked him to explain why the passengers in that car had been consigned to suffer. There is nothing to be done when the temperature *outdoors* is 85 degrees, and indoors the air conditioner has broken down; obviously when that happens there is nothing to do, except perhaps curse the day that one was born. But when the temperature outdoors is below freezing, it takes a positive act of will on somebody's part to set the temperature *indoors* at 85. Somewhere a valve was turned too far, a furnace overstoked, a thermostat maladjusted: something that could easily be remedied by turning off the heat and allowing the great outdoors to come indoors. All this is so obvious. What is not obvious is what has happened to the American people.

4   It isn't just the commuters, whom we have come to visualize as a supine breed who have got onto the trick of suspending their sensory faculties twice a day while they submit to the creeping dissolution of the railroad industry. It isn't just they who have given up trying to rectify irrational vexations. It is the American people everywhere.

5   A few weeks ago at a large movie theatre I turned to my wife and said, "The picture is out of focus." "Be quiet," she answered. I obeyed. But a few minutes later I raised the point again, with mounting impatience. "It will be all right in a minute," she said apprehensively. (She would rather lose her eyesight than be around when I make one of my infrequent scenes.) I waited. It was *just* out of focus—not glaringly out, but out. My vision is 20-20, and I assume that is the vision, adjusted, of most people in the movie house. So, after hectoring my wife throughout the first reel, I finally prevailed upon her to admit that it *was* off, and very annoying. We then settled down, coming to rest on the presumption that: a) someone connected with the management of the theatre must soon notice the blur and make the correction; or b) that someone seated near the rear of the house would make the complaint in behalf of those of us up front; or c) that—any minute now—the entire house would explode into catcalls and foot stamping, calling dramatic attention to the irksome distortion.

6   What happened was nothing. The movie ended, as it had begun, just out of focus, and as we trooped out, we stretched our faces in a variety of contortions to accustom the eye to the shock of normal focus.

7   I think it is safe to say that everybody suffered on that occasion. And I think it is safe to assume that everyone was expecting someone else to take the initiative in going back to speak to the manager. And it is probably true even that if we had supposed the movie would run right through with the blurred image, someone surely would have summoned up the purposive indignation to get up out of his seat and file his complaint.

8   But notice that no one did. And the reason no one did is because we are all increasingly anxious in America to be unobtrusive, we are reluctant to make our voices heard, hesitant about claiming our rights; we are afraid that our cause is unjust, or that if it is not unjust, that it is ambiguous; or if not even that, that it is too trivial to justify the horrors of a confrontation with Authority; we will sit in an oven or endure a racking headache before undertaking a head-on, I'm-here-to-tell-you complaint. That tendency to passive compliance, to a heedless endurance is something to keep one's eyes on—in sharp focus.

9   I myself can occasionally summon the courage to complain, but I cannot, as I have intimated, complain softly. My own instinct is so strong to let the thing ride, to forget about it—to expect that someone will take the matter up, when the grievance is collective, in my behalf—that it is only when the provocation is at a very special key, whose vibrations touch simultaneously a complexus of nerves, allergies, and passions, that I catch fire and find the reserves of courage and assertiveness to speak up. When that happens, I get quite carried away. My blood gets hot, my brow wet, I become unbearably and unconscionably sarcastic and bellicose: I am girded for a total showdown.

10 Why should that be? Why could not I (or anyone else) on that railroad coach have said simply to the conductor, "Sir,"—I take that back: that sounds sarcastic—"Conductor, would you be good enough to turn down the heat? I am extremely hot. In fact, I tend to get hot every time the temperature reaches 85 degrees—" Strike that last sentence. Just end it with the simple statement that you are extremely hot, and let the conductor infer the cause.

11 Every New Year's Eve I resolve to do something about the Milquetoast in me and vow to speak up, calmly, for my rights, and for the betterment of our society, on every appropriate occasion. Entering last New Year's Eve I was fortified in my resolve because that morning at breakfast I had had to ask the waitress three times for a glass of milk. She finally brought it—after I had finished my eggs, which is when I don't want it any more. I did not have the manliness to order her to take the milk back, but settled instead for a cowardly sulk, and ostentatiously refused to drink the milk—though I later paid for it—rather than state plainly to the hostess, as I should have, why I had not drunk it, and would not pay for it.

12 So by the time the New Year ushered out the Old, riding in on my morning's indignation and stimulated by the gastric juices of resolution that flow so faithfully on New Year's Eve, I rendered my vow. Henceforward I would conquer my shyness, my despicable disposition to supineness. I would speak out like a man against the unnecessary annoyances of our time.

13 Forty-eight hours later, I was standing in line at the ski-repair store in Pico Peak, Vermont. All I needed, to get on with my skiing, was the loan, for one minute, of a small screwdriver, to tighten a loose binding. Behind the counter in the workshop were two men. One was industriously engaged in servicing the complicated requirements of a young lady at the head of the line, and obviously he would be tied up for quite a while. The other—"Jiggs," his workmate called him—was a middle-aged man, who sat in a chair puffing a pipe, exchanging small talk with his working partner. My pulse began its telltale acceleration. The minutes ticked on. I stared at the idle shopkeeper, hoping to shame him into action, but he was impervious to my telepathic reproof and continued his small talk with his friend, brazenly insensitive to the nervous demands of six good men who were raring to ski.

14 Suddenly my New Year's Eve resolution struck me. It was now or never. I broke from my place in line and marched to the counter. I was going to control myself. I dug my nails into my palms. My effort was only partially successful:

15 "If you are not too busy," I said icily, "would you mind handing me a screwdriver?"

16 Work stopped and everyone turned his eyes on me, and I experienced that mortification I always feel when I am the center of centripetal shafts of curiosity, resentment, perplexity.

17 But the worst was yet to come. "I am sorry, sir," said Jiggs deferentially, moving the pipe from his mouth. "I am not supposed to move. I have just had a heart attack." That was the signal for a great whirring noise that descended from heaven. We looked, stricken, out the window, and it appeared as though a cyclone had suddenly focused on the snowy courtyard between the shop

and the ski lift. Suddenly a gigantic Army helicopter materialized, and hovered down to a landing. Two men jumped out of the plane carrying a stretcher, tore into the ski shop, and lifted the shopkeeper onto the stretcher. Jiggs bade his companion good-by, was whisked out the door, into the plane, up to the heavens, down—we learned—to a nearby Army hospital. I looked up manfully—into a score of man-eating eyes. I put the experience down as a reversal.

18   As I write this, on an airplane, I have run out of paper and need to reach into my briefcase under my legs for more. I cannot do this until my empty lunch tray is removed from my lap. I arrested the stewardess as she passed empty-handed down the aisle on the way to the kitchen to fetch the lunch trays for the passengers up forward who haven't been served yet. "Would you please take my tray?" "Just a *moment,* sir," she said, and marched on sternly. Shall I tell her that since she is headed for the kitchen *anyway,* it cannot delay the feeding of the other passengers by the two seconds necessary to stash away my empty tray? Or remind her that not fifteen minutes ago she spoke unctuously into the loudspeaker the words undoubtedly devised by the airline's highly paid public-relations counselor: "If there is anything I or Miss French can do for you to make your trip more enjoyable, *please* let us—" I have run out of paper.

19   I think the observable reluctance of the majority of Americans to assert themselves in minor matters is related to our increased sense of helplessness in an age of technology and centralized political and economic power. For generations, Americans who were too hot, or too cold, got up and did something about it. Now we call the plumber, or the electrician, or the furnace man. The habit of looking after our own needs obviously had something to do with the assertiveness that characterized the American family familiar to readers of American literature. With the technification of life goes our direct responsibility for our material environment, and we are conditioned to adopt a position of helplessness not only as regards the broken air conditioner, but as regards the overheated train. It takes an expert to fix the former, but not the latter: yet these distinctions, as we withdraw into helplessness, tend to fade away.

20   Our notorious political apathy is a related phenomenon. Every year, whether the Republican or the Democratic Party is in office, more and more power drains away from the individual to feed vast reservoirs in far-off places; and we have less and less say about the shape of events which shape our future. From this aberration of personal power comes the sense of resignation with which we accept the political dispensations of a powerful government whose hold upon us continues to increase.

21   An editor of a national weekly news magazine told me a few years ago that as few as a dozen letters of protest against an editorial stance of his magazine was enough to convene a plenipotentiary meeting of the board of editors to review policy. "So few people complain, or make their voices heard," he explained to me, "that we assume a dozen letters represent the inarticulated views of thousands of readers." In the past ten years, he said, the volume of mail has noticeably decreased, even though the circulation of his magazine has risen.

22　　When our voices are finally mute, when we have finally suppressed the natural instinct to complain, whether the vexation is trivial or grave, we shall have become automatons, incapable of feeling. When Premier Khrushchev first came to this country late in 1959 he was primed, we are informed, to experience the bitter resentment of the American people against his tyranny, against his persecutions, against the movement which is responsible for the then great number of American deaths in Korea, for billions in taxes every year, and for life everlasting on the brink of disasters; but Khrushchev was pleasantly surprised, and reported back to the Russian people that he had been met with overwhelming cordiality (read: apathy), except, to be sure, for "a few fascists who followed me around with their wretched posters, and should be . . . horsewhipped."

23　　I may be crazy, but I say there would have been lots more posters in a society where train temperatures in the dead of winter are not allowed to climb up to 85 degrees without complaint.

● Vocabulary

commutation (2)	ambiguous (8)	unctuously (18)
sibilant (2)	heedless (8)	technification (19)
stupor (2)	bellicose (9)	notorious (20)
gauntlet (3)	girded (9)	reservoirs (20)
consigned (3)	impervious (13)	aberration (20)
supine (4)	telepathic (13)	dispensations (20)
dissolution (4)	mortification (16)	plenipotentiary (21)
vexations (4)	centripetal (16)	inarticulated (21)
hectoring (5)	deferentially (17)	automatons (22)
unobtrusive (8)		

● The Facts

1. What illustrations form the backdrop for Buckley's argument? Summarize each in one sentence.

2. Whom does the author blame for being excessively shy about speaking up when something irritating could easily be mended?

3. Basically, what is Buckley's view of the American people? What has happened to them?

4. Why, according to the author, do large groups of people suffer blatant discomforts or even injustices without anyone making a move to rectify them?

5. Why doesn't the author complain about collective inconveniences? Does his reason resonate with you? Why or why not?

● The Strategies

1. How does the author's language reveal his intellectual level? To whom would this essay appeal? Who would have trouble reading to the end of the essay?

2. How does the title of the essay relate to its content and purpose?

3. Where is the main point of the argument best stated? Does it call for some kind of action or is it merely descriptive?

4. What image does the author use to describe how much his wife hates his infrequent outbursts of temper? (See paragraph 5.) What is your reaction to this image?

5. Why does the author end his essay with such a brief and ambiguous paragraph? Is he praising fascism or communism, or does he have something else in mind? Explain your answer.

● The Issues

1. Do you agree with Buckley's argument that the American people are too passive in their response to conditions that need changing? If you agree, then add a few examples of your own; if you disagree, give some examples of when an individual or a group of people have spoken up and demanded change.

2. Why do you think commuters might be considered a particularly "supine breed"? Explain the term and give reasons for your answer.

3. How does the author relate technology to the lack of initiative he sees in Americans? Do you agree with his observation? What other factors might be responsible?

4. Since the anthologizing of Buckley's essay in 2004, have you seen a change in our national character? For instance, have you noticed an increase in people's resistance to a top-heavy government or to being slaves to machinery?

5. What kind of response do you usually reveal in a situation where many people are uncomfortable yet no one complains? Like the author, do you complain only when your anger reaches the boiling point, or are you assertive enough to complain while you are still calm and collected? What kinds of situations compel you to complain? Are there some situations not important enough to warrant your complaint? Give specific examples of each.

● Suggestions for Writing

1. Write an essay refuting Buckley's argument by stating that Americans stand up for their individual rights more than most other citizens in the world. Use the guidelines for argumentation offered in this chapter. Be sure to anticipate the opposition, and avoid logical fallacies.

2. Write an argument supporting the thesis that freedom of speech is a mighty privilege that must never be abused. Use the guidelines for argumentation offered in this chapter. Be sure to anticipate the opposition, and avoid logical fallacies.

A Modest Proposal

For Preventing the Children of Poor People from Being a Burden to Their Parents or the Country and for Making Them Beneficial to the Public

JONATHAN SWIFT

Rhetorical Thumbnail

Purpose: to rail against the English for their brutal treatment of the Irish

Audience: eighteenth-century reader of pamphlets

Language: standard eighteenth-century English

Strategy: portrays the landlords as insatiable beasts intent on devouring Irish tenants; affects the pose of a reasonable man anxious to find a solution to the problem

Jonathan Swift (1667–1745) is considered one of the greatest satirists in the English language. He was born in Dublin and educated at Trinity College. His satirical masterpiece, *Gulliver's Travels*, was published in 1726, by which time Swift was already regarded by the Irish as a national hero for his *Drapier's Letters* (1724). Originally published as a pamphlet, "A Modest Proposal" first appeared in 1729.

In this famous satire, Swift proposes a savage solution to Irish poverty and the historical indifference of the English to it.

• • •

1   It is a melancholy object to those who walk through this great town, or travel in the country, when they see the streets, the roads, and cabin doors crowded with beggars of the female sex followed by three, four, or six children, all in rags and importuning every passenger for an alms. These mothers, instead of being able to work for their honest livelihood, are forced to employ all their time in strolling, to beg sustenance for their helpless infants, who, as they grow up, either turn thieves for want of work or leave their dear native country to fight for the Pretender in Spain or sell themselves to the Barbadoes.[1]

2   I think it is agreed by all parties that this prodigious number of children, in the arms or on the backs or at the heels of their mothers and frequently of their fathers, is in the present deplorable state of the kingdom a very great additional grievance, and therefore whoever could find out a fair, cheap, and

---

[1]Swift refers to the exiled Stuart claimant of the English throne, and to the custom of poor emigrants to commit themselves to work for a number of years to pay off their transportation to a colony.—ED

easy method of making these children sound and useful members of the commonwealth would deserve so well of the public as to have his statue set up for a preserver of the nation.

3   But my intention is very far from being confined to provide only for the children of professed beggars; it is of a much greater extent, and shall take in the whole number of infants at a certain age who are born of parents in effect as little able to support them as those who demand our charity in the streets.

4   As to my own part, having turned my thoughts for many years upon this important subject and maturely weighed the several schemes of other projectors, I have always found them grossly mistaken in their computation. It is true, a child just dropped from its dam may be supported by her milk for a solar year, with little other nourishment, at the most not above the value of two shillings, which the mother may certainly get, or the value in scraps, by her lawful occupation of begging; and it is exactly at one year old that I propose to provide for them in such a manner as, instead of being a charge upon their parents or the parish or wanting food and raiment for the rest of their lives, they shall on the contrary contribute to the feeding, and partly to the clothing, of many thousands.

5   There is likewise another great advantage in my scheme, that it will prevent those voluntary abortions and that horrid practice of women murdering their bastard children, alas! too frequent among us, sacrificing the poor innocent babes, I doubt more to avoid the expense than the shame, which would move tears and pity in the most savage and inhuman breast.

6   The number of souls in this kingdom being usually reckoned one million and a half, of these I calculate there may be about two hundred thousand couples whose wives are breeders, from which number I subtract thirty thousand couples who are able to maintain their own children (although I apprehend there cannot be so many, under the present distresses of the kingdom); but this being granted, there will remain a hundred and seventy thousand breeders. I again subtract fifty thousand for those women who miscarry or whose children die by accident or disease within the year. There only remain a hundred and twenty thousand children of poor parents annually born. The question therefore is how this number shall be reared and provided for, which, as I have already said, under the present situation of affairs is utterly impossible by all the methods hitherto proposed. For we can neither employ them in handicraft or agriculture; we neither build houses (I mean in the country) nor cultivate land; they can very seldom pick up a livelihood by stealing, till they arrive at six years old, except where they are of towardly parts, although I confess they learn the rudiments much earlier, during which time they can, however, be properly looked upon only as probationers; as I have been informed by a principal gentleman in the County of Cavan who protested to me that he never knew above one or two instances under the age of six, even in a part of the kingdom so renowned for the quickest proficiency in that art.

7   I am assured by our merchants that a boy or a girl before twelve years old is no saleable commodity, and even when they come to this age they will not yield above three pounds or three pounds and a half a crown at most on the exchange, which cannot turn to account either to the parents or the kingdom, the charge of nutriment and rags having been at least four times that value.

8   I shall now, therefore, humbly propose my own thoughts, which I hope will not be liable to the least objection.

9   I have been assured by a very knowing American of my acquaintance in London that a young, healthy child well nursed is, at a year old, a most delicious, nourishing, and wholesome food, whether stewed, roasted, baked, or boiled; and I make no doubt that it will equally serve in a fricassee or a ragout.

10   I do therefore humbly offer it to public consideration that of the hundred and twenty thousand children already computed, twenty thousand may be reserved for breed, whereof only one fourth part to be males, which is more than we allow to sheep, black cattle, or swine; and my reason is that these children are seldom the fruits of marriage, a circumstance not much regarded by our savages; therefore one male will be sufficient to serve four females. That the remaining hundred thousand may, at a year old, be offered in sale to the persons of quality and fortune through the kingdom, always advising the mother to let them suck plentifully in the last month, so as to render them plump and fat for a good table. A child will make two dishes at an entertainment for friends; and when the family dines alone, the fore-or hind-quarter will make a reasonable dish, and seasoned with a little pepper or salt, will be very good boiled on the fourth day, especially in winter. I have reckoned, upon a medium, that a child just born will weigh twelve pounds, and in a solar year, if tolerably nursed, will increase to twenty-eight pounds.

11   I grant this food will be somewhat dear, and therefore very proper for the landlords, who, as they have already devoured most of the parents, seem to have the best title to the children.

12   Infant's flesh will be in season throughout the year, but more plentifully in March and a little before and after; for we are told by a grave author, an eminent French physician, that fish being a prolific diet, there are more children born in Roman Catholic countries about nine months after Lent than at any other season; therefore, reckoning a year after Lent, the markets will be more glutted than usual, because the number of Popish infants is at least three to one in this kingdom; and therefore it will have one other collateral advantage, by lessening the number of Papists among us. I have already computed the charge of nursing a beggar's child (in which list I reckon all cottagers, laborers, and four fifths of the farmers) to be about two shillings per annum, rags included; and I believe no gentleman would repine to give ten shillings for the carcass of a good fat child, which, as I have said, will make four dishes for excellent nutritive meat, when he has only some particular friend or his own family to dine with him. Thus the squire will learn to be a good landlord and grow popular among his tenants; the mother will have eight shillings net profit and be fit for work till she produces another child.

13   Those who are more thrifty (as I must confess the times require) may flay the carcass, the skin of which, artificially dressed, will make admirable gloves for ladies and summer boots for fine gentlemen.

14   As to our city of Dublin, shambles[2] may be appointed for this purpose in the most convenient parts of it; and butchers, we may be assured, will not be

---

[2]Slaughterhouses.—ED

wanting, although I rather recommend buying the children alive than dressing them hot from the knife as we do roasting pigs.

15   A very worthy person, a true lover of his country, and whose virtues I highly esteem, was lately pleased in discoursing on this matter to offer a refinement upon my scheme. He said that many gentlemen of his kingdom having of late destroyed their deer, he conceived that the want of venison might be well supplied by the bodies of young lads and maidens, not exceeding fourteen years of age nor under twelve, so great a number of both sexes in every country being now ready to starve for want of work and service; and these to be disposed of by their parents if alive, or otherwise by their nearest relations. But with due deference to so excellent a friend and so deserving a patriot, I cannot be altogether in his sentiments; for as to the males, my American acquaintance assured me, from frequent experience, that their flesh was generally tough and lean, like that of our schoolboys, by continual exercise, and their taste disagreeable; and to fatten them would not answer the charge. Then as to the females, it would, I think, with humble submission, be a loss to the public, because they would soon become breeders themselves, and besides, it is not improbable that some scrupulous people might be apt to censure such a practice (although indeed very unjustly) as a little bordering upon cruelty, which, I confess, has always been with me the strongest objection against any project, however so well intended.

16   But in order to justify my friend, he confessed that this expedient was put into his head by the famous Psalmanazar, a native of the island Formosa, who came from thence to London above twenty years ago and in conversation told my friend that in his country, when any young person happened to be put to death, the executioner sold the carcass to persons of quality as a prime dainty and that in his time the body of a plump girl of fifteen, who was crucified for an attempt to poison the emperor, was sold to his imperial Majesty's prime minister of state and other great mandarins of the court in joints from the gibbet at four hundred crowns. Neither, indeed, can I deny that if the same use were made of several plump young girls in this town who, without one single groat to their fortunes, cannot stir abroad without a chair, and appear at playhouse and assemblies in foreign fineries which they never will pay for, the kingdom would not be the worse.

17   Some persons of a desponding spirit are in great concern about that vast number of poor people who are aged, diseased, or maimed, and I have been desired to employ my thoughts what course may be taken to ease the nation of so grievous an encumbrance. But I am not in the least pain upon the matter, because it is very well known that they are every day dying and rotting by cold, and famine, and filth, and vermin, as fast as can be reasonably expected. And as to the young laborers, they are now in almost as hopeful a condition; they cannot get work and consequently pine away for want of nourishment to a degree that if at any time they are accidentally hired to common labor, they have not strength to perform it; and thus the country and themselves are happily delivered from the evils to come.

18   I have too long digressed and therefore shall return to my subject. I think the advantages by the proposal which I have made are obvious and many, as well as of the highest importance.

19   For first, as I have already observed, it would greatly lessen the number of Papists, with whom we are yearly overrun, being the principal breeders of the nation as well as our most dangerous enemies, and who stay at home on purpose to deliver the kingdom to the Pretender, hoping to take their advantage by the absence of so many good Protestants, who have chosen rather to leave their country than stay at home and pay tithes, against their conscience, to an Episcopal curate.

20   Secondly, the poorer tenants will have something valuable of their own which by law may be made liable to distress and help to pay their landlord's rent, their corn and cattle being already seized and money a thing unknown.

21   Thirdly, whereas the maintenance of a hundred thousand children from two years old and upward cannot be computed at less than ten shillings apiece per annum, the nation's stock will thereby be increased fifty thousand pounds per annum, beside the profit of a new dish introduced to the tables of all gentlemen of fortune in the kingdom who have any refinement in taste. And the money will circulate among ourselves, the goods being entirely of our own growth and manufacture.

22   Fourthly, the constant breeders, beside the gain of eight shillings sterling per annum by the sale of their children, will be rid of the charge of maintaining them after the first year.

23   Fifthly, this food would likewise bring great custom to taverns, where the vintners will certainly be so prudent as to procure the best receipt for dressing it to perfection and consequently have their houses frequented by all the fine gentlemen who justly value themselves upon their knowledge in good eating; and a skillful cook who understands how to oblige his guests will contrive to make it as expensive as they please.

24   Sixthly, this would be a great inducement to marriage, which all wise nations have either encouraged by rewards or enforced by laws and penalties. It would increase the care and tenderness of mothers toward their children when they were sure of a settlement for life to the poor babes, provided in some sort by the public, to their annual profit or expense. We could see an honest emulation among the married women, which of them could bring the fattest child to the market. Men would become as fond of their wives during the time of their pregnancy as they are now of their mares in foal, their cows in calf, or sows when they are ready to farrow, nor offer to beat or kick them (as is too frequent a practice) for fear of a miscarriage.

25   Many other advantages might be enumerated. For instance, the addition of some thousand carcasses in our exportation of barreled beef; the propagation of swine's flesh and improvement in the art of making good bacon, so much wanted among us by the great destruction of pigs, too frequent at our table, which are no way comparable in taste or magnificence to a well-grown fat yearling child, which, roasted whole, will make a considerable figure at a lord mayor's feast or any other public entertainment. But this and many others I omit, being studious of brevity.

26   Supposing that one thousand families in this city would be constant customers for infant's flesh, beside others who might have it at merry-meetings,

particularly at weddings and christenings, I compute that Dublin would take off annually about twenty thousand carcasses and the rest of the kingdom (where probably they will be sold somewhat cheaper) the remaining eighty thousand.

27   I can think of no one objection that will possibly be raised against this proposal unless it should be urged that the number of people will be thereby much lessened in the kingdom. This I freely own, and it was indeed one principal design in offering it to the world. I desire the reader will observe that I calculate my remedy for this one individual kingdom of Ireland and for no other that ever was, is, or I think ever can be, upon earth. Therefore let no man talk to me of other expedients; of taxing our absentees at five shillings a pound; of using neither clothes nor household furniture except what is of our own growth and manufacture; of utterly rejecting the materials and instruments that promote foreign luxury; of curing the expensiveness of pride, vanity, idleness, and gaming in our women; of introducing a vein of parsimony, prudence, and temperance; of learning to love our country, in the want of which we differ even from Laplanders and the inhabitants of Tupinamba; of quitting our animosities and factions, nor acting any longer like the Jews, who were murdering one another at the very moment their city was taken; of being a little cautious not to sell our country and conscience for nothing; of teaching landlords to have at least one degree of mercy toward their tenants; lastly, of putting a spirit of honesty, industry, and skill into our shop-keepers, who, if a resolution could now be taken to buy only our native goods, would immediately unite to cheat and exact upon us in the price, the measure, and the goodness, nor could ever yet be brought to make one fair proposal of just dealing, though often and earnestly invited to it.

28   Therefore, I repeat, let no man talk to me of these and the like expedients till he has at least some glimpse of hope that there will be ever some hearty and sincere attempt to put them in practice.

29   But as to myself, having been wearied out for many years with offering vain, idle, visionary thoughts and at length utterly despairing of success, I fortunately fell upon this proposal, which, as it is wholly new, so it has something solid and real, of no expense and little trouble, full in our own power, and whereby we can incur no danger in disobliging England. For this kind of commodity will not bear exportation, the flesh being of too tender a consistence to admit a long continuance in salt, although perhaps I could name a country which would be glad to eat up our whole nation without it.

30   After all, I am not so violently bent upon my own opinion as to reject any offer proposed by wise men which shall be found equally innocent, cheap, easy, and effectual. But before some thing of that kind shall be advanced in contradiction to my scheme and offering a better, I desire the author or authors will be pleased maturely to consider two points: first, as things now stand, how they will be able to find food and raiment for a hundred thousand useless mouths and backs; and secondly, there being a round million of creatures in human figure throughout this kingdom whose whole subsistence, put into a common stock, would leave them in debt two millions of pounds sterling, adding those who are beggars by profession to the bulk of farmers, cottagers, and laborers, with the wives and children who are beggars in effect, I desire those

politicians who dislike my overture, and may perhaps be so bold as to attempt an answer, that they will first ask the parents of these mortals whether they would not at this day think it a great happiness to have been sold for food at a year old in the manner I prescribe, and thereby have avoided such a perpetual scene of misfortunes as they have since gone through by the oppression of landlords, the impossibility of paying rent without money or trade, the want of common sustenance, with neither house nor clothes to cover them from the inclemencies of the weather, and the most inevitable prospect of entailing the like of greater miseries upon their breed forever.

31   I profess in the sincerity of my heart that I have not the least personal interest in endeavoring to promote this necessary work, having no other motive than the public good of my country, by advancing our trade, providing for infants, relieving the poor, and giving some pleasure to the rich. I have no children by which I can propose to get a single penny, the youngest being nine years old and my wife past childbearing.

● Vocabulary

importuning (1)	censure (15)	propagation (25)
sustenance (1)	gibbet (16)	parsimony (27)
prodigious (2)	encumbrance (17)	overture (30)
proficiency (6)	digressed (18)	inclemencies (30)
collateral (12)		

● The Facts

1. On what premise is "A Modest Proposal" based? What is the chief assumption of its argument?
2. Reread paragraph 11. Why do the landlords have "the best title to the children"?
3. Swift's satire redefines children in economic terms. What does this say about his view of the society in which he lived?
4. What does the satire imply about religious feelings in Ireland during Swift's time?
5. Given the state of affairs as the author describes them, is his argument logical? Explain.

● The Strategies

1. What is the effect of the word *Modest* in the title?
2. Swift describes people with words like breeder, dam, carcass, and yearling child. What are the effects of these words?
3. Satire usually provides hints of the true state of things as it proposes its own alternatives. How does Swift hint at the true state of things? Give examples.
4. How would you characterize the tone of this piece?
5. Reread the final paragraph. What is its purpose?

● The Issues

1. Do you consider satire an effective way to call attention to social ills? Why or why not?

2. Which paragraphs reveal Swift's real suggestions for improving the economic condition of the Irish? How do these paragraphs fit into the general scheme of Swift's essay?

3. How persuasive do you consider this essay? Would a straightforward essay be more effective? Why or why not?

4. Is Swift's essay simply a literary masterpiece to be studied within its context, or does it have a message for us today?

5. What condition existing in our country today would make an excellent subject for the kind of satire used by Swift? What satirical proposal can you suggest?

● Suggestions for Writing

1. Infer from "A Modest Proposal" the state of life in Ireland during Swift's time. Do some additional research online if needed and write an essay about the treatment of the poor in Swift's day. Make specific references to the article to justify your inferences and give proper credit for any other source you use.

2. Using your answer to question 5, under the Issues, write a satirical proposal for curing some aspect of today's society.

A Nation in Need of Vacation

STEVE RUSHIN

> ### Rhetorical Thumbnail
>
> **Purpose:**   to argue that Americans need more vacation time in order to be more productive
>
> **Audience:**   magazine readers who are curious about the value of vacations
>
> **Language:**   standard English with a relaxed and witty approach
>
> **Strategy:**   cites as backing for the argument various studies that show the benefits of taking vacations

Steven Rushin (b. 1966) is considered one of the best sports writers in our country. After graduating from Marquette University in 1988, he joined the staff of *Sports Illustrated,* where he worked for nineteen years. In addition to his widely read essays on sports and travel, Rushin has written several books, including a travelogue, *Road Swing* (1998), and a collection of his travel and sports essays, *The Caddie Was a Reindeer: And Other Tales of Extreme Recreation* (2005). In 2006, Rushin was named the Sportswriter of the Year by the National Sportswriters and Sportscasters Association . His essays have appeared in *Time* magazine and the *New York Times.*

Don't let the agile style of the writer lessen the serious point of this essay—namely that vacations are hugely beneficial to anyone hounded by a serious work ethic. Ponder his claim that Americans would be more productive if they took more time off to vacation.

• • •

1   The word *vacation* comes from the Latin *vacatio,* or "freedom from duty," and by happy coincidence the first liberating stop for many vacationers is something called a duty-free shop. When a flight attendant wheels that trolley down the hushed aisle of a darkened airplane, she is not just whispering a sales pitch but telling you, the holidaygoer, what you have suddenly become: "Duty-free . . . duty-free . . . duty-free." When I vacation, I vacate: vacate the house, vacate the office, vacate the state, vacate the country. Vacation requires a metaphorical gulf—and preferably an actual one—between the vacationer and home. *Vacation home,* to me, is an oxymoron. There's a reason it's called Getting Away From It All. Going on vacation requires, above all else, going.

2   I like to get as far away as possible and bring along lots of books, themselves a form of escape, so that I'm now twice removed, like a distant cousin or the multiply deposed Haitian President Jean-Bertrand Aristide.

3   And yet, if statistics are to be believed, I am a freak: an American who loves—an American who takes—his vacation. My fellow citizens are the least vacationing people in the industrialized world. We receive, on average, 14 days of vacation a year, and no legally mandated paid leave. Even the Japanese average 17.5 days off annually, and they have a word—*karoshi*—for working oneself to death. American English, by contrast, has given the world the phrase *working vacation,* a favorite of brush-clearing, woodchopping U.S. presidents who know voters are not sympathetic to the concept of time off.

4   Possessed by guilt, ambition, and responsibility—by duty, that is—we are either afraid to or unable to unplug, which is why some hotels now offer to seize your PDA at check-in, the way prisons seize shoelaces and belts. It's really for our own good: We can't be trusted with our BlackBerries and laptops and iPhones. We literally can't be left to our own devices.

5   And we still don't take what little vacation we're offered: We use only 11 days of our annual allotment. The U.S. Bureau of Labor Statistics estimates that Americans leave 439 million vacation days unused every year. That's 1.2 million years—nearly the span of time from the discovery of fire to the present day—annually abandoned, melted down in the crucible of the cubicle.

6   More than a third of U.S. workers take fewer than seven days of vacation a year. By contrast, the French—who gave us the word *leisure* and perfected it as a concept—get 36 days and take 94 percent of them. In England (24 vacation days), *leisure* and *pleasure* rhyme. In the United States, *leisure* rhymes with *seizure.*

7   The truth is, leisure helps reduce seizures. Researchers at the State University of New York at Oswego studied 12,000 middle-aged men and concluded that guys who took annual vacations reduced their risk of death from heart disease by 30 percent. A study published in the *Wisconsin Medical Journal* stated

that women who vacation at least twice a year are less depressed than women who vacation every other year. And why wouldn't they be?

8   Historically, it's been more difficult for a woman to experience *vacatio*—to feel entirely duty-free. Or entirely doody-free: My mother always seemed to be changing diapers on the station wagon tailgate at some windswept scenic overlook. Half a century ago Anne Morrow Lindbergh, who along with her husband helped spark dreams of taking flight from home and responsibility, wrote: "By and large, mothers and housewives are the only workers who do not have regular time off. They are the great vacationless class."

9   I come from a long line of vacationers, and I know the salutary benefits of a holiday. My father took us away every summer, always leaving under cover of darkness, so that for the first several hours of every trip we rolled across the country like a band of fugitives. In doing so, he forged in each of his five children a love of travel, to say nothing of a castiron bladder.

10   From the beginning of time, and across cultural boundaries, humans have had wanderlust, often with the emphasis on the second half of that compound word. Jimmy Buffett sees the romantic possibilities when freedom from duty and duty-free booze conspire: "The weather is here, I wish you were beautiful/ My thoughts aren't too clear but don't run away/My girlfriend's a bore, my job is too dutiful/Hell nobody's perfect, would you like to play?"

11   It's a nearly universal human impulse. And so another bard—of Avon, not Margaritaville—was writing the very same sentiments some 400 years earlier in *As You Like It:* "Come woo me, woo me; for now I am in a holiday humour, and like enough to consent."

12   So humor me—"holiday humour" me—and consent. We are One Nation in Need of Vacation. Studies show that Americans would be more productive with increased time off. Some companies are now mandating that employees take their vacations. In short, it's not just your right to annually abdicate duty. It's your duty.

"A Nation in Need of a Vacation" by Steve Rushin appeared in ENCOMPASS MAGAZINE, July 2008. Reprinted with permission from Steve Rushin.

● Vocabulary

vacate (1)	devices (4)	fugitives (9)
metaphorical (1)	salutary (9)	mandating (12)
oxymoron (1)		

● The Facts

1. What is the difference between a metaphorical gulf and an actual gulf? Which of the two does a vacation require?

2. In paragraph 1, what is the meaning of the quotation "Duty-free . . . duty free . . . duty-free"? How does the quotation apply to people heading for a vacation?

3. According to the author, how many vacation days do Americans leave unused per year? What source is used for this statistic?

4. What is the truth about the connection between health and vacations (see paragraph 7)? Does this connection seem believable? Support your answer with evidence from your own observations.

5. Why is the author so knowledgeable about the benefits of holiday trips? Do you agree or disagree with him? Give reasons for your answer.

● The Strategies

1. Steve Rushin is famous for his delightful sense of humor. How and where is this humor revealed in the essay? Point out some specific passages.

2. The author likes to use unusual word rhymes. Where are such rhymes found in this essay? What, if anything, do these rhymes add?

3. How does the author add a serious component to his essay? Which technique indicates that the writer has researched the subject of the benefits of vacations?

4. Who is the "bard of Avon" referred to in paragraph 11? How is the bard's identify clarified?

5. Who is Jimmy Buffett? Why is his verse quoted?

● The Issues

1. What is the thesis of the essay? Where is it stated? How effective is the placement?

2. How well did the author argue his point? Were you convinced? Why or why not?

3. Do you agree with the author that Americans would be more productive if they had more time off? Do your relatives and friends tend to be workaholics, hedonists, or somewhere in between? What is your opinion of the importance of vacations?

4. Why do you think that vacation time for women is crucial in keeping them from getting depressed? Are women different from men in this respect? Clarify your answer.

5. What, in your opinion, are the salutary benefits of vacations? For instance, what benefits are derived from Camp David, the official Presidential vacation site in the Catoctin Mountains of Maryland? Use examples from your own observations of your family, friends, or public figures.

● Suggestions for Writing

1. Write an essay arguing that vacations are particularly necessary for people in stressful jobs. Base your argument on a sound premise, supported by accurate facts. Use vivid examples if helpful, and cite expert sources to support your views.

2. Argue either for or against generous vacation time paid by employers to their workers. Cite expert opinions and examples to support your thesis.

The Pregnancy Trap

GERRY GARIBALDI

> ## Rhetorical Thumbnail
>
> **Purpose:** to argue that we the public creates an atmosphere that is too easy on pregnant teenagers
>
> **Audience:** educated readers
>
> **Language:** standard English laced with a few informal expressions
>
> **Strategy:** cites some experts and his own personal experience with students in his classes

Gerry Garibaldi (b. 1952) spent twenty-five years as a Hollywood film executive and writer, but recently left this career to teach English at an urban high school in Connecticut, where he observed firsthand the pressing educational problems that cost our nation money and mental stress. Despite his full-time teaching job, he finds time to write provocative essays about such matters as affirmative action, discrimination, and teenage pregnancies. Among his best-known essays are "Conspiracy of Dunces: In Schools Male Behavior Is New Pathology," "Gender-based Admissions to Medical School," and "How the Schools Short-change Boys." The essay below was originally written as a longer piece for the *City Journal* (Winter 2011).

Reading this essay may offend the bleeding hearts of people who remember the "Scarlet A" days when young girls who got pregnant were snubbed and hidden away from public—avoided by their friends and lied about by relatives who were too ashamed to admit that one of their own had humiliated the family by being immoral. The offspring of these girls were called "illegitimate," and their social standing was tarnished. Over the last few decades, as society has taken a more humane approach to teenage pregnancies, becoming a "single mom" not only has become acceptable, but in some circles it has acquired an oddly glamorous veneer. This laissez-faire *approach has gone too far, claims the author of the essay that follows. He fears that school officials and parents are becoming so warmly fuzzy toward teenage pregnancies that they have turned a safety net for the most vulnerable into a hammock. Where do you stand on the issue? That is the question you need to answer after studying Garibaldi's essay.*

• • •

1   In my short time as a teacher in Connecticut, I have muddled through President Bush's No Child Left Behind act, which tied federal funding of schools to various reforms, and through President Obama's Race to the Top initiative, which does much the same thing, though with different benchmarks. Thanks to the Feds, urban schools like mine are swimming in money. Our facility is state-of-the-art,

thanks to a recent $40 million face-lift, with gleaming new hallways and bathrooms and a fully computerized library.

2   Here's my prediction: The money, the reforms, the gleaming porcelain, the hopeful rhetoric about saving our children—all of it will have a limited impact, at best, on most city schoolchildren. Urban teachers face an intractable problem, one that we cannot spend or even teach our way out of: teen pregnancy. This year, all of my favorite girls are pregnant, four in all, future unwed mothers every one. There will be no innovation in this quarter, no race to the top. Personal moral accountability is the electrified rail that no politician wants to touch.

3   My first encounter with teen pregnancy was a girl named Nicole, a pretty 15-year-old who had rings on every finger and great looped earrings and a red pen with fluffy pink feathers and a heart that lit up when she wrote with it.

4   My main gripe with Nicole was that she fell asleep in class. Each morning—bang!—her head hit the desk. Nicole's unmarried mother, it turned out, worked nights, so Nicole would slip out with friends every evening, sometimes staying out until 3 a.m., and then show up in class exhausted, surly, and hungry.

5   After I made a dozen calls home, her mother finally got back to me. Your daughter is staying out late, I reported. The voice at the other end of the phone sounded abashed and bone-weary. "I know, I know, I'm sorry," she repeated over and over. "I'll talk to her. I'm sorry."

6   For a short time, things got better. Encouraged, I hectored and cajoled and praised Nicole's every small effort. She was an innately bright girl who might, if I dragged her by the heels, eventually survive the rigors of a community college.

7   Then one morning, her head dropped again. I rapped my knuckles on her desk. "Leave me alone, mister," she said. "I feel sick."

8   There was a sly exchange of looks among the other girls in class, a giggle or two, and then one of them said, "She's pregnant, Mr. Garibaldi."

9   She lifted her face and smiled at her friends, then dropped her head back down. A moment later she vomited, and I dispatched her to the nurse. In the years since, I've escorted girls whose water has just broken, their legs trembling and wobbly, to the principal's office, where their condition barely raises an eyebrow.

10   In our society, perversely, we celebrate the unwed mother as a heroic figure, like a fireman or a police officer. During the last presidential election, much was made of Obama's mother, who was a single parent. Movie stars and pop singers flaunt their daddy-less babies like fishing trophies.

11   None of this is lost on my students. In today's urban high school, there is no shame or social ostracism when girls become pregnant. Their friends throw baby showers at which meager little gifts are given. After delivery, the girls return to school with baby pictures on their cell phones or slipped into their binders.

12   Teenage girls like Nicole qualify for a vast array of welfare benefits from the state and federal governments: medical coverage when they become pregnant (called Healthy Start); later, medical insurance for the family (Husky

Healthcare); child care (Care 4 Kids); Section 8 housing subsidies; the Supplemental Nutrition Assistance Program; cash assistance.

13   In theory, this provision of services is humane and defensible, an essential safety net for the most vulnerable—children who have children. In practice it is a monolithic public endorsement of single motherhood—one that has turned our urban high schools into puppy mills. The safety net has become a hammock.

14   The young father almost always greets the pregnancy with adolescent excitement, as if a baby were a new Xbox game. In Nicole's case, the father's name was David. David manfully walked Nicole to class each morning and gave her a kiss at the door. I had him in homeroom and asked if he planned to marry her. "No" was his frank answer.

15   Boys without fathers, like David, cultivate an overweening bravado to overcome a deeper sense of vulnerability. There's a he-man thing to getting a girl pregnant that marks you as an adult in the eyes of your equally unmoored peers. But a boy's interest in his child quickly vanishes. When I ask girls if the father is helping out with the baby, they shrug. "I don't care if he does or not," I've heard too often.

16   As for girls without fathers, you walk on eggshells with them. You broker remarks, you negotiate insults, all the while trying to pull them along on a slender thread. Their anger toward male authority can be lacerating.

17   With Nicole, I dug in. In journalism class, I brought up the subject of teen pregnancy and suggested that she and a friend of hers, Maria, write a piece together about their experiences. They hesitated; I pressed the matter. "Do you think getting pregnant when you're a teenager is a good thing or a bad thing?"

18   "Depends," Nicole replied.

19   "On what?"

20   "My mom and my grandma both got pregnant when they were teens, and they're good mothers."

21   "Nobody gets married anymore, mister," Maria and another mother, Shanice, chime in. "You're just picking on us because we have kids."

22   As much as Nicole is aware of her mother's sacrifices, she is equally proud of her mother's choice to keep her. It's locked away in her heart like a cameo. The talk turns to her mother's loyalty and love, and soon the class rises in a choir to mom's defense.

23   "Fine," I say. "If that's your position, like any good journalist, you have to back up your arguments with facts and statistics."

24   As do most of my 11th-graders, Nicole reads at a fifth-grade level, which means I must peruse the articles and statistics along with her. She counts the number of pages before she reads. With my persistent nudging, she and Maria begin to pull out statistics: 63 percent of all suicides are individuals from single-parent households. The same is true for 75 percent of adolescents in chemical-dependency hospitals, and for more than half of all youths incarcerated for criminal acts.

25   "I don't want to write about this!" Nicole complains.

26   "Why?"

27   "Nobody wants to read it."

28   Maria, in particular, rebels. She wants to recast the article in a rosier vein and talk about how happy her son makes her. A father myself, I understand a parent's love. Our talk turns more sweetly to teething cures, diaper rashes, and solid food. I suggest ways of incorporating that love into the piece, while also hoping that some of these grim statistics have gotten through to the girls.

29   As morbid as it sounds, the students take an interest in obituary writing. I have them write their own obits, fictional biographies that foretell the arc of their lives. From Nicole's, I learn that her mother was 16 when she had Nicole, her father 14. After high school, the fictional Nicole went on to have four more kids whom she loved dearly and who loved her dearly. She died of old age in her bed, leaving six grandchildren.

30   "Nicole, you never got married?" I remarked.

31   "No," she responded with a note of obstinacy in her voice.

32   "I think you would make a wonderful wife for someone."

33   "I *would* make a good wife," she replied. "But I'm not going to get married."

34   As Nicole entered her third trimester, she had a minor complication with her pregnancy and disappeared for nearly two weeks. She returned, pale and far behind in my classes. She no longer had to report to two classes: physical education and a science lab where strong chemicals were used. Since openings in my schedule coincided with the vacant spots, I was asked to be her chaperone.

35   For five weeks, Nicole became my shadow. If I had cafeteria duty, she'd trot along. I'd buy her a candy bar and she'd plop down on the seat beside me. I'd escort her on her restroom runs, and wait for her outside the door.

36   The father in me wanted to be protective and kind, but Nicole was becoming too connected with me. She blew off assignments regularly now. Life had allowed her to slide before, through every year of her education, as others in her life had slid—starting with her father, whom she barely recalled.

37   Nicole failed both my classes, but when she returned the following year, she was in good spirits. The birth of her son had gone well. She had a heart-adorned album full of photos of her boy. Things were settled, she said. She was going to work hard this year; she felt motivated, even eager. And by year's end, her reading level had indeed risen nearly two grades—but it was still far below what she would need to score as proficient.

38   The path for young, unwed mothers—and for their children—can be brutal. I once had a student named Jasmine, who had given birth over the summer. One day, I observed her staring off mulishly into space for nearly the entire period, not hearing a word I said and ignoring her assignment. At the end of class, I took her aside and asked, with some irritation, what the matter was.

39   Her eyes welled with tears. "I gave my son to his father to look after yesterday. When I picked him up, he had bruises on his head and a cut." Her son was 6 months old.

40   Honestly? I just wanted that day to go by. But we have a duty to our students, both moral and legal. "You have to be a brave mama and report him," I said. I led her to the office and to the school social worker, and I tipped off the campus trooper. Even with that support, she backed off from filing a complaint and shortly afterward dropped out of school to be with her baby.

41   My students often become curious about my personal life. The question most frequently asked is, "Do you have kids?"

42   "Two," I say.

43   The next question is always heartbreaking.

44   "Do they live with you?"

45   Every fall, new education theories arrive, born like orchids in the hothouses of big-time university education departments. Urban teachers are always first in line for each new bloom. We've been retrofitted as teachers a dozen times over. This year's innovation is the Data Wall, a strategy in which teachers must test endlessly in order to produce data about students' progress. The Obama administration has spent lavishly to ensure that professional consultants monitor its implementation.

46   Every year, the national statistics summon a fresh chorus of outrage at the failure of urban public schools. Next year, I fear, will be little different.

"The Pregnancy Trap" by Gerry Garibaldi was originally published in CITY JOURNAL, Winter 2011 issue. Reprinted with permission from City Journal.

● Vocabulary

benchmarks (1)	ostracism (11)	peruse (24)
intractable (2)	monolithic (13)	proficient (37)
surly (4)	bravado (15)	mulishly (38)
hectored (6)	unmoored (15)	
flaunt (10)	lacerating (16)	

● The Facts

1. How does Garibaldi begin his essay? What does the beginning tell us? What connection does the beginning have with the point he is trying to make?

2. What prediction does the author make? What reason does he give for his prediction? Does this reason seem logical to you? Why or why not?

3. Who is Nicole, and what role does she play in this essay? Would some appropriate statistics be more convincing than Nicole's example? Cite the advantage, if any, of citing one specific experience over numerous statistics.

4. What are the grim statistics pulled from articles read by Maria and Nicole? How do the two girls react to the statistics? What might you advise these two girls if you were their teacher?

5. What happened to Jasmine's baby boy when she left him with his father? How old was the baby? How did this incident affect Jasmine's education? What is your opinion of Jasmine's decision?

● The Strategies

1. How does the author achieve a sense of drama as he develops his thesis? Does this strategy add or detract from the seriousness of the problem being analyzed? Give reasons for your answer.

2. In paragraph 12, what rhetorical strategy is used? How does this strategy help the reader? Be specific in your answer.

3. What simile (a figure of speech comparing two items, using the word *like*) is used in each of these paragraphs: 10, 22, and 45? Explain the use of each simile and be prepared to state how they boost the writing.

4. Why does the author use the word "Trap" in his title? Explain the use of this word. Is it appropriate in terms of the author's purpose? Give reasons for your answer.

5. What is the latest government innovation concerning education? What is the author's purpose in mentioning the innovation? Is this a good strategy? Explain your answer.

● The Issues

1. Piercing to the heart of the teenage educational catastrophe described, what ingredient is missing, according to the author, in order to make any headway in curing the problem? Where in the essay is the problem diagnosed? What is your reaction to the author's view? Defend, dispute, or quality his opinion.

2. Paragraph 12 mentions a list of welfare benefits for which pregnant teenage girls can qualify. Do you think the government should continue these benefits? If not, why not? If yes, to what extent and under what circumstances?

3. What explanation can you provide for the comments made by the author in paragraph 16? Clarify the phrases "walk on eggshells," "broker remarks," and "negotiate insults."

4. What does the author mean when he states that Nicole was becoming "too connected" with him? Does this seem like a realistic problem? How should it be overcome? How would you deal with such a problem as you tried to be helpful to the girl?

5. Do you think that many of the girls who become teenage mothers make the kind of mothers you would want for your child? What might be their strengths and what might be their weaknesses?

● Suggestions for Writing

1. After researching the Internet on the topic of teenage pregnancies, write a paper in which you provide your answer to this widespread problem. Begin with a well-worded thesis and base your argument on pertinent and logical premises. Use expert testimony and valid statistics if necessary. When using ideas from other people, synthesize them and integrate them smoothly into your own text, giving credit where credit is due.

2. Write an essay of approximately 500 words, explaining what kind of mother you consider ideal. Use anecdotes about mothers you have admired or quote from periodicals and books.

ISSUE FOR CRITICAL THINKING AND DEBATE: HOMELESSNESS

Homelessness would seem to be a nondebatable issue. Everyone is against it, at least in principle. The debate begins not on whether or not homelessness is terrible—everyone agrees that it is—but on its causes. The division of opinion is predictably political: Conservatives, as a whole, blame homelessness on lapses and addictions in the individual; liberals tend to blame economic causes.

Adding to the muddle is the blurry definition of homelessness. Is a person who lives in a government-funded shelter, such as a hotel that houses the poor through a system of voucher payments from the state, homeless? Or is the homeless person one with no permanent residence, who sleeps on the street, in a car, or in a bus station? Most government statistics count both groups among the homeless. Yet, government-funded housing, as some critics point out, may be drawing people who had been doubling up with family members into the ranks of the counted homeless. The result is that the more the government funds shelters for the homeless, the greater the homeless population seems to grow.

How many people are homeless in America? No one knows for sure. Homelessness advocates say there are three million. Other studies have put the figure at around 400,000. A recent study indicated that every night in the United States about 760,000 people experience homelessness. In its 2008 Report to Congress, the U.S. Department of Housing and Urban Development (HUD) indicated that on a single night 56 percent of homeless people were sheltered and 44 percent were unsheltered. Of the unsheltered homeless, a staggering 30 percent were persons in households with children. Thanks to HUD's ongoing efforts to address the special needs of the chronically homeless, the number of this subpopulation has declined 11.5 percent since 2005. Despite such minuscule hopeful signs, the speculation is that nearly 1 percent of American families, even in a robust economy, will go through episodes of homelessness within a year (The Urban Institute: available online at http://www.urban.org/news/pressrel/ pr000201.html). These figures—whether high or low—are difficult to trust because they are always based on different methods of counting. Added to the roster of the uncountable are the so-called "invisible homeless," who have no residence of their own but live in makeshift arrangements with relatives.

The three essays in this section typify the debate about homelessness. The first essay, by well-known journalist Anna Quindlen, argues in poetic language that the need for a home is a deep human hunger and that one of the saddest aspects of today's world is that too many people have no home to call their own. The other point of view is represented by a columnist who examines the complexities behind the homeless problem and shows us an example, Greg, who ended up being homeless because of a change in Boston's rent control laws. The student essay, written by a female who observed several homeless people sleeping on the streets of her neighborhood, laments the loss of family solidarity in the days when uncles, aunts, or cousins would take in family members who were down on their luck with no place to live and nothing to eat.

Which view of the causes of homelessness is accurate? It is impossible to say. Certainly, one can imagine a scenario where an individual, even a family, can fall on hard times that result in homelessness. Yet anyone who lives in a city also knows from plain observation that many dysfunctional, tormented souls haunt the streets. Why homelessness exists in such an affluent country as ours may be impossible to explain, but one thing is certain: It should not exist.

"Listen, Mister. Parasites have to eat, too, you know."

Homeless

ANNA QUINDLEN

Anna Quindlen (b. 1952) is a Pulitzer Prize-winning journalist, novelist, and writer of children's books. Her trademark sense of humor, often including satire, has delighted audiences all over the United States. As a columnist for *The New York Times* from 1981 to 1984, Quindlen was only the third woman in the paper's history to write a regular column for the prestigious Op-Ed page. In 1995, she left the paper to devote herself to writing novels. Today she writes regularly for *Newsweek* magazine. Among Quindlen's best-selling novels are the following: *One True Thing* (1994), *Black and Blue* (1998), *Rise and Shine* (2006), and *Every Last One* (2010). Several of her novels were turned into popular motion pictures.

Although it is impossible to quantify accurately the amount of homeless people in America, we see them begging at entrances or exits to freeways, and we see them crowding the sidewalks of large cities. Moreover, we are told by the Coalition for the Homeless and other charitable organizations that more than half of homeless people are mentally ill or suffer from substance abuse. As you study Quindlen's essay, try to figure out what can be done by individuals as well as organizations to improve the lot of people who have no home.

• • •

1   Her name was Ann, and we met in the Port Authority Bus Terminal several Januaries ago. I was doing a story on homeless people. She said I was wasting my time talking to her; she was just passing through, although she'd been passing through for more than two weeks. To prove to me that this was true, she rummaged through a tote bag and a manila envelope and finally unfolded a sheet of typing paper and brought out her photographs.

2   They were not pictures of family, or friends, or even a dog or cat, its eyes brown-red in the flashbulb's light. They were pictures of a house. It was like a thousand houses in a hundred towns, not suburb, not city, but somewhere in between, with aluminum siding and a chain-link fence, a narrow driveway running up to a one-car garage and a patch of back yard. The house was yellow. I looked on the back for a date or a name, but neither was there. There was no need for discussion. I knew what she was trying to tell me, for it was something I had often felt. She was not adrift, alone, anonymous, although her bags and her raincoat with the grime shadowing its creases had made me believe she was. She had a house, or at least once upon a time had had one. Inside were curtains, a couch, a stove, potholders. You are where you live. She was somebody.

3   I've never been very good at looking at the big picture, taking the global view, and I've always been a person with an overactive sense of place, the legacy of an Irish grandfather. So it is natural that the thing that seems most wrong with the world to me right now is that there are so many people with no homes. I'm not simply talking about shelter from the elements or three square meals a day or a mailing address to which the welfare people can send the check— although I know that all these are important for survival. I'm talking

about a home, about precisely those kinds of feelings that have wound up in cross-stitch and French knots on samplers over the years.

4   Home is where the heart is. There's no place like it. I love my home with a ferocity totally out of proportion to its appearance or location. I love dumb things about it: the hot-water heater, the plastic rack you drain dishes in, the roof over my head, which occasionally leaks. And yet it is precisely those dumb things that make it what it is—a place of certainty, stability, predictability, privacy, for me and for my family. It is where I live. What more can you say about a place than that? That is everything.

5   Yet it is something that we have been edging away from gradually during my lifetime and the lifetimes of my parents and grandparents. There was a time when where you lived often was where you worked and where you grew the food you ate and even where you were buried. When that era passed, where you lived at least was where your parents had lived and where you would live with your children when you became enfeebled. Then, suddenly, where you lived was where you lived for three years, until you could move on to something else and something else again.

6   And so we have come to something else again, to children who do not understand what it means to go to their rooms because they have never had a room, to men and women whose fantasy is a wall they can paint a color of their own choosing, to old people reduced to sitting on moldedplastic chairs, their skin blue-white in the lights of a bus station, who pull pictures of houses out of their bags. Homes have stopped being homes. Now they are real estate.

7   People find it curious that those without homes would rather sleep sitting up on benches or huddled in doorways than go to shelters. Certainly some prefer to do so because they are emotionally ill, because they have been locked in before and they are damned if they will be locked in again. Others are afraid of the violence and trouble they may find there. But some seem to want something that is not available in shelters, and they will not compromise, not for a cot, or oatmeal, or a shower with special soap that kills the bugs. "One room," a woman with a baby who was sleeping on her sister's floor once told me, "painted blue." That was the crux of it: not size or location, but pride of ownership. Painted blue.

8   This is a difficult problem, and some wise and compassionate people are working hard at it. But in the main I think we work around it, just as we walk around it when it is lying on the sidewalk or sitting in the bus terminal—the problem, that is. It has been customary to take people's pain and lessen our own participation in it by turning it into an issue, not a collection of human beings. We turn an adjective into a noun: the poor, not poor people; the homeless, not Ann or the man who lives in the box or the woman who sleeps on the subway grate.

9   Sometimes I think we would be better off if we forgot about the broad strokes and concentrated on the details. Here is a woman without a bureau. There is a man with no mirror, no wall to hang it on. They are not the homeless. They are people who have no homes. No drawer that holds the spoons. No window to look out upon the world. My God. That is everything.

● Vocabulary

rummaged (1)	ferocity (4)	molded (6)
adrift (2)	predictability (4)	crux (7)
samplers (3)	enfeebled (5)	

● The Facts

1. Where did the author meet Ann? What significance does the place hold? What was Ann trying to prove by revealing the contents of a manila envelope hidden away in her tote bag? How is the content related to the thesis of the essay?
2. Why does the author mention what was NOT inside Ann's bag before she describes what WAS inside? What is the most relevant item described? Why was there no need to discuss what was inside the folded sheet of typing paper?
3. In paragraph 6, what does the author mean when she says that nowadays children "do not understand what it means to go to their rooms because they have never had a room." In this case, what are the connotations of the "room"?
4. How do you respond to the author's allegation in paragraph 8 that we tend to lessen our involvement in people's pain by turning social problems into issues rather than into individual cases of misery? Try to challenge the author by citing instances that show a concern for the individual.
5. Why do some homeless people prefer to sleep sitting on a bench, cramped inside a cardboard box, or huddled in doorways rather than go to a shelter? The author mentions "pride of ownership" as a reason for not compromising by using a public shelter. What other reasons have been proposed? Which reason makes the most sense to you?

● The Strategies

1. What two self-criticisms does the author offer in paragraph 3? On whom does she blame the second fault? Do you consider these serious character flaws or something else? Explain your answer.
2. Do you agree that we as a society tend to "turn an adjective into a noun"? What other adjectives besides "poor" and "homeless" have we turned into nouns and with what results? Present some examples and explain the effect.
3. How do you interpret the author's use of "cross stitch" and "French knots" as images of home? Look up the word "sampler" in a dictionary if you are baffled by these images.
4. How does the color blue (see paragraph 7) fit into the main point the author is attempting to advance? Explain the importance of color in this particular example.
5. How were you affected by the opening sentence of the essay? Do you find it appealing or do you wish she had opened straight away with her thesis? Give specific reasons for your answer.

● The Issues

1. Quindlen's essay ends with the gripping exclamation, "My God. That is everything." If this exclamation pierces to the heart of Quindlen's thesis, then what is her thesis? What other word is directly connected with *everything*? Explain in your own words how Quindlen sees the tragic crux of homelessness.

2. What are some facts you yourself have observed that would either support, deny, or qualify the changes Quindlen addresses in paragraph 5? In other words, do you accept wholeheartedly her view that family ties have weakened or become irrelevant over the years, or do you see evidence that family ties are remaining strong but perhaps based on a different foundation than that of the past? Explain your response.

3. What is your interpretation of the author's claim that "Homes have stopped being homes. Now they are real estate"? Would you rather rent or own a place in which to rear your family? Give reasons for your answer.

4. According to the author (see paragraph 8), some "wise and compassionate people" have dedicated themselves to solving the problem of the homeless. What organizations or individuals do you believe to be actively working on this problem? Describe them and their activities.

5. Who in your experience qualifies for the term "homeless"? If you know of someone, describe the causes of this particular instance of homelessness. Could it have been avoided? How? What is your response to people sitting on city streets or at the entrances of freeways begging for money? What about the fellow who held up a sign warning, "THIS COULD BE YOU." What is your reply?

● Suggestions for Writing

1. Write an essay about the emotions—good or bad—you connect with your current home. Describe in vivid details what you love or hate about it. Find a key word (e.g., stability/insecurity, predictability/uncertainty, private/public, cozy/cold, etc.) to reflect the reason for your emotions.

2. With the help of some research, write a paper in which you gauge the present problem of taking care of the homeless in our country (or in some other county with which you are familiar). Cite important statistics if available and use expert testimony to bolster your argument.

David Doody/Index Stock Imagery/PhotoLibrary

● Why does a shopping cart become "home"?

The Homeless Lack a Political Voice, But Not American Ideals

MATT LYNCH

Matt Lynch writes a column for *University Wire.*

Exactly who are the homeless and how did they get that way? The answer you get depends on whom you ask. Conservatives maintain that the homeless mainly consist of people with addiction problems or those who are mentally ill. Liberals reply that anyone can become homeless during difficult economic times, that elements of bad luck and bad timing are often responsible for homelessness. These two points of view have a radical effect not only on our attitudes toward the homeless but on government policy. If we believe that people become homeless because of bad economics, we are inclined to help. If we think that addiction is to blame, we are more inclined to punish. This writer demonstrates that the stereotypes about the homeless are often off the mark and hollow.

● ● ●

1   Greg is a conservative's dream.

2   He wakes up every morning before 6:00 A.M., showers, eats breakfast, and dons a suit and tie. He goes to his office job every day, puts in more than forty hours per week, saves his money and doesn't drink. He gets back in time for dinner, watches the news and is in bed by 10:00 P.M.

3   Greg is not his real name. Homeless shelter volunteers are not permitted to give out the names of those staying in the facility, for fear of discrimination. It's a fear that is well-founded.

4   The prevailing attitudes toward the homeless in America are not particularly sympathetic. Most people view them as a minor annoyance; their only exposure to the homeless comes when someone on the street bothers them for change. Many would characterize them as a bunch of degenerates and alcoholics, fully deserving of their unfortunate fate.

5   If they would only get themselves together and get a job like everyone else, most say, they wouldn't find themselves in this predicament.

6   But it's a bit more complicated than that.

7   Homelessness in the wealthiest nation on earth is caused by a variety of factors and they are not always the result of repeated bad judgment by those who are homeless. For Greg, it came from the skyrocketing rents and housing prices in Boston, which did away with rent-control laws in 1997.

8   For others, it comes from an untimely lay-off and a lack of close relatives to take them in. Some, like a former Boston College basketball player and account coordinator whose story appeared in a recent *Boston Globe* column, just made one mistake—in his case, incurring the wrath of the I.R.S.

9   Walking into a homeless shelter in Cambridge, Massachusetts, the shelter where Greg sleeps, is not setting foot into the armpit of society. It's more akin to walking into a hospital waiting room: residents play cards, watch the news or read magazines. At dinnertime, they are as orderly and polite as anyone else.

10   The shelter is dry; anyone who is intoxicated is turned away at the door. Fights and rude language are no more common than in the rest of society. Residents are early to bed and early to rise, and strive to look as presentable as everyone else.

11   For most at this shelter, homelessness is not a career. They have fallen on hard times, and are trying to pull themselves up by their bootstraps. Anyone who buys into the American work ethic, particularly politicians, should be proud.

12   Yet efforts to help the homeless remain woefully under-funded, and the only legislation that deals with homelessness—the oft-amended McKinney-Vento Bill of 1987—addresses the effects rather than the causes of the problem. The National Coalition for the Homeless called for $4.3 billion for their efforts in the 2002 budget, an amount it says will still leave many of its programs without adequate funding. Bush requested just over half that amount for efforts to help the homeless.

13   In today's political climate, this is not surprising. Requests for homeless programs are seen as bleeding-heart-liberal garbage, further evidence of the liberals' tax-and-spend nature. They do not understand that efforts to help the homeless are compatible with the historical, mythical allure of America: the opportunity to start over, to begin anew. It brought colonists here as the continent was being settled, and it brought them to the frontier as the country grew.

14   But the frontier is gone; those with economic troubles can no longer escape to the West. Greg will probably escape homelessness through his shelter's progressive work-contract program, but he is one of the lucky ones.

15   Today's economy is struggling, and most homeless shelters do not have enough beds to go around. Not all of them have the resources for the kind of work-contract program Greg takes part in. Few can offer the necessary treatment for diseases that sometimes contribute to homelessness, namely mental illness and alcoholism.

16   Unfortunately, the problem will probably not be addressed until stereotypes disappear, until those begging on the street are no longer taken to represent the group as a whole, until people understand that those who are homeless often appear no different than anyone else. Most strive for the same goals and possess the same virtue, but do not have the same luck.

17   Politicians must change their attitudes, as well. They do deal with the effects of homelessness; no one enjoys hearing stories of the homeless freezing to death in winter months, and usually there are places for them to stay for some period of time. But the politicians need to get over their instinctive reactions against funding programs and address the roots of homelessness by helping people out of it.

18   The cause is not a hopeless one; it has simply never been given the resources it needs and deserves. Republicans and Democrats alike must recognize that though the homeless lack a strong political voice in this country, most do not lack its ideals.

From THE BADGER HERALD, February 14, 2002. Reprinted by permission of The BADGER HERALD.

● Vocabulary

prevailing (4)   woefully (12)   allure (13)
degenerates (4)   mythical (13)   stereotypes (16)

● The Facts

1. What is it that makes Greg a conservative's dream? Do you agree that he is a conservative's dream? Why or why not?

2. What is the prevailing attitude toward homelessness, according to the author? What is your own attitude?

3. What is the reason for Greg's homeless condition? What other reasons, besides irresponsibility and drug abuse, can you cite for the homelessness of certain people?

4. What institution does Greg's shelter resemble? What factors contribute to the resemblance?

5. According to the author, programs to help the homeless reflect the American Dream. What is the American Dream, and how can government programs help the homeless achieve it?

● The Strategies

1. What is the author's thesis, and where is it stated?

2. How does the author try to capture your attention at the start of his essay? How successful is he? What other effective introduction can you suggest?

3. What figures of speech does the author use to enliven his language? Name at least two and explain the meaning of each.

4. In paragraph 13, what effect does the expression "historical, mythical allure" create? Explain why you think the author used this phrase.

5. Why does the author insist that real help for the homeless cannot come until we get rid of stereotyping? What does stereotyping do to retard the general cause of helping the homeless?

● The Issues

1. What plan for helping people like Greg would you propose if you were mayor of your city or governor of your state? How would you propose to fund your plan?

2. What is the best method of demolishing established stereotypes—whether of the homeless, of certain ethnic groups, or of class levels?

3. In paragraph 12, the author mentions that current legislation deals with the effects, rather than the roots, of homelessness. What effects does he have in mind? What is the difference between cause and effect in this case?

4. How is the pursuit of the American Dream different today from, say, two centuries ago? What can we do to help the homeless pursue the American Dream?

5. Do you agree with the notion that anyone in a homeless shelter has the right to live there anonymously in order to avoid discrimination? Explain your answer.

● Suggestions for Writing

1. Write a proposal in which you suggest practical ways of helping the homeless reestablish themselves.

2. Write an essay in which you describe how a friend, relative, or acquaintance lost all possessions and the living conditions that this person was forced to accept. If help was offered, mention that as well.

Punctuation Workshop
Quotation Marks ("")

1. **Put quotation marks around the exact words of a speaker:**

   He said, "I'll buy the house."

2. **Begin every full quotation with a capital letter. If a quotation is broken, the second part does not begin with a capital letter unless it is a new sentence:**

   "You are an angel," Guido whispered, "and I want to marry you."

   "Some people feel," said the woman. "Others think."

   Set off with a comma the identification of the person who is speaking unless a question mark or exclamation mark is needed:

   "You need to learn how to use a computer," he told his grandfather.

   "Are you satisfied with your life?" she asked.

3. **When you are writing a dialogue, begin a new paragraph with each change of speaker:**

   "It never occurred to me that I might have a half-brother," he muttered.

   "Why not? It seemed so obvious to us," she said.

   If a speaker takes up more than one paragraph, put quotation marks at the beginning of each new paragraph. Use one set of quotation marks at the end of the last paragraph.

Antoinette Poodt

Furman University

People Out on a Limb

Homelessness is an epidemic in our country, but just how many people are homeless is unclear. One estimate says that 600,000 people are chronically homeless and another 700,000 sometimes homeless. A large number of the homeless are blacks and some 40 percent are veterans. The homeless are not lazy as some people think. Ninety percent of them once held jobs, and 15 to 20 percent of them are currently employed but unable to afford a home. In another chilling statistic, it was found that 40 percent of the homeless are entire families ("Ending Homelessness").

So what is the cause of homelessness? Some of the explanations suggest it is economic, and some suggest it is individual circumstances. But one cause of homelessness is almost certainly deinstitutionalization, or the releasing of patients from mental hospitals. In the early '70s, with the emergence of psychoactive drugs, deinstitutionalizing the homeless appeared to be a good way to save money and a way of giving freedom to people whose mental illnesses had trapped them in institutions such as asylums. Unfortunately, releasing the mentally ill into the streets and expecting them to function as responsible citizens turned out to be a pipe dream. Many of the mentally ill had developed "institutionalism," which means they had become used to living a life that had been over-regulated (Lamb). In a nutshell, people who were released on the streets were incapable of taking care of themselves.

As a society, many of us are unsure what we think about the homeless. The typical reaction is either one of pity or of condemnation. Yet, if we live in an urban area, the likelihood is great that our lives will intersect with the homeless people who hang out around our neighborhood. For the past year, for example, an elderly woman who was obviously mentally ill had been sleeping in a public garage near where I park. Some of my coworkers were so familiar with her that they would greet her by name. Some brought her food; some gave her money. When I worked late, I often saw her curled up asleep on pieces of cardboard laid out on the floor. One morning she was found dead in the same spot where she had always slept.

The attitude of my town towards the homeless is mixed. Because many of the homeless are dirty and smell from living outdoors, and because many of them are aggressive panhandlers, the city council often instructs the police to jail the homeless for vagrancy and keep them out of sight of the tourists. The police, themselves, are inconsistent in their treatment of the homeless. For example, there's a post office near work with two rooms filled with only post boxes. A homeless man sleeps in one of the rooms when the weather is bad. An older police officer cruising past will often turn a blind eye, but will make certain that the man is gone before daybreak. On the other hand, when the older police officer is off duty, other police officers drive the homeless man away from this makeshift shelter.

Not so long ago Americans had extended families who acted as a safety net against homelessness. If a family member fell on bad times, the unfortunate one would be welcomed into the home of an aunt or uncle or cousin and given shelter until he or she got on his or her feet. That sense of obligation to the extended family is rarely practiced anymore. Today's family generally consists of mom, pop, and children. We do not always feel a sense of obligation or responsibility for anyone else in the family. This shift has made the government a last resort. But government benefits have taken more cuts in the past three years than in the past twenty-five years. Rent has also risen substantially in the past few years, making the issue hit closer to home than many ever imagined. As a college student, who is earning below the poverty line, who cannot afford housing on her own, and who receives little or no government benefits, I can empathize with the homeless. When it comes right down to it, the only difference between me and a homeless person is that I have a family who cares.

It is easy for me to sit in judgment when I see a "bum" on the side of the street and think to myself that he should get a job, because I am not in his position. Usually as I walk past this helpless-looking unkempt creature, whose possessions are bundled in crude wrapping, I mutter to myself, "There, but for the grace of God, go I." And I sometimes even add a more secular thanksgiving, "There, but for the love of my family, go I."

Works Cited

"Ending Homelessness in America." *Mental Health Association.* Mental Health Assn., 2005. Web. 22 June 2005.

Lamb, H. Richard. "Deinstitutionalization and the Homeless Mentally Ill." *Interactivist.* N.p., June 2005. Web. 22 June 2005.

How I Write

Writing has always been a challenge for me, and it is usually very difficult for me to get started. Once I get the introduction down, however, the rest of the paper usually flows. Before I begin writing, I gather information about my topic, which I get from the Internet or the library. Then I go to my computer and begin typing. I cannot write in pen or pencil, and then type a paper. Instead, I type as I write. This is easier for me because it is simple to make corrections as I go along. When writing a paper or essay, I usually begin with a story, quote, or statement that will grab the reader's attention. Then, taking into account the audience and depending on the type of writing I am to do, I follow with an outline covering specific points. If the paper is a story about me, or something I am very familiar with, I do not follow an outline.

After I write the first draft, I begin with a spell check followed by a computer grammar check. Then I print out the paper and do at least three to five revisions. Once I think the paper is good, I give it to someone else to read. I feel that I do much better on a paper when I spend a few days revising it instead of writing, revising, and turning it in all in one day. When I leave a paper for a while, and then go back to look at it, I see new things that I can do to improve it. Once I have made all the revisions, I read it over one more time and then turn it in.

How I Wrote This Essay

I began this paper by doing research to get some facts on the homeless. It took me a while to figure out what spin I was going to take. I actually started this essay three or four times before I found the spin I wanted to use. Once I got started on the one I wanted, the essay flowed for me. After a very rough first draft, I revised the paper six times. Then I had my mom read it over to make any last-minute changes. While doing my corrections, my improvements were more instinctive than made for any specific reason. When I thought I could not change the paper any more, I printed out the last copy.

My Writing Tip

One word of wisdom I can give to fellow writers is to learn to type on a computer as they write. Being a college student, I do not know where I would find the time if I had to write, say, in pen or pencil, and then type. Corrections are so much quicker and easier to make when you can see them on the computer screen. It saves so much time, leading to less stress and hence better writing.

Another tip I would give is not to follow a cookie-cutter style of writing. Find your style, become comfortable with it, and use it whenever you write. Do not let one teacher discourage your writing ability because he or she doesn't like your style. We all have our own style. Write in your own style and your paper will turn out better than if you try to write like everyone else. In other words, trust your own personality.

● CHAPTER WRITING ASSIGNMENTS

1. Write an essay arguing the point that religion is a conditioned reflex.

2. Write an argument opposing or supporting a recent legislative action imposed by our government.

3. Write an argument pointing out the benefits or the dangers of our political parties becoming more and more polarized.

4. Should a belief in intelligent creation be taught along with Darwin's theory of evolution? Write an argument answering this question.

5. Write an essay suggesting ways of achieving sexual equality.

● TERM PAPER SUGGESTIONS

Investigate the major arguments related to any one of the following subjects:

a. The influence of the church in our country today

b. Animal experimentation

c. Better care for the poor

d. Increased emphasis on physical fitness

e. Careful monitoring of the ecosystems on our planet

f. Equal rights for women (or some other population group)

g. Maintaining ethnic identities in a pluralistic environment

h. Improved local and federal response to natural disasters

i. The need for a national health program that provides funding for long-term health care

● WRITING ASSIGNMENTS FOR A SPECIFIC AUDIENCE

1. Write an essay arguing for a campus completely free of smoking. Your audience consists of the readers of your college paper. State your proposition clearly and support it with convincing evidence about the hazards of secondhand smoke.

2. Write an essay in which you argue that movies often portray minorities inaccurately or offensively. Be specific with your facts and examples.

● IMAGE GALLERY WRITING ASSIGNMENT

Visit pages IG-27–IG-29 of our image gallery and study all three images dealing with homelessness. Then choose the image that most appeals to you. Answer the questions and do the writing assignment.

Pointer from a Pro

READ WELL, WRITE WELL

Back in the '20s there was no rivalry between people who watched movies and those who read. Technology was an art form. We watched movies, but we also read. No one supervised our reading. We were on our own. We civilized ourselves. We found or made a mental and imaginative life. Because we could read, we learned also to write. From watching Charlie Chaplin in *The Gold Rush* to reading Jack London's stories was a short step. If the woods were filled with readers gone astray, among those readers there were probably writers as well.

—Saul Bellow

The parallel today is our present world of technology. If you can watch TV, your computer, your iPad, or any other modern electronic device and then segue from there to a book or an article, you can probably become part of the minority of "highbrows" who write well, for research continues to draw a close connection between people who read and people who write.

17
Combining the Modes

What Combining the Modes Does

The rhetorical modes are an idealization. In the rough-and-tumble writing of the everyday world, they exist only in hit-or-miss practice. It is possible to find a paragraph or even an entire essay that is written strictly in one mode; it is far more typical to find essays that blend the modes rather than observe them faithfully. Writing, a creative art, is nothing if not unpredictable.

Here are two examples that illustrate what we mean. The first is a paragraph that we would say was developed by *illustration.* It opens with the traditional topic sentence (highlighted), which it then supports with a series of examples.

Considerations of what makes for good English or bad English are to an uncomfortably large extent matters of prejudice and conditioning. Until the eighteenth century it was correct to say "you was" if you were referring to one person. It sounds odd today, but the logic is impeccable. *Was* is a singular verb and *were* a plural one. Why should *you* take a plural verb when the sense is clearly singular? The answer—surprise, surprise—is that Robert Lowth[1] didn't like it. "I'm hurrying, are I not?" is hopelessly ungrammatical, but "I'm hurrying, aren't I?"—merely a contraction of the same words—is perfect English. *Many* is almost always a plural (as in "Many people were there"), but not when it is followed by *a,* as in "Many a man was there." There's no inherent reason why these things should be so. They are not defensible in terms of grammar. They are because they are.

—Bill Bryson, *The Mother Tongue: English and How It Got That Way*

---

[1]An amateur grammarian whose influential book, *A Short Introduction to English Grammar* (1762), enshrined many of the stupid rules of English usage still observed today.

Here, however, is an example of a mixed-mode paragraph that is even more typical of everyday writing:

causal
analysis
illustration

comparison
argument

> English grammar is so complex and confusing for the one very simple reason that its rules and terminology are based on Latin—a language with which it has precious little in common. In Latin, to take one example, it is not possible to split an infinitive. So in English, the early authorities decided, it should not be possible to split an infinitive either. But there is no reason why we shouldn't, any more than we should forsake instant coffee and air travel because they weren't available to the Romans. Making English grammar conform to Latin rules is like asking people to play baseball using the rules of football. It is a patent absurdity. But once this insane notion became established grammarians found themselves having to draw up ever more complicated and circular arguments to accommodate the inconsistencies. As Burchfield notes in *The English Language,* one authority, F. Th. Visser, found it necessary to devote 200 pages to discussing just one aspect of the present participle. That is as crazy as it is amazing.

—Bill Bryson, *The Mother Tongue: English and How It Got That Way*

The writer begins with a causal analysis, gives an illustration, makes a comparison, and then develops an argument.

This is exactly how writers actually write. They treat the rhetorical modes the way a baker might treat a cookie cutter. The object is to produce cookies, not exalt the cutter. It is the same with the rhetorical modes—they exist to make writing easier for beginners. When you're no longer a beginner, you will discard them.

When to Combine the Modes

Combining modes is a tactic many writers follow, especially for long and complex subjects. You should use a combination of modes only when you feel comfortable with it and when your subject is a particularly demanding one that requires a complex form. If you're ranging far afield on an unfamiliar topic, you may not wish to follow any strict pattern and might prefer to improvise as you go along. This is the ideal time to combine the rhetorical modes.

How to Use Combined Modes

The key in writing a mixed-mode essay is to stick to the point and use ample transitions. Essays that are written in a combination of modes have a tendency to either drift from the point or to be herky-jerky rather than smooth. Writers overcome these tendencies by using the techniques of paragraph writing covered in Chapter 7 (now would be a good time to review this material). If you use transitions to guide the reader from one point to the next and if you faithfully stick to your announced topic, your mixed-mode essays will read as smoothly as anything you've ever written in any single pattern. Here is an example of a mixed-mode paragraph that sticks to the point. The writer is discussing the implements that the Arawak Indians, who lived in Jamaica at the time of Columbus, used in their daily lives. He begins with a description, moves to a process, and ends with a definition. He is able to do all of these things without losing the reader because his focus is so tight and his transitions skillful.

> Apart from earthen pots and other utensils, the main items of furniture were hammocks and wooden stools. The hammock was an Indian invention (even the original name, which was *hamac*), one which was not known in Europe before the discovery of the West Indies. These hammocks were made either of cotton string "open-work," or of a length of woven cotton cloth, sometimes dyed in bright colours. Jamaica was well known at that period for the cultivation of cotton, and much of the women's time was spent spinning and weaving it. In fact Jamaica supplied hammocks and cotton cloth to Cuba and Haiti for some time after those islands had been occupied by Spain, and the Spaniards themselves had sail-cloth made in Jamaica. Because of this, one of the many suggested origins of the name *Jamaica* attempts to link it with the Indian word for hammock and to prove that it means "land of cotton." The name Jamaica is of great interest. Some of the early Spanish historians, substituting X for J as they often did, write the name *Xaymaca,* but it also appears in its present form in a work published as early as 1511. Columbus called the island *St. Jago* (Santiago), but as with the other islands of the Greater Antilles, the Indian name has survived the Spanish. It is commonly thought that Xaymaca in the Arawak language meant "land of springs," but since the discoverers do not give the meaning of the name (as they do in the case of various place-names in Haiti) it is possible that the meaning had already been forgotten by the Indians themselves.
>
> —Clinton V. Black, *The Story of Jamaica*

Notice the repetition of the word *hammocks,* the variant forms of *Jamaica,* and the writer's use of the transitional sentence "The name Jamaica is of great interest." These little transitional touches are designed to nudge the reader along the writer's line of thought.

To sum up, if you do not now do it, eventually you will find yourself commonly writing essays that conform more to the mixed-mode pattern than to any other. The rhetorical modes are useful tools for the beginning writer, but less so for the veteran. As you make your way through school, you, too, will become a practiced writer who has outgrown them.

EXAMPLES

Shrew—The Littlest Mammal

ALAN DEVOE

Rhetorical Thumbnail

Purpose: to inform us about the life habits of the littlest mammal

Audience: educated readers

Language: academic English

Strategy: covers the life cycle of the shrew from birth to death

Alan DeVoe (1909–1955) wrote many naturalist essays that were much admired by his readers. He also contributed widely to numerous magazines, among them the *American Mercury, Audubon,* and *Readers' Digest.* Additionally, he was the author of numerous books, including *Phudd Hill* (1937), *Down to Earth* (1940), and *This Fascinating Animal World* (1951).

DeVoe's description of the tiniest mammal, the shrew, tells us how this frenzied little beast got its reputation for ferocity. The shrew, having features similar to those of a mouse, is so rabid about pursuing its one mission in life—to eat—that it will attack animals twice its size. DeVoe uses paragraphs of different modes to portray the life cycle of this tiny creature whose nature is driven by a giant appetite.

• • •

1   The zoological Class to which we human beings belong is the Mammalia. There has been some dispute as to whether we possess immortal souls and the capacity for a unique kind of intellection, but we do possess unquestionably the ". . . four-chambered heart, double circulatory system, thoracic cavity separated from abdominal cavity by muscular diaphragm, and habit of bearing the young alive and nursing them at the breast" which classically establish our membership in that group of warm-blooded animals which are guessed to have come into being on the planet some hundred-odd million years ago.

2   It is today a large and various group, this mammalian kindred. With some of our fellow-mammals it is not hard to feel relationship: with apes, for instance, or with the small sad-eyed monkeys that we keep for our beguilement as flea-bitten captives in our pet shops. But with others of the group our tie is less apparent; and the reason, often enough, is disparity of size and shape. It is such disparity, no doubt, that prevents our having much fellow-feeling for the hundred-ton sulphur-bottomed whales that plunge through the deep waters of both Pacific and Atlantic, though whales' blood is warmed as ours is, and the

females of their kind have milky teats; and likewise it is doubtless in part because we have two legs and attain to some seventy inches of height that we do not take as much account as otherwise we might of the little animal that is at the opposite end of the mammal size-scale: the little four-footed mammal that is rather smaller than a milkweed pod and not as heavy as a cecropia cocoon.

3   This tiniest of mammals is the minute beast called a shrew. A man need go to no great trouble to look at it, as he must to see a whale; he can find it now in the nearest country woodlot. Despite its tininess a shrew is still after a fashion a relative of ours; and on that account, even if on no other, should merit a little knowing.

4   In the narrow twisting earth-burrow dug by a mouse or a mole the least of the mammals is usually born. Its fellows in the litter may number four or five, and they lie together in the warm subterranean darkness of their tiny nest chamber in a little group whose whole bulk is scarcely that of a walnut. The infant shrew, relative of whales and elephants and us, is no more than a squirming pink speck of warm-fleshed animal aliveness. Totally defenseless and unequipped for life, it can only nuzzle the tiny dugs of its mother, wriggle tightly against its brothers to feel the warmth of the litter, and for many hours of the twenty-four lie asleep in the curled head-to-toes position of a minuscule foetus.

5   The baby shrew remains a long time in the birth-chamber. The size of even an adult shrew is very nearly the smallest possible for mammalian existence, and the young one cannot venture out into the world of adult activity until it has almost completely matured. Until then, therefore, it stays in the warm darkness of the burrow, knowing the universe only as a heat of other little bodies, a pungence of roots and grasses, a periodic sound of tiny chittering squeakings when its mother enters the burrow after foraging-trips, bringing food. She brings in mostly insects—small lady-beetles whose brittle spotted wing-covers must be removed before they can be eaten, soft-bodied caterpillars, ants, and worms. The young shrew, after its weaning has come about, acquires the way of taking this new food between its slim delicate forepaws, fingered like little hands, and in the under-earth darkness nibbles away the wing-covers and chitinous body-shells as adroitly as a squirrel removes the husk from a nut.

6   When at last the time comes for the young shrew to leave its birthplace, it has grown very nearly as large as its mother and has developed all the adult shrew-endowments. It looks, now, not unlike a mouse, save that its muzzle is more sharply pointed, but a mouse reduced in size to extreme miniature. The whole length of its soft-furred little body is only a fraction more than two inches, compared to the four-inch length of even the smallest of the white-footed woods-mice; its tail is less than half as long as a mouse's. The uniquely little body is covered with dense soft hair, sepia above and a paler buffy color underneath—a covering of fur so fine and close that the shrew's ears are nearly invisible in it, and the infinitesimal eyes are scarcely to be discerned. The shrew's hands and feet are white, smaller and more delicate than any other beast's; white also is the underside of the minute furry tail. The whole body, by its softness of coat and coloring and its tininess of bulk, seems far from kinship

with the tough strong bodies of the greater mammals. But it is blood-brother to these, all the same; warm blood courses in it; the shrew is as much mammal as a wolf. It sets forth, with its unparalleledly tiny physical equipments, to live as adventurous a life as any of its greater warm-blooded relatives.

7   The life-adventure of Man, "the medium-sized mammal," is shaped by such diverse motives and impulsions that it is difficult to say what may be the most powerful of the driving urges that direct it. In the life-adventure of the littlest mammal, the shrew, the driving urge is very plain and single: it is hunger. Like hummingbirds, smallest of the aves, this smallest of the mammals lives at a tremendous pitch of nervous intensity. The shrew's little body quite literally quivers with the vibrance of life-force that is in it; from tiny pointed snout to tailtip the shrew is ever in a taut furor of aliveness. Its body-surface, like a hummingbird's, is maximally extensive in relation to its minimal weight; its metabolism must proceed with immense rapidity; to sustain the quivering nervous aliveness of its mite of warm flesh it must contrive a food-intake that is almost constant. It is possible on that account to tell the shrew's life-story almost wholly in terms of its feeding. The shrew's life has other ingredients, of course—the seeking of its small mate, the various rituals of copulating and sleeping and dung-dropping and the rest, that are common to all mammal lives—but it is the process of feeding that is central and primary, and that is the distinguishing preoccupation of the littlest mammal all its days.

8   The shrew haunts mostly moist thick-growing places, the banks of streams and the undergrowth of damp woods, and it hunts particularly actively at night. Scuttling on its pattery little feet among the fallen leaves, scrabbling in the leaf-mould in a frenzy of tiny investigation, it looks ceaselessly for food. Not a rodent, like a mouse, but an insectivore, it seizes chiefly on such creatures as crickets, grasshoppers, moths, and ants, devouring each victim with nervous eagerness and at once rushing on with quivering haste, tiny muzzle incessantly a-twitch, to look for further provender.

9   Not infrequently the insects discoverable in the shrew's quick scampering little sallies through the darkness are inadequate to nourish it, so quick is its digestion and so intense the nervous energy it must sustain. When this is the case, the shrew widens its diet-range, to include seeds or berries or earthworms or any other sustenance that it can stuff with its little shivering forepaws into its tiny muzzle. It widens its diet to include meat; it becomes a furious and desperate carnivore. It patters through the grass-runways of the meadow-mice, sniffing and quivering; it darts to the nest of a deer-mouse. And presently, finding deer-mouse or meadowmouse, it plunges into a wild attack on this "prey" that is twice its size. The shrew fights with a kind of mad recklessness; it becomes a leaping, twisting, chittering, squeaking speck of hungering fury. Quite generally, when the battle is over, the shrew has won. Its thirty-two pinpoint teeth are sharp and strong, and the wild fury of its attack takes the victim by surprise. For a little while, after victory, the shrew's relentless body-needs are appeased. For a little while, but only a little; and then the furry speck must go pattering and scuttling forth into the night again, sniffing for food and quivering with need.

10   That is the pattern of shrew-life: a hunting and a hungering that never stops, an endless preoccupied catering to the demands of the kind of metabolism which unique mammalian smallness necessitates. The littlest mammal is a mammal in all ways; it breathes and sleeps and mates and possibly exults, as others do; but chiefly, as the price of unique tininess, it engages in restless never-ending search for something to eat.

11   The way of a shrew's dying is sometimes curious. Sometimes, of course, it dies in battle, when the larger prey which it has tackled proves too strong. Sometimes it dies of starvation; it can starve in a matter of hours. But often it is set upon by one of the big predators—some fox or lynx or man. When that happens, it is usually not the clutch of fingers or the snap of the carnivorous jaws that kills the shrew. The shrew is usually dead before that. At the first instant of a lynx's pounce—at the first touch of a human hand against the shrew's tiny quivering body—the shrew is apt to shiver in a quick violent spasm, and then lie still in death. The littlest of the mammals dies, as often as not, of simple nervous shock.

From THIS FASCINATING ANIMAL WORLD, 1951

Vocabulary

beguilement (2)	infinitesimal (6)	extensive (7)
disparity (2)	discerned (6)	contrive (7)
minuscule (4)	diverse (7)	provender (8)
chitinous (5)	impulsions (7)	exults (10)
adroitly (5)		

The Facts

1. About which zoological fact is the author sure? About which element is he less sure? Why is he so much more sure about one than the other?

2. Where is the shrew usually born? What does this tell us about shrew parents?

3. In terms of its impulses, how does the shrew differ from its other mammal relatives? What causes this difference?

4. If the shrew can't find enough insects to feed its hunger, what will it do?

5. If insects and vegetation are not available, what will the shrew do to get the food it so badly needs to stay alive? What attitude does the shrew convey? How do you view this attitude?

The Strategies

1. This essay reveals the use of more than one rhetorical mode. What modes other than description are used? Try to name these modes paragraph by paragraph.

2. What dominant impression of the shrew did you receive from this essay?

3. What is the purpose of the quotation in the opening paragraph? What, if anything, does it add to the essay?

4. Of what help is paragraph 10 as you learn about the shrew?

5. Why does the author sprinkle specialized terms throughout the essay (e.g., *cecropia, cocoon, chitinous body shells*)? How do these terms affect the author's style?

● The Issues

1. The author declares a kinship among whales, monkeys, shrews, and humans. Of the nonhuman mammals, which do you feel closest to? Why? Of all animals, which one would you prefer to have as a pet? Why?

2. Do you agree with the author that because the shrew is related to us, we should know something about this mammal? Give reasons for your answer. What other reasons are there to encourage us to learn more about animals?

3. If a woman is called a "shrew," what is meant by the label? What connection can you see between this metaphor and the tiniest mammal?

4. Do you think that laboratory experiments on the mammalian shrew would be justified if the purpose were to benefit humans?

5. What is the largest mammal? Where have you seen this mammal other than in pictures? How do you react toward it?

● Suggestions for Writing

1. Describe the most interesting animal you have ever observed. If needed, use more than one rhetorical mode for this assignment.

2. Choose one of the following creatures and write an essay describing in what ways it is superior to human beings: lion, tiger, cat, dog, eagle, snake, or ant.

Will Spelling Count?

JACK CONNOR

Rhetorical Thumbnail

Purpose: to convince readers that good writing is hard work and demands control of details like spelling

Audience: English teachers and students

Language: standard English, written with an authoritative voice

Strategy: draws a humorous self-portrait and shows the effects of counting or not counting spelling

Jack Connor grew up in New Jersey and received his PhD from the University of Florida. For many years he taught English in the Department of Humanities and Communications at Drexel University in Philadelphia. It is interesting to note that in 2003, the freshman composition teachers of Drexel University created a *Handbook for Freshman Writing* to help new teachers teach their classes effectively.

For those students who have always been anxious about the mechanics in their compositions, Connor offers an answer. Although his essay mainly focuses on the importance of

spelling, his journey of discovery can be applied to other aspects of writing, such as grammar, organization, clarity of purpose, and style. The point is that writing requires meticulous effort, so keep that in mind as you read about Connor's experiences in the college classroom.

• • •

1   "Will spelling count?" In my first year of teaching freshman composition I had a little act I performed whenever a student asked that inevitable question. Frowning, taking my pipe out of my mouth, and hesitating, I would try to look like a man coming down from some higher mental plane. Then, with what I hoped sounded like a mixture of confidence and disdain, I would answer, "No. Of course it won't."

2   In that first year, I was convinced that to have a significant effect on my students' writing I had to demonstrate that I was not the stereotypical English teacher: a fussbudget who would pick through their essays in search of misspellings and trivial errors. I intended to inspire students in my classes to write the kinds of papers the unconventional teachers I had read about—John Holt, A. S. Neill, Herbert Kohl, and Ken Macrorie—had inspired: papers bristling with life, written by the students with their inner voices.

3   It was not to be. Week after week students handed in papers that had obviously been dashed off in 30 or 40 minutes. By the end of the year I realized my mistake: I had been too subtle; I had not made it clear enough that mine was a revolutionary way to teach writing.

4   So, in my second year, I answered the question with a 50-minute lecture. I quoted education theories, told several semifictional stories of my student days, and recited some entirely fictional statistics—all of which argued that people write better when they don't worry about spelling.

5   "What you have to do is write honestly about things you care about," I told them. "Don't interrupt your thoughts to check your spelling."

6   That lecture—and other strategic changes I made in my teaching style that second year—had no noticeable effect. Once again, almost all the papers were dull, predictable, and carelessly done. My students didn't understand that writing could be an act of self-exploration and discovery.

7   They wrote essays of two kinds: unorganized narratives with such titles as "My First Drunk" or "How to Roll a Joint at 70 m.p.h." and fourth-hand, insipid arguments with such titles as "Capital Punishment Is Murder" or "The Space Race—What a Waste."

8   Since assigning topics or imposing organizational schemes would mark me as just another conventional English teacher, killing any chance I had to inspire my students to discover their inner voices, I tried to proceed indirectly—with class discussions on subjects I thought would make good topics: the latest editorial in the student newspaper, the problems of communicating with parents and friends, political apathy, the sights and sounds of the campus. However, although I could sometimes get a "lively" discussion going, it was obvious that the students saw these exchanges not as relevant to their writing but as a painless way to spend the 50 minutes. They sat up and took note only to ask

me about the mechanical details of the next assignment: "How many words does it have to be?" "How much do you take off for late papers?" "Is it O.K. to write in blue ink?"

9   It was in that year that I began to be embarrassed by my students' course evaluations. They usually gave me top grades in every category and then wrote something such as, "This was a great class because the teacher understood that students in this university have a lot of other things to worry about besides his particular course."

10   By the start of the third year, I was wondering whether the education theorists had known what they were talking about. When the usual question came, I equivocated and told them they could decide questions about spelling for themselves.

11   It was a low point. By that time a couple of hundred freshmen had passed through my composition classes, but I could not have named one who had discovered himself as a writer because of my teaching. Of the few A+ papers in my files, half were written by students who could have written an A+ paper the first day of class; the rest were happy accidents, written by students in moments of inspiration they were unable to repeat.

12   That year, one student wrote in his evaluation, "This was a very good course because the teacher believed college students are mature enough to make their own decisions about things like whether spelling is important. It isn't important to me. I'm going to let my secretary take care of my spelling."

13   I knew it was time for a radical change. I was going to have to give up trying to teach my students that writing could be an act of self-exploration; I would have to concentrate on teaching a truth more essential to their education: Writing is hard work.

14   In the summer before my fourth year, I wrote a ten-page syllabus, two pages of which were given over to the old questions and my new answers:

Q: Is blue ink acceptable?
A: No. In fact, handwriting is unacceptable. All papers in this course must be typed.
Q: What about students who can't type?
A: This course will provide them with an opportunity to learn.
Q: Why do papers have to be typed?
A: Because in the real world adults type when they want to put serious communications in writing.
Q: What if we can't hand a paper in on time?
A: Hand it in as soon as possible. It will be marked "late."
Q: What if we have a legitimate excuse?
A: Keep it to yourself. My job is to evaluate your writing, not your excuses.

15   Knowing the eternal question would come up the first day, I had my best answer in reserve. When one of the students asked it after my introductory talk, I crossed my arms and let them have it.

16   "The best answer to that question is an analogy: Imagine a team of college basketball players meeting their coach for the first time. The coach distributes a book outlining the plays he will be teaching them, and then talks to them about how the practices will be organized, what he thinks his role should be, and what he considers their responsibilities to be. When he has finished, the first question is, 'Will dribbling count?'"

17   The student who asked the question dropped the course, as did a couple of others who didn't like their first impressions of me and my nasty syllabus. But my new tone, and the classroom style it forced me to adopt, had several excellent consequences:

18   I stopped trying to make the class interesting. No more lively discussions on the sights and sounds of the campus—or anything else that wasn't directly related to helping my students write better this week than they had last week.

19   I learned to keep oral analysis and commentary to a minimum, because it disappeared into the air over my classroom. I put all directions and suggestions in writing, and tried to note on each of the papers submitted where the writer had followed my advice and where he had not.

20   The students spent more and more time pushing their pens across paper in class: writing thesis statements, writing drafts of introductory paragraphs, listing ten concrete words (five from last week's essay, five they thought they could use in next week's), working to arrange a sentence or two from their last essay into a parallel structure.

21   I stopped hoping to find in the weekly pile of papers evidence of some student writing with his inner voice. Inspired papers continued to appear at the old rate (about one in a hundred), but I no longer looked to them for proof of my effectiveness as a teacher.

22   A new kind of paper appeared in the weekly pile: well organized, mechanically polished, and clearly a second or third draft. Although some of them were titled "My First Drunk" and "The Space Race—What a Waste," I could read them attentively and praise their strengths sincerely.

23   Finally, I received some negative comments in the course evaluations: "I did not enjoy this class. The teacher was too finicky and graded too hard."

24   After four years of teaching I had learned that, given my particular skills, I had to leave consciousness-raising to other teachers. My first three years had been unsuccessful because I had been too intent on playing the guru, and I couldn't pull it off. The role I adopted that fourth year was not one I was comfortable with—Ken Macrorie is a hero of mine, not Vince Lombardi—but I could pull it off. And, more important, the tyrannical coach was a character my students recognized, and they understood what would be expected of them.

25   Last year, on my way to a different university, I decided to modify the role a little. The new syllabus has the old rules, but—while still playing the traditional authoritarian—I have changed my tone to that of a man sure of what he wants his students to do, certain they can do it, but too cool to be nasty about it.

26   This year, I have a little act I perform whenever a student asks, "Will spelling count?" Frowning, taking my pipe out of my mouth, and hesitating a moment, I try to look like a man coming down from some higher plane. Then, with

what I hope sounds like a mixture of confidence and disdain, I reply, "Yes. Of course it will."

"Will Spelling Count" by Jack Connor appeared in THE CHRONICLE OF HIGHER EDUCATION, June 2, 1980. Reprinted with permission from the author.

● Vocabulary

inevitable (1)	apathy (8)	analogy (16)
disdain (1)	equivocated (10)	oral (19)
stereotypical (2)	radical (13)	guru (24)
strategic (6)	legitimate (14)	authoritarian (25)
insipid (7)		

● The Facts

1. What conspicuous change did the author make in his approach to teaching composition? How long did it take him to make that change?

2. What were the typical questions asked by students about their essays? Try to add some current questions to the list.

3. What two kinds of essays did Connor receive from his students? Do you think teachers still receive these kinds of essays today? Explain your answer.

4. What is Connor's ultimate answer to the question posed in the title of the essay? Do you think most composition teachers today would give the same answer?

5. What reason does Connor offer for his requirement that students type their papers? Does his reason still hold true today?

● The Strategies

1. How does the author's essay come full circle in the end? How effective is this strategy? What does it bring to the essay?

2. How is paragraph 14 different from the other paragraphs? What does it do for the essay?

3. What is the purpose of paragraphs 19 to 23? What would the essay lose if these paragraphs were deleted?

4. What descriptive details in Connor's essay no longer fit the current group of English teachers? What details could be added that probably did not exist at the time of Connor's writing? Which of Connor's observations are still prevalent in composition classes?

5. How does Connor indicate the passage of time? What is remarkable about his pacing?

● The Issues

1. What is the thesis of Connor's essay? Is it entirely limited to spelling? If not, what more expanded thesis does he develop?

2. Do you agree with Connor that writing is hard work? (See paragraph 13.) Or does writing for you flow easily as your fingers fly across the computer keyboard? Evaluate the ease or difficulty with which you write.

3. Which kind of professor do you value most—the cool guru who helps you through self-discovery or the teacher who teaches with lucid objectives that he or she tries to achieve in class? Describe the kind of English teacher you consider ideal.

4. Do you think that lively class discussions are useful to the writing process or are they "a painless way to spend 50 minutes"? (See paragraph 8.) Explain your answer with appropriate evidence to support your point.

5. After studying this essay, how convinced are you by the author's views? Is his essay still relevant to today's freshman composition students? Or has the computer rendered his ideas beside the point? Do not simply answer yes or no, but give reasons for each of your answers.

● Suggestions for Writing

1. Write an essay offering your opinion on the importance of mechanics and grammar in writing English. In other words, ask yourself if it is more important to express a profound and important thought than to write correctly. Support your thesis with strong examples.

2. Write an essay in which you describe the changes that have taken place in freshman composition courses over the last ten years. Consider these innovations: (1) interactive computers that allow you to communicate after class with your teacher; (2) submitting your papers electronically to the teacher; (3) doing library research on the Internet; (4) using spelling and grammar checks on your computer.

Once More to the Lake

E. B. WHITE

Rhetorical Thumbnail

Purpose: on the face of it, to relate a traditional family holiday

Audience: educated readers

Language: standard English, written in an elegant style

Strategy: lulls the reader into a mood of quiet reminiscence—and then drops the bombshell

Elwyn Brooks White (1899–1985) was one of the wittiest and most admired observers of contemporary American society. As a member of *The New Yorker* magazine staff, he wrote a number of essays for the section called "Talk of the Town"; some of these essays have been collected in *The Wild Flag* (1946) and *Writings from* The New Yorker (1991). With James Thurber, White wrote *Is Sex Necessary?* (1929). His other well-known works include *One Man's Meat* (1942), *Here Is New York* (1949), and two beloved children books, *Stuart Little* (1945) and *Charlotte's Web* (1952).

This essay ends with a bang, not a whimper. The writer tackles what might seem at first glance a humdrum subject—an annual vacation trip to a lake—and describes in evocative and lovely prose the carefree summer days he spent hiking and fishing with his son. Then, at the very end, the true meaning of the essay is revealed.

• • •

August 1941

1   One summer, along about 1904, my father rented a camp on a lake in Maine and took us all there for the month of August. We all got ringworm from some kittens and had to rub Pond's Extract on our arms and legs night and morning, and my father rolled over in a canoe with all his clothes on; but outside of that the vacation was a success and from then on none of us ever thought there was any place in the world like that lake in Maine. We returned summer after summer—always on August 1 for one month. I have since become a salt-water man, but sometimes in summer there are days when the restlessness of the tides and the fearful cold of the sea water and the incessant wind that blows across the afternoon and into the evening make me wish for the placidity of a lake in the woods. A few weeks ago this feeling got so strong I bought myself a couple of bass hooks and a spinner and returned to the lake where we used to go, for a week's fishing and to revisit old haunts.

2   I took along my son, who had never had any fresh water up his nose and who had seen lily pads only from train windows. On the journey over to the lake I began to wonder what it would be like. I wondered how time would have marred this unique, this holy spot—the coves and streams, the hills that the sun set behind, the camps and the paths behind the camps. I was sure that the tarred road would have found it out, and I wondered in what other ways it would be desolated. It is strange how much you can remember about places like that once you allow your mind to return into the grooves that lead back. You remember one thing, and that suddenly reminds you of another thing. I guess I remembered clearest of all the early mornings, when the lake was cool and motionless, remembered how the bedroom smelled of the lumber it was made of and of the wet woods whose scent entered through the screen. The partitions in the camp were thin and did not extend clear to the top of the rooms, and as I was always the first up I would dress softly so as not to wake the others, and sneak out into the sweet outdoors and start out in the canoe, keeping close along the shore in the long shadows of the pines. I remembered being very careful never to rub my paddle against the gunwale for fear of disturbing the stillness of the cathedral.

3   The lake had never been what you would call a wild lake. There were cottages sprinkled around the shores, and it was in farming country although the shores of the lake were quite heavily wooded. Some of the cottages were owned by nearby farmers, and you would live at the shore and eat your meals at the farmhouse. That's what our family did. But although it wasn't wild, it was a fairly large and undisturbed lake and there were places in it that, to a child at least, seemed infinitely remote and primeval.

4   I was right about the tar: it led to within half a mile of the shore. But when I got back there, with my boy, and we settled into a camp near a farmhouse and into the kind of summertime I had known, I could tell that it was going to be pretty much the same as it had been before—I knew it, lying in bed the first morning smelling the bedroom and hearing the boy sneak quietly out and go off along the shore in a boat. I began to sustain the illusion that he was I, and therefore, by simple transposition, that I was my father. This sensation persisted, kept cropping up all the time we were there. It was not an entirely new feeling, but in this setting it grew much stronger. I seemed to be living a dual existence. I would be in the middle of some simple act, I would be picking up a bait box or laying down a table fork, or I would be saying something and suddenly it would be not I but my father who was saying the words or making the gesture. It gave me a creepy sensation.

5   We went fishing the first morning. I felt the same damp moss covering the worms in the bait can, and saw the dragonfly alight on the tip of my rod as it hovered a few inches from the surface of the water. It was the arrival of this fly that convinced me beyond any doubt that everything was as it always had been, that the years were a mirage and that there had been no years. The small waves were the same, chucking the rowboat under the chin as we fished at anchor, and the boat was the same boat, the same color green and the ribs broken in the same places, and under the floorboards the same fresh water leavings and débris—the dead helgramite, the wisps of moss, the rusty discarded fishhook, the dried blood from yesterday's catch. We stared silently at the tips of our rods, at the dragonflies that came and went. I lowered the tip of mine into the water, tentatively, pensively dislodging the fly, which darted two feet away, poised, darted two feet back, and came to rest again a little farther up the rod. There had been no years between the ducking of this dragonfly and the other one—the one that was part of memory. I looked at the boy, who was silently watching his fly, and it was my hands that held his rod, my eyes watching. I felt dizzy and didn't know which rod I was at the end of.

6   We caught two bass, hauling them in briskly as though they were mackerel, pulling them over the side of the boat in a businesslike manner without any landing net, and stunning them with a blow on the back of the head. When we got back for a swim before lunch, the lake was exactly where we had left it, the same number of inches from the dock, and there was only the merest suggestion of a breeze. This seemed an utterly enchanted sea, this lake you could leave to its own devices for a few hours and come back to, and find that it had not stirred, this constant and trustworthy body of water. In the shallows, the dark, water-soaked sticks and twigs, smooth and old, were undulating in clusters on the bottom against the clean ribbed sand, and the track of the mussel was plain. A school of minnows swam by, each minnow with its small individual shadow, doubling the attendance, so clear and sharp in the sunlight. Some of the other campers were in swimming, along the shore, one of them with a cake of soap, and the water felt thin and clear and unsubstantial. Over the years there had been this person with the cake of soap, this cultist, and here he was. There had been no years.

7   Up to the farmhouse to dinner through the teeming dusty field, the road under our sneakers was only a two-track road. The middle track was missing, the one with the marks of the hooves and the splotches of dried, flaky manure. There had always been three tracks to choose from in choosing which track to walk in; now the choice was narrowed down to two. For a moment I missed terribly the middle alternative. But the way led past the tennis court, and something about the way it lay there in the sun reassured me; the tape had loosened along the backline, the alleys were green with plantains and other weeds, and the net (installed in June and removed in September) sagged in the dry noon, and the whole place steamed with midday heat and hunger and emptiness. There was a choice of pie for dessert, and one was blueberry and one was apple, and the waitresses were the same country girls, there having been no passage of time, only the illusion of it as in a dropped curtain—the waitresses were still fifteen; their hair had been washed, that was the only difference—they had been to the movies and seen the pretty girls with the clean hair.

8   Summertime, oh, summertime, pattern of life indelible with fade-proof lake, the wood unshatterable, the pasture with the sweetfern and the juniper forever and ever, summer without end; this was the background, and the life along the shore was the design, the cottages with their innocent and tranquil design, their tiny docks with the flagpole and the American flag floating against the white clouds in the blue sky, the little paths over the roots of the trees leading from camp to camp and the paths leading back to the outhouses and the can of lime for sprinkling, and at the souvenir counters at the store the miniature birch-bark canoes and the postcards that showed things looking a little better than they looked. This was the American family at play, escaping the city heat, wondering whether the newcomers in the camp at the head of the cove were "common" or "nice," wondering whether it was true that the people who drove up for Sunday dinner at the farmhouse were turned away because there wasn't enough chicken.

9   It seemed to me, as I kept remembering all this, that those times and those summers had been infinitely precious and worth saving. There had been jollity and peace and goodness. The arriving (at the beginning of August) had been so big a business in itself, at the railway station the farm wagon drawn up, the first smell of the pine-laden air, the first glimpse of the smiling farmer, and the great importance of the trunks and your father's enormous authority in such matters and the feel of the wagon under you for the long ten-mile haul, and at the top of the last long hill catching the first view of the lake after eleven months of not seeing this cherished body of water. The shouts and cries of the other campers when they saw you, and the trunks to be unpacked, to give up their rich burden. (Arriving was less exciting nowadays, when you sneaked up in your car and parked it under a tree near the camp and took out the bags and in five minutes it was all over, no fuss, no loud wonderful fuss about trunks.)

10   Peace and goodness and jollity. The only thing that was wrong now, really, was the sound of the place, an unfamiliar nervous sound of the outboard motors. This was the note that jarred, the one thing that would sometimes break the illusion and set the years moving. In those other summertimes all motors

were inboard; and when they were at a little distance, the noise they made was a sedative, an ingredient of summer sleep. They were one-cylinder and two-cylinder engines, and some were make-and-break and some were jumpspark, but they all made a sleepy sound across the lake. The one-lungers throbbed and fluttered, and the twin-cylinder ones purred and purred, and that was a quiet sound, too. But now the campers all had outboards. In the daytime, in the hot mornings, these motors made a petulant, irritable sound; at night in the still evening when the afterglow lit the water, they whined about one's ears like mosquitoes. My boy loved our rented outboard, and his great desire was to achieve single-handed mastery over it, and authority, and he soon learned the trick of choking it a little (but not too much), and the adjustment of the needle valve. Watching him I would remember the things you could do with the old one-cylinder engine with the heavy flywheel, how you could have it eating out of your hand if you got really close to it spiritually. Motorboats in those days didn't have clutches, and you would make a landing by shutting off the motor at the proper time and coasting in with a dead rudder. But there was a way of reversing them, if you learned the trick, by cutting the switch and putting it on again exactly on the final dying revolution of the flywheel, so that it would kick back against compression and begin reversing. Approaching a dock in a strong following breeze, it was difficult to slow up sufficiently by the ordinary coast-ing method, and if a boy felt he had complete mastery over his motor, he was tempted to keep it running beyond its time and then reverse it a few feet from the dock. It took a cool nerve, because if you threw the switch a twentieth of a second too soon you would catch the flywheel when it still had speed enough to go up past center, and the boat would leap ahead, charging bull-fashion at the dock.

11   We had a good week at the camp. The bass were biting well and the sun shone endlessly, day after day. We would be tired at night and lie down in the accumulated heat of the little bedrooms after the long hot day and the breeze would stir almost imperceptibly outside and the smell of the swamp drift in through the rusty screens. Sleep would come easily and in the morning the red squirrel would be on the roof, tapping out his gay routine. I kept remembering everything, lying in bed in the mornings—the small steamboat that had a long rounded stern like the lip of a Ubangi, and how quietly she ran on the moonlight sails, when the older boys played their mandolins and the girls sang and we ate doughnuts dipped in sugar, and how sweet the music was on the water in the shining night, and what it had felt like to think about girls then. After break-fast we would go up to the store and the things were in the same place—the minnows in a bottle, the plugs and spinners disarranged and pawed over by the youngsters from the boys' camp, the Fig Newtons and the Beeman's gum. Out-side, the road was tarred and cars stood in front of the store. Inside, all was just as it had always been, except there was more Coca-Cola and not so much Moxie and root beer and birch beer and sarsaparilla. We would walk out with the bottle of pop apiece and sometimes the pop would backfire up our noses and hurt. We explored the streams, quietly, where the turtles slid off the sunny logs and dug their way into the soft bottom; and we lay on the town wharf and fed worms to

the tame bass. Everywhere we went I had trouble making out which was I, the one walking at my side, the one walking in my pants.

12   One afternoon while we were at that lake a thunderstorm came up. It was like the revival of an old melodrama that I had seen long ago with childish awe. The second-act climax of the drama of the electrical disturbance over a lake in America had not changed in any important respect. This was the big scene, still the big scene. The whole thing was so familiar, the first feeling of oppression and heat and a general air around camp of not wanting to go very far away. In midafternoon (it was all the same) a curious darkening of the sky, and a lull in everything that had made life tick; and then the way the boats suddenly swung the other way at their moorings with the coming of a breeze out of the new quarter, and the premonitory rumble. Then the kettle drum, then the snare, then the bass drum and cymbals, then crackling light against the dark, and the gods grinning and licking their chops in the hills. Afterward the calm, the rain steadily rustling in the calm lake, the return of light and hope and spirits, and the campers running out in joy and relief to go swimming in the rain, their bright cries perpetuating the deathless joke about how they were getting simply drenched, and the children screaming with delight at the new sensation of bathing in the rain, and the joke about getting drenched linking the generations in a strong indestructible chain. And the comedian who waded in carrying an umbrella.

13   When the others went swimming my son said he was going in, too. He pulled his dripping trunks from the line where they had hung all through the shower and wrung them out. Languidly, and with no thought of going in, I watched him, his hard little body, skinny and bare, saw him wince slightly as he pulled up around his vitals the small, soggy, icy garment. As he buckled the swollen belt, suddenly my groin felt the chill of death.

● Vocabulary

incessant (1)	pensively (5)	indelible (8)
desolated (2)	undulating (6)	sedative (10)
primeval (3)	unsubstantial (6)	imperceptibly (11)
transposition (4)	cultist (6)	premonitory (12)
tentatively (5)		

● The Facts

1. How old was White when he first went to the lake with his father? How old was he when he took his own son there?

2. What illusion did White begin to sustain on hearing his own son sneaking out to go down to the boat on the lake?

3. What changes did the author notice in the road leading from the lake to the farmhouse? What did these changes say about the passing of time?

4. What difference did the author note between the way guests arrived at the lake in his own boyhood days and their arrival now?

5. What experience precipitated White's realization that time had passed, that he was no longer young, that he was mortal?

● The Strategies

1. Aside from description, what other mode of development is implicitly part of the structure of this essay? What is the purpose of holding back the true meaning of the essay until the final paragraph?

2. In paragraph 2, White writes that he "was sure that the tarred road would have found it [the lake] out." What is odd about the phrasing of this sentence? What do you think White was trying to achieve in phrasing it that way?

3. Examine the author's boyhood recollections of the lake (paragraph 2). To which of our senses do his details and images appeal?

4. Examine the description of the fishing boat in paragraph 5. How does White manage to convey such a vivid picture of the boat?

5. In what part of his body did White feel the chill of death? In the context of the essay, why is this such an appropriate place?

● The Issues

1. In paragraph 2, why does White refer to the lake as a "holy spot"? What is the connotation of this term, given that the place was not a religious shrine? What, in your life, would be a similar spot? Give reasons for your choice.

2. The author states that he missed the "middle track" of the road leading up to the farmhouse for dinner. Try to imagine yourself in a similar situation forty years hence. What vehicles of transportation, not yet commonly used, might invade your road then?

3. What is the social implication of the words *common* and *nice* in paragraph 8? Have times changed, or are these distinctions still made?

4. Not everyone would have reacted in the way the author describes his own reaction in the final sentence of the essay. What might be another realistic reaction?

5. What are some clear signs in your life to indicate that you are not immortal? What are your feelings about these signs?

● Suggestions for Writing

1. Write a mixed-pattern essay about some aspect of life that troubles you. Feel free to describe, narrate, give examples, cite causes, or use any other rhetorical pattern that would support your main point.

2. Write an essay in any rhetorical pattern about which aspect of life gives you the most hope for a decent future. Consider such aspects as global security, cultural advances, personal relationships, and a purpose-driven life.

ISSUE FOR CRITICAL THINKING AND DEBATE: THE NEW TECHNOLOGY

Every era of human history is characterized by its own technology. Even primitive peoples with nothing but simple tools are capable of evolving a technology for coping with their environment. Take the example of the Arawak Indians, a Stone Age people who once inhabited Central America and the West Indies. They had no metal for making fishhooks, but they still came up with a unique way of fishing, using the remora or sucker fish, which uses its suckers to fasten itself to other fish and suck out their nutrients. The remora was kept hungry in captivity and taken to sea, where it was released with a string tied around its tail. As soon as it had fastened itself to another fish, the remora was pulled to the surface, the fish pried from its suckers, and the still-hungry hunter thrown overboard to seek more prey. One can imagine the shrieks of something like "Eureka!" the first time this technology was used successfully.

Technology today is a complex mesh of mathematics, engineering, computer chips, and old-fashioned ingenuity. For the most part, it feeds us and clothes us and allows us to live in relative comfort. But there is a penalty attached to many kinds of technology. The technology of atomic power, for example, while generating electricity for millions, leaves behind radioactive waste that will continue to be deadly to life for hundreds, even thousands, of years. The stuff keeps piling up, usually in secluded caves until one day we shall run out of room—then what will we do? Who can forget the horrendous accident at the Chernobyl nuclear plant in Russia on April 26, 1986, which came within a hairsbreadth of core meltdown and required the evacuation of over 60,000 people, many of whom had to permanently abandon their homes? And what of the frightening explosions in various plants at Yamuguchi Daiichi, Japan, when several nuclear plants exploded after a 9.9 earthquake, followed by a demonic tsunami, hit Japan on March 18, 2011? It took months to calculate the range of damage that might occur globally.

The invention of the internal combustion engine equipped humankind with the splendid vehicles we see today on the roads. But we have paid a heavy price in air pollution and motor vehicle accident mortality. Even with 100,000 horses passing in and out of the cramped roads of nineteenth-century London, depositing tons of manure on the streets daily, the environment was still cleaner then than it is today.

The speed at which new technology increases is downright bewildering. We are warned that by the time students seeking a degree in electronics finish their first two years of college, half of the information they acquired will already be outdated. According to a Sony video produced in 2011, more than a trillion Internet devices existed at that time, with the number growing exponentially. To contemplate the future is inconceivable. Here are some further statistics provided by Sony:

70 million people use MySpace every month.
1 out of every 8 married couples met online.

174 million users visit Facebook every day.

YouTube is the most watched video in the world.

The total number of text messages sent daily exceeds the number of people on our planet.

At the speed with which new technology is changing, these statistics will be outdated by the time they are published.

Young people exult in the new technology whereas old people shake their heads, wondering if this mad rush to acquire the latest gadget is not a sign of cultural decline as they observe reading skills and interaction with people being corroded.

The technology of communication has evolved in a special way. Some people call it *social networking;* others call it *the Apps,* short for *applications.* Whatever the label used, the reference is to computer software that can run on the Internet, computer, cell phone, or other computer device. We recognize this software by names like Facebook, MySpace, Twitter, iPhone, iPad, Kindle, YouTube, GPS, and many other descriptive brands.

Over the centuries, technology has had its enemies, who insist that its price is too high. Probably the best example from history is the movement of the Luddites from 1811 to 1816. The Luddites were artisans who objected to the technological improvements in the English textile industry because they thought their way of life threatened by the new super-efficient looms. Mobs of them roamed the English countryside destroying textile manufacturing facilities and machinery. The movement was violently suppressed by 12,000 troops sent by Parliament, its ringleaders captured and either hanged or deported to Australia. Still, even today the Luddite spirit lingers in our attitude toward new technology. With the evidence before our own eyes, these misgivings are understandable.

The three essayists whose work follows bring different perspectives to the issue. The first, an MIT graduate, takes smug satisfaction in making do with a minimal technology. He ecstatically peals off the accomplishments of his abstinence: no television, no computer, no VCR, an old car that he seldom uses, preferring to ride a bicycle to the library to do research or to shop. Yet he admits benefiting from some modern technology, such as vaccines, refrigerators, and sanitary water. He doesn't understand why the press fusses over him as if he'd done something spectacular. In return for his austerity, he has more time to spend with his kids. Meanwhile he has written a popular book on the topic of giving up technology. The next writer is a former English teacher who worries that the new devices can become addictive and turn people into mindless robots who have lost the treasured skill of personal communication and human intimacy. In a way, these two writers typify popular reactions to technology. One prides himself on using only a rudimentary amount of technology in his lifestyle. The other quails at the destruction of intimate relationships. The student essay was written by Charlie Sorenson, a Harvard student who values the Internet as "an incredible tool with an enormous capacity to help one learn."

In this debate there are no right or wrong answers, no absolutes that tell us what we should or should not do. Earth is the only place we have to live. If technology can make Mother Earth better, we should embrace it. If its adaptation means further polluting our home planet, we must think long and hard about the consequences.

Glamour Girls
by Marisa Marchetto

© Marisa Acocella Marchetto/The New Yorker Collection/www.cartoonbank.com

No Technology? No Problem

ERIC BRENDE

Eric Brende (1965?) has earned degrees from Yale, Washburn University, and MIT. He is best known for his popular book, *Better Off: Flipping the Switch on Technology* (2004), which describes how he and his wife learned to love simple pleasures after living for 18 months with an Amish couple they met by chance. The experiment convinced the Brendes to adopt the simple life that uses as few technologies as possible. Today they continue to live simply in an old-town section of St. Louis, Missouri, where Eric makes his living as a rickshaw driver and soap maker. The essay below was reprinted from "What Matters," a guest opinion column, written for the October 2004 issue of Infinite Connection: MIT Alumni Journal.

Much of the author's life has been an experiment to see if cell phones, BlackBerrys, computers, wide-screen TVs, and SUVs have made life better. His purpose was to answer the question "What is the least we need to achieve the most?"

• • •

1   As MIT graduates go, I realize I am unusual. I run a rickshaw service in downtown St. Louis, where I live. I make soap at home, and my wife sells it at the local farmer's market on Saturdays. We travel on foot or by bicycle to get the day's errands done and tote our groceries in capacious, foldable rear bike-baskets, carting our children behind using "Trail-A-Bikes," attachments that convert an adult bicycle into a tandem for a child.

2   Either one of my sons or myself mows our yard with a hand-powered cutting cylinder. My wife, assisted by our children, does the laundry using an old-fashioned, swing-handled washing tub. We don't have a computer, television, or VCR, although we do listen to the radio and drive a car when the need arises (a 1983 Honda Accord). I will go to the library by bicycle, and use the Internet at times.

3   I recently returned from a three-week tour promoting a book I wrote about how we live and how much we learned after spending eighteen months in an Amish-style community. Press outlets, radio stations, bookstores, and the public hungrily ate up what I had to offer. The book is now in a third printing. Everyone was fascinated by the thought of something so radical, so singular, so counter-cultural. Many people admired my "bravery," my "pioneering spirit," my "self-control", wondering how I or my wife or my children could endure such privation. Many called my ideas thought-provoking and—although they weren't ready to put them in practice just yet or so radically—they would mull over the possibilities.

4   And yet, now that I've lived like this for almost twelve years, I must ask—who is really being brave, radical, or extreme? Is it I? Or is it the people who marvel at me? Compared with the vast majority of earthlings down through history, I am hardly deprived. I use generous amounts of technology. For all my "austerity," I still benefit from major historic advances like sanitary water, vaccines, plentiful food supplies (shipped in from the countryside by high-speed vehicles), many mass-manufactured goods, and select forms of automation, such as electric fans, a small refrigerator, a dehumidifier in my basement, a digital piano, and, as mentioned, sometimes a car and a computer. And with this degree of usage, I enjoy a balanced life, blending family with work, and leave ample leisure to write books and articles, play music, and visit relatives. Because our costs are so low, even though I make hardly anything, I have enough disposable income to dine out fairly often and take my wife to the movies or a show. We can't afford to live in a ritzy neighborhood, but our inexpensive urban setting is compact, walkable, and architecturally pleasing.

5   Compared to the world's silent majority, I am markedly better off, even pampered, and I don't consider myself radical or extreme in my practices. It is the Americans around me. I am merely wading in technology. They are drowning in it, dog-paddling to keep their heads above water. If a certain amount of something is good, it does not follow that lots of it is. King Midas tried a famous alchemical experiment, and we know what happened: he learned that too much of a good thing is not a good thing.

6   Today, in my eyes, most of our personal and economic activities, our hustle and bustle, our coming and going, spring from the need to undo or counteract the effects of a tidal wave of technology.

7   In the workplace, technology is an economic weapon necessary to keep even with the competition, namely other technological advances. Few are particularly thrilled at the technology itself. As skilled workers become obsolete, they are replaced as if they were machine parts. The constant turnover in jobs creates social instability and expensive retraining programs which, as President Bush accurately points out, are the keys to success in the changing global economy, but which also consume vast amounts of time, effort, and money, while undermining family life and neighborhoods. Bush bragged in a presidential debate that during his term he increased the education budget by forty-nine percent, and did so mostly for the sake of the economy. The extravagant cost, of course, can only be borne by us in the form of taxes or tuition, and we must work that much harder.

8   In our communities, a mass-migration has been under way for decades, from urban cores and inner suburbs to outer rings, spawning fabulous public works projects unparalleled in world history—monumental freeway interchanges, parking lots, malls—together with a burgeoning population of motorcars, which from 1969 to 1995 alone in the United States multiplied six times faster than the human population. All those transportation costs alone total to one sixth of our nation's annual income. And all for what?

9   Largely to escape the effects of cars themselves, together with other obnoxious technologies—the cumulative noise, pollution, congestion, and menace accompanying a rapidly expanding artificial environment. Human beings, understandably seek out safety and serenity in a world of turbulence. But the more they try to escape from that maelstrom, the worse it gets. For the only means of escape from cars appears to be—cars.

10   Building new houses instead of restoring old ones, traveling hours each day in a vehicle, paying for the sundry other technologies—all this takes money which translates into human labor, probably the better part of the workday for most Americans. But there is another sort of costly compensation that technology foments. When it goes too far, it often does for us something we'd be better off doing ourselves. It encroaches on our own vital human functions, and when it does, we must go back and regain them. We must dog-paddle lest the upsurge in technology close over our very human identity. Dog-paddling, the improvised struggle for self-recovery, is quite taxing, and creates a multiplicity of flailing motions from what once was a single integrated experience.

11   Too much technology deprives us of needed physical activity. Hence the unique, modern oddity: the self-imposed exercise regimen. After sitting motionless all day, people jog around the block. They drive to the gym. They mount treadmills. They create work for themselves to make up for the work their labor-savers saved them. It has gotten to the point where some people perform hand-squeezing routines since computer keyboards do not offer the physical resistance they need and can lead to carpal tunnel syndrome. (Also, studies show that, for the sake of one's lower back, it is better to work as a

longshoreman than in an office.) As ridiculous as these compensations may appear, shrinking away from remedial physical exercise brings even worse consequences. One triple-bypass operation costs at least $100,000 and, besides being horrific in itself, raises everyone's insurance premiums, forcing us back on the technological treadmill for another round of penance.

12   Television and computers reduce face-to-face human interactions with similar results: the quest to create "quality time" with family and friends. Nobody ever used this phrase before technology became so dominant. Now time is so short that most parents carry around a vague feeling of guilt over how little of it they spend with their children, so they must manufacture opportunities for it. When time permits. The inability to spend enough time with loved ones is a dark cloud hanging over everyone's head. Yet in a world of time-saving devices, everyone complains there's not enough time.

13   Multimedia devices also erode and atrophy human mental powers and skills, like reading and, perhaps because these are even harder to recover or even identify, these losses can contribute to a vague sense of uselessness which our antidepressants have not been able to cure. If technology is all but living our lives for us, why live at all?

14   I agree that becoming technologically deprived can be a danger but it is not I who is at risk. In a world superabundant in gadgets and gizmos, the richest among us are those who have mastered the delicate art of thinning out the excess, making way for the expression of their full humanity. If anything, I may still have some thinning to do.

15   As for the rest of you: Will the real extremists please stand up? Living without so much technology may be less radical than you think. It certainly is a lot easier.

"No Technology? No Problem" by Eric Brende. From WHAT MATTERS? MIT ALUMNI JOURNAL, October 2004 issue. Reprinted with permission from MIT Alumni Association.

● Vocabulary

capacious (1)	maelstrom (9)	deprived (14)
austerity (4)	sundry (10)	gizmos (14)
obsolete (7)	foments (10)	extremists (15)
turbulence (9)	penance (11)	

● The Facts

1. How does the author currently make a living? How do you know that this is not his only income?

2. What three modern items does the author admit to using? If you were to retain only three modern technological advancements, what would they be? Give reasons for your choices.

3. What was the reading public's first reaction to Brende's book describing his experiment with the simple life? What is your reaction?

4. What does the author like most about the way he and his family have lived for more than a decade? Do the advantages he cites appeal to you enough to give up your present lifestyle? Explain your answer.

5. What happens when skilled workers in our technological society become obsolete? What is the ultimate effect on our society?

● The Strategies

1. On which rhetorical strategies does the author rely mostly? Point out some obvious examples. How useful are these strategies?

2. Where in the essay does the author use figures of speech? Choose one you consider particularly remarkable and explain its meaning.

3. Paragraph 7 ends in a question. Where does the author answer the question? How effective is his placement of the answer?

4. What do all of the examples in paragraph 10 prove? What irony is involved? Do you agree with the author's attitude about these examples?

5. What does the author mean by the "dark cloud" hanging over everyone's head? How can this dark cloud be lifted?

● The Issues

1. Does true happiness lie in shunning modern technology? Or, can you conceive of living happily in a society where televisions, computers, cell phones, BlackBerrys, iPods, and high-powered cars are a daily component of life?

2. If you were to thin down your life by getting rid of certain technological gadgets, which ones would you discard and which ones would you keep? Give a rationale for your choices.

3. Who do you think is more radical and extreme—the author or those individuals who are glued to their technological lifestyles?

4. What is the point of the allusion to King Midas in paragraph 4? Do you agree with this point? If not, why not?

5. Which part, if any, of Brende's lifestyle do you consider worth espousing? Consider his reference to rebuilding old houses, riding bicycles to work, doing physical work around the house, refurbishing the inner city rather than escaping into the suburbs, and reducing the cost of technologies by thinning them down.

● Suggestions for Writing

1. Create a diary entry for one day in which you describe each time you use a piece of technological equipment. Try to avoid a dull recitation by injecting humor and vivid scenes into your writing.

2. Write an essay criticizing Brende's lifestyle and praising the virtues of our technological society.

Beware the Apps!

LACRETA SCOTT

Lacreta Scott is an accomplished public speaker and writer. Now retired, for twenty years she was an English professor and administrator at Cerritos College in Norwalk, California. Since 2001, she has written a monthly column, "Life Lessons," for several southern California newspapers. She is active in foster youth and homeless shelter programs.

The essay that follows addresses everyone who is so intrigued by new technology that it seems to be their end-all of each day. Do you spend most of your time playing video games, texting your friends, writing on your Facebook wall, watching YouTube videos, tweeting, or reading the messages posted by your friends? Do you become fidgety when you are out of range of your cell phone? Then "Here Come the Apps!" is meant for you as a reminder that a rich life exists somewhere beyond the apps.

• • •

1   Already I am too late. The Apps are with us. Texting, Tweeting, E-mailing, Etc-ing. They are fixtures in our lives. And they are already showing up in cartoons. A young couple at dinner, phones in hand, look over at an older couple

and the woman says to the man, " I hope that when we are old, we don't sit at a restaurant not texting!" I recall saying very similar words to my husband when we were young, "I hope that when we are old, we won't sit at a restaurant not *talking.*"

2   Not talking can cost you the chance at a good relationship. A young man tells me of a recent evening with a good-looking young woman. He was eager to date this woman. He arranged a dinner at a high-end place and was all set to go. But the date did not go well. The conversation lagged. Finally, she looked at him apologetically and said, "I am better at texting than talking." She blew her chance. In my young male friend's mind, the evening was wasted, and he never called her again.

3   I have seen, and you have seen, two people at lunch, talking, but not to each other. Each is talking into a cell phone to absent third parties. And we have all seen people walking along beside each other, similarly distant. Another common sight is someone walking along, ignoring the sounds of nature or of the city, with a hands-free device in his ear. Sometimes I think he is talking to me, so I try to answer! No. He is off in another land, not present in the moment in this place, for he is talking to another person, perhaps far away, on his cell.

4   Far be it from me to decry technological advancement. I am not a Luddite. These nineteenth century British textile workers, alarmed at changes the industrial revolution brought, smashed mechanized looms. I am not about to destroy any device that makes life easier. I love E-mail. I am more intimate now with distant friends and family, all because of E-mail. I can write them whenever I feel like it and not have to worry about interrupting them with a phone call. I can Instant Message them and be really in touch. I used to hate writing letters, not the writing itself, but all that stuff about finding a stamp and getting the letter to the post office and other inconveniences of snail mail; all that is gone.

5   I also keep my cell phone handy in case I need to call 911, or in case I am running late and need to call whoever is waiting on me to explain. I also used to get lost all the time. Now I just put the address into my GPS and away I go. I used to be concerned that the encyclopedia we bought would be outdated as soon as it landed on our bookshelves. Now I use the Web to search for information. I used to have to hunt for parking when I went shopping. Now I do most of my shopping on-line from my computer at home. I sometimes buy my groceries this way.

6   Hooray for the new world!

7   But this new world has brought a burden to personal relationships. We can be rude and not even notice it. We can numb ourselves from relating to real flesh and blood. Recently we visited with another couple. It was hard to talk with them as he was so engrossed in his new iPhone, and she was doing I-don't-know-what with her hand-held device. Now and then, they looked up, but basically they were off in space somewhere. They probably thought we had a good evening; we did not.

8   It is easy to become absorbed in mindless surfing, whether on a desktop, a laptop, or a smart phone. We can play games absentmindedly.

9   One woman complains, "My husband is jealous of my iPhone. I try hard not to use it in bed." One man laments that he and his wife have very little time together because they both work during the day at their jobs. He explains that he is lonely. When the couple is finally through with the day's obligations, there she sits, checking her e-mail or playing games on her phone. In defense, he watches TV.

10   Love of technology can slip up on us. Soon using our devices becomes addictive. We tune out others around us. There we sit, robotically clicking or tap-tap-tapping, and we don't even know others are in the room. We occasionally look up dazedly to see that our companion has fallen asleep from boredom or is mechanically pressing on the TV remote, trying to find some stimulation somewhere.

11   And so our evenings are spent. Gone are discussions about the day each has had. Gone are the Scrabble games played with real wooden tiles. Gone are the arguments that brought out vital issues, fostered new understandings, and circulated fresh air into being together. Gone is our bond.

12   And we may not even know it. Who will confess to jealousy of an inanimate object? Few will even know what they are jealous of. What they are really jealous of is attention.

13   How can such problems be solved? First, the non-texting/surfing partner has to be honest and tell of the hurt. Admitting hurt is difficult because it exposes one's vulnerability. It may be that the other person has been unaware of the problem and will make a strong effort to reform. But if the partner becomes very defensive about the issue of surfing and texting, then getting more help is a good idea, maybe even professional counseling.

14   A second solution is easier all around. The texting/surfing partner can just stop. Easy? Not really! Ever try to stop smoking? Addiction is addiction, whatever form it takes. But ending an addiction has so many benefits. I encourage you, even if your partner has not said a word, just to put aside the apps when you are together and see what happens.

15   If you feel all jittery and clammy at the prospect of putting away your various devices when with another person, you probably ought to see a therapist. You are in trouble, and you didn't even know it!

16   I am serious, folks. The effects of these apps on a life can be lethal.

Reprinted with permission from Lacreta Scott.

● Vocabulary

fixtures (1)	decry (4)	lethal (16)
device (3)	encyclopedia (5)	

● The Facts

1. What does the author mean when she says she is "too late"? What event has she missed? Explain the intent of this phrase.

2. What words spoken by the female on her first date with a man eager to meet her ruined her chances for a good relationship? Would those words have had the same effect on you? Explain your answer.

3. Do the experiences described in paragraph 3 seem as common as the author claims, or are they merely exceptions experienced mainly in large cities? From your observation, how accurate and recognizable are the author's examples?

4. What is a Luddite? Is it good or bad to be one? Explain the label briefly and evaluate whether or not a Luddite has any value to society.

5. What, according to the author, is the first step in healing the breech that has ruined a relationship due to the addictive use of apps? What other steps would you recommend?

● The Strategies

1. How does the title link with the content of the essay? What other title might have an impact or grab the reader's attention?

2. What tone does the author establish between the reader and herself? How effective is the tone? What does it achieve?

3. If you were to create an outline of this essay, what would be its major entries? In other words, what major topics organize the essay? List them in writing. How do they help the reader?

4. What strategy does the author use to introduce the solution to the problem described in the essay? Evaluate the effectiveness of this strategy. Why does it work or fail to work?

5. Reread the final sentence. Do you consider it conclusive or does it leave you hanging in limbo? What response does the author hope to receive from you? What is your actual response?

● The Issues

1. Of the applications mentioned in this essay, which one do you consider to have the most prestigious future in our global society? Explain by using examples why you deem this particular app of such great consequence.

2. Why do you think the author did not mention Google in her essay? Speculate on why she might have left out this popular search engine. If you have a favorite app that was not mentioned, describe its use and its societal significance.

3. Of all the devices of the new technology, which would you least want to relinquish? Make a good argument for its excellent contribution to improving our world in general and your life in particular.

4. Does it seem realistic to you that a husband or wife could become jealous of a spouse's texting habit? Do you consider texting more threatening than telephoning? Explain your answer.

5. How would you expand on paragraph 6—"Hooray for the new world!"? Try to challenge the idea that the new apps are lethal to personal relationships by portraying them as the Prometheus of modern life. (Look up "Prometheus" if you aren't familiar with this name.)

● Suggestions for Writing

1. As an attention-grabbing writing assignment, text a cell phone message, full of the customary abbreviations, to your best friend, accepting an invitation to his or her family's Fourth of July picnic. Then write that same message in regular, well-crafted English.

2. Write an essay in which you either defend or attack the use of chatspeak, lol-speak, or any other shortcut slang in formal school assignments. Support your argument with evidence and logic.

Stumped by monotonous sentences? Exit on page 709, at the **Editing Booth!**

Punctuation Workshop
Using Other Punctuation with Quotation Marks

1. **Periods and commas go inside quotations marks; semicolons and colons go outside.**

   "Gilberto," she insisted, "let's do some rope climbing."
   He lectured on "Terrorism in Spain"; I immediately thought of the story "Flight 66": It seemed to follow the lecturer's claims.

2. **Question marks, exclamation points, or dashes that apply only to the quoted material go inside the quotation marks. Otherwise, they go outside:**

   INSIDE: The Senator asked, "Who will pay for it?"

   OUTSIDE: Which of the senators asked, "Who will pay for it"? (Do not use double quotation marks for questions within questions.)

   INSIDE: The crowd shouted, "No more lies!"

   OUTSIDE: Stop playing Bob Marley's "Crazy Baldhead"!

   INSIDE: "Materialism—the greed for things—" insists my father, "is bad."

   OUTSIDE: The article said, "You may be at risk for cancer"—something to think about.

3. **Put quotation marks around titles of small works, such as stories, essays, newspaper or magazine articles, poems, songs, and book chapters.**

   "Design" (poem by Robert Frost)

   "The Annihilation of Fish" is a short story that became a cult movie.

   "My Brown-eyed Girl" was a big hit for Van Morrison.

   "The Rainbow Coalition" (Chapter 20) discusses blended families.

4. **Either quotation marks or italics can be used in definitions:**

   The word "aquiline" means "related to eagles."

   or

   The word *aquiline* means related to *eagles*.

Student Corner

Charlie Sorensen
Harvard University
　　Thoughts about the Internet

I'm worried I waste too much time. Like many of you reading this, I'm a student. I'm a college freshman to be precise, and I've had my share of trouble managing on my own for the very first time. The intensity of the pressure to do well at school is insane. Unless I'm spending every waking second buried in a textbook or writing an essay, I feel like a lackluster student. I feel like I'm doing something wrong. Or bad. I can tell myself that this is an unreasonable way to think. And I know that it is. But I can't shake the feeling.

Virtually every student I know suffers the same feeling. In a way, we feel torn. On the one hand, we never work as much or as hard as we are telling ourselves we should; yet, on the other hand, we crave time without obligation—"free time" to ourselves. I'm a part of this ambivalent crowd, and as such, I am particularly susceptible to the seduction of the Internet. I'm going to go ahead and say that I waste 80% of my time on the Internet.

A lot has been said about the distracted nature of my generation. And while I won't disagree that many of us, myself included, have issues holding our concentration from time to time, I don't think exploring the Internet should be considered a social problem. The Internet is an incredible tool with an enormous capacity to help one learn. It's been a great benefit in my life. In other words, the pros outweigh the cons.

Just think about everything that we can do now that just a generation ago was science fiction. As a student, the Internet is my number one resource tool. Sure, I'm distracted from time to time, but I can't imagine being a student twenty years ago. How slow must it have been doing research in those days! When I use the Internet, a search query can turn up hundreds of results from authentic sources on any topic imaginable. For example, this semester I'm taking a course on

Sorensen   2

Albert Einstein and twentieth-century physics, a topic about which
I know next to nothing. In my readings I came across references to
a group known as the "Vienna Circle." A quick search on Google,
and in only a couple of minutes I have sources to tell me who these
philosophers like Moritz Schlick were, and why they are important.
The Internet is also the best tool I have for staying in touch with all the
friends and family who make it easier for me to be away from home
and face a brave new world. E-mail and social networking Web sites
help me maintain friendships that I'm afraid I might otherwise lose.

When I mull over the role of the Internet, it's hard not to be in awe
of the volumes of information available to anyone with a computer
and an Internet connection. The entire world opens up to you. I can
share my experiences with someone on the other side of the globe,
and get a glimpse into a life I never otherwise would see. I work hard
in the classroom, of course. There's nothing more valuable than a
good education that includes stimulating lectures or rousing classroom
discussions. But I value what I learn everyday searching through the
Web just as much as what I learn in a classroom. The Internet is the
home to the world's most astonishing communities, and if you know
where to look, you can learn more online than anywhere else. If there
is such a thing as "Internet addiction," then maybe I'm an addict. The
Internet is rounding out the best education I could hope to get.

How I Write

It always helps to create an outline first—even if it's the roughest of sketches,
as mine usually is. I used to be a writer who sat down and wrote without
sketch or design. My first instinct is still to sit down and write the first
thoughts that come to mind. But I've learned that taking a couple of minutes
to organize ideas and get the focus of my essay down on paper improves my
essay.

How I Wrote This Essay

Working off the idea that the Internet is a force for good, I quickly mapped out a set of points explaining why I felt this way. I asked myself if I thought I could shape a convincing argument from these points. I asked myself if there were points that could get in the way of my argument. I planned an outline that incorporated these counterarguments in the introduction. The rest of the outline fell into place, and from there it was mostly a matter of copying the outline over into my essay, and shaping my points into an ordered argument.

My Writing Tip

The most difficult part of writing, in my experience, is getting that first sentence down. The best lesson I ever learned was how important it is to simply start. Get it down on paper. Write, write, and write! After I get that first draft down, then the essay writing really begins. Until then, the most important thing to do is place your ideas down on paper. Once you've done that, it is much easier to rewrite your sentences and reform your essay into the one you want.

● CHAPTER WRITING ASSIGNMENTS

1. Write an essay about your favorite Internet site.
2. Write an imaginative essay that predicts and describes useful gadgets yet to be invented.
3. Who is your favorite actor for playing the "heavy" or a villain in movies? Write an essay that vividly describes the skills that makes this actor dominate the screen as an ill-famed scoundrel.
4. Write an essay about the job you would least like to have. Make this job unappealing to your reader.
5. Write an essay in which you argue that the latest new technology has opened the door into an entirely new world that would seem like outer space to our ancestors.
6. Write an essay about your favorite board game, emphasizing the lure or excitement of this particular pastime.

● **WRITING ASSIGNMENTS FOR A SPECIFIC AUDIENCE**

1. Write to the Internal Revenue Service, outlining your expenses for a semester of school. Make these expenses seem indispensable and therefore nontaxable.
2. Explain baseball to a foreigner who has never heard of the game.

● **IMAGE GALLERY WRITING ASSIGNMENT**

Visit pages IG-30–IG-32 of our image gallery and study all three images dealing with the new technology. Then choose the image that most appeals to you. Answer the questions and do the writing assignment.

Pointer from a Pro **AVOID NOUN CLUSTERS (NOUN+NOUN+NOUN)**

Never use a series of nouns to modify another noun. If you do, your writing will fade into deadly haziness. Note these examples that should make any reader cringe:

Medication maintenance level evaluation procedures

Automobile tire durability guidelines

Training needs assessment review

—Joseph P. Williams

PART THREE

Rewriting Your Writing

The Editing Booth

Inside the Editing Booth, you will find information on the following topics:

Revising

Editing

Revising is part of writing. Few writers are so expert that they can produce what they are after on the first try.

—William Strunk, Jr., and E. B. White

Rewriting is a necessary part of the composing process. That a writer's best comes gushing out spontaneously at the first and only sitting is true only in some rare instances. Most of the time, it must be coaxed out of the pen, drop by drop (or on the computer, keystroke by keystroke), by labored rereading and rewriting. Rewriting means reviewing what you have written and making changes to your text. These steps may be broadly classified as revising and editing.

Revising literally means "seeing again." You take a second look at your paragraphs, sentences, and words and change them until they express your intended meaning. You make major changes to the essay's structure, sentences, and paragraphs. You are trying to stick to a thesis, present evidence in a logical order, and project a tone appropriate to your audience. Accomplishing any of these three tasks may require you to move or insert paragraphs, cut out sentences, add transitions, rewrite your essay's beginning or ending, or even do more research.

Editing, on the other hand, means focusing your rewriting efforts mainly on individual words and sentences. It entails making small changes to the text, often with an eye to improving syntax and overall smoothness. It means choosing a better synonym, correcting a misspelling, inventing a sharper image, improving punctuation, conforming to a specific format, and pruning unnecessary words or phrases.

Both revising and editing are important parts of any rewriting effort. And although it is true that revising usually comes before editing, even this sequence does not necessarily always apply. You may find yourself making small changes to individual words and sentences when you go over your text the first time. On a second reading, you may find an obvious defect missed earlier, causing you to make major changes in the material. As with writing, rewriting is hard to segment into absolute steps.

REVISING

Essential to all rewriting is careful and purposeful rereading. You reread your work with an eye on its intended audience and overall purpose. As you reread what you have written, you ask yourself whether your audience is likely to understand it. You ask yourself whether this paragraph, sentence, or word is appropriate, whether this passage makes your views emphatic and plain. You read with pen in hand or fingers on the keyboard, slashing away here and there, scribbling in the margins, striking out and rewriting some sentences. And as you progress through multiple rereadings, your text will gradually begin to get better.

But the key is rereading, and its importance to a writer cannot be overstated. If you wish to write well, you must be willing to reread your work constantly. You must reread it not only when it is done, but also while you are doing it. If you should even become temporarily stuck—and virtually every writer occasionally does—don't stare vacantly into space or at the ceiling. Reread your work from the beginning. If no new ideas occur to you and you're still stuck, reread your work again. Sooner or later you will see where your text made a lurch in the wrong direction and be able to correct it.

Writing and rewriting are part of the recursive pattern of composing. Some revising to your rough plan or purpose will take place in your head even before you have scribbled a first draft. But most will occur immediately after or during the act of composition. You will set down a sentence or two on the page, glance at it, and see a way to make it better. Or you will write a paragraph, begin another and become stuck, then go back to the first and insert some details or transitional material. Regardless of your personal method of composing, once you have finished your first draft, you should begin the formal process of revising by rereading it. As an example of what we mean by revising, consider the following student paper in its first draft. The writer was asked to indicate through marginal comments the changes she proposed to make. Since this section emphasizes revising, as opposed to editing, we have corrected the errors that would have been caught in the editing process and have left only those that could be improved through revising. In the next part of this chapter, we shall stress editing.

The Exploitation of Endangered Wildlife

The fascination with endangered wildlife within the affluent nations of the world increases the market for illegal poaching and exporting of wildlife goods. Wildlife is big business. Exotic-bird collectors will pay as much as $10,000 for a hyacinth macaw. At Saks Fifth Avenue in New York a pair of cowboy boots, trimmed in lizard skin, will sell for $900. A Christian Dior coat, made from only the belly fur of seventeen lynx cats, will cost a staggering $100,000. These are rather mild examples of what is being done with animals stolen from wildlife retreats across the world.

Move to end of paragraph.

For stronger opening, begin here.

Of course, it's not that anyone cares if people spend their thousands on nonessentials. Instead, the act of murdering innocent and lovely animals for vanity's sake is an irreversible and despicable crime. For example, the baby seals, so prized for their exquisitely soft furs, are repeatedly beaten over the head with heavy clubs until they lie spread out on the ground, unconscious. To the poachers who routinely do the butchering, death is not relevant to this ugly scenario, nor are humane methods of killing. All they care about is the blood money extracted from the skins of these helpless little creatures. Another example is the thousands of wild birds imported live from Brazil and Australia. Since these countries have laws banning such exports, each cage of birds is smuggled aboard the smugglers' boat and has a weight attached to it. In case of being spotted by some police official, the cages can easily be thrown overboard, and no implicating evidence will remain. Still another species of endangered wildlife being exploited is the elephant. Investigators have found as many as twenty of these enormous pachyderms, gunned down with automatic weapons or shot with poison darts,

Delete: adds nothing. Is too informal.

More commentary needed here. Add a transition.

of...

How often? For what purpose?

Where? Add detail.

lying close together as if they were victims of some cruel genocide. Their tusks have been carved from their heads and carried away, leaving the bloody carcasses to rot and waste away on the plains.

Be more direct.

The irreversible effect of this illegal murdering could mean the extinction of many exotic wildlife species. In the seventeen century, 13,200 species of mammals and birds were known, but today more than 130 species have gone. An estimated 240 more are considered seriously endangered. Almost all of the cases can be traced to human activity.

Add a transition.

It's not because we needed these animals for food, nor because their unique traits could help us find cures for diseases, nor because killing them taught us anything relevant, except that perhaps when they are gone forever, taking with them their natural mystery, beauty, and grace, then we may learn how ignorant we have been.

Rewrite to make stronger appeal to reader's sense of fair play. Make more coherent.

Following is the revised version of the first draft:

The Exploitation of Endangered Wildlife

Wildlife is big business. Exotic-bird collectors will pay as much as $10,000 for a hyacinth macaw. At Saks Fifth Avenue in New York a pair of cowboy boots, trimmed in lizard skin, will sell for $900. A Christian Dior coat, made from only the belly fur of seventeen lynx cats, will cost a staggering $100,000. These are rather mild examples of what is being done with animals stolen from wildlife retreats across the world. The fascination with endangered wildlife within the affluent nations of the world increases the market for illegal poaching and exporting of wildlife goods.

The act of murdering innocent and lovely animals for vanity's sake is an irreversible and despicable crime. It is a way of saying that animals have no feelings and that human beings have the right to plunder and kill the lower orders if doing so will enhance the human lifestyle. For example, the baby seals, so prized for their exquisitely soft furs, are repeatedly beaten over the head with heavy clubs until they lie spread out on the ground, unconscious. To the poachers who routinely do the butchering, death is not relevant to this ugly scenario, nor are humane methods of killing. All they care about is the blood money extracted from the skins of these helpless little creatures. Another example of this savage and unnecessary rape is the thousands of wild birds imported yearly live from Brazil and Australia—to end up either in cages gracing the living rooms of tycoons who like to collect birds, or as ornaments on sweaters and hats of rich and fashion-conscious women. But since most countries have laws banning such exports, each cage of birds is smuggled aboard the smugglers' boat and has a weight attached to it. In case of being spotted by some police official, the cages can easily be thrown overboard, and no implicating evidence will remain. Still another species of endangered wildlife being exploited is the elephant. Investigators in West Africa have found as many as twenty of these enormous pachyderms, gunned down with automatic weapons or shot with poison darts, lying close together as if they were victims of some cruel genocide. Their tusks have been carved from their heads and carried away, leaving the bloody carcasses to rot and waste away on the plains.

The irreversible effect of this illegal murdering will certainly eventually lead to the extinction of many exotic wildlife species. Already time has witnessed the demise of many exotic animals. In the seventeen century, 13,200 species of mammals and birds were known, but today more than 130 species are extinct. An estimated 240 more are considered seriously endangered. In almost all cases, the extinction can be traced to greedy plunder by human beings. And the tragic part is that we did not commit the plunder because we needed these animals for food, nor because their unique traits could help us find cures for diseases, nor because killing them taught us anything useful. But perhaps when they are gone forever—taking with them their natural mystery, beauty, and grace—then we may see how ignorant and foolish we were. Then we will realize, much too late, that we sold our birthright for a mess of pottage.

EDITING

After revising—in most cases—comes editing. You now concentrate on the smaller elements of your writing—on individual words and sentences—with the goal of improving them. Again, careful editing begins with close rereading. You remember whom you are writing for and why, and you use your intended audience and purpose to judge the suitability of both your syntax and diction.

What follows is a checklist of some fundamental rules of editing. Have your own work in front of you as you go over this list. If your writing suffers from mechanical problems, such as fragments, comma splices, and dangling modifiers, you should consult a good grammar handbook.

Rule 1: Make Your Title Descriptive

The title of a paper should describe its content. Avoid puffy, exotic titles like this one on a paper dealing with the use of fantasy in Keats's poetry:

> **Poor:** Keats: The High Priest of Poetry
>
> **Rewrite:** The Use of Fantasy in Keats's Poetry

Rule 2: Begin with a Simple Sentence

It is stylistically good sense to open your paper with a short and simple sentence. A long and involved opening will repel, rather than attract, a reader:

> **Poor:** The problem that has come up again and again before various workers in the social sciences, and especially before sociologists and anthropologists, and one that has been debated at length in the journals of both disciplines as well as in the classrooms of various universities and colleges across the country, and one to which various answers, none satisfactory, have been proposed, is this: Are social scientists politically neutral, or are they *ipso facto* committed by their research?

To open with such a cumbersome sentence is like compelling a friend to view a landscape through a dirty windowpane. It is better to begin with an easily grasped sentence:

> **Rewrite:** The question is this: Are social scientists politically neutral, or are they committed by their research?

Rule 3: Prune Deadwood

Deadwood refers to any word, phrase, or sentence that adds bulk without meaning. It accumulates wherever the writing is roundabout and indistinct. Some styles of writing are so vested in wordiness that it is impossible to assign blame to any single word or phrase:

> **Poor:** There are many factors contributing to the deficiencies of my writing, the most outstanding being my unwillingness to work.
>
> **Rewrite:** I write badly mainly because I am lazy.
>
> **Poor:** Anthropologists carrying their studies of primate behavior deep into the tropical forests of Malaysia contribute, through the pursuit of their specialized interest, to the one field that in fact gives us our broadest perspective of human beings.
>
> **Rewrite:** Anthropologists add to our knowledge of human beings by studying primate behavior in the forests of Malaysia.

The solution to wordiness is to be plain and direct—to state your ideas without fluff or pretension.

Aside from wordiness there are other, more specific kinds of deadwood:

a. Cut *there are* and *there is* whenever possible, thereby tightening a sentence.

> **Poor:** There are many reasons why businesses fail.
>
> **Rewrite:** Businesses fail for many reasons.
>
> **Poor:** There is a cause for every effect.
>
> **Rewrite:** Every effect has a cause.

b. Cut *I think, I believe,* and *in my opinion.* Such phrases make the writer sound insecure.

> **Poor:** I think that Freud's approach to psychology is too dominated by sex.
>
> **Rewrite:** Freud's approach to psychology is too dominated by sex.
>
> **Poor:** I believe that women should be paid as much as men for the same work.
>
> **Rewrite:** Women should be paid as much as men for the same work.
>
> **Poor:** In my opinion, marriage is a dying institution.
>
> **Rewrite:** Marriage is a dying institution.

c. Cut all euphemistic expressions.

> **Poor:** He went to Vietnam and paid the supreme sacrifice.
>
> **Rewrite:** He was killed in Vietnam.
>
> **Poor:** Last year for the first time I exercised the right of citizens on Election Day.
>
> **Rewrite:** Last year I voted for the first time.

d. Cut *-wise, -ly,* and *-type* word endings. Such words, easily concocted from adverbs and adjectives, have become popular in college writing, but they add bulk, not meaning.

> **Poor:** Moneywise, she just didn't know how to be careful.
>
> **Rewrite:** She didn't know how to be careful with her money.
>
> **Poor:** Firstly, let me point out some economic problems.
>
> **Rewrite:** First, let me point out some economic problems.
>
> **Poor:** A jealous-type man annoys me.
>
> **Rewrite:** A jealous man annoys me.

e. Eliminate all redundant phrases or expressions. Here are some typical examples, followed by possible substitutes:

Redundancy	*Rewrite*
bright in color	bright
large in size	large
old in age	old
shiny appearance	shiny
in this day and age	today
true and accurate	accurate (*or* true)
important essentials	essentials
end result	result
terrible tragedy	tragedy
free gift	gift
unexpected surprise	surprise
each and every	each (*or* every)
beginning preparation	preparation
basic and fundamental	basic (*or* fundamental)

In the preceding cases, all you have to do is cross out the words that *do not add* any meaning.

Another kind of redundancy is the use of ready-made phrases that could be replaced by a single word:

Ready-Made Phrase	*Rewrite*
owing to the fact that	because
plus the fact that	and
regardless of the fact that	although
in the event that	if
in a situation in which	when
concerning the matter of	about
it is necessary that	must
has the capacity for	can
it could happen that	may, can, could, might
prior to	before
at the present time	now (*or* today)
at this point in time	now (*or* today)
as of this date	today
in this day and age	nowadays
in an accurate manner	accurately
in a satisfactory manner	satisfactorily
subsequent to	after
along the lines of	like

Unfortunately, we cannot give you an exhaustive list of all unnecessary phrases. Only by a thorough rereading of your text can you spot these redundancies.

However, some chronic redundancies are caused by such words as *process, field, area, systems,* and *subject* being unnecessarily attached by the preposition *of* to certain nouns. Usually these words and the preposition can be eliminated with no damage whatsoever to your meaning and a considerable lightening of your style. Here are some examples:

> The *process of law* is not free of faults.
> The *field of education* needs creative minds.
> Some incompetence exists in the *area of medicine.*
> People employed in *systems of management* make good salaries.
> They know little about the *subject of mathematics.*

In each case, if you delete the "of" phrase, the redundancy disappears:

> The law is not free of faults.
> Education needs creative minds.
> Some incompetence exists in medicine.
> People employed in management make good salaries.
> They know little about mathematics.

Context, activity, concept, factor, and *problem* are similar offenders.

f. Cut all preamble phrases such as *the reason why . . . is that.*

> **Poor:** The reason why wars are fought is that nations are not equally rich.
> **Rewrite:** Wars are fought because nations are not equally rich.
> **Poor:** The thing I wanted to say is that history has shown the human being to be a social predator.
> **Rewrite:** History has shown the human being to be a social predator.
> **Poor:** The point I was trying to make is that reality is sometimes confused with fantasy in Keats's poetry.
> **Rewrite:** Reality is sometimes confused with fantasy in Keats's poetry.

In all such cases the rewrite principle is the same: lift out the heart of the idea and state it plainly.

g. Cut most rhetorical questions.

> **Poor:** That illusion, though deceptive, is more consoling and less hostile to human needs than reality appears to be a central theme in Keats's poetry. Why would anyone feel this way? Why did Keats himself feel this way? Possibly because he had tuberculosis and knew he was going to waste away and die.

Rewrite: That illusion, though deceptive, is more consoling and less hostile to human needs than reality appears to be a central theme in Keats's poetry. Keats possibly felt this way because he had tuberculosis and knew he was going to waste away and die.

Rule 4: Do Not Overexplain

Poor: Some critics sneered at Keats for being an apothecary-surgeon, which is what he was trained for.

Rewrite: Some critics sneered at Keats for being an apothecary-surgeon.

If Keats was an apothecary-surgeon, then that is obviously what he was trained to be.

Poor: As president of the company, which is an executive-type position, he never scheduled work for himself during April.

Rewrite: As president of the company, he never scheduled work for himself during April.

The term *president* already lets the reader know that the position is an executive one.

Poor: The car is blue in color and costs $18,000 in price.

Rewrite: The car is blue and costs $18,000.

That blue is a color and that $18,000 is the price are self-evident.

Rule 5: Be Specific

Lack of specific detail will infect your prose with a pallid vagueness.

Poor: The effect of the scenery was lovely and added a charming touch to the play.

Rewrite: The scenery, which consisted of an autumn country landscape painted on four flats extended to cover the entire background of the stage, added a charming touch to the play.

Being specific is simply calling things by their proper names. In speech, it might pass as cute to call things *thingamajigs* or *thingamabobs* or *widgets,* but in prose, any sort of vagueness caused by the writer's not calling things by their proper names will leave a bad impression. Consider the following examples:

Poor: James Boswell, the famous writer, died from living badly.

Rewrite: James Boswell, the famous biographer, died of uremia following a gonorrheal infection.

The writer of the second sentence, who has simply named Boswell's terminal infection, appears more competent than the writer of the first.

> **Poor:** Browning wrote poetry in which a speaker talked either to himself or to someone else.
>
> **Rewrite:** Browning wrote *dramatic monologues.*

In the first sentence, for want of a name, the writer is forced into a roundabout description of the kind of poetry Browning wrote. A little research on Browning would have yielded the term *dramatic monologue.*

Rule 6: Avoid Trite Expressions

Some words, phrases, or expressions through overuse have become unbearably hackneyed and should be avoided. Following are some of the most glaring offenders.

> in conclusion, I wish to say
>
> last, but by no means least
>
> slowly but surely
>
> to the bitter end
>
> it goes without saying
>
> by leaps and bounds
>
> few and far between
>
> in the final analysis

Rule 7: Use the Active Voice

The active voice is more vigorous and understandable than the passive because it allows the subject of a sentence to stand in its familiar position in front of the verb: for example, "I took a walk." The subject *I* occupies the position immediately in front of the verb *took.* The same sentence in the passive voice denies this familiar immediacy between subject and verb, "A walk was taken by me." The subject and verb stand at opposite ends of the sentence, with *by* intervening between them. In some passive constructions, the subject is even dropped:

> Information about the suspect could not be obtained.

By whom, you might ask. The answer is not evident in this sentence. Because of this tendency to implicate no one as the doer of an action, the passive voice enjoys widespread use among bureaucratic writers. Notice how converting the above sentence to the active voice not only makes the sentence more vigorous, but also makes some agency or person its subject and, therefore, responsible:

The police could not obtain any information about the suspect.

The strongest argument to be given for using the active instead of the passive voice, however, is the simplest one: the active voice is easier to read and understand. Here are some more examples of the passive voice, followed by appropriate revisions:

Passive: Her makeup was applied in thick, daubing strokes by her.
Active: She applied her makeup in thick, daubing strokes.
Passive: To see their hero in person was the fans' most cherished dream.
Active: The fans' most cherished dream was to see their hero in person.
Passive: It was determined by the committee that the new tax law would benefit middle-income people.
Active: The committee determined that the new tax law would benefit middle-income people.
Passive: My last trip to Jamaica will always be remembered.
Active: I shall always remember my last trip to Jamaica.

The use of the passive voice is stylistically justified only when an action or the object of an action is more important than the subject:

There, before our eyes, two human beings were burned alive by gasoline flames.

In this case the object, *human beings,* is more important than the subject, *gasoline flames,* and the passive voice is therefore effective. Here are two more examples of the passive voice appropriately used:

Cancer-producing particles are released into the atmosphere by spray guns applying asbestos during building construction.

In this context, cancer-producing particles are more important than spray guns.

Widespread death and injury were caused when 20,000 tons of TNT were dropped on Hiroshima in an atomic bomb.

Obviously the human dead and injured are more important than the atomic bomb.

Rule 8: Make Your Statements Positive

Statements that hedge, hesitate, or falter in the way they are worded tend to infuse your style with indecision. Whenever possible, word your statements positively:

Poor: He was not at all a rich man.

Rewrite: He was a poor man.

Poor: *The Cherry Orchard* is not a strong play; it does not usually sweep the audience along.

Rewrite: *The Cherry Orchard* is a weak play that usually bores its audience.

Poor: A not uncommon occurrence is for rain to fall this time of the year.

Rewrite: It commonly rains this time of the year.

Rule 9: Keep to One Tense

Once you have decided to summarize an action or event in one tense, you must thereafter stick to that tense. Don't start in the past and shift to the present, nor start in the present and shift to the past. Notice the corrections in the following passage.

Here is what I saw: For two acts the ballerina pirouetted, leapt, and floated

like a silver swallow; then suddenly, she ~~falls~~ *fell* to the ground like a heavy

boulder. Her leg ~~is~~ *was* fractured. For years before I observed this spectacular

drama, I *had* often heard of this artist's brilliant career. Now I ~~am~~ *was* watching her final performance.

Rule 10: Place Key Words at the Beginning or End of a Sentence

Poor: Workers today have forgotten the meaning of the word *quality,* so most craftsmen tell us.

Rewrite: Workers today, so most craftsmen tell us, have forgotten the meaning of the word *quality.*

Poor: Generally speaking, *wars* turn civilized nations into barbaric tribes.

Rewrite: *Wars,* generally speaking, turn civilized nations into barbaric tribes.

Rule 11: Prune Multiple *Ofs*

A double *of* construction is tolerable; a triple *of* construction is not.

> **Poor:** The opinions *of* the members *of* this panel *of* students are their own.
>
> **Rewrite:** The opinions expressed by this panel of students are their own.

A good way to break up an *of* construction is to add another verb. In the preceding example the verb *expressed* is inserted in the sentence.

Rule 12: Break Up Noun Clusters

A noun cluster is any string of noun + adjective combinations occurring at length without a verb. The cluster is usually preceded by either *the* or *a*. Noun clusters contribute a tone of unarguable objectivity to prose and have consequently found favor in the writing styles of textbooks, the government, and the social sciences. Note the italicized noun clusters in the following:

> **Poor:** We therefore recommend *the use of local authorities for the collection of information on this issue.*
>
> **Poor:** *The increased specialization and complexity of multicellular organisms* resulted from evolution *according to the principles of random variation and natural selection.*
>
> **Poor:** *The general lessening of the work role in our society* does not mean that we have abandoned the work basis for many of our values.
>
> **Poor:** One cannot doubt *the existence of polarized groups in America.*

The test for a noun cluster is whether or not it can be replaced by a single pronoun. Each of the above can be.

To rewrite noun clusters, convert one or more of the nouns to an equivalent verb form:

> **Better:** We therefore recommend *using* local authorities *to collect* information on this issue.
>
> **Better:** Multicellular organisms *specialized and evolved* in complexity by the principles of random variation and natural selection.
>
> **Better:** Because people today *work* less than they used to is no reason to believe that we have abandoned work as a basis for many of our values.
>
> **Better:** One cannot doubt that polarized groups *exist* in America.

Noun clusters clot the flow of a sentence. Avoid them by being generous in your use of verbs.

Rule 13: Use Exclamation Points Sparingly

The exclamation point should be used rarely and only when urgency or strong emotion is being expressed, as in the following:

This is what we fought our wars for!

Hooray! They found the prize!

Otherwise, it adds a forced breeziness to your prose.

We must have urban renewal; and we must have it now!

One cannot construct a science with unreliable instruments!

Rule 14: Vary Your Sentences

Do not begin two sentences in a row with the same word or phrase unless you are deliberately aiming for an effect.

Poor: The true Keats scholar is as familiar with the poet's life as with his poetry and can instantly relate any stage of the two. The true Keats scholar has a tendency to use Keats's poetry to explicate his life, and to use his life to explicate his poetry.

Rewrite: Scholars of Keats know the poet's life as well as they know his poetry and can instantly relate any stage of the two. They use Keats's poetry to explain his life, and his life to explain his poetry.

In addition to varying the words, vary the length of your sentences.

Poor: The man was angry and wanted his money back. But the officer would not give it back and told him to leave. That made the man angrier, and he threatened to call the police.

Rewrite: The man was angry; he wanted his money back. But the officer would not give it back to him, and told him to leave, which made the man angrier. He threatened to call the police.

The rewrite is more effective because the sentences have a greater variety in length and style.

Rule 15: Keep Your Point of View Consistent

If you begin a sentence by referring to yourself first as "I" and then as "one," you have made the error known as shift in point of view. Such shifts can occur because of the several ways in which you can refer to yourself, your audience, and people in general. You can refer to yourself as *the writer, I,* or *we.* You can refer to your audience as *you, we,* or *all of us.* You can refer to people in general as *people, one,* and *they.* The rule is that once you have chosen your point of view, it must remain consistent:

Poor: Do not buy Oriental rugs at an auction, because if we do, we may get cheated.

Better: Do not buy Oriental rugs at an auction, because if you do, you may get cheated.

Poor: I try to take good care of my car, for when one does not, they usually pay a big price.

Better: I try to take good care of my car, for when I do not, I usually pay a big price.

Poor: Everyone stood aghast when I told them about the accident.

Better: They all stood aghast when I told them about the accident.

Rule 16: Use Standard Words

College students can be unrelenting in their invention of newfangled vocabulary and often fall prey to the excesses of neologisms—new or coined words. Voguish words fade as quickly as they appear. By the time this book sees print, such words as *tight, trippin',* and *skeezy* will have begun to sound dated and old-fashioned. You should use neologisms sparingly—if at all—in your writing. Instead, draw your primary stock of words from the vocabulary established over the centuries. Remember, too, standard words must be written in standard spelling. Double-check any doubtful spelling in a dictionary.

Rule 17: End with Impact

The ending of your essay should clinch your argument, summarize your main point, reassert your thesis, urge some kind of action, or suggest a solution. Avoid committing the following common errors in your ending:

a. Endings that are trite:

> In conclusion I wish to say . . .
> And now to summarize . . .

Such endings are too obvious. If your essay has been properly developed, no special announcement of the conclusion is necessary.

b. Endings that introduce a new idea:

> Wealth, position, and friends, then, made him what he is today, although his father's death may also have influenced him.

If an idea has not been covered earlier, do not give in to the temptation to introduce it as a novelty item in the final paragraph.

c. Endings that are superfluous:

> And so these are my thoughts on the subject.
> As you can see, my essay proves that carbohydrates are bad for our health.

From these thoughts you will clearly see that Diaghilev was a dominant figure in modern ballet.

These endings do not reflect thoughtfulness on the part of the writer; they are useless in an essay.

EDITING AN ACTUAL ESSAY

Following is the first draft of a student paper, with revisions marked in boldface. In the left margin is the corresponding number of the rule in this section that has been broken.

Rule 1	*The Loss of Horror in Horror Movies* ~~Goose Pimples, Where Are You?~~
Rule 6	*Audiences* ~~For various and sundry reasons,~~ áudiences are no longer
	scared as they once were by the old-fashioned horror
	movies. Over the years people have been exposed to
Rule 5	*vampires, werewolves, zombies, and mummies* so many ~~monsters~~ that such creatures have lost their
Rule 3g	effectiveness as objects of terror. ~~Why do you think this~~
	~~happened?~~
	Lack of novelty has produced indifference. Originally, a
	movie monster, such as the one created by Frankenstein,
	terrified audiences simply because the concept of a man
Rule 9/3e	*was* creating human life ~~is~~ new. ~~Plus the fact that~~ Frankenstein's
	monster had a sinister plausibility that people of the 1930s
	had not experienced. But then the public was inundated by

2

a deluge of other film monsters as studios tried to capitalize

on the success of the original. Gradually audiences grew

bored as these creations became trite and shopworn.

Fearing loss of business, ambitious movie producers

Rule 3d   tried to invent fresh ~~type~~, grisly shapes that would lure

moviegoers back into the theaters. But their attempts

had no effect on a public surfeited with horror, so

Frankenstein's monster, Wolfman, and Dracula eventually

became comic creatures in Abbott and Costello films.

Rule 3e   Most modern horror films fail *to produce* ~~in the production of~~

genuine, goose-pimply terror in their audiences. Of course,

it may be argued that films like *The Exorcist* and *Jaws*

Rule 5   scared many people—even to the point of ~~great fear~~ *hysterical screams*. But

these films relied heavily on shock rather than on fear.

Rule 8   Shock ~~and fear are not the same~~ *differs from fear.* Genuine fear involves

the unknown or the unseen. ~~Genuine fear~~ *It* seduces the

Rule 14   imagination into fantastic realms~~.~~ ~~Genuine fear appeals~~ *and appeals*

to our innate store of nightmares. But shock is merely

synonymous with repulsion. People are shocked when

they see something they don't want to see. For example,

3

the scene of a man being devoured by a shark will shock.

The flaw here is that the shock value of such a scene

Rule 16   serves more to ~~give the creeps or the heebie jeebies~~ *repulse or offend* than

to frighten.

Today shock devices are used far too frequently in

motion pictures; yet, the sad truth is that these graphic

displays of blood and gore lack imagination. In older horror

movies, the audience was not privy to the horrible details

Rule 7   of murder. Scenes ~~which~~ merely suggested evil ~~were used~~

instead, and the ~~details were supplied by the audience's~~ *audience's imagination supplied the details.*

Rule 4   ~~imagination.~~ This approach is more effective ~~in its results~~

than shock because it spurs the viewers to conjure up

their own images of the unseen. The old movie formulas

did not have to use shock devices, such as bloody

murders, to achieve a pinnacle of horror. Unfortunately,

today's audiences have become "shockproof" in the

Rule 5   sense that it takes ~~more and more~~ *bigger and more bizarre doses of horror* to scare them.

Rule 17a   ~~In conclusion, horror~~ movies ~~have truly lost their effect~~. *One wonders what the ultimate horror movie will be.*

Here is the polished version of the paper, ready to be submitted to the instructor.

The Loss of Horror in Horror Movies

Audiences are no longer scared as they once were by the old-fashioned horror movies. Over the years people have been exposed to so many vampires, werewolves, zombies, and mummies that such creatures have lost their effectiveness as objects of terror.

Lack of novelty has produced indifference. Originally, a movie monster, such as the one created by Frankenstein, terrified audiences simply because the concept of a man creating a human life was new. Frankenstein's monster had a sinister plausibility that people of the 1930s had not experienced. But then the public was inundated by a deluge of other film monsters as studios tried to capitalize on the success of the original. Gradually audiences grew bored as these creations became trite and shopworn. Fearing loss of business, ambitious movie producers tried to invent fresh, grisly shapes that would lure moviegoers back into the theaters. But their attempts had no effect on a public surfeited with horror, so Frankenstein's monster, Wolfman, and Dracula eventually became comic creatures in Abbott and Costello films.

Most modern horror films fail to produce genuine, goose-pimply terror in their audiences. Of course, it may be argued that films like *The Exorcist* and *Jaws* scared many people—even to the point of hysterical screams. But these films relied heavily on shock rather than on fear. Shock differs from fear. Genuine fear involves the unknown or the unseen. It seduces the imagination into fantastic realms and appeals to our innate store of nightmares. But *shock* is merely synonymous with repulsion. People are shocked when they see something they don't want to see. For example, the scene of a man being devoured by a shark will shock. The flaw here is that the shock value of such a scene serves more to repulse or offend than to frighten.

2

Today shock devices are used far too frequently in motion pictures; yet, the sad truth is that these graphic displays of blood and gore lack imagination. In older horror movies, the audience was not privy to the horrible details of murder. Scenes merely suggested evil instead, and the audience's imagination supplied the details. This approach is more effective than shock because it spurs the viewers to conjure up their own images of the unseen. The old movie formulas did not have to use shock devices, such as bloody murders, to achieve a pinnacle of horror. Unfortunately, today's audiences have become "shockproof" in the sense that it takes bigger and more bizarre doses of horror to scare them. One wonders what the ultimate horror movie will be.

● Exercises

1. What follows is the opening paragraph of a student essay. Revise it to improve its effectiveness. Remember that your lead sentence should captivate your audience.

> Wars are always destructive and rarely worth the devastation they cause. Today, Europe is still recuperating from World War II. Endless statistics attempt to project what would happen if a nuclear war were to break out today; yet, nobody really knows the actual effects. The most accurate picture to date was provided by the bombing of Hiroshima in 1945. This terrible historical event provided actual evidence of what a super weapon has the capability of accomplishing. For the first time the world saw the greatest disaster ever created by man. The effects were unforgettably horrifying and disastrous. No one had bargained for the ensuing nightmare.

2. From the following pairs, choose the more descriptive title.
   a. (1) The Dreadful Nightmare of 1945
      (2) The Crippling Effects of the Atom Bomb on Hiroshima
   b. (1) Whence Did We Come and Why Are We Here?
      (2) What Is Philosophy?
   c. (1) China and Europe: Two Different Cultures
      (2) Dynamic Growth versus Static Social Principles
   d. (1) The People of the Black Moccasin
      (2) The Plains Culture of the Blackfoot Indians
   e. (1) Francisco Pizarro, Conqueror of Peru
      (2) Mighty Conquistador of the New World

3. Rid the following sentences of all deadwood:
   a. There are many ways in which light can be diffracted.
   b. No one has the right, in my opinion, to dictate to another human being whom to worship.
   c. Educationwise Will Rogers never did go to college.
   d. It has been said many times that power corrupts.
   e. There were thousands of teachers who attended the conference.
   f. The attitude-adjustment hour will begin at 5:00 P.M. and will be "no host."

4. Eliminate all redundant or imprecise phrases from the following sentences. Rewrite passages if necessary.
   a. Owing to the fact that it rained, Napoleon was defeated at Waterloo.
   b. We asked for a full and complete list of the passengers.
   c. One-man-one-vote should be a basic and fundamental reality of any political system.
   d. The room is square in shape, pale blue in color, and cheerful in appearance.
   e. The custodian was fired on the grounds that he slept on the job.
   f. A huge celebration marked the occasion of Martin Luther King's birthday.
   g. Those engaged in the profession of writing should be the guardians of grammar.

5. Rewrite the following sentences in the active voice:

  a. From early times on stucco was used by the Romans as a finish for important buildings.
  b. Immortality was not believed in by the Sadducees of Jerusalem.
  c. The *Brahmanas,* originally written in Sanskrit, were produced by Indian priests.
  d. Chewing mouths are used by termites to eat wood.
  e. A good time was had by all of us.
  f. Sometimes no symptoms are exhibited by victims of trichinosis.

6. Rewrite the following sentences to break up the noun clusters:

  a. The way to avoid a worsening future fuel crisis is the construction of a mass transportation system and the investing in quality insulation.
  b. The inspecting of the chemical-disposal plant was never accomplished.
  c. One can hope for the existence of an afterlife.
  d. The making of great strides by medical technology gives hope to people with incurable heart diseases.
  e. The development of a good ear is necessary to the writing of effective prose.

7. Rewrite the following sentences to correct an inconsistent point of view or shift in tense:

  a. They left early for the big city of San Francisco. Once there, they take the cable car to the top of Nob Hill. At five in the evening, they eat at a restaurant on the wharf.
  b. One must have respect for the flag of our country. If you don't, how can we expect others to respect it?
  c. Swarms of bees attacked him, so he quickly hides his face inside his heavy wool jacket.
  d. If one has ever lived by the sea, you always tend to miss the roar of the waves and the sound of seagulls.

Special Writing Projects

Why English Instructors Assign Research Papers

Students rarely greet the research paper with joy, but it still remains one of the most important college assignments. Writing one entails thinking critically about a subject, tracking down and evaluating facts for relevance and truth, organizing materials in support of a thesis, and cultivating a readable style. Success in college depends largely on the acquisition of these skills, which are also essential for accomplishment in business, the major professions, and even in private life. Salespeople often research a market and analyze it for trends; lawyers track down facts and organize them when preparing briefs and contracts; journalists depend on investigative research to gather material for stories. Engineers, nurses, secretaries, actors, architects, insurance agents—members of virtually all the professions—rely on the research techniques exemplified in this chapter.

How to Choose Your Topic

Typically, English instructors grant students the freedom to choose their own research topics, thus promoting exploration and self-discovery. If such a choice is indeed available to you, we recommend some preliminary browsing through the library until you come across a subject that arouses your curiosity—be it primitive Indians, the reign of the last empress of China, some influential sports figure, the complexities of the

New York Stock Exchange, children's psychological problems, or the fiction or poetry of a modern writer. Here are some tips on finding a suitable topic:

1. **Work with a familiar subject.** For instance, you may have been fascinated by historical attempts of the super-rich to manipulate the U.S. economy, such as the Gould-Fisk scheme to corner gold in 1869, with the consequent Black Friday market panic. Now you must find out more about Jay Gould, who became symbolic of autocratic business practices and was hated by most American businesspeople. Research will supply the necessary information.

2. **If familiarity fails, try an entirely new area.** Perhaps you have always wanted to learn about Lenin's philosophy of government, genetic engineering, stem cell technology, evolution in the Paleozoic era, the Roman empress Galla Placidia, the causes of earthquakes, pre-Columbian art, or the historical causes for the political unrest in the Middle East. A research paper finally gives you the opportunity to do so.

3. **Books, magazines, newspapers, and the Internet can suggest possible topics.** The library is a gold mine of hidden information. Browse through books, magazines, and newspapers. Some topic of interest is bound to leap out at you. Looking at secondary sources online is probably today's most popular way of finding research material. However, since anyone—from a well-known writer to a smart elementary school student—can place material on the Web, it is best to base your research on databases that are maintained by professionals. Some of these databases may even contain indexes that will allow you to download interesting material at no charge. The process of finding information on the Internet is always the same: access a search engine such as Google and enter a topic in the search slot. The computer will then search databases and Web sites on your topic and present a list of matching items. For example, we did a Google search on "illegal immigrants" and in less than a second got 2,380,000 hits. If you are new to computer research, ask for assistance from the librarian.

Avoid topics for which a single source can provide all the needed information; those that require no development but end as soon as started; those so popular that virtually everything about them has already been written and said; those so controversial that you have only fresh fuel to add to the already raging fire; or those decidedly unsuited to your audience, such as a paper advocating radical revision of the U.S. Constitution written for an instructor who is a conservative Republican.

How to Narrow Your Subject

Good research papers deal with topics of modest and workable proportions. To attempt a paper on the galaxies of the universe or on World War II is to attempt the impossible. A simple but practical way to narrow your subject is to subdivide it into progressively smaller units until you reach a topic specific enough for a paper. The following diagram on the sport of fencing illustrates what we mean:

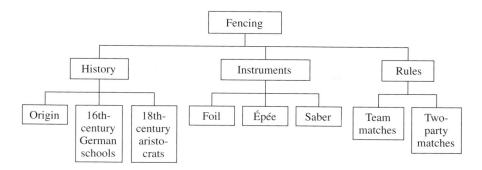

Any of the entries found on the lowest subdivision are properly narrowed subjects. For instance, you could write a useful paper on the sixteenth-century German schools that taught fencing to European gentlemen, on the use of the saber in fencing, or on the rules of modern team fencing. But a paper just on fencing would be overambitious and tricky to write.

Another point to bear in mind is that unlike the typical class-written paper, in which you must first formulate a thesis and then write the text, in the research paper you gather evidence, study it, and only then deduce a thesis. The assembled facts, statistics, graphs, schematics, arguments, expert testimony, and so on will suggest a topic that will be your thesis. What you learn in this process of writing the research paper is not only how to write but also how to infer a reasonable conclusion from a body of evidence.

The Process of Writing the Paper

You have narrowed your subject. You do not yet have a thesis or a definite topic, but you have a likely subject area to explore. You can do it in these simple steps:

1. **Find and Evaluate Sources** To do this, you must spend time in a library, which is your systematized retrieval network. Materials for your subject will most likely be found in electronic databases that have replaced the card catalog and are instantaneously linked to other sources that may be a thousand miles away. Most library storage systems are straightforward and easy to use—if there's something about the one at your school that you don't understand, ask your friendly librarian. You evaluate each source by scanning titles, tables of contents, chapter headings, or article summaries. Check the date of publication to make sure the information in the source is still valid. As you work, write down information on a possible source on its own bibliography card, providing the information necessary for easy retrieval. Some students prefer to record this information on a laptop but we still recommend that you use bibliography cards such as the one shown here.

   The most important part of Internet research is to evaluate the accuracy and dependability of sources. Here are some guidelines for evaluating Internet sources:

813.409   *College Library*

Sch.

Schneider, Robert W. Five Novelists of the

   Progressive Era.

   New York: Columbia University Press, 1965

Chapter 5 evaluates the novels of Winston Churchill, stating why

they were loved by contemporaries but scorned by succeeding generations.

- Check the reliability of the source. Since the World Wide Web grows bigger and more complex daily, some of the sources are bogus. We suggest that you stick to Web sites that end in *.org* (nonprofit organization), *.gov* (government entity), or *.edu* (educational body), since they are usually reliable.

- Check the dates of the sources to make sure that the information is not outdated.

- Check the authors of the material you have found by logging in their names on the Internet. Their biographies will tell you about their credentials, contributions, and reputations. For instance, if the author is a seasoned journalist reporting for the *New York Times* or the *Wall Street Journal,* you can be reassured that he or she is most likely a credible source.

2. **Take Notes** Using your electronic notebook or pile of bibliography cards, retrieve the books, magazines, pamphlets, and other identified sources and place them in front of you. Skim each source to get the drift of its content. Decide if it contains material relevant enough to warrant a more detailed reading. Once you have skimmed your sources, you can start taking four basic kinds of notes:

   a. **summary**—record the gist of a passage

   b. **paraphrase**—restate in your own words what the source says

   c. **direct quotation**—copy the exact words of a source

   d. **personal comments**—express your own views on the subject or source

Handwrite your notes on cards or type them on your computer and print them out on sheets of paper, which can be easily shuffled or discarded when you get down to the business of writing the paper. For easier reorganization of your notes, restrict each card or page to a single idea. To guard against unintentional plagiarism, copy down only exact quotations from your sources, and note these direct quotations as such, while digesting and expressing all other ideas in your own words. At some point in this stage (it varies from paper to paper), a thesis will occur to you. When it does, write it down for permanent reference. This will be the starting point for your paper.

Plagiarism Plagiarism is the willful or accidental stealing of someone else's writing. To help you understand the ins and outs of plagiarism, here are first the original source passage and then three passages about the American poet Walt Whitman, two of them plagiarized and one of them not.

Original Passage

Even when Whitman was working at his career as a newspaperman, his casualness threatened his advancement. As the owners of the New York *Aurora* fired him from the editorial staff, they accused him in print of "loaf-erism," describing him as "the laziest fellow who ever undertook to edit a city paper." Whitman never reformed. It remained his custom as editor to have the paper made up and ready for printing by noon, then to be off for a swim, a stroll, or a ride down Broadway on a horse-car. Even when working at that leisurely pace, he was complaining in the columns of the Brooklyn *Daily Eagle* that "most editors have far, far too much to do."

Plagiarized (Version 1)

During his career as a newspaperman, Walt Whitman was considered a loafer because his bosses felt that he didn't spend enough time in the newspaper office. In fact, he was fired from the editorial staff of the *Aurora* and labeled "the laziest fellow who ever undertook to edit a city paper." Being fired did not change Whitman, who always felt that editors worked much too hard. It remained his custom as editor to have the paper made up and ready for printing by noon, then to be off for a swim, a stroll, or a ride down Broadway on a horse car.

This is blatant plagiarism. The student has not acknowledged any source for the comments made about Whitman, in effect taking credit for them himself. Even the quotation is not documented.

Plagiarized (Version 2)

Whitman was considered a lazy loafer by the owners of the New York *Aurora* who employed him. They even fired him from their editorial staff and called him "the laziest fellow who ever undertook to edit a city paper." Whitman never reformed. He continued his habit of having the newspaper ready for printing by noon so that he could be off on some adventure of his own—a swim, a stroll, or a ride down Broadway in a horse carriage (Bridgman vii, viii).

This is the "Works Cited" information:

> Bridgman, Richard. Introduction. *Leaves of Grass*. By Walt Whitman. San Francisco: Chandler, 1968. Print.

Despite correct documentation, this passage is still plagiarized because the student has retained too much of the original source's wording, leaving the impression that it is his own.

Not Plagiarized

According to most of Walt Whitman's biographers, the poet did not have a compulsive or ambitious personality as far as his career as a journalist was concerned. In fact, "as the owners of the New York *Aurora* fired him from the editorial staff, they accused him in print of 'loaferism,' describing him as 'the laziest fellow who ever undertook to edit a city paper'" (Bridgman vii, viii).

Reading Whitman's own letters to friends or studying his poetry makes one aware that part of Whitman's philosophy was that a worthwhile life included both partying and working.

The "Works Cited" page then contains this entry:

> Bridgman, Richard. Introduction. *Leaves of Grass*. By Walt Whitman. San Francisco: Chandler, 1968. Print.

This passage is not plagiarized. The documentation is accurate and the ideas found in the original source are properly paraphrased. Remember that it is not enough to simply cite a source. If you're quoting from it, you should use quotation marks. If you're paraphrasing its material, you must do a true paraphrase. Whether you find material on the Internet or in a library book, you should never plagiarize. To avoid plagiarism, follow these rules meticulously:

- Acknowledge any idea taken from another source.
- Place quoted passages inside quotation marks.
- Provide a bibliographic entry at the end of the paper for every source used in your text.

You do not, however, have to document everything. Facts that are common knowledge need no documentation (example: "Abraham Lincoln was shot by John Wilkes Booth"). As a rule, a piece of information that has appeared in five standard sources can be considered common knowledge and needs no documentation.

3. **Write the First Draft** With a jumble of notes strewn on your desk, you may feel bewildered about what to include or exclude as you tackle your first draft. This may be the time for an outline, which can be adjusted later to fit your paper, or your paper can subsequently be adjusted to fit your outline.

In any case, by now you should have become something of an expert on your subject. Using your outline, start composing your first draft. As you write, you will be backing up your own opinions and views with source material uncovered by your research and recorded in your notes.

4. **Use Proper Documentation** Except for statements that are common knowledge, all information taken from your sources—whether quoted, paraphrased, or summarized—must be accompanied by a source citation given in parentheses and conforming to the proper format. We provide two sample papers in this chapter—one in the Modern Language Association (MLA) format, the other in the American Psychological Association (APA) format. Use the MLA author-work format if your instructor tells you to do so or if your paper is on a subject in the liberal arts or humanities, such as literature, philosophy, history, religion, or fine arts. For a paper in a more scientific field, such as psychology, sociology, or anthropology, the APA author-date format should be used. Always check with your instructor about the documentation format that is expected and appropriate. One caution: Do *not* mix styles.

The two annotated student papers represented in this part serve as general models and illustrate many of the documenting problems you are likely to encounter. For more complex citations, we recommend that you consult a style sheet or a research paper handbook. Both MLA and APA have gone to a system of parenthetical documentation, which gives brief but specific information about the sources within the text itself. The MLA style cites the author's surname or the title of a work, followed by a page number; the APA style cites the author's surname, followed by a date and a page number. In both styles, the author's name, work, and date can be omitted from the parentheses if they have already been supplied within the text. The rule of thumb is this: If the citation cannot be smoothly worked into the text, it should be supplied within parentheses. This kind of parenthetical documentation is obviously simpler than footnotes or endnotes because the citation can be given as the paper is being written rather than being tediously repeated in the text, the note, and the bibliography.

Flexibility in citations is a characteristic of both the MLA and APA styles. For example, you might choose to cite the author's name in the text while putting the page (MLA) or year and page (APA) in parentheses:

MLA Example

In her autobiography, Agatha Christie admits that often she felt the physical presence of Hercule Poirot (263).

APA Example

According to *800-Cocaine* by Mark S. Gold (1985, p. 21), cocaine has exploded into a business with brand names.

Or you might choose to include the title or author(s) of the citation in the parentheses:

MLA Example

The author began to realize how much she liked Poirot and how much a part of her life he had become (Christie 263).

APA Example

During the airing of ABC's *Good Morning, America* (Ross & Bronkowski, 1986), case histories were analyzed in an extremely serious tone.

In any case, the overriding aim should be to cite the necessary information without interrupting the flow of the text. What cannot be worked elegantly into the text is cited within parentheses.

This textbook does not have the space to pack in examples of every possible source you might use in your research. Aside from common sources, such as a periodical article or a book by one author, your investigation may lead you to include periodicals or books by multiple authors, edited volumes, scholarly journals, anthologies, translations, government documents, legal works, organizational papers, graphics, emails, blogs, tweets, anonymous works, published or personal interviews, and a whole stack of other sources that require meticulous citations. We offer only the most common variations. The following two guide books, for purchase online or in college bookstores, offer precise answers to most questions students have concerning citation or documentation formats:

Lester, James D., and James D. Lester, Jr. *Writing Research Papers: A Complete Guide,* 14th ed. New York: Pearson, 2012.

Winkler, Anthony C., and Jo Ray McCuen-Metherell. *Writing the Research Paper: A Handbook,* 8th ed. Boston: Cengage, 2012.

By typing "MLA Style" or "APA Style" into your Web browser, you can also receive free help from several online sources. One of the most helpful comes from the Online Writing Lab at Purdue University, which offers extensive advice on how to use the MLA style or APA style for properly formatted college research papers. To date, Purdue has allowed students to download their guidelines without paying a fee.

Preparing "Works Cited" or "References"

The sources cited in your text must be alphabetically listed in full at the end of your paper. In the MLA style of documentation, the list is titled "Works Cited"; in the APA style, it is titled "References." Both styles require the same general information, but differ slightly in details of capitalization and order. MLA entries, for example, begin with a surname, followed by the author's full (first) name; on the other hand, APA requires a surname, followed only by the initial letters of the author's first and middle names. In MLA entries, the author's name is followed by the title of the work, whereas in APA entries, the author's name is followed by the date. Both APA and MLA entries use hanging indentations (second and subsequent lines are indented one-half inch). Other differences are also minor: MLA requires titles of periodicals or books to be italicized, articles or chapters to be placed within quotation marks, and all principal words of a title to be capitalized (articles, prepositions, coordinating conjunctions, and the "to" in infinitives are not capitalized if they fall in the middle of a title). On the other hand, APA italicizes the titles of magazines and books but uses no quotation marks around the titles of chapters or articles within these longer works. APA capitalizes only the first word of an article or book title, the first word of a subtitle (if there is one), and any proper nouns; all other words are lowercase. For titles of periodicals, MLA capitalizes all principal words. See the sample student papers for specific examples of how to handle various bibliographic matters. Here are two typical examples that will allow you to see the difference between MLA and APA bibliographic listings for an article in a periodical:

MLA: Ripley, Amanda. "What Makes a Great Teacher?" *The Atlantic* Jan.–Feb. 2010: 58–66. Print.

Note that the MLA style now requires all "Works Cited" entries to include the medium of publication used. Most entries will be listed as **Print** or **Web** sources; however, other possibilities are **Film, CD-ROM,** or **DVD.** The MLA style no longer requires writers to provide URLs for Web entries. Nonetheless, if your instructor insists on them, provide them in angle brackets at the end of the entry, and end with a period, as follows: <http://classics.mit.edu/>.

APA: Dixit, J. (2010, January). Heartbreak and home runs: The power of first experiences. *Psychology Today, 43,* 61–69.

Here are two further examples to indicate the difference between MLA and APA when listing a book:

MLA: Martel, Yann. *Beatrice and Virgil.* New York: Spiegel, 2011. Print.

APA: Moyers, W. C. (2006). *Broken: My story of addiction and redemption.* New York, NY: Viking.

Online sources require a special format. In MLA style the "Works Cited" reference for a Web page should include the following elements: name of the author or editor of the project or database, if available; italicized title of the project or database; electronic publication information, including version number (if relevant and not part of the title); publisher of the project or database; date of electronic publication or of the latest update; medium (Web); and date of access. MLA no longer requires the use of URLs in "Works Cited" entries. Because Web addresses can change often and because documents sometimes appear in multiple places on the Web, MLA explains that most readers can find electronic sources through title or author searches via Internet search engines. If your instructor does require the URL, place it within angle brackets (< >) after the date of access.

APA style for online sources requires a retrieval statement at the end of the reference item—with a date, if the information is likely to change, as with Wikis—such as the following: "Retrieved January 23, 2011, from http://apa.org/journals/webref.html" or "Retrieved from www.apa.org/psycarticles/." If an article has a DOI (Digital Object Identifier), include it in your citation rather than the URL.

When using electronic sources, it is always a good idea to keep personal copies of information. Get in the habit of printing out or saving Web pages and articles in PDF format for future reference. Also, you might use the Bookmark function on your Web browser in order to return to documents more easily.

Writing the Final Copy

Revising and editing your paper is the final step. Do not be easy on yourself. Pretend that the paper is someone else's and badly in need of work. Check for logical progression, completeness of development, and mechanical correctness. The only way to produce an excellent paper is to pore over it paragraph by paragraph looking for weaknesses or faults. After careful review and editing, prepare the final copy using one of the formats exemplified by the two student papers. If you are following the APA format, you will also need to write an abstract summarizing your findings (see student sample, pages 755–773). Remember that the appearance of a paper can add to or detract from its quality. Here are some important tips on manuscript appearance:

1. Use 8.5″ × 11″ white paper. Double-space throughout the paper.

2. Except for page numbers, use one-inch margins at the top, bottom, and sides of the paper. (For page numbers, see item 6.)

3. Avoid fancy fonts such as script. Times New Roman 12 pt. is preferred.

4. If required, place a balanced and uncluttered outline before the text of the paper. Double-space throughout the outline.

5. APA papers require a title page. For MLA papers do not use a title page unless your instructor requires one. Instead, put your name, instructor's name, course number, and date on the first page of the outline, repeating this information in the upper left-hand corner of the first page of the text. The title should be centered and double-spaced below the date. (See sample papers.)

6. Number pages consecutively throughout the paper itself (see item 1 below, regarding the outline for an MLA paper) in the upper right-hand corner, 1/2 inch from the top border. Do not follow page numbers with hyphens, parentheses, periods, or other characters. Number the first page of the paper with an Arabic "1", and continue numbering pages consecutively throughout the paper, including "Works Cited" or "References" list.

7. Double-check the appropriate format (MLA or APA) for citing and documenting. Once again, we point out that you can use the online writing lab at Purdue University free of charge to find listings of all possible citations—both within your text and in "Works Cited" or "References."

8. Note that APA papers feature an abstract and a running header. (See sample paper.)

ANNOTATED STUDENT RESEARCH PAPER

Modern Language Association (MLA) Style

(1) *The first page seen by your reader is usually the first page of your paper; however, some teachers require an outline to precede the first page. If so, paginate the outline with small Roman numerals (i, ii, iii ...). Place your name in the top left-hand margin, followed by your instructor's name, the course number, and the date the paper is due.

See the sample outline on the next page. If you are using an outline, begin with a thesis, consisting of a single declarative sentence preceded by the word *Thesis*. The rest of the outline follows the rules for correct sentence outlining. Some instructors allow topic outlines, which consist of phrases rather than full sentences. Do not make the outline too long. A sound rule is to have one page of outline for every five pages of writing. The outline leaves out the details of the paper, mentioning only major points.

(2) Center the title (as well as the subtitle) of your paper. A good title should tell the reader what the paper is about. Double-space throughout the entire paper.

---

*The Arabic numerals in the left margin of the student paper correspond to the comments on the facing page.

1 → Stephanie Hollingsworth

Professor Dekker

English 101

30 September 2011

2 →Choosing Single Motherhood: A Sign of Modern Times?

Thesis: Increases in educational and career opportunities for women, advances in medical technology, and diminishing social stigma all contribute to the rising number of women who are choosing to become single mothers.

I. Women are waiting longer to start families.

  A. A shift in women's consciousness has occurred since the 1960s.

   1. Marriage is no longer a necessary component to childbearing.

   2. The use of birth control gave women more choices over when or even if to get pregnant.

  B. There are more opportunities for women today.

   1. More women are taking advantage of higher education.

   2. The number of career opportunities for women has increased.

  C. Women are more willing to wait for the right partner.

   1. Personal fulfillment plays a higher role in the consciousness of today's woman.

   2. Many of today's women are children of divorce and would like to avoid that situation in their own marriages.

  D. Waiting longer creates concern for some women who fear the biological clock's ticking.

II. Advances in fertility technology are providing women with more options as to when and how to have a child.
  A. Women can have children later in life.
  B. Single women have the option of conceiving a child through donor insemination.
III. The social stigma of a single woman having a child has diminished.
  A. More adults today are children of divorce and therefore more tolerant of single parenting.
  B. The formation of support groups for single mothers has given single parenting a boost.
IV. Although many critics argue that single mothering by choice represents a breakdown of traditional family values, some studies indicate otherwise.
  A. Critics fear that the traditional nuclear family is quickly becoming the exception.
  B. Some studies argue that a father is not necessary for the healthy upbringing of a child.
    1. These studies show that children do not necessarily fare better when a father is present.
    2. Many fathers spend less than two and a half hours a day with their children.

(1) Place your last name and page # in upper right corner of each page, 1/2 inch from top border.

(2) Use Times New Roman 12 pt. or similar font that is easy to read.

(3) Give your name, instructor's name, course number, and date.

(4) Center the title of your paper.

(5) Double space throughout the entire paper.

(6) Margins are 1 inch left, right and bottom.

(7) Margin are 1 inch left, right and bottom

(8) You may use figures when the paper features many numbers. Very large numbers can be expressed by a combination of words and figures (11 million bricks), but be consistent.

(9) In-text citation to a specific source in "Works Cited."

(10) The thesis statement appears in its conventional position, at the end of the first paragraph.

(11) In-text citation for two separate works.

(12) Throughout this paragraph, the student does not use any direct quotation, but simply synthesizes Band, Bailey, and Jeweler's ideas and restates them in his own words, keeping the rhetorical style consistent.

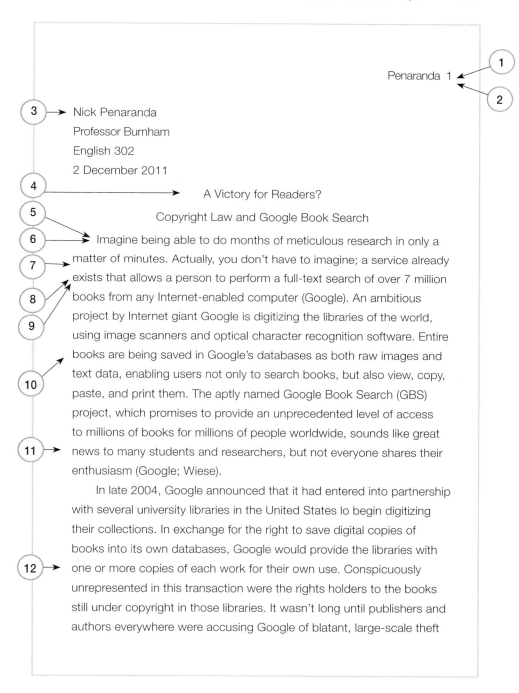

Penaranda 1

Nick Penaranda
Professor Burnham
English 302
2 December 2011

A Victory for Readers?

Copyright Law and Google Book Search

Imagine being able to do months of meticulous research in only a matter of minutes. Actually, you don't have to imagine; a service already exists that allows a person to perform a full-text search of over 7 million books from any Internet-enabled computer (Google). An ambitious project by Internet giant Google is digitizing the libraries of the world, using image scanners and optical character recognition software. Entire books are being saved in Google's databases as both raw images and text data, enabling users not only to search books, but also view, copy, paste, and print them. The aptly named Google Book Search (GBS) project, which promises to provide an unprecedented level of access to millions of books for millions of people worldwide, sounds like great news to many students and researchers, but not everyone shares their enthusiasm (Google; Wiese).

In late 2004, Google announced that it had entered into partnership with several university libraries in the United States lo begin digitizing their collections. In exchange for the right to save digital copies of books into its own databases, Google would provide the libraries with one or more copies of each work for their own use. Conspicuously unrepresented in this transaction were the rights holders to the books still under copyright in those libraries. It wasn't long until publishers and authors everywhere were accusing Google of blatant, large-scale theft

13 In-text citation for three works. The Jeweler citation has a page reference because it is a print document. Whenever you cite authors from different works, provide enough information to direct the reader to the correct source.

14 Italicize names of books, plays, long poems, television shows, newspapers, magazines, websites, databases, art, Films and record albums are also italized.

15 Use ellipsis points (three equally spaced periods) to indicate an omission within at quotation.

16 Use the phrase "qtd. in" when quoting an author from another source. In this case, Verba is quoted in Hafner's work.

17 Use brackets to indicate explanatory interpolations within quotations.

18 Notice how the student smoothly integrates quotation, paraphrase, and personal commentary throughout this entire paragraph—proving that he has synthesized the original materia and understands it.

19 Leave a 1-inch margin from the bottom of page.

Penaranda 2

13 ▸ of their intellectual property. Google's 2004 announcement would spark
one of the largest copyright and fair-use debates that the Internet era
has ever seen (Band; Bailey; Jeweler 95–96).

Sidney Verba, former chairman of the board of Harvard University
Press, Harvard political science professor, author or co-author of

14 ▸ over 15 books, and now director of the Harvard University Library,
has a unique perspective on GBS. In an interview for the *New York
Times* in 2005 he discussed the concerns of publishers regarding

15 ▸ GBS: "Scanning the whole text |makes publishers very nervous. . . .
They have to be assured that there will be security, that no one will

16 ▸ hack in and steal contents, or sell it to someone" (qtd. in Hafner). In
addition, because some of his books are still in print, he says that
he understands writers' concerns that GBS may disrupt their books'
markets. Despite this, he believes that GBS will ultimately do more good
than harm, and eventually agreed to give Google access to Harvard
University Library's seven million volumes (Hafner).

On the other hand, one publisher, Rowman & Littlefield, opted
out of GBS entirely. Jed Lyons, president and CEO of the publishing

17 ▸ company, called Google's project "an outrageous rip-off," and added,
"[Google is] flagrantly violating U.S. copyright law" (qtd. in Albanese).

18 ▸ More specifically, Lyons was referring lo Google's backwards method of
obtaining permission. Traditionally, the burden of obtaining permission
is the user's. Google, on the other hand, has assumed that it has
permission and has given publishers and other rights holders a chance
to opt out. He. like many other publishers and authors, felt that Google
was going too far with GBS (Albanese).

And so, approximately one year after Google first announced its
then-named Google Print project, two major lawsuits were filed against
it. The first was a class action lawsuit filed by the Author's Guild and a

19 ▸ handful of authors, representing individual rights holders. McGraw-Hill

(20) The word *except* is italicized for emphasis.

(21) In-text citation for a U.S. government code.

(22) Here the student uses both quotation and paraphrase in a passage that requires accurate reflections from a legal code. For clarity, the guidelines are numbered, but only the first is directly quoted, presumably because it is the most important.

and several other publishers filed a second lawsuit a month later to represent publishers' interests. Both lawsuits claimed that Google, in creating and retaining digital copies of works to which the plaintiffs held rights, infringed on their copyrights. The plaintiffs of these two lawsuits believed that Google was committed only to increasing its revenue, regardless of copyright laws. In addition, they claimed that GBS would devalue their product or otherwise harm their market. They wanted the courts to order Google to destroy its collection and to declare such activity illegal ("Author's Guild"; "McGraw-Hill").

In response, Google claimed that their right to provide GBS is first and foremost protected under the First Amendment. Specifically, it claimed that its searchable digital library constitutes fair use and that no express permission was required from the rights holders. Further, it also claimed that only a portion of works are protected by copyright, and even that some works are unprotectable under U.S. copyright law. Google also fired back at some of the rights holders, claiming that some of them "have engaged in copyright misuse and have unclean hands" ("Author's Guild"). It also felt that GBS, by providing links to places where book search results could be purchased, could only benefit book markets. Predictably, Google wanted the courts to reward the plaintiffs nothing and declare that GBS was within copyright laws ("Author's Guild").

Il should be noted that Google's defense relied almost exclusively on the notion of "fair use." According to copyright law, all manner of reproduction, distribution, or displaying of intellectual property are the exclusive rights of the owner, *except* when its use falls within a set of guidelines set forth in the United States Code. When a party is accused of copyright infringement, courts are specifically instructed to consider (1) "the purpose and character of the use" (USC 107); (2) what the copyrighted material is, e.g., textbook or painting; (3) how much of the work was used; and (4) how the use will affect the copyrighted material's market or value. Beyond these four guidelines, courts have

(23) Names of legal cases are italicized.

(24) If a quotation runs more than four lines, indent an additional 1/2 inch with no quotation marks except for a quotation within the quotation (note "for the public good?").

(25) This long paragraph serves as a fine example of how to alternate between quoting, paraphrasing, and using personal commentary. By fully synthesizing the background material and making it his own, the student has avoided a choppy style and has maintained the integrity of his research.

Penaranda 4

little else on which to base their decisions. One can quickly see how the charges brought against Google are difficult and highly subjective matters to arbitrate (USC 106–107; Jeweler, 97).

Should publishers and authors have to give up their copyrights for Google's and, by extension, students and researchers' benefit? Or should Google be required to compensate rights holders for its digital copies? To date, there is no clear-cut answer. Like many other issues, this one is subject to "case law." or legal precedents created by past court decisions which guide future rulings. Unfortunately, there have never been disputes of this type, scale or scope until now (Kohler). A few cases in the past

23 → have been only slightly similar, for instance, *Kelly v. Arriba Soft Corp.,* in which the court ruled that "Internet search engines' [image] indexing activities constitute a fair use" (Jeweler 97). Thus, both the court and the litigants have a very limited historical guide to rely on. Perhaps this is the reason that, at the time of this writing, neither lawsuit has been settled in court ("Author's Guild"; "McGraw-Hill").

The murky book settlement has caused hundreds of blogs, tweets, and other comments to be posted in cyber space. One typical blogger's reaction is in the form of a question:

24 → Why can't the public just buy in-print books outside the Settlement, and buy out-of-print books from used booksellers or take them out of the library? The libraries who lent the books for scanning will also lend them for inter-library loan. Why is it that the creators of the works are not supposed to have any say in what is done "for the public good?" (Grimble) Legal matters aside, Google states that one of its motivations behind GBS is to "ensure the ongoing accessibility of out-of-print books . . .

25 → to protect mankind's cultural history" (Google). At least to some extent, publishers and authors agree with this end, and their agreement has

26 Use parentheses to enclose nonessential or supplementary material within the text.

Penaranda 5

allowed the parties to negotiate a settlement out-of-court. This settlement includes, among other things, provisions for rights holders to exclude their work from CBS and for the establishment of a non-profit organization to guarantee the rights of authors, publishers and others whose work is indexed. Perhaps most significantly, it outlines how rights holders will be able to profit from the inclusion of their works in GBS. The settlement distinguishes books into three categories: Books that

(26) → are in-print and under copyright, out-of-print but still under copyright, and those that are out-of-copyright (i.e., public domain). The first two types of books will have limited previews, enabling users to flip through them "just like you'd browse them at a bookstore or library" (Google). In addition, GBS will provide a means to purchase full versions of copyrighted books, while full versions of out-of-copyright books will be available free of charge. Lastly, GBS also intends to make physical copies of books more accessible, by pointing users to where they can get their hands on actual print versions of search results. Rights holders are poised to reach a bigger market for books that are in print and to rediscover markets for out-of-print books. Libraries and bookstores will enjoy greater patronage and advertisement, respectively. Lastly, Google will undoubtedly see increased traffic and thus increased revenue (Google; Kohler).

But what does it all mean for those not immediately invested in GBS? For starters, it means that anyone in search of an old, out-of-print book won't have to dig through used book store or library shelves, provided, of course, that the author didn't opt to turn his or her book's listing off in GBS. It means that students who are lucky enough to attend a university that purchases a GBS subscription, or anyone who happens to live near a subscribing library, will have access to full versions of millions of books, new and old. It means that some books that,

(27) The paper ends by restating the thesis. It also includes a quotation, which at first glance might seem to diminish some of the student author's sway; however, the quotation happens to come from the co-founder of Google; thus, it lends a sense of final authority to the paper.

until recently, could only be found in a handful of libraries in the world, are now accessible to anyone with an Internet connection (Google).

Like the legal struggle that its inception sparked, GBS's contribution to the accessibility of knowledge is unprecedented. It's hard to imagine what the Internet would be like without search engines like Google, and soon it may be just as hard to imagine what doing research would be like without digital libraries like GBS. The GBS settlement, though still awaiting court approval, stands to usher in a new era in publishing. In much the same way that iTunes changed the music industry for artists and record companies, GBS could potentially rock the literary world for publishers and authors. But perhaps most exciting of all, "the real victors are all the readers," said Sergey Brin, co-founder of Google. "The tremendous wealth of knowledge that lies within the books of the world will now be at their fingertips" (qtd. in Google).

27 →

(28) The "Works Cited" list follows the MLA rules for citing references. Most of the references are to works from a database or a web site. The date following the word "Web" is when the student retrieved the article from the web site. The other date is the date of publication.

(29) Center the title "Works Cited."

(30) Arrange sources alphabetically by the author's last name, or if there is no author, by the first word in the citation.

(31) Indent each source 1 inch from the border, double space, and indent second and consecutive lines—1/2 inch.

(32) Include the medium of each source: print, Web, CD, DVD, television, radio, film, email, performance, etc.

Penaranda 7

Works Cited

Albanese, Andrew. "Publisher: No Thanks, Google," *Library Journal.*
Libraryjoumal.com, 1 Nov. 2005: n.p. Web. 21 Nov. 2011.

"Author's Guild et al. v. Google Inc." *Justia.com*. Justia, 2009. Web. 12
Nov. 2011.

Bailey, Charles W., Jr. "Google Book Search Bibliography." *Digital-
scholarship.org,* Digital Scholarship. 14 Sep. 2009. Web. 6
Nov. 2011.

Band, J. "The Google Library Project: Both Sides of the Story."
*Plagiary: Cross-Disciplinary Studies in Plagiarism, Fabrication, and
Falsification,* 1 (2006): 1–17. Web. 12 Nov. 2011.

Google, Inc. "Google Books Settlement Agreement." *Google.com.*
Google, 2009. Web. 12 Nov. 2011.

Grimble, Frances. Blog. *The Laboratorium* Web. 22 Nov. 2011.

Hafner, Katie. "At Harvard, a Man, a Plan, and a Scanner." *New York
Times* 21 Nov. 2005: n.p. *Nytimes.com*. Web. 21 Nov. 2011.

Jeweler, Robin. "The Google Book Search Project: Is Online Indexing a
Fair Use Under Copyright Law?" *Focus on the Internet.* Ed. B. G.
Kutais. New York: Nova Science Publishers, 2006. 95-100. Print.

Kohler, David. "This Town Ain't Big Enough for the Both of Us—Or is it?
Reflections on Copyright, the First Amendment and Google's Use
of Others' Content." *Duke Law & Technology Review* 5, (2007): n.p.
Social Science Research Network. Web. 8 Nov. 2011.

"McGraw-Hill et al. v. Google Inc." *Justia.com*. Justia, 2009. Web. 12
Nov. 2011.

(33) Include the URL only if the instructor requires it, or if the source is difficult to find without it.

Penaranda 8

Peritz, Rudolph J.R. and Marc Miller. "GBS: An Introduction to
     Competition Concerns in the Google Books Settlement." *The
     laboratorium*. Web. 21 Nov. 2011. <hltp://laboratoritum.net/
     archives/2010/03/21/gbs_an_introduction_to_competition_
     concerns...>
United States Copyright Law, Section 106: Exclusive Rights in
     Copyrighted Works. Amended 1990.
United States Copyright Law, Section 107: Limitations on Exclusive
     Rights: Fair Use. Amended 1990.
Wiese, Katie. "The Pens and The Keys: Controversy over Google Books
     and Scholar." *Echoditto*. 31 July 2009: n.p. Web. 6 Nov. 2011.

33

ANNOTATED STUDENT RESEARCH PAPER

American Psychological Association (APA) Style

Running Head: Development of a Scale 1

Development of a Scale to
Detect Sexual Harassers:
The Potential Harasser Scale (PHS)

Leanne M. Masden
and
Rebecca B. Winkler
DePaul University

(1) The Abstract should not exceed 120 words. Any numbers present in the Abstract should appear as Arabic numerals (except a number that begins a sentence).

①   → Abstract

The current study was an attempt to design a scale to detect one's propensity to sexually harass women. The Likelihood to Sexually Harass (LSH) scale designed by Pryor (1987) was used as a starting point in probing the characteristics held by men who sexually harass women. Using existing research, an initial scale was designed and tested on a pilot sample of men known to the authors. After the scale was completed by the participants, statistics were calculated and explored to determine which items needed to be retained and which needed to be dropped. Following these analyses, the Potential Harasser Scale (PHS) was determined to be statistically sound and ready for future use.

(2) This is a typical citation, appearing at the sentence's conclusion and followed by a period. This work has three authors.

(3) Because the information mentioned in this sentence is derived from three different sources, the paper's authors have chosen to place each citation adjacent to the corresponding element. Note that the first citation identifies a source with two authors, the second citation has three authors, and the third citation has one author.

Development of a Scale to Detect Sexual Harassers: The Potential
Harasser Scale (PHS)

Our interest in the current topic was first sparked as a result of sexual
harassment being the focus of one team member's master's thesis.
Current estimates state that approximately one out of every two women

2 ➤ will be sexually harassed at least once during her working or educational
life (Fitzgerald, Swan, & Magley, 1997). But why do so many women
experience sexual harassment? Researchers have found evidence to
support a power threat motive for offenders, whereby women who
possess certain characteristics that would put them in direct competition
with men for resources are more likely to be harassed, apparently
in an attempt to dissuade them from entering the male-dominated
sphere of privilege and power. Some such female characteristics are

3 ➤ having egalitarian sex-role attitudes (Dall'Ara & Maass, 1999), being
single, having more education and longer tenure within the organization
(DeCoster, Estes, & Mueller, 1999), and being young (Gruber, 1998).
However, there is not pure consensus in the field regarding the effect of
age on the risk of being sexually harassed (O'Connell & Korabik, 2000).
Because men are more likely than women to be perpetrators of sexual
harassment (Fitzgerald, Magley, Drasgow, & Waldo, 1999), this particular
population will be the focus of the present study.

During the initial research process, we discovered the Likelihood
to Sexually Harass (LSH) scale, originally developed by Pryor (1987).
This scale was designed to measure one's propensity to sexually harass
based on the possession of certain characteristics that perpetrators of
sexual harassment tend to have.

(4)   Because the authors are mentioned in the sentence, a citation is not necessary at the sentence's conclusion.

(5)   The paper's first-level internal heading appears centered, using bold uppercase and lowercase.

(6)   The paper's second-level internal heading appears flush with the left margin, using bold uppercase and lowercase.

This scale gave us the direction we needed to conduct further research in order to identify the relevant constructs this topic contained. Luckily, the LSH scale has generated a fair amount of research as a result of others attempting to find exactly what constructs this scale measures. For example, Driscoll, Kelly, and Henderson (1998) found that men who scored high on the LSH also held more traditional views toward women, more negative views toward women, and had a more masculine personality. Other researchers also found that aggression, acceptance of interpersonal violence, fraternity affiliation, and sex-role stereotyping were related to scoring high on the LSH (Lackie & de Man, 1997). In addition, Pryor (1987) showed that men scoring high on the LSH found it more difficult to view things from another's perspective and had higher authoritarian beliefs. As a result of this research, we now knew what we needed to include when we started to develop our own Potential Harasser Scale (PHS).

Method

Item and Scale Development

After reading the relevant research on our topic, we decided that our scale should include eight dimensions plus a few demographic questions. We also decided that each dimension should have four items. Our eight dimensions were as follows: aggression, sex role stereotyping (i.e., holding traditional views toward women), egalitarianism/negative views toward women, masculinity, acceptance of interpersonal violence, lack of empathy, authoritarianism, and hostile environment behaviors.

The first seven dimensions were derived from the current literature on the topic of sexual harassment and related concepts. However, the last dimension was developed to fill a gap in the existing LSH scale. The LSH scale is designed to detect sexual harassers who exhibit *quid pro quo* behaviors, meaning those who attempt to exchange sexual favors for work-related promotions or other advantages (Pryor, 1987). However, this focus fails to address other forms of sexual harassment, such as hostile environment behaviors. This type of sexual harassment is considered to be less severe but even more pervasive (Fitzgerald, Gelfand, & Drasgow, 1995). Therefore, we thought it would be important to attempt to capture this dimension in our PHS instrument.

We also included a few demographic questions to see if age, race, or marital status were related to one's potential to sexually harass. In addition, a short section about fraternity membership and extent of one's involvement were included as a result of this affiliation being significantly related in previous research (Lackie & de Man, 1997). Therefore, our total scale had 37 items, 32 in the actual scale and 5 demographic questions. Furthermore, we renamed our instrument the *Personal Beliefs Questionnaire* so that those who completed our instrument would not be alerted to what it was attempting to measure.

Characteristics of the Pilot Sample

We recruited male classmates, co-workers, fathers, and significant others to complete our scale. As a result of our efforts, we had 14 respondents. All of them were Caucasian with the exception of one Hispanic. In addition, three individuals in our sample were married, five were single, and six currently lived with a partner.

Our respondents ranged in age from 23 to 60, with a mean age of 30.28. Concerning fraternity affiliation, 35.7 percent of our sample were members of a fraternity, and 40 percent reported being "very involved."

Results

Results of Preliminary Item Analyses

First, we cleaned the data by looking at the frequencies and descriptive statistics. All values were within the expected range, so we considered our data to be clean. By taking a closer look at our means and standard deviations, we immediately noticed some items had extremely low standard deviations. For example, item 11 asks about one's acceptance of domestic violence. Whether the answers reflected socially desirable responses due to lack of anonymity with only 14 respondents or true beliefs, everyone in our sample strongly disagreed with the appropriateness of hitting one's spouse.

We scanned the correlation matrix including all of our items, and with the exception of item 11, which had no correlations due to its lack of variance, every other item exhibited at least one theoretically meaningful correlation with another item. For example, two items relating to aggression were significantly correlated (i.e., "I am an aggressive driver" and "I enjoy playing sports with a lot of physical contact"). The only items that were not significantly correlated with anything else on the scale were those that tapped into fraternity affiliation and involvement.

We also ran an intraclass correlation analysis to determine our scale's internal consistency. As a result, our Cronbach's alpha was $r = .8069$, which shows that our scale had high internal consistency.

(7) The authors refer the reader to the Appendix, which appears at the paper's conclusion and following the References.

Final Scale Revision

Based on our initial item analyses, we determined that a few changes could be made that would improve our scale's psychometric properties. Therefore, we removed the items on fraternity affiliation and involvement. Although previous research has shown these constructs to be related to one's likelihood to sexually harass (Lackie & de Man, 1997), our analyses showed that these items were the only ones that were not significantly correlated to any other item in our scale. Since these items were in the demographics section, they were not included in the intraclass correlation analysis. Therefore, this analysis was not re-run, because no improvement would have been noted here.

Although traditional scale construction theory would normally guide us to remove a few other items due to their low standard deviations, we decided that the low variance on these items was most likely due to the restrictions placed on us by our small sample. If we were to administer our scale to a greater number of people in a more anonymous setting, perhaps we would not see the same restricted variance due to the greater chance of people answering truthfully. In our small and familiar sample, we found many answers that may have been driven by a socially desirable and appropriate manner of responding. See the Appendix for the final version of the PHS.

7 →

Discussion

This project taught us many valuable lessons. To begin with, we were pleased with the fact that we were able to construct a theoretically meaningful instrument that also displayed desirable psychometric properties, such as our high Cronbach's alpha. In addition, it was

DEVELOPMENT OF A SCALE 8

an interesting experience to design items that fit into our proposed dimensions. We also had a fun time piloting it on our sample and gathering the reactions from our participants, in addition to analyzing their answers to draw the relevant conclusions on our new tool. However, there are also many things we would have done differently had this been a "real world" project.

First, merely masking our scale's true intent by designing a new label did not do much to mask the content and what we were trying to measure. Our participants (especially our classmates) could tell by the transparency of many of our items what we were aiming for. In addition, although we believe our sample to be well-educated and fairly liberal overall in their views toward women, they all still knew that we would be analyzing their responses and would probably be able to tell who was who if we really wanted to. Therefore, there may have been some socially desirable responding that caused many of our items to have low variances.

Some improvements in methodology could prevent this type of responding from occurring. For example, administering this scale in a more anonymous format with many other respondents (e.g., in an auditorium setting) would probably allow more truthful answers to emerge. Furthermore, if the scale items could be embedded within a larger instrument, the aim of the Potential Harasser Scale would also be less obvious. Overall, however, we were pleased with both the process and the results.

During the course of this project, we each also attempted to contact a publisher who had designed a relevant scale. One person contacted the company Risk and Needs Assessment, Inc., to obtain their Sexual Adjustment Inventory. The other person contacted Sigma Assessment Systems to obtain their Sex-Role Egalitarianism Scale.

DEVELOPMENT OF A SCALE 9

Both of us were successful in our endeavors and did not have to endure any trouble at all. One team member simply called the publisher and received a sample packet in a matter of days that included one test book, two answer sheets, one training manual, one example report, and a computer disk that provided the scoring key program. The other person emailed the publisher and received a sample brochure in the mail a few days later. Therefore, the ease in contacting the publishers was about equal between the two team members, but the amount of scale information given varied greatly.

In summary, working on this project allowed us to put into action much of the theory that we have spent the past ten weeks learning. It was interesting to us to experience the process of developing a scale as well as learning to deal with some of the pitfalls that inevitably occur with not having a large group of people we don't know to pilot our instrument on.

However, all in all, we think we will be better survey and test developers in the future as a result of constructing the Potential Harasser Scale.

(8) The list of references appears on a separate page (or pages), with the heading "References" centered at the top of the page. All references cited in the text must appear in the Reference list; and each entry in the Reference list must be cited in the text of the paper. Note that APA now prefers italicizing titles of books, magazines, and journals over underlining.

(9) References with the same first author and different second, third, or fourth authors are alphabetized by the surname of the second author (or, if the second author is the same in the two references, the surname of the third).

⑧ ——————————————▶   References

Dall'Ara, E., & Maass, A. (1999). Studying sexual harassment in the
 laboratory: Are egalitarian women at higher risk? *Sex Roles,
 41*(9/10), 681–704. Retrieved December 9, 2011, from Proquest
 Education Complete database.

DeCoster, S., Estes, S. B., & Mueller, C.W. (1999). Routine activities and
 sexual harassment in the workplace. *Work and Occupations, 26*(1),
 21–49.

Driscoll, D. M., Kelly, J. R., & Henderson, W. L. (1998). Can perceivers
 identify likelihood to sexually harass? *Sex Roles, 38*(7/8), 557–588.

⑨ ▶ Fitzgerald, L. F., Gelfand, M. J., & Drasgow, F. (1995). Measuring sexual
 harassment: Theoretical and psychometric advances. *Basic and
 Applied Social Psychology, 17,* 425–427.

Fitzgerald, L. F., Magley, V. J., Drasgow, F., & Waldo, C. R. (1999).
 Measuring sexual harassment in the military: The sexual
 experiences questionnaire (SEQ-DoD). *Military Psychology, 11*(3),
 243–263. Retrieved December 9, 2011, from Academic Search
 Elite database.

Fitzgerald, L. F., Swan, S., & Magley ,V. J. (1997). But was it really
 sexual harassment? Legal, behavioral, and psychological definitions
 of the workplace victimization of women. W. O'Donohue (Ed.),
 Sexual harassment: Theory, research, and treatment (pp. 5–28).
 Boston: Allyn & Bacon.

Gruber, J. E. (1998). The impact of male work environments and
 organizational policies on women's experiences of sexual
 harassment. *Gender and Society, 12*(3), 301–320.

Lackie, L., & de Man, A. F. (1997). Correlates of sexual aggression among male university students. *Sex Roles, 37*(5/6), 451–457.

O'Connell, C. E., & Korabik, K. (2000). Sexual harassment: The relationship of personal vulnerability, work context, perpetrator status, and type of harassment to outcomes. *Journal of Vocational Behavior, 56,* 299–329.

Pryor, J. B. (1987). Sexual harassment proclivities in men. *Sex Roles, 17*(5/6), 269–290.

(10) If the paper has only one appendix, label it "Appendix." If your paper has more than one appendix, label each one with a capital letter (e.g., "Appendix A," "Appendix B"). Provide a title for each appendix.

DEVELOPMENT OF A SCALE 12

10 ────────────────────────▶

Appendix

Personal Beliefs Questionnaire

Please rate how strongly you agree or disagree with the following statements using the scale provided below. Please answer all questions honestly; note that all of your answers will remain anonymous.

1 = Strongly Disagree

2 = Disagree

3 = Neither Agree nor Disagree

4 = Agree

5 = Strongly Agree

1. Being around strong women makes me uncomfortable.	1	2	3	4	5
2. I am an aggressive driver (e.g., I cut people off, honk the horn often).	1	2	3	4	5
3. I believe some women are to blame for being raped (e.g., by wearing sexy clothes, flirting, etc.).	1	2	3	4	5
4. I believe that every citizen should have the right to carry a gun.	1	2	3	4	5
5. I believe that it is important for a woman to take care of her body so that she looks good for her man.	1	2	3	4	5
6. I believe that it is important to volunteer time or donate money to help others in need.	1	2	3	4	5

1 = Strongly Disagree

2 = Disagree

3 = Neither Agree nor Disagree

4 = Agree

5 = Strongly Agree

7. I believe that men should be the primary   1   2   3   4   5
breadwinners for their families.

8. I believe that most homeless people are   1   2   3   4   5
still homeless because they are lazy.

9. I believe that people should respect their   1   2   3   4   5
place within an organizational hierarchy.

10. I believe that some women are still paid   1   2   3   4   5
less than men for doing the same work.

11. I believe that sometimes it is OK for a   1   2   3   4   5
husband to hit his wife.

12. I believe that too many women are   1   2   3   4   5
focusing too much on their careers,
to the detriment of their families.

13. I believe that too many women are   1   2   3   4   5
trying to enter occupations that are
better suited for men.

14. I believe that women should be primarily   1   2   3   4   5
responsible for taking care of children.

15. I believe that women should not play   1   2   3   4   5
sports with a lot of physical contact
(e.g., football).

DEVELOPMENT OF A SCALE   14

1 = Strongly Disagree

2 = Disagree

3 = Neither Agree nor Disagree

4 = Agree

5 = Strongly Agree

16. I display pictures of naked/near naked   1   2   3   4   5
women at work/school.

17. I do not question the decisions made   1   2   3   4   5
by the President.

18. I enjoy cooking for others.   1   2   3   4   5

19. I enjoy magazines that display pictures   1   2   3   4   5
of scantily clad women.

20. I enjoy participating in cultural events   1   2   3   4   5
(e.g., attending dramatic plays, museums,
poetry readings).

21. I enjoy playing sports with a lot   1   2   3   4   5
of physical contact.

22. I enjoy playing video games that allow   1   2   3   4   5
you to fight and kill others.

23. I enjoy watching action movies with scenes   1   2   3   4   5
involving car crashes, fights, and guns.

24. I flirt with women at my place of   1   2   3   4   5
work/school.

25. I often get into fights.   1   2   3   4   5

26. I tell lewd jokes at work/school.   1   2   3   4   5

DEVELOPMENT OF A SCALE 15

1 = Strongly Disagree

2 = Disagree

3 = Neither Agree nor Disagree

4 = Agree

5 = Strongly Agree

27. I tend to raise my voice when I am upset.   1   2   3   4   5

28. I think it is important to obey   1   2   3   4   5
authority figures.

29. I try to put myself in others' shoes to   1   2   3   4   5
help me understand their situation.

30. In spousal disagreements, I believe that   1   2   3   4   5
the man should have the final say.

31. Watching the nightly news   1   2   3   4   5
can be depressing.

32. When it comes to asking a girl for a date,   1   2   3   4   5
I don't take no for an answer.

DEVELOPMENT OF A SCALE 16

Demographics

33. How old are you?_____

34. What is your race? Check one.

☐ Caucasian   ☐ African American   ☐ Hispanic

☐ Asian   ☐ Native American   Other_____

35. Please indicate your marital status. Check one.

☐ Married   ☐ Single   ☐ Divorced

☐ Widowed   ☐ Living with partner

36. Did you belong to a fraternity? Circle one.   Yes   No

If so, how involved were you? Circle one.

Not at all involved   Somewhat involved   Very involved

How to Write a Paper about Literature

Literature is a difficult subject to write about. First, it is a subject about which there is no shortage of opinions. A famous play such as *Hamlet,* for instance, has been so thoroughly studied and interpreted that it would take a tome or two to collect everything that has been written about it. Beginning writers must therefore always live in dread that what they have to say about a work may be blasphemously contrary to established opinion.

Second, the beginning writer is often unaware of the tradition or era into which a piece of literature falls. Yet to write intelligently about a piece of literature, a student must be able to distinguish the qualities of its literary tradition from the properties singular to the particular work. It is nearly impossible, for instance, to write comprehensibly about the work of a Romantic poet unless one knows something about the disposition of Romanticism.

However, the beginning student is rarely called upon to perform any such feat of interpretation. Instead, what an instructor generally wishes to evoke from a student writer is simply an intelligent exploration of a work's meaning, along with a straightforward discussion of one or two of its techniques. The student might therefore be asked to analyze the meaning of a sonnet and to comment briefly on its prosody, to discuss the theme of a short story and to examine the actions and attitudes of a principal character, or to explain the social customs upon which a certain play is based.

Even so, there are numerous pitfalls awaiting the beginning commentator on literature. The first of these is a tendency to emote over a literary favorite. Students who fall victim to this trait mistake sentimentality for judgment, and write enthusiastically about how much they like a particular work. But this is not what the instructor is generally looking for in a student's essay. What is desired is not an outpouring of affection, but the careful expression of critical judgment.

A second mistake beginning students of literature often make is assuming that one opinion about a literary piece is as valid and as good as another. It is only in literature classes that one finds such extreme democracy. Geologists do not assume that one opinion about a rock is the same as another, nor do chemists or astronomers blithely accept every theory about chemicals and planets. This fallacious view of criticism has its origin in the mistaken belief that one's primary reaction toward literature is emotional. But the emotional response evoked by the literary work is not what a writing assignment is designed to draw out of a student. Instead, what the instructor is looking for is reasoned opinion based on a close reading of the text. Disagreements in interpretation can then be referred to the text, and evidence can be gathered to support one view over another. It is very much like two lawyers getting together to interpret the fine print on a contract. It is not at all like two people trying to reconcile their differing reactions to anchovy pizza. Interpretations that cannot be supported by the text may be judged farfetched or simply wrong; those that can be supported may be judged *more* right.

But perhaps the most common mistake of the student-critic is a tendency to serve up inconsistent, unproven, and fanciful interpretations of the literary work. Often, these take the guise of rather exotic meanings that the student has inferred and for which scanty (if any) evidence exists. In its most extreme form, this tendency leads to rampant symbol hunting, whereby the writer finds complex and knotty meanings bristling behind the most innocent statements. The only known cure is the insistence that all interpretations be grounded in material taken from the text itself. If you have devised an ingenious explanation or reading of a work, be certain that you can point to specific passages from it that support your interpretations, and always make sure that other passages do not contradict your thesis.

The In-Class Essay on Literature

Often, students are asked to analyze and interpret literature in class-written essays. The literary work may consist of a poem, a passage from a novel being read by the class, a short story, or a play. Depending on how the assignment is worded, the student may be required to find and express the theme, analyze an action, interpret a symbol, or comment on form.

Finding and Expressing a Theme   The theme of a literary work is its central or dominant idea, its comment on life. Finding and expressing this idea involves a form of literary algebra that requires students to think logically from cause to effect. Of course, writers say more than any summary theme can possibly express; finding a theme should not involve smothering a writer's work under a crude and simplistic summary. Instead, in the summary you should compress into a few brief sentences what you interpret as the emphasis of the work.

Consider the poem "Design" (p. 591). A moth has been found dead in a spider's web spun on a heal-all flower. The poet wonders what could have brought the moth to this particular flower, where a web was spun and a spider was waiting. Why didn't the moth go to another, safer flower? This apparently trivial discovery leads the poem to speculate that destiny operates in random and mysterious ways, which is more or less the central emphasis or theme of the poem.

This theme can, of course, be stated in several ways. So, for that matter, can the theme of any poem or other literary work. What you must do, after you have deciphered the theme of the work, is to make a statement and prove it. Proof can be supplied by quoting lines and passages from the work. The instructor can then reconstruct the process of thinking behind your conclusion. If you have misinterpreted the work, the proof allows the instructor to see how your misreading occurred.

Analyzing Character and Action   Fictional characters behave according to the same hopes, fears, hates, and loves that motivate real people, but the characters of fiction are found in exotic dilemmas real people hardly ever encounter.

Consequently, fiction provides us with an opportunity to ponder how common people might react in uncommon situations; we can then draw moral lessons, psychological principles, and philosophical insights from their behavior. Without fiction, we would remain hemmed in by the narrow horizons of reality and experience.

By asking you to write an essay explaining why a certain character performed a certain action, your instructor is fostering valuable skills of social analysis. If you can understand the rage and jealousy of Othello or the isolated pride of Hester Prynne, you are better equipped to understand these emotions in yourself or in your acquaintances.

When you state that a certain character behaves a certain way, the burden of proof is on you. It is not enough to say that Hamlet was indecisive or weak, or that Lear was overweening and arrogant, or that the unidentified male character in "Hills Like White Elephants" is petty and selfish. In every instance, you must quote passages that prove your interpretation.

Interpreting Symbols   In its most literal sense, a symbol is a thing that stands for something beyond itself. The dove is a symbol of peace; the flag is the symbol of a country. In literature, a symbol is created when an author invests an object, an idea, or an action with a significance far beyond itself. A person may also be treated in such a way as to symbolize a class or a group of people.

Most of the time, symbolism is implicit in literature. The reader is left to unravel the meaning of the symbol. Indeed, the effect of a symbol would otherwise be ruined by preachiness. But occasionally an author will come out and say what a certain symbol means. For instance, in "Ars Poetica" (p. 437), the poet tells us explicitly that "An empty doorway and a maple leaf" are symbols that stand for "all the history of grief." In the interpretation of symbols, it is less a matter of who is right or wrong than of who has proven a point and who has not. Symbols rarely have cut-and-dried, unarguable meanings. Considerable variation in the interpretation of symbols is not only possible, but extremely likely. Whatever your interpretation, however, it must be supported by material quoted from the text.

Commenting on Form   For the most part, this type of assignment applies to poetry, where the student has numerous opportunities to express knowledge of the terms and concepts of prosody. (Fiction and drama contain fewer nameable techniques.) In writing about a poem, you may be asked to describe its verse form or its meter, or to label and identify various tropes and figures of speech.

Wherever possible, use the formal names of any techniques present in a work. If you know that the poem you are analyzing is an Italian sonnet, it does no harm to say so. If you know that a certain action in a play occurs in its *denouement*, you should not be bashful about using that term. If a story begins *in media res* and then proceeds in *flashbacks*, you should say so. Your use of such labels will show an instructor that you have not only mastered the meaning of the work but have also grasped its form.

In summary, when writing about literature, you should do more than simply ascribe a certain interpretation to the literary work. Your prime purpose should be to prove that your reading of the work is reasonable and logical. Passages from the work should be liberally quoted to support your paper's interpretation of it. Above all, never assume that any reading of a work, no matter how unsupported or farfetched, will do.

Bear one thing in mind before you begin to write your paper: Famous literary works, especially works regarded as classics, have been thoroughly studied to the point where prevailing opinion on them has assumed the character of orthodoxy. What may seem to you a brilliant insight may, in fact, be nothing more than what critics have been saying about the writer and his or her works for years. Saying that Hemingway's male characters suffer from *machismo* is a little like the anthropology student opining that humans are bipedal. Both remarks are undoubtedly true, but they are neither original nor insightful. You should, therefore, check out the prevailing critical opinions on a writer before attempting to dogmatize on your own.

ANNOTATED LITERARY PAPER

The following literary paper is one student's response to the following assignment: "Write a 500-word critical analysis of Eudora Welty's 'A Worn Path,' focusing on character, action, mood, setting, and literary techniques such as diction, figurative language, and symbolism. Choose those strategies that best illumine the theme of the narrative." (See this essay on pp. 299–305.)

(1) The introductory paragraph captures the reader's attention by creating a "jewel" metaphor. It also presents the reviewer's unqualified literary judgment—that "A Worn Path" is an excellent, moving story.

(2) Paragraph two provides a summary of the story's literal level, allowing even the uninitiated reader to comprehend the reviewer's comments and interpretations.

Douglas B. Inman
Professor McCuen-Metherell
English 102
15 March 2011

A Worn but Lightly Traveled Path

1 ⟶ In this day when mediocrity is praised as inspiration and chaos as art, it is refreshing to find among the literary dung heaps a jewel, shining and glittering and making one forget, for the moment, the overwhelming stench and filth that threatens to suffocate and squeeze the very life from one's literary soul. Eudora Welty's "A Worn Path" is such a rare jewel. Here is a story that exudes craftsmanship from every pore. It is filled with finely turned phrases, distinctly vivid imagery, and carefully constructed moods; but, more importantly, it tells its story well, communicating on many different levels. Ms. Welty demonstrates a firm command of the art of storytelling, and the way she weaves this particular tapestry of words will convince the reader that here is a lady who could turn a sow's ear into silk.

2 ⟶ "A Worn Path" is the portrait of Phoenix Jackson, an old Negro woman, seen making a trip to town to retrieve badly needed medicine for her ailing grandchild. Burdened by age and faced with obstacles, she nevertheless presses on, stoically pursuing her goal. On the most obvious level, this is the story of an eccentric but delightful woman whose spirit belies her advanced years. She makes the long and arduous trip to town despite the great distance, the many obstacles she encounters, and an encroaching senility that gently touches the soul of the reader. She climbs hills, crosses a creek by way of a suspended log, crawls under a barbed wire fence, marches through fields, confronts a stray dog, and comes to grips with exhaustion, hallucinations, and a failing memory. And throughout these ordeals, the author reveals a character filled with pride and dignity.

(3) The third paragraph begins the most important part of this critical review. The student has chosen to focus on the symbolic level of the story. For him, the importance of the narrative lies in its relationship to the history of black freedom in America.

(4) Here, as in several other passages, the reviewer carefully quotes from the story in order to bolster his argument—that the plight of Phoenix Jackson is also the history of blacks in America. Notice that each quotation is smoothly integrated into the main text of the essay. Note also that when Phoenix Jackson, the character, is speaking, the student writer uses single quotation marks within double quotation marks. But when the student is quoting the narrator, he uses double quotation marks only. In this way the reader can distinguish what the narrator says from what the character says in monologue or dialogue.

(5) The reviewer is straightforward in his explication of the thorn bush as a significant individual symbol within the total allegorical framework.

(6,7) Two more symbols—the marble cake and the scarecrow—are interpreted.

3 ━━➤ But there is another story here, one played out on a much deeper level. It is the story of black people in America, and their struggle for freedom and equality. The path Phoenix follows is the road of life for her people, and the obstacles she encounters on the way become the challenges of being black.

4 ━━➤ For instance, she comes to a hill. "'Seems like there is chains about my feet, time I get this far,'" she says, and we know that it is the hill out of slavery that she must climb. And she does it, although "'something,'" white people perhaps, "'pleads I should stay.'" And when she gets to the top, she turns and gives a "full, severe look behind her where she had come." Doubtless this action represents the black race scrutinizing in retrospect some especially difficult scene in the drama of their freedom. Phoenix encounters opposition to her newfound freedom **5** ➤ in the form of a thorny bush, and here her dress is a symbol of that freedom, as she struggles to free herself from the thorns without tearing her garment. But she maintains her dignity, showing no spite for the thorns, saying "'you doing your appointed work. Never want to let folks past—.'" And finally, trembling from the experience, "she stood free."

But freedom for blacks is an elusive thing, as the reader understands **6** ➤ when a small boy seems to bring Phoenix a slice of marble-cake, "but when she went to take it there was just her own hand in the air." Like the cake, freedom for the blacks has historically often been a seductive picture that seemed real; yet, when the blacks tried to claim it, it dissolved back into fantasy.

Phoenix passes through the childhood of her race when she traverses fields of "withered cotton" and "dead corn." She encounters **7** ➤ "something tall, black, and skinny," and it is both a scarecrow and the image of slavery past. "'Who be you the ghost of?'" she asks, but there is only silence and the scarecrow dancing in the wind. And here Phoenix is the Negro of the past giving way to the future, as she intones, 'Dance, old scarecrow, while I dancing with you.'"

8 The reviewer alludes to Egyptian mythology in order to draw attention to the special significance of the heroine's name.

9 The reviewer points out other bird symbols and interprets them. Even the little grandson is seen as a bird symbol. Again, quotations from the story are used as primary sources to support the reviewer's claims.

10 The reviewer begins to summarize by focusing on the mood of the story, calling it "optimistic." In other words, the summary appraisal is that this is a story of hope and triumph, not of bitterness and despair.

Inman 3

In this story, birds are used repeatedly to symbolize freedom.

8 → The character's very name, Phoenix, is an illustration of this strategy, for the phoenix was a bird in Egyptian mythology which, every five hundred years, would consume itself in fire and then rise renewed from the ashes, as blacks rose from slavery after the Civil War. Other bird

9 → symbols occur. For instance, Phoenix comes to a place where quail are walking about, and she tells them, as she would young Negroes, "'Walk pretty. This is the easy place. This is the easy going,'" referring to the new time of freedom after the Civil War. And when she encounters a white hunter, she sees in his sack a bobwhite, "with its beak hooked bitterly to show it was dead," indicating that even though slavery has been abolished, whites still managed to oppress blacks, and the struggle for black freedom is not yet complete.

Phoenix's grandson represents the new generation of blacks who never knew slavery, but still feel its impact, and he too is portrayed as a bird of freedom. "'He suffer and it don't seem to put him back at all. He got a sweet look. He going to last. He wear a little patch quilt and peep out, holding his mouth open like a little bird,'" she tells a nurse in town.

10 → Overall, the story is an optimistic outlook on the black experience. Though much of the action focuses on earlier hardship, it ends with hope for the future, as can be seen when Phoenix finally reaches town. There, it is Christmastime, while during her journey it is simply a cold December day. In town, dozens of black children whirl around her in the street, bells are ringing, and colorful lights abound. "'Here I be,'" she says, indicating the end of the journey, the attaining of freedom and new life. And already the past is being forgotten; all the slavery, the fight for freedom, the long and painful road to happiness is but a dim memory. "'It was my memory had left me,'" she says near the end, "'There I sat and forgot why I made my long trip.'"

"'Forgot?'" asks the nurse. "'After you came so far?'"

(11) The final paragraph makes the point that it is Phoenix Jackson, the heroine and major character of the story, who gives the story its meaning and beauty. The concluding sentence brings the analysis full circle by using the same jewel/gem metaphor used in the introduction.

Inman 4

11 →   This is the story of a courageous and dignified old woman on a long journey, but it is also the story of a courageous and dignified race, and their long struggle for freedom and equality. With wonderful artistry, Eudora Welty takes the reader along, to travel this worn path of struggle that has been trudged by so many people over the ages. She shows the dignity in the struggle and the hope of a new generation. And she does so with the craftsmanship of a fine watchmaker. One cannot help but be changed in some way by this beautiful story. "A Worn Path" is truly a gem.

● ## Exercises to help you learn how to synthesize someone else's work into your own writing.

The purpose of each exercise is to merge someone else's expression into your own writing without having your style lurch or stagger. While the smoothness we seek is not always easy to achieve, practice helps you improve.

1. On the Internet, find some biographical information on Jawalharlal Nehru, the first Prime Minister of India following its independence from England in 1947. After reading some of Nehru's public statements, write a passage in which you declare in your own words what Nehru's primary goals were for India. Since Nehru's words are in public domain, you will not need to attribute a secondary source to them.

2. Read "Kinds of Discipline" by John Holt (pp. 526–529) and restate the three kinds of disciplines he proposes by using them in the introduction to a paper about the lack of discipline in children today. Give Holt credit for his classification, but synthesize his ideas and reflect them, rather than quote him precisely.

3. Through some Internet sleuthing, find out what Libya was like before Moammar Kadafi took over. Then, write a paragraph pointing out the upheaval and violence that preceded his rule. Cite one or two experts on Libya, but summarize their words, turning them into a natural part of your own writing rather than quoting them verbatim.

4. In preparation for a research paper on stuttering, study paragraphs 16 and 17 of "My Strangled Speech" by Dan Slater. Then, compare the ancient explanations of stuttering with modern ones. You may refer to Slater by quoting him directly or by absorbing his ideas and then stating them in your own words, but either way, give him credit where credit is due.

5. For an APA-style paper on how the high school grades of athletes compare with the grades of nonathletes, assimilate the following statistics into a smooth sentence that indicates your understanding of the statistics. Use those statistics that strike you as the most reliable and least biased.

   • High school students who participate in sports have an average 2.61 GPA compared with an average 2.39 GPA for those who do not participate (from the Iowa High School Athletic Association, n.d.).

   • According to a recent Indiana University study, high school athletes have a 3.05 average GPA whereas high school nonathletes have a 2.54 average GPA.

   • High school athletes have higher grades, lower drop-out rates, and attend college more often than nonathletes (from a recent survey by the Women's Sports Foundation).

   • A study of 22,000 students conducted at the University of Colorado in 1999 indicates that students who participate in sports have an overall significantly higher grade-point average than those who do not.

6. Review paragraph 26 of "Breast Cancer No. 2" by Margaret Overton and quote from it in order to establish how physicians often deal with the daily horror of watching bodies being wounded, destroyed, hurt, or disfigured . Use only those words that pierce to the heart of the medical doctor's quandary.

7. For a paper on the future of computer dating, review "The Truth About Online Dating" by Robert Epstein—especially his concluding paragraphs. Track down the ideas by Andrew Fiore (alluded to in paragraph 32) or some other expert on dating to see what psychologists have to say concerning this future possibility. Quote or summarize, but make sure that you have digested the writer's statement so you can present it smoothly in your own words.

8. In preparation for a research paper on bullying, surf the Internet for recent cases in which bullying caused serious consequences, including death. Summarize in your own words the essence of what happened in each case. Then write an introduction leading up to your thesis statement. If a direct quotation strengthens your thesis, use it, but do not pawn it off as your own or quote it out of context.

9. Integrate the following quotation into a paragraph about our modern world: "The picture of a meaningless world, and a meaningless human life, is, I think the basic theme of much modern art and literature" (W. T. Stace, p. 222). You may support, challenge, or qualify this quotation, but use it as the nub of your paragraph—knitting it into your writing so that it fits there naturally.

10. Paraphrase the following quotation, preserving the tone and mood of the original. Retain exceptional words or phrases of the original by enclosing them in quotation marks. Use approximately the same number of words as the original and be sure to give credit to the original source:

The shrew haunts mostly moist thick-growing places, the banks of streams and the undergrowth of damp woods, and it hunts particularly actively at night. Scuttling on its pattery little feet among the fallen leaves, scrabbling in the leaf-mould in a frenzy of tiny investigation, it looks ceaselessly for food. Not a rodent, like a mouse, but an insectivore, it seizes chiefly on such creatures as crickets, grasshoppers, moths, and ants, devouring each victim with nervous eagerness and at once rushing on with quivering haste, tiny muzzle incessantly a-twitch, to look for further provender (from "The Littlest Mammal" by Alan DeVoe, p. 660).

● Part IV Suggestions for Writing

The topics listed below are not meant to be used as compulsory assignments, but to spark off some ideas of your own. Use the suggestions only if they appeal to you or your instructor.

1. Using the MLA style, write a five- to eight-page research paper on one of the following topics: Pay attention to the advice put forward in this chapter.

   a. The importance of studying the classics in literature

   b. Har´ry Potter (or some other contemporary literary character) as an emerging hero

    c. The treatment of women in Muslim countries

    d. Mandatory sentencing—fair or unfair?

    e. How altruism can shape character

    f. The need for government-funded stem cell research

    g. Analyzing the relationship between plot and character in a favorite novel

    h. The rise of social networking (e.g., Face book, You Tube)

    i. Religious faith and politics

    j. A critical analysis of one of the following influential female writers: Maya Angelou, Pearl S. Buck, Kate Chopin, Sandra Cisneros, Willa Cather, Isak Dinesen, Shirley Jackson, Harper Lee, Doris Lessing, Mary McCarthy, Carson McCullers, Flannery O'Connor, Tillie Olson, Katherine Anne Porter, Gertrude Stein, Alice Walker, Eudora Welty, Virginia Woolf

2. Using the APA style, write a five- to eight-page paper on one of the following topics. Pay attention to the advice put forward in this chapter:

    a. Eating disorders among teenagers

    b. The effects of loneliness and purposelessness on the elderly

    c. The growing rate of divorce in our society

    d. Gender roles in the United States or a foreign country

    e. Climate experimentation

    f. The need for anger management

    g. Exploring one of the latest anthropological findings (e.g., leeches in Rwanda, the Japanese Ainu, continued search for the Abominable Snowman, Ghengis Khan's tomb, prehuman tools, female infidelity in anthropology, fossil finds that trace our ancestry)

    h. Facilitating death in the universal health care system

    i. Dealing with addictions

    j. The psychology of cartoons

● Suggestions for a thesis-driven research paper

1. Write a research paper, following the format suggested by your instructor. Above all, choose a topic in which you have a genuine interest. The following titles and restricted theses are presented to stimulate your own investigation.

Title	*Thesis*
"A Look at Thomas Wolfe"	The inconsistencies in Thomas Wolfe's writing can be directly attributed to constant family conflicts, to his doubts concerning his country's economic stability, and to his fear of not being accepted by his reading public.
"American Architectural Development"	The development of American architecture was greatly attenuated until the eighteenth century because of the lack of adequate transportation and manufacturing facilities, and because city life had not formed prior to that century.

"Wordsworth and Coleridge: Their Diverse Philosophies"	Although Wordsworth and Coleridge were both Romantic poets, they believed in two completely different philosophies of nature.
"Why Jazz Was What We Wanted"	Various trends led to the rise, development, and recognition of jazz as an important part of American musical culture during the nineteenth and twentieth centuries.
"The Influence of Imagism on Twentieth-Century Poetry"	Imagism, a self-restricted movement, has greatly influenced twentieth-century poetry.
"Automation and Employment"	The current fear of humans being displaced by machines, or what alarmists term the "automation hysteria," is based on insubstantial reports.
"Needed: A New Definition of Insanity"	Our courts need a better definition of insanity because neither the M'Naghten Rule nor the psychological definition is adequate.
"The Proud Sioux"	The Sioux Indians, although confined to a shabby reservation, still fought on stubbornly against their captors—the white man and his hard-to-accept peace terms.
"Women's Fashions after the World Wars"	The First and the Second World Wars had significant effects on women's fashions in America.
"Charlie Chaplin"	Various factors made Charlie Chaplin the master of silent movies.
"The Funnies"	Today's funnies reflect a change in America's attitude toward violence, ethnic minorities, and ecology.
"The Decline of the Mayans"	The four most popular theories that have been advanced to explain the abrupt end of the Mayan civilization are the effects of natural disaster, physical weaknesses, detrimental social changes, and foreign influence.
"Relief Paintings in Egyptian Mastabas"	The relief paintings found in the mastabas depict the everyday life of the Egyptian people.
"Athena"	The goddess Athena bestowed her favors not on those who worshipped her, but on those who fought for their own beliefs.
"Goldfish"	Originally from China, goldfish have been bred into one of the most beautiful and marketable species of fish.

2. Choosing any poem or short story in this book, write a literary analysis focusing on theme, character, action, or form.

Glossary

abstract Said of words or phrases denoting ideas, qualities, and conditions that exist but cannot be seen. *Love,* for example, is an abstract term; so are *happiness, beauty,* and *patriotism.* The opposites of abstract terms are concrete ones—words that refer to things that are tangible, visible, or otherwise physically evident. *Hunger* is abstract, but *hamburger* is concrete. The best writing blends the abstract with the concrete, with concrete terms used in greater proportion to clarify abstract ones. Writing that is too steeped in abstract words or terms tends to be vague and unfocused.

ad hominem argument A fallacious argument that attacks the integrity or character of an opponent rather than the merits of an issue. (*Ad hominem* is Latin for "to the man....") It is also informally known as "mud-slinging....

ad populum argument A fallacious argument that appeals to the passions and prejudices of a group rather than to its reason. (*Ad populum* is Latin for "to the people....) An appeal, for instance, to support an issue because it's "the American Way... is an *ad populum* argument.

allusion A casual reference to some famous literary work, historical figure, or event. For example, to say that a friend "has the patience of Job... means that he is as enduring as the biblical figure of that name. Allusions must be used with care lest the audience miss their meaning.

ambiguity A word or an expression having two or more possible meanings is said to be ambiguous. Ambiguity is a characteristic of some of the best poetry, but it is not a desired trait of expository writing, which should clearly state what the writer means.

analogy A comparison that attempts to explain one idea or thing by likening it to another. Analogy is useful if handled properly, but it can be a source of confusion if the compared items are basically unlike.

argumentation A writer's attempt to convince the reader of a point. It is based on appeals to reason, evidence proving the argument, and sometimes emotion to persuade. Some arguments attempt merely to prove a point, but others go beyond proving to inciting the reader to action. At the heart of all argumentation lies a debatable issue.

audience The group for whom a work is intended. For a writer, the audience is the reader whom the writer desires to persuade, inform, or entertain. Common sense tells us that a writer should always write to the level and needs of the particular audience for whom the writing is meant. For example, if you are writing for an unlettered audience, it is pointless to cram your writing with many literary allusions whose meanings will likely be misunderstood.

balance In a sentence, a characteristic of symmetry between phrases, clauses, and other grammatical parts. For example, the sentence "I love Jamaica for its weather, its lovely scenery, and its people... is balanced. This sentence—"I love Jamaica for its weather, its lovely scenery, and because its people are friendly...—is not. See also **parallelism.**

causal analysis A mode of developing an essay in which the writer's chief aim is to analyze cause or predict effect.

cliché A stale image or expression, and the bane of good expository writing. "White as a ghost... is a cliché; so is "busy as a bee.... Some clever writers can produce an effect by occasionally inserting a cliché in their prose, but most simply invent a fresh image rather than cull one from the public stock.

coherence   The principle of clarity and logical adherence to a topic that binds together all parts of a composition. A coherent essay is one whose parts—sentences, paragraphs, pages—are logically fused into a whole. Its opposite is an incoherent essay—one that is jumbled, illogical, and unclear.

colloquialism   A word or expression acceptable in informal usage but inappropriate in formal discourse. A given word may have a standard as well as a colloquial meaning. *Bug,* for example, is standard when used to refer to an insect, but when it is used to designate a virus—for example, "She's at home recovering from a bug…óthe word is a colloquialism.

comparison/contrast   A rhetorical mode used to develop essays that systematically match two items for similarities and differences. See the comparison/contrast essay examples in Chapter 13.

conclusion   The final paragraph or paragraphs that sum up an essay and bring it to a close. Effective conclusions vary widely, but common tacks used by writers to end their essays include summing up what has been said, suggesting what ought to be done, specifying consequences that are likely to occur, restating the beginning, and taking the reader by surprise with an unexpected ending. Most important of all, however, is to end the essay artfully and quietly in a way that emphasizes your main point without staging a grand show for the reader's benefit.

concrete   Said of words or terms denoting objects or conditions that are palpable, visible, or otherwise evident to the senses. *Concrete* is the opposite of *abstract.* The difference between the two is a matter of degree. *Illness,* for example, is abstract; *ulcer* is concrete; "sick in the stomach… falls somewhere between the two. The best writing usually expresses abstract propositions in concrete terms.

connotation   The implication or emotional overtones of a word rather than its literal meaning. *Lion,* used in a literal sense, denotes a beast (see **denotation**). But to say that Winston Churchill had "the heart of a lion… is to use the connotative or implied meaning of *lion.*

critical thinking (or reading)   The attempt to understand and judge the underlying assumptions of a claim. It involves the following steps: (1) *analysis*—looking at the components that support a claim; (2) *synthesis*—blending the components analyzed into a new, original claim; (3) *evaluation*—judging or assessing a claim.

deduction   Something inferred or concluded. Deductive reasoning moves from the general to the specific.

denotation   The specific and literal meaning of a word, as found in the dictionary. The opposite of *connotation.*

description   A rhetorical mode used to develop an essay whose primary aim is to depict a scene, person, thing, or idea. Descriptive writing evokes the look, feel, sound, and sense of events, people, or things. See Chapter 9 for instructions on writing a descriptive essay.

diction   The choice of words a writer uses in an essay or other writing. Implicit in the idea of diction is a vast vocabulary of synonyms—words that have more or less equivalent meanings. If only one word existed for every idea or condition, diction would not exist. But because we have a choice of words with various shades of meaning, a writer can and does choose among words to express ideas. The diction of skilled writers is determined by the audience and occasion of their writing.

division and classification   A rhetorical mode for developing an essay whose chief aim is to identify the parts of a whole. A division and classification essay is often an exercise in logical thinking. See, for example, "Thinking as a Hobby,… by William Golding, in Chapter 14.

documentation   In a research paper, the support provided for an assertion, theory, or idea, consisting of references to the works of other writers. Different styles of documentation exist. Most disciplines now use the parenthetical style of documentation—see the sample research paper, "Choosing Single Motherhood: A Sign of

Modern Times,... in Part Four—where citations are made within the text of the paper rather than in footnotes or endnotes.

dominant impression   The central theme around which a descriptive passage is organized. For example, a description of an airport lobby would most likely use the dominant impression of rush and bustle, which it would support with specific detail, even though the lobby may contain pockets of peace and tranquility. Likewise, a description of Cyrano de Bergerac—the famous dramatic lover whose nose was horrendously long—would focus on his nose rather than on an inconspicuous part of his face.

emotion, appeal to   An appeal to feelings rather than to strict reason; a legitimate ploy in an argument as long as it is not excessively and exclusively used.

emphasis   A rhetorical principle that requires stress to be given to important elements in an essay. Emphasis may be given to an idea in various parts of a composition. In a sentence, words may be emphasized by placing them at the beginning or end or by judiciously italicizing them. In a paragraph, ideas may be emphasized by repetition or by the accumulation of specific detail.

essay   From the French word *essai,* or "attempt,... the essay is a short prose discussion of a single topic. Essays are sometimes classified as formal or informal. A formal essay is aphoristic, structured, and serious. An informal essay is personal, revelatory, humorous, and somewhat loosely structured.

evidence   The logical bases or supports for an assertion or idea. Logical arguments consist of at least three elements: propositions, reasoning, and evidence. The first of these consists of the ideas that the writer advocates or defends. The logical links by which the argument is advanced make up the second. The statistics, facts, anecdotes, and testimonial support provided by the writer in defense of the idea constitute the evidence. In a research paper, evidence consisting of paraphrases or quotations from the works of other writers must be documented in a footnote, endnote, or parenthetical reference. See also **argumentation** and/or **documentation.**

example   An instance that is representative of an idea or claim or that otherwise illustrates it. The example mode of development is used in essays that make a claim and then prove it by citing similar and supporting cases. See, for example, the essays in Chapter 11.

exposition   Writing whose chief aim is to explain. Most college composition assignments are expository.

figurative   Said of a word or expression used in a nonliteral way. For example, the expression "to go the last mile... may have nothing at all to do with geographical distance, but may mean to complete a task or job.

focus   In an essay, the concentration or emphasis on a certain subject or topic.

generalization   A statement that asserts some broad truth based on a knowledge of specific cases. For instance, the statement "big cars are gas guzzlers... is a generalization about individual cars. Generalizations are the products of inductive reasoning, whereby a basic truth may be inferred about a class after experience with a representative number of its members. However, one should beware of rash or faulty generalizations—those made on insufficient experience or evidence. It was once thought, for example, that scurvy sufferers were malingerers, which led the British navy to the policy of flogging the victims of scurvy aboard its ships. Later, medical research showed that the lethargy of scurvy victims was an effect rather than the cause of the disease. The real cause was found to be a lack of vitamin C in their diet.

image   A phrase or expression that evokes a picture or describes a scene. An image may be either literal, in which case it depicts what something looks like, or figurative, in which case an expression is used that likens the thing described to something else (e.g., "My love is like a red, red rose...").

induction   A form of reasoning that proceeds from specific instances to a general inference or conclusion. Inductive reasoning is the cornerstone of the scientific method, which begins by examining representative cases and then infers some law or theory to explain them as a whole. See Chapter 14.

interparagraph   Between paragraphs. A comparison/contrast, for example, may be drawn between several paragraphs rather than within a single paragraph. For an example of an interparagraph comparison/contrast, see Chapter 7.

intraparagraph   Within a single paragraph. For an example of an intraparagraph comparison/contrast, see Chapter 7.

inversion   The reversal of the normal order of words in a sentence to achieve some desired effect, usually emphasis. Inversion is a technique long used in poetry, although most modern poets shun it as too artificial. For examples of inversion, see Shakespeare's "That Time of Year… (Sonnet 73) in Chapter 6.

irony   The use of language in such a way that apparent meaning contrasts sharply with real meaning. One famous example (in Shakespeare's *Julius Caesar*) is Antony's description of Brutus as "an honorable man…: Because Brutus was one of Caesar's assassins, Antony meant just the opposite. Irony is a softer form of sarcasm and shares with it the same contrast between apparent and real meaning.

jargon   The specialized or technical language of a trade, profession, class, or other group of people. Jargon is sometimes useful, but when used thoughtlessly it can become meaningless expression bordering on gibberish, as in the following sentence from a psychology text: "Her male sibling's excessive psychogenic outbursts were instrumental in causing her to decompensate emotionally…. A clearer statement would be the following: "Her brother's temper eventually caused her to have a nervous breakdown….

literal   *Literal* and *figurative* are two opposing characteristics of language. Literal meaning is a statement about something rendered in common, factual terms: "Good writers must be aggressive and daring…. Figurative meaning is clouded in an image: "Good writers must stick out their necks…. See **figurative.**

logical fallacies   Errors in reasoning used by speakers or writers, sometimes in order to dupe their audiences. Most logical fallacies are based on insufficient evidence ("All redheads are passionate lovers…) or on irrelevant information ("Don't let him do the surgery; he cheats on his wife…) or on faulty reasoning ("If you don't quit smoking, you'll die of lung cancer…).

metaphor   A figurative image that implies a similarity between things otherwise dissimilar, such as the poet Robert Frost's statement "I have been acquainted with the night,… meaning that he has suffered despair.

mood of a story   The pervading impression made on the feelings of the reader. For instance, Edgar Allan Poe often created a mood of horror in his short stories. A mood can be gloomy, sad, joyful, bitter, frightening, and so forth.

mood of verbs   A verb form expressing the manner or condition of the action. The moods of verbs are *indicative* (statements or questions), *imperative* (requests or commands), and *subjunctive* (expressions of doubt, wishes, probabilities, and conditions contrary to fact).

narrative   An account of events that happened. A narrative organizes material on the basis of chronological order or pattern, stressing the sequence of events and pacing these events according to the emphasis desired. Narration is often distinguished from three other modes of writing: argumentation, description, and exposition. See "How to Write a Narrative… in Chapter 8.

objective and subjective   Two attitudes toward writing. In *objective* writing, the author tries to present the material fairly and without bias; in *subjective* writing, the author stresses personal responses and interpretations. For instance, news reporting should be objective, whereas poetry can be subjective.

pacing The speed at which a piece of writing moves along. Pacing depends on the balance between summarizing action and representing the action in detail. See "How to Write a Narrative… in Chapter 8.

parallelism The principle of coherent writing requiring that coordinate elements be given the same grammatical form, as in Daniel Webster's dictum, "I was born an American; I will live an American; I will die an American.…

paraphrase A restatement of a text or passage in another form or in other words, often to clarify the meaning. Paraphrase is commonly used in research papers to assimilate the research into a single style of writing and thereby avoid a choppy effect. See also **plagiarism.**

personification Attributing human qualities to objects, abstractions, or animals: "'Tis beauty calls and glory leads the way.…

plagiarism Copying words from a source and then passing them off as one's own. Plagiarism is considered dishonest scholarship. Every writer is obligated to acknowledge ideas or concepts that represent someone else's thinking.

point of view The perspective from which a piece of writing is developed. In nonfiction, the point of view is usually the author's. In fiction, the point of view can be first- or third-person. In the first-person point of view, the author becomes part of the narrative and refers to him- or herself as "I.… In the third-person point of view, the narrator simply observes the action of the story. Third-person narration is either *omniscient* (the narrator knows everything about all of the characters) or *limited* (the narrator knows only those things that might be apparent to a sensitive observer).

premise An assertion or statement that is the basis for an argument. See **syllogism.**

process A type of development in writing that stresses how a sequence of steps produces a certain effect. For instance, explaining to the reader all of the steps involved in balancing a checkbook would be a *process* essay. See Chapter 10 for examples of process writing.

purpose The commitment on the part of authors to explain what they plan to write about. Purpose is an essential part of unity and coherence. Most teachers require students to write a statement of purpose, also called a *thesis*: "I intend to argue that our Federal Post Office needs a complete overhaul.…

red herring A side issue introduced into an argument to distract from the main argument. It is a common device of politicians: "Abortion may be a woman's individual right, but have you considered the danger of the many germ-infested abortion clinics?… Here the side issue of dirty clinics clouds the ethical issue of having an abortion.

repetition A final review of all of the main points in a piece of writing; also known as *recapitulation*. In skillful writing, repetition is a means of emphasizing important words and ideas, of binding together the sentences in a passage, and of creating an effective conclusion. Its purpose is to accumulate a climactic impact or to cast new light on the material being presented.

rhetoric The art of using persuasive language. This is accomplished through the author's diction and sentence structure.

rhetorical question A question posed with no expectation of receiving an answer. This device is often used in public speaking to launch or further discussion. For example, a speaker might say, "What is the meaning of life, anyway?… as a way of nudging a talk toward a discussion of ethics.

satire Often an attack on a person. Also the use of wit and humor to ridicule society's weaknesses so as to correct them. In literature, two types of satire have been recognized: *Horatian satire*, which is gentle and smiling, and *Juvenalian satire*, which is sharp and biting.

simile A figure of speech that, like the metaphor, implies a similarity between things otherwise dissimilar. The simile, however, always uses *like, as*, or *so* to introduce the comparison: "My word is like a steel plate, never to be broken.…

slang   The casual vocabulary used by specific groups or cultures, especially students—usually considered inappropriate for formal writing. In today's technological culture of text messaging, chat speak has developed as a particular kind of slang. Examples are LOL (laughing out loud), IMHO (In my humble opinion), or OMG (Oh, my God).

slanting   The characteristic of selecting facts, words, or emphasis to achieve a preconceived intent:

favorable intent: "Although the Senator looks bored, when it comes time to vote, she is on the right side of the issue....

unfavorable intent: "The Senator may vote on the right side of issues, but she always looks bored....

specific   A way of referring to the level of abstraction in words; the opposite of *general*. A *general* word refers to a group or class, whereas a *specific* word refers to a member of a group or class. Thus, the word *nature* is general, the word *tree* more specific, and the word *oak* even more specific. The thesis of an essay is general, but the details supporting that thesis are specific. See also **abstract** and **concrete.**

Standard English   The English of educated speakers and writers. Any attempt to define Standard English is controversial because no two speakers of English speak exactly alike. What is usually meant by "Standard English... is what one's grammar book dictates.

statement of purpose   What an author is trying to tell an audience; the main idea of an essay. Traditionally, what distinguishes a statement of purpose from a *thesis* is wording, not content. A statement of purpose includes words such as "My purpose is . . .." and "In this paper I intend to . . .. A statement of purpose is often the lead sentence of an essay. See Chapter 5.

straw man   An opposing point of view, set up so that it can easily be refuted. This is a common strategy used in debate.

style   The expression of an author's individuality through the use of words, sentence patterns, and selection of details.

Our advice to fledgling writers is to develop a style that combines sincerity with clarity.

subordination   Expressing in a dependent clause, phrase, or single word any idea that is not significant enough to be expressed in a main clause or an independent sentence:

lacking subordination: John wrote his research paper on Thomas Jefferson; he was interested in this great statesman.

with subordination: Because John was interested in Thomas Jefferson, he wrote his research paper on this great statesman.

syllogism   In formal logic, the pattern by which a deductive argument is expressed:

All men are mortal. (major premise)

John Smith is a man. (minor premise)

Therefore John Smith is mortal. (conclusion)

symbol   An object or action that in its particular context represents something else. For instance, in Ernest Hemingway's novel *A Farewell to Arms,* the rain represents impending disaster because when it rains something terrible happens.

synonym   A word or phrase that has the same meaning as another. For instance, the words *imprisonment* and *incarceration* are synonyms. The phrases "fall short... and "miss the mark... are synonymous.

syntax   The order of words in a sentence and their relationships to each other. Good syntax requires correct grammar as well as effective sentence patterns, including unity, coherence, and emphasis.

theme   See **thesis.**

thesis   The basic idea of an essay, usually stated in a single sentence. In expository and argumentative writing, the thesis (or *theme*) is the unifying force that every word, sentence, and paragraph of the essay must support.

tone   The reflection of the writer's attitude toward subject and audience. The tone can be personal or impersonal, formal or informal, objective or subjective, or expressed in irony, sarcasm, anger, humor, satire, hyperbole, or understatement.

topic sentence The *topic sentence* is to a paragraph what the *thesis* or *theme* is to the entire essay—that is, it expresses the paragraph's central idea.

transition Words, phrases, sentences, or even paragraphs that indicate connections between the writer's ideas. These transitions provide landmarks to guide readers from one idea to the next. The following are some standard transitional devices:

time: soon, immediately, afterward, later, meanwhile, in the meantime

place: nearby, on the opposite side, further back, beyond

result: as a result, therefore, thus, as a consequence

comparison: similarly, likewise, also

contrast: on the other hand, in contrast, nevertheless, but, yet, otherwise

addition: furthermore, moreover, in addition, and, first, second, third, finally

example: for example, for instance, to illustrate, as a matter of fact, on the whole, in other words.

understatement Deliberately representing something as less than it is in order to stress its magnitude. Also called *litotes.* A good writer will restrain the impulse to hammer home a point and will use understatement instead. An example is the following line from Oscar Wilde's play *The Importance of Being Earnest:* "To lose one parent, Mr. Worthing, may be regarded as a misfortune; to lose both looks like carelessness...."

unity The characteristic in writing of having all parts contribute to an overall effect. An essay or paragraph is described as having *unity* when all of its sentences develop one central idea. The worst enemy of unity is irrelevant material. A good rule is to delete all sentences that do not advance or prove the thesis or topic sentence of an essay.

voice The presence or the sound of self chosen by an author. Most good writing sounds like someone delivering a message. The aim in good student writing is to sound natural. Of course, the voice will be affected by the audience and occasion for writing. See Chapter 4, "What Is a Writer's Voice?...

Index